THE STUDY OF CULTURE

AT A DISTANCE

Edited by **Margaret Mead**
and **Rhoda Métraux**

THE UNIVERSITY OF CHICAGO PRESS
CHICAGO & LONDON

PART of the material in the theoretical sections

was originally given

in the Josiah Mason Lectures

delivered by Margaret Mead

at the University of Birmingham

October–November 1949

The University of Chicago Press, Chicago 60637
The University of Chicago Press, Ltd., London

International Standard Book Number: 0-226-51508-7
Library of Congress Catalog Card Number: 53-13135
Copyright 1953 by The University of Chicago
All rights reserved. Published 1953
Fifth Impression 1971
Printed in the United States of America

TO RUTH FULTON BENEDICT

who inaugurated
Columbia University
Research in Contemporary Cultures

ACKNOWLEDGMENTS

This Manual is based on the researches inaugurated by the late Professor Ruth Benedict, under the title of Columbia University Research in Contemporary Cultures, under a grant from the Human Resources Division, Office of Naval Research, and according to the terms of the contract, reproduction in whole or in part is permitted for any purpose of the U. S. Government. The research was continued in a series of successor projects under the auspices of the American Museum of Natural History -- Studies in Soviet Culture, conducted on behalf of the Rand Corporation, and Studies in Contemporary Cultures, conducted partly under the Office of Naval Research, partly under the Center for International Studies, Massachusetts Institute of Technology. In its present form the Manual is a very much condensed version of a preliminary draft presented to the Office of Naval Research in the autumn of 1951.

Our obligations are manifold: to the inspiration and leadership of Ruth Benedict; to the conveners of the several groups, Conrad Arensberg (East European Jews), Sula Benet (Poland), Ruth Bunzel (China), Geoffrey Gorer (France and Russia), David Rodnick (Czechoslovakia), Martha Wolfenstein (Child Study);[1] to those who have contributed to this Manual both in attributed and anonymous contributions; to those who contributed to the draft version of the Manual and who, although not represented here by any contribution, helped to define its form and content; to all of the participants in the projects, not all of whom can be included by name; and to all our informants and special consultants who gave unsparingly to the research through sympathy with its aims: a better understanding of the peoples of the modern world and the development of methods for making this understanding more precise.

The permanent records of these projects are in the custody of the Institute for Intercultural Studies, 15 West 77th Street, New York City, where they are available for consultation by professional workers.

In this Manual all unpublished documents from the files of the projects have been referred to in footnotes by the original document numbers by which they can be located in the files;[2] they are not included in the general bibliography. Publications which are project-connected are double-starred in the bibliography.

---

1. Geoffrey Gorer was succeeded by Margaret Mead in the Russian group and by Rhoda Métraux in the French group. Conrad Arensberg was succeeded by Margaret Mead in the Jewish group. Margaret Mead was the convener of the Syrian group, of the General Seminar, and of the successor project seminars.

2. In Columbia University Research in Contemporary Cultures documents are filed by culture: RCC-CH (China), RCC-F (France), RCC-J (Jewish), RCC-P (Poland), RCC-R (Russia), RCC-S (Syria); minutes of meetings are filed by culture and date. SSC stand for Studies in Soviet Culture. All documents are filed chronologically by date.

In Parts Three and Four and in one section of Part Five of the Manual, all members of the project have been referred to by code symbol (cf. Introduction pages for details of this procedure). Throughout the Manual all editorial insertions -- as contrasted to those in the original materials -- are indicated by brackets.

In the preparation of the Manual special thanks are due to Ruth Bunzel and to Natalie Joffe, who generously put at our disposal their detailed knowledge of the research materials in the files of Columbia University Research in Contemporary Cultures and thereby lightened the task of making selections, and to Barbara Harris, Claire Jacobson, Mary Keller, and Leila Lee, who worked untiringly over the details of this volume in its various stages of preparation. Thanks are due also to Bella Weitzner of the American Museum of Natural History for the details of departmental hospitality.

Thanks are due to the following publishers, authors, and copyright holders for the privilege of reproducing the materials indicated: American Imago, for "Trends in Affectlessness," by Nathan Leites, which is reproduced it its entirety; Chanticleer Press, New York, for passages by Geoffrey Gorer from The People of Great Russia, by Geoffrey Gorer and John Rickman; Institute for Intercultural Studies, New York, for selections from "An Analysis of the Nazi Film Hitlerjunge Quex," by Gregory Bateson, and from "Rumanian Culture and Behavior" and "Thai Culture and Behavior," both by Ruth Benedict; Institute for Religious and Social Studies, New York, for selections from "A Case History in Cross-National Communications," by Margaret Mead, which appeared in The Communication of Ideas, edited by Lyman Bryson; W. W. Norton and Co., New York, for a passage by Gregory Bateson from Communication, The Social Matrix of Psychiatry, by Jurgen Ruesch and Gregory Bateson; Rorschach Research Exchange and Journal of Projective Techniques, for a portion of "Some Aspects of Personality of Chinese as Revealed by the Rorschach Test," by Theordora M. Abel and Francis L. K. Hsu; Society for the Psychological Study of Social Issues, for a selection from "Morale and National Character," by Gregory Bateson, which appeared in National Morale, edited by Goodwin Watson; The New York Academy of Sciences, for passages from "Cultural and Thematic Analysis of Fictional Films," by Gregory Bateson, and from "Themes in Japanese Culture," by Geoffrey Gorer, both of which appeared in the Transactions, Series 2. "The Soviet Image of Corruption," by Martha Wolfenstein, is based on work done for the Center for International Studies, Massachusetts Institute of Technology.

CONTENTS

PART ONE: INTRODUCTION

x

CONTENTS

APPENDIXES

BIBLIOGRAPHY

INDEX

PART ONE

INTRODUCTION

THE STUDY OF CULTURE AT A DISTANCE

Margaret Mead

I. The Purpose and Scope of This Manual

This Manual is concerned with methods that have been developed during the last decade for analyzing the cultural regularities in the characters of individuals who are members of societies which are inaccessible to direct observation. This inaccessibility may be spatial because a state of active warfare exists -- as was the case with Japan and Germany in the early 1940s; or it may be -- as is now the case with the Soviet Union and Communist China -- due to barriers to travel and research. Or the inaccessibility may be temporal, since the society we wish to study may no longer exist. It may have been physically destroyed and the survivors scattered, as is the case with the East European Jewish small towns; it may have been altered by drastic revolutionary changes, as is the case in Indonesia and Thailand. We then face a situation in which we have access on the one hand to many living and articulate individuals whose character was formed in the inaccessible society and on the other hand to large amounts of other sorts of material -- books, newspapers, periodicals, films, works of popular and fine art, diaries, letters -- the sort of materials with which the social historian has learned to deal without the benefit of interviews with living persons. By combining the methods of the historian with those of the anthropologist, who is accustomed to work without any documented time perspective, we have developed this new approach.

It is important to realize, however, that the value of this method lies in the extent to which it gives us access to information which we need and can get in no other way, not in its suitability for theoretical purposes. Anthropologists who wish the best research conditions for their theoretical problems must continue to go to living primitive societies; historians who wish to work on problems of method or theory will correspondingly choose the best-documented periods. This method is applicable when it is essential, either for exigent political reasons or in order to obtain background for some other piece of work, to know something about a period or a culture that is not accessible but from which there are still living representatives who can be interviewed. By extension, we may hope that some of the methodological insights can be used in the interpretation of periods so remote in time that no living representative can be found, but for which the simultaneous handling of document and informant will have provided a new model of analysis. However this may be, it is certain that for the rest of the twentieth century we shall be dealing with types of change that are so rapid and so revolutionary that we shall be in continual need of methods for reconstructing the cultures of a quarter of a century or even ten years ago.

The pioneer work with this method has been done during the last decade in the political contexts provided by World War II and the post-World War II divided world. It has been focused on national groups -- on the attempt do discover cultural regularities in the behavior of members of nation-states that are to be referred to their having been reared within a given nation or to having migrated and lived in the new home long enough to take on its cultural forms -- and so it has come to be called the study of national character. This focus on national cultures has been dictated by an interest in the role of nationally originating behavior in warfare, policy making, domestic educational and morale-building campaigns, and so on. The method is, however, equally suitable for the study of the regional version of a national culture or of a group like the East European Jews, whose communities stretched across several national boundaries. With appropriate redefinitions, the same methods can be used to explore the occupationally regular behavior of sailors from many countries, or the vocationally regular behavior of members of a religious order distributed in many countries. The national emphasis in our studies has been the exigent one that they were studies designed to help national governments to deal with members of other nations who were also behaving nationally, as members of armies, negotiating commissions, and so on. However, in order to cover all the uses to which the method may be put, the term cultural character structure is perhaps more appropriate.

The study of the cultural character structure of members of a complex literate contemporary society is a formidable undertaking, especially when it must be pursued away from the living society. For the multitude of cross-checking observations that a single fieldworker can make in a community, it is necessary to substitute a group of research workers diversified by sex, temperament, and habits of mind who by their interaction can provide a kind of substitute for the interaction of members of the culture being studied. For such research work, we need not only a group that is diversified, but also a variety of disciplinary skills -- interviewing skills, skill in analyzing documents or objects of art, skill in identifying psychodynamic patterns and relating these patterns to the institutions of the culture. And we need research workers with special kinds of knowledge -- of child development, of pedagogical practices, of the labor movement, of the legal system, or of the history of the literature or the art of a given country.

So this Manual is primarily a manual on interdisciplinary research practices as they apply particularly to the study of cultural character structure in cultures that are spatially or temporally inaccessible. It is designed for the use of research workers who are already trained in one of the disciplines drawn upon in the combined methodology. It is assumed that a research worker who is receiving training comparable to that for the Ph.D. in cultural anthropology, clinical psychology, dynamically oriented child development, psychologically oriented psychiatry, psychologically oriented history, culturally and psycholgically oriented literary criticism, or modern linguistics, should be able to use the general method outlined in this Manual, with special reliance on his or her own discipline.

No attempt will be made to discuss the general principles of anthropology, dynamic psychology, learning theory, and so on. Each of these subjects has far too extensive a literature and methodology of its own to make this a practicable procedure. Furthermore, any summary treatment of the theory or methods of any of these disciplines would lead to an illusory sense that the study of culture at a distance, or of the character structure of members of such a culture, can be approached without a complete grounding in at least one of them. The discussions in this Manual will be confined to indicating ways in which the theory and practice of these different disciplines interrelate in this particular type of inquiry, with such bibliographical references as may make it possible for the experienced research worker to follow through on any particular methodological approach.

The study of contemporary societies where field work is possible -- as in the work of Warner and others (Yankee City Series, 1941-), Hughes (1943), Riesman (1950, 1952), the community studies sponsored by the Unesco Tensions project, and so on -- calls for a large number of additional techniques. Everything that is said in this Manual about interviewing individuals or analyzing documentary or artistic materials is applicable to such field studies; but the other techniques that can be used -- direct observation of child-rearing practices, mapping of networks of relationships, observation of group behavior, and so on -- will not be discussed here, as none of them can be used in studies made at a distance. Although informants' reports on child-rearing practices provide one very useful clue in the study of cultural character structure, we have purposely not devoted a section to the study of child rearing in order to emphasize the importance of observation for such research. However, throughout the materials presented in this Manual a systematic model of child development is assumed, for while such a model is a convenient alternative in the study of living societies, it is essential where the observation of a living society is impossible.[1]

For those who wish to gain some impression of the methods used in this kind of work but who do not wish to learn to do it themselves, the Manual may be sampled selectively. It is, however, primarily designed for students who are learning to interview or who are learning to analyze films or literature, and, at a different level, for those who are responsible for the organization of group research dealing with human behavior when the group includes members of different disciplines.

Experimentation over the last five years with teaching graduate and post-

_____

1.   A volume on methods and results in the study of child-rearing practices is
     in preparation by Margaret Mead and Martha Wolfenstein.

doctoral students and with inducting senior members of different disciplines into this approach, combined with careful attention to the criticisms and misunderstandings of the method, suggest that the major dangers in this field are facile imitation and too pat and inappropriate applications of theory. There is very serious danger that in the attempt to standardize the approach, the importance of adjusting the research method to each unique body of material and the significance of each worker's individual style will be lost. In an attempt to prevent this happening, this Manual gives no prescriptions beyond statements of mini-mum requirements of training or procedure, and presents instead series of excerpts from work in progress in order that the research worker may identify with the process rather than with the product. In doing so, it is assumed that the Manual is not for use in isolation, but is rather supplementary to an apprentice type of training for students working together or under supervision. From it the student should be able to learn, not exactly how to conduct a set of interviews, but what interviews of this sort are like and what kinds of interviews may be expected to yield fruitful results. (This includes the acceptance of long patches of dull and unrewarding stuff, since the directed interview -- which attempts to short-circuit verbosity -- cannot yield the same kind of material.) The material suggests how to go about analyzing films, but not the particular steps or the particular themes to look for, and ways in which literary materials may be related to other types of material. It is meant to be suggestive, stimulating, to build up in the student -- who is also working on some aspect of the whole problem -- a model of the flexible adaptation to the unique character of each body of cultural material.

The materials in this Manual have been chosen from the work of those who participated in the Columbia University Research in Contemporary Cultures inaugurated by Dr. Ruth Benedict, and in a series of successor projects,[2] between 1947 and 1953, involving a group of more than 120 people who represented fourteen disciplines, sixteen nationalities, and varied in age from the early twenties to the late fifties and in level of training from occasional very gifted undergraduates to senior members of their profession with experience in half a dozen cultures. This group of people worked together -- some over the entire period, some for only a few months -- on a series of cultures: China, Czecho-slovakia, the East European Jews before World War II, France, Great Russia before 1917, Poland, Syria, Germany, and contemporary Soviet culture, with brief preliminary explorations of Italian culture, Spanish culture, and so on. Some of these studies have been published as monographs or as individual articles and these have been indicated in the Bibliography so that students may, if they wish, read the finished study first and then return to the detailed pieces of work shown in this Manual.

---

2.   Studies in Soviet Culture (American Museum of Natural History), and Studies in Contemporary Cultures A and B (American Museum of Natural History).

The study of a complex modern national culture when approached by the methods that have been developed for the study of national cultures at a distance may be divided into four stages:

1. An exploratory stage, in which a set of hypotheses is developed

2. A confirmatory stage, in which these hypotheses are tested out on a variety of available materials, in samples designed to prevent biased selection

3. A stage of quantification, in which proportional relationships within cultural materials or among members of, or groups in, a society are established by sampling methods

4. A stage of experimental verification, in which change experiments are performed with the hypotheses that have been developed and of which the proportional relationships have been quantified

Stage 3 is only partly possible when an inaccessible culture at a distance is studied, i.e. we may sample a particular type of cultural product -- such as all the issues of a given periodical for a specified period of time -- but we cannot sample the number of persons who respond in a specified way to that periodical. Stage 4 may also be impossible if nationals from the nation in question are not available.

This Manual is primarily concerned with Stage 1, with the development of a first set of hypotheses about a culture which has never been explored from this point of view. In this first exploratory stage, the type of material used is far less important than the congeniality between the particular research worker and the type of material. Here, too, attention has to be focused upon the specific use that an investigator of a given cast of mind, habit of work, and disciplinary background will make of informants, or film analysis, or any material. The Manual is arranged to exemplify this relationship between the idiosyncratic style of the research worker, the record of work in progress, and the type of results that emerge.

For those who will turn to this Manual not with a view to using the method themselves but for help in understanding the results which come from the use of the method, it is important to stress that every canon and precept insisted upon in this Manual has probably been violated often by all the principal workers in the field. We have quite literally had to learn from our mistakes, and because of the speed with which the field has expanded, our new awarenesses come right on the heels of our most recent errors.

Because we are working on contemporary cultures, the processes of research and communication are interwoven in a different way from that which obtains when basic research is done far from possible specific and immediate application. Results in this field have to be made intelligible to policy makers, to experts, and to technicians who are laymen to the disciplines used. Such results become automatically available to other laymen and a part of the climate of opinion within which further work has to be done. This means that the use of the research becomes, in a sense, an integral part of the research method itself.

To emphasize this point, certain unorthodoxies have been introduced into the presentation: comments upon the communication consequences of certain methods of reporting research results, discussions of the value of including in a research team a naïve observer, both for the research contribution and for the communication contribution, and other such matters, are interspersed advisedly in the discussions of theory and practice. Theory and practice are, furthermore, discussed together, and a discussion of the necessary specific abilities of research workers in this field precedes any general discussion of the methods employed and the conventional methods upon which these new methods have been modeled. These choices are based upon the belief that a manual must embody in its over-all organization the type of procedure that is recommended; such a blending of choice of research method, ways of reporting results, and insistence upon special types of experience and skills is regarded by the authors as integral to this particular method.

In Part One of this Manual, I have attempted to deal with some of the main theoretical issues involved in this kind of work, to indicate how the concepts of the different disciplines fit together, and to indicate some of the principal pitfalls both in doing the research and in communicating it to others.

Part Two is a unified statement by Geoffrey Gorer -- who has done more than any other anthropologist to develop the study of national character -- of those aspects of the problem which he regards as of major importance. Work in this field is still so subject to stylistic differences among research workers that it has seemed important to us to have individual contributions from those who have been most interested in developing it: Gregory Bateson, Ruth Benedict, Geoffrey Gorer, Nathan Leites, Rhoda Métraux, Martha Wolfenstein, and myself.[3]

Part Three is a discussion of the way we worked as groups, and the special advantages and problems of working in groups. Although this discussion is slanted specifically to studies of culture, it applies in large part to the organi-

---

3.   As in so many other aspects of his varied activities, it is impossible to represent simply the enormous contribution Lawrence K. Frank has made to this field since his inauguration of the Yale Seminar (in the early 1930s) with students from different nations, and his stimulation of the initial activities of the Institute for Intercultural Studies. Nor has it been possible to represent the role played by Philip Mosely in bridging the gap between history and living field work, which has been expressed in such interdisciplinary efforts as his contribution to the American Historical Association's 1939 program, published as The Cultural Approach to History (Ware, 1940), and in his participation in the 1949-52 phases of our research on Soviet culture. Those who entered this field initially through Columbia University Research in Contemporary Cultures are most unevenly represented in the Manual because some pieces of work fitted the design of the Manual and others did not, and many brilliant contributions could not be used because of considerations of space.

zation of all research in which members of different disciplines dealing with human behavior work together. It is supplemented by an Appendix A, which deals with some of the details of financing and organization relevant to group research, particularly group research that is government-financed.

Part Four is devoted to the core of the method -- the long, free, carefully recorded interviews with informants, individually, in pairs, or in groups. It is prefaced by selections written by members of the research project acting as self-appointed informants, in which the need of the research -- rather than the presence of the interviewer -- was the stimulus. It then goes on to a series of interviews selected from those recorded in the project files, arranged to show counterpoint between different cultures and the contrasting styles of different interviewers.

Part Five, on written and oral literature, deals less fully with the ways in which the imagery and themes in folklore and literature can be used. The illustrations range from an analysis of traditional tales to Nathan Leites's intensive study of the response of reviewers to the complex work of Camus.

In Part Six, Martha Wolfenstein deals with the treatment of theme and image as they are found in films. This section is more extensive than that on literature, as films, being group products, have proved to be more immediately useful for the analysis of culture than have individual literary works.

Part Seven is a short discussion of the use of projective tests, brief because it was the experience of the project that while projective tests are a valuable tool for those who are more accustomed to their use than to free interviewing, they provide nothing that cannot be provided by skilled interviewing and have the additional disadvantage of furnishing us with far less cultural content for the time expended.

In Part Eight, Rhoda Métraux discusses some of the problems involved in studies of culture at a distance for the anthropologist who works with resonating imagery or themes.

In Part Nine, we present an illustration of working from an original abstract scheme -- end linkage analysis as developed by Gregory Bateson -- through applications of the scheme in four different cultures.

Part Ten gives a variety of examples in which materials derived from the kinds of research illustrated by the preceding sections have been organized to apply to particular problems or situations.

The Bibliography, which contains all published work to which reference is made throughout the Manual, has been so organized that the student can find also the principal work that has been done in this field.

In the preparation of the Manual, I have taken responsibility for the total design, and Rhoda Métraux the responsibility for the detailed work of selecting the most suitable material from the voluminous minutes of the group seminars and the 118 volumes of interviews and other materials prepared by Columbia

University Research in Contemporary Cultures. Because it was desirable to protect the identity of some of our participants who come from countries overseas, and some of our informants whose identity might have been revealed by naming the interviewer, all participants in the project as well as all informants have been given code numbers. This makes it possible to follow the same participant from one seminar or one interview to another when detailed work is being done on method. It cannot be stressed too strongly that this anonymity does not mean any lessened emphasis on the individual style of the research worker, which must always be taken into account in understanding his or her work. This anonymity is rather an explicit statement of the responsibility of the anthropologist to protect his informants and to make his final statements impersonal and anonymous.

II. The Needed Skills and Their Place in Cultural Analysis

This method is called anthropological because it has been developed by extension from methods used by anthropologists in primitive societies and is rooted in certain methodological assumptions that are basic to anthropological work. The skills involved are not, however, primarily anthropological skills, but are rather skills shared among a number of disciplines: the skill of delineating patterns of personality -- of individuals, or periods, or cultures -- by following clues provided in what can somewhat loosely be called symbolic behavior. In these delineations the research worker's own perception is used as a searching device to pick out from the mass of behavior being analyzed -- written or spoken words, gesture systems, ritual idiom, kinship usage, figures of speech, arrangements of space in architecture or design, dance patterns, cosmologies -- systematic relationships that give clues to the way in which individuals, or members of an artistic school, or the representatives of a period in literary history, or the members of a whole culture, organize their experience. Such delineations may be made by a psychoanalyst listening to an individual patient; by a political-science content analyst who uses as his "listening device" the recurrence of political symbols; by a literary analyst working out the recurrent clusters in Shakespeare's imagery; by an anthropologist finding the form of a kinship system that the native perceives only as a series of separate terms for different relatives; by a linguist working out the grammar of the language of a people who have no written language and no concepts of grammatical form; by a historian who finds indications of membership in an esoteric secret society concealed within a popular dramatic presentation. They have in common the aim of describing and analyzing behavior that is not conscious and accessible to the individual or the people whose symbolic system is being scrutinized. The levels of inaccessibility may vary enormously. Thus where some speakers of primitive languages lack the simplest grammatical concepts with which literate speakers of Western European languages operate

-- and to analyze their speech into units like "a sentence," or "a word," or "a verb" introduces a level of analysis of which they are unaware -- analyses of cadence and the handling of cadence through superscripts introduce a comparable new level of awareness to English speakers (Trager and Smith, 1951). Some primitive peoples can explain their own kinship system immediately by drawing diagrams as complete and accurate as the anthropologist prides himself on having drawn for people with a less systematic awareness of their own behavior; the problem then shifts to an analysis of the way systematization is handled in the more articulate culture, and this again taps a level of unawareness.

Special native gifts in the handling of imagery and the perception of pattern are necessary for work of this sort; additionally, a great deal of training is required. A young psychiatrist learning to be a psychoanalyst, a clinical psychologist learning to interpret projective tests, an anthropologist sent to the field to sort out from a mass of unfamiliar and unorganized behavior patterns that are not discriminated by the people themselves -- all these are undergoing training in this sort of pattern analysis.

For the study of culture at a distance, however, additional capacities are needed, because in every case the research worker who uses a particular kind of material -- interviews, films, art forms, games, slang, and so on -- is required to go beyond his or her source material, to delineate in terms of a larger whole, the culture, that is, the total shared, learned behavior of the members of the group or society or period being studied. In historical studies this has been called the historical imagination -- the ability to reconstruct from a set of parchments, epitaphs on gravestones, lists of purchases by a steward for a manor, or of expenditures for the costumes worn in a morality play, the life of a long-past period as a whole. For such reconstruction, the student must be able to move from one set of clues to another, so that if he has a painting that shows the costumes worn in a period, a list of expenditures for stuffs, a list of the foods that were sold in the shops, a few bars of religious music, a knowledge of the climate, a calendar, he will be able to see, hear, and smell a thronged medieval street down which a Whitsunday procession passed. Only so, by fitting together separate sets of clues or traces into a reconstructed living whole, can the parts be made meaningful. But the student of contemporary affairs in an accessible community, whether he is an anthropologist, a sociologist, a political scientist, or a historian, has no such problem. If he wants to know about a parade he can go to it, use his senses on the spot or supplement them with moving pictures and sound recordings. He need, in fact, have no imagination in the sense that I am using the word here, as the ability to re-create -- in the absence either of the once experienced or of the never fully experienced living scene -- an artist at work, a people on holiday, a synod in session. Although the subject has been very little studied, there are apparently very great differences in this particular respect among people who otherwise share many aspects of the trained analytical mind. The anthropologist who on his return from a field trip knows only what is in his notes, although they were originally taken in a context of immediate sensory participation, or the historian who insists on a rigid cataloguing and analysis of surviving documents and who never "goes beyond the documents" even to include information that is writ large in the gargoyles outside the library inside which he is poring over the documents -- such research workers, who do not work with a reconstructive imagination, tend to brand as "intuitive," "brilliant," and "unsystematic" those who can put these different types of evidence together. This is the more likely to occur because until very recently workers who were most skilled at such reconstructions tended to guard their skill by refusing to analyze it. So the systematic psychologist who is attempting to understand whether there is any method in the way the psychoanalyst or the literary critic works may give up in despair and say "they have no methods." And here we who work with these methods face a situation where we actually must lift ourselves by our bootstraps, for only those individuals who have this type of disciplined ability to use their reconstructive imagination can perceive and analyze adequately this particular skill. Only those who habitually use multiple clues, filing subliminal impressions, holding in memory partially perceived behavior sequences that become meaningful only after some later act -- only they have the disciplined equipment for analyzing other research workers whose methods are, to borrow a figure from the field of computing machines, analogical and not digital.[4]

One important component in the use of the reconstructive imagination is experience. It has been said that for the social scientist "experience has to be substituted for rigor." This means, in effect, that acuteness of the ear or the eye is progressively disciplined by experience -- that the experienced psychiatrist can diagnose far more rapidly than the inexperienced as the patient before him presents him with clues so faint that they can only be perceived

---

4. Cf. Ruesch and Bateson (1951). In Chapter VII, "Information and Codification," Bateson discusses digital and analogic codification as follows (pp. 170-71):
    "First, there is what the engineers call 'digital' codification. This is the method used in the ordinary desk calculating machine, which is made up of interlocking cogs and is essentially a counting mechanism which counts the teeth of the cogs and how many times they rotate in complex interaction. In this type of codification the input already differs very profoundly from the external events about which the machine is 'thinking.' In fact, for such machines it is necessary to have a human being who will codify the external events in terms of their arithmetical <u>relations</u> and feed this codification into the machine in an appropriate manner which defines what problem the machine is to solve.
    "Second, there is the type of calculating machine which the engineers call 'analogic.' In these machines the external events about which the machine is to think are represented in the machine by a recognizable model. For example, a wind tunnel is a thinking machine of this kind. In such ma-

against a background of knowledge of other patients; that one can make out
faint ink-blurred letters in a known language that will have no form at all if
written in an unknown language. The art analyst who looks at a first picture
from a strange period or a strange culture, the anthropologist on his first field
trip, has no such models to refer to, and faint, partial, inexplicit, incomplete
indicators are missed. This accumulation of models, against which increasingly smaller clues become significant, is roughly what is provided by "experience"
-- which may include having read thousands of documents from a given period
or having looked at thousands of answers to Card VI on the Thematic Apperception Test. As a research worker or a clinician builds up such a skill, a kind of
deutero learning (Bateson, 1942) also takes place: he learns something about the
relationship between experience and a fresh observation, he knows what he has
to know before he can be certain that he is making a correct analytical statement.

Training for linguistic work may be used as a model of preparation for the
exercise of this type of skill. If one is to be a linguist who is to work with living
languages, one must first have a very good ear, a capacity to hear in sequential
patterns, and an ability to reproduce the sound made, analyzing the while the
sequence of acts that one goes through to make it. No known instrument is a
substitute for this specific human skill. Recordings may make communication
easier; they can be made by individuals without linguistic skill for the use of
individuals having such skills; they are better communication between linguists
than the most delicate notations that have been devised. But actually to analyze
a new language, or a new problem in a known language, this specific linguistic
skill is needed.

Additionally, the linguist needs a knowledge of the way sounds are formed,
of the phonetic regularities that systematize our understanding of shifts -- such
as those described in Grimm's law -- and of phonemic regularities, perception
of which systematizes our understanding of the steps by which the babble of an

---

chines changes in the external system can be represented by corresponding
changes in the internal model, and the results of such changes can then be
observed. Whether any analogic mechanisms exist in the human central
nervous system is exceedingly doubtful, but subjectively we think that we
form images of the external world, and these images seem to aid us in our
thinking. The nature of these conscious images is, however, obscure, and
in any case it is difficult to imagine the operation of any true analogic model
in a system such as the central nervous system, which has no moving parts.
Apart from the central nervous system, however, there is a possibility that
the whole moving body may be used as an analogic component. It is probable, for example, that some people empathize the emotions of others by
kinesthetic imitation. In this type of thinking, the body would be an experimental analogue, a model, which copies changes in the other person, and the
conclusions from such experimental copying would be derived by the more
digital central nervous system which receives proprioceptive cues. It is
also certain that human beings often use parts of the external world as
analogic models to aid them in solving their own internal problems."

infant is organized into progressively more finely discernible units (Jakobson, 1939). He then needs to know a great deal about the formal ways in which different languages have met like problems, which problems all languages must meet, and which possibilities are elaborated in some languages and omitted entirely in others. From such study, the linguist builds up a formal model of "language" that is very different from the model used even by the highly literate European who speaks half a dozen European languages, and also a set of submodels against which he can immediately test the as yet unorganized material from a new language. From these, he knows, for instance, that a language may include the type of qualifiers that we call "adverbs" in the verb only, so that all the distinctions that we make by the use of adverbs like "fast" and "slow" are made instead by a verb comparable to "walk" or "run"; that "gender" may not be sex gender or formal gender assimilated to gender, but may be purely formal, or may be based on or assimilated to categories of shape or use. He will expect that any language he finds will be systematically related to phonetic and phonemic regularities and to the symbolization function of the human central nervous system, the necessities of human thought, and the necessities of human communication between human beings and within each human being. He will expect, for example, groups of phenomena to be classified together, although one people may have one word for "snow" whether it is hard or soft, falling or melting, while another people may have a different word for "snow" of each type. He will thus work with an open-endedness that is based upon a scientific knowledge of phonetics and phonemics, which are themselves systematic because they are based in human physiology and anatomy, and upon a scholarly knowledge of the forms of many languages, against which new perceptions are possible.

It cannot be too strongly stressed that the perception of the new is in itself partly a function of the extent to which one is aware in detail of what one already knows. New Guinea natives who have never seen an airplane close to will perceive differences in the shapes of airplanes, because their perception of shape has been disciplined by the observation of birds or fish in movement; but they will not perceive differences in the construction of engines, because they have no knowledge of engines.

Vivid illustrations of differences in this type of perception are provided by the responses that psychologists, as compared with anthropologists, make when confronted with members of a new culture. It has been a frequent experience of mine to discuss with psychologists their first experiences among American Indians when they have gone out without anthropological training but with a "belief" in cultural differences. Their first response is surprise that these people are "so human," "so like us." The descriptions of behavior that they bring back are likely to contain nothing that would make it possible to place the tribe in question, though it is often possible to place the tribe within the larger culture area of "American Indians." Contrastingly, in anthropological description the specific form of the traditional tribal culture will appear, even though the clues have become very faint -- i.e. where once a horse was given away, today a buffalo nickel is wagered -- but the pattern of the larger culture area will be taken for granted, as will the "human" psychological similarities. Again, in contrast, when the analyst skillful in delineating dynamic themes looks at cultures that appear very different to the anthropologist, whose attention is focused upon differences, thematic similarities will immediately emerge -- in the ways in which hostility is handled or the relationship between father and son is resolved, and so on. The additional recognition that certain behaviors, such as extremely dependent intimacy and extreme avoidance of intimacy, can be two expressions of the same attitude opens up at once an entirely new area of perception in understanding the work of an individual,[5] or in recognizing the common elements in the practices of two tribes (as in totemic arrangements, where one tribe insist that all members of a clan eat their own totem, while the next tribe absolutely forbid their ever touching it).

Ability to see and hear and, finally, to fit the new into a pattern is thus a function of natural ability plus training, knowledge, and a disciplined capacity to hold in abeyance partial perceptions. Anthropologists especially, but to some extent all those who do exploratory work in this field, are continually constructing schemes of analysis that fit all the material to date but that must be held in readiness for reorganization when new material is presented.[6]

Some anthropologists have preferred to work on the assumption that there are a limited number of variables which, while still unknown, will one day underlie a body of theory about human behavior as a developing science of human behavior makes it increasingly possible to refer patterns of culture to regularities in human growth and development and to the functioning of the human nervous system, and they are able to refer these in turn to regularities in the whole world of living things and possibly also to patterning in inorganic life. This on the whole is true of those anthropologists who received their original training in the natural sciences, although sometimes there is a reaction to natural-science training in the form of a special insistence upon the role of historical accident. Franz Boas's basic objection to psychoanalytic theory was that it did not make systematic provision for historical accident within its theoretical structure. Other anthropologists, like Ruth Benedict and Alfred Kroeber, have been struck by the great variety of cultural forms and are inclined to impute a kind of open-ended regularity that would never result in an analogue of the periodic table.

---

5. As, for instance, in Nicolas Calas's interpretations of Bosch's reversals of the texts on which his symbolic paintings are based (Calas, n.d., in preparation).
6. Cf. the discussion of the way in which Gregory Bateson's original scheme of schismogenic analysis had to be altered to include the Balinese material (Bateson, 1935, 1936, 1949). Cf. also a reconsideration of previously collected material on Manus (Mead, 1949a, Notes; Mead, 1951a).

In summary, this Manual is designed as a series of suggestions for research workers on cultures at a distance in time or space who are already thoroughly trained in some relevant discipline, and who have the particular type of imagination required to work from small partial pieces of material when it is impossible to study the society -- the organized group of people who embody the culture -- and impossible to participate in the living scene with its complexity of available sensory clues. Some of the obfuscation that surrounds this field may be dispelled by the recognition that in the analysis of any part of living human behavior, specific skills are required as well as general scientific and scholarly training; that just as linguistics requires a special ear and a special capacity to analyze phonetic production, so comparable abilities to see, to empathize posture and gesture, to fit together sequences of any kind of image, to follow a series of partially completed images, and so on, are needed for each sort of cultural analysis. Our willingness to recognize linguistics as science, in spite of the very specialized skill requirements, is partly due to the fact that "language" is an area of cultural behavior that has been singled out historically as "learnable," "teachable," and "analyzable." The addition of mechanical methods of recording and of determination of pitch, and the like, were all that was necessary to ensure in the minds of practitioners of other disciplines who continued to be blithely unaware of the details a belief that it was "scientific," and in the linguists themselves a somewhat isolated picture of their own methods, which led them to think of linguistics as "scientific" because it could produce an analysis of regularities that other people accepted, and to think of the analysis of the rest of culture as somehow of a different order. It is the contention of this Manual that all cultural behavior is mediated by human beings who not only hear and speak and communicate through words, but also use all their senses, in ways that are equally systematic, to see and to project what they see in concrete forms -- in design, costume, and architecture -- and to communicate through the mutual perception of visual images; to taste and smell and to pattern their capacities to taste and smell, so that the traditional cuisine of a people can be as distinctive and as organized as a language.

But full understanding of the methods used is dependent on the acceptance of skill within a framework of scientific assumption and scholarly knowledge -- and not a relegation of imagination to an unanalyzable limbo called "the artistic" or "the intuitive." Understanding depends also upon a recognition that all cultural behavior is as systematic as linguistic behavior -- that just as the "same sound" may recur in many languages, but its position in each will be discriminatable, describable, and distinctive, so too the position of the "same gesture" (e.g. a handshake) or the "same food" (e.g. roast pig) or the "same roof type" is distinguishable. The details, devised by human beings to meet human needs, are recurrently similar within a long history of contact and borrowing, within

the limitations imposed by the human organism, within the patterns imposed by
the logic of manufacture in which raw materials are turned into finished products, within the limitations and potentialities of the whole of the natural world
-- the hardness of steel, the malleability of gold, the fertility of the soil, the
migration habits of fish, the smaller and larger periodicities of temperature
and climate. Within great areas of the earth's surface, within long periods of
history, there will be organizations of human behavior that have developed "in
contact," whether the contact came from the members of one tribe trying to
imitate the finished forms of a basket the making of which they have never
seen, or through the Roman colonizers who introduced a large part of Roman
civilization into Britain. But within such discriminatable areas or periods
there will be patterns: in the traditional behavior of guilds of goldsmiths, or
Welsh miners, or Polish peasants, or the haute bourgeoisie of the Hanseatic
cities, there will be patterns; and within each individual there will be a distinguishable pattern. Any item of a Western European-American individual's
behavior may be referred, culturally speaking, to his acting within a technological history that began with the use of an unworked stone as a tool; to his
acting within the Graeco-Roman tradition, including those local traditional
components which may be referred to cultural elements that predated the
Roman conquest; to his acting within the particular identified nation-state of
which he is a member -- France, Belgium, the Netherlands, Argentina; to his
origin or habituated residence in a region -- Provence, Yorkshire, California;
to his special class position as a peasant, an unskilled worker, a landed gentleman, a white-collar worker; to his occupation as a lawyer, a fisherman, an
actor; to his particular family and the interaction between the living members
and the role of the remembered dead and the anticipated unborn; and finally,
to his own particular life history as an individual with given capacities -- born
slightly deaf, learning to speak two languages as a child, taking a degree at the
Sorbonne, marrying a Brazilian, becoming a proficient chess-player, and so
on. Which of these organizations a given item of behavior will be referred to
is a matter of level of analysis, but not of the presence or absence of pattern.
This is present and discernible by methods that can be taught and learned by
individuals who have the capacity to put them into effect.

Our present tendency to regard only those activities as "scientific" which
can be performed with equal skill by any individual with an IQ of over 130, and
as "an art" any activity in which one individual with an IQ of over 130 excels
another -- this tendency is a peculiar cultural by-product of an age that has
become intoxicated with the rewards of measurement, intoxicated to the point
of extreme danger. For while man's humanity is enhanced by the quantifying
methods of the natural sciences, his humanity is denigrated when human beings
are treated as interchangeable ciphers in monolithic schemes in which, in

human affairs, the distinctiveness of the individual human being, of each human culture, each period of history -- and each scientist -- is ignored or denied.

III. Theory and Practice
1. Theory and Methods Derived from Anthropology

The framework of theory and practice within which this method has developed draws in broad outlines of method on cultural anthropology, but in content on a number of sciences, particularly dynamic psychology, especially as practiced clinically; studies of growth and development, including concepts drawn from embryology; studies of constitution and temperament; learning theory; experiments in change; theories of group behavior, ecology, and cybernetics.

Cultural anthropology itself has developed on the basis of a tradition of classical scholarship in such fields as analysis of Greek ritual, Biblical criticism, Indo-European linguistics, analyses of European folklore on the one hand, and on the basis of scientific investigations of primitive cultures on the other. Its major distinctive feature is that while it includes the traditional recognition of human culture as a historical development, transmitted from one generation to another and from one people to another by human contact or records of human behavior, it also includes a recognition of the biological bases of human behavior. It seeks to explain any given culture not only in terms of antecedent cultures and the identifiable modifications of tradition introduced by identifiable individuals or groups, but also by referring a given culture to the basic mammalian inheritance of those human beings who embody it, to their specifically human inheritance, and to the specific ways in which their needs as living creatures, their needs as mammals, and their needs as members of Homo sapiens are met. A cultural anthropologist like Malinowski will stop at this point, will derive his "human needs" from a comparative study of human cultures, and will then discuss the institutional arrangements by which these needs are satisfied in each culture. A student of personality in culture, the wider field to which the study of cultures at a distance belongs, will be interested in the specific detailed ways in which individuals within a given historical tradition, and with a common human endowment, learn the particular ways of a given culture and by their learning perpetuate that culture in others.

The details of this process will be different, depending upon whether we are studying the way an infant learns its culture, receiving its first impressions while it is helpless and inexperienced, and relating the sequence of learning to the regularities in the human growth process, or whether we are studying the way in which an adult who already embodies one culture learns another. The first process of culturation, which is parallel with the socialization of the child, has been much more studied than the second, and has provided a model for the analysis of adult character structure. Methodologically, one can study culturally regular character structure by following the sequences of learning and by co-ordinating the details of this process with the total adult behavior -- showing

how in given cultures the fears and uncertainties, the trust and the optimistic
expectation that there will always be enough or the pessimistic belief that one
will always have to give more than one receives, that are regularly developed
in early childhood can be traced in the fantasies, individual and group, of the
adult members of each society. Or one can also explore a culture by oneself
going through -- rapidly -- a somewhat comparable sequence of learning, as
when a European child of fourteen or fifteen who does not speak English enters
an American public school and completes the whole curriculum up to its own
age level in a year or two. Here the immigrant child uses its own already
learned knowledge of reading, writing, and arithmethic as a clue to what is
happening in the new culture, and also experiences something of the sequence
in which its age mates will have learned the culture both are now to share.
Such a condensed experience, in which sequential learning is, as it were,
divorced from some of the accretions of developmental confusions and misunderstandings with which a child pursues its first learnings, results in a grasp
of the form of the new culture that may often appear as a peculiarly beautifully
structured set of insights when expressed in statements about the new culture
(see for example, the work of such men as Joseph Conrad, Frank Tannenbaum,
and Kurt Lewin). But it may also appear as caricature when it is expressed
in behavior, as in the case of cosmopolitan Europeans who learn with what appears to be almost "dishonest" celerity the language and modes of behavior of
another culture. "These refugees," complains an honest Australian merchant,
whose honesty includes the fact that he knows no culture but his own and believes all others to be both inferior and unlearnable, "these refugees come
over here and in three months they speak the language and do business as well
as I can. They can't come by it honestly."

This highlights an additional factor in the situation; namely, the extent to
which those who learn a new culture as adults have been prepared for this
learning by the culture in which they grew up, and the extent to which the
members of the culture into which they go are prepared to have adults learn
their culture. East European Jews were prepared to speak more than one
language and to adjust to a variety of non-Jewish societies. Americans are
prepared to have adult European immigrants become "Americanized," and will
accept them to the extent that they become so. (Cf. Gorer, 1948, Chapter VIII,
"More Equal than Others.") The English, on the other hand, regard culture as
something that is very slowly and painfully learned, and while often less
critical of foreigners than Americans are, do not expect them to become English. The French regard their civilisation as something that can be taught and
learned and that can, therefore, be more or less shared in by literate members
of other societies; but just as the Frenchman who goes abroad never wholly
ceases to be "French," so also the immigrant to France can never become
wholly "French." A foreigner can be a friend of France; to be French is to be

born of French parents in a French milieu (Métraux and Mead, 1953). People
who grow up regarding a series of linguistic variants as one language will
expect (if they speak English) to be able to communicate with inhabitants of
West Virginia, Johannesburg, Melbourne, Vancouver, Glasgow, Wellington, and
Cornwall. Without the central expectation that people in all these places speak
a language called "English," there would be far more difficulty in actual communication, just as it is diffucult for an American who learns "Polish" rather
than "Polish as a Slavic language" also to learn Czech. When both peoples, the
immigrants and the members of the country into which the migration takes
place, share a framework of expectation about learning a culture as an adult,
a kind of marginal purgatory is formed in which the immigrant is given a
place, complete with its own subcultural forms, which actually acts as a pre-
ventive of any sort of complete learning of the new culture. [7]

So we assume that cultures are systems of learned behavior shared by the
members of a group, in which the principal model is a complete society, lasting
through many generations, in which learning within the family during im-
maturity is the expected method of induction, and in which the total system is
dependent upon the stimulus provided by the behavior of infants and children
who have learned how to provide that stimulus to their elders, as well as by the
way in which elders behave to juniors. This is the basic model in human experience, as well as in anthropological theory, and following at least some of
these sequences within a culture facilitates the learning by an immigrant and
also the learning by the anthropologist. Those individuals who have learned to
learn languages, so that the acquisition of another Scandinavian or Romance or
Slavic language is for them a matter of a few months, presumably have established a "set" in which the original process of learning to speak a first language
has been schematized and condensed within the culturally regular expectation
that languages can be learned. Present evidence suggests that the acquisition
of literacy (Mead, 1946a, 1947b) is also dependent upon some such process,
either learning the original principles of symbolization in the mother tongue,
or in one of the languages spoken by the parents and regarded as the appropriate
language for the acquisition of literacy -- as is the case, for instance, in Germany and Italy and German Switzerland, where literate persons continue to
speak a localized dialect to children and to one another.

These questions of ways in which a culture is learned have been discussed
at some length because they are particularly relevant not only to this method,
indicating the extent to which childhood learning is relied upon to give a clue to
adult character structure, but also to the acceptance and the application of this

---

7.   Cf. especially Gregory Bateson's discussion of pidgin English in New
     Guinea (Bateson, 1944a), and the extent to which a lingua franca may pre-
     vent -- while appearing to facilitate -- communication between members
     of two different cultures.

method. Inevitably, analysis by members of one culture of the "national character" of any people who are at a distance in space, or who are of another period
in the history of another country, will be subjected to the mediation of persons
who to some degree share the culture of both. This is inevitable. It would be
impossible to translate The Chrysanthemum and the Sword (Benedict, 1946a)
into Japanese without the assistance of Japanese who know English or of Eng-
lish-speaking persons who know Japanese. Yet this very circumstance intro-
tudes a new factor into the situation. The accuracy of the conclusions drawn
depended originally upon acts of learning of a new culture other than one's own,
whether performed by the anthropologist or the interpreter or the translator.
If other such mediating persons -- anthropologists, historians, political
scientists -- feel that any aspect of their own contemporary culture-straddling
or culture-sharing position, in which they have a deep personal investment,
is called into question by the analysis, they will resist it.

This resistance to analyses of a culture from which one comes but which
one has partly left, or of a culture one has just embraced as a full member, is
likely to be particularly strongly expressed if the description of the culture is
couched in terms of the way it is learned by a growing child. The adult who
embraces a new culture wishes neither to have reactivated in him the process
by which he learned the culture that he has left nor to have delineated for him
the process by which others -- the "natives" but not he, the "immigrant" --
learned the new culture. Here again we have a dilemma that is intrinsic to the
method and which it is the responsibility of those who use the method to deal
with.

Disciplined cross-cultural experience is essential to become an anthropologist or to work on contemporary studies of national character -- this
experience, incidentally, does not make one an anthropologist. This cross-
cultural experience may be handled with very low emotional tone if it consists
in expeditions from a modern society in which one has strong personal ties and
commitments to primitive tribes where the possibilities are very slight of
genuine personal involvement in significant human relations, in the system of
prestige and reward, or in a symbolic system within which one might become a
creative artist or a religious prophet or a political reformer. The matter is
very different, however, when individuals move, often under the pressure of
political or economic circumstances, from one modern country to another
where all the possibilities of commitment, intermarriage, friendship, parenthood, political advancement, artistic activity, and so on are available. The
situation is roughly comparable to the different degrees of involvement of a
psychiatrist who treats a stranger in a psychotic episode and a psychiatrist
who might attempt to treat his own wife in a psychotic episode. The psychiatrist can send his wife to another psychiatrist. But if we are to increase our
cross-cultural understandings, the very individuals who are deeply involved by

residence, work, and personal relations -- either actually or potentially --
with the people whom they are studying must carry out the study of the culture.
And for acceptance of the results specific safeguards against nonacceptance
must be developed in each case.

I shall treat first the anthropological concepts which are used in this approach and then discuss the way in which theories of dynamic psychology, child
development, learning, and cybernetics are interrelated with them.

The major abstractions which this approach uses are culture and character structure. "Culture" is the term applied to the total shared, learned
behavior of a society or a subgroup, so we may speak of "a culture," using the
term for the whole, or of an item of behavior as "cultural," referring this item
to the whole. The model situation on which the anthropological concept of culture is based is that of the total learned, shared behavior of a functionally
autonomous society that has maintained its existence through a sufficient number of generations so that each stage of the life span of an individual is included within the system. Such learned behavior, when studied, has been found
to be systematic, and this systematization can be referred to the uniformities
in the structure and the functioning of the human beings who embody the culture. While the content of any particular culture has to be referred to a long
series of historical events, many of them fortuitous from the standpoint of any
given culture, the form in which this historically determined content will be
expressed, will -- given a sufficiently long period of time -- become systematic
and, as such, will be comparable with the same formal aspects of other cultures.

This concept of culture, once developed on relatively static primitive
societies, has proved useful, when suitably modified, to the study of groups
that do not have all the characteristics of the primitive societies on which the
concept was developed. Any one of these characteristics -- e.g. coexistence
with a functioning autonomous society, stability over time, inclusion of behavior
appropriate for all age periods -- may be absent, and still, if its absence is
systematically allowed for, the concept of culture may be used. However, any
one of these extended and to some extent analogical uses of the concept involves
a series of choices which sometimes have serious methodological implications.
Some social scientists are willing to use the term, when properly specified, for
the behavior that is specific to one family among many, or to the inhabitants of
a given small community, or to a given occupational group, or even to a group
of people who have been together for a few weeks -- for instance, on a cruise
ship.

At some point a line must be drawn in the selection of those groups to
whom a specific "culture" may be usably imputed, and some other concept,
such as "group atmosphere" (the term used by Kurt Lewin and his coworkers;

cf. Lewin, 1948) or "ethos" (as used by Bateson),[8] must be used instead. In making a decision as to whether and where this line is to be drawn, a useful criterion to hold in mind is that of learning and the extent to which this learning -- by a new member of the group -- approximates the learning of an individual who is born into and reared in a given group. The usefulness of the concept will then be found to be proportionate to the type of learning required. For instance, while a single sex school may be less like a whole society in one formal characteristic of representativeness of the entire range of age and sex necessary for reproduction and persistence, nevertheless in the type of learning required of new members, it may be more like such a society than, for example, a small village would be.

A second criterion of usefulness is the extent to which the whole behavior of any specified group is included. If a given subgroup, such as an occupational group, a boarding school, a single community, is described in such a way as to include all the learned shared behavior of the constituent members, both that which is special to this particular group and that which is shared with some larger group -- for example, not only the special jargon or technical vocabulary but also the language spoken -- then it becomes more useful to refer to its particular version of the culture of the wider group as a subculture. The unique features of such a group may then be treated either within a framework of historical analysis or as a special version of more widespread practices -- such as the handling of slang or jargon or ritual in that particular culture.

The distinction between culture and subculture must be made in another way if time rather than position within a larger group is to be considered. If we wish to speak of the culture of a period in a given society or in a group of interacting societies, then the assumption is implicit that members of that society -- or group of societies -- will participate differentially in that particular culture, elderly people having to relearn behavior that young children are learning for the first time.

Rather than engaging in controversy over which extensions of the term "culture" should and should not be made, it seems best to recommend that the model from which the concept is derived should be so kept in mind that the application of the term other than to the total shared learned behavior of a functioning autonomous society over a time span that includes many generations should always be qualified. Then the size of the group or the length of the period studied, culturally, will be a methodological question related to the particular problem to be investigaged. So the study of national cultures that are neither homogeneous nor relatively unchanging is determined by the requirements of an applied science in which the aim is to make recommendations

---

8.   Cf. Bateson (1936), "Examples of Ethos in English Culture," especially the discussion of the St. John's College high table (pp. 119-22).

on the <u>national level</u>, or to make predictions about the behavior of individuals acting in <u>nationally</u> defined contexts.

However the group to be studied is defined, care must be taken to specify the larger wholes to which the behavior of its members is being referred. It is necessary, for example, to distinguish such frames of reference as "peonage in an industrialized Western world," or "historical Afro-American tradition," from "the culture of the United States," when the behavior of a group of Negro sharecroppers in the American Southeast is being analyzed. Any <u>unannounced</u> change in the larger framework that is invoked distorts the material, just as any other change in observational standpoint does.

This handling of the culture, whether of a small community or of a nation as a whole, can be seen from several points of view. When, in addition to studying the culture, one is also studying a society -- the actual living group of human beings -- the analysis is complicated by considerations of function and also by criteria for establishing significant boundaries. It has therefore been suggested that the significant cultural field within which all observations should be placed is the largest within which a change in any one part produces a change in another; this may be further qualified by saying "for the purposes of the particular analysis." If, for example, the culture of a white community in the Tennessee mountains is being studied, events outside that community -- in the state, the nation, and the Western world -- would be treated as outside the system and would be considered only when they were represented inside it. A change in style of comic books, a national selective-service law, a flood originating in another state, would be considered only if and when children within the community were able to buy and read the comic books, or young men were drawn away by the draft, or precautions were taken against the spread of the flood. Sufficient methodological rigor makes such an analysis quite practicable. At the same time, it is essential that the size of the larger cultural whole to which each detail is being referred be chosen in a way that is meaningful for the problem being investigated. Karl Deutsch (1950b) has suggested ways in which communication flow could be treated very much as watersheds are handled, so that the communication boundaries between France and Switzerland -- in contradistinction to the political boundaries -- might be discriminated; or areas of economic interdependence that cross national boundaries might be discriminated out. Then, in terms of the type of problem, such an area could be used as the area of cultural analysis. (See also Richardson, 1941.)

The problem of the delimitation of choice can be handled in still another way. As an example, we were interested in comparing the style of British foreign relations and American foreign relations during World War II. Here it was found useful to discriminate the social class in each country from which the foreign-relations personnel were drawn or upon whose behavior the behavior of the members was modeled. The foreign-relations behavior was then placed against the background of the culturally class-typed behavior, this class-typed behavior in turn placed within the whole of American culture on the one hand and of British culture on the other. Thus the different ways in which the two groups treated the idea of partnership -- in Britain based on a games model, in which the two partners were regarded as symmetrically related for the duration of the game, boasting and grieving for each other's errors; in the United States based on a business model, in which each partner brought different resources and skills, and each claimed his own contribution -- could be used to illuminate the confusions that arose during the war over reporting each country's contributions in the other country.[9]

But whatever the area or the period chosen, it must be clearly circumscribed and adhered to, and events that arise outside the system must be treated differently from those which arise inside. While increased understanding of the greatest area and the deepest time undoubtedly contributes to an analysis, it can be carried to inappropriate lengths. A case in point is the difference between the extent to which the village of Bajoeng Gedé (Bateson and Mead, 1942) was affected by world events in 1934, during the period of Dutch colonialism, and the extent to which world events would have to be taken into consideration after the

---

9.   Cf. Mead (1948a), for the following (pp. 227-28):
     "The phrase proud of, so galling to American ears, was a British way of boasting on behalf of the Americans. The whole problem of how Americans should speak of English achievement and British of American was a particularly ticklish one through the war. After repeated instances of the degree of misunderstanding which was generated by the way in which each ally spoke of its own allied efforts, Geoffrey Gorer and I worked out a phrasing in terms of the conceptions of partnership which provided a form of clarification suitable for lecturing and teaching.
     "All through the war the United States and Britain were spoken of as 'partners,' a word which is common to both languages. But the British associated the word when applied to international affairs with a sports concept, with the tennis partner, who, for the duration of the game is treated like oneself, whose successes one acclaims and whose failures one grieves over. It was possible to invoke from the memories of anyone who had played deck tennis with British partners the continuous, 'Good shot, partner!' 'Hard luck, partner!' which is an inseparable part of the verbal etiquette of the game.
     "The American, seeing international relationships primarily in a business context, associated the word 'partner' with a business partnership, in which the relationship is conventionally asymmetrical; one partner putting up the funds, the other providing the brains or the entry, but neither committed to a social relationship with the other, with an expectation of the partnership lasting until it is disrupted by disagreement or death, and with no obligation on either to boast for or grief for the other partner. So a careful British attempt to boast for their partners, as in the case of the great emphasis given to the American contribution to bringing down the buzz bombs, was met by the Americans, not by a little piece of symmetrical vicarious boasting, about, say, the landing platforms, but instead by blowups in the American papers of what the British had said about the buzz bombs. This produced inevitable confusion, and even some abortive attempts on the part of the British to do their own boasting."

formation of the Indonesian Republic. In the past, the villagers were affected by events outside Bali as passively as they would have been affected by an earthquake; now they themselves are part of a larger whole and can by their own actions make changes within this whole.

The reference of each item of observation to such a larger whole is essential to preserve the proportions within it. From this point of view, the isolated statement that the people of a given country go to church "often" or "twice a week" or "once a year" is quite without meaning until we know also what other groups are attended, with what regularity, whether there are family prayers in the home, whether residences are so scattered and roads so bad that all communication is broken off during half the year, whether people work so hard that they only gather after harvest, and so on. By ordering the material on any culture in larger sections, such as making a living, education, associational memberships, these relationships can be defined and any item can be placed within the whole context, even though a detailed study is being made of only one aspect of the behavior. [10]

Traditional anthropology has provided two methodological tools for analyzing cultures comparatively that have been adapted for use in the study of national character, principally by Ruth Benedict. These are the culture-area approach and the culture trait.

The culture area is an anthropological method of holding history constant (Bateson, 1944b). As used in American anthropology, a culture area is an area within which all the component societies share substantially the same historical tradition, and therefore presumably have had access to a common cultural content. The forms that any aspect of this tradition take will vary within the area, and this variation can be regarded as one form of information about the particular culture studied. If it is possible, by the use of Carbon 14, or by historical records, to date these (e.g. to date when American Indians of a particular area first learned to cultivate corn, or when Christianity was introduced into the Roman Empire, or when the idea of representative government was disseminated in Europe), then, by studying the way in which -- in a given culture -- such a shared possibility is handled certain aspects of that particular culture can be more precisely defined.

In anthropological analysis, when culture is handled without formal reference to the psychological functioning of the human carriers, cultural behavior is divided into traits, the smallest convenient unit suitable for the analysis of the area of diffusion under discussion. Then we may treat as a

---

10. It is one of the serious results of the research use of the Human Relations Area Files (Yale University) that this basic rule is constantly violated, as claims are made that an item or a complex of behavior has been studied in "194 cultures" (Ford and Beach, 1951) -- which is quite obviously impossible, except by collating bits of disassociated information that have been dissected out of imperfectly defined wholes which are never referred to again.

trait <u>woodworking</u>, or <u>wooden pillows</u>, or even <u>wooden pillows with legs</u>. When this method of analysis divorces the cultural item both from the human beings who use it and from other "traits" which, taken together, make up a culture, it is unsuitable for personality in culture analysis. However, if a trait that is widespread in some area of the world is analyzed in relation to its proportional and qualitative position in several cultures in the same area -- so that the peculiar handling of the dowry in one of several dowry-using cultures, or of retirement of the landowning male parent in the peasant economy of all Europe or Eastern Europe is followed through -- this becomes a useful method. The French emphasis on preserving family property intact may then be compared with the Italian prodigality in the face of smaller resources, but only if each of these is placed within the whole framework of French and Italian cultures (Benedict, 1946b).

The use of the culture-area approach with a detailed treatment of the way a particular trait or a functional cluster of traits -- called in technical anthropological work a <u>culture complex</u> -- appeared in the several cultures of the area was pioneered by Ruth Benedict's analyses (1922, 1923, 1928) of the differential acceptance of peyote and alcohol and significance of the vision quest -- both historically available forms of behavior -- by different American Indian tribes within the same culture area.

In the study of national character, the culture-area approach has several specific uses. It is an excellent device for pointing up the probable emphases in a culture on which the material on individuals is very poor, as was, for instance, the case for Burma (Gorer, 1943b) and to some extent for Japan (Benedict 1946a). Attitudes within the family may be inferred where the inheritance system is known in detail; attitudes toward the individual may be derived where it is known that reincarnation has disappeared from a shared religious system in which reincarnation has been historically important. Material on the attitudes toward the relative importance of different age and family roles may be found by a study of the way in which the members of the Christian Holy Family and the Trinity are represented in the iconography of different Christian cultures -- as one culture emphasizes the crucified Christ, another the young Christ in the temple questioning His elders, a third the infant Christ in His mother's arms, while a fourth represents the Trinity as three bearded young men of the same appearance. When such material is combined with a detailed analysis of the culture, it is exceedingly useful in pointing up contrasts within an area, especially for exploration, for identifying the possible lines of conflict or agreement, and for communications with laymen. Thus American and British behavior can be analyzed in terms of a shared concept of "fair play" to point up significant differences in the way the two cultures define relationships of strength and weakness; for instance, the American phrase "don't give a sucker an even break" is seen by the British as harsh and overbearing and unsportsmanlike, while to Americans it appears a necessary protection against the inroads of the overprotected invading younger group (Mead 1948a).

The actual significance of any piece of symbolism -- whether it be lifting the bride over the doorstep, a folk tale, a method of ordaining a religious practitioner -- is brought into much sharper relief when the practice is seen against a wider distribution. So the Russian tale of Prince Ivan and the Witch Baby contains elements that are exceedingly deviant from the standpoint of this tale, which is simply a local variant of one of the most widespread folk tales in the world -- the magic flight. (In the Russian version, the witch is a baby with iron teeth and the hero escapes not by throwing protective obstacles on the path behind him, but by using the objects, which are transformed into obstacles, to augment the strength of others who subsequently protect him.) These deviant elements assume far more significance when placed in the context of the widespread versions of the tale. Conversely, a knowledge of the distribution of a plot or a ritual guards the interpreter from overinterpreting the meaning of the particular detail without supporting evidence. Psychological interpretations that do not take distributions into account are likely to use as demonstration, or even as proof, some very widespread detail that is unconvincing even if the interpretation is perfectly sound."

All cultural analysis is comparative. It is assumed that without comparison culture would be imperceptible to the individual, who would not be able to distinguish between cultural behavior, such as expressions of anger symbolized by the clenched fist or the arm retracted in a spear-throwing position, and biologically given, unlearned behavior, such as the grasping reflex, because both would appear to be the "natural" behavior of human beings. So, through comparison, patrilineal organization becomes distinguishable when we find examples of matrilineal and bilateral organization; monogamy is named and distinguished from polygyny, and polygamy from polyandry; incest taboos that include all members of own clan are distinguished from those that include only members of own family; classification of color by hue is differentiated from

---

11. By observing the particular rules of credibility of adjacent disciplines, resistance to these findings can be reduced. For example, if the presentation of the Trinity in Russian icnonography as three identical young men is to be commented upon, this should be done with the comment that this usage is also to be found in other Greek Orthodox art, and it is noted for congruence with other aspects of Great Russian character as having been preserved unaltered. It is, of course, impossible to reiterate in every case that historical factors of this sort have been taken into account; a systematic statement that this has been done, a demonstration that the research worker knows the implications of distributions, and an occasional careful reference must, as a rule, suffice, and yet will not be a protection against arbitrary attacks that the research worker has "ignored history."

classification by saturation; the arbitrary character of the seven-day week is recognized against three-day market weeks or five-day weeks, and so on. Here again, as no people who have been observed could have lived in isolation, all our knowledge of human cultures is based on peoples who have made some comparisons between themselves and their neighbors -- the island people, the coastal people, the inland people, the people of the next province, the people of the forest or the hills or the plains. As in the case of linguistics, a scientific analysis is preceded by a folk recognition of difference that is often accompanied by assumptions of superiority, differential divine ordination of events, or priority in time. Then one group of people will be seen by another as backward, or their customs will be regarded as devised by the Devil, or by some minor saint, after the Lord wearied of creation. Descriptive terms like "matriliny" and "dual organization" and "totemism" and "sympathetic magic" include the other cultures within which the like form has been identified and also the other cultures within which contrasting forms have been described and identified. Statements of absence -- such as "the bride is married without a dowry" -- either refer to a view of marriage customs for the world, in which dowry and bride price are treated as recurrent variants, or refer to the fact that the people whose culture is being described live in an area or derive from a cultural area within which dowries are or were given. When anthropologists were a small, quite homogeneous group who had read most of each other's work and shared the same set of theoretical assumptions, the referent of any comparative statement was usually quite clear to the technical reader, who knew that some statement about vision quest would be expected in any description of a North American Plains Indian culture, but would not necessarily be included in a description of religious usage in some South Sea island culture, unless that culture belonged to an area on which no other work had been done, when recourse would be had -- for purposes of negative definition -- to a world-wide frame of reference.

Let us consider, for instance, this statement: "The people of the Southeastern United States have an inclusive and exclusive first person and second person plural pronoun." This is significant within the framework of the English language, which lacks such a distinction, and within the framework of American social organization, where the particular extended family type of feuding of the Southern mountains contrasts with the absence of this institution in the rest of the country. The usage would possibly go unnoticed by an analyst who was not familiar with inclusive and exclusive pronouns and their social use in other unrelated cultures elsewhere in the world.

When anthropologists began to write for readers from other disciplines, the habits of the in-group, with whom communication had been highly stylized, still prevailed, and the specificity of the comparative reference -- to the culture of the reader, the writer, or the historical past, or the whole geographical area -- was often imperceptible to the reader, even though specified by the anthropologist.

We may now return for a moment to the methodological model that an anthropologist uses: work within a defined whole and the handling of every detail in the twofold reference to this defined whole and to other cultural wholes with which comparison is made. If these practices are held in mind, they can facilitate comprehension by the reader new to the material and communication from the writer unused to the exposition of such material to readers beyond his particular field. Then, for any single observation quoted from the files of a study of culture at a distance, two questions may be asked: To what cultural whole does the statement apply? With what cultural whole is a comparison being made?

So, for instance, taking the statement, "It has been claimed that Russians are subject to wide swings of mood," one may ask, first: "To what whole did the term Russians refer (Great Russia? European Russia? the Soviet Union? and at what period of history?)?" And second, one may ask: "With what wholes were the Russians being compared (the people of the Caucasus? other Slavic peoples? peoples of Eastern Europe? other European peoples? other Christian peoples? other nonindustrialized peoples? other feudal societies?)?"

If these questions are asked, they will be a way of directing the attention of the reader to the fact that they have been answered by the anthropological writer and that the answer has been neglected by the reader. If the method of exposition is one in which the level of comparison frequently shifts, as is likely to be the case -- unless consciously checked -- when a senior anthropologist of wide cross-cultural experience is writing, then it is necessary to find the actual antecedent statement that defined the level within which the statement was made. Statements about culture can no more be torn from their context than an item of culture can be interpreted without the cultural context. Consider, for example, this statement: "Then his wife picked up his left boot and began to chew it." Made about an Eskimo woman, this is a statement of wifely devotion; made about an American, it would be highly indicative of intoxication, starvation, or psychosis -- again depending upon the context -- but not of wifely devotion.

Because this is an analogical method of research, [12] in which a human being -- representative of a very specialized version of the mid-twentieth century American scientific culture, working with other members of this same specialized group -- is the instrument through which an analysis is made of other cultures, the basic theoretical assumptions with which the research worker operates are pertinent both to the research workers themselves and to the interpretation of their results. Therefore it is safest to assume that even the

12. In the sense described in footnote 4, p. 12.

simplest, apparently factual statement -- e.g. "There were twenty-five houses in the hamlet of X" -- is made in a context that makes this number larger than or smaller than in other hamlets within the country or the tribe or at the period. It is not the sort of result that is obtained automatically by ticking off the occurrence or nonoccurrence of a "house" in spaces on an IBM card. [13]

Discussions of culture within this necessary comparative context involve three kinds of qualifications, each of which needs to be watched carefully. These are indicated (1) by such phrases as "most of the members of Culture X ..." or "only a few of the members of Culture X..."; (2) by phrases that include degrees of regularity over time, such as "the harvest is usually celebrated by ..."; (3) by statements of intensity, such as "the father's treatment of the child is very severe." The experienced anthropologist makes such statements advisedly, but particular care needs to be taken in this applied field to respect the usages of other disciplines. In the first place, it is necessary to recognize the difference between the methods that can be used to establish those aspects of a culture which apply to all members of the group concerned and the methods that are needed to establish the proportions of frequencies with which different members of the group manifest facets of the culturally regular behavior.

For whatever unit the term the culture is being used, it is possible by the judicious use of competent informants [14] to establish a set of regularities that will apply to every member of the group with two sorts of exceptions. These exceptions are (1) those which are derivable from the nature of the regularity discussed; i.e. a statement about the cadence of speech would exclude the deaf-mute; and (2) those which require a complete knowledge of the individual case and cannot be expected to be discovered by any form of sampling; i.e. the idiosyncracies in the behavior of the one child in an entire tribe who refused to suck and yet was kept alive by the accident of a passing trader who taught the mother to dip a bit of bark cloth in coconut milk; or peculiarities in the dreams of an Eskimo who had been taken to an international exposition. The analytical unit for the establishment of those regularities which apply to all the members of the culture, within the limits just given, is an identified act

---

13. This is further complicated by the fact that when even the simplest descriptive statement is phrased in the language of the observer, it refers to the concepts of his culture. A "village of 25 houses" in certain communities may contain several times that number of separate residential structures, which, however, are not classified by natives as "houses" because they are not the permanent residences of family units. A "house" in China may be a large compound containing many separate units, whereas in Zuni a "house" is any room with four walls and a roof, and a family jointly occupying four interconnecting rooms will say, "We own four houses."
14. For a discussion of these methods, see below, "The Single Informant," p. 41ff.

performed by an identified person at an identified place and at an identified time in an identified context. The regularities in these items of behavior may be uniformities ("in this culture, a knife and a fork are used in formal meals"), or they may be complex regularities ("in this culture, eating with a knife and a fork is regarded as upper-class behavior, while eating with a knife alone is regarded as lower-class"; or "while steel knives are now used as a tool in everyday life, an obsidian knife is still used for circumcision"; or "dreams of carving knives occur in the dreams of middle-aged depressed patients"; or "small boys are given large knives of their own as soon as they are big enough to go to the fields by themselves"). Such regularities are organized into larger statements about class, or ceremonial, or dream symbolism, or childhood independence.

Examination of these different sorts of regularity reveals at once that they do not refer to the actual overt behavior of all members of the society, and that their frequency of occurrence will be different for different individuals or groups. But if the statement is to hold for the whole culture, then these differences in incidence and frequency must be subsumed under the general statements in such a way that the behavior of those who do not perform a particular act, or do not show a particular symptom, or do not manifest a particular belief, nevertheless is included -- although it may be at an implicit or an unconscious level— in the regularity (of which the behavior they do not show is one possibility).

For example, the statement that "in American culture success is emphasized" includes not only attitudes toward the successful and the unsuccessful, but also the attitudes of those who repudiate the emphasis upon success -- a repudiation unlike that in a culture where success is not emphasized. If the statement is correct for American culture, then any segment of American behavior of requisite size (the size being determined in relation to the nature of the particular statement) will reveal this emphasis upon success at some level, explicitly or implicitly by negation, by the handling of a sequence of descriptive detail, and so on.

By what may seem to be a paradox, it is a great deal easier to establish those culture-wide regularities which apply to all members of a culture -- subject to the limitations already stated -- than it is to establish the proportions of the population who manifest one specific behavior rather than another among the possible set of behaviors that are subsumed under the regularity statement. This is equally true for statements of frequency and statements of intensity. To illustrate: A very small number of informants is required to establish that in American culture the word for male parent is "father." But to establish which groups in American society use "father" as a term of address, in what contexts the word is given more or less emotional weight, or the significance of its recurrence in a conversation, requires enormously detailed work, in combination with the most modern sampling methods. Yet even if both methods are used, the statement "Most male members of the lower middle class in region X frequently refer to the male parent as 'pop' except in situations of extreme stress, when 'father' is used," does not have the same sort of completeness of reference as the statement that "'Father' is the word for male parent in American culture." For this reason, it is advisable to be exceedingly careful to specify either the source of a quantifying statement, such as "most" or "frequently," or the comparative referents of a qualifying statement, such as "extreme stress." Although it is true that where quantifying methods have been used, as in Linton's study of material culture relationships in Polynesia (Linton, 1923), or Kluckhohn's study of the amount of time Navaho Indians spent on ceremonial (Kluckhohn, 1938), the results have been in close accord with the judgments earlier anthropologists had made, it is still important to maintain the distinction between a "most" and a "frequent" that is derived from inspection or experience and one that is derived from a statistically valid sample. [15]

We may now turn to the concept of cultural character structure, the regularities in the intrapsychic organization of the individual members of a given society that are to be attributed to these individuals having been reared within that culture.

In the study of culture, the behavior of individuals is examined in order to make statements about the shared culture that are of such a nature that they can be discussed without invoking any specific theory of learning or of psychodynamics. Furthermore, methodologically, each item from which the description of the culture is built could, theoretically, have been obtained from a dif-

---

15. Attention may be called here to the contradictory results that are obtained when a cultural statement is qualified by giving only one part of the whole statement, as, for instance, when it is said that "many Americans suspect the British of Machiavellian intentions." This attitude towards Britain is only one of a complex of attitudes, which include a high and a low valuation of Machiavellianism as well as a high and a low valuation of the alleged superiority of the British in this particular respect.

The lay reader who is not a specialist in social-science methods will react to this statement either by identification -- if this is his attitude -- or by exclusion, saying in effect, "Many Americans, but not I." But in either case his acceptance of the statement will in all likelihood be readier than if the anthropologist had stressed the actual regularity; namely, "Some articulate attitude towards Great Britain is a component of the American sense of nationality." For a certain number of Americans will express this regularity by denial.

However, the qualified, partial statement will evoke a very different response from the trained social scientist, who -- if he also wishes to deny the particular manifestation of American national attitudes towards Great Britain -- will attack the basis of the statement by demanding to know what the sample was on which it was based.

This illustration merely points up the difficulties of communication in this field and the number of precautions that are necessary if all effort is not to be negated by different types of nonacceptance.

ferent member of the culture, providing his exact position in the culture was adequately specified. In studying the cultural character structure of members of a culture, however, we attempt to specify the psychodynamic regularities. Methodologically, this means a type of research that examines in detail the way in which individuals who are fully identified in terms of constitution, accidents of experience, social placement, and so on experience their culture from birth to death. Such a research method is, of course, not practicable, and we substitute for it (1) cross-sectional studies of individuals at different developmental stages studied simultaneously; (2) retrospective life histories of selected individuals; (3) detailed records of segments of individual lives; (4) detailed analyses of the creative products of individual efforts; (5) the psychoanalysis of individuals. Regularities found in any one of these selected segments are integrated, through the invocation of psychodynamic and developmental theories, with the systematic child-rearing practices, the patterns of interpersonal relations, the symbolic products, and so on of the culture.

Stated in another way, all the types of data needed for the specification of cultural character structure can be used for the study of a culture, although certain of the methods used to obtain them may be uneconomical in that they are low in details of cultural content. [16] However, for the study of cultural character structure we need special kinds of data in which a large number of items of behavior can be referred to a single organism in order that the intrapsychic organization that has been developed in the course of learning the culture may be revealed.

The same sort of reference to a primary model and possibilities of extrapolation has to be made here as in the use of the concept of culture. The concept of cultural character structure has been developed by the study of the learning that proceeds from earliest infancy, but the experience of the immigrant who as he learns a new culture takes on part of the character structure that the members of the new culture themselves learned as children shows certain similarities to childhood learning, as was briefly discussed earlier in this section. The use of the concept of cultural character structure, involving as it does the systematic theoretical structure of several other disciplines, improves the chance of correct prediction of the behavior of members of other cultures by providing more ways of organizing fragmentary material and ways of cross-checking hypotheses based upon such fragmentary materials.

2. Theory and Methods Derived from Other Disciplines

The study of culture at a distance, although it has been developed primarily by anthropologists, has also drawn extensively upon two other fields: psychoanalytic theory and practice, and child development. This use of theory

---

16. This is conspicuously true of projective tests such as the Rorschach Test.

from outside anthropology proper has gone on for many years in the work of
some of the antnropologists who have participated, and for any complete
account it is necessary to consider the history of the culture and personality.
theory, which was given an initial stimulus and has been fostered through the
last twenty-five years by Lawrence K. Frank. [17]

Two other approaches have become progressively prominent in this field:
the use of interaction analysis, [18] and the use of change experiments as an
exploratory tool. [19]

If the field is classified by methods rather than by theories, we may distinguish different emphases: [20] the use of the life history (Dollard, 1935;
Kluckhohn, in Gottschalk, Kluckhohn, and Angell, 1945; Kardiner and Dubois,
in Dubois, 1944); the observation of children and of parent-child interaction
(Erikson, 1950a; Gorer, 1938, 1940; Mead 1946b, 1949a, Mead and MacGregor,
1951); the use of projective tests (Dubois and Oberholzer, in Dubois, 1944;

17. From the Social Science Research Council Symposiums on Culture and
    Personality in 1928 and 1929 (cf. Proceedings, First Colloquium, 1928;
    Proceedings, Second Colloquium, 1930) and the establishment of the Yale
    Seminar under the leadership of Edward Sapir and John Dollard, in 1932,
    through the initial work of the Council on Intercultural Relations (now
    Institute for Intercultural Studies) in 1940, to the setting up of Research
    in Contemporary Cultures in 1947.
        Through the years different anthropologists have branched out from
    strictly anthropological studies in a variety of ways: e.g. Ruth Benedict's
    interest in cultures as configurations embodying different possible organ-
    izations of personality; Irving Hallowell's interest in the use of Rorschach
    techniques; Robert Lowie's interest in studying historical variations
    through German culture, etc. (Three volumes of collected essays give a
    fair picture of the development in the field: Haring, 1948; Kluckhohn and
    Murray, 1948; and Newcomb and Hartley, 1947.)
        Through the years, work has also been initiated from the psycho-
    analytic side by Erikson, Fromm, Plant, Sullivan, and Kardiner in co-op-
    eration with Benedict, Bunzel, Dubois, Dollard, Kroeber, Linton, Mead, and
    Sapir. The whole development is heavily indebted to those workers who
    have combined the skills of anthropological or sociological analysis with
    the practice of psychoanalytic techique -- Dollard, Erikson, Fromm, and
    Lasswell.
        The application of this emerging body of theory to problems of national
    character -- of enemy, allies, and own population -- is principally asso-
    ciated with the work of Bateson, Benedict, Gorer, Kluckhohn, Leighton,
    Leites, Mead, R. Métraux, with Gorer playing a pioneering role in his
    study of Japanese character (1942, 1943a).
18. Under the study of interaction, there is Sullivan's theory of personal re-
    lations (1940-1945; 1948); Bateson's theory of schismogenesis (1935;
    1936; 1949); Lasswell's specification of the position of the observer (1937);
    Chapple's chronographic method of isolating invariants in behavior (1940;
    1949; Chapple and Vaughn, 1944); Mead's study of parent-child inter-
    action (1949a; Mead and Macgregor, 1951); also Frank (1939a) and Plant
    (1937).
19. The study of change as an exploratory tool in this field is associated with
    Bateson (1935; Ruesch and Bateson, 1951); Benedict (1928); Lasswell
    (1935; 1948a; Lasswell and Kaplan, 1950); Mead (1940b; 1947f; 1949d);
    Erikson (1945). The actual use of experiment was developed by Kurt
    Lewin's group, particularly Bavelas.
20. The references given here are meant to be suggestive, not complete.

Hallowell, 1945, 1951; and in the Indian Personality and Administration Research project, e.g. Laura Thompson, 1950); the analysis of historical or cultural material in psychoanalytic terms (Brickner, 1943; Fromm, 1941, 1948;
Kardiner, 1939, 1945; Riesman, 1950, 1952); the use of play techniques in the
field (Levy, 1937; J. and Z. Henry, 1944); the use of the intensive psychoanalytically oriented interview (Devereux, 1951; Dollard, 1935, 1943, Gorer,
1950b, Gorer and Rickman, 1949, Róheim, 1950); the use of screening questionnaires (Brickner, 1942; Dicks, 1950; Levy, 1946 and 1948; Schaffner, 1948;
also Hohman and Schaffner, 1947); the analysis of myths and literary materials (Bateson, 1937; Benedict, 1935; N. Calas, in prep.; Gorer, 1941, 1950a;
Kardiner, 1939; Lasswell, 1948b, 1951; Leites, 1947, 1951; Rank, 1912, 1914);
the analysis of drama, ritual, and film (Bateson, 1943, 1945; Gorer, 1943b;
Wolfenstein and Leites, 1950; Róheim, 1930, 1934, 1943, 1945).

   The contributions from psychoanalytic theory, learning theory, child
development, and interaction theory have been expressed best in the interdisciplinary work which has been done in this field, and it would be too large
an undertaking to try to outline the entire position here. The student is advised
to follow the clues provided in the references in this section, realizing that
each significant contributor to the field has added new theory as the theory and
methods developed elsewhere were applied in the anthropological setting. [21]
There are, of course, instances where anthropological field work has been used
merely to illustrate principles of learning theory or psychoanalytic theory.
(Cf. Dubois, 1944; Whiting, 1941; Holmberg, 1950; and much but not all the work
of Róheim.)

   It is by following the theory in its application to cultural materials that the
method is learned, and I shall merely summarize here -- for the benefit of
those who wish to use this Manual as a reference book on the method without
themselves expecting to use the method for research -- my understanding of
the principles and theoretical positions that are used from other fields.

21. The student can go, for example, from Bateson's paper on deutero learning
     (1942c), from Miller and Dollard (1941) and Dollard and Miller (1950),
     to Hilgard and Marquis (1940); or from Wolfenstein and Leites (1950) or
     Erikson's chapter on the Ego (in 1950a) to Anna Freud (1946); or from
     R. Métraux' section on imagery in this Manual to Armstrong (1946) and to
     Sharpe (1937, 1950); or from Mead (1935, 1940a) to Róheim (1932) to
     Abrahams (1909, 1912, 1942), to Freud (1938, 1940-50); or from Gorer's
     swaddling analysis (in Gorer and Rickman, 1949) to Klein (1948) and to
     Freud.
       The research worker whose primary training lies in one of the other
     disciplines may wish to reverse this order, going for instance, for psycho-
     analytic theory from Sharpe (1937, 1950) or Marie Bonaparte (1933) to
     Gorer (1940, 42, 49); or from Freud (1938; 1940-50) to Erikson (1950a), to
     Bateson and Mead (1942). Students who have been trained in political and
     sociological analysis may wish to go from Weber (1930) to Fromm (1941,
     1948), to Mead (1937), or from Warner et al (Yankee City series, 1941,
     1942, 1945, 1947) to Davis and B. and M. Gardner (1941) and Dollard (1937).
     Students trained in literary analysis may wish to start from Spurgeon (1935)
     and Armstrong (1946), and go to Sharpe (1950), to Leites (1947), etc.

From psychoanalytic theory and practice, it is accepted that a large part of psychic life is inaccessible to the acculturated and functioning individual in any society, and that the degree and type of inaccessibility -- as delimited by the methods which are necessary to make any given item or memory or affect accessible -- can be used as significant information on the previous experience of members of a culture (that is, the response of individuals to the patterned child-rearing practices) and on the present organization of the personality. Interviews and various types of group productions -- rituals, myths, films, popular art -- are analyzed in accordance with this assumption. The methods shift with developing psychoanalytic theory and practice, but the assumption basic to this method has been that during life the individual's character structure is so shaped by his experience that certain parts remain unconscious.

The second theoretical assumption taken from psychoanalysis, which is supported by observations of children by child analysts as well as by the constructions based on the productions of adult patients, is that the child learns to relate itself to other people and to the world around it through the use of its body, in a successive series of adaptations appropriate for different stages of growth. As different cultures emphasize different zones or different modes -- intake, elimination, etc. -- these institutionalized emphases can be analyzed in conjunction with clinical findings and child-rearing procedures. (Cf. Erikson, 1950, Chapter II, Figs. 1-5.)

From psychoanalytic theory we also get a series of tools for studying symbolic productions, modeled on analysis of what Freud called the "primary process." It seems probable that for cross-cultural purposes it will be useful to distinguish three separate aspects (cf. Mead, 1951c) of the primary process: (1) the primary process as characteristic of "the unconscious" in members of our Western European civilization; (2) the types of cognitive association based on body-modeled thought, which Margaret Lowenfeld (1951) has called the "proto-system," and which Ella Sharpe (1937) has related to the figures of speech of traditional rhetoric -- simile, metaphor, metonymy, synecdoche, etc. (the part for the whole, the whole for the part, the container for the thing contained, the cause for the effect, etc.); (3) types of affective association based on common affect, the grouping together of a series of unrelated objects or persons because they are feared, or hated, or loved, etc. Preliminary exploration suggests that the type of process characteristic of the unconscious may vary from culture to culture. In Trobriand culture (cf. Lee, 1940, 1949, 1950), for example, cause-and-effect "reality" thinking is disallowed consciously, but seems to persist "unconsciously" to guide the Trobriand native in utilizing natural sequences that he denies verbally.

To the anthropological assumption that culture is learned, learning theory brings tools by which the learning process can be followed out step by step. Early anthropological workers were content to invoke concepts like "imitation"

or "habit," and it is to the combination of learning experiments and psycho-
analysis that we owe our methods of analyzing how culture is learned. From
learning theory comes the emphasis on detail, on stimulus-response sequences,
on types of reinforcement, so that the whole process of embodying a culture
can be dissected into interactive sequences in which cues are exchanged between the growing child and others in his society. (Cf. Dollard and Miller,
1950; Gorer, 1940.)

While learning experiments have provided the analytical tools for discriminating the steps in any learning sequence, psychonalysis has provided the
theoretical background for understanding the significance in character formation of different sorts of learning. Learning theory permits us to discriminate
between instrumental reward and instrumental avoidance; psychoanalytic theory
traces the implications of such differences for ego formation. Learning theory
places the hunger drive or the sex drive in experimental contexts; psycho-
analysis demonstrates the differential effects of discipline that is focused in
the period when the child's contacts with the world are primarily mediated by
one or another organ zone. Learning theory discriminates between punishment
and reward; psychoanalytic theory traces the counterpart in character formation -- in degrees of repression of parts of experience into unconsciousness,
and the nature of the defenses that are set up against memories that are too
painful or tendencies that have inappropriate appeal for the approved adult
personality (cf. Mead, 1940b, 1949c, 1950a).

Learning theory and psychoanalytic theory can be combined in a genetic
sequence, so that the nature of the learning situation is related to the unfolding
sequence of the child's maturation (Erikson's epigenesis), and can be corrected
and checked by developmental studies of growth of the Gesell type (cf. Gesell
et al. 1943, 1945, 1946; Mead, 1947c).

Or the learning experience can be taken for granted in a description of
adult culturally patterned behavior, and one can study the steps by which a new
culture or a new ideology is learned -- as when, for example, an adult Chinese
peasant becomes a Communist, or when a middle-aged Syrian man emigrates
to the United States. However, it must be recognized that any statement of the
dynamics of adult character, however synchronically stated, includes in it a
theory of learning during maturation. Descriptions of cultural character that
do not have recourse to discussions of child-rearing practices are often more
congenial to social scientists who are imperfectly acquainted with Freudian
theory, but actually, underlying each sentence of description of adult character
there is awareness of the relevance of systematic theory of childhood learning
(cf. especially Hebb, 1949).

We get from learning theory tools for analyzing stimulus-response sequences; from developmental studies of growth, tools for identifying chronological sequences and the potentialities of each stage of maturation; and from

psychoanalytic theory, a way of weighting the significance of the type of learning -- what was learned, when, from whom, with what sanctions -- and for
analyzing symbolic cultural expressions. However, these three disciplines
focus on the life history of the single organism, delineating sequences that,
because of the nature of the life history, are one-way sequences; in the past
this led to the construction of theories of causation that were general in pre-
quantum physics (cf. Frank, 1951). By focusing on the growth of the child, the
development of the ego, it was necessary to locate in the individual organism
some sort of "energy" or "dynamism" that could be used as an explanatory
principle -- the "drives" of learning theory and the "libido" of orthodox Freudian theory. [22]

Correctives for this kind of treatment have come from two sides. From
the cultural anthropologist has come the recognition that cultural forms emerge
from other cultural forms. Stated genetically, this means that parents and
children are a continuously interactive system, not a one-way system in which
the child (impelled upward by a set of specific drives) simply meets a series
of obstacles (in the form of institutions) that, if it is sufficiently mutilated by
them, it will then proceed to alter. The historian has maintained the position
of interaction, but because historians have kept their biological and psychological theories implicit, their effective communication with those who are
oriented to psychoanalytic and learning theory has been impeded, since they
have not traced out the changes within human beings as institutions have
changed.

This lack of any systematic inclusion of psychobiological theory in work in
history and economics is vividly demonstrated by the misunderstanding of
work on national character. For when the anthropologist traces the way a
human infant is reared by Russian parents, embodying a specific historically
developed set of Russian attitudes, so as to grow up in its turn as a Russian,
this is interpreted by many social scientists as a statement that the way a
Russian baby is reared is the cause of Russian culture (e.g. Shub, 1950; Berger, 1951). This misunderstanding is perhaps due equally to an absence of
psychobiological orientation on the part of the social sciences and to the persistence among social scientists of outmoded physical-science models of
cause and effect.

A second corrective in the form of new physical-science models has been
very useful in dealing with these conceptions of cause and effect. The corrective has come from the field of cybernetics, which has focused upon the

---

22. Dollard et al (1939), Alexander (1942), and Kardiner's handling of culture
    as a projection of infantile experience (1939 and 1945) are examples of
    this type of theoretical treatment.

mathematics of self-corrective mechanisms.[23] By using these models, especially the models drawn from the field of communication engineering and computation machines, it has been possible to emphasize analyses of behavior in which the focus is not upon the amount or the source of the energy, but upon the nature of the network within which that energy is utilized, and possible by studies of interactive systems to institute analyses in which effects feed back as causes. In the study of culture, this means that attention is focused upon the entire network of human relationships among human beings in different stages of maturation, the properties of the network being doubly defined by the historically determined culture and by the biological nature of the human species. The child's behavior is then seen not only as shaped and molded by what its parents do to it, but also as itself providing a stimulus to the next parental act. Thus we are given tools for analyzing cultural change, for identifying how any change in such an interactive system -- in the leadership behavior or in the willingness or capacity of a subordinate to take direction -- will be reflected in minute, specific, eventually discriminatable changes throughout the behavior of other members of the society. For those who prefer biological to mechanical models, Cannon's concept of homeostasis (1929, 1932), the work of Claude Bernard (1878), or the concept of reversibility in psychosomatic medicine (Mead, 1947d), have the same corrective possibilities.

Recognition of all human interaction systems as systems within which each individual affects the other -- so that the observer is part of the situation he observes -- has been essential to the development of this whole field of research. There has been an increasing allowance for the role of the observer in psychoanalytic theory on the one hand and in anthropological theory on the other (Lasswell, 1937, 1948; Mead, 1949b; Reusch and Bateson, 1951). [24] It is important to stress, however, that although the therapeutical framework of this kind of research draws heavily on research in these other fields and necessarily adjusts to new findings in these fields, it is not simply an additive collection of theories from different fields. The contributions of each are integrated within the concept of cultural character structure.

---

23. On problems of cybernetics, cf. Bateson, in Reusch and Bateson (1951); Deutsch (1950a); Frank, Hutchinson, et al. (1948); von Foerster (1951); Wiener (1948, 1950).
24. There have also been setbacks in practice that deny this interaction between observer and observed; e.g. the attempt to introduce "objectivity" into material by having three judges rate an account and then averaging the ratings (see, for instance, research reported by J. W. M. Whiting in his paper "A Cross-Cultural Test of the Freudian Theory of Fixation," given at the December 1952 meeting of the American Anthropological Association); the adoption of concealed roles for purposes of observation (as in a study in which an anthropologist lived as a "patient" in a mental hospital); or the use of subjects who falsify their perceptions in an experimental situation (Asch, 1951).

IV. Anthropological Models for the Study of Culture at a Distance

1. The Single Informant

The anthropologist has carried over into the study of culture at a distance
and of national character structure two sets of field procedures that have to be
understood if the use of interview materials in this method are to be understood. These are: (1) the use of single informants on a broken culture whose
members no longer function as a living society, and (2) the method of studying
a living culture by living in a community small enough so that every individual
in it can be known and every event that involves the whole community can be
recorded. The first is the method that was developed in the early days of work
with American Indians; the second has been used by British and American
anthropologists, particularly during the last thirty-five years, in the study of
living societies that either were still relatively intact or that had settled down
to a new, culture-contacted stability -- as is the case with many of the Indians
in the United States Southwest and in Central America. Although these
two methods have succeeded each other in time, some anthropologists have
used both -- either successively or because of the difference in the situations
of the peoples studied. [25] The use of the second method has tended to alter our
theory of the way the first should be used.

I propose to discuss the two methods as if the investigator were studying a
tribe from an area about which nothing had been written and as if he himself
were simply equipped with a general knowledge of what sorts of human cultural
behavior to look for. In the discussion of the single informant, I shall include
the use of several single informants; that is, representatives of a given van-
ished way of life who work individually with the anthropologist and who are not
related to one another in any way; i.e. the informants who have never been part
of the same social organization unit and have not shared the same event complex.

Each informant, then, must be considered individually. From an articulate,
willing, and verbal informant -- say a man of seventy who went on the last
buffalo hunt as a young man of twenty-five -- the anthropologist learned the
language and collected the general outlines of the culture and statements about
rituals and how they were performed, or else the names of rituals and such
statements about them as that "only the members of Clan X (or of the Y society,
or men who had had a vision of the Q) knew the secret of these rituals." If the

---

25. The following are examples of the anthropologists who have used both
     methods: Malinowski in his work on the Mailu (1915), where he did not
     speak the language and depended upon informants and interpreters, and
     his work on the Trobriands (1922, 1927, 1935); Reo Fortune's work in Dobu
     (1932a), using the second method, followed by his work on Omaha Indians
     (1932b), where he necessarily had to shift to the first; Alfred Métraux's
     work on Easter Island (1940) and his recent work in Haiti (1951).

informant could describe the ritual as one that had been taught him or the performance of which he had witnessed, this was positive cultural information -- always subject to various lacunae of uncertainty, for he might have heard about a ritual of another tribe, or he might have gone on a visit and have seen it in another camp circle. Considerations of <u>congruence</u> (how the ritual fitted with other cultural elements) and of <u>probability</u> (whether the informant had, as a boy, lived in an area where he could have seen rituals of other tribes) were both taken into account. [26]

If one has single informants who say that the punishment for murder, for instance, is ceremonial banishment, one would then ask for actual cases -- by name, clan, band, etc., and would place the instances cited carefully within the social structure and within the type of time record that the informant used. Surrounding episodes would be integrated with these accounts. However, from such statements it would still be possible only to state that informants related instances of banishment for murder. If in the course of further intensive interviewing murders were mentioned for which the murderer was not banished,

---

26. I shall quote here, in slightly abbreviated form, a statement in an unpublished manuscript by Ella Deloria, a Dakota Indian anthropologist trained by Franz Boas, as she evaluates a statement made by an aged Santee woman informant on wife-buying procedures, in terms of its credibility as compared with general usage among Yanktons, Santees, and Tetons:

"<u>Informant speaking:</u> It was very hard to be a young unmarried female in those days because of the restrictions under which girls lived. But they endured them without rebelling, not knowing anything else. Of course not every girl obeyed the rules.... Forget about them, I am not speaking about their kind.

"Let us suppose now that a worthy young man is ready to marry. He has achieved enough success to be reckoned a <u>man</u> and acquired enough property to start a home and family. So he sends gifts to the parents of the girl he has chosen. He has never talked with her....

"A paid messenger takes his gifts to the girl's home and leaves them outside the doorway. This is the first outward act. However, it is no surprise prise to the parents because messages have already been carried to and fro by the go-between, and an understanding reached.... [The girl] does not know what she will feel, for she has not seen the man. Until she does, she remains maidenly passive and deferential towards her parents' wise planning for her....

"The parents now reciprocate with return gifts sent to the man's tipi as a sign of acceptance.... Even if the preliminary steps had been kept secret, now, by the open exchange of gifts, the whole thing is publicized and the community becomes highly interested as it prepares for the ceremony. This becomes an active group affair in which as many young men and women as possible take part, forming two sections that will oppose each other in a sham battle over the girl. The women try to withhold her while the men help the groom to capture her. They make two lines facing each other, with the girl in the middle of the men. On signal the lines approach facing each other, but come to a halt at a distance. (Informant indicated what appeared to be about a hundred yards.)

"Suddenly, all the men make a dash after the girl while the women surround her and run away with her. There follows a wild struggle between protectors and pursuers. This always ends in the girl's being taken -- or there would be no marriage. Now here is the part that will amaze you.

and no informant could give an actual instance in which he or she had seen
banishment, this would also be taken into account. It would still not be safe to
say that banishment did not occur. Instead one could say: In this culture,
banishment is recognized as a punishment for murder, but informants could not
give any eyewitness accounts, although eyewitness accounts were given of other
types of punishment for murder.

In addition to checking on the informant's memory of actual occurrences,
and cross-checking among anecdotes and within the same genealogy (in time
the anthropologist gets to know both very well, so that he can relate a new
statement to "the winter Little Crow lost three horses," or can ask quickly:
"Was that your mother's younger brother?") the anthropologist learns the
personality of the informant as an informant -- which sorts of things he remembers and which he fails to observe, his conceits and biases, blind spots
and overemphases. Then each statement he makes can be qualified: "He would
not have noticed"; "He would have tended to blame the old men"; "He would have
taken the folklore version literally."

The man who succeeds in wresting the girl away from the women places
her on his back, as small children were carried, and starts to run with
her. Behind him run two men, each of whom shoulders one of her legs!
Thus she is borne prone to her husband. The rest of the men follow in a
triumphant procession. When the girl is delivered to her bridal tipi, the
marriage 'ceremony' is over. It would seem very funny and strange to
us. But in those days it was a great honor for a girl to be carried in this
way to her marriage....
I cannot say how long ago this custom was followed. My grandmother
told me. Her grandmother told her." [End of informan'ts narrative.]
Miss Deloria then comments:
"There are some startling differences here from the wife-buying already recorded. (1) All the frenzied and 'immodest' features -- rushing the
maiden though she is withheld from the males by the females, carrying
her off on a man's back, and especially with men holding her legs --
would be unthinkable in the typical Dakota marriage, where the bride
moved with utmost dignity and deliberation at all times. (2) The parents,
it appears, were the sole arbiters and the girl had no voice. There is no
indication that she was consulted at all. (3) They sent gifts back immediately as a sign of acceptance. (4) Large segments of the community took
part in the marriage. This especially is radically contrary to the procedure
as I have reported it, wherein the principals were left strictly to themselves
after their relatives had helped all they could with preparations.
"The narrator did not say this, but one may wonder if the way in which
the two sexes grouped and pitted against each other in a sham battle over
the bride might not be related to the custom of joking relatives opposing one
another with words only. If so, the modification of the custom tended
towards refinement. If we could know that those groups who actually fought
over the bride were joking relatives only, then this would be a reasonable
guess. We do not know this. The narrator did not know. To other Dakotas
with whom I discussed this story, it seemed utterly fantastic for men and
women to struggle in actual battle, even as a 'ceremony.' They were accustomed only to the casual bantering with their joking relatives. Even
the most careless do not lay hands on each other, as a rule. That is regarded as going too far."

Work with a good informant, even in a living culture where one is also participating in the ongoing life of the community and can draw upon half a hundred commentators on an event, runs into a great many intensive hours. In the end, when the anthropologist writes up his material, every statement attributed to the informant has been judged and weighed against the informant's life history and against internal congruence among his statements, has been cross-checked against the same genealogy and event sequences as these were referred to again and again, and has been qualified by a knowledge of the personality of the informant. In traditional anthropological work, only a modicum of this information is, or can be, published.[27]

Thus each informant is known to the anthropologist in a way to which the word "interview" -- as it is used by students of modern society -- gives no adequate clue. This is pointed up by questions frequently asked of the anthropologist: "On how many interviews is this material based?" or, "How many informants said this?" or, "How representative were your informants?" Each informant is a representative of his culture when his sex, family history, intelligence, type of experience in and outside his culture, and his relationship to the anthropologist are taken fully and properly into account. The word "interview," on the other hand, conjures up single sessions with different informants, each of whom is asked standardized questions about a subject on which the interviewer himself is not required to have special competence, and where all that is known about the respondent is the just-acquired data for the questionnaire sheet: age, sex, marital status, place of birth, and so on. The contrast in the relation to the informant in these two situations may also be compared to the difference between a letter written by an unknown person -- identified only by date and nationality -- in which it is said that Benjamin Franklin had made a speech of a given sort and a properly authenticated document of the speech itself. In this situation, one does not ask "How many documents?" but "What is the document?" The primary question in anthropological research is not "How many informants?" but "What kind of informants did you have?" And it seems better to state that in some forms of reconstructive ethnology, and in all work with single informants when a culture at a distance is being studied, the informant technique is used rather than to say that the work is based on interviewing.

One other very important difference between "work with a good informant" and "an interview" is worth stressing here. Where the emphasis is upon number of interviews, so that a sample may be obtained of characteristic responses of individuals who can be placed in special categories, in general the interviewer not only is not related to the respondent beyond the exigencies of the half-hour

27. I have published one such statement in the detailed description of the individuals who made up the village of Alitoa (Mead, 1947e).

or even four-hour interrogation, but he also is not related to the material about which he is inquiring. If a schedule is used, he will in time, of course, get used to the kind of answers that respondents of a given category may be expected to give and will then probe harder when an atypical answer is given. In the exploratory deep interview in which the expert interviewer is searching for categories for questionnaire-building, the interviewer will be looking for some kind of whole, but usually even this operation is necessarily short-lived and heavily affected by the requirement of breaking down whatever is perceived into a usable schedule. In contrast, the anthropologist, who works with an informant through long hours of following out leads and recording a great diversity of material, is trying to construct a picture of a whole. Each phrase -- "The old man kept a bundle, so I couldn't shout," or "But he couldn't go, he belonged to the other half," or "I was hungry while the others ate, because my brother-in-law was there" -- taken down as its occurs and recurs, suggests and may later confirm the formal structure of the sanctity of the tipis of men who keep sacred bundles, the presence of a dual organization, the custom of treating brothers-in-law with great respect, which includes not eating in their presence. And the informant likewise learns to take into account what the anthropologist knows and, over time, alters his statements to take more and more for granted. So from the first fortuitous statement that comes up as part of a folk tale or in a dictated text, through a systematic exploration to the time when the informant comments only, "He was his brother-in-law" -- that is, from the period when the informant is unaware that he is communicating, through the period when he and the anthropologist struggle to define what is communicated -- what is a bundle? or what is avoidance behavior? -- to the point at which the two work within this accepted and understood context, there is a steady progression. As the informant says, "You remember that Little Bear was his 'little father,'" or "You remember I told you about that man who disappeared in Prague in 1937," each tone of voice serves to build the picture more firmly. As the construction of the whole slowly emerges in his mind, the investigator reaches out and includes the new item, the new tone of voice, putting it in its place as it is given by an informant himself increasingly conscious of that whole.

This is the model of anthropologist-informant relationship, of the way Boas worked with George Hunt (1897), Radin with Crashing Thunder (1920), Ruth Bunzel with Nick (1932), and I myself with Unabelin (1949b).[28] The society within which each of us worked was broken down or was unknown in different degrees, and consequently discussions with informants were differently related to ongoing events that could be independently checked.

---

28. Unabelin came from a village I never visited.

Almost all anthropologists have one or more informants with whom they work on a given culture with great intensity over a long time, to whom they go to get difficult points elucidated, on whom they depend for long, complex accounts of ritual and mythology, for dictated texts, or for elaborate genealogies. This relationship becomes a model one to which all less intensive informant contacts are referred. Yet it is never certain that any member of the culture with whom one talks for the first time may not "become an informant," and furthermore, each item of information is habitually referred to the social placement of the speaker. This means that the single interview conducted by an anthropologist is different from the single interview in a series of single interviews by a professional interviewer in American society, although it has something in common with a first interview between a psychoanalyst and a possible patient. Each item of information -- conveyed by words, posture, tone -- is reacted to, checked, and put in place in relation to other knowledge of the culture, and helps to form a picture of the informant himself -- his social position, experience, ability to report, tendency to exaggerate or to slur, and so on. The interview is seen by the anthropologist, almost inevitably because of the model on which it is based, as a first interview in a long relationship and therefore -- even when it is an only interview -- it differs conspicuously from the interview that is accepted as a singleton. With these considerations in mind, it should be clear why the questions "How many informants?" or "How many interviews?" have to be considered in a very different context.

The question is less "How many?" than "What informants?" and "How good were they?" To the question, How many informants are necessary? the answer may be given: To build even a formal structural picture of a culture that is not seen -- either because it no longer exists or because it is inaccessible -- one needs at least one informant from each area of life the tone of which differs from other areas in the same culture. I say "tone" advisedly, because it may well be that there are twenty clans with twenty sets of secrets, but although the content will differ, the tone in which the secret is held will be the same. Then, to build a formal model of the culture, it is not necessary to know the actual content of all the clan secrets. If the informant can state his relationship to his own clan secrets and can provide evidence that this is duplicated in the others, one does not need an informant from each of the twenty clans. The major categories for each of which at least one informant is needed are: sex, age (that is, an informant should have experienced the different ages, so that an old man may report for a young one, but a young man can rarely report for an old one), class, caste, technically differentiated occupations (such as mining or fishing) or professions (priest, artist, and so on). For large cultures with subcultural regional differentiations, it is desirable to have informants from different villages or provinces to cancel out local elaborations; if these are missing, then the localization of any concrete information must be proportionately stressed.

One good informant is usually able to provide, over time, a diagram of the culture that will make clear to the anthropologist just how many kinds of informants he should have. Where no informant is available for a given category (no women, no shamans, no urban workers, no Roman Catholic priests, no army officers, no high officials in the NKVD), this lack is systematically allowed for in any statement about the whole. Information from the available informants is usually sufficient to indicate how serious the lack is. For example, if it is customary for laymen to witness religious ceremonies, the absence of an informant who is a religious practitioner is less serious when ceremonies are being discussed than it is in cultures where laymen do not witness ceremonies and all lay people speak only from hearsay. A first task in beginning work on a new culture is to delineate these areas and their degrees of inaccessibility, recognizing the while that certain types of inaccessibility will never be tapped by the informant method without observation on a living society. Behavior that is unverbalized and which only occurs in situations of interaction -- as, for example, the way in which the women who have been banished from a male ceremony behave when a boy enters the house -- is so unlikely to be given by an informant that it would be a waste of effort to try to get such material from informants directly.

When work is being done on a modern culture through the informant method, there is often one serious difficulty, in that the research worker knows something about the culture in question, may have traveled briefly in the country, and may have read novels, seen plays, and known members of the culture professionally, and so on. In order to attain the degree of sharpness of listening that makes every detail of an informant's account usable, it is desirable to have as complete ignorance as possible of the culture on which exploration is beginning. The experienced worker may to a degree approximate this blankness through previous experience in working on completely unknown cultures. For the less experienced, actual ignorance is desirable, even though it is admittedly a difficult condition to meet satisfactorily. [29]

We may now turn to the second anthropological model in which a small complete living community is used for analysis instead of the one or more well-placed and deeply known informants, each of whom is a representative of the way in which the culture is embodied in someone of that sociological position, experience, temperament, character structure, age, and sex. This second method is sometimes referred to as "participant observation," but the term can be misleading, as it suggests that the anthropologist becomes a part of the

29. In a research team studying a culture at a distance, the inclusion both of individuals who are naïve in the sense of being initially ignorant of the culture and of individuals who are members of the culture, but have not worked on cultural analysis, is a special development of this situation.

community in some inconspicuous and disguised form. Actually, the anthropologist who lives in a native community does become part of it, but in so doing
he changes the form of the community, provides new employment, new sources
of material objects; his house may become a sort of club -- "somewhere to go"
-- and his role as dispenser of simple medical remedies or recorder of
economic transactions may be fitted into the existing structure. What is essential, however, is that the anthropologist work for a consecutive stretch of time
within a community where the network of interrelationships can be known, and
the responses to events of people of different sociological categories and different personalities, individually and in groups, can be followed. Here one
learns to understand a culture not simply as it is embodied in individuals, but
in the society that functions through the cultural forms. Just as in exploratory
work with an individual informant knowledge of the culture and knowledge of the
individual informant proceed side by side, so also when one studies a living
society, knowledge of the actual people and their interrelationships and knowledge of the cultural forms within which they are acting proceed and unfold together. Information about an individual is interpreted against two types of information -- the knowledge that a certain man "lives in the last house in the
village," and that "widowers who live alone are believed to be sorcerers."
It is possible then to study such problems as retrospective falsification by comparing informants' accounts of events that were actually witnessed at the time
and six months later, or by rechecking the reasons people gave why they
attended a ceremony, and so on. This is, of course, the ideal way to study a
culture, especially if it is possible to return at intervals of about ten years over
a period of thirty or forty years. [30]

This Manual will include a short section on the basic procedures followed
in the study of the small community because, like the models of working with
individual informants, they form a model for work on culture at a distance, and
because there is no systematic statement in print, except as methods are
stated in isolated monographs that are read only by anthropologists. If one has
to learn a culture and to know a community together, then when there is no
community but only material on the culture, a model of the possible community
is present in one's mind, guiding one's questions, structuring one's imagination
in a way that is less likely to occur if the worker has never studied a living
community. [31]   Furthermore, working within living communities enormously
increases one's ability to use informants who can be observed interacting not

---

30. Clyde Kluckhohn's Navaho studies have been carried on for almost a quarter
    of a century in order to provide this kind of background depth.
31. A case in point is the work of the East European Jewish group, in which
    the social structure of the shtetl, the small Jewish community, was recon-
    structed from informants' accounts. For examples of work by the East
    European Jewish group in this Manual, cf. Part Three, pages 123-31;
    Part Four, pages 198-205; and Part Nine, pages 386-89. Cf. also
    Zborowski and Herzog (1952).

only with the anthropologist, but also with their relatives, wives, equals, superiors, and subordinates -- each observation forming a context within which the information given as an informant can be checked. The difference in the utilization is comparable to that between a patient whose life situation is known only through psychiatric interviews and one on whom careful social case work has been done in which home visits have been included.

For the research worker who has had experience within living communities and who subsequently works only with the individual informant, this earlier experience becomes one facet of his later work with informants. However, all methodological statements about the relationship between the account of a culture that can be built up by working with selected informants and that which can be arrived at by living in a community and making a set of supporting observations -- all these must be made at present on the basis of anthropological experience with different cultures, with different types of situations. An experiment that might (and might not) be crucial would be to conduct two simultaneous investigations of one modern culture upon which no work of this type had been done (for example, a modern Latin American culture), sending an individual or a team into the field and matching the work done with a study made by an individual or a team at a distance where only individual informants and written and other types of cultural products were available for analysis. Yet while such an experiment might increase the acceptability of the methods used to study culture at a distance as well as our knowledge of the pitfalls inherent in studying a particular kind of culture at a distance, it must still be recognized that there are very great differences among cultures in their susceptibility to verbal report. An extensive use of moving pictures and plastic as well as graphic cultural products might in part compensate for this difference between cultures. It would, however, be unfortunate if the search for higher credibility should result in any insistence upon standardization of method that would destroy the essence of this approach -- the capacity of trained investigators to adapt themselves to a new culture by using, in each case, methods of investigation that must also be partly new.

2. The Study of Living Communities

A section on the study of living communities is included in this Manual not because culture at a distance can ever be studied in this way, but because it is the accepted anthropological field method and, as such, provides a model against which the substitute and necessarily less satisfactory methods for studying culture at a distance can be measured. It is a method that could conceivably be applied to the study of small enclaves of immigrants; but it has not yet been demonstrated how fruitful for these purposes the study of such small enclaves can be. Most such enclaves are nonrepresentative of the emigration from a country, and are held together by religious sect ties or by peculiar ex-

ploitive arrangements, or in some other way. In the United States, less so in
Canada, the maintenance of the enclave is, in a sense, socially abnormal. No
study has yet been made comparing the advantages of using individual informants of many kinds or of working in an enclave situation for the study of culture
at a distance.

The first step in the study of a living community in which the network of
relationships among identified persons is to be mapped is to demarcate the
community, clearly and definitely. The ideal situation is a village of less than
500 people; a larger number is virtually impossible to handle. The village
should be sufficiently isolated from other villages so that all entrances by
members of other villages and all trips to other villages can be matters of
comment. The community chosen should also have as much economic, social,
and political autonomy as is congruent with its representativeness for the
culture as a whole. The actual structure of the village will be a significant
factor in the size of the group the fieldworker can manage -- for the closer and
more compactly the people live, the more events can be followed (e.g. if there
is only one road through a village, the anthropologist can build his house in the
middle of the village, on this road, and all strangers must pass his door). [32]
Events in a village located in a lagoon and approached by canoe are far more
difficult to keep track of (e.g. village of Peri, Admiralty Islands). [33] A village
that has several formal exits (e.g. Bajoeng Gedé, in Bali)[34] is midway in ease
of work between a lagoon village and a village with a single entrance. If there
are courtyards that are surrounded by high walls, or if life is lived inside
closed doors, it will require more work to keep track of fewer people. These
are the kinds of consideration that have to borne in mind when the village is
initially chosen; in addition, one must consider the place of the village in relation to other villages -- whether it is placed centrally or near a border, how
it is related to larger administrative units, and so on.

Once chosen, the village, or, where this is impossible, the ward or neighborhood, to be studied must be investigated to see what categories of observation can be made inclusive. Some are, of course, quite simple. The village
must be mapped to scale and all residences, as well as any other buildings --
men's house, temple, post office -- must be noted. Roads, lanes, and customary rights of way must be indicated. A census must be taken of each household,
and the genealogical connections between households must be worked out. [35]
Not only must the relationships between households -- by location, consanguin-

---

32. For the plan of a village of this type, cf. Mead (1938), Fig. 25, Plan of
     Alitoa Village (p. 236).
33. Cf. Mead (1930), Appendix V. Diagram of the village showing house owner-
     ship, clan membership, residence (pp. 327-31).
34. Cf. Bateson and Mead (1942), Plate 1. Bajoeng Gedé: Village and temples
     (pp. 56-57). Cf. also Mead and Macgregor (1951), Chapter III, Part 1.
35. Cf. Radcliffe-Brown (1930) for a convenient cursive method of recording
     genealogies in field notes.

ity, and marriage -- be worked out, but also the body of information that must
be known about each household must be distinguished. This information will
vary for each culture studied, but should include landownership, occupation,
offices held in the village or in wider structures, the origin of each individual
(native to the village, married in, an immigrant, etc.), religious and club affiliations, rank, caste, and so on. In one community it may be important to know
who keeps a "god" in the house temple; in another, who owns a horse; in a
third, which houses have menstrual huts; in a fourth, which houses have elec-
tricity; in a fifth, who has made a pilgrimage to Mecca. Whatever categories
are determined upon as relevant, these must then be included in the data on
every single household in the community. The community itself, as a whole,
is taken as a suitable sample -- of its type -- of the whole culture and of the
functioning of the society at the village level. Within the village, the basis of
the network must then be evenly mapped.

The same principle must be adopted in relation to the event sequence that
is recorded. In one village, every birth will affect the whole village; in others,
a birth may be so unimportant that it is almost impossible to persuade the
people that one wants to hear about it. In the first, a record of every birth as
it occurs will be needed; in the second, one gets as good records of birth as
one can. In some cultures, the arrival of any stranger will have repercussions
throughout the community; in others, strangers come and go unheeded. An act
of magic or divination may be relevant to the whole group, or it may be entirely
private. The anthropologist records every event he hears of until he finds
which are the events of which he may expect to be able to get a complete record. These, then, are almost by definition the events of which cognizance is
taken by the whole community, so that if one is working in close touch with
people somewhere in the village, one is bound to hear about them. Once it has
been determined which events are important and are practicable to record,
then all events of that category must be recorded, and any lapses in the recording procedure -- due to absence or illness -- should also be noted. An event
sequence over a limited period of time is thus set up within which one can place
each note, each informant's comment, each narration of a myth, or photograph
of a temper tantrum. All records can then be made against time, with a diary
which serves as an index. If photographs are used, the time of putting a film
into the camera and of taking it out is recorded on the tail of the film or on the
Cine film box, so that these form a continuous record and can also be fitted
into the time sequence. Then any statement that is subsequently made about
the culture can be placed in terms of a group whose relationships at a given
level, in space and over time, are known.

Within this larger structure, smaller segments may be selected for
minute analysis. Out of 100 courtyards, five may be mapped in finer detail.
Out of ten death ceremonies, one may be recorded in far more detail than

others. Out of twenty-five performances of the same trance club, the process
of going in and coming out of trance in two may be recorded -- not in minutes,
but in seconds. But each ceremony, each courtyard, each behavior at a birth,
is studied in this context, so that it can be referred to a whole that is systematically known at a defined level. This makes it possible for certain kinds of
negative statements to have meaning -- as when an informant says that dual
marriage to sisters, or turning over land to the eldest son, is the custom, but
a complete survey of the whole village by the anthropologist reveals not a
single case where this has actually been done.

The anthropologist thus selects a spatial situation that is as self-contained
as is practical in terms of his goals. Within this self-contained situation, over
a specified length of time, he creates a homogeneous framework for his observations. He still remains dependent upon the occurrence of death, birth,
marriage, crime, misfortune, for a chance to see certain manifestations of the
culture, but whatever he does see, he can place in context.

Such a system makes it possible to pick at random a photograph out of a
large series and supply from one's notes the particular context in which it was
taken, who was there, what was happening, what else was happening on the same
day, what had happened the week before of village-wide importance in the same
family, and so on. Such questions as "Was the child's nervousness to be attributed to the illness of the grandmother who died on the second day of that week?"
can be explored retrospectively, as the death of the grandmother will also have
been recorded. An informant's account of suspicions of his wife on a given
occasion can be correlated with notes which mentioned that the wife had slipped
out of a group at a ceremony on that day. A dream can be tied in with a quarrel
in a neighbor's house. The choice of detail that is filled out within the framework depends upon the specific culture and also upon the problem and the style
of the investigator. What remains constant is the systematic provision of a
framework in time and space.

All events that occur outside the village network, however much impact
they may have upon it, are treated as external to the system, so that news that
someone has died in another village is a relevant item, but the anthropologist
will not expect to go to the other village to confirm the death. A rumor that
there is an epidemic in another part of the island, in response to which special
exorcist ceremonies are held, is important, but whether such an epidemic was
raging or not is not treated as of the same order of relevance. This is equally
true of events that happened outside -- that is, happened before -- the period of
investigation. An informant's statement that five years ago his father, now
dead, beat him is an item of information about the informant at the time of
speaking and is not comparable with the anthropologist's observation of a man
beating a child. A statement made to the anthropologist that last week his
father threatened to beat him is of yet a different order. The anthropologist

can see the father, he can talk with the father, he can observe other behavior of the informant, and of the informant and his father. He will, however, still not know whether such a threat took place, but the informant's statement about the threat will have a better temporal contextual quality. [36]

The essence of the study of a living community is that it provides multi-faceted material, so that report, observation, retrospective comment, the difference between oratio obliqua and oratio recta, explicit social behavior and inarticulate social behavior, can all be integrated. It is a living model, so recorded that the as yet unanalyzed variables are faithfully retained. To the anthropologist with field training who must work with partial material, with fragments, the model of the living community is like the paleontologist's systematic view of the skeleton of a type of extinct animal; when he is confronted with a few bones, he is able to reconstruct the animal with a fair chance of accuracy.

---

36. In the study of culture at a distance, individual informants often make statements about the history and politics of their country which have no more standing than such a reported act of a father, now dead, in a New Guinea society. The anthropologist will treat them in the same way, placing the comments against his knowledge of the informant, as material on the way such an informant sees his history, not as expert objective reporting by a trained person. The content of the statement, may, however, sound very similar to the expert report, and the critic, acquainted with what he believes to be the facts, as agreed upon by the experts in the field, will feel that the entire anthropological report is discredited because the investigator has listened to such "incorrect" statements. Or the psychiatrist or clinician, unschooled in handling social data except introspectively, may report such statements by informants as if they had been validated by the accepted social-science methods. It is important to keep clear that when, for example, a Soviet displaced person reports that before he or she ran away or became permanently disaffected, all the military, or all the officers, or all the NKVD, or all the commissars, etc., had already run away -- this is not interpreted as a statement about who ran away, but as a statement about the type of justification that ex-Soviet citizens advance when they say that they themselves did run away. This is not even a statement that the anthropologist accepts the informant's claim that he did run away, but rather a statement that when such a displaced person claimed to have run away, he also claimed that higher responsible officials had run away first.

PART TWO

NATIONAL CHARACTER

NATIONAL CHARACTER: THEORY AND PRACTICE

Geoffrey Gorer

I

The term "national character" suffers from considerable ambiguity, in great part owing to the historical situation in which the term was first introduced. The initial studies that were labeled studies in national character were made under the stress of World War II, when practical aims (e.g. a framework for psychological warfare) were more urgent than theoretical precision. The term has persisted, despite its ambiguities and imprecision, for want of a clearer alternative. "National" must be understood as referring to a society possessing a culture at an identified space and an identified time, and not necessarily to a nation-state. "Social character" would be more accurate, but the term is already in current usage to designate the stimulus value of an individual (or individuals) in contact with his fellows. "Basic character" and similar terms carry a suggestion of primacy that does not seem to be warranted by the available facts or theories.

The term "national character" would appear to carry three connotations, which are partly complementary and partly contrasting:

1. National character isolates and analyzes the principal motives or predispositions which can be deduced from the behavior of the personnel of a society at a given time and place.

2. National character describes the means by which these motives and predispositions are elicited and maintained in the majority of the new members who are added to the society by birth, so that a society continues its culture longer than a single generation.

3. National character also refers to the ideal image of themselves in the light of which individuals assess and pass judgment upon themselves and their neighbors, and on the basis of which they reward and punish their children, for the manifestation or nonmanifestation of given traits and attitudes.

Considerable confusion, which will not be completely clarified in this paper, has resulted from the fact that the term "national character" carries these different connotations, above all that it refers both to the analysis of observed behavior (connotation 1), which tends to be phrased in concepts that are partly or completely unknown to the actors (unconscious motives), and also to the description of ideal behavior (connotation 3), which is by definition known to the actors, and concerning which they are, or can be, fully articulate. The relationship between ideals and conduct is not a simple one; for although they do not usually coincide in a one-to-one relationship, the ideal may be considered

57

to influence conduct both in the choice of alternatives of behavior and in the negative judgments by the self and/or others (guilt, shame, ostracism, or other sanctions) when conduct deviates sharply from ideals.

Furthermore, the ideal character is the chief conscious criterion used by adults in the education (socialization) of children, in the meting out of praise or blame, reward or punishment, and thence in influencing the development, both conscious and unconscious, of the growing child and so impinging on connotation 2. National character (connotations 1 and 2) cannot be fully described without taking into account the ideal character (connotation 3). Confusion is likely to occur if a description is partly in terms of connotation 1, the analysis of behavior, and partly in terms of connotation 3, ideals; and also if in connotation 3, ideals are described as if they were identical with behavior (connotation 1).

It would of course be desirable to have three separate terms for these different connotations; but a short paper such as this does not seem the appropriate place for the introduction of neologisms. Within the scope of this paper, the phrase "national character" without qualifications is intended to carry connotation 1 only. Connotation 2 is nearly always made clear by its context, by its reference to infants, children, or education. The epithet "ideal" will be introduced to designate connotation 3.

II

National character is considered to be an integral aspect of social anthropology. It describes the organization of motives and predispositions within a society, as other aspects of social anthropology describe the organization of persons and objects in patterned behavior (institutions). Since the term "culture" carries even more ambiguous connotations than the term "national character," it would seem useful to define the way in which I intend to use the term.

I define culture as primarily mental or psychological, as nonbiological learned behavior ultimately derivable from the nerves and brain cells of the personnel comprising a given society at a given time. This does not mean that material objects are excluded from the concept of culture, but the various activities that transform, say a lump of clay into a decorated pot, take place if, and only if, a living person has learned the requisite skills and then externalizes what he has learned. Consequently I reject the Platonic or quasi-Platonic concept of culture that has been held by so many of the most distinguished anthropologists; in this Platonic concept culture is treated as though it had a transcendental existence of a different nature from that of the persons who manifest a given culture at a given time, and culture dictates or forbids, approves or condemns, activities in a quasi-supernatural manner. Such sentences seem to me to be either tautologous or meaningless.

Cultural behavior is learned behavior. For purposes of discussion, learning can be divided into two categories: (1) learning situations in which certainly the teacher and usually the pupil are conscious and can be articulate about what is being taught, and (2) learning that is not articulate or verbalized, which the teacher (if there is one) may not be conscious of teaching, and which may not be imparted or deliberately conceptualized as a total concept. A simple illustration could be the acquisition of the vocabulary and the syntax of one's native language. The vocabulary is consciously taught; answers are given to the child's questions What is this? or What does that mean? but the syntax is never taught at all, and is indeed very seldom articulately known. Faults of syntax may be corrected in an arbitrary fashion, because "they sound wrong" or "people don't talk like that"; but the overwhelming bulk of humanity acquire the syntax of their native language completely and accurately without being able to be in any way articulate concerning what they have learned or taught, ignorant of the rules and exceptions they exemplify, and indeed without being aware that syntax exists.

If this analogy can be carried a little further, the studies of national character so far made have been overwhelmingly studies of psychological syntax, of the regularities and modifications underlying observable behavior, and the way in which these regularities are acquired. The study of the acquisition of vocabulary -- of habits and skills concerning which teacher and taught could be articulate -- is an equally legitimate object of study; but, with the partial exception of Bateson and Mead's Balinese Character (1942), it has not been pursued by those anthropologists who have made studies of national character.

In common with all the other branches of sociology and anthropology (with the exception of physical anthropology), the scientific results of the study of national character consists of a series of normative statements. A normative statement does not imply universality, is not meant to be applicable to every member of the society being investigated; it does imply that members of a given society at a given place and at a given time act consistently in relation to certain norms or ideals of behavior, which may or may not be explicit. If an anthropologist reports that a society practices polygyny, has matrilocal residence, has decorated pottery, and consults oracles, this does not imply that every male has more than one wife, that every male lives in his wife's house, that every artisan paints designs on clay pots, or that everybody consults oracles before every undertaking. It implies at most that those practices are performed by some of the members of the society and are accepted by the remainder, that such actions are positively sanctioned, and that others are, or might be, negatively sanctioned. Similarly, statements about national character try to define and isolate those attitudes and predispositions which are manifested by the most representative and approved-of members of the society the nonmanifestation of which in others is criticized or punished.

Cultures are described by normative sentences. The anthropologist treats his observations of objects, of behavior, of relationships, and the statements he has recorded, as items in a series; from each series he derives the type; and

the sentences in which he defines or describes the type contribute to the
description of the culture.

All cultural statements are normative statements. Illustrations that
demonstrate a range of variation have relevance only in reference to an expressed or implied norm. If this were not the case, the description of a culture
would be impossible, for the observations that any anthropologist can make on
any subject are only an infinitesimal sample of the number of similar observations that could be made during the existence of a society.

Every normative sentence involves the problem of establishing a type for
the series in question. Although this problem arises every time a scientific
statement is made, few scientists are explicit about the techniques they use for
this operation. There are in fact a variety of such techniques.

Historically, the earliest method for establishing a type was to pronounce
the first example seen, collected, or fully described as the type, establishing
the type by primacy only. This was the method used by the pioneer botanists
and zoologists of the eighteenth century, and it has never been entirely discarded; thus one of the scientific losses of World War II was the destruction
of several German botanical collections that contained many "type specimens."
This method is still used in certain branches of anthropology, notably paleontology; most of the disputes that vex the students of early man are concerned
with the relationship of newly found specimens to the type specimens. When
units in the series are rare, the employment of this method is almost inevitable.
In cultural anthropology this method is no longer in general use; in earlier days
it was employed for such phenomena as totemism, matriarchy, and similar un-
European social devices; discussions of "atypical" or "atrophied" totemism and
the like refer implicitly to the type specimen fully described.

The second method that was evolved for establishing the type for a series
may be called the "arithmetic" method. When members of a series differ from
one another in a single measurable feature, or in a number of measurable
features all of which are directly correlated with one another, it is possible to
discover the mean object by measurement and establish that as the type. This
is the method used by most physical anthropologists, and is applicable to such
physical characteristics as height or hair color, and to the psychological
characteristics that are susceptible to measurement, such as tone discrimination or rating on the Stanford-Binet tests. In point of fact, it is extremely rare
in the organic world to find a series in which all the variables are directly
correlated, and the "arithmetic" type can be established only by ignoring all the
variables except the one under discussion. If there are two or more independent variables susceptible to measurement, and if all are exemplified by all
the members of the series, it is possible to determine arithmetically the mean
for each variable, and then to establish as the type the unit that exhibits all the
means. Or if, as commonly happens, such a unit does not exist, the scientist

describes an ideal unit exhibiting all the means. In such a case the type established for the series does not correspond with any single member of the series. This type may perhaps be called the "platonic" type. It is a method much used in archeology and by students of material culture. It is also in increasing use among modern physical anthropologists.

Cultural anthropologists have developed a special variation of the "platonic" type for series of which each member displays some features in common and some idiosyncratic features, by establishing the type as a combination of all the features that are present in any of the members, so that the type is more complex than any member of the series. Thus the kinship system that an anthropologist establishes for a given society is likely to have more features or categories than any of the family units that make up the series for which he is establishing the type.

Finally, there are those series in which the variables are not susceptible to mensuration; or in which there are so many variables that mensuration is not practicable; or in which each member demonstrates a number of idiosyncratic features as well as certain features in common. Archeologists and anthropologists dealing in material culture are faced with this problem as soon as the artifacts become complex or "artistic"; for example, if they are dealing with elaborately patterned textiles or basketwork, or decorated pots. In such cases the type is established by aesthetic judgment, either immediate or considered. Greek, Chinese, and Peruvian pottery, to take well-known examples, are so varied in form or decoration that practically every object is unique; but specialists in these objects have established a number of series and types, so that there is comparatively rarely any dispute concerning the assignment of a new specimen to a given series located in space and time. The type for these series generally contains fewer features than any single member of the series; it is generally determined by a combination of features, and not a summation; and this combination of features is apprehended aesthetically, either immediately and without verbalization, or after consideration.

Since social activities cannot by their nature be materially and contemporaneously before the eyes of the anthropologist, the apprehension of the psychological patterns that underlie social behavior must be considered. But as a concept, the analysis of national character has much in common with the analysis of, say, the style of decorated pottery. The type (the national character) possesses fewer features than any member of the series (the individual characters composing the society being studied); and this type is determined by the combination of features and not by their summation; it is the combination that determines the unique character, for each separate feature may be found in other societies. The apprehension of national character, like the apprehension of style, is probably dependent on the presence of certain idiosyncracies and sensitivities of which the origin is so far as obscure as, for example, that of a "true" ear. Without a true ear, no amount of application will enable a researcher to record non-European music, or the phonemes of a strange tongue; but neither will the true ear record these without application and study. For the study of national character a quasi-aesthetic ability to recognize pattern is probably a prerequisite; but this ability can be adequately exercised only within the framework of cultural anthropology and individual psychology.[1]

III

The study of national character resembles, then, all the other branches of social anthropology in that it presents its conclusions in normative sentences phrased by the investigator. These sentences define the type the anthropologist has derived from the series of data collected by him in the field. The method by which data are assigned to one or more series is ultimately dependent on the anthropological hypotheses employed by the investigator.

None of the accepted hypotheses and none of the conventional types of data are rejected by the student of national character. There are, however, two further principles that are fundamental to this type of research, one of which is not stressed (though tacitly acknowledged) in social anthropology without an interest in national character, and the second of which is often disputed. These are the principle of social continuity and the principle of congruence.

The principle of social continuity is one of the basic postulates of anthropology, the fact that societies continue though their personnel changes. This carries the implication that the characters and the predispositions of the new recruits to the society do not differ in any marked or consistent degree from those whose ranks they join or whose places they fill. If there were marked and consistent differences in character and predisposition in each generation, one would expect continual oscillations in the form and the function of the component institutions of all societies, and continuous conflict between generations. Observation shows that both these situations are uncommon; the statement that "you can't change human nature," which has been reported in different forms from so many societies, suggests that the universal experience is that character and predispositions are less amenable to permanent alteration than social forms and institutions. This should not be taken to imply that national character and shared predispositions are immutable; but it seems more usual for change to be gradual than for it to be sudden and catastrophic. The chief exception to this generalization would appear to be those societies which induce in the majority of their members wishes that cannot be gratified for the majority of members within the existing social institutions. Thus if a society develops as a necessity for self-esteem the accumulation of property, and possesses social institutions or natural resources of such a nature that the majority cannot accumulate property

---

1.   I am indebted to Professor Cornelius Osgood of Yale University for drawing my attention to the problem of establishing types, and also for many ideas in the preceding paragraphs.

to the degree necessary for self-esteem, one could then expect sudden changes in institutional forms that might be followed by changed wishes concerning accumulation.

It is on the basis of social continuity that the assumption is made that in any given society (or portion of society, where the society is large enough to be differentiated by regions or classes or a combination of both) the observable adults shared experiences and vicissitudes of childhood similar to those which observable infants and children are now undergoing; and further, that observable infants and children will grow up to have shared predispositions and characters similar to those of the observable adults. This assumption of recapitulation would seem to be the basic assumption of the study of national character, and is the assumption that divides the study of national character from the study of individual psychology. In the study of the individual, childhood experiences have to be reconstituted by anamnesic material from the individual and from those older people who may have been witnesses of his experiences; in the study of national character -- of the predispositions common to members of a society -- it is assumed (a) that these shared adult predispositions are related to shared earlier experiences, and (b) that these shared earlier experiences are of the same nature as those experiences now being shared by the contemporary infants and children. This postulate is at present unproved; but it would be capable of proof or disproof if societies in which the vicissitudes of childhood and the predispositions of adults have been adequately described were to be revisited after the lapse of a generation.

The principle of congruence is a convenient label for the fact (first demonstrated by Ruth Benedict) that the goals of the various institutions which make up a society are coherently related to one another; that if the end results of institutional activities are inspected, they will be seen to fall into patterns in which a small number of themes are dominant; that if the results of the activities of the personnel are inspected, they will be seen to gratify a relatively small number of wishes besides those biologically necessary for survival and reproduction. These themes or wishes are congruent with one another; that is to say, they are not mutually contradictory in their results, nor do they demand sudden changes in predisposition as the personnel moves from institution to institution. When changes in predisposition are demanded for change of status or for certain specialized institutions, they are habitually induced by socially organized withdrawal and retraining; when formalized, such retraining is labeled rite de passage.

In complex societies, or societies in rapid transition, it may happen that one institution may demand behavior and predispositions that are incongruous with the behavior and predispositions demanded from the remaining institutions; in such a case one can expect the incongruous institution to be explicitly resented and the personnel involved to be in emotional conflict, with the probable

development of neurotic symptoms. An example of such an incongruous institution would be the demand for strict superordination and subordination in the
army of a society whose other institutions stressed egalitarianism.

The establishment and recognition of congruence in varied situations and
activities, and the verbalization of the themes or predispositions such congruence illustrates, form probably the most disputed aspect of "national
character" social anthropology, and the one which excites most indignation and
repudiation from other anthropologists. The perception of congruence (it may
be admitted) involves an intuitive, or quasi-aesthetic, technique of analysis,
and so is to a certain extent dependent on idiosyncratic gifts; but so is any
other branch of anthropology. And although aesthetic perception is not consistently employed in other types of social anthropology, it has long been in
respected use in certain aspects of archeology and the study of material culture.

IV

To obtain the data from which the national character of a society can be
deduced, all the habitual skills and techniques of social anthropology are useful,
but the most essential are skill in interviewing and conscientiousness in recording. The skilled interviewer will be able to elicit expressions of spontaneous emotion as well as formal statements from his informants, and the
conscientious recorder will note these, however inexplicable or insignificant
they may appear at the time. It is to a great extent by such spontaneous
emotional expressions -- eagerness, embarrassment, secretiveness, boasting,
laughter, etc. -- that clues can be discovered which will indicate the chief
areas of emotional stress, especially those areas where the demands of social
conformity conflict with individual wishes. In the course of a field trip the
equivalent of a psychological and sociological case history can be built up for
each informant -- ideally for each individual in the community being studied.
The language in which such notes are made is a matter of individual preference
and skill; but as a general rule I feel it preferable not to employ technical
terms derived from the psychological studies of individuals in our society:
I think it preferable to note "X enjoys telling tales of cruelty" rather than
"X enjoys sadistic fantasies," "Y seems to want to order people about" rather
than "Y has marked authoritarian traits." Although such notes lack the appearance of scientific precision, they permit a flexibility of interpretation that the
more technical terms inhibit.

It seems to be a general experience with anthropologists that the most
willing informants are in some measure deviants from the cultural norm,
whether this deviance be psychological or sociological. The person who finds
most interest in talking to foreigners and giving up his time to them is likely
to be a person who for some reason or other does not find adequate satisfactions in his own position in his own society. Consequently there is always a

risk that the individual(s) whom the fieldworker knows most intimately will not be representative of the community as a whole. Thus among the Lepchas (Gorer, 1938) my most willing and articulate informant, Kurma, had had an unusual early life -- he had been adopted as a small boy and then had run away from his adoptive parents -- and manifested a desire to assert himself and appear of importance that was not in any way typical of his fellows. As an informant on the formal aspects of his culture he was extremely clear and precise, but his emotional responses and judgments were idiosyncratic rather than typical.

Where they can be elicited, judgments on the conduct of others -- whether they are members of the same society or of alien societies -- are extremely revealing; they indicate both the ideals the speakers have of themselves and often the fears they have of their own impulses; for the greatest indignation is often shown for the greatest (albeit unconscious) temptation. Similarly, the occasions for jokes and the subjects for laughter, the origin, development, and reconciliation of quarrels, the changing friendliness or formality of relations between identified individuals, all contribute important psychological data.

Such briefly is the additional material the student of national character needs to collect in the field. I have stressed the term "additional," for such material can only be interpreted against a background of the social structure and normative institutional behavior of the society under investigation. An analysis of the psychological functions of an institution can be performed only when the institution has been thoroughly described; and it is the institutions, the social structure, that determine the framework within which both national and individual character must be manifested.

By the psychological function of an institution I mean the way in which the institution is envisaged by the personnel and the expectations or predispositions that the personnel bring to it. Thus the Lepchas shared with many of their neighbors elaborate rules of levirate and sororate marriage and potential marriage partners; they interpreted these rules as devices for protecting the weak against the strong, the younger against the older. About a generation ago they imported cardemum as a money crop from their neighbors the Nepali, together with the religious observances deemed necessary for its successful cultivation. Among the Nepali the women are considered ritually unclean when menstruating, and a menstruating woman will blast the cardamum crop if she enters the field. Among the Lepchas, where the women suffer under no other ritual disadvantages, this prohibition was adopted; but the Lepchas gave as an explanation the fact that the cardamum dislikes all strong smells; it would also wilt if soap or onions were taken into the field. Thus, although formally the religious observations connected with cardamum cultivation stressed the blasting effect of women among both the Nepali and the Lepchas, the psychological function of the prohibition among the former reinforced the general attitude towards women as an inferior and dangerous group, whereas among the latter it was reduced to a rule of horticulture that in no way reflected on women outside the specific situation. Similarly, the men's secret tamberan cult, which exists in many cultures in New Guinea, can have the psychological function of keeping the uninitiated women and children in terror and subjection, or that of protecting the uninitiated women and children from supernatural dangers; it can be used by the older members as an excuse for humiliating and exploiting the younger, or as a means of succor and education.

The psychological functions of institutions are basic data for the analysis of national character. Indeed, Dr. Ruth Benedict (1934, 1946a, 1946b, 1949) relied almost entirely on this aspect of analysis, stressing particularly the different psychological functions of formally similar institutions within a culture area. It is particularly through the psychological functions of institutions that the previously mentioned principle of congruence is demonstrated.

As the field work continues, the psychological functions of the institutions can be phrased with increasing precision and clarity, the ideal personality for each age and sex (and possibly class and region) that people use as a model for themselves and a standard by which to judge others will become increasingly clear and full, emotional responses will indicate areas of tension and concentration, and the case histories or descriptions of individuals will show the range of personality within the society and particularize the more approved from the less approved, the well-adapted from the deviant; and as these components become clear, tentative statements can be made concerning the shared motives or predispositions operative in the members of the society.

The ideal would be for such statements to be made in fairly definitive form before the field trip is completed, or, even better, in an interval between field trips, so that the formulations could be tested against subsequent behavior; but in most cases there are many practical difficulties in the way, and it may be only after notes have been studied at leisure that important generalizations can be made. Thus in my own case I did not realize till some months after being in the field that the most deviant Lepchas had all been adopted as children, and that of the six men who had been adopted in childhood, five were markedly maladjusted. The discovery of this fact made me reconsider all my material on the relations between parents and growing children (among the Lepchas adoption normally took place between the ages of seven and nine) and illumined the seeming contradiction of the independence of boys of this age with the dependence most of the younger adult men tended to show. My notes were full enough for me to venture a reformulation with some feeling of security; but how much more satisfactory it would have been if I could have checked this reformulation against further observation.

So far, I have made no mention of the observation of children. I believe that it is possible to get all the essential data for an analysis of national character from the observation and analysis of adult behavior within the social structure. If this information is full and detailed enough, it should be possible to reconstitute with considerable accuracy the vicissitudes of childhood, whereas it is impossible to interpret the outcome of childhood experiences without a knowledge of the social structure. The observation of childhood training lessens the area of speculation, and may suggest potentialities that the social structure does not develop, the possible psychological dynamics of change.

Technically, the observation of children and their treatment in primitive society differs from similar observations in our own society only in detail. The language, the composition of the food, the clothes, the household arrangements, are obviously different, but the techniques of observing and noting what is done to the child and how it responds are similar. Of course, both the treatment and the response may be without analogue in our own society; but though this may make for complexities of theoretical implications, it should not impinge on the field work.

I think the employment of tests -- whether standardized or open-ended -- insofar as they are related to universal growth patterns and an approximation to laboratory conditions, is legitimate in the study of primitive children, and has the usefulness of providing fully comparable data. With adults, I am more doubtful of the utility of tests; with the exception of the Rorschach and its derivatives nearly all current psychological tests are culture-limited, and the application of tests would seem to risk distorting the anthropologist's relationship with his informants to the detriment of all other field work.

In the observation of primitive children it is especially important to keep the principle of social continuity in mind. Few field trips last much more than twelve months to two years, and so it is generally impossible to observe the same children in all the different phases of maturation. Consequently, if there is marked contrast in the behavior of groups of children of different ages (or ordinal position in the family), it is necessary to be very alert for the experiences that may motivate such transformations. These may be of short duration, and may or may not be formalized. Thus among the Navaho children as described by Leighton and Kluckhohn (1947), the change from infantile optimism to childish withdrawal seems to be mediated by the sudden weaning and banishment from the parental home for a few days. Among the Hopi, as suggested by Simmons (1942), a pantomime of physical castration, performed by an older man standing in the relationship of a "joking" grandfather, would seem to play a similarly important role.

The data of the returned fieldworker can then be divided into three categories: (1) the psychological functions of the institutions, (2) the emotional response of the adults, and (3) the experiences and vicissitudes of the children. It is then a matter of trial and error in analyzing and interpreting these data so as to arrive at statements that can link the obervations together and account for the exceptions and deviations. These statements should preferably follow the principle of economy, and should be compatible with accepted theories of human motivation. They should be so phrased that they can be applicable to a wider range of situations and experiences than those observed during the field trip. If the statements have been correctly deduced, it should be possible to use them to predict the responses of members of the society being studied to novel situations of groups -- not of individuals. Such predictions would be the test of the accuracy of those statements which describe the national character of the people being studied.

V

It will probably have been noted that in the very summary description in the preceding section of field-work techniques and data to be collected I have made no mention of psychological or psychoanalytical qualifications. As far as my own experience and understanding go, such qualifications are not necessary or useful in the field,[2] except in the very general way in which such qualifications will improve the quality of the fieldworker as interviewer by lessening or making conscious his own anxieties and blind spots, by increasing his awareness of the possible relevance of spontaneous behavior on the part of his informants, and by increased self-consciousness of the investigator's role and his influence on the investigation. The conditions under which psychological and psychoanalytical work are performed in our own society cannot be approximated in the field, owing to the absence of laboratory conditions, of privacy, and, in the case of psychoanalysis, of motives in the people being studied adequate for the prolonged and painful collaboration necessary for depth analysis.

In my view, psychological theory takes its major place in the study of national character as an explanation (or hypothesis) of the links between observed series of behavior, or, to use a mathematical simile rather loosely, as "transformation equations." Observation supplies the data: The same people (or the same persons) engage in behavior A and behavior B, say X and do Y. What underlying theme or themes can be hypothesized to link these apparently disparate or contradictory or congruent observations? Some of these explanations will be external, material, but some will also be endopsychic, unless it is assumed that the whole personnel of a society is under constraint, or acting as automata. These endopsychic explanations must be found in scientific psychology.

---

2.   In this sentence I am using "in the field" in a very restricted sense, to signify the actual interviewing or participation, the collecting of data. There are, of course, periods when the anthropologist is geographically in the field, but when he is engaged in studying and organizing his notes and observations; in these periods psychological or psychoanalytical knowledge is obviously relevant.

Scientific psychology has been established and developed by specialists working in a small group of related societies -- above all Germany and Austria, England and the United States -- and practically all their evidence has been based on the behavior of inhabitants of these countries. Anthropologists are not equipped to develop an alternative scientific psychology (supposing such a thing were possible), and consequently they have to employ the concepts developed within this limited area. In applying psychological concepts to unrelated societies with different customs and attitudes, it is necessary to try to distinguish those concepts which appear to have universal validity -- because they are based on human physiology, maturation, and methods of learning -- from those concepts which derive from the culture of a specific society or small group of societies. In this section I will try to outline briefly the concepts that appear to me to have universal validity, and to indicate those which, while operative in our own society, do not appear to be manifested in all societies.

For the purpose of analysis, the motives of any individual at a given time can be described as the combination of the cues provided by the contemporary environment and of the predispositions of the individual resulting from his experiences from birth to the moment of investigation. Of course in no circumstances can all the contemporary cues, nor all the past experiences, be known or described; and although the theoretical ideal is a total description, it is only the cues and experiences subjectively considered most important by the individual, or theoretically considered relevant by the observer, that can be included in even the most detailed description.

The cues provided by the contemporary environment may be further subdivided into internal and external. The internal cues are those arising from the rhythms of physiology, and are assumed to be similar for all human beings of similar constitution, age, sex, and health. The external environment comprises, besides the natural environment (whether modified or not by human activity), the implements that are the object of the study of material culture, and the social structure that is the object of the study of social anthropology (Murdock, 1949). The predispositions, insofar as they are shared, are the object of the study of national character. Thus the study of national character is supplementary to the other branches of social anthropology; it is neither an alternative to nor a substitute for them.

The concept of predispositions implies a historical view of the development of human personality. Although the genetic variations of physique and temperament are not denied, it is assumed that variations are distributed "at random," and can be ignored in the study of the predispositions common to a group. This is almost certainly an oversimplification, particularly when dealing with the small inbred groups that comprise most primitive tribes; but scientific modification of this viewpoint is dependent on advances in human genetics. Until the geneticists have determined the qualities of physique and temperament that are controlled by heredity, and the manner in which they are inherited, the anthropologist cannot safety develop hypotheses involving such variables.

The historical view of personality is an elaboration of the concept of the "law of effect" as developed by Thorndike (1932) and Hull (1943). In its most simplified form this assumes that every activity or experience on the part of the individual produces a permanent and definite change or effect (presumably neurophysiological) in the individual, which will determine, to a certain degree, his future activity or predispositions. In the classical experiment of rats running mazes, a successful run will result in an increment of "habit strength," which will render more likely a successful run (with fewer hesitations, false turnings, etc.) on the second trial, and so continuously, with habit strength increasing on an exponential curve until all behavior that does not lead to the goal is eliminated.

But besides learning to run a particular maze, or a similar task, the experimental animal also learns about learning -- what Gregory Bateson (1942c) has called "deutero learning" and Dr. Harry F. Harlow "learning sets" (Harlow, 1949, 1950; Meyer and Harlow, 1949).

Dr. Harlow, whose work was done with monkeys, has shown that if the problem, rather than the trial, is taken as the unit to be investigated, monkeys develop learning sets in an orderly manner, the ability to solve novel problems steadily increasing with experience. Before the formation of a discrimination learning set, a single training trial produces negligible gain; after the formation of a discrimination learning set a single trial constitutes problem solution. These data clearly show that animals can gradually learn insight (Harlow, 1949, p. 56).

Dr. Harlow's published work indicates, and a personal communication confirms, that the acquisition of a learning set renders what might be called reverse learning more difficult: "The importance of response to oddity patterning is also indicated by the great difficulty encountered in training monkeys to respond either in opposition to, or without relation to, the oddity principle" (Meyer and Harlow, 1949, p. 461). In other words, the acquisition of learning about one type of problem solution facilitates the application of similar solutions to novel problems, and inhibits the application of reversed or unrelated solutions.

These experiments with laboratory animals are a paradigm of, rather than a parallel with, human learning. It is assumed, however, that the law of effect and the law of learning sets are equally applicable to mice and men, although the demonstration of these laws is not possible in the case of human beings. These concepts can be used in the field only as a guide to thinking; in the laboratory they can be measured with considerable precision.

In learning theory the increment of habit strength (or decrement in inhibition) is directly correlated with the strength (amount) of reinforcement. Under laboratory conditions this can be strictly controlled within a single continuum (quantity of food, strength of electric shock, etc.), but even within a laboratory, equivalents cannot be established between different continua; it is not possible to state that so many amps of shock are the equivalent of so many pellets of food.

I find it useful to make the assumption that with human beings the maximum of pain is quantitatively considerably greater than the maximum of pleasure, that the quantum of reward is such that numerous repetitions are necessary to establish a habit based on reward, whereas very few repetitions of punishment are necessary (or in extreme cases only one) to establish (videlicet, extinguish) a habit. On the behaviorist level, this is a restatement of the Freudian concept of trauma. With this concept of the greater habit-forming potentiality of pain, it becomes inevitable that more emphasis tends to be placed on the restrictive rather than the permissive customs in a given society.

It appears that the processes of maturation outlined by Freud and his followers are biologically determined, and therefore occur in all human beings. For all neonates the mouth has primacy as an organ of pleasure and displeasure and for expressiveness; with teething, the mouth can also become a (symbolic) organ of destruction. Towards the end of the first year of life the anal sphincter and the feces become invested with importance, followed in turn by the genitalia. There would appear to be a biologically determined first phase of sexuality that terminates some time between the fourth and sixth year.

Besides the importance of the mucosi, the control and exercise of the striped muscles would seem to be of considerable psychological importance, especially from the sixth month to about the end of the second year. Since muscular control and movement are not normally inhibited during this period in the cultures from which Freud drew his patients, this aspect has not been developed in Freudian theory. (However, cf. Hartmann, Kris, and Loewenstein, 1949, especially pp. 22-23.)

Although the processes of maturation are biologically determined, their vicissitudes depend on individual modifications of the cultural norms. In all societies in which the child-rearing practices have been studied, it has been found that there are articulately recognized norms of child care, and that although practice is not uniform, deviations from the norm are relatively slight, particularly in comparison with the norms of different cultures.

It is assumed that the thought processes of infants and young children are biologically determined, and are of the same nature in all societies, irrespective of culture. Although not so described by Freud, it is assumed that these preverbal thought processes demonstrate the mechanisms ascribed by Freud to the id. In the primary system there is an absence of logical constructs, so that contradictory attitudes can be held simultaneously about the same objects, a failure to distinguish between parts and wholes, a failure to distinguish between wish and action, a confusion concerning the symbol and the thing symbolized. This system is characterized by unmodifiability of its all-or-nothing demands and attitudes, inadequate or no concepts of time, space, and direction. It is assumed that these mechanisms continue to operate in human dreaming; and that the other mechanisms of the dream that Freud has outlined -- condensation, displacement, symbolization, dramatization, secondary elaboration -- are found in different degrees in the dreams of all human beings. It is also assumed that these mechanisms are operative in most mythologies.

Although introjection is probably a universal mechanism in infancy, it is assumed that the developed ethical superego described by Freud and his associates is a derivative of specific cultural behavior and does not occur in all societies. Although it is not possible to state categorically all the necessary conditions for the development of an ethical superego, it appears that a sine qua non is that parents and parent substitutes should reward and punish the young child, give or withdraw love, for the child's conformity (or nonconformity) to explicitly stated norms of correct behavior. If the norms are not stated, or if the parents either maintain an even tone towards the children or reward and punish them capriciously and not in relation to the child's conformity to ideal behavior, the child will not be likely to develop the type of superego described in psychoanalytic literature. Where such internal sanctions are weak, external sanctions are likely to be strong. It is convenient to speak of internal sanctions as "guilt" and external sanctions as "shame";[3] both these mechanisms probably exist in every sane human being, but societies appear to differ considerably in the extent to which they invoke one or the other mechanism. It is thus convenient to speak of a "shame-guilt continuum" and to describe societies placing most emphasis towards one end or the other of the continuum. In societies that place most emphasis on shame it appears general to find suicide as a socially recognized method of dealing with voiced blame, or of vindicating one's innocence. When societies with their major reliance on shame develop a state, the sanctions employed by the state are likely to be severe and arbitrary when compared with those employed by states in which guilt is a major mechanism of social control.

Similarly, it is assumed that the development of the Oedipus conflict is dependent (a) on the typical composition of the family in a given society, (b) on the attitude of the parents towards the child, (c) on the permissiveness or restriction placed on the manifestations of childish sexuality, and (d) on the permissiveness or restriction placed on the verbalization of childish aggression. If the family consists of more than one adult of each sex, if the attitude of the parents is without intensity, if childish sexuality and verbal aggression are not treated as serious (or "wicked"), it would seem probable that the child will pass the Oedipus stage without severe conflicts. There is not sufficient evidence to state that in any society children do not go through an Oedipal phase, in which they desire exclusive possession of the parent of opposite sex; but

---

3.   "Shame" is understood to include "pride"; when the major sanction is the opinion of external others, conformity may be motivated by fear of others' blame or by hope of others' praise.

there are societies where the individuals studied do not appear to exhibit the derivatives of an unresolved Oedipus situation such as fill Occidental clinical literature.

Similarly, castration anxiety would seem to be closely correlated with the social attitude to infantile sexuality, and the extent to which modesty is enjoined and practiced so that the genitals of the other sex have to be "discovered." Penis envy would appear also to be dependent on modesty, and on the amount of deference accorded to women in a given society. Falling in love, or "object love," apparently occurs in some cases in all societies, but societies appear to differ very considerably in the extent to which such behavior is considered normal or abnormal, desirable or undesirable, whether attempts are made to elicit it in all the members of the society at an appropriate age or to deny its existence and treat it as morbid.

Homosexual behavior may be enjoined on all the members of a society at a given period of their lives (or of one sex in the society), may be manifested by some members and approved by the remainder, manifested by some members and disapproved by the remainder, or may not be manifested at all. It appears that there is some correlation between the incidence of homosexuality and the extent of contrast between the expected behavior and the assumed temperaments of men and women; the greater the contrast (stated in terms of "all men do ..." "no true woman does ..." etc.), the greater the incidence of homosexual behavior.

There is no clear evidence to show whether "sadism", "masochism," or "sadomasochism" are cross-cultural biologically based categories or whether they are culturally limited, dependent on the social treatment of infantile strivings or wishes. Overt sexual sadism and masochism have been reported from very few non-Occidental societies.[4]

VI

Is it possible to describe the national character of a society when the functioning society cannot be observed? There are two types of situation where this has been attempted: (1) when the society has disintegrated before the visit of the anthropologist (e.g. the Marquesans, and most of the Plains Indian and Californian Indian societies); and (2) when the society, though functioning, cannot be visited by the anthropologist (e.g. Japan 1941-45, the USSR). Under such adverse circumstances any statement about the society must be in the nature of a reconstruction, bearing a parallel resemblance to the living society as a paleontologist's reconstruction of an extinct animal bears a resemblance to a zoologist's observations. Although, if a choice were available, every scientist should prefer the zoologist's observations, paleontology is not therefore discredited.

---

4. Apart from the problem of the universality of sadomasochism, it seems clear that the term "sadism" is often misapplied when describing the callous behavior of non-Occidentals.

This analogy can be pushed somewhat further. The paleontologist can never reconstruct the sounds of the animal, and very rarely its color; he can establish the skeleton with considerable precision, the musculature nearly as well, and can make deductions about the probable feeding habits and methods of reproduction.

If the anthropologist is dependent on the reminiscence of haphazardly selected informants, on records and symbolic material, he cannot, I believe, make an adequate reconstruction of the social structure; for its adequate description, the actual (as opposed to the symbolic or ideal) behavior of the personnel of a functioning society demands observation as well as interviewing. The formal elements of the institutions can generally be reconstituted with some accuracy from the records of literate societies, and from allusions in symbolic material, but their functioning cannot be.

Another possibly useful analogy is the attempt -- made an several occasions by psychoanalysts -- to reconstruct the personality of a dead (or otherwise un-interviewable) man on the basis of his literary remains and the reminiscences of people who knew him; with ingenuity it is possible to establish the main unconscious motives (id and superego drives), but not unrecorded conscious ego behavior. One can determine with considerable probability the attitude of X to food and hunger, to incorporating and fears of depletion, but not what he actually had to eat, how it was prepared, and at what times it was eaten. One can state Y's attitudes to money, to saving and spending, but not the techniques of banking or borrowing that he employed.

Although analogies are dangerous, I think there will always and inevitably be the same or similar gaps in the reconstruction of a society distant in space (the analysis of a society without observation) as in the reconstruction of a society distant in time (the analysis of a dead society, history). The principal themes may be successfully isolated and illustrated, the antecedent causes for subsequent results deduced, but the actual functioning of the society (how people went about their lives) can be reconstructed only to the extent that there are available contemporary records (ultimately founded on particpant observation) or anlayses. Similarly, the variations in behavior that (at least to a very large extent) make for regional and class differences would appear to escape such reconstruction. It is hardly conceivable, for example, that the Italy of the classical period of Imperial Rome had fewer regional variations of dialect, cuisine, costume, and physique than contemporary Italy, but I know of no evidence by which such variations could be reconstituted.

Of the three categories into which I divided the data of the fieldworker, the anthropologist working away from a society with informants has only one: the emotional responses of the adults, of the informants, as shown in their behavior to the interviewer and to other people, and recalled by them in reminiscences. These emotional responses are the basic data from which deductions concerning shared motivations can be drawn. All the information given by informants can be considered psychologically relevant; its objective truth can be determined only by other evidence. Thus the fact that Japanese mothers emphasize the fragility of Japanese houses and the damage that untrained babies can do (even to distorting the house by stepping on the lintel) is psychologically relevant to the attitudes held by the informants towards physical control and the relationship of the individual to his environment; factually, the statement was almost certainly incorrect.

From a series of informants there will gradually become clear areas of anxiety and freedom from anxiety, tension and relaxation, intensity and indifference, embarrassment and boasting, that can be identified as relevant and shared. It is unlikely that as manifest content they will appear to be coherently related.

Although the vicissitudes of childhood cannot be observed, the beliefs and reminiscences of adults about their own childhood and the childhood of their compatriots can be elicited. Here too the objective truth often cannot be ascertained, though in complex societies it is often possible to obtain a check by comparing the statements of aliens with the statements of natives. An Occidental mother who has had her children cared for by a native nurse is usually very articulate concerning the practices of the latter. There may also be available verbal or pictorial records of pediatrics made by members of the society being studied. In this way a scheme of the principal shared vicissitudes of childhood can be reconstructed, though the validity of this scheme can never be complete.

There is a third source of material on complex societies that is not present at all, or only in relatively rudimentary forms, in primitive societies. This is symbolic material -- literature, drama, cinema, painting, sculpture -- that purports to depict the society being investigated. Such symbolic material is susceptible to a variety of analytic techniques: the tendency of the work as a whole -- the moral or message -- can be deduced and stated; the subjects of crisis or drama can be catalogued; individual characters (in narratives) can be studied to demonstrate what motives are consciously considered to be the sources of what action, what types of behavior are commended and what disapproved of; the actual choice of symbols, the type of relationship between symbol and referent, can be studied for consistent pattern; and above all, the silences and omissions can give most important clues. Where motives are thought to be self-evident, so that the author, writing for his compatriots, feels it unnecessary to explain his characters' behavior, it can be assumed that this presumption is shared by the readers. In popular books, plays, and films what is "self-evident" to the audience is most revealing to the analyst.

Where material on social structure is available, it is often possible to make deductions of the psychological function of the institutions from the form

of the institutions, particularly as to the expectations of subordination and superordination, of reliability and untrustworthiness, of authority and submission.

To return to the analogy of paleontology, data from the sources indicated
above can be considered the analogues to the bones, teeth, and fossil impressions with which the paleontologist works. Principles of psychology and anthropology replace the principles of anatomy and physiology in assigning position and function to the various elements available. As with the paleontologist's
reconstruction, a major test of its accuracy is that further findings can be immediately incorporated; if they cannot be, the reconstruction is wrong. In the
same way news reporting, independent researches by others, further informants, provide a check on the accuracy of the reconstructed national character;
but until the living society is studied by a psychologically trained anthropologist it will only be a partial reconstruction, of which the justification is its
practical utility in the absence of alternative and more accurate descriptions.

VII[5]

I approach the attempt to describe the national character of a society
without being in the territory of that society by the assumption of a highly self-
conscious ignorance. This ignorance has to be much more self-conscious than
in the case of field work. In the field every sight and experience emphasizes
this ignorance and also produces material to modify it; when one is relying on
interviews with exiles and emigrants and symbolic material (books, pictures,
films, etc.), this ignorance must be constantly kept in the forefront of the mind.
By ignorance I mean that I ignore, for the time being, any ideas, impressions,
or prejudices I may have acquired through visits to the country in question,
acquaintance with members of the society being investigated, experience or recollections of their works of art, literature, and music, reactions to newspaper
reports of the behavior of that nation's government, and so on. Subsequently, I
may use any or all of this material to test hypotheses developed in the course
of the work; but my initial position is that I know nothing whatsoever about the
society I am investigating.

Although I assume that I know nothing about the society under investigation,
I assume that I know certain laws about societies in general and about human
beings in general, and that my task is to discover the particular manifestations
of these general laws in the present instance. Following Malinowski, though
maybe with modifications, I assume that every society, from the simplest to the
most complex, possesses the same basic institutions and cultural imperatives,
and that these institutions are intelligible only in terms of the needs -- basic and
learned -- that they satisfy; following what I believe to be the basic underlying
assumptions of Freud and Hull, I assume that human behavior is understand-

---

5.   This section is reprinted (with brief omissions) from Gorer and Rickman
      (1949, pp. 198-211).

able, and is derived from the operation of the laws of learning on the innate biological drives and processes of physical maturation which are common to all human beings. When I made the initial study of national character away from that nation's territory (the study of the Japanese in 1941) I developed a set of twelve postulates; with the possible exception of postulate 7 (the assumption that fear and anger are not innate), my subsequent experience and study have not led me to abandon them, and I will therefore repeat them here:

1. Human behavior is understandable: with sufficient evidence it is possible to explain any observed behavior, however incongruous isolated items may appear.

2. Human behavior is predominantly learned. Although the human infant may be born with some instincts and is born with some basic biological drives whose satisfaction is necessary to its survival, it is the treatment which the infant receives from other members of the society into which it is born, and its experiences of its environment, which through the gratification or frustration of its needs enables it to learn new needs and the new methods of gratification. (In this context I should perhaps state that I assume that, in a large society, genetic peculiarities do not involve any major inherent psychological differences in comparison with other large societies.)

3. In all societies the behavior of the component individuals of similar age, sex, and status shows a relative uniformity in similar situations. This is equally true in unformulated and unverbalized situations.

4. All societies have an ideal adult character (or characters, depending on sex and status) which is of major importance for parents and other adults in authority in selecting which items of children's behavior to reward, and which to punish.

5. Habits are established by differential reward and punishment (indulgence and deprivation) chiefly meted out by other members of the society.

6. The habits established early in the life of the individual influence all subsequent learning, and therefore the experiences of childhood are of predominant importance.

7. The chief learning in early childhood consists of the modifications of the innate drives of hunger, thirst, optimum-temperature seeking, pain avoidance, sex and excretion, and of the (possibly secondary) drives of fear and anger (anxiety and aggression) and of the biological derivatives of maturation, which are demanded by the adult members of the society; consequently a knowledge of the types of modifications imposed, the means by which they are imposed, and the times at which they are imposed, is of major importance in the derivation of adult behavior.

8. Since in the greatest number of societies it is predominantly the parents who reward and punish their children, the attitudes of the child to his father and mother, and, to a lesser degree, to his brothers and sisters, will become

the prototypes of his attitudes towards all subsequently met people. In societies where the disciplinary role is normally taken by adults other than the biological parents, the attitudes towards such adults also become of major importance.

9. Except in situations of the greatest physiological stress, adult behavior is motivated by learned (derived, secondary) drives or wishes superimposed upon the primary biological drives.

10. Many of these wishes are unverbalized or unconscious, since the rewards and punishments which established the habits of which these wishes are the motives were undergone in early childhood, before the acquisition of speech, or because the verbalization of these wishes was very severely punished; consequently people very often cannot express their motives in words, and the motives have to be deduced from the observations of what satisfactions are actually obtained from different courses of behavior.

11. When these wishes, acquired through early learning, are shared by a majority of the population, some social institutions will eventually be developed to gratify them; and institutions which originate in other societies and are then subsequently adopted will be modified to congruence with these wishes (to the extent that this is possible without impeding the gratification of the primary drives).

12. In a homogeneous society the cultural patterns of superordination and subordination, of arrogance and deference, will tend to show a certain consistency in all institutions, from the family to the religious and political organizations; and consequently the patterns of behavior demanded in all these institutions will mutually reinforce each other.[6]

A reproach to studies of this nature which is frequently voiced is that they ignore the influence of history, economics, geography, and similar "impersonal" phenomena. To my mind, this reproach would only be justified if any claim, overt or implied, were made that studies of national character were meant to describe all the phenomena of a nation's life; as far as the studies I have made are concerned, all that is attempted is the isolation and description of the main motives of the majority of the population over and above those rational ones which are gratified by the operation of the institutions which historical accident and technological development have produced at a given time.

For example, marketing (the exchange of goods or services) performs similar basic functions in all societies; I try to isolate what specific functions, beyond the acquisition of articles of use, prestige or profit, marketing has for members of a given society. Anybody who has done shopping in a number of dif-

---

6. These postulates were originally mimeographed, late 1941, in the Institute of
    Human Relations, Yale University; reissued in Gorer (1942); subsequently
    published in Gorer (1943a and 1946); a few verbal modifications have been
    made here.

ferent countries will know that these are very various: in one society the pleasure may be in skill in bargaining, so that the vendor feels defrauded if his first
asking price is paid without demur; in another the vendor may feel gratified if
he has passed off an imperfect article at a high price, while in yet another he
may get greater satisfaction from an experienced and discriminating buyer who
manifests his appreciation and knowledge of the vendor's skill and taste; and so
on, with a very great number of variations and permutations. I consider it my
business to isolate this psychological "surplus value" and to attempt to bring it
into relationship with other similar manifestations; the description of the operation of the market as an economic institution I leave to the specialists in such
matters. If it is necessary to the development of my argument I may quote from
some recognized authority on the subject; but I have not the training to conduct
independent research; and I assume that the recognized authorities are as available to interested readers as they are to me.

The case of history is parallel. I do not question for a moment the importance of historical developments, but the study of these is not my specialty. I
am interested in how members of a society interpret their own history, and in
some cases have made great use of this, but I have nothing original to contribute
to history as such. . . .

The history of religion and theology will tell how and when Roman Catholicism, for example, was adopted in different countries, and the formulation of its
dogmas. I want to understand why, in the religious pictures and statues of one
country, great emphasis is placed on Jesus as an infant or child, and the Virgin
Mary as a young girl; in another on Jesus as a mature and bearded man, and
Mary as a mature and maternal woman; in a third on Jesus as tortured and crucified, Mary as an older and grieving woman. All these figures are contained in
Roman Catholicism; my interest is to discover what psychological mechanisms
have influenced the choice in any given case.

My usual, and preferred, method of modifying my total ignorance of the national character of the people I am investigating is by long interviews with members of that society. Although clues can be found and hypotheses developed by
an analytic reading of books and other symbolic material, I personally prefer to
use such material for confirming (or disproving) hypotheses deduced from interviews, and for providing additional evidence.

Who my earlier informants are is usually a matter of chance. I have been
fortunate, so far, in always having friends who have had friends or acquaintances
of the nationality I am interested in, who have given me introductions. These
first informants in turn give me introductions to their compatriots. As the research progresses, I may feel the need for interviewing people who occupy (have
occupied) certain positions in their society; in that case I enlist the assistance
of anybody whom I think capable of helping me; or, if I know that a person of the
type I am interested in exists, write directly. . . .

Since studies of this nature are inevitably qualitative and not quantitative --
to use an analogy from biology, they are anatomic, not taxonomic -- and since it
is impossible to produce any reliable quantitative and statistical results[7], I do
not pay much attention to the "sociological" representativeness of my informants,
though I try to get them from as many varied social milieus as possible, and of
all ages and both sexes. I try to get as much of a "scatter" as possible, but make
no attempt to make this scatter proportionate. In most cases the risk I have to
guard against is "reverse" proportions; often the largest portion of the resident
population -- the peasants and factory workers -- is quite inadequately represented in the migrant population.

I work on the assumption that any individual who has passed his or her childhood and adolescence as a full participant of his culture is a typical representative of his culture and manifests its national character, whatever his or her
individual characteristic attitudes, quirks, vicissitudes or occupation may be.
This may appear paradoxical, since we are all deeply and intimately aware of
differences between individuals; but in the same way and at the same time, as
people acquire their mother tongue, they acquire their national character. To
pursue this analogy further, different people have very different vocabularies
and different manners of speaking, sometimes different accents; one may use the
language fluently and skillfully, while another may barely make himself understood; one may use the language poetically and imaginatively, whereas another
may only make flat and dry statements; some may stammer, some lisp, some
speak ungrammatically; and each speaker has an individual voice and intonation
which his friends usually recognize without ambiguity. It needs a very analytically minded person to be conscious of the fact (so obvious to a foreigner) that
he and his friends and family all speak the same language, with its highly complicated and idiosyncratic rules of grammer and syntax, and probably speak it
in a way which identifies them by class, or region, or both. Without perhaps full
verbalization, people recognize and stress the differences of timbre, speech
rhythm, and turn of phrase which give each person his speaking individuality;
but they completely ignore the far larger identity of language and accent which
characterizes every one in the group and the group itself and (linguistically
speaking) completely differentiates it from groups of very similar social and individual composition in other societies, and often from similar groups in other
regions or classes of its own society.

The fact that a person has learned Russian (for example) as his mother
tongue means that his thoughts and concepts will be limited and defined by the
vocabulary and syntax of the language; in certain important ways he will view
and interpret the universe differently to the way he would do if he had been

---

7.   Statistics gathered by technicians for other purposes are of course employed
     when available.

brought up with English or Chinese or Eskimo as his mother tongue. Further, every Russian is an informant (technically a linguistic informant) on the Russian language; one may have a specialized technical vocabulary, another may speak with a peasant idiom, and so on; but if you want to learn Russian, and know none, any native-born Russian can be your informant or teacher, though you may learn more, and bétter, and more easily, from some than from others.

Analogies are dangerous traps for the unwary; but I am convinced that in this case the analogy is fundamentally accurate; that every deviation and variety of personal character is a deviation from the norm of the national character; even in the case of the neurotic and the physically handicapped this axiom holds good. Though I know of no work on the subject, I feel convinced that a study of deafness, for example, would show significant differences in different societies in the manner in which this affliction is endured and interpreted, and the way in which the sound of hearing respond to the deaf.

When I have a first interview with an informant, I always give briefly my reasons for troubling them, and on occasion a little of the theoretical background; in many cases I state my sincere belief that the study I am engaged on will tend to promote mutual understanding between their country and ourselves; and I always try to convey, even if I do not state it in so many words, my conviction that each informant has unique and valuable knowledge which only he (or she) is capable of providing. Then, unless the informant has specialized knowledge on which I want to concentrate, I ask some quite general question: usually, in the case of mothers or grandmothers, how they brought up their children; in the case of men, or women without children, details of their schooling. From then on, I let the informant take charge of the conversation, filling in pauses by demands for further clarification; in the main part of the interview I only direct the conversation if the informant is indulging in excessive generalizations or entering political arguments. After a number of interviews, I always have a series of subjects which I want to check with every appropriate informant; if they have not come up spontaneously during the course of the interview, I bring them up at the very end, usually after the interview is formally over, and we have risen from our seats. I count the interview a failure, whatever the information gained, if it has not been for the informants an interesting and stimulating experience, which they wish to repeat in the near future. In most cases the informant's response is rather like Monsieur Jourdain's delighted discovery that he had been talking prose all his life; people are pleased to discover that their "ordinary" life can be so deeply interesting to a stranger.

Unless I have excessively nervous informants, I take the fullest possible notes (I do not know shorthand); I either have my notebook out at once, or use the first excuse of a foreign word or phrase to bring it out of my pocket. I have acquired the technique of writing -- almost illegibly to others, I must confess -- without looking down at the paper on which I am writing; none of my attention is distracted from my informant by this notetaking, and, as far as I can tell, it never worries the informant. My preferred situation is to interview two or three or more (up to about six) informants at once;[8] they stimulate and correct one another, forget that I am there, or nearly, and often evoke material which I would not envisage, or of a depth I should be unlikely to reach; and their behavior towards one another gives valuable additional data. In the case of professional people interviewed alone I like to have a shorthand typist (seated behind the informant and out of sight) to take down the interview verbatim. When I have taken down my own notes, I dictate or write as full as account of the interview as possible at the first opportunity.

I take these extremely full notes, always indicating my own questions, and any interruptions, whether from other informants or mechanical causes (telephones, doorbells, etc.), because two of the chief sources for getting hypotheses (as contrasted with data) are metaphors and the free association of ideas;[9] the juxtapositions of ideas or figures of speech have quite different significance if they are spontaneous or if they are elicited. When they are elicited, the means by which they are elicited may also be significant. This concentration on metaphor and association of ideas bears a slight resemblance to psychoanalysis, and would not have been developed without the practice of the psychoanalytic interview; but it is also not unlike the work of the classical detective of fiction, hunting for significant clues among the mass of data presented.

As far as possible, I avoid asking leading questions; but an elucidating technique which I have often found useful is the presentation of cross-cultural illustrations, either from the society in which the interview is taking place or from other societies which I know of from reading or investigation, and asking whether the informant's experience contains anything similar.

---

8.   I had thought that this preference for multiple interviews was a personal idiosyncracy; but further experience suggests that where observation of a living society is impossible, and the interview is the main source of data, a great deal of material will never appear if informants are interviewed always as individuals.
9.   Other topics which I find suggestive are jokes of all kinds, swearing, religious observances, obscenity, preoccupations about health, judgments or criticisms made of other individuals in the same society, criticisms of concrete aspects of foreign cultures.

PART   THREE

GROUP RESEARCH

A. THE ORGANIZATION OF GROUP RESEARCH

Margaret Mead

The methods discussed in this Manual are all designed for use in a research group. Individual research workers, fieldworkers going alone into living
cultures, may get help from the various techniques discussed, but as presented
here all these methods and types of material are seen as supplementary to each
other within a group setting in which each worker's research or insight, technical proficiency or experienced knowledge of an area, contributes to some whole --
the whole itself emerging from their combined work. Experience in these projects can therefore contribute in two ways: (1) to the development of group-
research procedures in the sciences of human behavior, and (2) to the development of group research in the study of culture.

By group research, I mean research in which two or more individuals
participate, all working with the same problem or with the same materials, the
concrete details of which are shared among them. I do not mean the ordinary
research seminar in which a number of students in a general field (e.g. Russian
studies) or interested in a general technical area (e.g. psychometrics or communication theory) meet to present individual materials or to exchange ideas.
In group research of the sort for which I am using the term, the group as a
whole approximates the individual research worker who, with a variety of different skills and capabilities, past experiences and sources of information,
confronts a new problem. As the individual research worker may check over
in his mind the desirability of using one method of approach or another, the
likelihood of one hypothesis being more fruitful, the usefulness of one rather
than another model, so the group among themselves engage in similar discussions. As the individual research worker who is to integrate findings from a
great variety of sources -- interviews, analyses of documents, test results,
observations of living persons' behavior -- must be familiar with all of these
or he cannot integrate them, so the group must work with shared materials.
When the materials collected exceed the capacity of the group members' powers of assimilation, the research deteriorates. As the individual research
worker checks immediate observation against memory, and corrects an
auditory impression with a cue given by gesture, so the various types of
sensitivity within the group must be brought into play, simultaneously and
rapidly cross-checking and illuminating each other.

Aside from the question of apprenticeship training, there is no excuse for
doing group research unless it is more fruitful than the work of one investigator in speed of work, or type of insight, or capacity to handle more complex
materials or to use -- fruitfully -- a greater variety of techniques. Group

85

or team research is the peculiar contribution of British and American science in the last twenty years. An understanding of the methods involved has been almost completely beclouded by the exigencies of war (out of which the British concept of operational research developed) and in the United States by the provincialism of scientists who have had to bring in members of other disciplines simply to supplement ignorances that they ought never to have had, and by fashions, such as the use of Rorschach tests for research. The question has been further confused by attempts to standardize several workers so that they will react identically to the same materials (cf. McClelland, 1951), treating them as substitutes for the machine which, ideally, will someday be able to do this, and by attempts to arrange individual and group research on a continuum and to ask whether a group gets better results than an individual (cf. Lorge, 1952, footnote p. 54), and in what ways such group superiority or inferiority is influenced by the way in which the group is organized (cf. Bavelas, 1951). These approaches treat individuals as if they were interchangeable with other educated human beings with scientific training and a high IQ.

But the kind of research with which this Manual is concerned is dependent not on the uniformities among intelligent, highly trained individuals, but upon the unique configuration of perception, training, and experience of the individual research worker. A group which attacks a problem in this field must be able to do something that the most gifted individual worker cannot do physically (because of factors of time or space, such as the need to be in two places at the same time or to collect two parallel sets of materials); or sociologically (because of age, sex, class, caste, sect, race, or nationality); or technically (because of lack of mastery or facility in techniques, such as statistical methods or photography); or psychologically (because the problem requires for its solution more dimensions than the most gifted individual is able to encompass, as, for example, if phonemic, morphemic, and discourse analysis are needed simultaneously to solve a linguistic problem); or historically (because specialization in the past in one area has automatically precluded expert knowledge of another, as field work in Africa excludes firsthand knowledge of Oceanic cultures, or concentration on Russian history excludes concentration on English poetry).

It will be seen from this summary that in group research we attempt to extend the abilities of the individual research worker in time and in space, in materials of which he could have collected any set but not all, in knowledge and experience that he might have acquired if he had not specialized in some other period or area; and also we attempt to complement roles and insights denied to him because of age, sex, and so on. The group atmosphere must then be such that each individual is able to welcome the extensions of his work and to use the insights and experience he (or she) never could have had alone. The extension aspect of the group primarily makes up for limitations in time

and space, enabling the individual whose appetite for knowledge and experience is gargantuan to gain access to materials and insights that he (or she) has
the capacity to use but not the time to collect. The complementary aspect is
primarily a matter of toleration of the incompleteness of each sex without the
other. Where the extension aspect merely expands individual possibilities,
the complementary aspect is an expansion not of the single research worker
but of male-female teams, or of teams that cross a generation, or unite an
exceedingly intuitive worker with a compulsively rigorous one.

In making decisions about whether a problem should be tackled by a group
or by an individual research worker, we can use the criteria of necesssity --
for field work in a living culture, no single worker of one sex ever gets as
comprehensive a picture as do workers of both sexes; of urgency -- for a
group working together may speed up processes that would be possible but
slow for the single worker; of practicality -- for group research workers cannot be ordered, like interchangeable units, from a personnel office, but must
be positively motivated towards the undertaking; and of congeniality -- providing group research settings for those individuals who prefer to work in
groups and who work best in groups. Once these criteria have been satisfied
(and failure to consider any one of them introduces conflict into the group),
the success of the enterprise may then be enormously facilitated by a series
of organizational procedures that seem to be somewhat, if not entirely, independent of personality differences.

Before discussing these organizational procedures, it seems useful to
give a history of the kinds of experience that lay back of the design of Columbia University Research in Contemporary Cultures. This was group research
designed to deal with problems which of necessity had to be studied by groups
-- as no culture can be properly studied by a single individual, and as the
organized materials on any modern culture are too manifold to be mastered
by any one individual -- working on problems whose urgency was recognized.
The design was practicable because there were available in New York City a
large number of differentially gifted people and representatives of other
cultures, who felt that they would find participation in group research congenial. The conditions for the planning of the project were Ruth Benedict's extreme permissiveness and hospitality towards variety in personal approach
and practice, and my own professional interest in the problem of co-operation
in research situations. She brought to the project a general willingness to let
anyone -- of no matter how unorthodox an approach or a professional background -- work in the project if that person was motivated to do so. The
conditions of the Office of Naval Research grant included experimentation with
method; this gave formal sanction to such expenditures as were necessary to
keep minutes of group meetings, and to variations in the way in which groups
were constructed so that they could be cross-compared. As the project in-

cluded provision for work by volunteers, both student and senior scientist, no considerations of budget limited Dr. Benedict's hospitality; the resulting diversity forced on the conveners of the various constituent research groups solutions and insights comparable to those with which all anthropologists -- who must forever adjust their methods to the living realities of a particular culture -- are familiar.

In planning the project, I drew on my own experience of having studied one primitive culture alone against a large background of published material; six cultures as a member of a husband-wife team; and one culture, Bali, as a member of a continuous team of three (husband-wife and literate native assistant) which interacted with two other two-member teams (women investigators with native assistants) and individual male specialists in studying large ceremonials or particular problems. Out of this field experience I had learned the value of investigations pursued parallel to each other when the findings were very frequently shared, and the dangers of any unshared data when one fieldworker was too engrossed to read the other's notes; the usefulness of time records and of line-numbered notes in keeping the work of several people -- or different kinds of material -- synchronized; and the way in which one kind of observation and one kind of analytical or synthetic capacity can complement another. I also learned how the interaction between informant and fieldworker, the response of the fieldworker to the members of a society, the way in which a native exploits differences between fieldworkers, and so on all provide invaluable data on the culture. This field experience with multipersonal research on whole cultures was supplemented by experience of various types of interdisciplinary research on special problems; i.e. the Hanover Seminar in 1934, the Adolescent Study in 1934-35, and the Family Study in 1940-41. Through these I had access to a great amount of material on the problems that arise when individuals are chosen for desciplinary reasons ("because we need a psychologist"), when therapeutically trained persons were asked to do research and withhold therapy, when hierarchies among disciplines conflicted with seniority or intelligence, when the anxieties of the agencies or foundations involved in the research hampered the work of the group. I learned the inevitable perils of research in which therapeutic practitioners combine with "pure" research workers; i.e. workers who lack therapeutic skills. I learned that most of the endless arguments about conceptual schemes, frames of reference, reliability of data, bias, protection of the patient or client, and so on, could be overcome if the torn and warring group actually got to work on some shared materials, if the group was focused on a common task and its members could communicate with one another in carrying out that task by reference to these shared materials, concretely, without implicating separate vocabularies or specialized conceptual schemes. If one could talk about "Mary," arguments about the Oedipus complex, or the bias of the observer, or the choice of cases, became tangible and could be resolved. My experience in these studies reinforced Dr. Benedict's hospitality. I was convinced that a member of any discipline who is genuinely interested in a problem and wants to work on it is far more valuable than someone brought in who is ignorant of the problem and only generally professionally motivated because someone feels that it is necessary to have a psychiatrist or a historian.

So Research in Contemporary Cultures was set up to welcome participants rather than to search for "research workers"; to permit any type of participation from full-time work by senior people to short-term part-time work, long-term part-time work, extensive volunteer work by students or seniors, student participation as part of course work or at student rates of payment; participation for a few weeks or throughout the project; change of status in any direction during the project; and uneven remuneration in terms of each situation or individual need rather than by categories. Except in the case of students enrolled in courses given by senior members, most of the 120 workers entered the project through personal or professional ties with some member of the project.

In order to prevent the development of any sort of hierarchical structure or of vested interests, a circular design was set up (cf. chart on page 90). As the chart shows, the entire project membership was integrated around project aims in a series of coequal circles -- the one inner group of circles organized by cultures (Chinese, Czech, French, etc.) and the outer group of circles organized by problems or methods (Clinical Methods, Child Study, Conveners' Group, etc.). It provided also for the organization of temporary groups to prepare a report on some particular problem (e.g. A Report on National Character, requested by the Working Group on Human Behavior under Conditions of Military Service, Research and Development Board). The plan was for each senior member to occupy at least two roles of differing status within the total research group (e.g. Dr. Benedict was not the director of the General Seminar, but acted merely as a member of it, and was the convener of the Czech group; Dr. Benet was the convener of the Polish group and a member of the Russian group; Dr. Abel was the convener of the Clinical group, acted as a clinical psychologist in the French and Chinese groups, and was a member of the Polish group). There were no titles that indicated prestige, but only those indicating different types of responsibility. As there were volunteers at every level, most of the competitive problems about budgeting did not arise. The administration of the project -- the typing and processing of materials -- was localized in at least three offices, so that competition for typists was minimized. Every participant, including the secretaries and typists, was expected to be interested in the project, to attend the General Seminar, and to be attached actively to one of the groups studying a particular culture.

The entire membership of the project met at the General Seminar every two weeks. In this seminar cross-culturally organized materials were presented.

CHART

RESEARCH IN CONTEMPORARY CULTURES

Structure of a Non-Hierarchical Organization

1947 - 1951

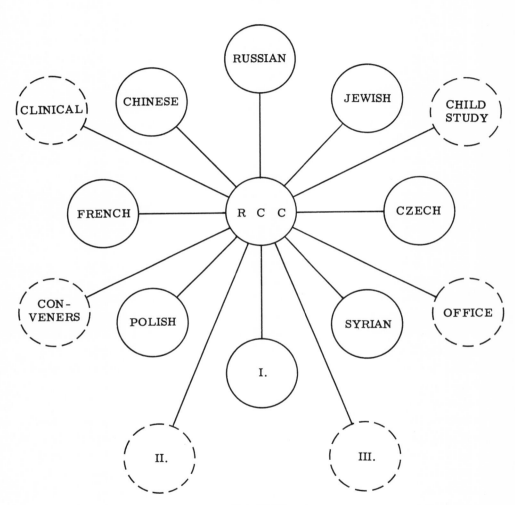

Key to Chart:

Central Circle: General Seminar

Closed Circles: Research groups on seven Cultures; and I -- Individual exploration

Open Circles: Cross-cutting Groups; and II -- Cross-cultural consultants
                 III - Professor Benedict's European
                 Seminar at Columbia University

Each research group worked with informants and with various types of source material on familial relationships, or the role of some particular relative, or on a topic like friendship or the stranger. Reports on this work were then presented in the General Seminar for discussion, to give contrasts on a common theme. Each group also presented -- sometimes through one person, sometimes through a panel of three or four who worked together -- reports on special aspects of their work. The seminar as a whole learned to know the different personalities of the members, so that the written records of groups other than their own became more fully available to them and they could experience the change in ethos as reports moved from one culture to another -- the easy communicability of Czech humor to a group meeting in America; the shift in ethos for the entire seminar when reporting by the Jewish group shifted from inside the shtetl (the small Jewish community) to attitudes to the goyim; the way Russian members nearly fell out of their chairs with laughter when attitudes towards money were presented which assigned particular bits of money ("the proceeds from the house Aunt Lida left me") to particular ends ("to pay for Susan's music lessons"), and so on.

These large seminar experiences were important in establishing communication within the project, building up a common vocabulary, and permitting the theoretically minded to go ahead faster because of the cross-cultural material. They also provided continual object lessons as members of X cultures talking about Y cultures spoke -- now as Greeks, now from the viewpoint of a French education, now as Russians, now recalling Polish training -- about a Chinese problem. Then the German ancestry and childhood training of two members would suddenly be revealed in a pedantic interchange of authority symbols; or one Russian would collaborate with another in building up an incipient "riot." The existence of such situations was an essential part of the procedure of training individuals and of the group functioning in the project. Verbatim records were made of all the General Seminar meetings and provide one part of the history of the project.

Through this seminar and informal meetings among conveners and other members of the project, constant exchange of research findings was possible, and the whole research was speeded up. Visiting specialists were welcomed at the General Seminar, and the project was equally open-ended at each level -- individuals who never attended the General Seminar could be invited to one or more group meetings; some few individuals working on other related projects in the city attended the General Seminar but were not members of any group. Every effort was made to make the organization a matter of focus and facilitation rather than a rigid form that dictated and narrowed research procedures and constricted the imagination.

Cultures were chosen on the basis of the state of knowledge of different areas, the crucial character of the area, the availability of informants, and

the availability of senior personnel familiar with the area. (Thus when Dr.
Benedict died, the plan to disband the Czech group (since two members of this
group were now pursuing research in Czechoslovakia) and replace it with a
Spanish group, which Dr. Benedict would have led, was abandoned; instead, a
Polish group, which Dr. Benet was free to lead, was substituted.)

Each group was organized differently, met on a different time schedule,
had a different composition. While it was felt that it was crucial to have members of the culture being studied within each group, this requirement was met
in various ways. The Chinese and Polish groups depended upon members who
were academically trained in the relevant sciences; the Russian group placed
a high dependence upon sophisticated, highly cultivated but academically untrained members. The French group was made up almost entirely of specialists who had nonspecialist experience of France, as students or residents.
The French group was the most academically homogeneous, the Syrian group
the least so. The East European Jewish group had no psychologist member,
the Syrian group had no historian, but the Chinese group included two psychiatric
practitioners representing different schools of psychoanalysis. Each group
planned its own work and responded to requests to present certain types of
material to the General Seminar.

A traditional anthropological method that influenced the development of
Research in Contemporary Cultures group methods was the anthropological
habit -- based on the practice of sending a single fieldworker to a relatively
little-known culture -- of controlling all the known material on a culture and
depending upon a single mind to integrate it. The anthropologist, like the
psychoanalyst, however carefully he records, must in the end rely upon a highly trained memory, for no practicable system of coding can break down the
materials of cultural observation into usable form for the thousands of cross
references that have to be made to arrive at a working hypothesis for the next
field-work question. Cross-referencing not only takes place between different
kinds of data -- genealogies, informants' accounts, myths, running observations,
photographs, and so on -- but also between different formal aspects -- tempo,
sequence, content, simple verbal similarities (a piece of slang, a figure of
speech, an item in an offering, an ornamental door handle). For the fieldworker, certainty in using his own memory as a "searching device" is greatly enhanced by his command of all the material and by his having no haunting doubts
about unread volumes that may be read by his critics and used to confound him,
not necessarily because they actually contradict his formulation, but because he
has not been able to incorporate some nuance, or an additional piece of symbolism, into his formulation. This habit of control of all the material -- exaggerated to an extreme in the case of the anthropologist who has worked alone
on an unknown culture -- is undoubtedly related to the special kind of certainty
that anthropologists often display. As scientists they of course expect their

formulations to be altered in the light of better theory and more information. But meanwhile this particular formulation is based on all the available knowledge analyzed in terms of what they regard as the best body of theory. If the work has been well done, objections raised by colleagues whose theoretical position was known when the work was done will not be expected to uncover new points, as these positions will have been taken into account. Members of other disciplines, trained to the partial approach to one aspect of a complex culture, are continually challenged by what they do not know -- not because it is at the moment unknowable, but because it deals with different materials, collected by different methods, though on the same society. Where the members of several disciplines have been combined into research teams without an anthropological slant, the members may spend months defending their respective points of view and demanding their own kind of data.

Anthropology is, furthermore, such a peculiar occupation that most anthropologists may be said to do their work out of a genuine interest in it. It has not yet reached the stage of professionalization in which shop talk is disapproved and practice is simply a way of attaining prestige and of making a living. While such motivations are becoming more frequent among graduate students, they are inadequate for sustained and good field work, which requires a total commitment from the fieldworker if results are to be obtained. Graduate students cannot, of course, always be relied upon to be motivated in such a clear way, but there is one very simple aspect of anthropological work -- whether in New York City or in central Africa -- that automatically eliminates those whose interest is not very deep: the need to work long and unconventional hours. The anthropologist must adapt to the ceremonial calendar, the event pattern, the occupational rhythms, and periods of freedom of his informants. In projects of this sort everyone works far more than the specified number of hours. They work evenings and Sundays, they go to films that are shown in the early hours of the morning in remote suburbs, and tolerate informants who arrive at midnight. These patterns also become institutionalized in the procedures of the group. Meetings are held in the evening so that some member or members who are otherwise engaged in the daytime can come; people turn their houses over to meetings; secretaries let their apartments be used as offices. The network of extra and informal obligations that develops is an expected outgrowth from the point of view of the field, where one works as a matter of course all one's waking time and at all hours.[1]

----

1. Disasters that would be comical if they were not tragic are likely to occur if anthropologists are put in charge of a project the staff of which has been recruited for reasons unrelated to any genuine interest in the problem, and who expect to observe ordinary hours and to give only a professionally adequate minimum to their jobs. This is particularly striking in work in a modern city where the participant begins to complain about "dates" or "duties to one's children." This situation -- which could not, of course,

Sharing in the use of materials was accomplished by having a duplicate open file located in two offices and by circulating new typed materials among the members of each group.

Each interviewer was asked to make out an "Informant Card" (see below) for each informant with whom he (or she) worked, and to preserve strictly the anonymity of the informant, who was referred to in the open records only by the code number given him (or her) by the individual interviewer (e.g. "Interview No. 5 with X's Informant 7," or "Rorschach of X's Informant 10"). Each individual had the responsibility of keeping the key to his own informant list (though several people might at various times work with the same inform- ant, all of them using the original code number for this informant).

Informant Card

Date of interview:

Country: Fieldworker: Informant Number: Date of write-up:

Sex: Local residence:
Age: Other parts of U.S. in
Occupation: which informant has lived:
Education:
Order of birth: (include age and sex of siblings)
Old World reference: (give region, class, etc. Place parents, if
        possible, e.g. mother: Catholic, Prague, singer; father: Prot-
        estant, village in X province, lawyer)
Age of leaving Old World: (include whether before or after marriage;
        whether children born before or after, etc.)
Culture contact notes: (e.g. 5 years as violinist with a French
        quartet; 2 years Army service in Pacific, etc.)
Marital history: (include any cultural points of reference for wife)
Children: (sex, age, birth order)
Personality comments:
Contact made through:

Interview numbers:

---

occur in the field -- can be partly compensated for by a project organi- zation that is equally holistic and human, which does not demand a strict accounting for hours from people who are known to be working twelve hours a day and using their personal resources, which gives people time off to deal with personal crises without question, which expects that some workers will sleep until ten in the morning and work until two in the morning, and recognizes that going to a party given by one member of the group may be more important at a given moment than recording another interview.

Each recorded interview also contained basic cultural identification data
on the first page (sex, age, place of birth, length of time in the United States --
visitor, born here, came as young man or as parent with two adolescent children, etc. -- marital status, religion, professional training), the kind and
inclusiveness of the detail given depending upon the culture (as it was important to know whether a given French informant was a Roman Catholic, a
Protestant, or a Jew; whether a given Jewish informant had been born in a
shtetl in Poland or in the Ukraine), and upon the individual informant (as it
was important to know whether an informant had been consulted as a specialist on some aspect of his own culture, etc.), and the specific point of observation (was the informant speaking of his own childhood in another culture, as a
father bringing up children born in the United States, as a grandparent living
in a household with Americanized grandchildren). Having such information in
abbreviated form meant that the reader did not have to go back to the Informant
Card each time an interview was consulted. Each recorded interview also
included the name of the interviewer.[2]

Thus each item of recorded information in the project contains double
identification: on the informant and on the interviewer. This identification was
maintained spontaneously in the research groups, for people would talk about
"A's lace merchant who said ..." or "B's interview with that diplomat ..." or
"C's second interview with the old junkman when he talked about the fountains
..." -- preserving intact the very necessary individuality of each piece of
information.

All material was recorded with line numbers, making possible rapid cross
reference during seminar and group discussions, as well as simplifying the
recording by the stenographer. Group research of this sort would be unman-
ageably clumsy without the use of line-numbered documents.

The dimension of time was also preserved, as the date of the interview,
and also the dates of discussions at group meetings and at general seminars,
were recorded and are available.

In the beginning of the project, abstracts were made of each interview, but
this procedure was later abandoned for the following reasons: It was very ex-

---

2. See Part Four, Work with Informants, for examples of the way essential
    data on the informant and on the circumstances of the interview were
    recorded for each interview. (In this Manual, however, the information
    has been abbreviated and the interviewer is identified only by a code
    number.) In each original interview (or other document), the interviewer's
    name, the date on which the interview was made, and that on which it was
    recorded by the interviewer are given. In the Index to the project files,
    running entries were made for each culture, in which every document
    was entered by document number (e.g. RCC-F 27), volume in which it
    was filed, code number of informant, name of interviewer, number of in-
    terview (e.g. Interview 10 with Informant 5), date of transcription for the
    files, and typist's name. The body of materials on each culture, includ-
    ing also minutes of group meetings and materials prepared for the Gen-
    eral Seminar, was filed in a separate set of volumes.

pensive in terms of both the necessary skills and the time involved. The abstracts were little used. There was an increasing recognition by those
responsible for the methodology that only those who knew all the material
could use any of the raw material (as distinct from organized discussion of the
raw material) competently; so when any worker was going over the material
for a special purpose, own notes taken on the original documents were preferred to any formal abstract that could be prepared in advance.

Certain other observations may be made on this problem of shared material. First, a method of processing that gives each participant a copy is to
be preferred to a few typewritten copies that have to be circulated.[3] Second, if there is too much emphasis on "finished" written results, group members are likely to concentrate more on increasing their own supply of materials
than upon attending to the work of others, and the integration is likely to be exploitive -- the more highly trained or highly motivated people using the separate
contributions of the less-trained members of the group. Third, it is necessary
to pay attention also to the proportion of written materials to be shared, in
terms of the time that the different participants have to read and to master
them. In general, a smaller amount of completely shared, well-discussed
material is to be preferred to masses of material only part of which is shared.
Where all participants in a group are employed full time on a project, it is possible to demand that material of any type or amount be read, but where some
participants are volunteers or are working part time, then a workable relationship between the amount and relevance of the material and the amount of
discussion is likely to develop.

A cross check on the effectiveness of the organization of Research in Contemporary Cultures was provided by two successor projects, Studies in Soviet
Culture[4] and Studies in Contemporary Cultures A, both of which I directed, and
which overlapped in time, personnel, and area with Research in Contemporary
Cultures. Both of these projects dealt with the Soviet Union and both were
directed towards what I have defined as stage 2 of national character structure
research, pinning down the general hypotheses in carefully selected, limited
samples of material.[5] In one of these projects we experimented with a type of
financing that made it possible to pay almost all the participants good salaries
for full-time work, with pressure for finished individual and group production.

---

3. In this the somewhat increased cost of materials and the use of clerical
    time must be weighed against the definite advantages of the participants
    having copies to work on in their own time and to annotate in their own way.
    A distinct advantage of processed as against typed materials is that the
    master copies can be preserved and used again at a later date if it is nec-
    essary to have more copies.
4. A detailed account of the membership of this group, including the sources
    of published materials used, is published in Mead (1951b), Appendices,
    passim.
5. Above, page 7.

This procedure, while guaranteeing a higher amount of productivity of finished work, increases tension, decreases sharing -- partly because of the unmanageable volume of the material -- and provides a setting for exploitive and competitive behavior. In the last project of this type, I returned to the design of Research in Contemporary Cultures -- combining a small number of competent but not necessarily senior full-time or part-time paid research workers and a large number of senior experts who volunteered their time for group discussions.

During the development of Research in Contemporary Cultures I realized that the groups we had set up -- which we had only very generally defined as optimally containing members of at least three cultures (including the culture being studied), both sexes, several disciplines, and several types of mind -- were actually a very special kind of tool where the study of an inaccessible culture is concerned. In the study of a living society, the single research worker is continually confronted by the interplay of persons of both sexes and of all ages, individuals of different statuses, minds of different types, all acting within the culture he is attempting to study. With inaccessible societies, this rich social interaction is unobtainable; we have at best interviews with a couple or a small group, observations in a foreign restaurant, the study of an a typical enclave. But by building a research group that is highly diversified, and whose members concentrate their analytical and intuitive abilities on single products -- an interview with one informant, the scenario of a single film -- we obtain a comparable richness by a reverse method.

During the years when the methods for studying cultures at a distance (in time or space) were being developed by anthropologists, we experimented with group extensions of the traditional informant method. The original work was begun in the autumn of 1940 in the Council on Intercultural Relations (later incorporated as the Institute for Intercultural Studies), using only exceedingly sophisticated informants -- psychiatrists, psychoanalysts, anthropologists, political scientists -- who were themselves representatives of the culture being studied. Here a type of interview situation was devised -- with two or more research workers questioning the informant -- in which the informant played a double role, relating parts of his or her own life history and then commenting upon it from the standpoint of own scientific discipline. These interviews were principally on German and Austria cultures.

Two other variants of the informant method were also developed. One of these was the method of asking specialists to work out new points about a culture they had previously studied, co-operating in a seminar setting in which each was struggling with the same theoretical problem. In the seminar, each specialist on a culture who had done either field work or else careful library work on the published material, acted, in a sense, as an informant of the other members of the group. As all were anthropologists, it was not multidisciplinary research, but was rather oriented to a single problem within a single discipline, using multicultural material. (Cf. Mead, 1937, Introduction).

The second method was the single or group interview of specialists -- in this case, doctors, nurses, dietitians, teachers, case workers, group members -- who had had some particular type of contact with members of a particular ethnic group. Such specialists might or might not belong to the group being studied, a circumstance that was systematically taken into account by placing the statements made by an American public health nurse about Italians side by side with statements made by an Italian public health nurse; allowance would also be made for the fact that the Italian nurse was of North Italian origin and was speaking about a Sicilian, or that she was of Sicilian origin herself.[6]

Both of these were anthropological methods also, as the cultural position of the expert informant, in either the individual or the group situation, was taken carefully into account in evaluating and organizing the material. The anthropologist's experience in judging each statement in terms of the cultural background and social position of the informant was used, rather then reference to expert status, academic training, or disciplinary position. That a nurse made one statement and a social case worker another was treated in terms not only of the culture of each -- in reference to the culture studied -- but also of the occupational position of each. So, for example, if an American case worker said that a Hungarian veteran of World War II was "resistant to efforts to give him help," case-work attitudes towards "willingness to receive help" -- with their occupational theory as well as their American cultural base -- would be allowed for.

A combination of these methods was used in the research seminar of the Family Study.[7] This was a group seminar with a set of shared materials on families of different ethnic backgrounds, in which the members of the seminar represented different professions and in which the occupational biases of each profession had to be taken into account.

All these research attempts provided insight into methods of group research where the participants were of different cultures or disciplines and studied shared materials on individuals or groups from still other cultures. At each level, individual personality and discipline had to be allowed for as the members of the group varied their roles, sometimes acting as informants while others made the allowances for their cultural acuities and myopias, sometimes reversing this process.

All this experience was reflected in the organizational plan of Research in Contemporary Cultures. Additionally, there seems to be some systematic relationship between the active participation of trained anthropological field-

---

6. This method was used extensively in developing the background materials for the National Research Council Committee on Food Habits between 1942 and 1945. Cf. Report of the Committee on Food Habits (1945).
7. A joint undertaking of the Community Service Society and the New York Hospital, 1940-42. Cf. Richardson (1945).

workers in a group and the tendency to follow a pattern that is derivative of the informant method. Each research group in Research in Contemporary Cultures showed this tendency towards interchangeability of roles -- accentuated, of course, in the case of group members from the society whose culture was being studied. However, these members quickly learned to reverse the procedure and to question the members from other societies, who a moment before had been acting as expert interrogators, about their cultural preoccupations.

The presence of members of the studied culture in the research group is also the way in which the ethical requirement of this type of research is under- written -- the requirement, namely, that statements made about a culture should be phrased in terms that are acceptable to members of that culture.[8] In practice, this means including in any statement made about a culture the cul- tural defenses against the recognition of the repressions that are necessary to support the culturally approved character structure.[9]

A correlate of existing cultural theory is the recognition that the enuncia- tion of a statement about a culture, one's own or another, has the potentiality of altering that culture, so that it is the anthropologist's ethical duty -- as it is the ethical duty of all those who do cultural analysis -- to take the responsibility for "all foreseeable events."[10]

In group situations where some members are psychoanalytically oriented and some, for other reasons, deal freely and easily with body imagery and un- conscious material while others resist all such material, a continuous check can be provided against phrasings that later, when published, arouse resentment from readers who are equally unequipped to deal with those parts of their per- sonality which their education has made unconscious. In Research in Contem- porary Cultures, however, it was found as time went on that the most recal- citrant came, within the group at least, to deal easily with the whole culture -- which meant dealing with the whole personality of members of that culture. The presence or absence of such recalcitrance is, of course, an important factor in the relative speed of work of a particular group, but it is nevertheless worth having such recalcitrance as a precaution. And if the research group is to exercise the functions of a microcosm of the larger culture being studied, it

---

8. I do not include here any obligation to satisfy those who have a specific political ax to grind and whose claims about another culture, phrased in such terms, call into question a detailed cultural study. I would include here, for example, objections to the claim that there were definite as- pects of German character structure that fitted Nazism, or that there are aspects of Russian character structure that make strong authority seem a necessity, objections to the culturally supported predictions about the behavior of Japanese troops if the Emperor were retained.
9. For a more detailed statement of this point, cf. Mead (1949a), Appendix on Method. For the type of misinterpretation to which it is liable, cf. Seward (1950), review of Male and Female.
10. Cf. Mead, Chapple, and Brown (1949). For an outline of the thinking that led up to this report, cf. Mead (1950b).

must periodically be renewed by the addition of new members who will be able --
for a while at least -- to challenge, with affect and conviction, the approach the
group has learned to take.

If such a research group is to function in this way, substituting for the diversity of a living society, there are certain minimum categories that may be
indicated, always keeping in mind that personal commitment to the project task
is more important than membership in any particular discipline:

1. Disciplinary backgrounds. An anthropologist with field training; a
clinician who is interested in people rather than tests; a historian who combines
a general formal knowledge of the period with a vivid interest in concrete detail
and an ability to recall documented concrete situations; someone interested in the
arts or in literature, with an interest in imagery and symbolism; someone familiar with the socioeconomic setting in at least one area in the culture (e.g. agriculture, industry, etc.). Research in the field of culture must contain within it,
in the assumptions of members of the research group, the possible types of assumption inherent in that culture at that period, so far as scientific and scholarly work is concerned, so that these two approaches both contribute to an increasing knowledge of culture.

2. Personal variations. Both sexes; some variety in age -- preferably a
generation span among those with experience of the culture; variations in personality -- individuals who prefer high-level abstractions: concrete thinkers, individuals who use different types of imagery, slow stubborn people for whom each
point has to be spelled out, and quick, darting minds.

3. Cultural requirements. Participants from at least three different cultures, one of which is the culture being studied, and where there are deep
divisions within the culture studied (as between Protestants, Catholics, Jews, and
Mohammedans; Mensheviks and Bolsheviks; gentry and peasantry; Westernized
and non-Westernized groups), represenatives of each of such major divisions are
desirable at some time during the work. It may not be feasible to have them in
the group together, but wherever possible, that is desirable. Different degrees
of sophistication are useful. The naïve individual, who will react with explosive
rejection or open amusement to statements that do not jibe with the expressions
of his own culture, is invaluable.

Additionally, each culture makes certain requirements as the style of rapport
varies -- e.g. with the Polish emphasis upon serious academic status, the Russian emphasis on rapport, the French emphasis on established frames of reference. As these are followed through, more interviewers of one type than of
another may be required.

Other requirements that vary considerably from one culture to another have
to do rather with the context within which work with informants can best be
carried on over time; optimal conditions of work with informants are dependent
upon the combined preferences of informant and interviewer. In the case of

each new culture, the conditions need to be subject to experimentation and must be handled with considerable flexibility, since the informant-interviewer relationship provides some of the most delicate clues to the culture.

B. FIVE ILLUSTRATIONS OF GROUPS AT WORK

Introduction

Rhoda Métraux

In this section of the Manual there are presented illustrations -- each a portion of a discussion that took place at one or two meetings -- of group work on France, pre-Soviet Great Russia, China, the East European Jewish shtetl, and Italy, five of the cultures studied in Research in Contemporary Cultures. All are taken from the recorded minutes of weekly or biweekly meetings and are reproduced here without textual alteration (except insofar as parts of the discussions have been omitted for reasons of conciseness and as the names of the individuals present have been replaced by code symbols).[1] Membership in the several groups was overlapping, since individuals participated in more than one study. Nevertheless, each selection represents a different style of work as at different periods the research was shaped by a different combination of participants and by the emphases of the culture studied. The first two selections, on France and on Russia, are from early stages of work -- in the project as well as on the particular culture; the next two, on China and on Jewish culture, are from summarizing periods, when large pieces of research were being brought together so that the group could consider the gaps and contradictions in the material and the special problems encountered by individual research workers; the last selection, on Italy, is an initial discussion by a group organized after three years' work on other cultures had been done, when it was possible to experiment with the use of complex combinations of materials as points of entry into a culture.

---

1. The minutes of these meetings vary -- especially in the early stages of the work, when the recording secretaries were not yet accustomed to the speech habits of the participants, etc. -- in the extent to which they can be regarded as strictly verbatim records. In later stages of the work it was found that only a secretary who had been involved in the work for a long time and who knew how each individual was likely to express himself (or herself) could match the pace of the group; this was done with considerable success. Even so -- since the minutes of meetings provided the members of a group with basic records of their mutual work -- the use of a recording machine (with the secretary listening to the discussion) became a virtual necessity. A chance remark, a series of images in a momentary aside, the precise phrasing of a comment in a rapid interchange among four or five speakers, might well give a clue to the understanding of material obtained weeks or months later. The examples of minutes of meetings given here were all stenographically recorded and illustrate both the increasing skills of the recorders and the need for extremely precise recording as the discussions themselves became more intricate.

These five selections on groups at work are so placed, prefacing the other illustrative materials in this volume, that the reader may get a sense both of the styles of work of different groups and of ways in which various kinds of source materials (interviews with informants, analyses of literary materials or films, etc.) were brought into play in the working situation. We have concentrated here upon presenting the small groups in discussions that require a minimum of annotation to be understood, so that attention can be focused upon approach and method.[2]

The selections are intended to be read both for the contrasts among them and, individually, in combination with other materials in this Manual on the same culture. So, for example, the French group discussion may be read together with the interview on French family relations and figures of fear (Part Four, Interview IV, pages 182-88), with the notes on father figures in two French films (Part Six, pages 289-91), and with the discussion of the role of the spectator, which was a much later elaboration of the problem of dyadic relations (Part Nine, pages 390-93); here the content of each paper is, to some extent, supplementary to the others. Or, reading for style of discussion rather than content, the Jewish group discussion may be read together with the two Jewish interviews (Part Four, pages 198-205), and, taken together, these may be compared with the discussions of the Chinese group and the interview with a Chinese scholar (Part Four, pages 192-98), which also, stylistically, form a unit. Or the Chinese group discussions and the same interview -- in all of which Chinese and non-Chinese participants were involved -- may be compared with the style of work in the analyses of themes in popular stories (Heyer, Part Five, pages 221-34) and in films (Weakland, Part Six, pages 292-95), where the initial research was done without a knowledge of the language and had to be supplemented by discussion and work with informants. Or, in terms of the work of particular individuals, one may compare the discussion by the Russian group with the work done by two members of that group, one of whom, 9F, acted as an informant on her culture for the group (Part Four, pages 162-69) and as an interviewer working within the culture (Part Four, pages 211-15); while the other, 27M, was working as an interviewer from a position outside (Part Four, pages 205-11). Or again, the style of working with new materials -- and the kinds of materials that were used initially -- may be compared in the French, Russian, and Italian groups.

---

2.   Ideally, a meeting of the General Seminar -- in which all members of the project met -- should have been included among these illustrations to give a full sense of the interplay among the participants and the use of various materials. However, the task of working through a properly annotated set of minutes of such a meeting -- which might involve 20 or 30 people as discussants -- would place an almost intolerable burden upon the reader who was unfamiliar with the faces and voices of the speakers and did not have access to the materials on which the discussion was based.

Within the common frame of reference, each group in Research in Contemporary Cultures developed an individual style and made somewhat different demands upon the participants. So, for example, the French group developed a rapid, diagrammatic way of fitting together materials from various sources that required continuous attention, for example, to levels of consciousness. In the Chinese group it was necessary to develop and maintain a very personal sense of mutual trust among all the participants in order to protect and facilitate the kind of intragroup interviewing that took place on topics of the most intimate concern to those involved, whether these concerned early childhood memories or philosophical attitudes. In this group it was also necessary to vary the pace so as to ensure the full participation of every member at every step. Work in the Jewish group required self-analysis and disciplined discussion of quite a different order, since most of the participants shared -- from the beginning -- a common set of attitudes towards the culture they were studying (though by no means a common set of opinions or altogether a common fund of background knowledge), and in many situations it was necessary to clarify the accepted attitudes and to locate blind spots through very detailed attention to shared materials.

However, it is important to recognize that the approach and the emphases of any one group in turn affected the work of each other group as insights obtained by one means in one group illuminated problems and suggested possible avenues of work to others. Thus because individuals worked in more than one group and because the groups worked together on specific problems in the General Seminar, and also because the working papers were available to everyone in the whole project, each group provided correctives for the others in terms of style, content, and awareness.

One caution in the use of this material is necesaary, which applies also to most of the illustrative material throughout this Manual. These group discussions are records of work in progress, not final results. Consequently, statements made by the participants in the discussion represent their thinking at the time, which may or may not have been substantiated by further research.

I. Formulation of a Working Hypothesis: French Dyadic Relationships[3]

One of the hypotheses first developed by the French group concerned the structuring of relationships in the French family. This hypothesis, as formulated in a preliminary report[4] based on five months' work by the group, was as follows:

A married couple, together with their children, constitute a _foyer_: a _foyer_ consists of a nexus of dyadic relationships -- relationships between pairs of individuals -- each of which by its existence gives strength, richness, and significance

---

3.   Unpublished document, French Group Meeting, October 21, 1947.
4.   Unpublished document RCC-F 123.

to the others. All relationships tend to be of an exclusive dyadic nature; valued emotional complexity develops in those situations where the whole group is interconnected through mutual dyadic relationships over a long stretch of time.

The discussion that follows is from the earliest stage of work by the French group. At this time there were available to the group about 100 interviews with French individuals, mainly on family life, and some data on masculine friendships, mainly from literary sources. For the purposes of this meeting, abstracts had been made from the interviews (all of which had been read by members of the group) on specific familial relations (i.e. father-son, father-daughter, mother-son, mother-daughter, and sibling relations). There are several references to these quotations (not included in this presentation) in the discussion.

This extract from a group discussion is given here as an illustration of the initial work of a group when it is attempting a first formulation of problems on which work will be done. For closely related materials on France in this Manual, cf. Part Four, "Interview with a French Couple: Dyadic Relations in the Foyer" (pages 182-88); and Part Six, "Notes on Two French Films" (pages 289-91). -- Ed.

[The group have been discussing interviewing problems. The discussion is picked up here as a new subject is introduced. A digression on the question of untranslatable words and on the linking-up of images has been omitted here.]

27M: I have here five copies of excerpts from 40F's interview on father-son, father-daughter relationships. The best are the father-son. All of them are ... concrete statements. I should be interested in any hypotheses people can make. They are all statements of identified Frenchman about their relationships with their fathers.

[Brief omission; discussion of a technical point.]

30F: I'm interested in the father as initiator of the boy's adult life. He tells him how to handle women. He tells him when he can go about and when he can't.

64F: The point is that he tells him how to spend money, not when.

30F: But until he tells him he can get married, he can't.

64F: The emphasis is on what you let him do, rather than the other way around.

46F: The question is -- is he ready to do it yet?

64F: The father is looking at the positive development of the son.

46F: The father leads, he doesn't discipline.

64F: It does say that the mother threatens to tell the father, but never does. (46F interrupts to say this was not the point made: the point was that the father leads.) I'm sorry, I thought you said leaves. But it stands out in sharp contrast to the betraying mother in Germany. The [German] mother says she won't tell the father, and does. It is a threat position and the uncovered amount of the threat is important to watch.

39F: I notice that fear and respect don't go together. The mother is respected, the father feared.

64F: Note that the father is urging the mother to be harsher. In Manus, the father urges the mother to be softer.

28M: Voice and tone must be gone into deeper.

27M: Yes, but this is just our first data. The father, while alive, controls the son; the son can't become adult as long as the father is alive.

64F: The father is always there as an old person, and you can never get rid of
him.

40F: In Poland, the father gives up at fifty.   [That is, is supposed to retire
then.] [5]

28M: You would have to follow this up in peasant, bourgeois ... [Part of this
comment was not recorded.]

27M: But this is only our first material.

64F: You've got to see the difference between thinking you know something and
getting your data. In the last statement [statement by an informant] notice the
series of words: "responsibility," then "tolerance" and "sympathy." Responsibility
tied up with something permissive. Then "liberal." What is the meaning of "liberal" in French? Then "disgust" and, on top of that, "unhealthy." It's a peculiar under-
pinning position. If you've kept in mind the possible structural relationships, it
is a peculiar sequence....

         [Discussion of these terms, their sequence as used, etc., omitted.]

27M: ... The role of the father as consultant is worth considering. What is the
father's position as decision-maker?

64F: The son consults him and he consults his wife.

46F: The mother protects the son, which assumes that there is intimacy of
communication between mother and son.

64F: We have the son going to the mother, the mother going to the father, the
mother not telling the father ... the son consulting the father, the father consulting
the mother. What would you ask your father's advice about? In an interview,
you would ask: "If your father hadn't been there, whom would you have asked?"
Are there noncommunication areas?

50F: There is total structure in the family and between any two individuals;
the tendency is to keep that strong. The father tells the child, then will tell the
mother, and vice versa....

64F: Making each of the personal relationships firm against the outside.

46F: The father may know something about the mother's position that he doesn't
want to pass on to the son.

27M: Looking out for all children's relationship.... The mother-son relationship is practically nonexistent outside childhood [in the material from these in-
formants] .

39F: Is that deviant?

64F: What is the mother-son relationship?

27M: I am interested in the femme de quarante ans (the woman of forty, quoting

---

5.   For an informant's discussion of this point, cf. Part Four, "Interview with
      a Polish Peasant Woman: Parents and Children" (pages 179-81). -- Ed.

this from a statement) -- the mother's best friend who is also the boy's sexual initiator....

64F: What is the relationship between the mother's best friend and the father's mistress as sexual initiators ...?

30F: The form is also important; if it's general, not specific, that's data. The contrast is important.

64F: 46F, doesn't the picture 50F is giving about keeping the relationship closed -- mother-son -- fit in with your hypotheses on friendship?

46F: Where anxieties about friends come out, it cuts into the pairs....

[There was then some further comment on men's friendships, especially as seen through literature, which was not recorded. There was then a brief discussion, not fully recorded, in which a suggestion was made that possibly in friendships each individual is analogous to the hub of a wheel, with the friendships radiating out.[6] It was then suggested -- with some blackboard drawings of family relationships to illustrate what was being said -- that possibly the father also is in a hub position in the family.]

64F: Methodologically, out of verbatim interviews we have selected concrete bits relative to a particular single-pair relationship -- out of the two spokes in a wheel position, the sides forming an unfinished triangle. 46F said that the father was the hub, which formed that into a series of triangles.... The father as consultant, and consulter also fits in.... 50F pointed out that each pair inside the relationship will keep the relationship on the same level.

50F: It's more of a square than a triangle, so as not to let the other sides collapse. Like this:

(She draws on the blackboard, adding a new figure.)

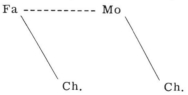

64F: [At present] we can handle only the figure of the triangle with the hub of the wheel. Those images are all important....

[End of discussion omitted here.]

II. Formulation of a Working Hypothesis: The Swaddling Hypothesis[7]

This was the third meeting of the nuclear research group on Great Russia, which was later much enlarged. The first meeting had dealt with subdivisions of the Soviet Union, with the self-classifications which Russians in the United States used, and with Stalin's attributed cultural position in Georgia. The second meeting had started with an analysis of a published document, "From Vratch," originally published anonymously and later reproduced as part of John Rickman's

---

6.   The hub-wheel image was later discarded as inappropriate to individual friendships, but recurred as a descriptive image for a series of linked friendships. -- Ed.

7.   Unpublished document, Russian Group Meeting, November 6, 1947.

contribution to The People of Great Russia (Gorer and Rickman, 1949). In the course of the discussion, 79M had reported some observations on Russian posture made at a rehearsal of a Russian dramatic group, and the question of swaddling as related to posture had first been suggested by Margaret Mead, an idea originally suggested to her by a comment on Russian gesture made by Elizabeth Mead Steig after a discussion with Dr. Lillian Malcove, in 1935, about the effect of cradleboards on character. Interviewing and analysis of Russian literature had already begun.

In Appendix I of The People of Great Russia Geoffrey Gorer has given a personal account of the developing of the swaddling hypothesis. This group meeting presents part of the context of interchange -- the flat, unequivocal statements of individual Russians, the invocation of material from other cultures, combined with reports of work with informants, which, together with a systematic theory of the psychobiological development of the child, led to the swaddling hypothesis.[8] Before this hypothesis went beyond the small group, an immense amount of work in interviewing, checking imagery in literature, consultation of contemporary photographic files and Soviet manuals of child rearing, was necessary. -- Ed.

[The preliminary comments of the members of the group, as they settled down to the meeting, have been omitted. The transcript of the group discussion begins as it is given here.]

27M remarked on the reluctance of his Russian informants to spell out their names; 9F, 47F, and 54F agreed that there is no spelling in Russia. They are never taught spelling.)

64F: How do you learn to spell?

9F: We don't. Russian is phonetic. When we are asked to spell, we simply sound out the different syllables of the words. It's impossible to spell.

64F: Are there people who are bad spellers?

9F: Yes.

64F: What do you do about them?

9F: You just teach them to learn the right way. The child is taught to read by syllables. He is taught to read first one-syllable words, then two-syllable words, then three-syllable words.

47F: (Illustrates with babushka.)

64F: Do you use initials the way we do here?

9F: Yes.

27M: No.

9F: Yes, we do.

64F: Would you use them on towels and watches?

9F: Yes.

47F: Yes, as monograms, not as initials.

27M: As monograms. You see, 64F, not as initials.

9F: Well, do you sign your name in initials?

---

8.   For further discussion of this hypothesis, cf. also Gorer (1949), Mead (1951e), which includes pictures of swaddling, and a paper by Mead presented at the annual meeting of the American Anthropological Association (1952), "The Swaddling Hypothesis and the Question of Scope" (to be published).

64F: Yes, we do! (Gives examples -- writing and signing notes.)

9F (rather surprised): Well then, how can you tell everybody apart?

79M: Then you teach in syllables, not in letters?

(General agreement.)

27M and 64F: There seems to be some difficulty in breaking things up into component parts.

64F: How does an old-fashioned Russian woman pass on a recipe?

9F: Some people remember it. Some have it written down.

64F: It it were written down, how would it be written?

9F: If a woman were just learning to cook, she would put down the ingredients.

27M: Would you say four lbs. of this and two lbs. of that?

9F: Yes, indeed. (Illustrates with detailed description, listing all the ingredients and quantities for recipe for pascha.)

(A few more questions asked on this topic; not recorded.)

64F: Let's move from cooking. Do any of you know parsing? Did you ever get
it?

47F: I know parsing, but not from Russian.

64F: You know what parsing is, don't you? (Illustrates. Midway in her explanation, 9F, 47F, and 54F agree that "this is grammar. Yes, we have it.")

64F: These two lines are dead. Cooking doesn't follow spelling....

79M: How about the fact that Russian is a Slavic language and started without
an alphabet ... ?

27M: I don't think we can go back ten centuries.

9F: With a few exeptions that you may meet, you ought to know how every
word is spelled.

79M: Is it an aural rather than an oral thing?

27M: No. It must be related to the fact that there was a period in your life
when you didn't know things and that is so unpleasant you are forgetting it.

9F: There is only one way that a word can be spelled in Russian.

     (There is some argument back and forth about this. 27M says that there
are, for instance, three "i's" and 9F says that each has a different sound and
cannot, therefore, be confused with the others.)

27M: No, I think it is that it is intolerable to remember when you didn't know
things.

64F: How is it to remember when you were sick -- or in prison, or in some
sort of disgrace? Do you forget these things?

54F: I remember only the times I was ill. They were the most pleasant and
the most comfortable. I had everything I wanted.

9F: Childhood was very dull.

27M: From my informants I get this: I remember food I didn't like. At

school food was unpleasant and I remember that. Somewhere outside you --
you remember; the expected -- you repress.

64F: 9F, what do you remember about your food?

9F: Oh, food was awful in childhood.

27M: My French informants remembered lots of good things to eat in their
childhood with gusto.

9F: In childhood! No, we didn't have good food until after twelve.

54F: We were forced to eat such unpleasant things. Kasha, for example. I
hated it.

27M: But now you like it, I suppose?

9F, 54F: Yes!

27M: There! You haven't changed the food. You've changed your attitudes.

9F: Milk! After ten we stopped drinking it. Everybody stops drinking it
after ten or twelve. Nobody liked it.

54F: I started here when I saw everybody drinking milk. But I still don't
like it.

64F: 79M, tell us that story about your [Russian] teacher.

79M: My Russian teacher was explaining bolshoi -- wide, high, etc. He
used gestures, but these were only with the forearms, the elbows were kept
bent and close to the body. (Illustrates.)

    (On 27M's suggestion, the conversation was turned to swaddling.)

64F (to 9F): Were you swaddled as a baby?

9F: Yes, I was. I was really swaddled!

64F: How was it put on?

9F: Once or twice a day. The baby was unwrapped to take fresh air or a
bath, or to kick around. A baby has to be wrapped stiffly for convenience' sake.
Otherwise he is hard to carry around. It is easy to handle a child when he is
swaddled and stiff.

64F: Was the swaddling done so that the head was stiff too?

9F: No, it was loose.

64F: Did you have to support it?

9F: No, there was a pillow prop behind its neck which held the head.

47F: I was not swaddled.

27M: Why not?

47F: I came of a medical family with progressive views.

27M (to 54F): And you?

54F: I was swaddled. I remember my sister was swaddled in a very tight
four-cornered cloth. I wasn't allowed to play with her when she wasn't
swaddled because she would break. But when she was swaddled, I was allowed
to play with her once or twice.

64F: Why do you swaddle a child -- besides the convenience?

9F: If you leave him alone he will sprain his arms or legs.

27M: Why the arms? Italians swaddle but leave the arms free.

54F: They would break their backs, or come out of joint.

64F: Were they swaddled at night?

9F: Yes. They could move at night, too, and therefore the same precautions had to be taken.

54F: Also, it could grow crooked.

9F: Yes, hunchback.

64F: If you unswaddle -- do children cry to get swaddled or unswaddled?

9F: I don't know.

27M: Babies cry because they are hungry, sleepy, teething, or just because they want to cry -- that's from my informants.

64F: But no relation to swaddling?

27M: No. However, I've got a negative statement.

64F: That's not useful. 9F, see what you can get on that. Does it cry for unswaddling or swaddling?

69M: This might be a good clue to movement restraint, hyperkinesis, expressiveness in conversation.

64F: Yes, but the American Indians brought up on boards have no expressiveness in conversation.

79M: Is that due to deprivation of emotion?

64F: Well, it might be. Up to what age are babies swaddled?

(Nobody remembers.)

27M: I ask, have you seen children crawling?

(Nobody answers.)

64F: What's the Russian word for creeping or crawling?

9F: Poltsi? Polzuchi restenye?

64F: Does a child crawl?

9F: Yes.

64F: Where?

9F: I can't remember seeing a child crawl. One never saw a child.

47F: They are in the nursery.

64F: What did you do in the nurseries?

54F: I was several years older than my sister but I can't remember seeing my sister crawling. I remember the nyanya (nurse) supporting her while she took a few steps.

64F: Are there no proverbs, no statements about a child crawling or creeping? Do you remember a child sitting on its backside and hitching along with its hands? (No one had such a memory.)

27M: I think they are unswaddled just before a year old, just before they ought to walk.

64F: What happens in that interval?

27M: They crawl a bit. The mother used the expression "on all fours like a bear."

47F, 9F: But that would be applied to anyone -- to a drunken man going upstairs too. I always walked upstairs on all fours. (They continue to recall the frequent times when they walked on all fours.)

64F: This is the first culture I've seen where it's so hard to find the babies!

54F: When I think now, we were kept out of the rooms where the adults were.

27M: Were you glued to your governesses? Where were you kept?

54F: In my early childhood, I was in my room. Later on, with my sister.

64F: What did you do in your room?

54F: I played, sewed for my dolls, made pictures.

64F: Sitting on the floor?

54F: Yes, I did. I hated my chair, so I sat on the floor.

27M: There was nobody with you?

54F: Yes, the maid would come and talk with us.

27M: Where was the room?

54F: Let me see. (She lists the rooms of the apartment as she tries to remember where the room was and succeeds only vaguely.)

64F (to 27M): Would you like to state your swaddling hypothesis? But first let's all think of all we can say on the subject so as not to inhibit.

54F: I do remember that when I was taken out of my room, it was to be exhibited. We had to perform. We hated it.

(Lots of agreement.)

64F: What did you have to perform?

54F: When I was very little, I had to recite poetry. Later on I had to play on the piano.

27M: What nationality were your governesses?

54F: All Russians.

27M: No English, no French?

9F: Oh, much later. We had French governesses later. All our nurses were Russian.

27M: Did your nurses have moods?

54F: And how! Mother used to say, "She is in a bad mood. Don't upset her."

9F: It was only the wet-nurse with me. They were afraid of souring her milk. The wet-nurses were always sick because they were peasants from the country and not used to the different food and habits. They were put in the national costume, too, instead of being allowed to wear their own bundling wrappings. (Describes the colorful costume.)

64F: Was there any intermediate stage where the hands were out and not swaddled?

27M: 46F tells a story of her husband's being taken to visit his grandmother in

Russia. His mother was being modern with the baby and feeding it from a bottle. On the train the bottle broke and the child almost starved. When they got to their destination, the grandmother was there with a large cloak. She immediately took the baby and wrapped it up tightly in it and said, "Now he is a real Russian baby."

64F (to 9F): Did you swaddle your children?

9F: No.

64F: You didn't even cover it with an extra blanket or two, just in case?

9F: No, I followed my doctor's directions.

64F: How about blanket coverings?

9F: No, I never covered my children all over with blankets.

64F: Did you think the swaddling more uncomfortable than the blankets?

9F: Yes. Everybody thought so too, but it was necessary for the baby to swaddle it. They pitied the poor thing, especially in the summer, but it had to be done.

54F: I remember now that later on my sister was swaddled in a large shawl only until her chest, but her arms were left free.

27M: Do you think Russian babies are ever hungry?

47F: You mean, did they ever get a chance to be hungry?

27M: Yes.

47F, 9F: They were given some chewed-up black bread wrapped in a piece of cotton cloth to suck on and that would keep them from getting too hungry.

47F: It's a variation of a nipple.

64F: Or the sugar-tit in the South.

54F: I think we were terribly overfed.

64F (to 27M): How about your swaddling hypothesis?

27M: The swaddling point first. This is my hypothesis. Russian children in the first year of life have no feeling of deprivation on the oral or anal level. They are thoroughly healthy children, to my knowledge. But they have this swaddling mingled with periods of freedom when they kick a lot. That's why the parents swaddle them, because they will kick a lot and not be able to sleep. That's how the idea develops that restraint is unbearable; yet one has enormous strength and one must be swaddled in order to keep one from breaking things.

64F: And that ties in with self-control later on.

27M: The need for control or lack of control -- that comes later. But I don't want to go on with this at the moment. I put this up as a hypothesis. I don't know if it's true.

79M: It's interesting.

27M: There is no other deprivation except this one of muscular activity.

64F: Is the swaddling stuff soft or harsh?

47F, 9F, 54F: Oh, soft.

64F: So that the immediate skin is comfortable?

27M: The muscles, not the skin. It's soft all over.

54F: Babies were overprotected from the cold.

27M: One more protection from unpleasant internal sensory perceptions.

64F: What was the bath like?

9F: The babies were bathed in a trough.

54F: A narrow one?

9F: No, like a deep platter.

64F: What temperature?

9F: A comfortable one. The wet-nurse used to test it with her elbow.

64F: So the child was never exposed to hot or cold water.

(General agreement that this was carefully avoided.)

64F (to 27M): How about teething? The two places in the first teething which are crucial points physiologically, how about them?

27M: I was told that the wet-nurse gets a present on the child's first tooth. But it doesn't matter which tooth.

64F: Is there a first teething crying crisis at six months and a second one at a year?

27M: My picture is not a crying crisis.

64F: Well, among the Balinese, at the first teething crying crisis the children often died. In this country we still expect a great deal of trouble.

47F: Not any more!

64F: Yes. Some pediatricians don't, but the baby still goes through it. How about Russia? Was the baby given anything to bite?

47F, 9F: Yes, arrowroot.

64F: Is it loose, on a string, around its neck, tied to something?

47F, 54F: Loose.

27M: It seems to me that the focus of ambivalence is not being able to do what you've got the power to do. Not father, not dirtiness, etc. As far as I know, it's unique, the conflict in the first year of your life is in the large muscles, not in the erogenous zones.

64F: Not unique. Fifty per cent of my cultures are not centered around zones.

27M: Is it centered on muscles?

64F: If it's the cradleboard. The point of a cradleboard is that it is believed to be comfortable by the parents. I suspect two things. One, the absence of the flat board is important. You've bound into but not onto anything. In this case -- the Russian -- it's best tied down, it can't move. No relationship except to the universe. That's the important contrast to the cradleboard position. And second, that everybody thinks the position is uncomfortable.

27M: I think that's putting it too high. You sleep well that way; you won't sleep without it.

64F: But do you want them to sleep well? All 9F's statements are that ...

9F (interrupting): But if the mother thought that the child was uncomfortable, she would take it out of the swaddling to give it a rest.

64F: The American Indian thinks that the child cries for the board.

9F: It's unthinkable that the child would cry for the swaddling.

64F: What about when the child gets wet? Does it get cold? Or does it remain warm?

9F, 47F, 54F: Oh, always warm.

(64F brings up cases of Siberian children where, among men, resentment exists against the mother because she may have left them out to freeze and caused later impotence.)

54F, 9F: Oh, no. People are always too hot. During the winter the windows are never opened. We were not taken out until seven or eight months.

54F (makes a comparison with Polish babies): -- but I think the Russian babies were more overfed than the Polish babies which were left crying for hours. There was very little contact with the Polish baby during feeding. It was hasty feeding.

64F: Is the baby nursed in its swaddling?

54F, 9F: It's unswaddled.

64F: That's important.

9F: Yes, unswaddled and wrapped in a little sheet.

64F: Would its hands be free?

9F: I don't know. But it wasn't kept stiff.

64F: You feel that the combination of being stiff and being nursed is wrong? It's in apposition to Indians who nurse on the board; oral gratification and board combined.

64F and 27M: We've got to pursue swaddling in every direction, including metaphors or any kind of figures of speech.

79M: If Russians feel it safe to be hemmed in, wouldn't the gratification of nursing while being penned in be reinforcing?

27M: Well, it's not a gratification, it's a protection. Russian gratification is orgiastic -- restraint and pleasure don't go together.

64F: It's fun to go all out and not be kept in.

(General agreement.)

⎡Consideration of a point on vocabulary brought about a shift of subject. The second half of this meeting has been omitted here. -- Ed.⎤

III. Intragroup Interviewing: On the Definition of Terms

Excerpts from two meetings of the Chinese group are presented here. Both are from a period during the second year's work on Chinese culture when the group was consolidating previous research and was working on the interrelationship of themes. At both meetings the discussions were focused upon the refinement of definitions, on which a great deal of work had been done.

The first excerpt, "The Chinese First Teacher," is taken from the minutes of a meeting at which the draft of a major report by one of the Chinese members of the group (69F) was being discussed by the whole group. The draft had been circulated among the members and was now being discussed, sentence by sentence, as various persons raised questions about phrasing, the meaning of terms, and so on. The general topic under discussion was the education of the Chinese child. In the excerpt given, questions are asked about two separate points.

The second excerpt, "Sincerity," is taken from the minutes of a meeting at which there was a discussion of themes in Chinese comic stories, jokes, and popular stories, in connection with research by members of the group on popular stories. The discussion then turns from a consideration of different kinds of themes to ways in which ideas are expressed and thus to a consideration of the meaning of sincerity.

These discussions are presented here particularly to illustrate the smooth interaction within the Chinese group between the Chinese and the non-Chinese members (who themselves came from different backgrounds -- American, German, Dutch, etc.) as they interviewed one another as a way of defining Chinese concepts and attitudes. The group had been at work for a long period and each person in it was accustomed to the approach of each other member. In terms of both content and style, these discussions may be compared with the autobiographical paper, "My Inner Self," and "Interview with a Chinese Scholar: Friendship," both in Part Four (pages 157-62, 192-98). -- Ed.

1. The Chinese First Teacher[9]

[The discussion is picked up here as a new point is raised.]

8F: One point -- the phraseology "The teacher opens up the child.... "

*69F: The teacher opens up the ignorance of the child.

8F: Is the ignorance inside the child, and you take it out, or is the child empty?

*69F: Ignorance --mung -- is an untaught child. He's a mess inside -- unorganized.

71M: But there is something inside, or nothing?

*69F: There is something, but it's all muddled up.

*6F: The teacher channels it.

73F: "Open up" is different from "channel."

*6F: I mean being guided along a certain road.

71M: But not emptiness?

*69F: No. A child is not something you pour things into. The teacher opens up the room and there is stuff in it, but not organized.

8F: The child has certain capacities and the teacher organizes them. Our metaphors of teaching have essentially to do with restraint: "As the twig is bent the tree will grow" or "to set footsteps in the right path."

71M: But we also pump something into the child.

*6F: Only the modern ideal of education in China has this idea.

73F: "Opening up" sounds like the child has a vista of something.... Is there any of that idea?

8F: No. Opening the gates of knowledge is opening up the subject, not the child.

71M: It's outside the child. There it's already inside.

---

9.   Unpublished document, Chinese Group Meeting, March 11, 1949. There were ten members of the group present, of whom eight took part in this discussion. The Chinese members of the group are indicated by an asterisk (*).

8F: Yes, it's the idea of order.

*45F: Man is born of the essence of heaven and earth and so has something in him. As he grows up, he has to learn the principles of tao and cultivate them.

*6F: Tao means guiding.

*69F: The story of creation is that in the beginning of the earth, it's a confusion. Then the light rises to the top of heaven and the earth settles; then the universe is found. For children, it may be the same thing.

                [Brief omission; *69F continues to read her report.]

*6F: Why does the drama on the stage always show the teacher as rather ridiculous?

*69F: Because we respect him but we don't like him.

*45F: He's a poor scholar.

*69F: And he's dirty.

8F: We get pictures of the first teacher as being poor, ridiculous, and having great difficulty in disciplining the children.

71M: We get a picture of the teacher not getting enough to eat. The children have to bring him some food. He goes around writing poems to be fed. He eats in the children's homes. I knew one teacher like that in my childhood [in Germany]. I thought him ridiculous.

8F: The interviews all tell of making mischief for the teacher.

*69F: But that doesn't mean we don't have respect for the teacher....

71M: It's the later teacher you respect....

8F: You have a parallel here with the East European Jewish material: the first teacher is a poor scholar -- a pathetic figure. The later teacher you respect.

71M: There is a dichotomy between the teacher you describe and the teacher we have information about.

*69F: For instance, we made fun of the teacher, too, but when we grew up we respected him.

71M: But there must be some ambivalence.

*69F: We persecuted the teacher a lot -- my brother and I. I put flies in his soup....

*6F: My brother would put medicine into the food to give the teacher dysentery.

*69F: Even croton oil. I remember catching three flies, pulling their wings off, and throwing them into the teacher's soup. When he saw them, he asked who did it, and when I said I did it, he rapped me on the palms.

39F: We have to make some reconciliation between respect and this mischief.

71M: What you tell us now is more important than the stereotypes we know.

*69F: But still we kowtowed to him before we left. You're afraid of him and you want to get something out of it.

71M: But there's a tremendous amount of rebellion in it.

*69F: Yes, but now we can even talk to him about it.

73F: In the Red Chamber[10] there is a fight in the school where the young teacher who has been left in charge of the children can't control them. They organize a gang against him.

*6F: Respect is inculcated by the parents long before the children get to the teacher.

*69F: Yes.

  8F: Do children ever play tricks on their parents?

 39F: You wouldn't put flies in your father's soup, would you?

*69F: Oh no!

 39F: It's very important the way the Chinese get their outlet. Because they are in balance. That's another wonderful area -- the teacher.

*6F: You respect the idea of the teacher, but not the person.

*69F: We used to compose eulogies to the dead and burn them before the teacher. And we would fold papers into the forms used to chase ghosts and burn them in front of the teacher. The teacher is not a parent. He's someone you respect, but he's far off.

 50F: It's more like the relation of the governess to children in England.

  8F: In the Russian group, they were discussing the techniques used in getting rid of people you don't like. One person said she told her mother, "I don't want a German governess." Her mother got her a German governess and she got rid of her by not paying attention -- no tricks, no bad disciplining problem....

*45F: The Chinese can't do that.

 71M: Did your brother also pull the wings off flies?

*69F: Yes.

 71M: That's very common. Did you torture animals, too?

*69F: Yes, we tortured animals. My brother once burned the shell of a tortoise to see if the head would come out.

        [Omission: further discussion on the handling of animals by Chinese children. A digression from the point is also omitted.]

71M [going back to the original point]: It's interesting how this aggression is displaced from human beings to animals.

  8F: Are there any household pets?

*69F: No pets. Cats and dogs are not house pets; the dog guards the house and the cat catches mice. The Chinese say you have to be either an American or a lunatic to talk to dogs or play with dogs.

 50F: Would a dog be allowed to get up in a chair?

*69F: No.

  8F: Do children tease household animals?

*69F: Yes.

 71M: The Pomo Indians throw stones at dogs.

---

10. Tsau Hsueh Chin (n.d.).

*69F: Chinese children do, too, when they see two dogs having intercourse.

*6F: But you don't throw stones at your own dogs and cats. They're part of the family. It seems that defenseless little animals and insects are very much liked by children, but older animals are neglected or mistreated.

71M: I notice you make a distinction between insects and animals.

*6F: You consider insects animals?

8F: Yes. You wouldn't consider birds animals?

*6F: No.

8F: How about fish? Are they treated kindly?

*6F: We play with them.

*45F: But we do harm insects without feeling. My brother would light a cigarette in a toad's mouth to see it explode. A toad is considered an insect. After you are punished by the teacher, you don't get sulky, like Western children. If the teacher says, "Read that," you read it.

39F: Because you couldn't go home to get sympathy.

*69F: You can't even go home and hide in the toilet room; there is no such room in the Chinese house.

71M: Is there ever a quarrel between teacher and parents?

*69F: No. The parents would be ashamed. You can't quarrel with the teacher unless you sever all connections with him -- unless you move away.

71M: But on the other hand, the teacher has such a low position. He depends on their help.

*69F: It's not such a low position. It's just that you don't give him money. Money must be given as something else, not as money.

*6F: But it's often so little -- in the villages.

*69F: Gifts of food are different. Now, even, in the universities, you pay tuition in rice.

71M: How do you explain the fact that on the one hand, the teacher has a distinguished position and on the other hand, they don't feed him enough?

*6F: He's a scholar.

*69F: Here even, you earn more money in business than in teaching.

*45F: Socially, he has a high position; economically, it's low.

39F: In Arab culture, the teacher who first teaches you is a shepherd. He has a low position. But after he has memorized the Koran he gets a great deal of respect.

8F: Poverty in China doesn't have the same meaning as in America.

*69F: No, the poorer you are, the higher you are. If you have money, you get no esteem [as a scholar] .

2. Sincerity[11]

[The discussion presented here is from the latter part of a group meeting, at a point when the group is discussing problems of humor. -- Ed.]

*6F: There was a great poet of the Tang Dynasty who composed a poem, wrote it out on paper, and threw it into the river to the crocodiles. The poem explained to the crocodiles why they should not harm people, and it ended with: "Crocodiles, if you have sense enough to read and understand this, you will get out." The story is that they did get out.

*69F: That's not a joke. It's serious and possible. When you're sincere, heaven and earth will be moved. The poet who wrote a letter sending away poverty is another one. He says: "Poverty, you have been with me long enough. Leave me now and don't come back." That is funny.

*45F: It brings back the classic Chinese wit. There is the story of the chief who is sent on a mission to another country. The king gives him gifts to take back home with him and he starts to laugh. When the king asks him why he is laughing, he says: "I was thinking of an incident that happened on my way here. I was passing a village and I saw a man praying. He had pork, rice, and wine before him, and he was praying for prosperity." The king understood then, and gave him triple the number of gifts.

7M: What is the difference between writing to the crocodiles and writing to poverty that makes the poverty one funny and the crocodile one not?

*69F: Poverty is something abstract; it's not like a fly that keeps buzzing around your eyes and annoying you.

*6F: It's personified.

*69F: Writing of lack of prosperity is not so interesting as sending away poverty.

*Inf. M: Sending away poverty is a personal thing. Writing to the crocodiles is doing something for the people.

*6F: It's a psychological piece of literature, to calm the people. You read it in school.

8F: Why do you read it in school -- for the moral point?

*6F: No, for its literary merit.

[Brief omission. The discussion turns from a consideration of classical models of stories to the problem of the language that is used.]

8F: ... I wanted to discuss methods of teaching. Everyone learns the same thing. What is a pleasant, cultured conversation?

*6F: What class? What period?

---

11. Unpublished document, Chinese Group Meeting, June 2, 1949. There were eight members of the group present and also a Chinese man (Informant M), who was a guest participant. The Chinese speakers are indicated by an asterisk (*).

*69F: For the North, modern period, it would be: "Eaten?" For the South: "Have you had your dinner yet?"

*Inf. M: In the North they use few words. The South Chinese say the North uses four words: "Who?" (meaning Who's there?) "I," "What doing?" (one word in Chinese), and "urinating."

*69F: Between men and women there's a difference in the way they speak. In Chinese schools, the servants bring hot water for washing the face in the morning. In men's dormitories, they would call to the servants, "Face water." In the women's dormitories, they would say, "(Name), will you please get face water for me to wash my face?"

*Inf. M: Women are more refined.

*69F: The North and the South are different.

*Inf. M: Do you think the North people are simple, straightforward, and the South are polite?

*45F: Except the Cantonese....

*69F: In Hupei Province, in the North, they're very crafty. That's bad in China. They have a nine-headed ....

*6F: There is more talking the other person down.

*Inf. M: In Honan (adjacent to Hupei), the people are stubborn ... the "Honan mule."

*6F: The Honanese fight instead of talking.

8F: When you say, "Sincerity will move the crocodiles" ... what do you mean by "sincerity?" What's the word?

*69F: Ch'eng is sincerity.

77M: The word "sincerity" was quite in vogue in Shanghai in 1935. To the Japs, when they said the Chinese were not sincere, they meant they were not following Jap orders. It became a joke.

8F: Who is a sincere person?

*Inf. M: With people from the North -- Shantung -- if he sees anything wrong in your home, he tells you about it. From the South -- Shanghai, etc. -- they explain it not so directly. The Northerner would think that not sincere.

77M: The Chinese consul in Malaya thought the overseas Chinese in Malaya were not sincere.

7M: Chinese girls think American girls are not sincere, because they will flatter you about your clothes.

*69F: The Dale Carnegie book is built on insincerity. He tells you to try to be sincere in your insincerity.

*45F: You should say what is in your heart.

39F: But if your heart tells you not to hurt a person -- you want to make that person feel happy, what would you say?

*69F: But if you tell a girl her dress is pretty, she'll wear it again.

*6F: I think it's taking the other person's point of view. You have to be considerate with sincerity. Sincerity without consideration is bluntness.

*45F: If I don't like the color of your dress, I don't have to say I don't like the color. I can say, "The color is nice, but may I suggest that you wear another color?"

34F: Would you actually say that to a friend?

*45F: Oh yes.

34F: In the same way that you would ask the price of a gift she had given you?

*69F: Oh yes. It's all right to ask. In your heart you want to know. If it is a good friend, then you ask. Then, if you think it's too much, you scold her. You say, "Why did you spend so much?"

8F: If someone asks you the price of something, do you tell the truth?

*69F: Oh yes. Once you're asked, how can you get out of it?

*Inf. M: We say, "I didn't spend much money."

8F: If someone asks the price of a new dress you're wearing, do you make it less or more?

*69F: Less, so they won't scold you for being extravagant.

*Inf. M: It depends on the motive. If you do me a favor, I present you with a gift to impress you, but I don't want you to know the price. If I spent too much, I don't say -- not to embarrass you.... Sometimes I will say it was given to me -- especially if it's an antique. I know a man who did that....

39F: But it was also understood that he had bought it?

*45F: In America, if you don't want to accept a gift, can you return it?

8F: No, it's a great insult. It would break up any relationship you had with the person. A girl will send back a man's gifts if she doesn't want to have anything to do with him. Our time sequence is different. We send the gift after the favor, not before.

*Inf. M: We do that too.

*45F: The Chinese can return a gift if it is sent to ask a favor.

8F: Is that humiliating?

*69F: No. You send it back with a note: "The treasure is returned with thanks."

8F: Here a person in public office can refuse gifts.

34F: On principle only.

8F: Yes, and some of them even instruct their wives not to accept gifts. Women should not accept very valuable gifts from men not related to them.

34F: It's not insulting to the man if a woman returns such a gift?

8F: No.

7M: Not to the woman either.

8F: In Zuni, my Zuni friends would give me gifts and then tell me, without my asking, what they had cost -- which was usually double the [actual] price -- and how hard it had been for them to get it and they wouldn't do it for anybody else, even their own children, but it was just to show me how much they loved me.

They flattered me and expected a return, but they were not impressed by my way of giving presents, which was to deflate the value. I would say: "It's just a trifle." And they believed me. The proper way for them would be to exaggerate.

[Brief omission]

39F: About gifts -- if someone has a shop, can he say, "Come in and select what you want"? I was once invited to go to [an expensive shop] and select any dress I wanted because I had helped place a girl there. I refused, of course. Do you have that in China?

*69F: Yes. That's in the bribing field..

39F: Yes, it's another category.

8F: The Chinese have even more widely the pattern of entertaining buyers. It extends even into public life in China; here it's only in business.

*69F: When the servants give us presents, we can't refuse.

8F: Is it humiliating to receive presents from inferiors?

*Inf. M: No.

77M: When I was in Shanghai I made a great mistake. I had a cook who said his uncle was sick and he wanted to go to Singapore to see him. I said, go. He stalled and kept saying the same thing, and finally left and didn't come back. Later I learned that he wanted a raise.

8F: That's the technique for asking for a raise in business.

39F: Is that sincere?

*69F: Yes. For other culture, it would not be sincere, but for us, yes.

8F: You never say to the boss: "I've been here two years, I think I deserve more money"?

*69F: No. Usually you resign, or let it be known you intend to resign.

*Inf. M: Usually you spread a rumor.

77M: Later I found out if my cook had really wanted to go to Singapore, he would have offered to find me a substitute. Since he didn't offer to find me a substitute, I should have understood that he wanted a raise.

8F: Is sincerity something you keep for your friends?

34F: How do you reconcile politeness with sincerity?

*6F: Politeness often covers up a lot of hostility. Overpoliteness may indicate you want some favor.

*69F: In the Red Chamber, Phoenix [a girl] is overpolite. She wants to succeed in her own purposes. She's not sincere.

*6F: If it covers up a desire to ask a favor, the other person will resent it. It implies an attack....

39F: What about the technique of cheating in exams? Is that sincere?

*69F: Yes, it's very sincere in purpose. You ask a friend to take the exam for you because you don't like the course and you would do better to spend your time on studies you need. Sincerity is inside. It is a matter of character. We all know which of our friends are sincere. We can't help it.

<u>8F</u>:   It has nothing to do with the means you use to achieve your end, provided your purpose is sincere.

IV: Relations between Men and Women: Has the Woman a Soul?

The two discussions from which excerpts are presented here took place towards the end of the second year of work on the culture of the East European Jewish <u>shtetl</u> (small town), at a time when the group was trying to work out the main points of disagreement and the gaps in the material on which it was necessary to concentrate in preparation for the writing up of the material.[12]

In contrast to the French group, where everyone had had some French experience but no one was French by birth and upbringing, and in contrast to the Chinese group, which was divided between those who were Chinese by birth and upbringing and those who (with one or two exceptions) had had no previous experience of Chinese culture, in the Jewish group most of the members had some experience, direct or indirect, of the culture they were studying. And in this group (as among Jewish informants) the warmest debates grew out of questions of interpretation. In this respect, these discussions further illustrate the way in which the cultural backgrounds of group members affect the style of work and how, in turn, the style of work is affected by the materials obtained on the culture. These discussions may be compared to the Italian group discussion that follows, for in both -- though here at a much later stage in the work -- an anthropologist (who in the Jewish group had not taken part in the research but who was familiar with the material) acts as a catalyst for the group as a whole.

The first discussion is taken from the minutes of a meeting at which the group discussed a series of problems; this excerpt is from the latter part of the meeting. The second excerpt is from a meeting that took place approximately six weeks later, when group members reported back on interviews on the special point raised -- Ed.

1. The Position of the Woman[13]

[The discussion is picked up as a new subject is introduced.]

<u>43F</u>:   How does a woman fit into the Covenant before she's married? When she's married, of course, she's taken in because of her husband.

<u>55M</u>:   No, a woman is not in the Covenant.

<u>35F</u>:   Then is she a non-Jew?

<u>55M</u>:   No, she doesn't have <u>olem habe</u> (the life to come).

<u>64F</u>:   What's the position of a male child before any ritual takes place? Is he incomplete?

<u>43F</u>:   We took that up before.

<u>55M</u>:   He's incomplete until the age of thirteen.

<u>64F</u>:   Is the male at thirteen analogous to the marriage of the woman?

<u>55M</u>:   No. The boy at thirteen becomes a complete Jew.

<u>64F</u>:   Whether the minute the boy is thirteen he's a complete Jewish man? You have born into this system two sexes, male and female. We get this in the Syrian group, American feminism sometimes influencing it. Now look, two

---

12. Cf. Zborowski and Herzog (1952); this book is based on the work of the
    East European Jewish group.
13. Unpublished document, East European Jewish Group Meeting, May 19,
    1949.

sexes are born. They pass through this world, and they pass through this world differently. The female reaches the highest point she can reach when she marries.

21F: The highest point is when she has a baby.

64F: Marriage is a beginning; even without a baby, a son, she has a certain theological position in relation to God and Heaven. That's her cycle of completion. If the male also starts low, and increases his theological and sociological status in life at thirteen, is that the highest he can reach?

55M: No, when he has a son, that's the highest.

64F: The stations up to the position of having a child are different. Less is expected of the woman and less is accorded her, but to say she doesn't exist is wrong.

21F: Does the woman lose her olem habe if she is divorced for sterility?

55M: I don't know.

57M: All you say is perfectly true for purposes of external discussion. There are two complete life careers and each reaches a climax, but each member of the community has a rank -- the system ranks the male over the female.

64F: That's perfectly clear, yes. But that's not the point I'm raising -- but the idea that a female doesn't exist. What happens if a female child dies?

57M: It isn't that she doesn't exist. She's incomplete.

43F: Well, for the male, if he has been circumcised he is complete, because if he dies he will go to olem habe.

55M: He is complete for God, but he didn't complete all his functions.

64F: What happens to a woman who hasn't been married? Where does she go?

55M: I don't know. The woman has been completely neglected up to now.

38F: He (55M) has said again and again he doesn't have material on the woman.

64F: I don't believe that if you were to go to the Jewish Theological Seminary and ask what happens to an unmarried woman who dies, they would say they don't know. I've seen disallowance of women in these groups in DP camps. It is conceivable that they don't have anything to do with anything -- as the rabbit doesn't have anything to do with a soul -- but I don't think you have proved it as yet.

55M: I think it's the exact situation as the rabbit.

21F: But a woman isn't soulless.

55M: If you take, for instance, the folklore about the Dybbuk -- you never hear about a female Dybbuk. It's a lost soul which can't find its place in Heaven. It migrates from one animal to another. But you never find a female Dybbuk. In the same way, there is never a curse about a woman's soul. There is always one reference: if she is married and if she helps her husband, she'll sit at his feet [in Heaven]; that is, if she helps him be good Jew.

64F: Does she get a soul when she's married?

55M: That's a problem. Nobody speaks about it. There is never a reference to it.

35M: Do you know of any version in which the Dybbuk entered a man instead of a woman?

55M: Yes, many.

43F (to 55M): Animals have no soul?

55M: That's right.

43F: I've had many informants tell me animal souls entered the bodies of men and women -- many, many stories, so obviously animals do have something.

64F: The material is incomplete at present. No one is criticizing 55M. We're studying a whole culture. If, as 43F says, lots of informants comment on animal souls, they exist.

43F: The word "soul" wasn't mentioned, it was "spirit."

57M: Why not examine the hypothesis that the soul is the end of a chain of completeness?

21F: It isn't. It appears at the moment of conception.

57M: But the emphasis is what happens to the completed ideal.

64F: Well, does the soul change?

57M: It completes itself.

55M: I would be extremely glad to have documentation, any information on women, on the female aspect of this culture. All the time of my work I couldn't find anything.

64F: I don't deny that at all.

55M: There is something in this culture which is just neglected. The problem doesn't exist. It's empty space.

64F: Then, if it's empty space, we're not dealing with anything simple, we're dealing with something much more complicated.

57M: They don't define categories in this culture. They define ideal total continuums. The soul is human....

64F: "Human" includes women?

57M: Of course.

64F: Along this continuum, within this total, there is a segment undescribed.

57M: It's not a segment, it's an incomplete part.

64F: What's the difference between a segment and a part?

57M: Women don't have enough of these holy attributes that complete the soul.

64F: Where is that said?

55M: There is a very striking omission of its being said. That's the point.

64F: That's entirely different from a hierarchy.

55M: You see, I don't find any reference to women having a soul; but I don't find any reference to women not having a soul.

57M: But you're using "hierarchy" in the Western sense.

64F: I quoted from you. You used "rank order."

57M: I've been trying to communicate a very different idea.

64F: Certainly the goy is not "completeness." They define it in detail. On the same basis you should get no dealing whatsoever with disallowed parts of life. You should talk only about sheyneh Yiden -- and prosteh Yiden[14] should be defined only by omission. They should never have attributes.

38F: They have lots of attributes.

21F: Yes, they have. They're brutal, ignorant, enjoy violence, sex, drinking. The sheyneh Yiden can't exist without the contrast of the prosteh Yiden.

38F: The absence of findings on women is entirely significant. It hooks up with what informants say.

57M: I'm trying to give you a hypothesis.

64F: I don't see that it applies to lower classes. The body, bad behavior, why should it apply to women? In the particulars that make up the ideal values you enumerate them, you talk about sheyneh Yiden. Enumerate all of these things. You enumerated bad things. The same with the Jew and the goy. Is there anything here like that, which would allow us to see the female as a series of incompletenesses?

21F: The woman is not a potential man, no matter what happens.

55M: The proster Yid can change.

64F: Is there any possibility that a woman can become a man?

55M: There was a case. A woman became a tsadik (thaumaturge). It was a so strange, they didn't know what to do about it. She had a synagogue, she behaved like a man. They formed a delegation and asked her to marry a man. She did and lost her status as a Rabbi. She was put back in her place.

57M: Has anybody any other hypothesis for handling details we know, and omissions?

55M: You remember we spoke about the body; how the body changes. The importance of the container changed with the growing up of the child. When the child is small, he is just a child, he is rosy and fat; when he goes to school, he is supposed to be pale and emaciated from study. The woman is always rosy and fat, she stays that way. Remember we spoke about kosher -- fit and unfit? She is just like good Jewish food, fat and meaty.

57M: In German culture you have the same thing. You wouldn't recognize a German woman being inferior to a male.

64F: If woman is incomplete, is she an incomplete idea, an incomplete male, in which the ideal is sexless? It is not answered.

38F: The situation of the whole picture would lead you to expect it to be complementary. Balance of man.

---

14. Cf. two interviews with Jewish informants on the subject of sheyneh and prosteh Yiden, Part Four (pages 198-205). -- Ed.

57M: Overt and covert. There are some ... in which you get a complement.
But 55M is talking about ideal timeless patterns.

64F: One of the troubles may be -- 43F raised this question: What is the
theological position of a woman before marriage? If she has no position?

21F: In the legends too; there is a long legend in Ginzberg (1909) defining why
woman is different from man -- man is clay, but woman is from bone; bone
stinks, clay is clean.

64F: That's by defining.

21F: It defines so explicitly.

38F: The legend suggests a dual explanation -- in a sense she is part of man,
a complementary part.

21F: Man is incomplete without his bone; he gets it back by marriage.

55M: The problem is definition and finding out what can be said and what is
found about woman.

43F: I said it was theological.

64F: In the theory of conception, woman has a soul; then she doesn't have a
soul after, or what?

57M: No, no; it's not yet complete.

55M: What about speaking about this kind of soul?

64F: We don't have data on it. Have you?

55M: A human being is created by God and has a soul. Every human being has
a soul. Every human has a soul -- you spoke about woman, woman has a soul.
The problem is what happens to the soul, how does it evolve, what happens to it
after death, and so forth. Now you stop; here you have a lack. We are not able
to complete. We know what happens to man's soul; we don't yet know what happens to woman's soul.

21F: We know what happens to a married woman's soul: she sits at her husband's feet.

55M: Conditionally. If she's a good wife. The fact that she's married doesn't
mean immediately that she goes to sit at her husband's feet.

43M: But he doesn't either.

55M: No, if he is no good he goes to Hell.

64F: Does his wife go with him?

55M: We don't know.

43F: Can souls be separated?

64F: You have data about house tamberan cultures.[15] What we are calling
the "ideal pattern" corresponds to the formal pattern of the initiatory cults. You
never get the true picture of the initiatory cult until you've studied the women as
well. If only men anthropologists study them, they say the women are scared,
but a woman can go along and see how the women behave -- they may giggle.

_____

15. Cultures in which there are men's societies with making-a-man cults.

About marriage -- to say that it's a cultural idea of completeness, vague in spots -- that can only be said when we find women have no views.

21F: Maybe they don't have the theory that women made up sacred writings.

64F: I wouldn't be surprised if that turned up.

35F: You have women judges in the Bible.

55M: Deborah wasn't a judge. She completed the male's picture here. That was a secondary role. She was the good woman exalting man to fight. One of the simplest things, I think, would be to just ask women, "What happens to your soul?" Just ask it straight.

21F: They might laugh at you and say: "I don't know, I'm not dead yet."

55M: You can't predict answers.

57M: I'm not saying it's not a whole apparatus. Subordination of scale of completeness.

64F: The top of the scale is complete?

57M: He is most complete when he is male.

21F: Married, with a son.

57M: That's the highest.

64F: If you have a scale of completeness and handle the female as a less complete person, you don't say the female is an incomplete male; you don't put her in the same continuum.

57M: You have the continuum of fulfillment of Jewish obligations.

64F: You may have it. It's not proved.

38F: It runs counter to our whole picture of the culture.

21F: Sex is the only status that is not achievable.

64F: The only ascribed status.

57M: Woman's soul is an incomplete soul.

21F: We don't know.

57M: That is a hypothesis. I say woman's soul is an incomplete soul.

55M: Not that woman has an incomplete soul; she has a different kind of soul.

57M: I want to see evidence for that.

55M: I will try to give you evidence. If it were the same kind of soul, it would be able to achieve higher and higher status, if it were incomplete. If it's a different kind of soul, as it is, it stays like it is. What confirms this point is the body. The woman's body never changes. In the Jewish male body there is a change in the not-physical. I would find it possible the soul is different. It's not incomplete. The whole idea of potentiality is absent here. About animals: we have descriptions of Jewish animals behaving just like Jews. They don't kill little birds. But what happened to the cat? He's supposed to be like a Jew. He has a different kind of soul. It's an animal's soul. In many primitive cultures you will find many different kinds of souls, not in the same category.

57M: I'm just trying to find by hypothesis how far it runs through here. It seems to me there is evidence here of absolute categories: animals, female,

Gentile, male, Jew. At least those five.

64F: Gentile is less absolute.

55M: We must make the point that all of these souls are complementary. Complementary to the total Jewishness.

57M: That's what I've been trying to say all morning.

64F: What you're trying to say is there is a concept of Jewishness with categories arranged around it. Only one-half of the category is a particular attribute and the other part is totality. Jewishness is a totality. Greed, un-Jewish, is a particular, So are you trying to construct a model -- ideal Jewish character -- out of which you can extract particulars so that Jewishness is a total? Any deviation is complementary.

57M: No, the following model: total of Jewishness ideal in which these five categories are ranked according to their possibility of achievement: animal, male, female, Jew, Gentile. We don't have to imply they are in in any order.

55M: In order to have a Jew, you have to have a Gentile; to have a man, you have to have a woman; to have a human, you have to have animals. It runs through Jewish culture.

57M: But the male human is the apex of this system.

38F: It seems to me this whole structure is in those pages we drew up....

64F: Complementary -- in which you need another part. As in Bali. What would a lion be without the forest? What would the forest be without a lion? Then the continuum statement is a class statement.

57M: You people forced me into "complementary."

64F: I think this is basic enough.

38F: We have agreed that for the most part the universe is not viewed as a series of dichotomies, that there are very few absolute categories. The few recognized were seen as complementary.

64F: Well, you say you agreed. 57M says he was forced into it.

57M: Complementary means to me occurring in pairs.

64F: It has nothing to do with pairs. It means you have contrast....

            [The conclusion of this discussion has been omitted here.]

2. Woman's Position Redefined[16]

[The subject of the woman's soul was brought up again at a group meeting six weeks later, when new material -- provided by interviews -- suggested a way in which the problem might be redefined. Only the relevant portion of the discussion is reproduced here. -- Ed.]

64F: I just want to say that I have had an interview on the subject of women's souls. The woman is about fifty-five, grew up in a Polish shtetl; her father was a considerable scholar. She was the favorite [child] and was allowed to do

---

16. Unpublished document, East European Jewish Group Meeting, June 29, 1949.

things that were supposed to be wrong for women. I asked her about souls, do women have souls? "Certainly, more than men." Do they go to Heaven? "Certainly." Then she said, "Oh, you mean that business about sitting at men's feet. Yes, they say that; they say if a man was a great scholar, women sit at their feet." What about spinsters? "There aren't any. I'd like to find a girl who was so sick she couldn't marry." What about a girl of fifteen who couldn't marry?

55M (interrupting): They would find someone. A girl who is a very bad cripple -- they would find another cripple to marry her to.

64F: Will she marry before puberty?

43F: There's a story about a woman who's engaged to a man; he has TB. She doesn't want to marry him. The final result is that she dies and he is still alive.

64F: We should have information about what happens to a girl who doesn't marry. Well, to continue the interview. She said, "Women have real souls and men have recognized souls."

48F: I think she's absolutely correct. We've been getting material to support that.

64F: That's a house tamberan culture.

55M: Your feeling is, she is sure she has a soul and will go to Heaven?

64F: Certainly.

38F: She thinks God recognizes that too?

64F: Yes.

55M: I spoke to a man. His first reaction was that women have souls. So I asked him, "I don't find anything about women's souls in the Talmud?" This confuses them. But they are convinced that women do have souls.

21F: I think you will find that women intrude on the male activities much more than men do on female activities.

64F: That's house tamberan too....

[The discussion was now dropped until further material on the point could be obtained. -- Ed.]

V. Themes in Italian Culture: A First Discussion[17]

The Italian group in Research in Contemporary Cultures was formed in 1950, when the larger project had been in operation for more than three years; a number of the participants in the new group had by then had considerable experience in the project working on at least one (but usually more than one) other culture and in the General Seminar. Under the circumstances, it was possible to select as a point of entry into the culture a combination of materials that was complex, with the expectation that it would provide rich clues for research.

At the first formal meeting of the newly organized Italian group, some portions of which are reproduced here, the group was presented with two contrasting types of materials: (1) a discussion of themes in Italian films by an analyst who was experienced in cross-cultural studies of films but had no systematic knowledge of Italian culture, and (2) spontaneous comments upon this discussion by an American anthropologist of Italian background who had recently made a

---

17. Unpublished document, Italian Group Meeting, January 27, 1950.

community study in Italy. Thus the group was presented with two very different kinds of insight as a preliminary step to research. The main participants in the discussion following on these presentations were two anthropologists (21F and 64F) who were familiar with the research methods, and two new group members (4F and 66F) who, because of their own background, were familiar with Italian life. In this situation, it is worth noting the kind of détail taken up by each -- the probing questions asked about the kin group, the tentative comparisons made, the image ("face") picked up by the anthropologists; the concrete material added by the others.

This group discussion is presented here primarily as an illustration of the way in which the point of entry into a culture can be selected in terms of the background, skills, and specific experiences of the research group.[18] -- Ed.

[The introductory part of this meeting has been omitted here.]

30F: These hypotheses are based on about fifteen Italian movies.[19] I realize that this is fantasy material and that the relation between this material and real life may be of any degree of indirectness. A special theme it is interesting to focus on is the image of the woman. It is easy to make the demarcation between the French and the Italian films on this basis. In both there is a sharp separation between the good and the bad woman, but each has a special way of styling it. In the French films, they are separated, but they tend to make a merger: the bad woman becomes more and more like the good woman; the seepage is all toward the bad woman, who is bad and sexy, but who then gains what is taken away from her and becomes interesting, while the good woman becomes uninteresting. It is just the opposite in the Italian movies. The bad woman becomes only a symbol of sexual gratification and is very boring. I think I can illustrate this best from the films. Has anyone seen Il Bandito? It is a good film to illustrate this, and typical of many. The good girl is identified with the sister. The sister is the model, and she should be virginal and must be protected.

[In Il Bandito] the hero comes back from the war, looks for his home, and finds only ruins. Meanwhile a song is heard: "A tisket, a tasket, my little yellow basket" -- sung in English in a pseudo-sophisticated little girl's voice. [A comment on Italian films is omitted.] The soldier then goes to a brothel, and is taken into a room. A girl comes in with her face averted, strikes a provocative pose, and when she turns around -- My God! It's his sister! It has terrific impact. The girl weeps and tells him how circumstances forced her into such a life.... So immediately he is going to rescue her. On the stairway, her pimp stops them and the two men fight. The pimp has a gun. The brother tries to wrest it from him; it goes off, and the girl is shot. The brother throws the pimp down the stairway and then runs to his sister, who is dead. He picks her up in his arms and

---

18. Because of unforeseen circumstances, the work of this group did not go beyond the stage of preliminary exploration.

19. The films were the following: Il Bandito, Sciuscia (Shoeshine), (Four Steps in the Clouds), Scampola, Un Giorno nella Vita, (Une Nuit avec Toi), (Open City), Furia, Giovinezza Scapigliata (Schoolgirl Diary), Paisan, (The Outcry), (Germany Year Zero), Sotto il Sole di Roma (Under the Sun of Rome), Molti Sogni per le Strada (Woman Trouble), (The Peddler and the Lady), (Bicycle Thief). Two of these were seen in Paris, the others in New York.

embraces her. The only time embracing a sister is allowed in these Italian films is when she is dead. It occurs in other films -- Un Giorno nella Vita -- a film about nuns. The nuns are all killed during an air raid and the bodies of the sisters are lying around all over. The Resistance fighters come back, and one of them picks up one of the sisters in his arms.

But to go back to the bad woman in films. [In Il Bandito] after the scene in the brothel, the hero joins a gang. There is a bad woman in the gang (played by Anna Magnani). She is a tough baby and her lover is running the gang. When the hero comes in, she is immediately attracted to him.

[Brief interruption omitted.]

... The hero easily becomes the bad woman's lover. It doesn't involve him emotionally at all. Then another sister figure emerges. As a soldier, the hero had been friends with an older soldier who had a preadolescent daughter. The hero has been a sort of absent uncle to this girl, sending her gifts, and so on. [The bad woman] sees the girl's picture and makes some sort of sarcastic remark about her. The hero becomes enraged and throws a glass of wine at her. It destroys their relationship. In the end the hero dies protecting the little girl; he is shot.

Following up the point about the consecration of the good girl -- there seems to be dramatic tension about the moment when a girl loses her virginity. The girl becomes the center of all sorts of disturbing events, and is apt to be surrounded by men. In the film One Night with You, a young girl is about to become engaged and several men get tangled up in something, and all land in the same jail cell. The girl is surrounded by men at the moment of coming into womanhood. The movie about the nuns -- Un Giorno nella Vita -- has a similar treatment of a young nun who thinks of leaving the convent.[20]

Loss of virtue, when it occurs in a man's life, is apt to be signified by his becoming a thief. There is just as much drama and feeling of hopelessness when a man becomes a thief as when a woman loses her virtue. The Bicycle Thief is a good example of this.

A girl is more likely to be led astray by a bad woman than by a bad man, as in Rossellini's Germany Year Zero.

There is another interesting point: the transformation of the good woman in passing from girlhood to womanhood. The young girl is sweet and gentle, but the woman after marriage is terribly scolding, terribly emotional, torrentially impulsive. She yells into the street. But she also has noble impulses. She is uncontrollably impulsive -- a veritable geyser of impulse. By our standards, she is less attractive. It reinforces again the fact that the ideal good woman is modeled on the sister rather than on the mother.

---

20. Cf. also Martha Wolfenstein, "Notes on an Italian Film, The Tragic Hunt," in Part Six, I, (pages 282-89), in which this theme is also central. -- Ed.

64F: One of the things we noticed in our adolescent study[21] was the solidarity of the women among the Italians, as contrasted with the Poles, where you couldn't get a Polish woman to tell another woman anything. There is also a thread of femininity tied into the girl's life. Birth and menstruation are tied together.... protecting the girl from menarche until childbirth. 30F's statement is not in any sense meant to be that Italy is like this, but that Italian films may provide us with clues worth following.

37M: I must make a few important points. In Italy there are tremendous variations of culture. 1. Instead of North and South, you have to divide Italy into cities, coast, and mountain towns, and look into the ethnic and political history of the town or region. 2. In the small towns, you have a literary culture -- an ancient culture built largely on fantasy and expressed through the popular theater. 3. The sense of the tragedy of life is pretty widely spread among all classes in Italy: "You can't escape life.".... [Details omitted.] 4. There is a tremendous telescoping of time. When speaking to the peasants you lose all sense of time.... [Illustrations omitted.] Thousands of peasants went to Syracuse to see the Greek dramas -- the classical theater -- and watched the plays as if they were happening today. 5. It is important to keep in mind the history of the Italian commune. In P--, you had a city within walls and the country outside. Inside the walls it was civilized. Outside the city walls it was wild. There you found organized bands of thieves. There was a distinctive culture in the city. Vestiges of this difference between the city and the suburbs and the countryside can be found today. Today you find elopement common outside the city -- that is, the boy and girl run off together and then go and live with the girl's mother until they can afford a marriage ceremony. A considerable time may elapse. You have elopements in the city too, but there the couple must get married immediately; outside they don't have to get married immediately. There is tremendous variation of culture patterns in other ways.

They do have the theater and the short story to present the dramatic side of life. One [theme] is the loss of virginity; another is the brother-sister relationship. But you must remember that there are class differences too. The peasant classes have a culture that is nearer to that of the landed gentry than that of the cities.

The position of the boy in the family is that of a potential father -- in a moral sense, of course. If the father dies, the oldest boy takes his place and orders his mother and sisters around. He may be only fourteen, but he assumes the role of the father. The brother-sister relationship is the ideal relationship between the sexes. There is great affection between brothers and sisters, but it is completely

---

21. The reference is to a study of adolescence conducted by the Caroline Zachry Institute of Human Development in New York City in the winter of 1946-47. Cf. Abel and Joffe (1950). -- Ed.

asexual. The sister assumes the position of the mother if the mother dies.

21F: Is that the oldest in terms of age, or the oldest unmarried child?

37M: They do recognize personal ability. Generally, it is the oldest girl or boy who takes the parent's place; but if the oldest one can't play the role, the one who can accepts it.

66F: In Italy the question would be academic anyway, because they all live under one roof.

4F: Generally the boys bring their wives home.

37M: Yes, where they have room. In Sicily and southern Italy they can't do that. Remember they live in towns, in very small houses, often in only one room. Only where there is extreme necessity do the married children live with the parents. ... [Omission.]

64F: But when the parents die after some of the children are married, will the oldest brother be head of the family?

37M: The oldest brother will still be head of the family and he will still have the say -- the responsibility; but at home the oldest boy left is head. Incidentally, the oldest son of the oldest brother is the titular head of the family on the death of his father and paternal uncles. The father is essentially a tyrant. -- in the classical meaning of the word. He represents authority and discipline. The sons eventually resent that authority. The mother has an entirely different role. The father is there by necessity and accident; the mother is there biologically. The real continuity is through the mother. The mother never loses the respect of her children, no matter what she does. In the story of Jesus and Mary, Mary is the eternal Mother who has to bear her Child in a manger and who sees her Son crucified. The experience of bearing a child in a manger is common to the peasants, but the tragedy is that the mother suffers for her children. Every boy is crucified; he is taken into the army.

To some degree you have in Sicily two cultures -- the man's and the woman's. The woman's culture is higher than the man's. Women are in closer contact with the priests and consequently get a certain wisdom from them.

64F: One culture is for the priests and the women and the other is for the men?

37M: Yes, one might make a point of that. The men are apart. They have their own clubs and political organizations. They never accompany the women to church. They have contact with the priests as teachers when they are young, but later they tend to become disassociated from the woman-priestly culture: men and women don't go to church together. In public men have little contact with women. But outside of the family circle the only contact that women have with men is with the priests.... [Omission.] During the war, the women who were left behind discovered they could earn their own living. In Sicily women do not work in the fields, except to help with the harvest, but during the war necessity forced them to go to work. (By the way, I found women informants very frank. They spoke to me openly even about sex.) They went into business. Then the men came back and they refused to let their wives and daughters continue working. The women were raging; the men didn't permit the women even though they themselves were unemployed. It would make them lose face. Generally in Sicily only merchants permit their women to work -- in the stores -- but there is an undercurrent of belief that merchants are Jews, not true Christians.

64F: What are the actual words in Italian [for loss of face] ?

37M: In the dialect, mala faccia -- "bad face."

66F (simultaneously): Brutta figura.

64F: Then they literally use the image of the face?

37M: This matter of the face is tremendously important. The brother has to protect his sister's honor because she possesses something -- her chastity -- which, if lost, cannot be retrieved. There, it is a very serious thing. A girl cannot get married if she is known to have lost her virginity.

21F: A man doesn't have to obey his sister as he does his mother, does he?

37M: The young boy is supposed to obey his elders, but the older he gets, the less he is inclined to obey them. He doesn't obey his mother either, except when she says: "Son, if you don't do this, I will die unhappy." The adolescent boy shows a strong inclination to disobey his mother except in extreme cases -- when she puts upon him the responsibility for her unhappiness or probable death. Remember though that women are not supposed to have the same knowledge of the rough and practical world as men do -- even as young boys do ... [Omission.]

... In the sixteen months I was in [Sicily] I never heard a single word against a mother, but a great deal against the father, on the part of the children. If the father mistreats the mother, the son might even kill his father. The ties between the child and mother are considered natural and inviolate. Between the child and father the ties are considered to be more social and formal.

The Sicilian peasant has somewhat the same attitude toward the nobles as the Negroes in the South have toward the whites. However, the cleavage is economic, not racial. Peasant boys are taught to defer to the upper classes. The father beats the hard facts of life into them. And I may say that the necessity to do this is extreme. A peasant in Sicily today works for four pounds of bread a week, and he works only half of the year. Winning and keeping the favor of the upper classes -- the employers -- is extremely important....

[Omission.]

When the brother assumes the father's role, he must become the disciplinarian and he must suppress affection.

64F: Is there any brother-sister avoidance before the death of the parents?

37M: No, but formerly there was. The firstborn son is very important to the mother; if he dies, she never forgets him. The relation between brothers and sisters is very affectionate, but formerly the oldest brother had to be addressed with the same term of respect as the father -- or a noble. Often a spiritual relationship exists between brothers, or brothers and sisters; they can promise to

be godfather or godmother to ⌊each other's⌋ children. After that they address
each other formally as <u>compare</u> (sponsor). It also happens between cousins.

<u>21F</u>:   Is there any taboo against the godparents of a child marrying?

<u>37M</u>:   I don't know, but I would say there is a taboo.

<u>21F</u>:   There is a taboo against it in Poland.

<u>64F</u>:   In Poland, the godparents can be people who were in love but didn't marry.

<u>37M</u>:   There is a special relationship of children to their paternal uncle, who is
also considered to be a potential father. You can't marry the children of uncles
-- parallel cousin marriage is incest -- that is, the children of two brothers.
But cross-cousin marriage -- with a child of mother's brother -- is permitted
and often arranged. The mother's brother looks after his sister's children because he is fond of his sister.

In spite of all the expression of love between brothers and sisters, the culture is not a sexy one. Women get much respect. They are perfectly safe on the
streets. There is no drive to violate women.

<u>64F</u>:   Did you have first-night rights in ancient Italy?

<u>37M</u>:   They had them centuries ago, but not any more. But you still may have
the situation of the wealthy man who makes it a condition with his peasant farmer
that he is to have access to the farmer's wife, and as compensation the farmer
will be permitted to advance, to rise, to prosper. Notice that he asks for access
to the man's wife, but not his daughter.

<u>66F</u>:   When that happens, does the man lose face, or does he just close his
eyes to it?

                              ⌊Omission.⌋

<u>37M</u>:   ... In Sicily, it is recognized that life is terribly hard; the man accepts
the situation. He loses face, but his disgrace is mitigated by this fact. He is
pitied rather than despised.

<u>21F</u>:   How does the woman's brother feel about it? Does he scold his brother-
in-law?

<u>37M</u>:   He resents it. He berates his brother-in-law, but he must accept it --
if the noble is tactless enough to make a public scandal of it.... There is a
tremendous necessity to keep up form; it is very important. Even atheists and
Communists will keep up the form of joining in processions and giving gifts to
the Church. You don't violate forms. It's patterned behavior. If a man's sister
is dead, he's got to show some grief and he has to embrace her. You must show
considerable grief if someone close to you dies. If his mother dies, a man sits
in his room and wails for two days.

<u>64F</u>:   Do they kiss the dead body farewell?

<u>37M</u>:   Yes, but children are protected from it. They try to get them away.

<u>30F</u>:   From what age?

<u>37M</u>:   A boy becomes of age when he begins to work -- at thirteen or fourteen.
In the upper classes, of course, it's like here.... In the poorer classes, a girl

of twelve or thirteen may act as a grown woman.

64F: What is the relationship of brothers-in-law?

37M: Not friendly, unless they are compares, which is an unextinguishable relationship -- a sworn relationship which they have had even as little boys. It is almost like a blood relationship and it persists throughout life, and woe to the one who violates it ....[Omission.] The compare has the freedom of the home.

21F: Does the priest have the same access to the house?

37M: Yes, but you have social control -- everyone knows; it prevents violation.

21F: Do brothers-in-law have the same access?

37M: No. Brothers have some say when the sister is to be married. But a man may have enmity and hatred for his brother-in-law all his life.

64F: One of the things that used to happen in this country among Italians was that the oldest daughter would not marry but would stay home and care for the younger children. In Sicily, does the oldest daughter have to be married before the others marry?

37M: They are usually married in order. But sometimes the oldest sister becomes a house nun. I think that in the cases you refer to, it was economic necessity that kept the oldest daughter unmarried. She was needed at home -- but also the family probably had not accumulated enough dowry to marry her off and by the time they did, she was too old to be wanted.

66F: [Regarding house nuns] In Sicily, not in Italy.

37M: It's common throughout the Catholic world....

64F: But the pattern of the oldest sister not marrying is there. Now, if a girl loses her virginity and it is publicly known, it is not necessary for her to have an illegitimate child to be disgraced?

37M: No. If the girl is caught openly in a compromising position.... If her brother discovers her, he may kill the man. If they have money, a marriage might be arranged. In Sicily things can always be arranged if there is money. However, the girl's lapse from virtue is never forgotten. [Omission.] Women enter marriage with no preparation.... In general, women informants told me women never experience any great pleasure from sexual intercourse. Wives must not appear too interested in passion; their primary function is to bear a child.

64F: It is more emphasizing maternity than de-sexualizing sex.

37M: Women are not exposed to sexual stimuli as they are here. There is no romantic ideal, but there is a deep sense of duty among the peasants that is confused with love. [Omission.]

64F: How about the point 30F made about theft for the man symbolizing loss of virtue for the woman? What can a man do ...

37M: There is very little thieving and practically none outside the large cities. An employer expects that an employee will take little things, but there is no real stealing. In the sixteen months I was there, the only thing I had stolen from me was a knife, which was taken by a gentleman; he was a kleptomaniac. However, the upper classes will tell you that the workmen and peasants are all thieves, though they continue to trust them. The peasants also accuse the upper classes of the same crime. Those who are actually thieves are well known by the neighbors and are treated as outcasts.

64F: But you said there were professional thieves....

37M: Yes, in the large cities.

64F: What happens in such a community if someone steals? Is he given extreme punishment?

37M: No. The general attitude is that he was impelled to do so by his nature -- poor guy. But he must be punished. If he is a peasant, he is beaten by the carabiniere and let go, if the crime is a trivial one and the victim doesn't prosecute. The sergeant of the carabiniere has great authority. If the thief belongs to the upper classes, things are arranged. Of course if the act is a serious one and is committed by a professional, the punishment is as severe as elsewhere, even though he is pitied.

21F: May I ask one question? Is it the thieving or the lost manhood, because he can no longer support his family, that is the disgrace?

30F: In the films, men who steal are represented as being at the point of desperation, but instead of trying to get clear, they hold their heads in their hands and say, "I'm a thief."

37M: But that is in the Christian tradition. These people are very heavily indoctrinated in Christian ethics. They have a terrible sense of guilt. To explain that would take a long time, but it goes back to classical times. There are no heroes. In my village the only "heroes" were a half-wit and a midget who didn't have sense enough to run away from danger. Saints are not heroes. They are reduced to very human dimensions. [Omission.] In all these stories, the audience reaction is important. The reaction even to a thief is "poor fellow."

30F: That's true about the other fellow, but for yourself -- no.

37M: No. The sense of guilt is very strong, particularly among men. Women don't have the same sense of guilt.

[Dialogue omitted.]

64F: ... This has been very interesting methodologically, because 30F has built up her hypotheses from thematic material. But this is a case where the treatment of the self and the treatment of others is different.... The interesting point is the audience reaction.

37M: Starting out with the poor guy who is knocked about by life. Every man is knocked around in some way. He lives on hope. [Omission.] Then he's frustrated. It doesn't happen. Well, that is the way life is. But there is always the possibility that the miracle may happen. In The Bicycle Thief the guy needs a job; he needs a bicycle for the job; he loses the bicycle and loses the job. For a moment he was uplifted; then he is let down. Poor guy! He is a prisoner of life.

64F: Belief in miracles is a sort of counterpoint against the misery of life.

37M: It's destiny. Destiny, for rich or poor, is inflexible. Some destiny is good -- but you can't avoid dying.

64F: But everything is a one-way progression.

37M: Italian literature deals with universal themes....

[The final part of the meeting, concerned with organizational details, is omitted.]

PART FOUR

WORK WITH INFORMANTS

A. INFORMANTS IN GROUP RESEARCH

Rhoda Métraux

Work with informants was central to all the studies made in Research in Contemporary Cultures. For essentially it is the long, free interviews, in which informant and interviewer work together over a period of time on problems of interest to both, and the microcosm of the relationship of informant to interviewer, which each interviewer must in his own way be able to recreate for other members of a research group, that provide the framework within which all the research materials are fitted together into a whole in the study of culture at a distance and, more especially, of national character structure. As it is used here, "work with informants" differs in meaning from and is to be distinguished both from the clinical and therapeutic interview or relationship and from what may be called "work with interviews,"[1] even though in practice all are in many respects overlapping. Since work with informants has already been discussed in this Manual, in the Introduction, I shall discuss first some of the things that it is <u>not</u> and then what it <u>is</u> in the same terms; then I shall comment briefly on the informant material included in this and other parts of the Manual. Without going into other, certainly equally important differences, I shall discuss only two that are common sources of confusion in discussions of interviewing as a research method -- the definition of the kind of problem on which one is working (as one way of distinguishing therapeutic work from work with informants) and the definition of the entity with which one is working (as one way of distinguishing work with interviews from work with informants).

Interviewing as it has been developed in recent years as a research method is based on several related general assumptions; i.e. that each individual is a unique entity (with consequent stress upon the total integration of the individual as well as upon the importance of individual differences); that there are linked regularities in the behavior of members of a group, in terms of which individuals in the group and the group itself can be defined; that direct interpersonal communication is a complex circular process of initiation and response that can provide

---

1. Examples of what is meant by work with interviews are the Gallup Poll type of interview in its many variations and the kinds of extended interview that were used, for instance, by the United States Bombing Survey in Germany in 1945 (1947) and other types of interview developed for the study of opinions and attitudes (among others, that developed for the Committee on Food Habits during World War II; cf. Métraux, 1943). I would include also much work that is done by means of questionnaires, as a form of indirect interviewing. As a single example of a study based on and combining work with various types of interviews, cf. S.A. Stouffer, <u>et al.</u>, <u>Studies in Social Psychology in World War II</u> (1949-50).

information with a kind of integration difficult to achieve by other means; and
so on. Depending upon the purpose for which the work is done, techniques of
interviewing vary very greatly in the ways in which they combine and emphasize
the possibilities of the method, and in the ways in which the problem is to be
defined.

In clinical and therapeutic interviews, as in work with informants, the relationship between "informant" and "interviewer" (however differently conceptualized) is of central importance. There is, however, a decisive difference in
the definition of the problem on which work is being done. In therapeutic relationships the problem is defined as primarily individual and personal to the
client or the analysand. In work with informants, on the contrary, however
personal the problem is or may become (and the handling of this question
places very great responsibility upon the interviewer, especially when he is
working with informants of a culture other than his own where both persons are
in the process of learning what is being communicated), it must be assumed by
interviewer and informant to be a problem in which both can take an objective
interest -- that discussions of, let us say the relationship of father and daughter, husband and wife, brother and sister, friend and friend, however much they
may draw on the informant's experience of one or more of these roles, are
motivated by a mutual interest in defining what these relationships mean to
others as well as to the informant (or to the interviewer!) himself.

In work with informants (as, in another way, in therapeutic interviews) it is
desirable, at least initially, to keep the possibilities of the informant-interviewer relationship open and to accommodate the relationship as far as possible
to the expectations of the informant. If this is not possible (and often it is not),
one should experiment with finding other types of relationship recognized by the
informant that are more adequately suited to the research situation. This will
vary from one culture to another and involves the use of different styles of interviewing by different kinds of interviewer in various situations and for various problems.[2] It does not preclude the use of already established relationships in the informant-interviewer situation -- on the contrary. It does mean,
however, that the fact that a daughter is interviewing her mother, a husband his
wife, a student his teacher, is part of the relevant information about these interviews, giving, for instance, indications about who can talk to whom about

---

2.   As one example, in Research in Contemporary Cultures, Chinese inter-
      viewers working over a longer time with particular Chinese informants
      found themselves becoming so involved in the whole system of mutual obli-
      gation (the validity of which they themselves accepted) that they -- and
      sometimes their families -- felt they could not extricate themselves. In
      this group it was found that, with some exceptions, it was wiser for Chinese
      interviewers to interview widely but not so intensively and for non-Chinese
      interviewers (of whom rather less was expected by Chinese informants) to
      do the long-term intensive interviews where informant and interviewer
      worked together for a year, or even two or three years.

what. The ways in which informants in different cultures redefine such an open relationship or use an already existing one can, of course, give major clues to definitions of interpersonal relations in these cultures. At the same time, these must be seen in terms of the research aim and the handling of the research problem in a partly impersonal manner. For instance, one must know and take into consideration whether when a sister is interviewing a brother, subjects can be discussed in an impersonal frame of reference that would ordinarily be embarrassing to both, or whether these are subjects brother and sister confide to each other about. Experience in work with informants in several cultures has shown also that it is advisable to include in the group of interviewers on a culture individuals of at least three cultures, so that one can be more certain that the relationships established and studied are not the product of one type of dyad (e.g. Chinese-American, French-American).

Especially the emphasis upon the individual as a specific, identified person (whether as informant or as interviewer) varies in different kinds of interviewing. Impersonalization of the interview situation is inevitable in work where, as an intermediate or final step, quantitative methods of analysis are used to organize the data (e.g. in the Gallup Poll type of interview) and also where, in qualitative analysis, the aim is to synthesize a mass of verbal material obtained from a large number of informants. The exigencies of quantitative methods of analysis -- the necessity (and desirability) of limiting the number of variables with which the analyst works, for instance, and the necessity of turning the raw verbal material into systematically comparable units that can be quantified -- decisively affects the work at every step (the planning of the interview, the handling of the interview situation, the kind and completeness of the recording, the categorization of the material by the analyst, etc.), determining both the kind of document that results from the actual interview and the kind of work that can be done with it. This applies as well to qualitative analyses -- though not in precisely the same ways -- where the analyst has no contact with interviewers or informants. Impersonalization of the interview does not preclude the necessity, for some types of work, of having interviewers with specific and highly specialized skills or informants who have been selected because they are qualified in very special ways, and it may necessitate very carefully planned standardization of the interview situation itself. It does mean, however, that once the specifications -- whatever they are -- have been met, the analyst need not, in considering how the details within an interview or among interviews are related, continually include in his thinking the particular individuals concerned. In some work with interviews, not only are informant and interviewer unknown to the analyst, but the two may be strangers to each other, whose interest in each other and in the problem is limited to the space of time in which the informant answers certain questions. Indeed, the interviewer can sometimes be regarded as a kind of evoking and recording device (replacing the anonymous questionnaire or some other method of obtaining information, because the data are not otherwise available, because a certain kind of rapport is necessary to obtain an answer, because it is necessary to test the limits of an answer, etc.); or the informant may be regarded as a combination of categories (e.g. a white, female, Protestant, public elementary schoolteacher aged 30-40, with an M.A. degree in Education) rather than as a person. An important problem in working with interview material is the extent to which informant and interviewer, knowing that only some of their behavior (the spoken word) will be recorded and considered, attend to or disregard other cues. (Occasionally these will be referred to directly in the interview, but sometimes they can only be inferred -- if that.[3]) Impersonalization may thus be carried very far into the interview situation itself; i.e. the responses of the particular interviewer to the particular informant in a rigidly scheduled interview may be limited to alterations of posture or gesture or to tone of voice (which may not, of course, be less meaningful to either or both than words); and the responses of all those involved are obviously exceedingly indirect in the case of questionnaires where each may -- in planning the questionnaire, in answering it, and in analyzing it -- come to think of the others (if they are all Americans) in terms of the impersonal but nonetheless meaningful "they."[4]

Several things follow from this impersonalization, some of which may be mentioned because of their relevance -- as contrast points -- to work with informants. First, there can be little question that in most cases where the focus is upon the recorded interview (rather than upon the persons who made it) it is desirable, especially when a large number of respondents are involved, for the interview itself to be styled so that interviewer and informant can -- since

---

3.   So, for instance, in a study of attitudes towards public housing, two young, experienced interviewers (who had actually previously taken part in government surveys in another part of the country) were continually asked by informants, "Do you come from the government?" or informants commented, "You have to be careful what you tell the government...." This particular question was never raised with other interviewers in the same study who were all undergraduate or graduate students, some of them working in war-housing areas as congested as those where worked the two who "looked like" other people the informants had seen coming from "the government." (Unpublished study made for the Committee on Food Habits, National Research Council, 1943). Or again, in a study made in Germany, where, for purposes of comparison, German interviewers were substituted for Americans but the circumstances of the interview situation (method of selecting informants, types of question, etc.) remained constant, one can infer from the kinds of reversals in the answers (compared to answers given in studies made by American interviewers) that German informants, were well aware that they were talking to Americans through other Germans; without reinterviewing, however, this is merely an inference based on a comparison of these and other materials. (Cf. Crespi, 1950.)

4.   This is of course not invariably the case; in long-term studies involving panels of correspondents, open-ended discussion questions and qualitative analyses, a community of interest may be built up. For one example, see the research reported by Herzog (1947).

their own personal styles are not to be taken into consideration -- accommodate themselves to it and the responses of all the informants can be judged in terms of a style that is known to the analyst. That is, it is desirable for interviewer and informant to be asked to act within a pattern, a determining part of which has been set in advance. This means, in effect, that those who are planning the interviews (and the analysis of them) must have, implicitly or explicitly, considerable advance knowledge of the kind of interview situation informant and interviewer will be able to interpret as a suitable one for giving and obtaining the kind of information that is sought, and they must be able to form hypotheses in advance about ways in which the content -- that is, the informants' responses -- can be categorized. This form of interviewing and analysis does not readily lend itself to exploratory work on a culture where the possible roles to which interviewer and informant can be assimilated are not known,[5] where the dynamics of question and answer (initiation and response) are not known, where the ways in which individuals categorize experience (and the kinds of imagery used to express experience) are not yet known.

Second, where there is a break between interviewer and informant on the one hand and the analyst on the other, one cannot attempt to reconstitute personality in the analysis of the interview material -- at least where one does not have a great many other sources of information -- on a new culture. At best, where the interview has been a sufficiently open and flexible one so that the interviewer, not bound by a schedule, has been able to respond in terms of the informant's own responses and there is a good deal of free-flowing content, one may through qualitative analysis get considerable insight into cultural regularities of behavior that can then be followed up with other sorts of work.[6]

---

5. A case in point may be cited where, during an early stage of exploratory work, a European refugee totally misinterpreted a formal interview situation into which she was brought without adequate preparation (as it turned out) and was asked to discuss her personal and professional life in some detail. In the interview, one person acted as interviewer and another as observer and recorder; neither was known to the informant except, rather vaguely, by name. As this setup followed a pattern of police interrogation to which she and many of her friends had been subjected in her own country (a fact the interviewers did not then know and so could not take pains to explain in other terms), the informant became extremely disturbed, and when the difficulty was finally made clear, several hours of explanation and reassurance were needed before the informant's confidence in her security was restored. This is an extreme, but certainly not a very unusual, example of the kind of thing that can happen.

6. One example of what is meant here is given in Part Three of this Manual, in the meeting of the French group (pages 104-07). One member of the group had had about 100 interviews with several French informants. These had been recorded and circulated among the members of the group and excerpts were made from them by the group convener for discussion at the meeting. However, the interviewer did not take part in the group discussion and had not yet been interviewed about the interviews or her relations to the informants. The group here was dealing with interviews, not work with informants; the situation changed later when the interviewer had had an opportunity, through discussion, to reconstruct for the group her relations to these informants, and so on.

Third, in work with interviews, when a new problem is raised that necessitates a revaluation of the whole or some part of it (whether this is one interview with each of 500 informants or 200 interviews with five different informants), the essential point of return is the <u>recorded interview itself.</u> In this respect, working with interviews is similar to work with any other documentary material: it is complete and fixed, and any new insights into the material depend upon alterations in the point of view or the approach or the knowledge of the analyst -- who may, in between an early and a later analysis, have tapped new sources of information that enable him to reinterpret or least interpret in greater detail the material which, very likely, prompted him to turn to other sources. The fixedness of the entity with which one is working -- the fact that one can return to it innumerable times, can break it down in ten different ways and each time, if necessary, reconstitute the same whole,[7] that one or twenty people can each analyze it, etc. -- is both the greatest advantage of and the final limitation upon work with interviews, as it is with work on any document. It is also the point of greatest contrast with work with informants.

For, essentially, in work with informants the point of return in each case -- whether one is considering a detail within the whole accumulated material or the whole in terms of a new question -- is the actual informant, or rather, the informant in his relationship to a specific interviewer. So in work with informants, the analyst must be someone who has continuous contact -- while the interviewing and work of analysis are proceeding -- with the informant-interviewer unit.

From this it follows that in group research, where one interviewer or at most two or three are likely to have direct communication with any one specific informant on a culture, it is necessary not only for the whole group to have continuous access to the entire recorded material (since it is assumed that each statement by informant and interviewer is related to all preceding ones) but also for the interviewer to act continuously as an informant to the group on the particular informant-interviewer relationship, so that the informant as a person and information about the problem discussed are mediated to other individuals in the group by a person with known training, professional skills, personal predilections, etc. Each interviewer (as also, as a matter of fact, each person working on any material) is, in this sense, a prism through which all look at the persons and the problems studied.[8] This means also, in reverse, that all the members of the group are, in a sense, informants to an interviewer on his own relation-

---

7.   The method of recording used in Bali in which theoretical insights are
     placed in a time record that includes photography greatly increases the
     possibility of a return to the same whole. Cf. Mead (1946b) and Mead and
     Macgregor (1951), Appendix I.
8.   The implications of this have been discussed by Dr. Mead both in the
     Introduction to this Manual and in Part Three on the organization of group
     research.

ships to his informants, for as one person will be more sensitive to gesture, another to tone of voice, another perhaps to pace, and so on, each tends to see his own informants in terms of these sensitivities and to alert others to unnoticed possibilities in these directions. This applies also, of course, to more formal aspects of the work, such as awareness of levels of consciousness, interest in plot or structure.

It is evident that although in work with informants one is attempting to work with the total personality, in work at a distance there are limitations in the extent to which this can be carried out, and that these limitations vary not only from one informant-interviewer relationship to another, but also from one culture to another (depending upon how these relationships can be interpreted in the culture). Nevertheless, if one is working on problems of personality -- or character structure -- it is necessary to maintain in the analysis of the material awareness of the individual personality insofar as it is known. This means that in group research the entity with which one is working is primarily the particular informant-interviewer relationship, but it includes also the whole group who are at work, for in the kind of group research discussed here, there is continuous interplay between the responses of informant and interviewer -- as each of these also responds to his own responses -- and between the responses of the interviewer and other members of the research group, which in turn feed back into following interviews.

Since this is true, and since it is necessary to give as free play as possible to each person involved, it is necessary for the interviews to be carried on in a highly disciplined fashion, but this discipline consists in continual accommodation to the total flow of information. Here again there is sharp contrast to other types of interviews that have been discussed (i.e. the impersonalized interview). It follows also that in order to conserve the richness and complexity of the material, analysis of work with informants is inevitably qualitative, depending for its results mainly upon insights into regularities in behavior and the ways in which details are interwoven in the whole.

Work with informants can be described, yet in the nature of the case, cannot be illustrated, but only demonstrated. Learning how to do work with informants depends primarily upon an apprenticeship type of training in which the apprentice learns by demonstration and by participation both as an informant for and an interviewer of more experienced interviewers in situations in which they can then analyze the content and the kind of relationship that developed. To develop flexibility in his own style, the apprentice requires variety in his training experience; for as the experienced interviewer adapts himself to the expectations of the informant (in the degree of formality, in the number and kinds of questions or mere exclamations needed to elicit answers and keep the interview going, even in the manner of recording his notes), so from one such interview the apprentice carries away as part of his learning about interviewing a

mirror version of his own expectations.[9] For practical reasons, he needs an
opportunity to work with several people whose adaptations will differ in terms
of their own style, and also to observe other informant-interviewer pairs (or
groups) at work. In group research, training also involves participation in group
discussions where several people are acting in the double roles of informant
and interviewer of one another.[10]

Since we cannot illustrate work with informants, this part of the Manual is
designed to show, through the presentation of a small number of interviews,
some variety in styles of work by interviewers and several kinds of informant-
interviewer relationship in different cultures (China, France, Poland, Syria, pre-
Soviet Great Russia, and the culture of the East European Jewish shtetl). In
addition, we are presenting three examples of work by members of research
groups who were acting as informants to the group by writing up for discussion
materials from their own experience. The thirteen selections represent work
by nine individuals, some of whom also appear as participants in group discussions in Part Three. Thus one may compare their work in two or three situations -- the work of one interviewer with a Syrian woman and a Syrian man (in
both of which interviews there is considerable awareness of posture and gesture,
for example) or of another interviewer with a French couple and with a Russian
actor. The selections are intended also to be read together with other materials
in the Manual -- the group discussions and the working papers on written
sources, films, and so on, but especially those which combine work on documentary materials with work with informants (e.g. Nelly Hoyt's analysis of imagery
in Russian bylini; the comparison of the film and the novel of The Young Guard
by Vera Schwarz (Alexandrova), where she herself is working from a position
within the culture she is discussing; and Martha Wolfenstein's discussion of
Soviet images of corruption; in other cases the work of analysis depended upon
similar combinations -- Virginia Heyer's analysis of popular Chinese tales,
John Weakland's two papers on Chinese films and on family images in Chinese
Communism, Leopold Haimson's analysis of Soviet chess -- but the informant
work is less apparent in the papers as written and presented here). No such
brief selection can illustrate the range of work by any one individual or by a
group doing research on one culture; the range of relationships established over
time between interviewers and informants; the kinds of interviewing problems
that had to be met and solved in a variety of circumstances; or the kinds of in-

---

9. I am indebted to Dr. Mead for this observation on training procedures.
10. For examples of two styles of intragroup interviewing, cf. Part Three of
    this Manual, the meetings of the Russian group (pages 107-15) and the Chinese
    group (pages 115-24). To these may be contrasted the Italian group dis-
    cussion (pages 131-40) where, at the first meeting of a new group, partici-
    pation was limited almost entirely to those who were presenting material
    and those members of the group who had already had considerable experi-
    ence of the method; their interaction in itself provided a demonstration
    to the others present.

terviewing -- and the length of time -- required to obtain comparable information in the several cultures studied. Nor is it possible to illustrate the subtle
changes in relationship that take place over time or when two interviewers work
with the same informant. At best, by selecting interviews both for likeness and
contrast, some of these points can be suggested.

In terms of content, the interviews have been selected so that comparisons
with other materials can be made and the reader, turning from one part of the
Manual to another, can see how these materials can be woven together into
statements about the culture.[11] So, for instance, one can compare the images
of the dangerous outsider that occur in an interview with a French couple (Interview IV) and the characterizations of the split-father image in two French
films and Nathan Leites's analysis of the viewpoint of an outsider in Camus's
novel L'Etranger. Or one may compare the discussion of friendship by a
Chinese informant (Interview VI) with the analysis of roles in the study of popular Chinese tales or in Cantonese films and the Chinese group discussion of
sincerity and the Chinese informant's description of her own "inner life." Or
again, one may compare the interview on friendship with the Chinese informant
(where the interviewer is an American and does not speak Chinese but knows
the informant well and is using as the basis of this interview material provided
by other informants) and another interview on the same subject with a French
informant (where both informant and interviewer are partly French, partly
American, speak French together, and so on). Or by comparing the excerpts
from essays by a Polish informant (who is a young, urban intellectual woman)
with the interview with an elderly Polish peasant woman (Interview III), one can
see consistencies of attitude that are included in the analysis of Polish attitudes
towards courage made by Sula Benet. Or one may compare the vigorous con-
tentiousness of the two pairs of Jewish informants (Interview VII and VIII) with
that of the Jewish group itself "acting," as one member of the group commented
to me, "like a group of Talmudic scholars each defending his own point."

In some cases the interviewer's notes on the interview situation and the
informant have been greatly curtailed for presentation here; in other cases
little was given (either because the informant was used for the first time and
the information was as yet meager or, on the contrary, because the relationship was a well-established one, known to the other members of the group).
Even so, they can help the situation come alive and make the contrasts more
apparent -- the formality of the French interviews (of which one took place in
an office, the other in a home); the studied concentration of the Syrian inform-

---

11. It is necessary, however, to repeat the caution already given, that as these
    are working papers isolated from their original context (many of them ex-
    cerpts) and records of work in progress, no detail, no statement by an in-
    formant, is to be regarded as necessarily objectively true except from the
    informant's own viewpoint at the time it was made.

ants, each of whom carried on the narration without a break in spite of numerous interruptions; the incorporation of the interviewer into the activities of the
home in the Jewish interviews; the free-flowing imagery of the single Russian
informant and the group of Russian informants where one (Interview IX) was
speaking to the interviewer for the first time and the others (Interview X) were
friends of many years' standing.

One interview, that with the Syrian man (Interview II), has been included
especially to illustrate how an informant may suddenly in the course of a long
and prosaic account give one a spontaneous symbolic statement of the greatest
possible value -- in this case moving from a tedious and fancified description
of his home to a description of a fountain, then to an image of the body and the
senses. Interviews can be carefully guided, as was, for instance, the Chinese
one where again and again the interviewer tests the interpretation of a point; or
the informants may be allowed to take the lead, the interviewer intervening only
enough to hold them to the subject, as was the case in the two Jewish interviews.
But in exploratory interviews such as all of these are, one cannot predict when
some entirely new point or one that pulls together details thus far quite unrelated will occur to an informant, or to the interviewer who is listening.

B. THREE ILLUSTRATIONS OF WRITTEN WORK BY INFORMANTS

I. Polish Personality[12]

These three personal essays, none of which is given here in its entirety, are from a series of brief papers written by one informant, 12F, on a variety of subjects related to Polish personality. The informant, a young woman, grew up and lived in Poland until the end of World War II. As a member of the Polish group in Research in Contemporary Cultures, she worked closely with the convener, who interviewed her at length about her own life. Then, taking as a starting point questions that had been raised in their conversations, the informant used these formulations (e.g. Does responsibility mean command?) as the subjects of essays in which she brought together the information at her disposal. In writing, she drew very freely upon her memories of her childhood in Poland, her recollections of her family -- especially her grandmother -- and of their and her friends. She herself interviewed other Poles and also drew upon these interviews in working out her views of the problems. These papers therefore stand in an intermediate position between the spontaneous autobiography and the interview where informant and interviewer are working together on a problem. Here the questions were, in the main, posed during interviews and discussions but were worked out with considerable independence by the informant, who put her information together in her own time and way. This method, agreed upon by two members of the culture being studied, is itself a reflection of an education in which the individual has been "indoctrinated to 'take responsibility by himself.'" (See below.)

In the viewpoint expressed -- i.e. the definition of personal responsibility and the emphasis upon the "hard" spirit -- these essays, written by an urban, educated young woman, may be compared to the statement of elderly peasant woman interviewed in Poland (cf. below, pages 179-81); and in style -- i.e. the transitions from the personal and individual to the Polish and the national -- they may be set beside the analysis of the culture made by Sula Benet (1952; for a brief excerpt from this study, cf. Part Ten, IV, pages 415-21). --Ed.

1. Does Responsibility Mean Command?

To peasant children responsibility is assigned much earlier than to the city children and to the children of landowners. They have to take full responsibility for younger brothers and sisters, sometimes as early as the age of three. Small children or babies are left with older children sometimes for the whole day. A three-year-old girl is allowed to "organize" the whole day of her younger sister. There are only a few suggestions from the parents on how this day should be spent.

When I was four or five years old my grandmother used to reprove me by saying, "Look at this peasant girl ... she is younger than you and she takes care of her small brother." There is a lot of admiration for the "hard education" given to peasant children; even the people who have contempt for "simple people" still admire their self-sufficiency, responsibility, hardness, and independence. "We are more and more soft," my grandmother used to repeat to me.

---

12. Unpublished documents RCC-P 91, 94, and 96. Informant 12F.

The consequences of lack of responsibility are often exaggerated. When I was four years old, I was supposed to take care of my young brother for one hour, one day. I did not take very good care of him, and when the nurse (mamka) came he was almost dead under the large pillow I had put over him while he was crying. This fact was a nightmare of my whole childhood. My grandmother repeated to me over and over again that I had no sense of responsibility, that I almost killed my brother.

Then I faced for the first time the idea of "punishment for sins" -- it was no longer a daily short family punishment, such as refusal of dessert, or standing in the corner; but it had a metaphysical meaning. First of all prison and afterward hell. Those who neglect their responsibilities will suffer the most horrible punishments. "Your brother almost died (as a matter of fact he was not dying at all). You were big enough to know how to behave in such a situation."

The child is obliged not only to listen to the orders of the parents but also to have command over the situation. The child has to realize that the worst may result from his neglecting assigned tasks: the person may die. I know my experience is not a peculiar one. The children who were educated in a different way -- who were not independent enough -- were teased by other children, and they were ridiculed by my parents and my grandmother.

A small boy (sometimes only three or four years old) should know that under difficult circumstances he has to protect his mother and young sister. The circumstances are difficult to predict. He has to have enough independence to manage unknown circumstances. The small boy is told by a father going away for a trip, "I leave you our mother -- remember to take good care of her." The girl is never asked to take care of mother. A boy is usually very proud when for the first time such a responsibility for a mother is assigned to him. The father tells him, "Now you are already a man." The boy is trained from an early age to substitute for his father as "head of family." The girl is trained to take care of younger brothers and sisters. When there is an older boy in the family and a younger girl, the boy is never asked to take care of a baby.

The child is told not only to make a good performance when the responsibility is assigned to him by parents or teachers, but he is indoctrinated to "take responsibility by himself." When the older boy passes a street where a struggle between younger children is going on, he should interfere. He should "help the weaker" -- this is his duty.

The child who is encouraged to hunt birds and animals is at the same time told to take care of a wounded bird or of a sick dog. In the same way he is supposed to take care of blind or crippled people whom he meets on his way. My grandmother and my nurses used to tell me that each of these poor sick individuals may be a disguised Christ, who appeared on my way to test my character.

A lack of responsibility is very much blamed in all social strata -- the man who does not take care of his family, the woman who does not take care of her children. The man may be drunk and he may lose his temper. "I understand the man," one Polish engineer told me, "who gets drunk and makes a baby on his wife -- it is all right, he has to live a full life. But later on he has to take the full responsibility." The conversation took place here in New York. The Polish engineer was criticizing a young American intellectual who did not take a job while his wife was pregnant. "This could not happen in Poland," he said. He also criticized him for the fact that he went to a party while his wife felt bad because of her pregnancy. "If he were a Polish peasant," he said, "the whole village would blame him and he could not behave in this way." One has to take the responsibility for his own acts, whatever these acts are. As a matter of fact, I think that the character of an act is seldom criticized in Poland -- the way one approaches it is criticized. Methods are more important than goals; one could say perhaps goals are only very vaguely prescribed, while the method of achieving these goals is under more strict social control. (One should check this hypothesis.) The taking of responsibility could be, I think, looked at as a part of these well-controlled methods of behavior....

There is a lot of admiration in Poland for individual responsibility and individual leadership, I think. The Polish national heroes are always solitary individuals who take on themselves whole responsibility. Many times they take on more than they can afford. This attitude was widely criticized in Poland after World War II, but it still has a great appeal for Poles. The director in a Polish office is, I think, a much more solitary individual than the director in an American office. I remember during the war one of the directors of the Warsaw Municipal Office (Magistrat); he was a simple clerk before the war and became director during September 1939. There was a lot of talk about his career. His own opinion and the opinion of others was that as a humanist (he was a historian) he was not afraid of taking responsibility which seemed too great to more specialized people: "He had a perspective"; "He was not a good tecnnician in any domain, but he had imagination."

During the war in Poland and during the Warsaw uprising I noticed that the "taking of responsibility" was greatly appreciated. Taking responsibility was understood as an ability to make decisions and to command people. One never inquired very much into the nature of these decisions. The lack of responsibility for the life of others was rarely criticized. The lack of responsibility for the idea, or rather for living according to ideals, was very much criticized.

The Polish Government in 1939 was very much criticized by all social strata for its failure to "stand for an idea"; very few people emphasized the point that in this way the Polish National Treasury was saved from German hands. There is a strong conviction one should "be an example" and remain with the people for whom "one is responsible." And one is responsible not only for small concrete groups but, many times, for millions, for the whole country. If one fails in this duty one can always repent. There was a lot of talk during the war in Poland about how

Rydz Smigly had repented. He apparently came back to Poland and became the
"humblest soldier" of the Polish Underground. There are many tales of this sort
in Polish history....

2. Attitudes toward Various Parts of the Body: the Upper Part, the Brain, the
Heart, Left and Right, the Lower Part

One could say, I think, that the upper part of the body is considered in Poland as "the noble part": breast, arms, head, forehead (a big forehead signifies
nobility and intelligence). People with a big head and necessarily a large forehead are considered more intelligent than people with a small head. People with
a small (low) forehead are suspected of being stupid, and even criminal. There
is quite a common belief that women have smaller brains than men. One has to
protect one's head carefully during the cold and during the hot days. The wearing
of hats is much more common in Poland than in America. Foreigners are often
surprised to see Polish children with covered heads.

The heart, together with the breast (in the case of men only), is considered
the seat of courage: "He has a lion's heart." It is not indecent to show "a nude
breast." One hears about men at war or at dueling fighting with the breast nude.
The tearing of one's shirt from one's breast is a sign of "honorable" despair
(for example, Rejtan). It is also a sign of protest under hopeless circumstances.
The man who is disappointed over his strongest beliefs may use this gesture as a
sign of protest. One speaks about a woman's breast with respect. It is much
more a symbol of maternity than a sexual organ. Speaking about beautiful
breasts of girls is considered very indecent.

The hands are strong, or helpful, or beautiful, or good. "Put your good hands
on my head" could be a part of a love dialogue in Poland. The right hand is more
important than the left one: "He is my right hand."

The lower part of the body is very "indecent." One should not speak about
it (excepting the legs, about which one speaks in Poland much as Americans
speak about beautiful breasts). The worst part of the body is, I think, the stomach.
One is supposed to conceal all stomach troubles. The man who would confess to
a stomachache in the presence of a woman would be looked at with disgust.

I think women's legs are the only part of the lower body which is defined as
sexually interesting and about which one is allowed to speak. Pretty legs are
considered the most important factor of sex appeal. This is probably only recent.
In the last century, beautiful arms played, I think, the role of pretty legs in the
twentieth century.

3. When is a Pole Allowed to Be Soft: Soft with Himself? Soft with Others?

I think it is allowed and approved to be soft toward a wounded soldier in a
hospital. He should not, however, be soft to himself even under such circumstances. He can be demanding and may feel he deserves all this, but he cannot be
weak. The wounded soldiers, and particularly officers, had everything at the beginning of the war in Ujazdowski Hospital. The wounded soldiers on a battlefield,

however, do not get much pity. The Polish song "How beautiful is war" says: "When the soldier falls down from his horse, his colleagues do not have any pity for him ... they trample him with their horses"; and they sing: "Sleep, dear colleague, in the dark grave....We wish you dreams about Poland."

One is allowed to be soft toward the Underground soldiers. Everything was given to them during the war, and they were allowed to be spoiled (the best beds, food, etc., were given to them at the cost of other people in the house). They were not allowed, however, to show any fear or even hesitation before the difficult tasks of Underground work. As a matter of fact, I think the Polish man is never allowed to be soft for himself. He has to be strong and well controlled, even in the last moments of his life. He may cry under certain circumstances, but never because of his own suffering or of personal defeat. He is allowed to cry because of the defeat of the country. The Mayor of Warsaw, Starzynski, was crying during the days of Warsaw's defeat in 1939. He remained in Warsaw and organized the defense until the last moment.

Courageous men are allowed to be soft toward themselves in this sense: "They lost in spite of their courage." "It was exterior defeat, but not moral defeat." The crying Starzynski was described with admiration even in the postwar Polish newspapers. The capitulating soldiers (it has to be so called "honorable defeat") were crying "like babies" and this was never criticized; it was, rather, admired by society.

Men are allowed to be soft toward women, children, and animals. Being masculine is often described in this way: "hard to himself and soft to all weak individuals."

The Poles (men and women) are also allowed to cry when the honor of the family is lost through no fault of their own. The parents of the girl who became Volksdeutsch cried, and this was largely approved.

The father is allowed to cry during moving family ceremonies like weddings, different anniversaries, or funerals.

II. My Inner Self[13]

The author of the following document is a young Chinese woman, the daughter of a public official of some prominence in one of China's port cities during the Nationalist era. Her father was born in an overseas Chinese community, was educated in China and the United States, and returned to China in early manhood to participate in the reorganization of China's government after the revolution of 1911. The informant herself lived in China until she was fifteen years old and left in advance of the Japanese occupation of her native town. After living for two years in a conservative Chinese family in a progressive South Seas community, she came to the United States to finish college, married an American-born Chinese, and at the time she joined Research in Contemporary Cultures was a graduate student.

At the time that these autobiographical notes were written, the informant had been working on the project for approximately two years. Her major contribution, in addition to participation in group discussions, had been a long and

---

13. Unpublished document RCC-CH 689. Informant 45F.

elaborate paper on the Chinese house. She wrote out these notes after the question of what "inner life" means to the Chinese had come up a number of times in the course of group discussions on China. About a week after handing in this document, the author remarked to the convener quite spontaneously and with considerable feeling, at the end of a meeting, "I have been thinking more about this inner life and do you know, I have lost it since coming to America." Asked why this was so, she replied: "I have no need for it any more. Here you can come right out with what is in your mind."

This recognition that adjustment to a new culture involves a reorganization of the total personality marked a stage in the informant's adaptation to American culture, to which she believed other work done on the project contributed. The writing of the paper on the Chinese house took her into an extended review of the basic works of Chinese philosophy, "because you cannot write intelligently about the Chinese house without describing <u>feng-shui</u> (the system of magic that governs the location and orientation of all structures in China) and you cannot describe <u>feng-shui</u> without describing how Chinese feel about man's relation to the universe." The paper when finished had a long philosophical introduction and a long philosophical conclusion, for which the author apologized. "I am sure that you will not want to publish all that, but I had to write it that way. I had to get these things written down. It plagued me; I couldn't sleep nights until I had gotten it straight." It was apparent that the work on the project was the means of working out a personal problem the precise nature of which did not become evident until somewhat later, but which concerned the relationship of the inform- ant to the two cultures to which she had been exposed. Stated symbolically, she had to work out her relationship to the universe before she could deal compe- tently with the location and orientation of her house. The notes on her "Inner Self" and the accompanying comments, besides telling us something about the inner life of a Chinese child, reveal one kind of experience that may be en- countered when one examines systematically the basic assumptions of one's own culture from a distance and in collaboration with others who, while sympathetic, do not share these assumptions.--Ed.

My inner self is my real self, my consciousness of awareness of being. It is a self not easily revealed to others and guarded unto myself as a basis of my secured well-being, especially in a society where truth is arrived at empiri- cally, not scientifically.

A typical example of this inner self as revealed in experience is the fol- lowing. I was eight at the time. My grandmother had just returned from Ameri- ca to join the family consisting of my parents, grandfather, elder sister, younger brother, and myself. Up to then my feeling toward Grandmother had been one of innocence and eager acceptance of her as a new experience in my young, sheltered life. The slightly American ways she brought with her, her com- paratively positive approach toward life (in comparison to my grandfather, who spent his old age in naïve philosophical bliss), her ability to help my sister and me in our Chinese, her introduction to us of Chinese juvenile literature (such as <u>Monkey</u>), and her readiness to tell us the history of the family (my grand- father and mother were the quiet type, my father was busy with his career, spending very little time with us children) -- all these created a favorable heroine image in my impressionable mind.

One day she remarked casually that at her age she needed glasses. Inno- cently I told her that probably my eyes were not so good either. "Why," I said, "the other day when I was walking into the bathroom (which had a window facing the door), I saw rings in the air coming toward me." (Scientifically, this phen-

omenon is attributed to the movement of the impurities in the fluid in the eyeballs.) She did not say anything to the remark and I forgot about the incident.

A few days passed. I entered the dining room one morning and found my
grandmother having breakfast with my father. The conversation was about
glasses, and observing my entrance into the room, my grandmother repeated
what I had told her about my eyes.

"Children should not open their mouths indiscreetly," my father said to me
sternly. "How could you have eye trouble at your age!" I felt terrible inside,
I wanted to say, "Why not?" Yet I could not find words to express my feeling,
so stirred was I by what seemed to me a frame-up. I stammered, "But it was
the truth," only to bring sterner remarks from Father. I bolted from the room.

My inner self was my best friend at such trying moments. I did not go to
Mother, nor did I tell my sister who was my closest companion. I felt ch'i
(filled with air or anger), which was only calmed down after a discourse I had
with myself. To me it was truth sacrificed by the fact that it was uttered by a
child. As for my grandmother, I thought her double face most hypocritical. I
took it as a warning not to be too open with her, or any other adult, again.

Such experiences helped to make a quiet child out of me, full of observations, feelings, and thoughts, but lacking in speech and action   Externally I
was passive, internally I was seldom inactive. Everything I observed, I "think
over in my heart" (hsin li hsien -- "heart within think"). Such thinking, however, was seldom translated into speech or action, partly because of the pressure from adults that children should not speak freely, and partly because of the
feeling that the battle is already won in your heart and exposure of it only
makes a small person out of you. This premeditation and reflection may be
partly responsible for the pungent speech I developed in my teens, speech that
was cutting and cold and somehow seemed uncontrolled by internal thoughts.
Of course there must be other reasons for this sarcasm, as we shall see later
in my relationship with other members of the family.

The earliest incident in my life in which I remember my inner self playing
a part occurred when I was about three and a half years old. The doctor was
giving me a vaccination while my mother tried to distract my attention with an
alarm clock. I knew exactly what was happening. I was not frightened by what
the doctor was doing, and I thought it foolish of my mother to attempt to distract me. However, I pretended that I was interested in the clock, whereas all
the time I kept an eye on the doctor.

My elder sister and I were constant companions when we were young. Our
parents were careful not to show partiality between us. As a matter of fact,
they always tried to give more consideration and attention to the child in the
less favorable position in order to help her along. This we understood very
well and as individuals we even co-operated with our parents.

I understand my sister was a demanding baby and very much attended to

by both my parents. When I was born the novelty had worn off, I was given to
the care of a wet-nurse -- a fact which my parents talked about in teasing
moods and which in turn made me feel rejected for many years to come. That
must have accounted partly for the tantrums I used to have before five, curable
only at the touch of Mother's hands. Before I was five, I had much childhood
sickness, and as a result was kept home much of the time. I was then the envy
of my sister. In later years, as our individuality developed we had our complaints of parental partiality, but these were complaints known only by our inner selves and very seldom expressed.

Our work, whether for home or school, was shared in good spirits. The
one who was better in one subject helped the other without condescension, and
the other accepted the help as freely as it was given. We never went to bed until the work of both was finished, and we took it as a duty to check on each
other's homework. Many a time our teachers in the American school which we
attended from the sixth to the eighth grades found we made similar mistakes
or had the same ideas -- actually those were mutual mistakes and ideas. This
mutual help is no doubt one of the dominant features of Chinese home life, but
here I wish to write of the consciousness of myself as a participant in such a
society.

I usually helped my sister in her English lessons, sometimes even to the
extent of rewriting a whole composition. But that was never made known to
others. Our report cards were compared by our parents; no praise was ever
given to the one with the higher marks, and whatever weak mark one had called
for a general lecture for both. I knew my parents sensed that my sister was
slower in her work; this, however, they attributed to good sense and steadiness.
They somehow always maintained that my sister knew what is right and wrong,
while I was temperamental, and that knowing what is right and wrong gives
character to a person, and that a fast mind is secondary to character. I often
held debates with my inner self over this observation of theirs. I conceded
that my sister had a strong mind, but I doubted if I lacked character of my own.
No doubt I betrayed my feeling through the sarcastic speech I developed in
this period, but in general I decided that the best way to correct such an attitude of my parents was through time and fortitude on my part. I figured that
if I should make a fuss of the situation (and this is not possible in a hierarchical
family like the Chinese), it only would prove the opposite of what I wanted to
prove. It would show narrow-mindedness, which I considered a base character.
"The sage looks like a fool" -- and I was bent to be that kind of sage. Furthermore, I was happy to see that through this debasement of myself, my sister
felt less inferior to me. What I did well in achievements she made up in her
superiority feeling in character. This attitude of my parents persisted through
our high school and college years. I had never attempted to correct it as I
felt it preserved better feeling all around. So far as I myself maintain inner

security afforded by my inner self -- in other words, so far as I know the reality -- my equilibrium is not disturbed. And so far as they like to hold onto a conception which makes them comfortable, I have no objection.

In the first Chinese girls' school we attended, a few boys were accepted in the lower grades. There was one boy in my class who sat next to me and who did many errands for me. My sister and I belonged to a gang which included my mother's stepsisters and brothers. One day the subject fell on boy and girl friends, and my sister told the group that the boy in my class was my boy friend. Actually it was not so, but I was embarrassed by the teasing that ensued. Inwardly I felt very bad about my sister, whose act, to me, spelled betrayal and lying to gain group acceptance at my expense.

Our maternal uncle was like an elder brother to us. He was entering college and was full of fun and spirit. He invented games for us, told us historical stories, helped us in our homework -- in fact we always felt he was more approachable than our overworked and much absent father. In his treatment of us sisters, it was apparent he had a partiality for me. I did not like the idea at all and so always tried to give my sister the benefit whenever possible. Many of Uncle's college friends became friends of the family; they too, to my annoyance, were attracted to me. I knew physical attraction is not man-made, and I felt God had done injustice to my sister. In time I developed some guilt feeling from this and compensated for it by being extra nice and sympathetic to my sister.

My sister had aimless tantrums until she was at least fourteen, and I was usually the victim of those fits. I never talked about those incidents, except sometimes to tease her when we were alone, and I doubt my parents ever knew half that went on behind our closed door. One time she gave me a punch so hard that I was out for a few seconds.

Relatives often lived with us. We rented two three-storied houses in a row in a lane. One of them was occupied by the family, the other was used partly as an office but chiefly as quarters for the men relatives who worked in Father's office. One of them was a young bachelor who was very fond of me. He used to greet me with kisses, a practice which was very modern considering the fact he was from the village, and which was discontinued as I grew older. When we were seven and eight, our parents were away for a whole year, and in that period my sister and I saw much of him. On Saturdays my sister usually made me ask him to take us to the movies. That presented great conflict to my inner heart. I wanted to go to the movies, but I also felt it inhuman of us to ask him to take us, considering the meager salary he made. The greatest guilt felt, however, sprang from the fact I felt my sister was making a prostitute out of me. I remember the relief I felt when our parents came home and took care of our week-end entertainment, but it was not completed until this relative moved out and got married.

My sister, a stepsister of my mother whom we called "little auntie," and

myself were week-end companions. Our alliance was considered by me anything
but holy. Under the domineering leadership of our "little auntie" we formed a
gang with her younger brothers and sister and did many wanton things. With
the group I felt perfectly happy, but with her and my sister, I often felt uneasy.
My sister and "little auntie" were of about the same age and they teamed up very
nicely. I was taken into this inner circle merely because I was part of a sisterly pair, and even then the two often teamed up to tease me (as in the case of the
boy friend incident).

One unpardonable incident I remember was their mischief toward the relative described above. That relative had in his room many calendar pictures of
seminudes. One Sunday we barged into his room in search of excitement. He
was practicing calligraphy, but we would give him no peace. We tried to get
him to tell us stories; he was not a good storyteller. We wanted to drag him
out to play with us; he insisted on practicing calligraphy. Disappointed, we were
on the verge of leaving when the two older girls decided to take it out on his
treasured pictures. With pens in hand, they began to make beauty spots all
over the pictures. Our relative, who at first dared not oppose us, as we were
Father's children, had to beg them to stop, with a forced smile on his flushed
face. I stood by while this went on; I did not want to have any part in it. I had
no aesthetic liking for the pictures, but I had respect for another's property and
did not think much of fun through destruction. I pleaded with the girls and only
succeeded after much effort. They had so much fun from their deed that they
forgot to make an issue of my pleading for the young man, and for that I was
thankful.

III. Russian Sensory Images[14]

The three papers included here are from a larger group on images associated with sensory experience, written by a Russian woman, an intellectual
who grew up in pre-Soviet Russia. The entire group was written spontaneously,
in response to a query about associations to a single term. The subject, here
acting as an expert informant, is a skilled and sensitive writer who early in her
work with Research in Contemporary Cultures wrote a long, vivid autobiography
that was extremely rich in details of family life and education in her home.
Work of this kind is important not only for its content, but also for its style --
for the way, for instance, in which the images cluster in each paper dealing with
a particular sense (hearing, touch, and smell), and for the way in which a single
inquiry related to one kind of sensory experience touched off the whole. In these
terms, these papers may be compared to the discussions of Russian imagery by
Nelly Hoyt (Part Five, pages 234-42 and 242-45), to the analysis of The Young
Guard by Vera Schwarz (Part Six, pages 297-302), and to the two Russian interviews, one of which was also done by this writer (below, pages 205-11 and
211-15). As a method of linguistic exploration, it may also be compared especially with the interview in this Manual with a Chinese informant on a series
of terms related to friendship (below, pages 192-98). --Ed.

---

14. Informant 9F. Unpublished documents RCC-R 232, 231, 233. The papers
    are not given in their entirety.

1. On the Sense of Touch

The dictionary of the Russian language (Dal, 1903) defines the sense of touch as follows: "In reality all five senses can be reduced to one -- the sense of touch. The tongue and palate sense the food; the ear, sound waves; the nose emanations; the eyes, rays of light." That is why in all textbooks the sense of touch is always mentioned first. It means to ascertain, to perceive, by body, hand, or fingers.

There are two words to express the idea "to feel." If one feels with some outer part of the body, it is ossyazat; but to feel without touching, without direct contact, is oschuschat. One can oschuschat physically, morally, or spiritually: "I feel (oschuschat) the cold or cold"; or "I feel (oschuschat) happiness." But when I feel something with my fingers, I ossyazat -- I don't really feel, I finger, grope.

Though there exists an adverb ossyasatelny (tangible), Russians avoid using it. I have never heard anybody using it, nor have I come across it in literature. Tangible evidence in Russian will be "material proof." Touch is not considered the right way of exploration. One does not have to finger a thing when one can see it with one's eyes. One of my ⌊Russian⌋ college professors complained that his students were "savages." When he showed them a bone, drawing their attention to a cavity, the majority of the students poked their fingers into it. Children were taught not to touch things. They learned very quickly, and when you handed a child something you wanted him to feel -- like a piece of velvet or a kitten -- the child picked it up and put it against his cheek.

The standard joke among lower-class people was for a man to ask a woman, "Nice calico you are wearing. How much did you pay a yard?" And under the pretext of feeling the material, he would pinch the woman.

Russians in general touch each other much less than Americans do. There is hardly any horseplay, slapping on the back, patting, fondling of children. The exception is when somebody is very happy or drunk. Then he hugs somebody. But that is not touching. He opens his arms wide as if to embrace the whole world, and then presses you against his breast. The breast is the dwelling place of the soul, and this gesture means that he has taken you to his heart.

Disgust of bodily contact with something dirty or disgusting is often expressed by people. The Russian language has two words for it: brezglivost and gadlivost. There is no equivalent in English. "Fastidiousness" implies exaggeration, and so does "aversion." There is no common everyday word in English to describe the feeling of not wanting to touch a snake, a filthy rag, or, spiritually, to employ low means to achieve an end. Russians use the two above-mentioned words very often, in many situations, and they are used by all classes.

2. On the Sense of Smells

Russians use two words for "to smell." One is an intransitive verb, pakhnut, and the other is a transitive verb, newkhat (to sniff). "The rose smells (packnet); I smell (newkhat) the rose." To smell (newkhat) is to make a conscious effort -- to sniff, to inhale the odor. It is used mostly in the imperative: "Do smell." Otherwise the expression is used: "Smells smoke" or "I feel the smell of smoke."

There is a Russian verb chuyat, which is something like "sensing." Dal's Dictionary of the Living Great Russian Language (1903) says: "To chuyat is to perceive by senses, feel, sensate, hear, smell, taste, but it does not include seeing." "The noun chutye is a capacity to chuyat, which refers to an indefinite feeling, to taste, touch and smell, but mostly to smell." "The heart chuyet a forthcoming calamity." "The cat chuyet whose meat she ate" (one feels before whom one is guilty). Chutye is intuition, instinct, presentiment, scent, hearing, nose, smell, feeling. "He has a good chutye" -- he has a good nose, he has a well-developed instinct. Higher animals have chutye, especially dogs. One does not say "the dog's sense of smell," one says "the dog's chutye." Common dogs sniff at footprints, but good hunting dogs have verkhnee chutye -- upper scent. They smell the air above the ground and follow the scent.

Pronukhat means to find out, to discover a secret, to sniff out something. Not to smell something means to be far away from it. "He did not smell the university" means that he was far from any education. "It is not for your pig's snout to smell lemons" means that you cannot even aspire to such things. To smell or sniff means to show curiosity, to scrutinize, to nose. "The pig sniffed the wind -- it smelled onions." "Don't sniff, you won't find out anything." "He smelled from where it smelled scorched" --·he found out the source of the trouble. "Sniff what it smells" is a threat. "Smells like fried" -- it is dangerous. "If it is not fried, it does not smell" means "how could one know in advance?" "Smells great events," or "smells calamity," or "smells jail" -- this may lead one to jail. Russians almost never use the expression "smells like"; they say, "It smells pine trees" or they use an adjective, "It had dog's smell." When a person goes far away and does not write or communicate with anybody, one says, "There is no rumor, no scent from him." "No matter how a low-class person washes himself, he still stinks." "He looks like a fox, but smells (like a) wolf."

Snuhatza means to understand each other and to unite to no good purpose. It is used also to mean to have a love-affair (it is a vulgar expression). Dogs' mating is referred to as snuhalis, because dogs sniff each other.

Peasants say dukh instead of odor. Dukh means "spirit," "ghost." Peasants will say "good dukh" or "bad dukh," "a bad dukh comes from him." Baba Yaga says, "It smells Russian dukh." People of all classes say, "Chtob dukhu tvoego tut ne bylo" ("Never let me feel your spirit" -- or your smell). It means "Never come here again."

Russians live surrounded by smells. Smells are part of life. Everything smells. Russian homes never have that bland sterile air that American homes have. In the autumn the windows of Russian homes are made fast. Storm win-

dows are put in and the space between the two windowpanes is filled with cotton
at the bottom. Then every crack is filled with putty, so that one cannot open a
window even if one wants to. There is an opening of one square foot at the top
of the window and this (fortochka) is open to air the room. Peasants' homes
do not have the fortochka, and so the only fresh air that comes in is from the
door. So the smells remain in homes, whether they are city homes or peasant
huts. If the odors become too pronounced, or if there is a sick person in the
family and the smell of medicines becomes too strong, then some kind of incense is used. It is called monashka (the nun)....

In this country, Russians complain that American fruits and vegetables do
not smell, and that flowers smell only faintly. Lack of aroma is especially
noticeable in cucumbers, a favorite Russian vegetable. They do not smell here;
neither do apples or strawberries. If you had a dish of strawberries or apples
on the table in Russia, you could smell them in the next room. The same with
flowers. They do not smell strong enough -- a bunch of violets could perfume
a whole room in Russia; here you have to stick your nose into the bunch to get
some aroma....

Russians expect things to smell, especially food. They complain that American food does not smell, has no strong aroma. "When you approach your house,
it is imperative that there be a smell from the kitchen.... Roast geese are masters of smell.... Don't say that. A duck or a grouse will spot a goose ten
moves.... The goose's bouquet lacks delicacy.... Young onions smell powerfully
when they begin to brown and sizzle so you can hear them all over the house"
(Chekov, 1903, "The Siren," Vol. I, p. 13).

Russians use one smell to kill another. When a person feels the excess of
alcohol during drinking, he often takes a crust of bread and smells it. That
kills the smell of spirits. Russians like game and eat a lot of it; they like the
strong smell of game. There was also a herring with dushkom (a little smell).
This smell came from a herring that was not very fresh but still not decomposed
-- just a little soft and with a strong odor.

Everything smells, and smells evoke emotions. The smell of smoke brought
by the wind tells the tired traveler that human habitation is near. There is the
bitter smell of polyn, a plant which smells exactly like sagebrush and evokes the
same emotions as sagebrush -- a feeling of toska (desiderium) and a desire to
cry. There is the smell of the first snow, of the first sticky leaves, the fleshy
smell of plowed earth, the smell of rain, the exciting smell of horses covered
with foam, the exotic sharp smell of wild animals, the damp cold smell of cats
on back staircases. When people write or tell about their childhood, they recall
the smell of Mother's hands, the smell of Father's favorite cologne, or soap, or
tobacco. Men also talk about the smell of the hands (palms) of the women they
loved, or the smell of women's hair. One Russian Don Juan insisted that
brunettes' bodies smelled stronger than blondes'. There is a strong male smell

that common women refer to as "goat smell." There is the smell of the sea, hay, furs, pine trees, fresh paint, theater's backstage, ladamum (church incense, associated with death), wax candles, heated human flesh, old books, Easter, Mother's shawl, the classroom smell of chalk and blackboard, train smoke, the March thaw -- all these, and a million others, Russians know and love. They feel that these are the smells of life itself. Russian poets always mentioned smells and one of them (Balmont) even insisted that the sun smells of grasses, pine tar, and earth.

In this country one can walk from one floor of a department store to another without being able to tell by smell what merchandise is being sold. In Russia every store smelled of its wares, and smelled strongly. A word can evoke a scent. Somebody said something, and "na menya pakhnulo starinoy" ("it brought the scent of older days"), or "pachnulo molodostyu" ("it brought the scent of youth").

Russians love perfume. As soon as a peasant woman comes to the city, she begins to use perfumes. Men like them, too. A chastushka (peasant song) of Soviet times says, "My beloved Vanya, pour over me Coty's perfume."

I do not know whether Russians have an acute sense of smell or whether everything smells stronger in Russia than in this country. Sometimes, though, people have a remarkable sense of smell. I know a Russian who can find a certain kind of mushroom in the forest by smell. This is very hard, because mushrooms are usually covered by decayed leaves; they are often hidden under them, and besides, the leaves themselves smell very strongly. And I remember how once I was returning home, in the country, with my little brother. He stopped at the gate, sniffed, and said, "Father must have come from the city. Horses and a carriage stood in front of the gate a few minutes ago. I can still smell them." He was right....

3. On the Sense of Hearing

Russians do not like silence. Silence is embarrassing. It is foreboding, oppressive, dismal. When there is a sudden silence, a lull in the conversation, somebody is bound to say, "A fool was born" and everybody hurries to fill the silence.

Silence is akin to death. The word glukhoy (deaf) means blocked up, walled up, made fast, without exit. A deaf grumble, a dissent -- means an indefinite, unintelligible, obscure grumble, A deaf sound -- an indistinct, dull sound. A deaf time -- a slack time, no movement, no action. A deaf village is a village far away from everything that happens in the world, a backward village. Deaf province is an expression to describe people who are far behind the times and have provincial manners.

Russians love the sound of their language. They consider it the best language in the world -- the most expressive, the softest, and the most musical....

The Russian language is very flexible and expressive. A slight intonation, an accent, can change the meaning of the sentence. By changing the ending of a word, one reveals the feeling toward the subject. If I am mad at my sister Maria, I will call her "Manka"; if I want to be nice to her, I will call her "Man-ichka." A small house (dom) can be domik, which means that it is small, pretty, and cozy; but I can say domishko about the same house, and it will show contempt for its smallness and insignificance.

These suffixes are not always standard. Many people invent them. In a humorous story by Teffy (1912), an elderly aunt says, "Must you always have your picnics-mikniks" (p. 191). The old lady knew that there was no word "miknik," but she was rich and so could indulge herself in making it up. When somebody mispronounces a word, he immediately reveals his class, his origin, and the part of Russia he comes from. When I interview a Russian, I some-times cannot place him, especially if he is a university graduate. To know him better, I have to know who his parents were, and to find it out, I switch the con-versation to childhood days. Then he has to use words he did not learn in the university and pronounces them in the way he used to do when he was a child. If he says mamka (mother), he comes from peasants; matz -- lower middle class; mamenka -- upper middle class; mamasha or matushka -- merchants. Intellectuals, upper burgeoisie, and gentry used mama. One of my informants, quite an educated man, pretended to belong to the aristocracy, but when he said titka instead of soska (the chewing cud used by infants), he revealed his peasant or-igin. Most Russian humorous stories, especially those by Zoschenko and Teffy, are impossible to translate because the humor consists in twisting the language. Every Russian likes to play with the language, to invent words and expressions and indulge in dialect fun. Words are made up without any regard to the roots. They are built on sounds; curse words are built on harsh sounds, endearing words on soft. In his "Communist March" the poet V. Mayakovsky (1928) wrote (p. 173), "Pile up a sound upon a sound. Forward, singing and whistling. We still have good letters: R, SH, SHCH."

... Children never asked the meaning of a word if the conversation was carried on by adults. They were sure to be answered, "If you know so much, you will grow old too soon." When children began to exchange information in school, they found out that words they said had quite a different meaning. When I was quite small, I heard Father and the Assistant Secretary of the Navy talk in whispers about La Perouse (the straits). That was during the Russo-Japan-ese War, and they played on the stock exchange, probably using military in-formation. Because they spoke in whispers, and because the word sounded like poos (a vulgar form of "stomach," a "belly"), I decided that "Laperoos" was a dirty word. Probably for a similar reason, one of my classmates thought that khryasht (gristle) was a curse word. The whole class liked her interpretation so much that we accepted it as a term of abuse for teachers we did not like....

Russians love to argue. When they argue, they interrupt each other, shout,

and try to have the last word. But they also love to listen. A young man in
love must be eloquent. A suitor who is not talkative is a bore. There is a famous Russian parody on European knighthood by Prutkov (1933):

Baron von Grinvalduss sits on a stone before the castle of Amalia. He sits and
keeps silent. Amalia refused the baron's hand, so he sits on the stone and keeps
silent. The barons are waging wars, the barons are giving big feasts, but Baron von Grinvalduss, this valiant knight, year after year sits on a stone before
the castle of Amalia. He sits there and keeps silent.

Russians admire a good storyteller. In the nursery it is nyanya (the nurse)
who tells fairy tales. In the kitchen there is always someone who has either
heard or read a good story. All the servants assemble around the person who
tells it and it is so quiet that one can hear a fly fly (a pin drop). In the drawing
room the center of attention is the person who can tell an interesting story and
tell it well. In school the most popular teachers were the teachers of literature
and history, because they could tell a good story. Some of the teachers were
very good narrators. They gave life to dull facts....

People used to go to concert halls (they still do) to hear skazitelnizy, usually old women from some faraway village in the government of Olonez or
Archangelsk, who recited by heart old Russian bylini (epics). In Russian theaters
in New York, besides a musician, a singer, and a dancer, there is always an
actor who either reads or recites a long story by heart. A few months ago I was
asked to tell the story of Kon-Tiki. There were about fifteen people in the dining room sitting around the table. It took me about two hours to tell the story
(I was holding the book in front of me; they asked me to because they were
afraid I would miss some episode). Some of the people were playing two-handed
canasta, some played solitaire, one woman was knitting, one man was fixing
everybody's cigarette lighters, one woman was drawing, the rest were just
drinking tea, but nobody said a word during the whole time. The only sounds
were exclamations of amazement, wonder, or praise. When I finished, an old
lady said to me, "If you come again across a book as interesting as this, please
let us know. We would like to hear it."

As long as the story is well told, most people do not care if it is true or not.
The proverb says: "If you don't like it, don't listen, but don't interfere with
the lying." Another says: "We are given two ears and only one mouth, so that
we should listen more and talk less."

"Listen" means to obey. "He does not move his ear" means that he does
not obey, does not pay any attention. Rumors are called slookhy -- "hearings."

Seeing is more rational than hearing. Hearing is more emotional. When
words fail, the sound carries the feeling. "This fine vague beauty of human
sorrow, which people are not able yet to understand and describe, and which
can be expressed only by music" (Chekov, 1907, "Doctors," Vol. III).

Hearing is inferior to seeing. This truth was constantly hammered into
our heads by our teacher of physics. When he made experiments in the class-

room, he insisted that we watch him carefully, asking girls with poor eyesight to come close to him and stand around the table. Then he would ask us to close our eyes and he imitated different sounds -- the yapping of a little dog, the voice of the principal, etc. Then he would say something like, "You see, you were fooled by sounds, but nobody can tell you that things expand from cold and contract from heat, because you just saw the opposite with your own eyes."

It appears that deaf and dumb people do not differ much from others. The classic story is Turgenev's "Mumu" (1898). In it, Gerasim, the deaf-mute, has very fine qualities -- he is kind, sensitive, and capable of great devotion People who avoided his company did it because they feared his superhuman strength.

Sounds appeal to emotions. One of the best attempts to describe sounds and their emotional appeal was made by the great Russian poet Foeth (1912; Vol. I, p. 297):

Don't expect a passionate song. These sounds are indistinct fantasies, a languid resonance of a string. Full of melancholy suffering, these sounds bring tender dreams. They flew in inringing droves and now sing in the clear height. I listen to them like a child. I don't know their meaning and I don't need to know. In the dark of night, a sad leaf whispers into the window of the bedroom. These whispers are not words, but under the light rustling of the birch, the head sinks into the realm of dreams.

Perhaps the desire to kill emotions prompted the last Russian saint, Serafim Sarovsky, to keep silent for over thirty-five years.

C. TEN ILLUSTRATIONS OF INTERVIEWS WITH INFORMANTS

I. Interview with a Syrian Woman: Life History[15]

Informant 25: about 40 years old; born in the United States; two years of college; married four times (first husband, Muslim, divorced; second and third husbands; Americans, Christians, divorced; fourth husband, Syrian-Egyptian); one daughter, Informant 26, present during interview.

Interviewer's note: ... Informant 25 was at her daughter's home and I was invited right into the kitchen. Informant 25 was helping to wash the dishes and fixing things for her daughter, whose glands on both sides of her ears [she had pierced them a few days before] were swollen and the ears very red. The baby [Informant 26's first child, a boy of about nine months] was there, sitting in his high chair. It was after two o'clock. The girl offered me some orange juice. There was Syrian bread and butter on the table and they offered that to me too. The baby had a big chicken drumstick in his hand. The two women would pluck pieces of meat from it and place them right in front of the baby on the tray of his high chair. Then the baby would take the meat in his mouth and eat it.

Interviewer: (I asked the informant to tell me about her childhood.) She started right away:

Inf. 25: Mine was exceptional as far as a daughter is treated. My mother had four daughters previous to my birth; none lived beyond fifteen years; two died at two and three years, the other two died at thirteen and fifteen. The girls that reached thirteen and fifteen were born in Syria. I had two brothers born in the old country who died at six and four. S---- died in this country and my brother A---- died when he was forty-six years old. He was born in the old country. He has been dead for four years now. (She tries to remember dates and says to her daughter, "You have been married for two years, honey.") At the time of my birth I had three brothers older than myself that were in this country. The oldest one was in South America.

My sister had just died at that time -- the last of the sisters. It was four months before my birth. (Informant 26 was reading the newspaper in the meantime, and spoke up: "How can a woman kill her daughter?" Informant 25 answered ("She's insane.") Upon my birth my mother didn't pay too much attention to me, nor did she give affection, such as she gave my brothers. Lack of affection on her side was given fully by my father. (The informant was speaking in a clear, distinct voice, just like someone lecturing, but when she spoke about her mother, her eyes would be open more wide than usual and there would be something stern about her face.) That's enough about my background.

The first thing I remember about the training of a child -- whenever my mother and father called or asked us to do something, we were supposed to an-

---

15. Interviewer 15F. Unpublished document RCC-S 4. This was the second of a series of interviews with Informant 25 and her daughter.

swer, "Na'am" (meaning Yes, sir, or Yes, ma'am, respectively) and always we
were taught to come right up to the speaker and listen carefully to what they
had to say without answering or asking questions until they had finished. Then,
if it was an order or a command, or some duty to do, you would say (and here
she smiled broadly): "I am ready and willing, Mother or Father." You executed the command and then he or she would say, "God bless you." I am afraid
that ofttimes we were superstitious about disobedience to our parents. We
were taught that disobedience to parents was wicked and God would frown upon
such wickedness. If you disobeyed -- you know, as a child would do, and run
away -- you would have proper time to think it over and you would come back
and say: "I'm sorry -- I'll not be wicked again if you'll bless me and forgive
me." Usually you ended up kissing their hand and putting it up to your forehead.
You were always taught to stand up when you were seated if an elderly person
entered, and not until they were seated would you sit down. All those things
seem so spotted ... so long since I have thought of them. Furthermore, when a
child is introduced to an adult he would kiss their hand as an act of respect.
Another thing was, when a child was seated at the table, he never began eating
or touching food until the father or mother began the blessing (bismillah)....
     [Omission: description of food and eating and meals.]
Inf. 25: I can remember that up to the time I was seven it was permissible, and
I was put to bed with my brothers.
Interviewer: How old were your brothers?
Inf. 25: Before they were twelve. After twelve, in my family at least, the boys
didn't have girls sleeping in the same bed with them. I remember that my
brothers, after coming from school, had some chores, like chopping wood,
bringing in coal, straightening fireplace and stove, carrying out ashes, going
to the store for miscellaneous items which they didn't have in the house. After
that they were free to play until suppertime. My being small, younger, I had
these three brothers older than myself. I was sent to play with them, but they
were to keep an eye on me. They didn't like it because I interfered with their
freedom of movement. I wouldn't run as fast as they; I tried, and they had to
carry me. (Laughs.) Once (and here she strikes a match) I can remember as
clearly as yesterday my mother wanted them to take care of me and they wanted
to go swimming. It was a warm Saturday afternoon. At that time they had no
such thing as swimming pools, but had creeks, pools, or the river proper. They
had built a sort of dam over a falls. We have falls in our home town and a
bridge passed over it. The train goes over it. This wasn't as popular for swimming as the old stone quarry, but they didn't trust taking me to the quarry lest
I fall into the falls that was some distance from the rocks. (The informant
stopped often, trying to make her sentences sound well finished. She seemed to
resent speaking in ordinary, everyday language.) So they went swimming above
the falls. They set me on top of the bridge. I imagine there was a foot-wide

railing off which they would dive into the water. They would probably swim out twenty feet and return, climb up the steel girders to where I was seated, come back, pat me on the head and say: "That's a good girl, don't move." It was near the train time and I heard the whistle of the train about two city blocks away. I became alarmed and stood up on the railing, shouting to my brothers. I lost my balance and fell into the water. The tide carried me right up to the edge of the dam. There were boards (showing with her outstretched hands) for the concrete to fill in. Fortunately for me, they were there. I was six years old then. I held on to them with both hands and started to scream. My two oldest brothers (thinks for a time) -- one was ten or eleven, the other eight or nine, couldn't have been any older than that -- came to my rescue.

[Omission: Describes how the train stopped and the trainmen jumped in river and rescued all the children. A trainman starts to take the children to the police station. The children escape and hide.]

... Then, after what seemed like hours, my brother said, "They must be gone." He went out himself to look around and they had truly gone. He took us out of there and sat us in the doorway and said, "Listen, we must keep this secret!" This was our first secret, because if they had learned what had happened that day, I would be kept prisoner. He made me believe that he was sorry for me and doing me a favor for not talking about what happened that day. Otherwise, if I told, they always could go out and play, because they were boys, and besides, they could say that I was lying and Mother would believe them, and she did believe him always -- the oldest brother. So I kept my secret, not daring to tell my mother that I had fallen into the river, but it wasn't a secret too long. It happened that a Syrian fellow -- a bachelor -- was fishing on the opposite side of the river and had seen me when I fell in. He also had witnessed the rescue, but not being able to swim, he did not come to help, but he hadn' seen my brothers swimming in the pool at the time. The story he told was absolutely twisted -- utterly out of perspective. He claimed that my brothers were sitting beside me, perhaps fishing, and I deliberately jumped in. I don't like him to this day. (The informant remembers, with the help of her daughter, his name, N----.) They risked their lives jumping after me. My mother, terrified at what a near-catastrophe had befallen her sons, gave me a sound whipping and sent me to bed. My brothers, who had listened to the recital of N----'s tale like two innocent cherubs, sat there just as innocently as could be. He would ask the boys, "Isn't that exactly what happened?" And my brother M----, acting as the spokesman, would say, "Of course, Uncle. I marvel at what wonderful eyesight you must have to have seen so far." It seems to me from the noise I could hear from my room that my mother had difficulty getting my brothers to eat their supper. I heard her say, "My dear sons, why aren't you eating?" First to answer was my brother H----. He said, "I am not hungry" -- just like that. From a sudden "ouch" I think M---- must have kicked him and he said to Mother, "After our sister's narrow escape -- how can we eat?" Such a devil! My mother said,

"You are a fine boy, my son. That girl is a wild one. Wait until her father comes, we'll see if he will condone her behavior of today." I think my brother's conscience bothered him and he said, "Is that necessary? Don't you think she has been punished enough?" Her reply was, "It's still necessary to relate the story to the father."

Two days later, when my father came home, I was still locked in my room, so she had a chance to tell him what exactly our friend N---- had told her.

(Interviewer's note: Here we were served food. We had chicken fried in crumbs, salad made of potatoes and onions. The baby was given a second chicken drumstick and he also ate some salad. They gave him everything with their hands, sometimes right into his mouth, sometimes into his hands. Whenever he dropped bread the mother lightly slapped his hand, lifted the bread, showed it to her child, and said "haram" (meaning, it's a sin). The food was not thrown away, but was given back to the baby to eat. We had two helpings each, and Informant 25 and Informant 26 ate with their hands, picking up food with the pieces of Syrian bread. After we had finished, Informant 25 continued.)

Inf. 25: My brothers tried that night, after she had fallen asleep, to bring food to me, but I refused and called them traitors. I was a very stubborn child anyway, especially with my mother, therefore for two days, until my father came, I refused to eat. My mother was quite alarmed by my refusal, fearing I would become ill and having my father blame her for punishing me so severely, so when my father came to my room he said, "Good morning, daughter." In a weak voice I answered, "Good morning, my father." And I came forward and kissed his hand. I know that my tears fell on his hand because he picked me up, sat me on his lap, and said, "Tears don't always help, child. I hear you have been a very bad girl." (She tried to remember her father's exact words.) "Don't you know it would have been a very bad thing if your brother would have perished trying to save you after your deliberate jump?" I didn't answer. "And didn't you think it was wicked of you to refuse to eat for two days?" Still I didn't answer. Then he commanded me to speak.

I put my head down and said, "It's a lie." He asked me, "What's a lie?" And he commanded that I look at him as I spoke. So I looked up and I said, "If I called all these people liars, would you believe me?" (While speaking, the informant didn't gesticulate. She held her head erect and looked straight ahead. There was no dreaminess in her attitude, but it was as though she saw things clearly in her mind.) Now my father was the kind of person that had always asked a direct and honest answer at all times from his family. Whenever one of us had done something wrong, and he asked, "Did you or did you not do such a deed?" if you answered honestly and told the truth, he was more apt to forgive the deed, after giving you a lecture, than if you had lied. If he knew you lied, there was no mercy tempered with justice. Justice you received, but mercy -- no! (She said this very emphatically.) Therefore when I asked the question -- would he believe me when I said they all lied? he looked directly into my eyes and said, "It would be hard to believe; however, tell me you side of the story." This I did. My father didn't say a word, stood up, took me by the hand into the living room where my brothers and mother were sitting. My father then called my two older brothers before him, related to them the story I had just told him. Before my brothers could answer, my mother said, "What an imagination this girl has. You must do something before she becomes too adept at lying." My father roared, "Quiet!" (Informant 25 always tries to use words that would aggrandize her father.) "I'll handle this myself, and I don't want another word from you until I've finished." (Here the informant sighed deeply.) My brothers, like myself, had never lied to my father when looking in his face; however, they were tired of being heroes at my expense, and they said, "Yes, Father, A---- has told the truth." I can hear my mother gasp to this day. (Here she lit another cigarette.) My father roared, "How dare you allow your sister to be victimized and punished in a manner which seems to be approved by you?" My brother said, "We don't know, Father -- all we know, we are very sorry." My father then forbade them swimming for the balance of the entire year. Furthermore, he told them he was taking me away until such time as they realized that the little sister in the house was something to be treasured, not something continually to blame. My brother started to cry, "Where are you taking her?" "To a good family out in the country who would like to have a little girl with them." They began to cry, but my father insisted and four days later ... (She stopped, and I asked, "Your mother?") My mother thought my father was acting very foolishly -- that it would make me all the more stubborn if he coddled me in that way. My father said, "If you divide your affection equally among your children, playing no favorites, this would not be necessary." My father at that time was a peddler, known and loved throughout the whole state. (Sighs.) His favorite friend was M----, an old German, who had come to this country at the same time as my father, in 1885. Both had homesteaded in South Dakota and found it a good state to live in.

[The latter part of this interview has been omitted. In it is recorded the informant's description of her life with the M---- family and her return home; an interruption by neighbors and the conversation that followed; a long account by the informant of an incident that parallels that in the first part of the interview; a discussion of pregnancy and infant deaths; etc.]

II. Interview with a Syrian Man: Life History[16]

Informant 35: about 60 years old; some education in Arabic; single; in United States since 1912; from Damascus; owner of junk store.

Interviewer's note: ... When I reached the corner where his store is, I saw him in front of the store. He saw me from a distance, started to smile, and looked very pleased. We went into the store and it looked a little more orderly than the time before.... I commented that it looked nice and that he seemed to have gotten plenty of new merchandise. It flattered him and, pointing to the lamp, he said, "That is already sold -- just waiting to be delivered." Then he disappeared at the back of his store, and emerged with two old shabby books. He placed them

---

16. Interviewer 15F. Unpublished document RCC-S 21. This was the second interview with Informant 35.

right on the small pieces of junk, turning the loose pages, and explaining to me that these were the books he had been reading during my absence and that he used to read them before. I understood that my informant wanted to appear before me in all his learning, so I prepared myself for his long talks and comments on the books....Then, after he was through with the books, he disappeared again into the back of the store and brought the old bench we had used during the first interview, placed it near the entrance, brought the same old feathery cushions, and then we were ready to start. In the meantime a little girl about three years old appeared in the doorway, sucking a piece of candy and looking up at him. I asked him if he liked children.

Inf. 35: I like children. Give them a penny to make them happy. (To the child, "But now I am busy. Scram!" The child left. He apologized to me for having forgotten my name.) Too much on my mind. Business bad, also marriage. You are not married, are you? (I answered that I wasn't. I was now sitting on the bench ready to take down notes. He took a stand by my side, facing the light, looking very small, slight, and old -- and poor.)

Interviewer: You never told me about your mother. Is she living?

Inf. 35: She's living -- absolutely (with determination). My mother, she hasn't got the patience though. When I come home from school, she ask me, 'Go do this. Go do that. Buy something. Go to cousin's house, borrow a kettle." I was in child way, but delayed. She got angry.. She had not got patience, and says, "When Father comes tonight I'll tell your father and next time you'll do what I want." When my father comes she tell him but it happened that instead of being reasonable, sure, and better way to think and treat the child, he hadn't got that patience either.

(A customer comes in and looks at some picture frames, but the informant is too interested in dictating to me. The customer leaves.)

Inf. 35: No, he hasn't got patience how to educate the child, how to make him think. He is a very educated man, but still everybody have some fault -- you know what I mean -- and that's the fault of my father. (His arms are folded, and he thinks.) That he happened -- when he started to hit not in a reasonable way. I remember that time when he carried me up. (Here he bends down and acts as if he is lifting something heavy, lifts his arms over his head and lowers them with force.) And throw me down. It's unbelievable. I was sick for three months. It was too much.

Interviewer: What did you do to get that punishment?

Inf. 35: Something (casually). I refused to go to my mother, or I am behind in my homework. Homework needs to be beaten, but not so much.

Interviewer: Did they beat the other children in the family?

Inf. 35: I was the only one they beat. Other children died, and my brother was one year old; my sister was about seven years old. I was ten or eleven. They didn't beat the sister -- no, no, because Mother was always fond of daughter. Majority fond of daughters. In the beginning Father enjoyed the kids, until four or five years old. After they started to go to school, six, seven years of age they went to school. He thought he was doing right. When I grow up I will be mannered well, but that was too much. He did not realize he did more bad than good by doing that.

⌈Omission: father's death; mother's remarriage and divorce from a man who "drinks too much."⌉

(As I sensed the odor of whisky around him, I asked cautiously, "Don't you ever drink -- just for fun?")

Inf. 35: Only lately. When I came to America and started to be free. (He has been in America since 1912). When I am not ashamed of one of my family -- you know what I mean. (He means that when one is in one's own country, one has to have definite standards of behavior because everyone knows one's family.) I started to drink when I had company. I enjoy friends, party, picnic, but all a-lone I don't drink. I enjoy company. I drink sometimes (hesitatingly). I don't drink over the limit. When I drink I feel nice and I know it's just enough for me. The drink is the best to examine a person's characteristics. You could see his action, his way to find out about him. When I drink I don't worry about any-thing. Only dancing, singing and laughing. If the whole world turned upside down, I don't care. I feel happy -- ye-ess -- and I am very sport when I drink. I spend money like anything. I feel like spend a lot of money. (He holds his hands behind his back.) If I really do, if I got money. (Here he had said too much about spending money and he wanted to make it clear that he spends it when he has it.) Yes. (Reminiscently.) God is great. (Hands slightly on his hips at the back. The gestures of the informant seemed to follow the trends of his thought, and I could not help being conscious of how he used them.)

⌈Omission: Further discussion of mother's second marriage; relations to father; description of father as "a big spender"; inheritance from father -- division among children, especially of a family house.⌉

Interviewer: Do you remember that house?

Inf. 35: Of course. Even I remember the house I have birth. That's my birth-place. The place my grandfather left for my father was the greatest house ever built, for my grandfather was very wealthy man. The house is built just inside the garden-like; there is a big, great garden, and the garden, for instance, four blocks square. And the house inside the garden was very great because my grandfather used to have very big family. He and his brother lived in the same house, because they used to tell us, my father and my mother, she say, "Was a big family," of my grandfather and his brother; was so big family that when they sit on dinner table was a group consist of about 200 persons. Three, four servants used to attend the service on the table. Because in those days colored servants were slaves. Would buy with money when children and raise them and use them as slaves....

⌈Omission: Fantasy description of slave markets and slaves; of last slave in the family.⌉

The house in shape (the informant thinks for some time): so difficult to find out beginning from the end. (He smiles, then begins to laugh.) If you get in that house, especially that house I remember, you don't know how to find your way to get out, because when you get in and slam the door, you see all doors around all alike, all same size, same shape, same design. That's why hard to find your way out. (He makes an indefinite gesture in the air with his hand.) Now I would like to draw it for you.

(I placed a notebook in front of him and was observing him as he was drawing. He first drew the square outline and put the dots in the corners, using a card as a ruler. In the meantime a customer came in, but the informant was not interested and told him to come later. Then he drew the inner square and joined the corners of the outer and inner squares. Last he drew a circle inside the squares. Then, turning to me, he said:)

Inf. 35: See, all round rooms. This is the entrance, this is fountain in the open, only the rooms have roofs, kitchen, only one flight. (He points to the different parts of the drawing.) This is the fountain. We have exceptional reception room. ⌊Brief omission: descriptions of rooms.⌉ The walls also, on walls all gold inlaid.

(A man comes in and inquires about the truck and the things he had already bought. The informant is more interested in dictating to me, so to help him out, I write down the address of the place and the customer leaves.)

Inf. 35: Yes, most of the walls in every room are decorated in poetry. Some of them from educated people. Some of them philosophers, and every room has different written in it. No two rooms alike, you see. (Thinks with his feet apart, then clears his throat.) Which most hand-carved with gold inlaid, everything hand-molded, laid with gold leaves, and beautiful designed flowers, all raised (shows with his hands). All carved. See, according to the history they say, very old house. Was the oldest and prettiest house since those days when built. You know what I mean? According to the history, because Damascus oldest and ancient city all over the world, which they discover the latest date, which is about 72,000 B.C. (I wrote down 7,200 B.C., thinking I had heard wrong, but the informant leaned down and added another zero, saying that it is 72,000 B.C.) Now the family (he walks to the drawing of the house), the house; even the fountain inside has a high-pressure water in the middle. Water raise so high from the ground level, about ten feet. And come out of volume of about two inches in diameter. Around the house is garden, all around the house. ⌊Omission: detailed description of garden with marble walks, of gates and windows with porches.⌉ They⌊the porches⌉all look alike, same size, same everything. (Grins.) And has always running water. Running water all the time, because Damascus has water, rivers. And they had that long time ago. They drank river water. That's why they have running water all the time. Seven rivers (draws it on the fountain). And this has faucet-like fountain (he steps back and looks at his drawing), has four fountains on each side. This fountain water run down and inside water run high. They look at it like beautiful scenery.

It's like nourishing body. Sure, the sight. What most nourishing to human body is those five senses. Those that most nourish the human body is the hear-

ing and sight and the feeling. When you look at something you admire. When
you admire it, you enjoy it. (He moves his hands with palm upward to and fro
and touches his chest.) When you hear something nice, like poetry by some
artist, it is nourishment to the human body. When you hearing beautiful voice
like great singer. If I don't hear it, I don't enjoy it. That's why people at all
the time made museums, parks, zoos, theaters and all those things that nourishing to the human body. Part of the life in the feeling, of course. Well, some
philosophers have argument about those two feelings -- hearing and sight.
Some say sight is more important to human beings than hearing, some say opposite. Even Harunu Rashid, one of those khaliphs from Beni Abbas. (Informant promenades to the door and back, stops, looks at the ground.) He was a very
great man about education. After he died, his son finished everything. Harunu
Rashid most interested in singing, pleasure. He used to drink, too. So he
brought to examine which is more important to human being, is the hearing or
the sight or the eyes. (He transfers balance from one foot to the other, arms
akimbo.) They brought forty mothers with forty babies on their arms, nursing
them. Before (arms crossed) they stopped nursing, they made the children very,
very hungry and they brought a music band, consist perhaps seven, eight pieces,
like ud [instrument like a huge mandolin] , guitar, banjo, violin. And they made
the children very hungry till all the children start to cry for their food. Then
the king, the khaliph, command the mothers to give the children their teats, because in those days they did not have no bottles. And while the children were
busy with their meals, the khaliph he commanded to start. Baby about three
months, he can't see -- because their sight is very weak, is not strong enough
yet -- but they can hear. Soon as the band start, some children leave their meal
and they turn around to find where is the music come from, such beautiful music, nourishing body. (The informant gesticulates in a lively way, showing how
the babies turn away from their mother's breast to listen, and then turn back
to grab the breasts. He makes gurgling sounds. He laughs.) Some of them,
they are too hungry, can't leave their meal, but they move their feet and hands
(moves his hands the way the babies move their feet), and they are so happy.
That proves that hearing is more important than the sight, because if you hear
things, right away attach to human mind and start to solve problem what does it
mean? East or West? The blind one can hear where voice come, he could get
along more than as if he deaf. And he could see. (Note how the informant now
goes back to the point where he started about the fountain. Although he digresses,
he goes back to the starting point.) By looking fountain, such beautiful clear
water comes, like crystal, especially when you have flowers and garden around,
plants, something pretty. We call it burka, the fountain....

[The last part of the interview, including a discussion of childhood friends,
has been omitted here.]

III. Interview with a Polish Peasant Woman: Parents and Children[17]

Informant S: peasant woman, 53 years old; a widow; locality, Rawski Powiat, Western Mazowsze, Poland.

Child Care

Interviewer: ?

S: The baby is given the breast for the first time three days after birth. Before that the milk is not good, because it so happens that two days before giving birth the parents have intercourse, because this is the way men are, and then the baby may die. This spoils the milk (S uses the word for "food"--Tr.) because the flow (presumably the semen--Tr.) would be taken in by the baby. The mother will get excited (sexually--Tr.) and this is bad (presumably for the baby--Tr.). If a woman menstruates into old age, fifty-three, for instance, she is more excited. One woman used to say, "My nature demands it and it will keep me healthier." And others said, "What does she need a man for while she has a husband in the army?" But there are such men who only want other men -- they are the bachelors. Usually it is a secret, but in the village everybody knows. But it isn't frequent. In our village there is one old bachelor who needs no one, but people are saying about him that he is the most decent because he needs no one.

Interviewer: When are you supposed to abstain from intercourse?

S: There is no special time indicated, but usually when the woman menstruates or forty days after the birth of the child.

Interviewer: How about young girls who sleep with boys?

S: Where don't you have such girls? In the olden times they used to do it, but not like at the present time. An illegitimate child brings shame, but some grandparents will take care of it; they send the daughter to work but she has to send money in (for the upkeep of the child--Tr.).

[Omission: details of feeding and weaning the infant.]

Interviewer: ?

S: The father doesn't take care of the baby. He never has time. The mother has to. And the father, it's up to him. During the holidays he may play a little with the child. But for him to help his wife, it would have to be a man who understands life.

Interviewer: ?

S: The child starts to crawl when he is about nine months old, if the parents are in good health. It gives much joy when he starts to walk, but don't let him go beyond the threshold, they say, "You'll learn first, then you'll run around."

_____

17. Interviewer 54F; translator 40F. Unpublished document RCC-P 70. This interview was made in Poland and was recorded in Polish. It was later translated and annotated for the use of other members of Research in Contemporary Cultures. For comparison, on attitudes towards the body and towards individual independence and responsibility, cf. "Polish Personality," above, pages 153-57.

Interviewer: ?

S: They don't teach the child how to walk, he holds onto the furniture.

Interviewer: ?

S: It is better not to rock the child because then he has a better head for learn-ing, but in the old times they used to rock. Even now they still have rocking cribs, but not too much.

[Omission: discussion of toilet training and attitudes of disgust.]

Property

Interviewer: ?

S: Ours is a large village, more than 400 houses. Three parts are relatively rich and one part poor. Good soil, when a man has 20 acres (morgi) he can live, and a rich owner has 40 acres. Before he had only 20 acres, but later he bought out a poor owner.

Interviewer: ?

S: About inheritance, when the father was well-off, the child got more, because a child cannot force his father. When the child was twenty or twenty-two years old, he already got the property. The child worked and when he was twenty years old he signed the annuity. A friend of mine (woman--Tr.) goes from house to house. Wherever she comes she does some work and they give her some-thing to eat. When she comes into a house, she first sits down in a corner. She doesn't go to church because she has no clothes. And she owns 15 acres, but her son works on the land. But she cannot get along with her daughter-in-law, and everybody knows that a son takes the part of his wife and not the part of his mother. Mothers are jealous of their daughters-in-law and this is why they can-not get along. Her son says to her, "Why do you go (to other people--Tr.)? Can't you eat here and take the cow to pasture?"[18] But she isn't so old as to eat and do no work. But it is hard life when one is old and can't work. A daughter as well as a son would say, "You've stayed here a week, go now to the other one" (another child--Tr.). She doesn't throw you out really, but God forbid to live to old age. It once happened in our village that a father gave his entire property to a son. The father was fifty-two years old. When they came back from the notary, the son who got the property started to beat his brothers and even hit his father. Three months later, when they could no longer stand it, the notary gave the property back to the father and said, "Now let the son 'hop' around the father." I am a widow and people are telling me, "Don't be foolish, don't give up your property." My son wants me to give up the land, but I refuse because I don't approve of his marriage. He says that he won't work the land if I don't make him the proprietor. This is because he doesn't want my other children to come to the house to eat. But if he were the proprietor, I couldn't give food to my other children. I'm praying to God not to live too long, because

---

18. Taking the cow to pasture is regarded as a child's task.--Ed.

it's the worst thing that could happen to anybody, to be dependent upon your children. I myself knew many dziady (word used for "grandfather," "old man," and "beggar"--Tr.) who gave their land to children. To be a dziad is a terrible shame, but it is even more of a shame to be one when one had property before and gave it away. Everybody marvels that I am capable of taking care of my property and need no one and am satisfied.[19]

Boys and Girls

Interviewer: ?

S: Children play all sorts of ball games, very little children play with pieces of wood or play "household." Bake bread.

Interviewer: ?

S: Those who take care of the geese play together (boys and girls--Tr.), but only until the time of the First Communion. After that, boys and girls play separately, because the priest tells them to. Every mother tells her daughter to keep away from the boys and dirty words. I told this to my daughter when she came from her first confession. I told them to both my daughters, but even so they both married for love. The young man says, "If you don't despise me, I'll like to become your son-in-law."

Interviewer: ?

S: When the young man learns that his bride is not a virgin he gets angry, but if she knows how to handle him (literally, how to live with him--Tr.) everything will be all right. No one knows about it, but she'll tell her mother, because mother is the best "secret-receiver" of the child. She won't tell it to the father, but she will tell it to the mother. A boy won't tell either of the parents. They talk very little with the parents. Most of the time they tell their friends. Sometimes a brother will tell his sister, but a sister won't tell her brother as much. A sister will often tell her mother on the brother. A girl friend will sometimes know more than the mother. A girl has one girl friend. But when she gets married, there is no more friendship. When a boy gets married, this also interferes with his friendships, because he now has the secrets with his wife. But one helps his friend.

[Brief omission.]

Interviewer: ?

S: When children are quarreling among themselves the parents interfere. Sisters are sometimes jealous, because the eldest one gets more because she is marriageable. Boys get along much better, because they don't care about clothes. Boys often say, "It's a pity that there are so many of us, there won't be much to divide." Everybody wants land.

---

19. Note how this phrasing echoes the informant's first comments about the "old bachelor who needs no one."--Ed.

IV. Interview with a French Couple: Dyadic Relations in the Foyer[20]

Informant 1: man, a self-made intellectual in the middle to late 40s, born in Charente-Inférieure, in the country, of petit bourgeois parents, who has lived very little in France since 1918....
Informant 2: (Informant 1's wife): born in Paris, but comes from much the same social milieu. She is obviously somewhat dominated by her husband, who maintains publicly that she is not an intellectual and cannot properly discuss sociological matters. She ... is neat and soignée in appearance.

Interviewer's note: Miss ---- (40F, also present at the interview) introduced me to M. and Mme.----, who arrived in this country three weeks ago.... The first 20 or 25 minutes were given over to establishing rapport by permitting Informant 1 to display his intellectual and other qualifications and to talk about his work. I then gave a brief outline of the work of the project, phrased in sociological terms comparable to those used by him earlier, and then started the interview proper by asking:

Interviewer: It seems to me that young French children go about by themselves very much less than young American children. Can you tell me what people say will happen to their children if they go about alone?

Inf. 1: In my part of the country it is quite regular, children are warned that if they are to go about alone the loup-garou or Ramponneau will get them.

Interviewer: ?

Inf. 1: This was in the Charente-Inférieure, but it is true of all the area between Bordeaux and the Massif Central.

Interviewer: ?

Inf. 1: Ramponneau is an evil spirit, pictured like an old beggar carrying a bag, with a pointed hat like magicians, and bearded. He's got a big bag on his back and children are told that he takes away naughty children.

Interviewer: ?

Inf. 1: The loup-garou is just a very big wolf which will eat up naughty children or children who go around by themselves. It has been fused with the apocalyptic bête de jeuvadin, which is the legend which has gone on since the thirteenth century.

Interviewer: ?

Inf. 2: No, in Paris they didn't say anything like that, but in the country we were told that the gendarmes would get us. (Inf. 1 concurs.) And we were also frightened of gens contrefaits (deformed people) and village idiots.

40F: ?

Inf. 2: No, we never played in the streets. We lived in the 15ème arrondissement [district of Paris] . I always went out with Mother until I was twelve years old.

---

20. Interviewer 27M. Unpublished document RCC-F 101. This was the first interview with these informants. It was conducted and notes were taken in French, but these were transcribed, as given here, in English. This interview followed on the French group discussion reproduced in this Manual (Part Three, pages 104-107); for purposes of comparison, cf. also "Notes on Two French Films" (Part Six, pages 289-91).

Interviewer: ?

Inf. 2: Mother impressed on me that if anybody spoke to me in the streets I was not to reply and not to follow them. When I was a child there was the notorious Soleilland case, and it had much impressed Mother and frightened her.

Interviewer: ?

Inf. 1 and Inf. 2   (replying almost together): Soleilland was a sadique (sadist) who had violated a little girl and cut her up in pieces. The case made a very great impression and all parents were frightened by it.

Inf. 2: We were also warned that gypsies would kidnap us and make us work in fair grounds. Generally, in my family, the children were très tenus (held in, controlled) up to fifteen or sixteen. If we were away from home at all, we had to give an exact account of where we had been. Mother would say, "You leave school at four and I expect you back at ten past four at the latest." We had to ask permission to go and visit friends.

40F: ?

Inf. 2: I always went out with my mother.

Interviewer: ?

Inf. 2: No, my father never took us out.

Inf. 1: I remember when I was a child there was an old man with a big sack who used to go around begging for money, for -- in those days -- for two sous you could get a loaf of stale bread, and he used to fill the sack with these loaves and feed them to the pigs. I was told that this sack held disobedient boys. (Reference to earlier discussion of Ramponneau.) I've always been cowardly at night and frightened of being alone. I remember that my mother used to go and visit her mother-in-law, and I used to say to her, "Don't tell me when you are going out, because then I won't be frightened."

Interviewer: ?

Inf. 1: I must have been five or six at the time.

Interviewer: If your father was at home, would that have been all right?

Inf. 1: My father ne comptait pas (was of no importance). I was very sensible (sensitive). I was an only son.

40F: ?

Inf. 2: Yes, I was an only child, too. You hardly need to ask that about the French. They are all only children. My father and mother were only children, too.

Inf. 1: On my father's side we were ten.

Inf. 2: When I was a child I used to visit my grandmother in the country, in the Massif Central Intérieur, and she made me very frightened of revenants (ghosts). I didn't dare go in front of a cemetery, and in fact I don't like to now.

Interviewer: What did she say the ghosts would do?

Inf. 2 (rather hesitant): I don't know -- take me away.

Inf. 1: They were <u>menaces imprécises</u> (vague threats).[21]

Inf. 2: The train used to go past a cemetery and each time it did so, I would shut my eyes tight.

Interviewer: ?

Inf. 2: No, I didn't mind in the daytime.

<u>40F</u>: Did you ever see a dead person?

Inf. 2: My grandfather died when I was seven or eight years old, but seeing him didn't have any effect on me (<u>ne me faisait rien</u>).

(There was now a short silence. The subject was apparently exhausted for the moment. I thereupon started a new subject.)

Interviewer: If you were found to have done something naughty, what would be done to you?

Inf. 2: That was quite simple. <u>On me donnait deux gifles</u> (I was given two slaps).

Inf. 1: That's right. <u>On nous giflait.</u> (We got slapped.)

Interviewer: On the ears?

Inf. 1 and Inf. 2: On the cheeks, tick-tock (illustrating this).

Inf. 1: In the school (Ecole Communale), they smacked you with a ruler on the tips of the fingers. That warmed you up on a cold morning.

Interviewer: ?

Inf. 1: For disobedience.

Inf. 2: I remember I broke a heap of plates and Mother slapped me on both cheeks. She told me that I'd remember not to break things again.

Interviewer: In America one of the big difficulties with children is that they often refuse to eat the food they are given. Did that ever happen to you?

Inf. 2: We always had to eat everything. When I was seven or eight, I said I didn't like turnip soup. I didn't like it because my father didn't and I wanted to be like him. Mother said, "I am going to give it to you every day for a month and you won't have anything else until you eat that."

Interviewer: ?

Inf. 2: Oh, I gave in long before the month was over. Mother wanted obedience (<u>voulait l'obéissance</u>) and respect. I wasn't allowed to talk at table.

Interviewer: Did your father punish you?

Inf. 2: No, Father never did.

Inf. 1: No, the father doesn't punish. He comes home tired from his work and wants his children to be quiet and <u>gentils</u> (amiable, "good children") so that he can rest himself. He gets interested in his children later; in his daughter, if pretty and well-dressed and <u>caline</u> (almost untranslatable word, but has some of the connotations of kittenish affection). He is proud of her and treats her <u>comme une petite aimée</u> (like a little sweetheart).

---

21. This phrase (<u>menace imprécise</u>) recurred in the responses of French informants to Rorschach test cards.--Ed.

Inf. 2: There is grande amitié (regard and affection) between fathers and daughters.

Interviewer: Would you say it was the same between mother and son?

Inf. 1: No, it's not the same (de la même façon) between mother and son. In that case, the question of maleness comes up. The mother thinks of her son as a man. She is proud of all his successes, particularly if he is successful with women.

Inf. 2: In the lower classes, the mother is really the servant of her sons.

Inf. 1: Twenty-five years ago, in the country the mother used to start out and serve her husband and the sons and the male servants at table, and would only sit down with the other women after the men had finished.

Interviewer: How old will the daughter be when the father takes more interest in her?

Inf. 1: If the girl is gentille and coquette, when she is eleven or twelve years old, when she becomes a woman. (Addressing this to his wife:) Do you remember that couple at Constantinople? He must have been a man of about thirty-eight and his daughter was fourteen or fifteen, and you would have said they were amant et maitresse (lovers) there was so much affection and tendresse. The mother was left quite outside.

Interviewer: Would you say this was rather exceptional?

Inf. 2: Perhaps it was exceptional, but it certainly wasn't unique. I've seen a lot of cases like it.

Interviewer: Do people make any remarks about it?

Inf. 1: No, there were no commentaires. Ca ne sortait pas des limites de bien-séance (it did not pass the limits of good breeding).

Interviewer: You've told us -- when a girl becomes a woman. When does a boy become a man?

Inf. 1: Oh, at six months or a year old.

Inf. 2: Yes, they are men from the moment they are born.

Inf. 1: A daughter becomes interesting if she is pretty, élégante, caline.

Inf. 2: Mothers are prouder of boys.

Inf. 1: They are proud of boys if they have lots of successes when they grow up. Mothers are particularly proud of their sons' successes with women.

Interviewer: Does it matter what sort of women they are successful with?

Inf. 1: No, what's important is that they should have lots of successes.

Inf. 2: It's better if they have successes with better-class women, smart and well dressed.

Interviewer: When I was a student in Paris, some of my companions told me that they had their first experiences with friends of their mothers,

Inf. 1: That's really the end of Romanticism. It may be true dans le grand monde, chic et dissolu (society, fashionable and dissolute), but it's not French. It's really a survival from the Romantic period, the tradition of de Musset and

Victor Hugo. It's quite exceptional.

Inf. 2: It's true boys often have their first affair with an older woman.

Inf. 1: That was the case with me.

Interviewer: ?

Inf. 1: No, it wasn't anybody my mother knew.

Inf. 2: Very often indeed it is with les bonnes (servantmaids).

Inf. 1: In the country the maid is often ordered by the father to sleep with the son. The maids are had by the father and the son. This is particularly true of girls from the Assistance Publique [state-owned foundling homes]. These girls are bétail qui couche (cattle for sleeping with) and if they refuse, they may be beaten and even smothered. They sometimes get killed.

Inf. 2: They are not often killed.

Inf. 1: It does happen.

Inf. 2: This treatment of girls from the Assistance Publique is une honte en France (a disgrace to France).

Inf. 1: You'll find thirteen-year-old girls given over to men fifty years old or more.

Inf. 1 and Inf. 2 (speaking together, very excited): If she complains, they say she is vicieuse, and if she complains and runs away, she is taken up by the gendarmes and sent to a maison de correction (reformatory).

Interviewer: Would you say this was general?

Inf. 1: It happens nine times out of ten. The father sleeps with her first and the son after. Now I'll tell you one very curious thing. The farmer's wife would make an enormous fuss if her husband had a mistress, but she doesn't mind at all, is not at all jealous, if he sleeps with a girl from the Assistance Publique. That seems quite natural. But if the girl was an ordinary servant, she would make a drame -- the maid would get herself given money and jewels and clothes.

Inf. 2: That's typical. The farmer's wife doesn't mind her husband being un-faithful. But she will make a scene if property were given away.

Interviewer: Is there anything like that in the towns?

Inf. 1: No, it's quite different. Girls from the Assistance Publique are not given jobs in town. The boys, maybe.

Inf. 2: They're given positions just like other servants. Nowadays they are treated just like anybody else.

Inf. 1: Yes, we had a girl from the Assistance Publique, a servant, but my father never slept with her, nor did I.

Interviewer: Did you know whom your father slept with?

Inf. 1: He slept with my mother (laughing).

Interviewer: But you said your father didn't sleep with this girl. Did your father ever talk to you about such things?

Inf. 1: No, my father was sérieux.

Interviewer: ?

Inf. 1: No, people don't talk about such matters between father and son, but my father didn't care about such things. He was much more interested in fishing and hunting.

40F: What was your father's position?

Inf. 1: He was called Sous-Ingénieur à la Marine.

(This was an awkward question. All the indications had been that Inf. 1 came from a fairly low social level and did not like to be reminded of it. I got back at once to the earlier situation by asking again about the relationships between father and son, and Informant 1 and Informant 2 both repeated that there was no intimité between fathers and sons. Children, they said, were brought up outside the interests and problems of their parents.)

Inf. 1: Although I was under age, I joined up when I was seventeen years old, and therefore immediately got la position d'homme (my majority). I have always been independent and left my family quite alone. I went to boarding school when I was fourteen years old, and after that I saw my parents very little.

Interviewer: Did many of the people whom you knew go to boarding school?

Inf. 1: Yes, among the bourgeoisie, the petite bourgeoisie, that is, lots of the boys went to boarding school, to the Ecole Supérieure when there was none like that in the neighborhood. Then we only saw our parents three mouths in the year.

Inf. 2: In general, il n'y a pas de confidences (there is no intimacy) between the children and parents. If the parents are in any difficulties, they try to hide them from the children.

(At this point the interview had to be stopped, as the informant had another engagement. A second meeting was arranged for in the near future.)

Interviewer's Summary of Significant Points

1. Inculcation of fear of strangers. Spontaneous mention of sexual mistreatment of children if they are not careful. Free association between fear and sexual mistreatment.

2. Very striking spontaneous statements on the quasi-sexual aspects of the relationship between father and adolescent daughter. This was not provoked in any way.

3. The free association, again, from the role of the mother to the sexual exploitation of the wretched girls from the Assistance Publique (a story which, incidentally, I had never heard about).

4. The absence of a significant role ascribed to the father in the education of the younger children. No difference apparently between town and country in this social class -- the petite bourgeoisie.

Interviewer's Queries

1. No evidence given as to the father-daughter relationship in the earlier years of life except Informant 2's statement that she wanted to model her

food tastes on her father's and her mother would not permit this. This needs considerable further investigation.

2. How far do the sexualization of fear and the fear aspects of sex coincide? (Note in this context that France is personified as feminine, and linguistically, invasion is equated with rape.)

3. As described here, the safeness of the home and the complete danger of complete strangers. Is there a neutral ground, and if so, how far does it extend?

V. Interview with a Young Frenchman: Friendship[22]

Informant 10: young man; student at an American university. Son of an American father (who fought in France in World War I) and a French mother, who divorced her husband and returned to France with her child. Informant served in the American Army in World War II; married a French girl.

Interviewer: I'm having a hard time getting a hypothesis on the way friendships are made in France.

Inf. 10: It's different. There is a difference from the way that they are made here. Let me see....

Interviewer: Do you mind if I take notes?

Inf. 10: Well, I don't know. You know, I would not like to be quoted. Who knows -- oh well!

Interviewer: No one will ever know who you are, who said these words. It will just be an anonymous Frenchman. It is the same for everyone.

Inf. 10: Well, all right. (There was much more persuading before he agreed.) I'll take notes too. There may be something interesting that will develop, you see. Now, let me begin. Let us begin with school friends. Well, in France there are more really close friends than there are here. However, the friend has got to be really close before you take him home. You make real friends in France and you try to keep them. You don't bring them home often. The home in France is a man's castle. Only once in a while do you bring them home. When they come, they never ask news of the women. It is the same as in Spain. In school -- you know, I went to boarding schools until I was fourteen years old. I resented it terribly. Even when I knew my mother could not do otherwise, I still felt she was wrong. (The mother had to work to support herself and her son.) Well, anyway I had some very good friends in school, just a few well-chosen ones. There was one especially -- we were always together. Well, in these relations which you make and which you value profoundly there is an element of passion. Real passion divorced of sexual implications. With the friends which

---

22. Interviewer 68F. Unpublished document RCC-F 191. Second interview with informant. The interviewer, a young married woman, was the daughter of French parents but had grown up abroad in a French milieu. Interviewer and informant both make direct and indirect comparisons between France and the United States. Interview was conducted in French and English and was transcribed in English.

you make when you are in school, the ones which you value, there is never any sex.

Interviewer: How old were you at the time?

Inf. 10: Nine. There may be a couple of boys sitting in a corner with a blanket on their knees masturbating. But you never do that with anyone you are fond of -- anyone who is your friend. If you choose someone to be your special friend, you never have anything which is sexual in your relationship -- jealousy, things like that, but never any kind of sex. You have sex relations with those who are not your friends. I remember I had a friend in school and once he took me home to spend the night with him. The old grandmother put us to bed. We slept in the same bed. She said, "Now turn your backs to each other." We did; there was no question in our minds. There is a kind of pudeur (modesty) in relations of this kind. We would never masturbate. This is a sacred relationship and independent of sex. We never have to say, "No, no...."

Between men and women -- When you date a girl and then want a little sexual intercourse with her, you speak about many things. Whether this is her first affair or not....With girls it is different where sex is concerned. Between friends (men and women) there can be a little love on the carnal side, that is O.K., but with men, there you can't have any sexual relations among friends. You know, when I was about fifteen, I read about André Gide -- he was a homosexual -- I loved the things he wrote, he was my hero. Corydon -- that was a book! Then I found out that he was a homosexual. I did not approve. That is terrible, really terrible.

Interviewer: Do you still have many of the friends you made in school?

Inf. 10: I went back to see them after the war. You know, I was in the American Army during the war. Well, I was disappointed in two out of the five. (?) Yes, the others I could not look up. Well, one had become a career doctor -- the one who had ideals, the same as I; and the other -- he was just an artist in Montmartre. That is the way it goes. There were some people in the hostel (youth hostel), who remained the same -- always the same. I would do anything for them. They were elderly people -- a couple, I remark here, of a similarity! The friends which I was able to keep were those who were already adult; the others I lost. I now have the feeling I never had any relation to them. I had some friends which I made in the Lycée V----. You know the Lycée V----? It really has the reputation for homosexual activities and tough guys. Even those friends were no longer there. You know, the criterion when you are a child and when you are older is different.

Interviewer: Do you think the friends you made [in France] were different from the ones you made here in school?

Inf. 10: You know, in France the friendships are very different from here. Friendships in France you don't enter into easily, there is so much less demonstration. This morning I received a letter from my wife (in France). In this, she mentioned that P---- (an American girl) came to visit her. "Elle (P----) a démontré de la grande affection" (She was very demonstrative). I can just see my wife. Cold and reserved, and P---- giving her a kiss. That is Anglo-Saxon, after all. You know, I was a good friend of her (P----'s) family before I married. A young bachelor -- and that is a traditional French picture, a culture all of its own. Well, P---- wanted to see what had become of me -- if I had changed or not. There, now she went to see my family. I can see my wife, how she might have been.

Interviewer: Why? It seems to me that there was much more demonstration in France than there ever was here.

Inf. 10: That is true. There is more. But it takes place in certain places and at certain times only. Now you take between girls and boys of a certain age -- well, when you are of the same age and young, you don't kiss. You have to be kissed by someone who is older -- like an older man who kisses you before you go on a trip, or something like coming back after a long absence. Then it is permissible to kiss. But you never kiss anyone who is your same age -- when you are young, in any case.[23]

Now my mother, she will kiss my wife when she sees her. That is right. But among women there is no demonstration of affection. I remember an old man who was my friend -- he was a famous writer -- and he came to see me off at the station. He kissed me in leaving. And -- well, that was correct.

You know, between friends we have a special pattern, we say: "Nous sommes de bons amis" (We are good friends -- masculine). And by this we mean a great deal. We mean that we can be counted upon. This kind of pattern can't be found between men and women. Between men and women, you must have sex. The woman asks for it, and the man gives it to her. They realize that these things are so. There is less sexual tension in a relationship between a man and a woman -- they realize the elements involved in the situation and start from there. Now here in America, they don't go in for that stuff -- that's what they think; all they do is to be hypocrites -- they hide the things from themselves, and the repercussions are greater. In France, you realize all of these things and you start from there. You bring the things -- the elements -- to the surface, and there you are. I have a little friend,[24] I see her from time to time.

---

23. Here is a clue to these demonstrations. In my opinion, two older men -- of 50 or so -- might gave each other an arm shake and a touch of the cheek. However, thinking back, this would never occur with girls my own age [early 20s]. It was the farthest thing from our minds to kiss. We would shake hands very formally and then dash off to do something together. On the other hand, in meeting a friend or relative near my parents' age, I would always extend my hand and turn my cheek for a kiss, first on one side and then on the other -- not kissing, just touching.--Int.

24. "Little friend" is a literal translation of petite amie, a phrase used to refer to a mistress, a girl usually of a lower social class than the man; it is not used to refer to someone of one's own social class--Ed.

We have sexual relations, and that is all. Then we speak of other things and the rest is finished.

Now with men it is different. You just don't mention sex at all. You bring to a well-defined situation the elements which are involved in it, nothing more. You don't bring in the elements which are dangerous or unnecessary.

Interviewer: How do you choose friends?

Inf. 10: Now let us take the choice of friends. Well, we say, "Tout le monde n'a pas la chance d'être né orphelin" (Not everyone has the good fortune to be born an orphan). That is very profound. We don't choose our friends haphazardly. We choose our friends as if they were ideal brothers or sisters. And the saying goes, "Je l'aime comme un frère -- comme une soeur" (I love him (her) like a brother -- like a sister). Then you have the feeling that this is a relation which is devoid of anything sexual -- it would be incest if you did ⌐not⌐.

Interviewer: How are friends -- say girl friends -- made? Or even boy friends, after introduction?

Inf. 10: You know, if you meet someone -- say my good friend so-an-so introduces me to someone -- in a café or some place like that. Afterward, if I want to see that person again, we will make a date for all of us together. You wouldn't go out with just one or the other, you would go out and be all together. If you invited just the one to whom you had been introduced, your friend would have the right to feel insulted. This you never do. Now, in the case of a girl -- well, there you just don't know exactly what to do. You have to be intuitive in those cases. You just can't take a person and accept the total case. But if it is your good friend who introduces you, then you never invite the one without the other.

But I repeat -- the friendship is an exclusive and durable thing. You do it and get into it because you have chosen this person as an ideal sibling. They say that you don't know your friend until you are in dutch, and that is true. The goal in choosing your friends is to complete or replace your home. Even in the relations with your professors -- there you consider the professor as if he were your father. He has that position for you. And you treat him with the same reverence and respect. There is a feeling of deference in your relations.

Interviewer: There are a few things which we've been able to see. First, one chooses one's friends as ideal siblings or parents. Second, there are very formalized and definite relationships. These relationships are well defined and demand certain emotions and no others. Sex is taboo and respect and dependability are primary requirements of the order which you might expect from either your father or your brother.

Inf. 10: That is true. And then you do things to make these relationships concrete. For instance, you might ask your best friend to be your witness at your marriage ceremony. This is an important thing -- not like here. You don't go out on the street and offer two bucks to the first guy who comes along. You do it with care and the recipient considers it an honor. The same thing, say with a godmother (marraine) or godfather (parrain) -- you hesitate in choosing, you do it with consideration. You cement the relationships which you have made.

There is one place where you make friendships disregarding class lines. You know, you have got to consider the kind of people with whom you make friends. You just can't make friends with everybody. Here they just say hello to someone on the street and they are immediately your friend. It is not so in France. You don't know to whom you talk. But in military life, in the army, you do make friends whom you keep. My uncle has lots of money. Yet when he goes to his club -- L'Amicale du 50ième -- there they are all good friends. (He raises his hand and arm in a kind of salute.) They meet and have a good time talking over old times and drinking and eating.

But these class lines are important. And the friends you make in your own class are the ones you keep.

VI. Interview with a Chinese Scholar: Friendship[25]

Informant 5: man 36 years old; married, one child; scholar; visitor in the United States from Shantung Province, North China.

Interviewer: (Asks the informant the meaning of peng-yu.)

Inf. 5: Both words mean "friend"; peng means friend and yu means friend; the compound means friend. You can say peng-yu, my friend, but you cannot say peng, friend, or yu, friend. I think this is in speaking language; but in some ancient books, sometimes they use one word; for example, Confucius' book Lun-yu. The book are notes by his students on his teachings.

Interviewer: What does lun mean?

Inf. 5: Lun means critical, discuss. (And yu?) Means language. In this book, Confucius say: Yu-peng-tze-yuan-fong-la -- have-friend-from-far-place-come. (Meaning?) "If you have a friend come here from a distance, are you not happy?" The full sentence is this. In this case, he uses the single word peng to talk about friendship. I read that book when I was young and this is the first paragraph, second sentence, in the book. (?) It may be that he speaks of friendship first because Confucius thinks it important.

Interviewer: When do you use peng-yu? With members of the family?

Inf. 5: No, my family is not "my friend."

---

25. Interviewer, 63F. Unpublished document RCC-CH 429. The interview, which is given in its entirety, is the eighth which the interviewer had with Informant 5. It is one of a series on the subject of friendship made by the interviewer with this and other informants at a time when the Chinese group was working on problems of relationships to persons outside the family. In this interview, the interviewer is working toward a definition of friendship, taking as a starting point vocabulary obtained through previous interviews made by herself and by other members of the Chinese group. For a discussion of related attitudes, cf. Chinese group meeting on "Sincerity," Part Three, pages 120-24.--Ed.

Interviewer: Not in any way, even in feeling?

Inf. 5: No, family is family; quite different.

Interviewer: They say here in the United States that a girl's mother is her best friend.

Inf. 5: Yes, I heard this in the movies. Sometimes a father calls his son "friend" and a son calls his father "friend." In China, we never do this, never call father or son "friend." (Mother?) No, never. (Brothers and sisters?) No, never. (Informant laughs.)

Interviewer: Why does my question make you laugh?

Inf. 5: It's quite different. (Why aren't members of family friends?) You know, family and relatives and friend different terms. (Different feeling?) Maybe feeling same. (How do you know?) If I have a cousin, he is my cousin; maybe we have a friendship. The feeling of friendship is higher than relative feeling; but still he is my cousin, he's not my friend. (Do you ever say, "He's my cousin and my friend"?) No, never. (?) If I do it, that is wrong. He's my cousin.

Interviewer: When I call my niece "my friend," she feels proud, more so than when I call her "my niece." How do you indicate that one of your relatives is more intimate than another, informally -- I don't mean formally?

Inf. 5: Yes, I understand, just in feeling. In this case, we say, "This is my relative." Maybe you can say in addition to "relative," some more words, for example, "I like him, he likes me." But we don't use the term "friend." Example: "This-is-my-relative-we-very-good." That means we love each other, we like each other.

Interviewer: When do you use this? How often?

Inf. 5: Oh ... if there is one of my relatives, family relatives -- maybe some relatives I don't like him; in some case, I like him. If we introduce relatives to another friend, I introduce him in this way. That means this person not only my relatives, but is my friend, but we don't use term "friend"! Never say, "This is my relative and my friend." This is in North China, Shantung Province; maybe in South China use the term "friend."

Interviewer: What age group? For example, children?

Inf. 5: No. Usually peng-yu about the same age. Because if someone is older, maybe he's your father's friend. Then you have to call him "uncle." You cannot call him "friend."

Interviewer: But if he doesn't know your father, but he's your father's age?

Inf. 5: If he knows you, in this case, he can be a friend to you. In this case we have a special term -- wong-nyang-dyo, "Forget-age-friend."

Interviewer: We don't have such a term.

Inf. 5: You don't have it? Well, because your friends don't regard age. But in China we regard the age -- generation. If he's older, he belongs to your father's generation; if he's younger, he belongs to your son's generation. (Do you use "forget-age-friend" to younger person?) Yes, same. (Is it used by men to wo-

men?) You can use it, but it is very scarce. (Shakes head.) In older society of
China, women only stay home. Friendship means social relations.

Interviewer: What about lao-peng-yu -- old friend?

Inf. 5: I think this term have two meanings. Lao means old friend and intimate
friend. Lao doesn't mean his age is old; friendship is old.

Interviewer: Men use this to women?

Inf. 5: No. In the older society, only the men have social relations and friendship is a term of social relationship. The women never. They don't use these
terms.

Interviewer: Neighbors?

Inf. 5: Ling-chu, close resident. (And friendship feeling?) Maybe they are
friends, but don't use the term. Older society, woman and friendship is funny!
Silly! Funny! (Laughs.) A woman cannot have a friend.

Interviewer: In your town, did your mother have any friends?

Inf. 5: No, she have only families, relatives, neighbors. (And your father?) My
father has his family, relatives and friends, and neighbors.

Interviewer: Who was closer to your mother, cousins, uncles, or neighbors?

Inf. 5: I think -- I tell you a proverb, then you can understand the relations.
Ching-tze, yuan-leo-chan; lin-chu-go-dan-chan: "Relatives-far-good; neighbor-
high-wall." (Explain that.) I explain. That means, the relatives who live far,
far away from you, the relationship between you and them will be good. The
neighbors maybe is your enemy, you know the wall is high. (We have a poet who
wrote "Good fences make good neighbors.") Yes, just the same! (What's the
other proverb?) Yuan-chin-bu-ry-chi-lin: "Far-relatives-not-as-good-as-
neighbor." You see, the two proverbs [are] quite different. The first one says
the far relatives good and neighbors bad. The second one says the far relatives
not as good as neighbors. The relations better among neighbors than among relatives. (?) That is according to your relationship. According to your real
relationship. My mother is very good. She has good neighbors and good relatives.

Interviewer: Do you remember your "uncles" -- father's friends?

Inf. 5: There were many.

Interviewer: Who are the "aunts"? Friends of whom?

Inf. 5: All my father's friends' wife, I call them "aunt."

Interviewer: Not single women?

Inf. 5: Not single women.

Interviewer: Mother's women neighbors?

Inf. 5: Same way. Call them "aunt."

Interviewer: What's the difference between father's friend's wife "aunt" and
mother's or father's woman neighbor "aunt." Same thing?

Inf. 5: Not same thing. My father's friends' wife, I always call them "aunt." But
some neighbors, maybe she call me "uncle." I don't know why. But in traditional

relations; maybe we have not relations [are not kin] -- but the old women call me sometimes "uncle" [or] "small uncle." Maybe we have some old, several generations, not so ancient, relations. Maybe his grandmother's grandmother is some relative of my grandfather's sister. (Laughter.) This way. If she belongs to lower generation, then she call me "uncle," even [if she is] older. That is interesting to you, I think. (Laughter.)

Interviewer: How does she know the relationship?

Inf. 5: By tradition. (Is it accurate?) I think. (Really?) Really. You know in small town, the people did not move so often, so maybe one family live in this house for many, many years. But somebody get his son very young; somebody get his son very old. Then after two generations, three generations, the neighbor at the same age, but not belongs to the same generation.

Interviewer: Then women don't have friends?

Inf. 5: Yes, if they do, that means silly, funny, strange.

Interviewer: Do you know women who call people "friends"?

Inf. 5: Not good women. Women who play Mah Jong call their women players "friends." (Lower-class women?) Yes, most of them belongs to the lower class. But that means funny. (Even among the lower class?) Yes, even. (Is it really friendship?) Uh--maybe, maybe not. All this in old society. In modern society, woman do this just as man. The man can have boy friend, girl friend; and the woman can have boy friend, girl friend, too.

Interviewer: Would you say there was some connection between attitudes of those lower-class women who call each other friends and the attitudes of modern men and women who now call each other friends interchangeably? Are both expressions of reaction against tradition? Do you understand?

Inf. 5: I understand. You are right. The upper class in traditional society want to keep -- I mean this older society, the upper class, want to keep the tradition because the upper classes get their privileges from the society; but the lower class get nothing, so it is easier to break the tradition. (And the "modern men and women" are members of what class?) Student. Maybe they belong to the upper class, but this higher class belong to the new society. (They have privileges?) Some connection; in different ways they all want to break with the old society. One is more definite -- the students.

Interviewer: We've strayed from "older friend." (Laughter.) When do you use it?

Inf. 5: I think I use this the same as [another informant] does, "familiar friend." Good feeling. (How different from peng-yu?) Lao-peng-yu still belongs to peng-yu. In conception we say it is peng-yu. But peng-yu may be not lao-peng-yu. You see? If I knew you yesterday today I introduce [you] as peng-yu, not as lao-peng-yu. (Time?) Yes, time is important in this word.

Interviewer: (Shows informant another word, hsin fu.)

Inf. 5: In my opinion, hsin fu not a friend, because friendship means something

equal. Equal relations. (What does this mean?) Hsin fu means the master and
his servant. We may say the servant is the hsin fu of his master.

Interviewer: And t'ung tsai chih i?

Inf. 5: That means a friend. (What kind of a friend?) I think this is some adjective term to modify the relationship of your friendship. That just means
"older friend".... (When do you use it? When you can get money from it? Is
this a special kind of friend?) This means a good friend. This means the degree of friend. In China we say common meaning, acquaintance, we are friends.
Maybe I may borrow some money from you but I have to return it to you. That
is common friend -- not a t'ung tsai chih i. But the best friend, most intimate
best friend, is chih chi. In China, if my head is necessary to you, let you take
my head away from me -- that is best, best friend, chih chi. You think, in this
case, life means nothing, property means nothing. So your money is my money,
my money is your money.

Interviewer: Is that stronger than family feeling?

Inf. 5: Yes, sometimes. Chih chi is speaking from feeling. T'ung tsai chih i is
financial relations between good friends. When good friends have t'ung tsai chih
i, they are usually chih chi, best friend.

Interviewer: Can you have financial relations between peng-yu?

Inf. 5: You can have t'ung tsai chih i with all peng-yu. Peng-yu is wide friend.
Chih chi is also a kind of peng-yu. In China, property belongs to the family;
usually; in family anything that belongs to me belongs to my wife and anything
that belongs to my wife belongs to me.

Interviewer: Is that a t'ung tsai chih i relationship?

Inf. 5: No, that's between friends. (Property belongs to friends?) No, borrow
and give, that's all.

Interviewer: (Asks about the meaning of chin-jou peng-yu.)

Inf. 5: That modify the peng-yu. (?) Not good friends. If you have money, he's
your friend. If you have wine, he drink. If you haven't he go away. (Are such
friends common?) You may say in China this common.

Interviewer: And chih chi friend?

Inf. 5: Common. (You have such friends?) Yes, I have. But I have not the
chin-jou peng-yu. I don't like such people. (How can you know them?) I can
know his personality. If I know his personality is not good, I don't have them.

Interviewer: What is good personality?

Inf. 5: Honesty -- good nature.

Interviewer: (Asks about meaning of chin-mi.)

Inf. 5: Intimate. Adjective. [Re another informant's definition:] Very good.
But chin means "dear" and mi means "close."[26] In modern society, chih chi

---

26. Note how the informant first praises and then corrects the definition given
    by the other informant. For other examples of this behavior, cf. discussion
    of Chinese group on "Sincerity" (Part Three, pages 120-24).--Ed.

used between men and women, men and men, woman and woman. (And chin-mi?)
The same. (In the old society?) Chih chi just between men and men. (And
chin mi?) This is adjective. You can use this to modify anything. My dear son,
my dear dog, my dear friend. Chin mi di peng-yu -- close and dear friend. (In
old society used between men and women?) No.

Interviewer: (Asks about meaning of t'ung chih.)

Inf. 5: I think this term have two meanings. One is relationship between members of a party, of a political party, especially political.

Interviewer: Friendship?

Inf. 5: Maybe there is a friendship. (Doesn't have to be a friendship?) Doesn't.
Maybe we belong to the same political party but we don't have to be friends. The
other means, people have same purpose, same aim. (Not friends?) In this way,
when people have the same purpose, they generally are friends. You like art
and I like art, we are t'ung chih, comrades. (Do these people become chih chi?)
You can, often.

Interviewer: (Asks the meaning of tung-chuan-nah.)

Inf. 5: Both-difficulty. Translated, if we happy, we happy together; if we're
poor, we're poor together. (Laughter.)

Interviewer: (Asks meaning of gun-kan-ku.)

Inf. 5: Both-happy-difficulty. Do you understand my translation? (When do
you use this?) With chih chi. (And with peng-yu?) You can, because chih chi
is also peng-yu. You don't separate the idea of chih chi from a friend, peng-yu.
Because chih chi is a kind of friend, most intimate, most know each other.
(Chih chi usually same sex, same age?) Usually. (Equals?) Yes. [Interviewer
notes an omission here.]

Interviewer: (Quotes a proverb relating power of horse to friendship.)

Inf. 5: We have that proverb in North China. I don't remember it very well. I
think the same meaning. Oh, I remember it! Liu-yo-dje-mah-li; jo-diu-diya-
cjen-jin-si: "The road-far-no-horse-power; (time) days-long-see-people-
mind (heart)."

Interviewer: ?

Inf. 5: If the way is far, far, then you can know the power or the energy of the
horse. You may know the man, after a long time. (How is this proverb related
to friendship?) That means friendship takes time.

Interviewer: Does peng-yu friendship take time?

Inf. 5: Peng-yu also takes time. (Then I cannot be your friend?) You can. Why
not? (Because it takes time!) I know, I understand what you mean. In this way,
you misunderstand the peng-yu and the chih chi. (In what way?) Usually we
say peng-yu, that means "friend and good relation." Sometimes, or usually, we
can call chih chi, peng-yu.

Interviewer: If you have two people with you who are your friends, how do you
introduce them?

Inf. 5: Oh, if you have two people, you cannot introduce them one as <u>chih chi</u> and the other as <u>peng-yu</u>. Same way.

Interviewer: But how can I be <u>peng-yu</u> if I don't know you a long time?

Inf. 5: Usually, the custom, I can tell from your manner whether we are friends. Let me say -- maybe I introduce you, <u>very serious</u>, I say "This is my friend." In this case you can only understand it from his manner. I may say in another case, "This is my best friend," he may not be as important a friend as the man I say, "This is my <u>friend.</u>" Oh, you cannot understand this!

Interviewer: I can.

Inf. 5: I say friend, two fundamental bases: one is time and the other is under-standing. Maybe some people know each other for many, many years, but they are not <u>chih chi,</u> they are not good friends. But maybe some people only talk once, they know each other, understand each other very, very deep. But gener-ally, the best friend have these two elements in it: time and understanding.

Interviewer: Does your best friend come from your same town? Do your father's best friends come from the same town?

Inf. 5: Maybe, maybe. (In the old way?) Usually from the same town, but not all.

Interviewer: Your father was an army man. Were his best friends army men?

Inf. 5: Yes, most of his best friends were army men.

Interviewer: How about your best friends -- students?

Inf. 5: Students. (Is that right?) That's true. (If he belonged to a political party, his best friend is likely to belong to the same one?) Yes.

VII. Interview with Two Jewish Men: <u>Sheyneh</u> and <u>Prosteh Yiden</u>[27]

Informant 20: 54 years old; born in S---- in White Russia; father a businessman; attended Cheder and later a Russian government school; left S---- when he was.25 years old; married in the United States and has two children; is a well-to-do dress manufacturer.

Informant 21: over 60 years old; born in K---- in White Russia; comes from a family of <u>Lamdonim</u> (students, learned people); attended <u>Cheder</u>, <u>Yeshiva</u> and Russian schools; came to the United States when he was 20 years old; married here and has two daughters (a son was recently killed in Israel); is a dress man-ufacturer.

Interviewer's note: I arranged to interview Informant 20 and made the appoint-ment through his daughter. Her first reaction to my request was, "He'll be an excellent informant. When my father starts talking, he doesn't stop." When I arrived at the house, Informant 20 was excited about the work I was doing and very anxious to start speaking. Before we began, he told me that he had invited a friend of his (Informant 21), whom he considered a very educated man and a "fine person," to take part in the interview.....Before I had a chance to start the

---

27. Interviewer 43F. Unpublished document RCC-JR 319. A first interview with both informants, conducted in Yiddish and later translated by the inter-viewer. This was a five-hour interview, from which only two excerpts are presented here: the opening passage, for the style of the two informants' communication with the interviewer, and a section near the end on <u>sheyneh</u> and <u>prosteh Yiden</u>. Cf. also Interview VIII, with two women, on the same subject (below, pages 203-15).

interview, Informant 20 asked for the questionnaire. I told him that I didn't have any, and that I just wanted him to talk about certain topics. He agreed that this method was a better one....

Informant 20 suggested that I interview him first and that I then start interviewing informant 21.

I explained to them that I wanted some information on Chassidim and Misnagdim. Informant 20 told me that he came from a Misnagdishe family, but that there was a large Chassidic group in S----(his home town), which he knew quite well. But the Misnagdim were in the majority in S----.

Inf. 20: My sister is married to a Chassid, and a pretty good one, too. (The sister was married in S----.)

Interviewer: What was the attitude of the family to that marriage?

Inf. 20: I don't remember anything being said against the marriage. Besides, he was a Veisser (white) Chassid and he knew better than the other Chassidim. He was a "Misnagdisher Chassid."

Interviewer: ?

Inf. 20: He didn't go to the Rebbe (Chassidic) or to the Hoif (the Chassidic Rabbi's house and yard) and on Yom Kippur when he wanted to have some fun and a good time, he went out with the Misnagdim.

Interviewer: Didn't the Misnagdim observe Yom Kippur?

Inf. 20: Certainly, but after Yom Kippur there was usually some sort of celebration and he would always be with us. To get back to my family's reaction to my sister's marriage. There was no reaction. Actually, Misnagdim never had a bad feeling against the individual Chassid. It was the opposite. If you want my personal opinion, Misnagdim were more cultured and more educated people. The Chassidim were too fanatic. And I'll tell you something, when it came to an important religious question, like about dietary laws or like that, even the Chassidim would come to the Rov -- the Rabbi.

At this point Informant 21 interrupted: You know a Rabbi or a Rov has to have Smichus Rabonus -- it's like a college degree -- and when he has that, he can decide on religious questions.

Inf. 20 (talking to Informant 21, and rather angrily): Look, Mr. A----, she knows that better than you. She wants my opinion. When your turn will come, you'll tell her.

Inf. 21: O.K., O.K., I was only trying to make it clearer. Maybe she doesn't know the difference between a Chassidic Rebbe and a Rabbi or Rov.

Inf. 20: Our Rov was very important. He went to Court even and what he decided was accepted by the Russian government. He was a personality. And when a governor came to visit the town, our Rov and the Misnagdim went to meet him, not the Chassidim. The Chassidic Rebbe in our town was Reb S----W----. He was a well-to-do man. He got a lot of money from the Chassidim, and also his sons, who became the Chassidic Rabbis after him, went into business and they were bankers. From his grandchildren, a few married Gentiles, and that's because of their environment.

Interviewer: Why do you think it was the environment?

Inf. 20: Because they didn't like the strictness and the orthodox way that they were brought up. The Chassidim were very old-fashioned. And our regular Rabbi, the Misnagdisher, he was Rabbi M---- O---- F----. He didn't get a penny for his work. And he used to work very hard. The train used to come in twice a day at seven A.M. and at seven P.M., and there would form a line in front of his house. He would answer problems and give Brachas (benedictions) the whole day. And he didn't get a penny for it. So how did he live -- you want to know? He was fortunate enough to have a rich son who supported him. Oh, he was a wonderful person....

[Omission: description of the Rabbi's activities.]

Inf. 20: ... He [the Rabbi] really had to know his work, because he could be examined by the people, and if they found out that he didn't know his work well, he lost his reputation. But the Chassidic Rabbi could be an ignoramus. He was never examined, and besides, his position was a hereditary one, so they usually were ignoramuses. It was like a dynasty. (He turns to Informant 21.) Do you agree?

Inf. 21: I don't agree, but I have a different story to tell. You finish yours first and then I'll talk. I don't want to interrupt. But one thing I'll add -- they were not all ignoramuses.

[Omission: a heated discussion between the two informants as they tried to characterize the Chassidim. The interviewer commented in her notes: "I realized that it was impossible to control the interview on this topic. I was now supposedly interviewing Informant 21, but Informant 20 would not let him talk, and if I asked a question it was ignored. He went on talking...." The interviewer therefore took advantage of a pause to change the topic.]

Interviewer's note: I told the two informants that I wanted to get some material on sheyneh and prosteh Yiden, and asked whether they could tell me something about that. Both of them immediately stated that in their shtetlakh (villages) they were not called sheyneh and prosteh Yiden, but Balebatishe and Haamoin (common, the masses).

Inf. 20: When you talk about sheyneh Yiden, you remind me of a joke. A man came from Bialystok, so somebody asked him: "Do you know Moisheh?" "No, there are a lot of Moishehs in Bialystok." "I mean Moisheh the scurvy-head." "No." "I mean Moisheh the scurvy-head with the rupture." "No" "I mean Moisheh, with the scurvy head, the rupture ... the blind man, you know." "Oh, you mean Moisheh the blind one. Oh, he's a feiner Yid" (a fine Jew).[28]

Interviewer: ?

Inf. 20: A Balebatisher Yid can be a worker, but he must be able to understand

---

28. It is significant that Informant 20 should spontaneously open the discussion of sheyneh and prosteh Yiden with this traditional story, told in many versions, which conveys to the Jewish listener the idea that true beauty (Sheynkeit) is of the mind and spirit and that Moisheh of Bialystok is a beautiful person. By so doing, the informant defines at the outset what to him is the essential quality of social distinction: intellectual beauty.--Ed.

a little and to learn a little. I remember when a Chazan (cantor) used to come
to town. And S---- used to have some of the best Chazanim. He used to pray
and sing in the Big Shul (synagogue). The Balebatishe Yiden of course had their
seats near the front. The Haamoin had to stand in the back. Of course they
couldn't hear the Chazan well. When it was over, they used to come out and say
that the Chazan was no good. He can't sing, he doesn't know his ivreh (Hebrew),
and nothing was right. Haamoin didn't even know how to criticize well. The
Balebatishe Yiden were able to criticize better. And of course you could never
please Haamoin. They were never satisfied and there were always fights (arguments was what he really meant) between them over such things as a Chazan.
The Balebatishe Yiden would pay for the Chazan to come and then the Haamoin
would criticize.

Interviewer: What were the fights about, usually?

Inf. 20: The Balebatishe Yiden would decide that the Big Shul had to be painted.
So Haamoin would yell: "Why do you have to paint the Big Shul? What's the
matter, you can't pray in an unpainted shul?" So you think they had to pay for
the painting? The Balebatishe Yiden paid for it.

Interviewer: Well, if they prayed in the Big Shul, don't they have some say in
the management of the Shul?

Inf. 20: They don't pray in the Big Shul. You see, there were a lot of shulen on
one or two of the streets. One next to the other. The tailors prayed in one shul,
the shoemakers in another, and so on. There was one Rabbi for the shulen,
and he would one day pray in one shul and the next day in another. Also, everybody could go from one shul into the next. You didn't have to pay for that. You
only had to pay for a seat in your particular shul. They used to come into the
Big Shul when they were through praying. Half the time they were drunk. You
know, you take a little bit of wine after you pray. So they used to take a few
glasses more, get a little high, and come visit in our shul. Then there was a
racket and a fuss. That's what I hated most about the Haamoin. But you couldn't
say that all the people who belonged to the Haamoin were like that. Some were
very nice and quiet.

Interviewer: What makes a proster Yid prost?

Inf. 20: The first and most important thing is background. I found out here as
well as in Warsaw, where I lived for awhile. The background of an individual
reveals itself no matter where he goes, and when you can trace that, you can
find out exactly where the person comes from -- Haamoin or Balebatishe family. A proster Jew can come here, he can make a lot of money, have an excellent business, drive in a beautiful car, and he can send his children to the university in Wisconsin (Informant 20 sent his daughter to the University of Wisconsin -- Int.), and he remains prost and his children too usually remain prost.
It takes many years until this prost-ness becomes erased. Of course, here in
America things are a little different. With the melting pot and the big cities,

you can change quicker. Recently I met a man who came from S----. He lives
in New Jersey and has a big business. I remember that in S---- his father was
a Meshugener (crazy man) and the children used to make fun of him in the streets.
And here this man has fine children and you would never realize their background. But if they lived in S----, it would react on him, his children, and his
grandchildren for a long time. They would always be Berl der Meshugenem's
kinder (Berl the crazy one's children). The shtetl (town) was too small, and if
you came originally from Haamoin, you usually remained there.

Interviewer: So how does a sheyner Yid get to be sheyn?

Inf. 20: Responsibility to the community, responsibility to the family, those are
important things which make a person sheyn.

Interviewer: If a man is learned but is a worker, is he a sheyner Yid or a
proster?

Inf. 21: When one is a learned Jew, then he can't be prost. But even a person
who is not learned is sometimes not prost. He may come from a Balebatishe
family but maybe for some reason or other he didn't get an education.

Inf. 20: When you come from a Balebatishe family, a spark of Balebatishkeit
always remains with you. And a proster Yid can become wealthy and give a lot
of money to the synagogue, but he still remains prost. Money doesn't change
that, and the sheyneh Yiden don't care to associate with them too much.

Interviewer: Did you associate with any prosteh Yiden?

Inf. 20: Sure, to me it didn't make any difference. I used to meet them at meetings of the movement and at school sometimes.

Interviewer: Did your parents associate with them?

Inf. 20: No, my parents were not very friendly with them. They used to call
them am harotzim (ignoramuses). My father used to refer to them as a sus
(horse) or a chamoir (donkey, ass). But if a proster Yid was an honest person,
they called him an orentlecher am haaretz (an honest ignoramus).

Inf. 21: May I say something? At home, in Europe, it was not like here. Here,
anybody can put on a nice suit or dress and you won't know where he comes
from or who he is. But in Europe there was a difference between the two groups.
A Balebatisher Yid is not a worker. He can learn a little, knows a little more
Torah, and has a little money. And so the Balebatishe Jews used to look down a
little on the prosteh Yiden. When it came to a Shidakh (marriage match) they
looked "crooked" (they frowned on) when there was too little Yichus.[29]

---

29. Yichus is one of the important concepts related to the social structure of the
shtetl, and is one of the more difficult to translate and define briefly.
Yichus has an approximate meaning of status and concerns learning, family
and gelt (money). In these discussions of prosteh and sheyneh Yiden (with
various informants) one purpose was to arrive at an adequate understanding of what was involved in Yichus, how it affected the family's and individual's position in the shtetl.--Ed.

My father was a <u>Magid</u> and the family in general were <u>Lamdonim</u> (learned people). But we didn't have very much money. In fact, we were poor. But it is not a question of money. My parents didn't look down upon <u>prosteh Yiden</u>, but nevertheless they always hoped for a good <u>Shidakh</u> (match) for their children.

<u>Inf. 20</u>: Of all the <u>Haamoin</u> in S----, those who were most <u>prost</u> were the butchers. And they had a lot of money too, because it is a good business. But they were so loud and vulgar. They always had to push their way into everything. And of all the <u>Haamoin</u>, they were the least educated. From their <u>shul</u>, you could hear the noise down the whole <u>shul hoif</u>....

[Brief omission with change of subject.]

<u>Inf. 21</u> (to Interviewer): May I ask you a personal question, if you don't mind?

<u>Interviewer</u>: (I said I didn't mind.)

<u>Inf. 21</u>: Where do you come from, where were you born?

<u>Interviewer</u>: I was born in Canada.

<u>Inf. 21</u>: So how come you speak Yiddish and write Yiddish?

<u>Interviewer</u>: (I explained my background to him.)

<u>Inf. 21</u>: You know, that gives me so much <u>nachas</u> (pleasure). You are a real <u>Yiddisheh tochter</u> (Jewish daughter).

[End of interview omitted here.]

VIII. Interview with Two Jewish Women: <u>Sheyneh</u> and <u>Prosteh Yiden</u>[30]

<u>Informant 18</u>: 51 years old; born in Galicia; educated in public and high schools and in a Zionist Hebrew school in home town, in night school in New York; in the United States since 1914; married 29 years; one son.
<u>Informant 22</u>: a friend of Informant 18, from a near-by village in Galicia.

<u>Interviewer's note</u>: ... she seemed rather delighted to be interviewed again. I arrived at the house at eight o'clock as I had arranged. Informant 18 was at that time busy cutting curtains for a friend of hers (Informant 22).... She asked if I had any objections if the other woman remained while I interviewed her. I said no, and was just about to begin interviewing when the bell rang.... One of her neighbors came in stating that she saw the light on and people walking in and out and there seemed to be a lot of commotion, so she had come in to see what was going on. She sat down and was offered coffee. I was offered coffee as well. Then Informant 18's husband arrived with a new type of sewing machine for the curtains. There was a demonstration and the three women watched eagerly....

The bell rang again and a woman who was selling a trousseau to Informant 18 for her son came in with her daughter, who is about twelve. I had met this woman previously ... and she asked whether I had any children yet. I said no. "So when are you going to have children?" she asked.... "Why don't you make your mother-in-law a grandmother already?"

The bell rang again and Informant 22's husband came in. He said, "I was coming from the dentist and I saw the light burning, so I came in." [Eventually the visitors left and the two men went for a walk. They later returned and

30. Interviewer 43F. Unpublished document RCC-JP 326. Third interview with Informant 18, first with Informant 22. The interview was conducted in Yiddish and later translated by the interviewer. The excerpt given occurs about half way through a five-hour interview. Cf. also Interview VII, with two men, on the same subject, immediately preceding.

joined in the interview.⌉ ... Informant 18 complained that this happend every
night and said that one of these days she was going to post a sign on the door
stating visiting hours. "They think," she said, "just because they are lonely,
everybody else is lonely too...."

I told the informant that I would like to get some material on Chassidim and
Misnagdim, and since she stems from a famous Chassidic family, perhaps she
could give me the information I need. Before I had a chance to ask a question,
she started to tell me about the C---- Rebbe. I tried to ask questions several
times, but she insisted that she must give me the background of the Rebbe and
his family before I could understand the whole picture.

⌈Omission: the informants' discussion of Chassidim and Misnagdim, and
of several other topics, has been omitted here. The women stopped talking
when the men returned from their walk, and the interviewer therefore changed
the topic.⌉

Interviewer: What is a proster Yid?

Inf. 18: A proster Yid is a worker, an illiterate person and a person who has no
Yichus.[31] And there are different grades of prosteh Yiden. Like take the
Balagoleh. Some of them were very prost, they were absolutely illiterate. Others could learn a little bit, so they were less prost, but still belonged to the
prosteh Yiden.

Inf. 22: They were not illiterate, because no matter how prost a Jew was, he
could still daven (pray). After all he still had to go to Cheder for a while.

Interviewer: Did your family ever associate with prosteh Yiden?

Inf. 18: No, never. My parents would say hello or how are you to a proster Yid,
but there was no friendship with them. And to marry into a family of prosteh
Yiden was considered hinteren Koved (beneath one's dignity). For example, in
the case of a Balebatishe (sheyneh) family where there were several daughters
and the father could not afford a dowry for them, then he would have to lower
himself and marry his daughters to people with less Yichus. Because that was
better than having your daughters remain alteh moiden (old maids). But that
only happened when they had no Nadan (dowry) and there were a few daughters.
When a family with Yichus had sons, they could shadchen zich (arrange a match)
with any family in the shtetl (small town). They could choose their Machatonim
(in-law family).

Inf. 22: Before the war, my family usually didn't associate with prosteh Yiden,
that is, the uneducated ones. But during the war, when things were so bad for
everyone, it really made no difference.

Interviewer: What makes prosteh Yiden prost?

Inf. 18: They have no background, no Yichus, and they knew nothing. They were
ignorant.

Interviewer: Were any of the Chassidim prosteh Yiden?

Inf. 18: Some of them were Chassidim, but very few that I know of.

Interviewer: Was an educated person who had no Yichus still a proster Yid?

---

31. See Footnote 29, page 202.--Ed.

Inf. 18: No matter how educated a person is, if he has no <u>Yichus,</u> he is low, he is still a <u>proster Yid.</u> A <u>sheyner Yid</u> must come from <u>Yichus,</u> and he remains a <u>sheyner Yid</u> -- he keeps up his background.

Inf. 22: I'm sorry, but to me a <u>sheyner Yid</u> was a Jew who could learn, who did good things, gave good advice, gave <u>Tzdokah</u> (charity), and who in general was a good Jew. And it made no difference if he had <u>Yichus</u> or not.

Inf. 18: No, you don't know what you're talking about. Very few Jews who had no <u>Yichus</u> could be <u>sheyneh Yiden.</u> A worker is not an aristocrat, and therefore he is not a <u>sheyner Yid.</u> Try and remember, in the <u>shtetl</u> people who were workers could not afford to send their children for very much education. When a boy became eight or nine years old, he was sent to study a <u>Melocheh</u> (trade) and to become a worker. The parents were only too glad to have him earn some money. Look at my husband. He was sent to work when he was ten because his father was poor and they needed help in the family. By <u>sheyneh Yiden</u> that didn't happen because they could almost always find enough money to keep their sons in <u>Cheder</u> or at <u>Yeshiveh.</u> In rare cases where a boy showed excellent talent for learning, so somebody would keep him in <u>Cheder.</u> But how often did that happen? There were only two kinds of <u>sheyneh Yiden.</u> Those who had <u>Yichus,</u> and those who were learned. Of course, if you had money, it helped a little.

(Informant 18 then suggested that we go into the kitchen and she would prepare coffee. The men remained in the living room and the two informants and I went into the kitchen.... The interveiw was continued where it had been interrupted when the men came home.)

[The final part of this interview has been omitted.]

IX. Interview with a Russian Actor: Interpretation of Roles[32]

Informant 22: man, about 55 years old; Greek Orthodox; educated at University of ----; in the United States since the 1930s.

Interviewer's note: The informant is a Russian character actor who recently played [a leading role in a Russian play]. I was impressed by his performance ... and therefore requested an interview with him.

Interviewer: (I explained only enough about the situation to make it clear to him that I was not a reporter, and then asked him what was the meaning of the gesture "when you nearly stroked the hair of X---- [another male character in the play] before you left him?")

---

32. Interviewer 27M. Unpublished document RCC-R 85. This was a first interview. Details of the actor's background, the name of the play, a description of the part played by the actor, etc., and the first 28 lines of the interview -- in which the informant analyzes the gesture discussed in terms of the part he plays -- have been omitted to protect the identity of the informant. This interview, in which interviewer and informant work very consciously with problems of gesture, may be contrasted -- on this point -- with Interviews I and II (pages 170-74, 174-78), where the interviewer attempts to record, without discussion of their meaning with the informants, significant posture-gesture images.

[Omission: the informant indicates that he regards the gesture as a paternal one and that he intended to suggest by using it at that point in the play
the multiplicity of emotions felt by the character he was portraying concerning
the person whose hair was nearly stroked.]

Interviewer: ?

Inf. 22: Oh yes, stroking the hair is a paternal gesture.

Interviewer: ?

Inf. 22: When the father is feeling most tender towards his child, he will stroke
his hair. He wouldn't kiss the child. A mother would do that.

Interviewer: ?

Inf. 22: Oh yes. The audience appreciate this point. They feel the sudden
warmth. In Russian nature this is most typical. There's only the breadth of the
split hair between cruel, coarse, abject brutality and the greatest warmth and
tenderness. The peasants will curse the Virgin Mary, and a moment later kiss
the hem of her dress. In the Civil War, which was in many ways more cruel
than the war of the Vendées, and that was on both sides, a friend told me about a
Red company in South Russia which was cleaning up the area, one of the most
cruel and pitiless groups in the whole Red Army. Well, one day this group came
to a burnt-out village, without a living soul, and suddenly they heard a baby crying and they looked and found a baby just a few weeks old, alive, lying beside
the corpse of his mother. Well, half-drunk and dirty bandits though they were,
they took the baby and then they asked, "Who will nurse this baby?" So they
invaded the next village and took a woman with a baby of the same age and killed
her husband and said to her, "Citizen, you must serve the Revolution." They
dragged this woman around with them several weeks and made her nurse her
own baby and the baby of the company. Although these were just primitive people, they took a pair of scales and used to weigh both babies on the balance
every day to make certain she was feeding the company baby properly. If the
company baby weighed less than hers did, they used to beat her for cheating,
but during the fighting they would all protect this woman and her two babies and
keep them in the rear. When they finally returned to Moscow, they gave the woman one of the highest awards and put her in an institution for orphanage, and made
her the chief nurse. Both the boys were brought up in this orphanage, and probably they are now important Soviet officials. This is just one example of the
mixture of the brutality and cruelty, and sympathy and warmth. In the midst of
the battle they were more engaged in protecting the babies than their own selves.

Interviewer: Would you tell me how you became an actor?

Inf. 22: It's my firm conviction that when I was very young, say three or four or
five, I was very silent and solitary. I started to read when I was three and had
an extraordinary memory, both optical and verbal, and I didn't like being disturbed when I was sitting in a corner of the library reading a book. The grown-
ups used to say to me, "Funny man, philosopher, what will you be when you
grow up?" And I used to say I'd like to be a bear. A bear seemed to me very

enviable because he cannot be disturbed and he is always comfortable. After that, I thought I wanted to be a vagabond. That would be when I was around ten or eleven, and at that time I was beautifully religious, and thought that one should think nothing of concrete reality. It seemed to me the ideal life would be to possess nothing but to be a vagabond, begging for food and living in the open fields. Then later I understood that it would not be so nice to be a vagabond, because it's not always sunny, there's sometimes snow, and people aren't always kind. After that I wanted to be a learned monk, and then when I read more I wanted to be a hero serving his country or humanity. My favorite image was St. Joan. When I was about fifteen or sixteen, I was always inventing comedies or little plays for my friends and my family, and even for the servants, if they would watch me. I would invent the movements and the costumes and so on, and I would play all sorts of things, not only human beings, both contemporary and medieval, but also animals and birds and even inanimate objects. I remember that once I played being a letterbox (standing up and illustrating). I was a letterbox that could read letters. All that, I understand now, was a drive to the theater. It's only as a character actor that you can be all people everywhere, a bear one day and a vagabond the next, a monk the day after and a hero the day after that. I felt that to live one life was not enough, I needed to live several.

Interviewer: Did you go to the theater much?

Inf. 22: Yes. Our family admired very much the Imperial Theatre. They were very great actors. And then the Moscow Art Theatre emerged as something new.

Interviewer: ?

Inf. 22: Yes. I thought a lot of the theater as a kid. A friend of the family was Directeur du plateau.[33] This man was a dear friend and used to let me go and look at the actors in the wings and sometimes I would go to the dressing rooms and just say a word of appreciation to the actors. We all gave our love to that theater. Stanislavsky learned from there -- an actress who belonged to that theater was really his coach. The Stanislavsky theater never attained such heights. They played especially Gogol and Ostrovsky. As young students of the university, several people worked their apprenticeships. When I was young I wanted to study and do serious and meticulous work. When I was sixteen or seventeen, I finished the classical gymnasium early -- because of my health I worked at home and only made my exams there. One had to get a special dispensation. I became a student at the ---- University when I was seventeen and studied philosophy and literature, and finished both with a doctor's diploma. I also worked in the theatrical school. I cracked up twice because of hard work.

---

33. There is no English or American equivalent to this position. In the Russian theater two men were in supreme charge, one of everything in front of the stage, and the other of everything behind the stage. The Chef du plateau was the latter and was nearest, perhaps, to the director in the American theater.--Int.

We worked for three years in the school, and then two years as apprentices, coming in on mob scenes and so on. After that, I knew all the methods and I began to get bored. This theater of Stanislavsky lacked magic. You no longer had an extraordinary evening, but felt something like you were looking through a keyhole. Stanislavsky abolished curtain calls because he said they destroyed the illusion, but I think that just the opposite is true. I say that in the theater there are three supreme A's: the Author, the Audience, and the Actor, and you can't have the theater without all three. I don't play _for_ the audience -- that is cheap and bad -- but _with_ the audience. There is no rivalry, no looking for effect, but pure sport. You send the ball to the audience and they send it back to you. If you lose the ball, that's your fault. But if the audience misses the ball, you win.

Interviewer: ?

Inf. 22: The audience misses the ball when you place it where they don't expect it and they are surprised. The most wonderful moment in the theater is when you surprise the audience. Often you surprise them with a new effect found in a moment. Although I study my parts with the greatest detail and meticulousness, I always leave about fifteen per cent of it unknown. What happens then depends on the audience and your own feelings, and then there is this great moment of surprise.[34]

Well, when I had been with Stanislavsky for some time, a new theater began to appear, Tyroff, a follower of Mayerholt, and he asked me to join him and also asked a young actress. He was not satisfied with what Stanislavsky was doing and wanted the theater to be romantic and colorful. This Kamerniy Theatre was founded in 1914. We opened with the Hindu play Shakuntala, which was a great surprise to the audience, and our repertoire consisted of that and plays by Molière, Calderon, Synge, and so on. I stayed there for ... years and then I gradually started becoming dissatisfied. Tyroff originally was using new methods, but gradually the methods became the goal instead of the means and the theater became mechanical, formalistic, and without promise....

[Omission: 33 lines in which the informant describes his further career, the fortunate "chance" that took him out of Russia, and various parts he played later in theaters in several European cities and in the United States.]

Inf. 22: ... and now I can play in English too. I prefer to write in English.

Interviewer: ?

Inf. 22: I dream in four languages, and that shows that it is your brain speaking for all the cast in your dreams. I often speak aloud in my sleep and my wife tells me in the morning, "You had a French dream last night" or "You had a Russian dream." For the most intimate things, like prayer, I speak in Russian, but I always swear in French. If I am dealing with very abstract and theoretical

---

34. Compare this actor's statement about his preferred relationship to his audience with the description of Soviet chess preferences in Haimson's "The Soviet Style of Chess," Part Ten, pages 421-31.--Ed.

points, I use German, but when I want to be precise and concise, then English. English is the most concise language. One page of English text is equivalent to two pages of German and three pages of Russian. In French it is the way you say a thing rather than what you say that matters.

Interviewer: ?

Inf. 22: Gestures come out of character. They are a physical language and one makes them instinctively. It is different for each specimen. I never make a mistake.

Interviewer: ?

Inf. 22: No. It's not conscious transformation, but inborn. I can fool my wife or even my most intimate friends if they can't see my face.

(Informant 22 then illustrated most convincingly the way different national-ities express different emotions. Unfortunately, this is impossible to describe.)

Inf. 22: There are two sorts of gestures: descriptive gestures and emotional gestures. Descriptive gestures are different for each nationality, but real emo-tional gestures are the same for all. I learned more about real emotional ges-tures from Isadora Duncan than from anyone else. Although the emotional ges-tures are the same, they differ for each nationality in scale and amount. Among the Anglo-Saxons they are very small, the Latins they are greater; but the great gestures are universal.

Interviewer: Were you taught these different gestures as a student?

Inf. 22: No. We were taught the mastery of the body, achieving a harmonious line and doing away with irregularity. It was nearer eurythmics, like the Dal-croze School, and then we were taught fencing and other physical skills. For two years I went to the circus and learned juggling and acrobatics. Until very re-cently I could do backward somersaults.

Interviewer: ?

Inf. 22: Applicants to the school were screened. There's a minimum of three years' training, but apprentices were given a little salary. The first year the training was on the voice, diction and articulation, but no scenes -- developing range and speed in articulation, and then dancing and fencing. The second year we'd do bits of plays, just one scene, to get used to dialogue. The third year we'd learn whole parts and give a school performance.

Interviewer: ?

Inf. 22: Oh yes, from the beginning. Students were always very interested in all the actors, in playing full parts. I'm always surprised that Americans who come and tell me that they want to act, when I ask them what part they want to play, they say they don't know. I should have thought all real actors would have had parts they would dream of playing.

Interviewer: ?

Inf. 22: Even when I was young I dreamed of playing Iago. He is not just black violence, but a stepchild of nature, a man who has never had love, and so is em-

bittered and has an unnatural desire to cause pain, to vindicate himself. You
know, I don't care about the result, or whether a thing happens. Sometimes the
deed precedes the cause; life runs backward to the cause. If a deed is evil but
done for a purpose, you must create the cause for expiation.

Interviewer: ?

Inf. 22: Othello is a child and very easy to play if the actor doesn't act. Othello
trusts everybody, and it is an insult to bring pain to him because he trusts
everybody. He gets mad easily, just like a child. He reacts without second
thought. He goes to battle without fear, like a child. You know our great poet
Pushkin was Othello, a real personification of Othello, all his life. He was
generous, noble, and trusting, and he was insulted and scorned.

Interviewer: ?

Inf. 22: No, the Stanislavsky training was not a waste of time. With it I have
remained safe all my life. I took things up like a sponge from everyone. I
even toured with a Japanese troupe because I admired the acting so much. But I
digested and adapted everything I took up in a spongelike way on the basis of
this five years of training. It's a fundamental which one cannot destroy. Any
audience I play with, what I try to send them are characterizations. It's how I
hold out my hand to human beings (with gesture). As a character actor my aim
is not to disguise myself, but to reveal myself as a human being, understandable
to all.

Interviewer: ?

Inf. 22: Yes, my parents did object to my being an actor. My mother died in
my infancy and I was brought up by other rich merchants. They were proud of
my intelligence and wanted me to be a writer or a professor. It was a big
shock to them and a big pain to them when I decided to become an actor. I owed
everything to them; I deceived them. Those rich bourgeois families, the way
they thought about the stage -- it was not quite shame.

Interviewer: (Referring to "revealing" himself as a character actor)?

Inf. 22: The core is always the same (putting his hand on his chest). But the
expression differs.... When you play a Frenchman, you think of all the past and
you begin to express yourself more exuberantly. When you are acting Racine,
you feel all the laces and cloth around the sleeve (making excellent French gestures). If you are playing a German you are never really relaxed in your body.
You communicate through all the physical means. I was very interested in looking at the news reels of the signing of the Peace Treaty with Japan. There were
the Americans, almost as if they were in sports dress, easy and relaxed; the
Russians with their epaulets and high collars -- you feel Alexander III and
Czarist Russia -- stiff, full of self-conscious pride; the French are almost
negligent, playing with their sticks; Englishmen -- he is always at home, with
his legs crossed. The Englishman carries with him wherever he goes a three-
foot square which he stands on, and he says, "This is England and I am at home

here." The German always with their inferiority burden somewhere in their self-satisfaction. They have fear and an inferiority complex. When Anglo-Saxons are at ease, they have a minimum of gestures, for they feel they have nothing to cover. The Germans always feel they have something to hide and are full of unnecessary gestures. They sweat so often, and that is because of muscular tension. You can see how they are always using their handkerchiefs, even if it is not hot. The French are playful and don't hide their Latin exuberance. They are sexually playful and get release from that.

Interviewer: ?

Inf. 22: The Russians suffer from self-consciousness. When they meet a stranger, they must do something. They can't sit relaxed, but play with cigarettes or matches, straighten their tie, feel around in their coat, and so on. This comes from a lack of being among people, a lack of ease with others.

Interviewer: Would you say that X----(referring to his role) was uneasy?

Inf. 22: No. He is highly trained, like a juggler.

Interviewer: What did that gesture mean when you reached out your hand toward the bowl of herring ... and your fingers quivered?

Inf. 22: X---- is a gourmet. He likes to eat very much, and what Russians like most of all isn't caviar or any other delicacy, but herrings. For Russians, eating is as sensual as any other pleasure -- they don't eat for hunger, but for pleasure. The terms "food" and "drink" are full of tender diminutives such as "little herring" or "father bread" -- Khlebushka.

(At this point the informant noticed that he was half an hour late for another appointment and regretfully left, asking to continue the conversation at another time.)

X. Interview with Four Russians: Images of Hate, Guilt, and Love[35]

Informants:

Mrs. A: 71 years old; nobility, former estate owner; intellectual; Russian Orthodox.

Mrs. B: about 55 years old; daughter of a priest; former ballerina; married four times.

Mrs. C: about 57 years old; daughter of a general; widow of a colonel; Russian Orthodox.

Mr. D: about 55 years old; actor; Russian Orthodox.

Mrs. A: I feel that he (informant's husband) hates me. He feels his guilt (vina) and he knows that I know it. For that he hates me. But when he does his work,

---

35. Interviewer 9F. Unpublished document RCC-R 157. The introductory portion of this interview was not recorded. This was an exploratory interview, made at a time when the Russian group was working on the problem of Russian attitudes toward guilt. The interviewer, herself a Russian (cf. "Russian Sensory Images," pages 162-69), is working, through conversation with a group of friends, toward definitions of terms (vina, zloba, zlost, etc.). The interview was made in Russian and later translated into English.

and when I don't reproach him, not only ⌐not⌐in words, but ⌐not⌐even in my
soul -- then he feels good towards me. But when he is lazy, I feel that he hates
me with all his soul.

Mrs. B: Yes, when one is not true to one's husband, one begins to hate him.
One feels guilty (vina).

Mrs. C: My sister hated her husband so much that we really believed she had
killed him. It was the first day of the revolution. They found him killed, and
decided that it was suicide. I never believed it. Of course, there was no police,
nothing, it was revolution, so everything passed unnoticeable. But I think she
killed him.

Interviewer: Why did she hate him?

Mrs. C: He was so nudny (a bore), a typical government official. So boring
(skuchny) and accuratny (neat, punctual). Mother was on his side. We all loved
him. Mother used to say to my sister that she has nothing to reproach him with,
that she should try to love him.

Mrs. B: I think she hated him because she was wrong (neprava). It was not his
guilt (vina) that he was so boring. She knew she was wrong. That's why she
hated him.

Mrs. C: I don't know. Maybe. I think she killed him and then pretended that she
found him dead, that he committed suicide.

Mrs. A: The same basis as in Anna Karenina. He (Vronsky) was irritable because she annoyed him with reproaches and jealousy. He ran away from her to
his friends and horse races. His conscience bothered him because he left her
alone, and in these moments he hated her. He felt his guilt (vina). Essentially,
he loved her deeply and she loved him, but she also tortured him.

Interviewer: What about hate in general, to other people?

Mrs. A: Mr. E---- hates everybody. How he obrushilsa (fell down) on Roosevelt. Everything is his fault, he was a Bolshevik, a dishonest man; he made a
fortune during the war. I asked him who told him that. But you know he cannot
reason logically. He is always boiling with rage (zlost). I know he loves me,
I am the only person in the whole world who is close to him. I know him since
he was nineteen. He was a poor student and had no friends in Petersburg. He
used to spend all his time in our house. I think he hates everybody because of
his unfortunate marriage. There was a girl in Chernigov. She was a frivolous
girl and became pregnant. They forced him to marry her to cover up somebody else's sin. His mother came to him and told him to get ready to go to the
wedding. He was so shy, he used to blush all the time. I don't know if he knew
whether this child was his or not. Maybe the child was born too early. She left
him a half a year later. He dragged the boy everywhere he went with the White
Army (Civil War, 1918-20). Then he left him in Siberia with some old man. He
never spoke about him, never sent him a package (of food).

Interviewer: Why do you think he hates you?

Mrs. A: I can feel it. He does a lot of petty nasty things to irritate me. If I ask him what he is reading, he answers, "A book," or pretends not to hear what I said. He is very rude to me. If he does not like the food, he pushes the plate away and raises his voice. Last summer he drove me to hysterics. I thought I am going to have another heart attack. I left the table and ran to my room, then to the garden. He ran after me. I shouted, "Leave me alone! I can't talk to you." He got down on his knees and kissed my hands. He kept repeating, "Auntie, Auntie, we are the closest people, we have lived such a long life together." It is my fault (vina) that I let him raspustitsa (loosen himself). My first husband knew how to handle him. Once he drove me nearly to hysterics. My husband took him by the collar and pushed him in the back with his knee. He shouted, "Get out of here!" Mr. E---- was like silk after that, for a long time.

Mrs. B: Killing is too good for him, for the sorrow he causes you. A man that is absolutely not needed by anybody. Nobody loves him, and he does not love anybody.

Mrs. A: He has no opinions of his own. When he lived with us, he was under the influence of my husband, and had decent liberal convictions. After he came back from D---- (another American city), I was surprised: he hates Roosevelt, he hates Jews, he is pro-Hitler. He is like a sausage: what you stuff him with -- this he carries around.

Interviewer: He sometimes tries to hurt my feelings by shpilki (literally "hairpins" -- sly hints), but I pretend not to understand them.

Mrs. B: That is the worst thing for him. He is afraid of you. He knows that you can put him in his place. That's why he is so careful to talk with respect to you, he does it even behind your back. He tried these hairpins (hints) to make you angry, and when you don't pay any attention, he feels unichtojen (destroyed, brought to nothing). You are too high for him. I also asked him once what is he reading, and he answered, "A book." I said, "Dope (durak), I know it's a book. What book?" He quieted down.

Mrs. A: He always worries that somebody will hurt his feelings. He is always ready to oshcheritsa (bristle like a cat). We once played "opinions." (This is a parlor game where one person chooses any noun for himself and leaves the room. The rest say their opinions about that noun. One person reads him all the opinions, and the person has three guesses. If he guesses right, that person goes out.) He (E----) named himself a "shoe." I said a shoe that chose a wrong mate. He got mad (obozlilsa), his bald spot got filled with blood, zlost (rage) sputtered from him. He shouted, "I don't allow anybody to discuss my personal life!" His zloba (rage) choked him.

Mrs. B: And remember, Dr. F---- called himself a "book" and his fiancée said, "A much-used, worn-out book from the public library." He did not feel hurt.

Mrs. C: My sister was also petty. She used to do nasty little things to annoy her husband. Mother advised him to give her a good beating, then she would have a real cause to be dissatisfied. But he would not do it. He was very goodhearted and loved her. And she treated him with such rudeness. If he would have slapped her face, she would have quieted down.

Interviewer: Do you think she could fall in love with him under favorable circumstances?

Mrs. C: If he would treat her right. One has to have a clean, deep soul to love a submissive person. Ennui! We can fall in love with strong men, criminals, men that are not true to us, men that we are afraid to lose. Look at the prostitutes, they all have kot (a pimp). He beats her, takes her money away, and she loves him with all her heart.

Interviewer: Do you think it is easier to fall in love with a strong person than a weak?

Mrs. B and Mrs. C: Yes.

Mrs. A: I'd rather love a weak person, where I feel that I am needed. But I think it is individual.

Mrs. C: No, I could not fall in love with a weak person. A meek one, yes. These meek people have terrific inner strength and sometimes they show it. A weak person is a nonentity (nichtojestvo).

Mrs. A: Love is so often mixed with hate. I just got a letter from G---- (her niece, recently divorced). She writes, "I read a review of H----'s book (her former husband). The review is very good, he probably wrote it himself...." And further, "He lives not far from here, probably with a new wife, may he be damned." Then she writes, "I went to the movies and saw an actor who reminded me of H----. What a terrible fate befell him in the picture. I got so upset that I cried all night." You see? She still loves him and hates him at the same time.

Mrs. B: She is a person that must respect a man she loves, and she could never respect him.

Interviewer: Can you recall an example of hate in literature?

Mr. D: May I put in a word? Or did the ladies decide already all the problems of the universe? You won't find much about hate in literature. Why? Because people who hated most were illiterate. All Russian ideas were expressed by a little group of intellectuals, and they would have felt sovestno (conscience) to confess that they hate. They even attributed their own noble feeling to the peasant, to the saintly, work-loving, much-martyred peasant, may he croak.

Mrs. B: How full of hate the peasants are! My father was a very popular priest, he used to cure klikushi (epileptics or hysterical peasant women; often considered saints or prophets or, most often, possessed by the devil). They used to bring klikushi to him from many places far away.

Mrs. A: I think hate is based on two things -- sex and envy. Mr. E---- has no sex life and he envies the Jews. What is there to envy? Look how well they got organized here, they help each other, they have institutions for their old people. And what can we organize? A drunken orgy or debauch?

Mrs. B: Yes, envy is the source of hate. I think it is the most common source of hate. But sometimes you feel hate from first sight, and the more you see the person, the more you hate him.

Mrs. A: That is not hate, that is nepryazu (dislike). Though I believe that you can dislike a person without a reason. You feel something vrajdebny (hostility).

Mr. D: I read recently Tolstoy's correspondence. He is so full of hate and zloba (rage) it is simply unbelievable.

Mrs. A: I never liked Tolstoy, I always thought that he was insincere with all his "plowing the land" and "poor little peasants." I am glad you agree with me.

[The discussion of Tolstoy continued, but was not recorded.]

PART FIVE

WRITTEN AND ORAL LITERATURE

WRITTEN AND ORAL LITERATURE

Introduction

Rhoda Métraux

The selections brought together here are intended to illustrate a variety of methods of work on different sorts of literary materials from three cultures. "Relations between Men and Women in Chinese Stories" by Virginia Heyer is a thematic analysis based on a group of published translations of popular tales some of which were read to Chinese informants who, in turn, gave the investigator versions of the tales they had heard or had seen performed in China. Nelly Hoyt's "The Image of the Leader in Soviet 'Post-October' Folklore" is an analysis of a single theme based on a comparison of published traditional and modern folk poetry. Her second contribution, "The 'Not-So: So' Images in Russian Folklore" is a discussion of a detail of structure in the same material. Both of these were written as working papers for group discussion. Leopold Haimson's "Russian 'Visual' Thinking" is an application of some of the same material. Nathan Leites's "Trends in Affectlessness" is a finished piece of work on a contemporary French novel in which are combined an analysis of the book itself and of statements about the book by a number of critics and reviewers. That this is the only example of such analysis which has been included is due mainly to the fact that working papers are likely to be extremely long and intricately organized and in many cases are so keyed into work by other members of a group that it is difficult to present selections from them out of the context of the group's work. The three selections, including a short excerpt from a group discussion, grouped together as "A Russian Double Image Cluster: 'Not-So: So'" are intended to suggest the process of association and synthesis that takes place as materials are used and re-evaluated over a period of time.

Six other contributions to this Manual are based in part on work with literary sources and should be considered together with those given here. In "An Analysis of the Soviet Film The Young Guard" Vera Schwarz (Alexandrova) compares the film version with earlier versions of the novel (Part Six, pages 295-302). "Male Dominance in Thai Culture" (Part Nine, pages 382-86) and "History as It Appears to the Rumanians" (Part Ten, pages 405-15), both by Ruth Benedict, are based on combined work with several types of literature and with informants. John Weakland's "Chinese Family Images in International Affairs" (Part Ten, pages 421-26) is a study using a variety of written sources in Chinese and in English translation (newspapers, autobiography, political writing, children's textbooks, etc.) together with extensive work with translator-informants. Leopold Haimson's

"The Soviet Style of Chess" (Part Ten, pages 421-31) is an example of work with technical literature and long, intensive work with a specialist on the subject. And finally, in "The Soviet Image of Corruption" (Part Ten, pages 431-48) Martha Wolfenstein combines a study of theme and imagery in a type of newspaper story with an analysis of comments on certain of the stories by Soviet DP informants.

These twelve selections, of which all but one are excerpts from larger pieces of research, can do no more than suggest how the work of analysis is done and ways in which techniques of analysis can be adapted to studies of cultures. For suggestions of how to go about the work, the reader may turn to other parts of the Manual, especially to Martha Wolfenstein's discussion of thematic analysis of fictional movies (Part Six, pages 267-80), to my own discussion of the use of multiple imagery (Part Eight, pages 343-62), and to Gregory Bateson's discussion of end-linkage analysis (Part Nine, pages 367-78), and to Margaret Mead's comments on the presentation of results (Part Ten, pages 397-400).

Here I shall add only one point, namely, that for a study of a culture the best results are likely to be obtained by the use of comparative methods and methods that combine work in more than one medium and in more than one modality. All the selections of work with literary materials in this Manual are illustrations of this. It is of importance for several reasons, only one of which is the necessity for intensive work with informants when one does not have a full grasp of the written language. The comparative method is, of course, an accepted, convenient device for highlighting the details of one's material and the only real problem is how to decide what kinds of comparisons are likely to be economical and constructive. However, comparative studies and work with combinations of materials have the special advantage for work on a culture of serving as interlocking devices for the research worker, helping him to get a sense of the larger and more complex units with which he is ultimately concerned. Thus one is concerned not with the way in which a specific writer develops plot or character or elaborates on a series of themes or uses particular images, nor only with the ways in which themes and images are expressed in paintings or in films, nor with the ideal version of the culture as it may be specifically presented in various sorts of materials, but rather with the interrelationships among all of these. Handled only as a separate unit, each piece of material must then be linked up to each other one; handled as integral parts of larger units, one creates multiple links so that the final organization is explicitly included in the ongoing process.

I. Relations between Men and Women in Chinese Stories[1]
Virginia Heyer

This paper is based on an analysis of the themes of sixty Chinese stories, in English translation, that are concerned with personal relations between men and women. The stories analyzed are of both folk and literary type; none are mythological. All contain strong elements of fantasy, such as the use of supernatural powers in the real world, the change from natural to supernatural, and the description of extraordinary occurrences. The stories analyzed were selected only for their subject matter and for their variety of plot. They represent a large part of the range of Chinese stories that are familiar to the author, by such criteria as level of literary accomplishment, social types of characters, religious and philosophical bases, and the use of supernaturalism and realism.

Abstracts of most of the stories were read to four Chinese men who were born and grew up in rural counties near Canton. They recognized almost all the stories; most had been told to them or they had seen them in operas performed in the villages, others they had read. The impression was gained that the lore was common, and that each theme appeared in many variations. The character types were always familiar, and sometimes the men would tell an entirely different story to illustrate a character type in one of the stories they were asked to identify. The conclusion was reached that the stories were part of the real projective system of the four men, and that an analysis of these stories was relevant to the character structure of Cantonese village men.

One of the most common male characters in Chinese popular literature is a type of young man which this paper will designate as the scholar. Frequently he is a scholar by occupation, but his characteristics typify many young men who are not scholars. He is a mild and docile man, never aggressive, often victimized by a more powerful man, by poverty, or by chance circumstances. Events happen to him, are not caused or manipulated by him, and he seldom takes any initiative in the unfolding of a plot. He lives with humility and piety and truthfulness, but beyond that he does not seek reward or adventure. He may be entertained, rewarded, harmed, sought by women, seduced; always he is a passive character.

His passivity and his misfortune frequently reach the extreme of failure, the scholar who has failed the official examinations being a common character. This failure is no reflection on his worth; it usually is assumed that a blind examiner has misjudged him. Failure is the result of aloofness from the circle of personal favors and bribery, which always secure official position, to the ideal ethical behavior of modesty and devotion to a study without worldly ambition: withdrawal to greater social passivity. Frequently the unsuccessful scholar has a fantasy experience in which recognition as a scholar, reward,

---

1.   Unpublished document RCC-CH 627. The article has been condensed for presentation here.

and position come to him through no effort of his own.

The scholar is described more intimately than is, for instance, the military man, who is another important character type in Chinese popular literature. The military man is old or middle-aged and has the power of position or money. He is often referred to as a tiger, which symbolizes ferocity and strength, and he may be cunning and exploitative. In contrast to him, the young scholar is a more human character, one who arouses the sympathy of the reader. The scholar's personal life is always the point of interest, particularly his relations with women or his marriage, whereas stories of military men concern their exploits in battles or intrigues. In a story of two generals, when their personal lives were brought into the plot, they suddenly began acting like the scholar type, as though the description of a man's personal life could be given only in terms of this passive characterization. (Cf. "Shee Yan Quai," in Lee, 1940.)

Upon first sight of a beautiful girl, the scholar falls helplessly in love, but at that point some obstacle frequently interferes: his parents may forbid him to marry the girl he loves, in which case he falls seriously ill, or he may not know how to make love, or he may decide he must resist the temptation of the girl, or some outside circumstances or misunderstanding may separate them before any intimacy. Stories of courtship difficulties are considered by Chinese informants to be true or possible, and informants often describe their own or friends' difficulties in courtship in the same terms. In this attitude there seems to be a ready identification with the young passive scholar in his troubles with women.

In contrast to the passivity of the scholar, many types of young women in the stories are extraordinarily assertive, independent, and capable of great accomplishments. The swordswoman is one of the most popular and notable of these women. She usually fights with a sword, thereby earning her title, and she will unhesitatingly kill her enemy with it. Through her intelligence, daring, and masterful strategies she often defeats a whole army and captures or kills its leader. She is a bold, fearless spirit, undaunted by circumstances that baffle and defeat men. She often has supernatural power, and with it accomplishes whatever she wants. Many stories tell of her avenging a man, whether friend or relative, or of saving his life.

Her unrestrained spirit and habits do not make her a fitting partner for marriage. Usually she does not marry in these stories, but continues on her independent and adventuresome way; when she does marry, she is required to change her personality. In an episode of a popular novel of the last century (Erh-nu ying-hsiung chuan, 1935, p.73),[2] an aggressive, powerful girl, whose distinctive weapon was the bow and arrow, was urged to marry a young man whose life she had previously saved and whom she had protected and cared for.

---

2. Analyzed by Dr. Hsien-chien Hu (unpublished document RCC-CH 567).

Before she could think of marrying, she had to be given family connections, and she had to exercise much control over her fierce untempered nature, allowing the modesty becoming to a young girl to govern her conduct.

The assertiveness and extraordinary abilities that are admired in the swordswoman, but kept in their proper sphere of supernatural wonder and transient military life, come threateningly close to the scholar in the common character of an <u>entrancing and dangerous woman</u>. This type of woman, who intrudes directly in the lives of lone and unsuspecting men, has an attractive and also a dangerous aspect, and is both real and supernatural. In one aspect she is beautiful and sexually exciting, available sexually, usually even taking the initiative in that direction. In her other aspect, she has supernatural power that enables her to appear and disappear at will, to change into a fox, snake, or ghost or other strange creature. She has the power to kill or cure, and to bring good or bad luck. Though the dangerous woman has supernatural abilities, she is not removed from the human sphere. She travels in disguise in the real world, indistinguishable from ordinary women; a man who becomes involved with her usually suspects nothing. A man may discover that his wife, to whom he has been married many years and who has borne him a son, has a supernatural aspect, and she may suddenly become dangerous to him. This danger is not a readily distinguishable and avoidable threat; rather it is a possible hidden characteristic of any woman. In her commonest role in stories, the dangerous woman appears to a young man, excites him, and becomes his regular sexual partner.

The result of sexual relations with a woman of this type is exhaustion or illness and often death; a man becomes weaker and weaker and finally wastes away. If death is averted, it is usually by the will and ministrations of the dangerous woman herself. In a story in which two ghost girls appear to a man in his secluded study and try to arouse him, he resists them for a long time and then says: 'Should you not love me, I would not dishonor two such lovely ones; and should you love men, why kill a free soul like me?" The cultural attitude that a man chooses whether or not he will dishonor the girl is contradicted, but not discarded, when he pleads with them not to kill him, as sexual contact inevitably would. In the same story the ghost girls help him when he is in trouble. To reward them he wants to share the couch of one. He says, 'Now I am ready to die for you." (Cf. "The Rebirth of Shiao-shieh," in Quong, 1946, p. 161.) The sexual threat is expressed by a fox woman: 'The reason why our kind incurs the revulsion of mankind is that we draw upon men's essence and thus harm them." (Cf. "Jenshih, or the Fox Lady," in Wang, 1944, p. 24.)

A deeper analysis of this anxiety on the part of the man can be sought in the imagery and symbolism through which the dangerous woman acts. In her hideous supernatural form some common features are a long tongue, long fingernails, a tall hat, a long tail instead of feet, and sharp jagged teeth. One form of dangerous woman, peculiar to South China, is the banana spirit. Some of these features suggest phallic imagery, and in an informant's drawing of the long tongue of one ghost woman this was particularly obvious. The sharp jagged teeth are very commonly described, and biting and sucking are often her means of destruction. One ghost sucks blood from the neck of her victim. (Cf. "The Corpse and the Blood Drinker," in Lee, 1940, p. 34.) A snake woman may bore a hole in her victim's head and suck out his brains. A proverb says, "Woman's mind is as much poison as snake's mouth." In a modern novel (Shaw, 1945, p. 179) the symbol of intercourse with an insatiable woman is her sucking the man's energy out of him. A precise meaning of this imagery is impossible to ascertain from the stories, but its constant use makes clear an association of sucking and biting with the woman's role in intercourse.

A specifically phallic meaning of the sword is found in the story "Yin-Niang the Swordswoman" (Wang, 1944, p. 98).[3] Yin-Niang, the ten-year-old daughter of a general,

was stolen from her home by a nun and did not return until five years later. When she returned she described how she had been taken to a cave where there were two other ten-year-old girls. The life they led was designed to strengthen them physically and they were taught special skills. The nun gave her a sword two feet long, and after a year of practice with it, she could kill monkeys, tigers, and leopards. After three years she could throw her sword to strike down eagles and hawks. By this time her sword had gradually shrunk to about five inches. The nun took her to a city and pointed out a man who had committed many unspecified crimes and told her to kill him with her sword. This she did. On another occasion the nun pointed out to her a man to kill, but since he was playing with a child, she waited until the child had gone away before killing him. The nun told her henceforth to take the child away herself and then kill the man.
The nun said to her: "I shall cut open the back of your head and conceal your dagger in there. You will suffer no harm and you can take out the dagger whenever you need it." The nun then brought her back to her father's house. Her father was very much afraid of her thereafter and complied with all her wishes, and allowed her to marry and bring home a man of her choice. She went into the employ of influential people, killing their enemies for them. When one of her patrons was threatened, she hid in his viscera and jumped out of his mouth after her presence had protected him from having his head cut off.

The training of the girls in the use of the sword came at the age of puberty, from ten to fifteen. Monkeys and tigers, which they were taught to kill, are usually symbols of strong men. The five-inch sword is very suggestive of the phallus, and the concealing of it in her body might indicate a fantasy of a woman who acted aggressively in genital contact. The symbolism of the story may be interpreted as the woman having a phallus with which she can kill men, and having the power to get inside a man to save him. In both acts she has the abilities of the man in sexual intercourse. She can use her ability aggressively or protectively.

---

3.   Abstracts of stories used illustratively in this paper give the full sequence of the main plot episodes. Some minor episodes and conventional beginnings and endings, which are unnecessary to the comprehension of the main plot, are omitted. Whenever possible the key words have been taken from the story and many phrases and passages are directly quoted without quotation marks.

Another story, "The Infection" (Eberhard, 1937, p. 133), shows a related idea:

It is a custom in Kwangtung that all grown-up girls should lie with a man before their marriage. In this way the man that was with her first receives the poison in her body and in a short time he is covered with red spots and great poisonous ulcers, which soon spread all over and kill him. This custom in Kwangtung is called "passing on the infection."

The daughter of a rich man had arrived at a marriageable age, but had not yet passed on the infection and was thus not wanted as a wife. The rich man called in Ma, a young man from Shaohsing who was reduced to being a beggar because of business difficulties, and offered him 100 dollars cash for having intercourse with his daughter. "Ma was delighted, because Shaohsing people consider the first night with a girl the most enjoyable, only he wondered why a beggar should be offered such a pleasure and be paid for it as well."

Ma fell in love with the girl, but she, not wishing to belong to him or to harm him, explained to him what would happen. She said also that she herself would fall ill if someone did not have intercourse with her. He wanted to sacrifice himself to save her, but she would not let him. She asked him to swear brotherhood with her and return home without sleeping with her. She said that she would become sick, her father would turn her out of the house, and she would beg her way to Ma's home and he must swear to receive her.

When, in a few years, her skin broke out in spots, her father was furious because she had deceived him, and he turned her out. She begged her way to the home of Ma, who in the meantime had become rich and had married. He was very kind to her and gave her shelter. She was almost dead of her disease when she became very thirsty and drank some wine into which a fiery red snake had fallen. The next morning she was cured, and soon Ma took her as his wife.

Another version of the ending was given by an informant:

Li-yu (the infected girl) sat down before the candle and fell into deep thought. Suddenly a big black snake swung down from the beam, hanging its head into a wine jar to get a drink, When it became full it fell into the jar and died. It scared Li-yu very much at first, but she figured that she would rather die than suffer from leprosy....She got some of the wine to drink, and then began to feel very itchy all over her body, so she rubbed her skin with the wine, and the more she did so, the more comfort she felt. Soon she was cured and became as beautiful as ever.

The "custom" is clear: The man is afraid of having sexual intercourse with his virgin bride, imagining that it will kill him. Furthermore, the woman can save herself from the disease only by killing a man in this manner. The episode of the snake drinking the wine seems to be a symbol of the sexual act necessary for the girl's cure, for the snake certainly seems to have a phallic meaning here. Of interest is the symbol of the snake taking a drink from the bowl. It is related to oral imagery of intercourse, such as a man tasting a woman's honey or eating from a dish (cf. Shaw, 1945, pp. 65-67). The male orgasm does not appear in the metaphor: the bowl contains the fluid, the snake sucks it and is poisoned, just as the man would have been poisoned by contact with the infected girl. Whereas, in the story of "Yin-Niang the Swordswoman" the woman had a phallic instrument, here she excretes the fluid in orgasm for the man to suck in. By both male functions she can kill.

It is interesting to see that here sucking is the sexual activity of the man, whereas previously mentioned stories have shown the woman sucking out his energy in sexual contact. Sucking is apparently an activity with a wide range of meaning, even carrying opposite associations. But in all cases noticed here it is an activity that constitutes an attack on the man.

The story "Ah-pao and Her Foolish Lover" (Quong, 1946, p. 17) expresses another idea along the same line:

A young and excellent scholar was considered a simpleton because he had six fingers. He sent a matchmaker to a beautiful girl, Ah-pao, and she said in ridicule, "If he cuts off his sixth finger, I'll marry him." He cut off the finger with great pain, but Ah-pao then said, "Tell him to cut off his foolishness." The scholar was hurt and decided to give up his suit. Later he saw her again and was so stricken by her beauty that his spirit followed her home and into her bed. A second time his spirit went to Ah-pao's room in the form of a parrot, and Ah-pao, impressed by his devotion, consented to marry him.

The scholar's act of cutting off his sixth finger and becoming a defenseless bird in order to win the woman is an acquiescence, even to the point of self-mutilation, to the woman's demands or conditions of marriage. The fact that the man is called a simpleton does not mean that this is a story of a despised or an abnormal man, though it may be a mask for the bluntness of the revelation. The storyteller points out that he is a scholar of distinction, though he has failed the examinations, and it has been remarked that his is not a ridiculed position. The highest rewards come to him in the course of the story, affirming his respected character: his wife's faithfulness brings him reincarnation, and he passes the examination (omitted from the abstract).

Cutting off the sixth finger suggests a symbol of castration, in which sense the activity of the woman and the inactivity of the man seen in previous stories here become the woman's demand that the man castrate himself and his acquiescence to her demand. The man's surrender of sexual power to the woman becomes complete. The image of a cut finger recurs in other stories, all of which allow its interpretation as a castration symbol. The dangerous female spirit of the banana tree is said to come from the blood of a man's cut finger,[4] or, interpreted, the power of the female spirit to kill comes from the man's castration.

In another story a man's mother eats a young carrot, an act the Buddhist religion forbids; her son, to disguise this transgression, cuts off his finger and buries it in the ground as a substitute for the carrot (cf. "Why the Carrot Is Red Inside," in Eberhard, 1937). In these three stories a man cuts off his finger, first, to subject himself to the will of the woman he wants to marry, second, to create the spirit of a woman who comes to seduce and kill him, and third, to show his devotion to his mother, becoming thereby a more perfect son to her.

The behavior of the young man when confronted by the dangerous woman is complete subjugation to her, the delegation of sexual initiative to her, even to the point of self-castration, with the imputation to her of an aggressive sexual power, even an aggressive sexual instrument. This behavior suggests that an in-

---

4.   An informant described this belief and told a story about a female banana spirit who slowly killed a scholar by her nightly visits.

vestigation of the role of the mother with her son might provide important clues. It is found that where mother and son are both important characters in a story, the mother almost invariably dominates her son. This is especially conspicuous in the role of the son-husband in the mother-in-law daughter-in-law conflict. Stories of a woman's cruelty to her daughter-in-law with the tacit or stated acquiescence of her son are very common. A story of a son who overtly tries to escape his mother's domination, but who twice loses the girl he loves and finds her only through his mother's help, was well known by informants and thought to be a true story. (Cf. "Engaged to a Nun," in Giles, 1908, p. 161.) "The King of the Bees" (Eberhard, 1937, p. 65) is an equally famous story:

A man worked at a palace a great distance from his home, but with a pair of magic shoes returned every night to sleep with his wife, his mother knowing nothing of this practice. The wife became pregnant and, to prove to her mother-in-law that she had not been receiving a lover, but her own husband, she stole one of her husband's magic shoes one night. With only one shoe her husband arrived late at the palace where he worked and so displeased the Emperor that he was beheaded. He took up his head and started home, and on the way asked a woman cutting grass, "Can grass go on living when it has been cut down?" She answered yes. He asked the same question of a woman cutting garlic, and she answered yes. When he reached his home, he asked his mother, "When a man's head is cut off, can he go on living?" His mother was horrified and answered, "No," and immediately her son fell dead.

His soul appeared to his wife and told her to keep his head in a caldron until worms appeared, to feed the worms every day and he would come to life. His wife dutifully did so until one day she had to return to her parents' house, so she asked her mother-in-law to feed the worms. The mother-in-law thought it a useless task, poured boiling water on the worms, and killed them. Then she threw them in the garden.

A bamboo shoot sprang up in that spot in the garden. The husband's spirit appeared to his wife again and told her to tend the bamboo shoot exactly one hundred days and then sell it for exactly one hundred dollars cash. On the ninety-ninth day the mother-in-law sold it for ninety-nine dollars, and it split when it was cut down. Thus again his reincarnation was prevented.

The practice of a man living and working far away from home, and leaving his wife to serve his mother as daughter-in-law as though her day-to-day function were as a daughter-in-law rather than a wife, is a fairly common one in China, and is frequently reflected in stories. It is a practice in Chinese life that contributes to and reflects personal estrangement of husband and wife and makes the man an obedient son, a son who brings his mother a daughter-in-law, but in his devotion does not replace mother with wife. The attempt in this story to counteract the practice was of no avail against the mother's domination. The mother caused her son's death, and three times prevented his reincarnation. Rebellion required magic power: the chances of overcoming the mother's will required reincarnation. Opposition to her control could not be visualized in simple human affairs or in the ordinary course of life. In this case, the son's rebellion against his mother's control is futile. Submission to the mother, acceptance of the mother's decision, acquiescence in the mother's tyranny over her daughter-in-law, are the pattern of most stories, but submission is granted with love and devotion. The most devoted son is he who will accept his mother's decision without question, and who will sacrifice himself for his mother. Many stories extolling a son's devotion to his mother tell of extreme suffering in the ten courts of the Buddhist underworld.

In a survey of historical stories of filial piety, Dr. Yu-ch'uan Wang found that piety of a son to his mother is the subject of over three times as many stories as is piety of a son to his father.[5] From a count of written works about fathers and mothers that express personal emotions, Dr. Wang concludes that

In literature, the Chinese sons have shown very little emotion toward their fathers, but very much emotion toward their mothers.[6]

The love between mother and son is reproduced in marriage in the story "The Predestined Couple" (Acton and Lee, 1941):

When To-shou was nine years old, he was betrothed to To-fu. To-shou later contracted leprosy and To-fu's mother demanded that her daughter's engagement to him be broken. Her husband dared not argue with her, nor did he want to propose the matter to his friend, the father of To-shou. But the father of To-shou heard of this feeling and proposed that the betrothal be broken. To-fu, however, refused to have it broken. To-shou himself offered to break the engagement and To-fu was so offended that she tried to commit suicide. She was saved and was allowed to marry To-shou.

She took care of him and "Except that she did not suckle him, her tenderness was that of a wet-nurse." But they could not consummate their marriage because of the disease. To-shou thought, I am on the verge of death, why should I spoil her virginity? and his wife thought, How could my husband endure the strain, exhausted from this terrible disease? Their abstinence did not seem necessary to To-shou's mother, and she tried to force the couple together, but was thwarted by To-fu's virtuous determination.

After three years To-shou visited a prophet who predicted his death after ten more years of affliction, so he decided to commit suicide, thinking: I have no fear of death; my sole regret is that my virtuous wife should have waited on me for three years without a single night's enjoyment. To-fu found him drinking arsenic and she seized the cup from him and drank the remainder. Both of them almost died, but were discovered in time to be given a medicine which made them vomit and bleed through their pores. To-shou discovered that losing the infected blood had cured him of leprosy and made him handsome again. They lived happily afterward and had two children.

The picture is one of self-imposed restraint from intercourse and preference for a relationship like that of mother and infant between the husband and the wife. It suggests the man's desire to regress to infancy when he is married,

---

5. Unpublished document RCC-CH 179.
6. This is further documented in a series of Thematic Apperception Tests which were collected from ten Cantonese village men between the ages of 25 and 45, who also showed intense emotion toward the mother and very little emotional response to the father.

  In Dr. Abel's analysis of Chinese Rorschach tests (unpublished document RCC-CH 610), she says of the responses to Card VII if 15 China-born males between 20 and 40 years: "These responses, although not conclusive, do suggest the possibility that the China-born male may be some way overwhelmed by a mother or female figure." About the responses to Card IV, the so-called father card, she says: "It would seem that the China-born males are more indirect than are the American-born males in projecting some expression of fear or retaliation....Perhaps the American-born males bring their problems of facing authoritarian figures closer to the surface of awareness than do the China-born males."

and the woman's preference of a mother's role to a wife's role. Though the marriage in this story was unproductive before the attempted suicide and cure and thus could not be considered successful, the love is described as ideal, and we are given some indication that a relationship between husband and wife which reproduced the mother-son relationship would be valued.

The theme of the young scholar's attachment to his mother and the threat of a sexually dangerous woman are often interwoven in stories. Usually, in stories where a man has experiences with two different women, one woman is protective and the other woman is dangerous. The protective woman is usually the first wife, or the first of two women who come to a lone man to gratify him. As well as being protective, she is associated in other ways with a mother figure. Placed in opposition to her, through their common interest in the man, is a young and beautiful girl who proves to be dangerous to him:

A young married man saw a pretty girl walk by carrying a large basket of fruit. He took her to live with him without his wife's knowledge. After a month he became very sick. One day he saw her as a horrible ghost who wore a painted skin; and as he watched she again transformed herself, "and then what was but a moment ago a hideous creature became the naked body of a young girl." He went to a wise old man who lived in the temple for help and the old man gave him some painted words to paste on the wall and a magic wand made of horses' tails to hang in his bedroom, and told him to sleep that night with his wife. He did so, though he only lay in bed terrified, and finally the female monster broke down the door, rushed in, ripped open his chest, and tore out his heart, liver, and intestines. The wife sought aid of the old man in the temple, who found the demon-spirit and reduced her to ashes by magic. The old man then told the wife about a crazy man who might restore her husband to life. She went to the crazy man and he did not listen to her, but he stroked her breasts and fondled her whole body. (In Giles's version he also beat her.)

The woman endured this treatment in the hope that her husband's life might be restored. Finally he said he would restore her husband's life if she would do three things: stay with him for one night as his wife, let him hold her in his arms and walk all around the village, and swallow a ball of blood and phlegm that he would cough up. The third task repelled her most, but she did it, and it was the only one she had to do. She went home and sat weeping over her husband's body and suddenly coughed up a human heart that fell into her husband's wound and restored him to life.[7]

The married man who secretly took a beautiful young girl for his pleasure was killed by her and restored to life by his wife. The beautiful girl who turned into a demon is familiar, but the character of the wife bears closer examination. The wife appears as a mother figure when she was possessed by the old crazy man, both because the crazy man demanded sexual rights with her,

---

7. "The Ghost Wife." This story is told in many versions. I have taken this abstract from the first and fullest of three versions in Lee (1940). In Giles (1908), it is entitled "The Painted Skin." Another version of this story given by an informant tells of the wife killing a cock and putting the cock's blood and heart into her dead husband's body to restore his life. The cock is used as a symbol of the man in absentee marriages as described by an informant, and is used in the initiation ceremonies to men's secret societies as mentioned in Giles (1908, p. 358, fn. 5). It is apparently the acquisition of a male symbol that effects the restoration of life.

and because by giving the younger man life he is figuratively his father. The
process of rebirth symbolizes conception and birth: the woman took the phlegm
of the crazy man into her mouth and later coughed up a live organ. It is interesting, too, that the old man in the temple advised the young man to sleep with
the nurturing wife to protect himself from the attractive but dangerous demon-
woman. In a story to be discussed later, as well as in other stories, the old
man in the temple or the old priest seems to represent the real mother as an
old woman, supervising the affairs of the younger generation.

The story "The Flower Maiden Shaing-yu" (Quong, 1946, p. 47) also tells
of two women and a scholar:

> The young scholar Huang lived in a monastery. One day he saw a beautiful
> girl, Shiang-yu, the spirit of a white peony, and in the evening she came to visit
> him. She said that she had been confined to the monastery by an Old Taoist priest.
> Huang cried, "Tell me his name and I will free you from this infamy," but the
> white peony spirit answered: "No need for that, he does me no harm. Besides,
> he allows me the opportunity of becoming intimate with such romantic scholars
> as yourself." Shiang-yu spent the night with Huang and came frequently after-
> ward.
> One day an old man dug up the flower that was Shiang-yu's spirit and took
> it home. The scholar heard that the flower died with the old man, and he
> mourned for her bitterly.... At the grave of Shiang-yu, also mourning, he found
> Shiang-yu's flower spirit sister, Chiang-shueh, a red camellia. Huang invited
> her to his study, but she said, "I will be your friend -- nothing more; intimate
> companionship by day and night, that I could not bear." But upon Huang's en-
> treaty she stayed the night and then disappeared for several days. When she re-
> appeared and Huang desired her, she said, "Must the joy of seeing each other
> always consist in this?" She would come sporadically and sometimes would not
> spend the night. Huang wanted to protect her from the old man who took Shiang-
> yu, but she refused to tell him where her flower spirit was planted, so he could
> do so. She continued to be capricious in her visits, which caused Huang much
> distress.
> Shiang-yu was restored because of Huang's love, but would remain only a
> spirit for one year while Huang had to tend her plant to ensure her final rebirth.
> Huang proposed taking her plant to his family home, but she refused, saying:
> "Everything has its appointed place in which to grow. I was not intended for your
> home, and should you insist, it may shorten my life. If you really love me there
> will come a time when we shall be together." Chiang-shueh had disappeared when
> Shiang-yu's spirit returned, saying: "You have come at the right time, my sis-
> ter. Your good man was bothering me to death." Huang wanted her, as Shiang-
> yu was only a spirit, and when he held her he felt nothing. Shiang-yu said, "If
> you truly want her to come, I can compel her," and she did so, Chiang-shueh ap-
> pearing petulantly. Eventually Shiang-yu was reborn and Chiang-shueh was very
> happy to be relieved of her duty of "acting as wife for another."

The contrasted characters of the first and the second woman -- of a kind
and attentive woman who never withdraws her love and a woman who is wanted
sexually, but comes and goes capriciously and is not available when wanted most,
who considers herself a substitute and without a permanent position -- are a
more realistic version of the two contrasted women in the last story. Chiang-
shueh is not dangerous, and does not kill the man as the demon-woman did, but
she does not satisfy him. Both Chiang-shueh and the demon-woman are most
important as erotic objects, not because of the man's devotion to them, and they
are both temporary partners. Shiang-yu, like the wife in the last story, is a
loving and devoted woman. She has been confined to the monastery by an old

man, and was taken away from Huang by an old man. The old man might conceivably be the projection of a father image; moreover, the control he has over Shiang-yu is analogous to that exercised by the head of a family over its female members.

In the Chinese family there are women other than the wife over whom the husband has control -- for instance his concubines, with whom the son might have, or wish to have, sexual experience -- but that Shiang-yu is identified with the mother is more specifically borne out in other passages. She is restored to the scholar after he has experienced more than a year of unsatisfying sexual relations with the capricious Chiang-shueh. While Huang is tending her so that she might be restored, Shiang-yu says: "Everything has its appointed place in which to grow. I was not intended for your home, and should you insist, it may shorten my life. If you really love me there will come a time when we shall be together." This seems to be a reference to the frequent situation in the Chinese family of the son after marriage continuing to direct his love toward his mother. The underlying scheme of that situation as represented in this story might be interpreted as a renewal of their strong relationship after he has performed his obligation to a sexual union with his wife, and after he has had a son.

The short period when Shiang-yu was dead and Huang was dependent on Chiang-shueh may signify the time from marriage to conception of the first child, and the year of working and waiting for Shiang-yu to be restored may be the fantasy representation of the time required for the birth of the child and its safe beginning of life. This interpretation of the meaning of the elapsed time can only be hypothetical, as there is no specific evidence in the descriptions of those periods that would point to it. However, after the promise of Shiang-yu's restoration and hypothetically after the first conception, Chiang-shueh, who never enjoyed submitting to Huang's desires, made herself unavailable to Huang, which could be taken to signify that it was no longer necessary for her to submit, since she had already conceived. When Huang complained, Shiang-yu said she could compel Chiang-shueh to come to him, as a mother could compel her daughter-in-law, and indeed as her duty to her son would require. Considering the emotion Huang feels, Shiang-yu is also treated as his mother. The love and devotion that Huang feels for Shiang-yu are described in Confucian discourses as emotions that a man feels for his mother. To his wife he is supposed to show rightness and justice, but not love.

In "The Guardian Immortal's Sleeve" (Quong, 1946, p. 243) the scholar Shang was in love with a singing girl named Hui-ko who was in the service of the Prince. Shang asked the help of a Taoist priest noted for his feats of magic. The priest held out his sleeve for Shang to enter. "He seemed to be in a cave, like an extensive hall, into which streamed a bright light. Inside were tables, seats, couches -- everything. Shang remained there, quite comfortable." The priest went to the palace and unobtrusively swept Hui-ko into his sleeve. "Shang sat in solitary meditation, when all of a sudden there came falling from the roof a beautiful woman.... Both were amazed and enraptured, and in extreme bliss they embraced." Suddenly five men entered and seized Hui-ko.

Several weeks later Shang again sought entrance into the priest's sleeve; altogether he entered there thrice. Then one day Hui-ko said, "Something stirs within my body...." After some months the priest came with the baby to Shang and told him to call his wife. Shang's wife was very virtuous and had only one living son, who later died. She was very glad about the new baby. The priest felt in his sleeve and brought out a baby boy, gently sleeping, with the naval cord not yet cut. Shang's wife took it tenderly in her arms, and it uttered its first cry.

The priest discarded his robe because it had spots of blood on it and told Shang to keep it, as it would have the power to make a difficult childbirth easy. Shang later did the Prince the favor of giving one of his favorite women some ashes from the priest's robe to make her delivery easy. The Prince offered a reward and Shang asked for Hui-ko. Hui-ko was then forty and the Prince, thinking her too old, wanted to give Shang a young girl, but Shang insisted on being given Hui-ko.

The priest's sleeve is used in this story as a symbol of the womb and vagina where the ecstatic experience occurs and where the son is conceived. Saving the blood-spotted robe reminds one of the Chinese custom of keeping the afterbirth in a jar under the bed, and keeping the open trousers worn during a delivery to be worn again for the next delivery, to make it easier.

The woman with whom Shang had sexual relations is again the second woman. He entered the mysterious sleeve only three times, or until a son was conceived. Thereafter he was separated from the erotic woman. The woman who cared for his son was not the dangerous woman whom he enjoyed, but his first wife, who had no sexual role in the story. She had borne children but they all died; thematically she is childless. Her function is to care for the baby, to produce the son every Chinese couple must have, while the sexual aspect of conceiving and bearing a son is fulfilled by another woman, and is surrounded with all the danger and unreality that are associated with the erotic woman. The necessary danger of sexual relations is kept outside of the family.

The singing girl did not come to live with Shang until she was forty, and then Shang refused to be given a young and attractive woman instead of her. It is a common theme of popular stories that the mother and son are separated from the father until the mother is middle-aged and the son grown up, or that the mother is separated from the father and son for as long a time.[8] This is again an avoidance of continued intimacy between a husband and wife during the period of sexual activity, an avoidance that is so often made possible in real life by the practice of leaving a wife with her mother-in-law while the man goes off to the city to work.

In the stories analyzed, two different types of women are consistently placed in contraposition to each other, the protective loving woman, and the dangerous erotic woman. The protective woman is associated with the mother most frequently by her relationship to a powerful or disliked old man, a father

---

8. For examples of such stories, cf. "The Lost Brother" and "Ta-nan in Search of His Father," in Giles (1908); also "The Long Lost Mother," in Lee (1940).

figure, who has control over her. She cares for the young man and protects him; she satisfies his sexual desires, but not at the expense of his well-being. In contrast to her is the younger woman, who is not as easily available for sexual relations as the first woman, who is unreliable or temporary, and who saps his strength or kills him violently.

Having isolated the types of female characters, we may look at the patterned use of these types and thereby gain some insight into the relation of these types of projection to reality. The protective woman may be seen as both a mother and a good wife. In "The Flower Maiden Shiang-yu" and "The Fox Maiden Lien-shiang" (Quong, 1946, p. 27; not analyzed in this paper) the young man had his first sexual experience with the protective woman, which might be associated with the mother's masturbation of the baby boy, a common practice in China, or with the preferred marriage with a girl who is a few years older than the boy who is chosen by the boy's mother, often from the mother's family, and who is strictly controlled after the marriage by the man's mother. The various social factors which determine that a boy's first sexual experience is likely to be with a protective (maternal) woman also contribute to the composite nature of the fantasy character. The fusion of mother and wife is apparent also in "The Ghost Wife," where the woman who gave the young man life also had the role of his wife. While the protective woman seems to be primarily a projection of the mother, she may appear in the position of wife, and thus may be considered a possible wife figure, an ideal of the wife.

The contrasted woman comes to the young man second, and serves principally a sexual function. This single function makes her role more clear than that of the protective woman. She may be the beautiful singing girl, or the concubine, or the wife as sexual partner. She clearly characterizes sexual relations as either dangerous for the man, although necessary to conception, or at best pleasurable, but contingent on the desires of the woman. The wife role lies between these two contrasted ideas of woman, sometimes seen as identified with the mother, sometimes associated with the pleasures and dangers of sex. The only character who does not have the qualities of either type is the wife in "The Guardian Immortal's Sleeve," whose role is simplified more than is possible in reality to the single function of raising the son. In Chinese fantasies of woman, only women who can be closely identified with a mother figure are able to integrate all the functions of a wife -- sexual gratification, procreation, and family role.

The sharp distinction of the protective and the dangerous woman is a literary pattern, but in several stories the two types of woman have been combined in one character. In "Ah-pao and Her Foolish Lover," the good wife demanded her husband's castration. In another story a son's devotion to his mother led him to cut off his finger. In "The Infection," the threat of the wife was expelled on a substitute and she became safe. The mothers or wives in these stories are

all strong, domineering women to whom the young man submits with devotion.
They embody the characteristics that are usually found allotted to two different
women. In uniting the two different female character types, these stories suggest that they are a projection of one woman, the real mother who controls and
protects, who is loved and feared, who is needed, but from whom the man would
like to escape.

The literary pattern of distinguishing the two female characters may be
seen as a split of the complex attitude of the Chinese son to his mother.[9] The
stylized mother figure is given qualities warmly remembered from childhood:
unconditional love, protection, and gratification. Exhaustive sexual excitement.
and destructiveness are projected onto the stranger, the second comer, the temporary woman. This split is a solution to the situation of being confronted only
with women who combine both aspects, a situation that is conceived as being
very threatening. It makes one category of women safe. The Chinese choice of
making the mother category safe and turning all suspicion against the erotic
category has given rise to the cultural practice of turning away from the wife and
remaining close to the mother, a practice which ramifies throughout the cultural
pattern.

II. The Image of the Leader in Soviet "Post-October" Folklore[10]

Nelly Schargo Hoyt

Russian folklore -- the legends, epics, laments, and songs handed down
from parent or nurse to child, from generation to generation of skaziteli, tellers
of tales -- has never been a static creation, frozen into permanent shape once
it has been told or sung to an attentive audience. It has been an ever growing,
changing, living thing, which grew as Russia grew and traveled as the men of
Rus traveled. The bogatyri, the demigods, of Kievan times -- Ilya Murometz,
Dobrinia Nikitich, and Alesha Popovich -- migrate to Moscow with the onslaught
of the Mongols, and Ilya Murometz, the "peasant's son," becomes the "old
Cossack." Sadko the Traveler and Ivan the Merchant's Son join the ranks of the
heroes when Novgorod becomes great and the tzars, Ivan the Terrible and Peter
the Great, enter the realm of folklore, historical figures in a gallery of demigods. The skaziteli responded to the existing situation, adapting their epic songs

---

9.   This has been suggested by Jane Belo in an unpublished article (RCC-CH
     587).
10. Somewhat condensed from unpublished document SSC-61. The analysis is
     based on an examination of available materials in Russian (for the princi-
     pal sources, cf. Mead, 1951b, pp. 127-28); the illustrative passages have
     been translated by the writer. For another discussion of Russian and
     Soviet poetry, cf. Bowra (1952); and for other translated examples of the
     "Post-October" folklore, cf. Sokolov (1950); both these books have been pub-
     lished since this article was written.--Ed.

to the changing milieu. As in the past important events were translated into the language of folklore, so too the October Revolution of 1917 created a fruitful soil in which a new folklore could bloom and live and enrich the old.

In this "growing folklore" as the Soviet folklorists call it, the tellers of tales and the ballad singers present the new byt, the new mode of life as it is seen and felt by the people. The kolkhoz (the collective farm), the building of the railroads, the interest of the Soviet government in the North Pole -- all these become the subject of legends. The new concepts and slogans of the Party pass into the folklore and are translated into auditory and visual images, images that can be understood by the people, by those who sing and those who listen, and it is through the folklore that the new heroes seem to become one with the lower masses.

Of the available Soviet folklore materials, the legends that have grown up around the leaders, Lenin and Stalin, are among the most interesting and rewarding. Here the old forms encompass something completely new -- a new type of bogatyr, a new hero, whose attributes and achievements seem to be different from the old legendary figures. What are they? How do they look? What is their relation to the peoples of the various republics, and how do they appear to them? These are some of the questions to which answers will be attempted below.

One of the most striking characteristics of these new heroes, Lenin and Stalin, is that they are at the same time extremely human, or perhaps humane, and completely superhuman. In their relationship to the masses their great humanity is continually stressed. They are affable (privetliv), they are tender (laskovy), they are full of love for the people, full of compassion for the suffering. They are remembered not for glorious deeds of war but for glorious deeds of peace. The Uzbek remember that Timur the Lame, Genghis Khan, Alexander the Great (or, as he is called, Ishkandar) were all great warriors, but they were destroyers. In contrast, Lenin,

> From desert made a garden, from death -- life,
> And he was more powerful than all these warriors taken together,
> Because alone, in eight years, he built what they had destroyed in a
>   thousand years. ("Warriors and Lenin," II)[11]

In their fight for the common people and in their relationship to them lies their humanity.

Stalin fought bravely for the people without sparing himself, while Lenin "burnt out his life on the flame of love" ("Flaming Lenin," Uzbek song, II). In big things as in small they are close to the people. Both Lenin and Stalin stay close to the people. Those who talk of Lenin had sat next to him, had boiled water with him, "had eaten bad biscuits with him and washed them down with tea" (I). Any-

---

11. For purposes of brevity, the three sources cited in this article will be referred to as follows: Kriukova, 1938 (I); Lenin and Stalin in the Poetry of the Peoples of the USSR, 1938 (II); Gorky, 1938 (III).

body can come to them, anybody can be received by them. Stalin, for instance,

> ... meets everyone tenderly,
> Speaks with all gaily,
> He leads them to his bright chambers,
> He makes them sit down at sculptured tables,
> At sculptured oaken tables,
> On soft chairs. ("Bylina about Stalin," III)

They come as friends, they are treated as friends, and "our friend" continually appears in the songs, whether they are of the Uzbeks, the Great Russians, or the Siberian tribes.

This friendliness, this closeness to the people, this sitting down together and drinking tea -- which to the Russian in general is the introduction to intimacy -- is the folklore interpretation of the Party's preoccupation with the closeness to the masses.[12] Lenin and Stalin, as leaders, have achieved it completely. This is their humanity. But in all their other aspects they are nonhuman, or rather, superhuman. They become completely identified with nature, are one with nature, almost natural manifestations. They can achieve things that the ancient heroes could not, and they possess the ultimate truth.

Physically, of course, there is no superhumanity in the leaders. They appear as the general bogatyr picture. If they were to be painted from the picture drawn in the legends, they would be exactly alike -- both with powerful shoulders, black curls, white hands and a white brow, and clear eyes. (The whiteness of the body in general is always associated with the good bogatyr, the hero who does good things. In one of the Ilya Murometz legends, the evil hunter, Sokolnik, is described as having a "black breast," while Ilya Murometz' breast is white.)

This is what they are in their human body. But actually they are much more than that. They not only control the forces of nature, they are the forces of nature. It is when they appear as a force of nature that their physical aspects become more distinct. Lenin, for instance, acquires eyebrows like mountain ranges and eyes burning with a blinding flame ("The Golden Dawn Is Lit," III). They become transmuted into the manifestations, the appearances, of nature; they become assimilated to them. When in a newspaper there appears a note speaking of "Stalin-tractor," it may seem strange and forced to Western eyes. But in the folklore, the leader figure becomes not only the machine, but also the rock of granite, the floe of ice, the golden dawn, the flame, the sun, the moon. Stalin and Lenin personify nature, they command nature, they control nature. Where Stalin walks, a spring will come to the surface, grass will grow, flowers will bloom, cities will rise ("Bylina about Stalin," III).

In all that is told and sung about the two leaders, there is a dual aspect. As manifestations of nature seen as such, they are all-permeating and all-powerful. As the friends of the humble, they are tender and gentle. It is continually "the

---

12. Cf., for instance, Stalin's speech at the 1937 Plenum of the Central Committee, which gave the formal construction to this tie with the masses.

haven and the avenger" image that comes up. Immensely big and yet of the same size as you or me or anybody, terribly fierce and yet tender, threatening and yet understanding. The image is in some way a Janus-like figure, terrible and immense when it turns outward, facing the danger, and full of love and kindness when it turns inward, facing the masses.

It is this ability to be small which makes it possible in the folklore to have these supernatural figures, who stand completely outside, be at the same time very dependent upon the people. In the folklore, the Antaeus image acquires a very concrete expression. The flaming bogatyr who appears to the poor Cirot hunter did not come from heaven or the bowels of the earth, though he did appear in a cloud, like the genii from Aladdin's lamp -- "He is the son of his own people, and therefore immensely powerful" ("The Golden Dawn," III); he draws his power from the people and the people are always there to protect him. When Stalin was sent to Siberia, the working people protected him so that he did not perish. When Lenin was in Siberia, it was the "muzhik Ivan" who came to him and said to him: "I shall save you from destruction, I shall free you from rapid death." After the Revolution, when the White armies were counterattacking, again the people saved Lenin. They carried him away "in their arms" (v okhapku -- an armful), shielding him from the guards; they made a tent to hide him and no one gave away the secret (I).

Here too we have the double aspect of the leader. He is superhuman, he represents the strength of the people, and yet he needs the people to shield him from harm. He is the expression of nature, he embodies Nature in her greatness, and yet he needs her protection. The Evenk hunter Dolbene wanted to kill Lenin as he was walking in the taiga, unprotected. He aimed at Lenin's head and the head disapppeared, he aimed at Lenin's back and the back disappeared. He aimed at Lenin's legs and only the footprints walked along.

> Dolbene thinks: Why didn't Vladimir have any head?
> I shielded it, says the fir tree.
> Why didn't Vladimir have any back?
> I shielded it, says the bogulnik (kind of tree).
> Why did Vladimir himself disappear?
> We shielded him, call the animals.
> ("Now There Is Light in the Taiga," III)

And so, though the leader may hold the sun and the moon, he is still indebted to the humble muzhik Ivan or to the fir tree.

Just as the leaders are of the people and yet outside the people, just as they are part of nature or are natural manifestations and yet dependent on nature's assistance, so their achievements partake of the tremendous and of the very small. To overthrow the world is nothing for them. To build in eight years what others destroyed in a thousand years is just an ordinary thing for Lenin. He blows away the power of the rulers in thundering strokes. He can direct the entire world at once, and both he and Stalin hold the sun and the moon and return it to the lightless tundra.

And at the same time their attention is turned to the smallest and the humblest man and to the smallest and the humblest matter. In Lenin's mind, which was great and immense, there was place for leadership as well as for the complaints of those who suffered. His hand chased timidity away from the people. And at the same time Lenin gave such material things as a jacket that fits, high boots that reach over the knees, and such spiritual things as articulateness, a sharp tongue to those who were dumb, and knowledge and learnedness to those minds were dark ("Fellow Khacho," an Armenian song, III).

All these seemingly contradictory things the leader can be at the same time. There is no contradiction in hating and loving at the same time, in being at the same time awesome and love-inspiring. Once again the leader is like the Janus figure. The different qualities are not directed toward the same end, are not used for the same goal. These apparent contradictions are in keeping with that portrait of the new generation elite members which appears in Fadeyev's novel The Young Guard (1945), and the huge demigod, whose eyebrows are like mountain ranges but who is at the same time like a child whom the people can cradle in their arms, is the folklore expression of that being who is at the same time dreamy and efficient, practical and full of flights of fancy, loving and good and merciless, with an open soul and merciless.

In such a way the folklore appropriates the formal Party concepts and makes them its own in ways that the masses -- the "dark masses" -- can grasp visually and really understand. This abstract leader figure which appears in the official literature, in speeches and in newspapers,[13] has become someone who is easily understood even though he may seem supernatural or superhuman. There seems to be a desire to translate all the abstractions visually. One of the most striking of such translations is probably the carrying of the word and the concept of bditelnost into folk literature.

Bditelnost (watchfulness) is one of the major qualities expected and demanded of the Party member, in the elite as well as in the ranks, from the member of the Komsomol and from Soviet citizens in general. It is a watchfulness directed inward as well as outward, and perhaps even more inward than toward the enemy without. Every Komsomol, for instance, is required to be bditelnii, and by that is meant that he must watch his fellow Komsomols for infractions of behavior as well as watch for possible enemies trying to attack from without. In Party leader speeches the concept or word bditelnost, bditelnii, occur continually. But that concept is a very abstract one. And it is a new one. Before the Revolution, this word did not carry the same affect at all. The synonyms for it were sledit, storozhit, okhraniat, which mean to watch over, to guard, to protect. When the word bditelni was used, one said bditelnoie oko, the watchful eye. This bditelnoie oko, this one watchful eye, has found its trans-

---

13. For a discussion of this figure, cf. Leites et al. (1951). -- Ed.

lation in the folklore, and the entire concept of bditelnost has become symbolized in the spyglass that translates the power of seeing all, within and without, at the same time. It is not the field glasses, but the spyglass, the telescope, the podzornaia truba (field glasses are called polevoi binokl), which is an extension of the watchful eye. The Red Army soldier who personifies Russia's armed might in a painting in the village of Palekh stands against a background of planes, trains, factories, tractors -- an immense figure, holding in his right hand the gun and in his left the spyglass, which is lifted to his eye. He personifies the watchfulness directed without. In general, it seems that the military leaders need this spyglass to exercise their watchfulness, to be able to exercise it. When Lenin calls on his leaders, or rather generals, to fight the White forces, Voroshilov is pictured as

> a wonderful knight, sitting on a white horse.
> He holds the reins in the left hand
> In the right hand he holds the spyglass. (I)

In the hands of the leader of the people, the vozhd, as Lenin and Stalin are called, the spyglass becomes more than just the power of watching the enemy without. It translates his all-seeingness, which is one of the superhuman qualities of the leader. It is true that he can have that quality even without the spyglass. After Bloody Sunday, Lenin races back to Russia and on horseback he stands on the "Vorobeiskie Mountains":

> Lenin looked, he saw
> All around how things were done:
> He saw the cut-off impetuous heads,
> They just lay around in the streets;
> He saw how the people were being destroyed,
> How they were being pushed into dark cellars,
> How they were being exiled far away,
> How all of Russia grew silent. (I)

This leader figure, seeing all with the naked eye and dominating the scene from above, reminds one of the battle scene on the lake in Eisenstein's film Alexander Nevski, with Nevski's figure standing alone on a rock, his head seemingly reaching the clouds, dominating the fierce battle on the flat expanse of the lake.

Thus the vozhd can be watchful, can be bditelnii, without the spyglass. But with the spyglass he can do much more. He not only sees all, he sees everybody, sees everything. And not only does he see everything, he hears everything, he knows "all our thoughts and little thoughts." The spyglass he holds in his hand has become a scepter that symbolizes his power. The Red soldier and even the general have to hold it to their eye to see. Stalin simply holds it in his hand, and his sharp glance sees everything and his sensitive ear hears everything:

> Beautiful is wonderful Moscow!
> Most beautiful is the Kremlin wall
> With its high towers,
> With its shining stars.

From one tower, day and night,
In his military dress,
Holding in his hands the little spyglass,
Looks and rules the country solicitously
The great leader, the tender father,
The glorious, the wise Stalin-light.
His sensitive ear hears everything,
His sharp glance sees everything,
How the people live, how they work.
                    ("Bylina about Stalin," III)

In the minds of the people, therefore, the watchfulness, so stressed in the
official Party language, becomes confused with the original meaning of the word
for "watching over, protecting." This is very much the feeling emphasized in
the tale "Knee-Length-Beard and the Clear Falcons" (Kriukova, 1937), which tells
of the Tcheliuskin expedition and of Stalin's personal supervision of the rescue
parties.

Another concept may also be traced in the symbolism of the folklore. An
old Russian saying is that truth is round: "pravda kruglaia." Something that is
round you can approach from many sides, but it is also something you can hold
in your hands, it is something that can be given to others to touch and to hold.
Lenin and Stalin, the two leaders, hold the truth. They not only know it, they
possess it and they can bring it to others, can enlighten others. (They thus
possess something that the ancient bogatyri did not have.) The two peasant
brothers who set out in search of truth appear in many of the old legends. They
reappear in the "Post-October" folklore. Having looked for the truth at the
landlord's, at the priest's, at the merchant's, one brother gives up the search;
the other brother goes to the factory. And there he hears: "There is only one
man who knows truth. This man's name is Lenin." And he goes to find Lenin.
Lenin says to him that he did well to go to the factory. "You hold truth in your
hands," says he. (Cf. "Lenin's Truth," III.) That intangible thing, truth, which
one set out to seek through the world, has become something so tangible now
that one can hold it in one's hands. It is like the sun, which Lenin returns to
the tribes of the dark tundra and which Stalin, after Lenin's death, brings to
them once more:

And he held in his powerful hand
Our golden sun.
He came down on the beach,
Put the sun on the ground,
Gave it a push and loudly bid it:
Go above the tundra,
Make life beautiful in the tundra.
                    ("The Song about the Returned Sun," Saam legend, II)

The relationship between Lenin and the people and Stalin and the people is
the same. But the feeling toward them is not quite identical. It is hard to find
any real difference, but it seems that Stalin is viewed as the father's son. He is
the "son of Lenin," great and wise like Lenin, and is carrying out a legacy,
Lenin's legacy. And Lenin is not dead. He lives on not only in Stalin's deeds,

but also in the sentiment of the people who have in their veins a drop of his blood and who

> ... go with Stalin as ⌊they⌋ went with Lenin,
> Speak to Stalin as ⌈they⌉ spoke to Lenin.
>> ("Everything Has Been Carried Out," Great Russian lament, III)

One bogatyr takes the place of another bogatyr to carry on the work. Only in one song is there a feeling of more equality between Lenin and Stalin:

> The ocean is blood brother to the ocean,
> Stalin is blood brother to Lenin.
>> (Ibid.)

One leader carrying on the works and carrying out the desires of another leader seems to leave the way open for a third leader who will continue the tradition. Lenin, then, as the original leader, the one who stands on top, is also the one credited with most power, and what he has been able to accomplish surpasses anything the ancient bogatyri could have done.

Such a leader as Lenin cannot brag. If he says he will do something, he will carry out his pledge. In The Legend about Lenin (I), we have a very old legendary theme transformed to fit the new hero image. In the ancient legend of Sviatogor, this hero -- feeling great strength coursing through his veins -- claims that he will lift up the earth. As he rides on, he sees a little purse lying on the ground. Trying to lift it, he finds it too heavy; he pulls and pulls, his knees buckle, he overstrains himself and dies in punishment for his bragging.

Young Lenin, too, feels great strength start up in him and he tells his mother:

> ... I hear great strength inside me....
> ... I know where to find the ring,
> I know how to turn the earth around,
> The entire earth, the entire Russia. (I)

And he performed the feat. The earth was turned over by him. But he did not stand alone. He called on the people and the people heard him:

> They would gather with all their heroic strength (bogatirskaia sila),
> They would take hold of the wonderful ring,
> It was hard to pull it out,
> They had to pull hard,
> With powerful force they pulled it out,
> They turned the glorious mother earth over
> On the other side, the just side. (I)

It was a superhuman feat, but not one carried out alone. Again the people stand in back of the leader with their own "heroic strength" and make the feat possible.

The people cannot be without the leader, who is their friend and their father, but neither can the leader be without the people, for he is also their child. Together they stand; separated they would fall. It seems that this is the main theme of the new folklore about the leader figure. It carries down into the masses the formal Party line and makes it possible for them to accept it.

When the Bolsheviks came into power, they brought with them a whole series of new words, of new meanings for old words, of new slogans. The new language was a bewildering experience for the masses. To understand the concepts, they had to try to make the language their own. In the folklore literature, which is the expression of the thought of the low masses, the former temny liud, the "dark people," the new language and the new concepts have been assimilated. In their expression we can find the meaning of the new byt.

III. A Russian Double Image Cluster: "Not-So: So"

The three brief selections that have been grouped together here are all concerned with a problem of form, illustrated in the first instance by a type of image found in the Russian bylini, folk poetry in the peasant epic tradition, and also adopted in popular Soviet poetry.

The first selection is a working memorandum describing and illustrating the type image as it occurred in the traditional poetry and in the "Post-October" folklore. It was prepared for a specific group discussion. The memorandum was written in 1949, when, in the course of a study of the bylini, the formal aspect of the images was recognized and (in another connection) related to forms of Russian thought. (See also the preceding article on "The Image of the Leader in Soviet 'Post-October' Folklore," which was part of the same study.)

The second selection is a passage from a discussion of the formal aspects of rumors in Russia, when one participant's description of the clustering of rumors recalled the work on imagery that had been done almost two years earlier, particularly the work on the 'not-so: so" image clusters.

The third selection is taken from a study of Russian thought processes. The writer was present at the group discussion of rumor, a passage from which is reproduced here, and immediately realized how the image form was related to the problem on which he was working and could be used to illustrate a particular point he wished to make. He then turned back to the original work on imagery.

This sequence, which in time covers slightly more than two years, is given as an illustration of the way in which in group work a detail can provide clues to new situations and problems and can be one of the links of relationship among several kinds of material. -- Ed.

1. The "Not-So: So" Images in Russian Folklore[14]
Nelly Schargo Hoyt

In looking at the imagery in order to find patterns, as you suggested, I have found only two, which I think you mentioned:

1. The image you called the "negative simile." This is very much like the constant epithet in the folklore: "It is not a cloud, it is the enemy" is constant; therefore enemies are like clouds, or evil is like a cloud. Or 'It is not the clear falcon" or 'It is not the eagle, it is the hero"; heroes are like the big birds, falcons or eagles. This old negative simile has grown in importance with the invention of the airplane, or rather with the use of the airplane in the Soviet Union, for now heroes really are "clear falcons" (cf. in particular the bylina, "Knee-Length-Beard and the Clear Falcons," by Kriukova, 1937). Not so often one finds that heroes are "not mountains" or "not the oak." That is the strength epithet (the mountainous snake of the Dobrinia legend, for instance). Grief is usually mentioned in connection with water or moving sands: 'Not the spring

---

14. Unpublished document RCC-R 234.

waters, Not the shifting sands running, Not the winds blowing." Death is the
sun going down: "Not the red sun went down:"

2. The other way the negative-positive statement seems to be used is in
describing what the hero actually did by stating what he did _not_ do first: "He
did not ask the watchman at the gate," or "He did _not_ enter the town wall by the
gate," or "The jester did _not_ sit down next to the prince." It is also used to
describe something by first saying what it is not: "Those were _not_ the houses of
boyars or peasants," etc.

This is definitely a poetic device and seems to be one of the distinctive
features of Russian poetry. I have asked several people what they saw when I
read some of the negative similes to them; except for two, they saw _both_ what
the hero is not (or what is not) and what the hero is, and so on: the cloud _and_
the enemy; the clear falcon _and_ the hero.

I do not know whether this is correct, and of course I have nothing to substantiate it, but my feeling is that this device makes the _bylina_ or song (it is
used in songs too) more colorful for the listeners because it gives something
through the images besides the mere description and thus heightens the interest.
It might be of the same order as the so-called _priskazki_ of the old fairy tales.
The taleteller starts with a long description of something and suddenly stops
and says, "This is not the tale, this is just the introduction, the tale is still
ahead." (The tale of the little hunchbacked horse has quite a few of these.) If
the _priskazka_ is good, then the people's interest is roused and their attention
will be sustained throughout the telling.

The other characteristic thing about most of the negative similes is that the
likeness is something taken out of nature: birds, trees, clouds, winds, water.
This helps, I think, to emphasize the closeness of the hero to the "wet earth,"
to nature, to the soil (in the actual physical sense) of Russia. As I say, these
are just guesses; I do not know whether they are of the pattern order you meant.

Illustrations:[15]

1. I did not leave my plow in the furrow
   Not for the passing traveler,
   But for the peasants and the villagers,
            ("Volga and Mikula," IV)
2. I am not a tzar or tzarevich,
   I am not a king or a king's son,
   Nor a strong powerful hero,
   I am the threatening and terrible death.
            ("Dobrinia and Death," IV)
3. She did not marry the prince, she did not marry the boyar,
   Nor the powerful Russian hero,
   But she married the brave Alesha Popovich,
            ("Dobrinia Away; Alesha Popovich," IV)

15. For purposes of brevity, the five sources from which illustrations have
    been selected will be referred to as follows: Kriukova, 1937 (I); Kriukova,
    1938 (II); Kriukova, 1941 (III); Latzko, 1911 (IV); Gorky, 1938 (V), The
    translations were made by the writer.

4. He did not enter the town wall by the gate,
    He passed the corner tower,
                    ("Dobrinia Away; Alesha Popovich," IV)

5. He did not ask the watchman at the gate,
    He did not ask the guards at the doors,
    He pushed everyone away;
                    ("Dobrinia Away; Alesha Popovich," IV)

6. The jester did not sit down next to the prince,
    The jester did not sit down opposite the prince,
    The jester sat down on the bench
    Opposite the princess.
                    ("Dobrinia Away; Alesha Popovich," IV)

7. These were not the houses of boyars or peasants,
    They were wonderful and amazing,
    They were made from ice.
                    (I)

8. The good lads did not go along the road or the path,
    They went through the forests and clean fields
                    (III)

9. He did not ask the guards at the gate
    But leaped across the Kremlin wall.
                    (III)

10. No small task have you thought up,
    Not a small, but a big task have you thought up
                    (II)

11. It isn't a small joke that you have started,
    Wait till it falls out of your hands!
                    (II)

12. That will not be for the brave lad's honor,
    Nor for the glorious knight's praise:
    To kill the tzar --
                    (II)

13. But Vladimir Ilich-light did not walk for long,
    He was caught, he was injured by the tzar's guard
                    (II)

14. Not the clear falcon came flying
    But on the road the leader came
                    (II)

15. Not the clear falcon was flying,
    As the falcon flew away in the clean field,
    So the hero rode away.
                    (II)

16. Not the eagle of the steppes started to fly.
    But our hero started to ride
                    (III)

17. Not the clear falcon flew around
    The glorious Stalin-light traveled around
                    ("Bylina about Stalin," V)

18. Not the white sea became agitated
    The young brave's heart started to beat.
                    ("Bylina about Stalin," V)

19. It was not a dark cloud rolling along,
    It was the merciless villain,
    The merciless villain, Dutov the general,
    And Kolchak, the admiral.
                    (III)

20. The oak does not bend to the earth,
    The leaves do not scatter,
    The son bows down before the father.
                    ("Ilya Murometz before the Town of Chernigov," IV)

21. But from that side, the western side,
    It is not noise that is heard,

It is not rain falling,
It is great thunder rolling.
                    ("Dobrinia and the Snake," IV)
22. The cold winds are not blowing,
    The shifting sands are not running,
    Again grief is rising,
    Like a black cloud.
                    ("Everything Has Been Carried Out," V)
23. That is not the green birch bending down in the field,
    Not the curly, green one bending over,
    That is the red flag unfurling over the grave,
                    (III)
24. Not the spring waters flow over,
    Not the waves unroll,
    The bright eyes are closed,
    The hot blood has congealed on his lips.
                    (II)

2. Rumor Cluster and Image Cluster: Detail from a Group Discussion[16]

101M: One of the things that comes to my mind was that the Soviet people as I knew them had the unusual capacity to hold a variety of conflicting or over-lapping rumors in solution at the same time. They could play with half a dozen overlapping rumors and believe all of them and none of them equally. I think perhaps that we tend in this country to say: Facts ... rumor ... and we play with a rumor perhaps and give it a definite outline and then either completely disregard the rumor or take it as a fact. In the Soviet mind the whole thing is much more confused and blurred and border-line, and [not] as sharp a distinc-tion between rumor and fact. At one moment they accept a series of rumors and don't necessarily choose any one of them and regard that one as the rumor.

64F: And they don't build into a single structure, but remain a series?

101M: ... Where there's a slight difference in the whole series, we tend to push it all together into a single focused image and they tend to see it as a whole series of possibiliities, any one of which or all of which may be true.

46F: On that point, does it depend on how crucial a situation it is for how large a series you are likely to have ... or keep suspended at once?

101M: I would say that the more dangerous a given situation, the wider the range of rumors which they accept, all of which or none of which may be true.

                    [Brief omission.]

31M: ... about this cluster or series of rumors, do you have the impression that these rumors are always connected, or tend to be connected, with the same feeling, or not? In other words, in your series of rumors, for example, if you have a certain hope, are they always connected with a positive hope in which you have a certain theory, or in terms of feeling, do they deal with alter-natives of feeling?

---

16. From a transcription of the verbatim minutes of a group meeting, SCC-A, July 10, 1951. The excerpt is taken from the middle part of the meeting; some discussion of other related points has been omitted here. -- Ed.

<u>101M</u>: I'd say that the variety of rumors can come out with exactly the same feelings. In other words, as related to emotional intensity.

<u>31M</u>:   And do they tend to be related to the same feeling?

<u>101M</u>: Oh yes.

[Brief omission.]

<u>102M</u>: I'd like to ask, When you talked about a whole class of rumors being held more or less in suspension or something of that sort, did you mean to imply that in this class there would be contradictory rumors?

<u>101M</u>: Oh yes. At the same time there would be rumors that there would be white bread on free sale at a high price next week and that there wouldn't be any bread at all. And they'd believe both.

<u>46F</u>:   Well, that fits in with a general point we got out of the <u>bylini</u> where you get a series of images -- what we then called the "Not-So: So" series. Nelly [Hoyt] found by interviewing, I believe, that people did hold <u>all</u> the images in suspension. For instance, "It is not the eagle, It is not the falcon, It is the hero." All the "nots" link together things that are related to the image you are trying to make. And so you have the "birch tree" and the "flag" and the dead hero -- and all sorts of things linked together. And all these "nots" were apparently present [as visual images], because if you gave people part of the image, they would say that visually they completed it. Or saw them both.

<u>102M</u>: Oh yes. It was in ... what is this girl? Who wrote it? 'The Black Pearl"? The poet describes her as "she didn't have the most beautiful breasts in the world, her teeth were not perfect pearls," and so on....

<u>46F</u>:   But here [in the Russian images] you have both at once -- here you have at one time the hero and the eagle, or whatever....

<u>64F</u>:   I don't think you've seen this particular point. But in the poetry you have a thing like this: "They were not two young eagles flying, They were two heroes riding," and you have <u>both</u> images. Or, 'It was not the birch tree bending, It was the flag." And the thing that it is <u>not</u> suggests the thing that it is.

[Discussion of metaphors in English and Russian poetry omitted.]

<u>64F</u>:   What we tend to do, then, what people using <u>English</u> imagery tend to do, is to say "the hero was <u>like</u> an eagle flying." You may get a sort of fleeting image of an eagle, but then you give the hero "eagleness." Now the striking thing in the [Russian] imagery we hit on -- what there was of it -- was that there was not a condensation, but that there was a simultaneous <u>set</u> of images, one thing it wasn't, and the other the thing it was.

3. Russian "Visual Thinking"[17]
Leopold H. Haimson

In comparison with the "objective" thinking characteristic of our society -- a type of thinking that is largely founded on motor activity and tactile manipula-

17. Reproduced from Haimson (1951).

tion of external objects [the "visual" thinking of Great Russians] was singularly
lacking in specificity (if evaluated on the basis of this criterion of manipulation).

On the other hand, viewed in the light of the categories of abstract thought
characteristic of our society,[18] it was deficient in logical simplicity, consistency, and completeness.

These "negative" characteristics were expressed (and, as we shall see,
continue to be expressed) in the day-to-day behavior of Great Russians; they
find very clear expression in the bylini, the folk ballads in the peasant epic
tradition. Examine, for example, the following lines from a bylina (Kriukova,
1945) about Lenin's life and death:

(1)   Not the red sun went down
(2)   Not behind the Vorobeiskii mountains
(3)   Not behind the stone Mother Moscow
(4)   Not behind the dark forests
(5)   Not behind the green gardens
(6)   Not behind the deep sea
(7)   Not behind the different towns
(8)   Not behind the villages and settlements
(9)   Not behind the quiet waters
(10) Our red sun rolled away
(11) And the heavenly moon
(12) And the dawn, the morning dawn
(13) And the evening star
(14) The red sun sank away
(15) Into the earth, the wet mother earth
(16) It is laid down as in a grave,
(17) Thus Ilich lies.

In our eyes, the first nine lines of this poem fail to build up any cognitive
order; they fail to establish any organized cognitive image. None of the individual objects to which each of these lines refers appears essential to the cognitive meaning of the poem as a whole, and the order in which they are introduced
could be endlessly shuffled without affecting the cognitive meaning. Only from
line (10) to line (13) is a logical sequence introduced, and no sooner has this
logic been established than it is arbitrarily abandoned. While the red sun is
sinking away into the wet mother earth, the moon, the dawn, and the evening
star -- which the poet has evoked in the preceding three lines -- are left hanging in mid-air, It is as if four balls were thrown into the air, and only one
dropped, while the other three soared on.

---

18. In contemporary American society, these categories of abstract thought
    are ultimately derived from the sensations that arise in the process of
    motor activity and tactile manipulation. Partly because it is largely re-
    pressed after childhood, visual imagery seems to constitute only a second-
    ary source for abstract thought.

By the specificity criteria of objective thinking, by the logical categories of abstract thought, the poem is a failure. But the writer is appealing to another kind of logic, to a logic of emotion. His aim is to build up a total response adequate to the subject with which he is dealing, and in this he does not fail.

With each individual image, with each individual line, he attempts to evoke a new feeling, a new and distinctive response,[19] until he has built up in the reader a veritable conglomerate, a veritable symphony of feelings, the range and volume of which are adequate to the fact introduced in the poem's last line, the fact of Lenin's death.

It is in the light of the cognitive standards we have outlined here that Western observers have commented on the early childhood characteristics of traditional Russian thinking, that they have pointed at its tendency toward reversibility, its lack of specificity, its readiness to equate a whole and a part, the outside and the inside of an object -- cognitive characteristics the nearest replicas of which are indeed to be found in some Western societies in the earliest phases of personality development.

IV. Trends in Affectlessness[20]

Nathan Leites

Albert Camus's The Stranger[21] is one of the most prominent post-1939 French novels, and one which has been widely regarded as conveying a new "philosophical" message. This paper is not concerned with the connections between the novel and the philosophical writings of the author (in particular Le mythe de Sisyphe, 1942). It attempts to trace relationships between the novel and certain trends in the temper of the age. In doing so, it offers a psychological interpretation of the content of the novel[22] and confronts this interpretation with those of a sample of American critics.[23]

---

19. Each image is kept distinct by the use of the "not - not" device, which is traditional in Russian folklore poetry and habitual in Soviet moralizing. Thus simultaneity is preserved without contamination.
20. Reproduced from Leites (1947).
21. L'Étranger, Paris, 1942. Translated by Stuart Gilbert, New York, 1946. All page references are to the American edition. All underlinings in quotations are supplied.
22. Dr. Martha Wolfenstein's suggestions have contributed to a number of points in this matter.
23. The following critics were considered: John Cournos, New York Sun, April 11, 1946; Clip Boutell, New York Post, April 15, 1946: Jex Martin, Jr., Chicago Sun, April 14, 1946; Richard Sullivan, Chicago Tribune, April 14, 1946; George Robbins, Chicago Daily News, April 24, 1946; Time Magazine, May 20, 1948; Newsweek, April 15, 1946; Charles Poore, New York Times, April 11, 1946; John L. Brown, New York Times, April 14, 1946; Lewis Gannett, New York Herald Tribune, April 13, 1946; Justin O'Brien, New York Herald Tribune, April 14, 1946; Max Lerner, PM, April 22, 1946; Richard Plant, Saturday Review of Literature, May 18, 1946; Nicola Chiaromonte, New Republic, April 29, 1946; Edmund Wilson, The New Yorker, April 13, 1946; Katherine Hoskins, Partisan Review, Winter, 1946; Albert J. Guerard, Foreground, Winter, 1946.

The outline of the plot is as follows: Meursault, a small French clerk in Algiers, receives news of his mother's death; he attends her funeral; he begins an affair and becomes engaged; he kills, under a blazing sun, without any adequate conscious motivation the brother of an Arab prostitite whose pimp he vaguely knows; he is condemned to death and will presently be executed. He is the narrator.

Three attitudes may be taken towards the hero. First, that he is the incarnation of a metaphysical affirmation which is known to be held by the author. Thus Justin O'Brien, (New York Herald Tribune, April 14, 1946) quotes a passage from Camus's Le mythe de Sisyphe ("The world that can be explained ... even with false reasons is a familiar world. But in a universe ... deprived of illusions and enlightenment, man feels himself a stranger.... This divorce between man and his life ... is ... the feeling of absurdity"), and says, "Here is the key to the novel. Meursault, the unintentional murderer, enacts a parable of man's fate. Since there is ... free will, he must have been free to kill or not to kill. But he cannot see it that way; if there was no other coercion, there was that of the dazzling sun."

Second, the hero may be considered unintelligible. Thus Edmund Wilson, (The New Yorker, April 13, 1946) says about the hero that "as a human being he seems to me incredible; his behavior is never explained or made plausible.... The queer state of mind of the protagonist ...[is] never accounted for."

Critics have tended to take one, or both, of these positions. A third position, which shall be set forth here, is that Meursault's behavior is largely intelligible....

The novel contains only few explicit indications -- almost entirely overlooked even by the sophisticated critics -- about the hero's past. But these few are quite significant. As to his father, "I never set eyes on him" (p. 138). As to his mother, "For years she'd never had a word to say to me and I could see she was moping with no one to talk to" (p. 58); "... neither Mother nor I expected much of one another (n'attendions plus rien l'un de l'autre)" (p. 109). "As a student I'd had plenty of ambition.... But when I had to drop my studies, I very soon realized all that was pretty futile (sans importance réelle)" (p. 52). The child and the adolescent are thus shown as reacting with withdrawal of conscious affect in intrapersonal relations (that is, the relations between the various components of the self) and in interpersonal relations. He is thus reacting to the guilty rage induced by the severe deprivations which were imposed by an absent father, an indifferent mother, and a withholding wider environment.

It is this characteristic defense which the hero perpetuates and elaborates in his adult life, and which gives his personality -- conveyed in a style appropriate to this dominant trait -- its particular aura. I shall now discuss the various major manifestations of the hero's affectlessness.

Firstly, and most obviously, the hero is usually rather clearly aware of the absence or weakness of affects in response to intrapersonal and interpersonal stimuli.[24] "I could truthfully say I'd been quite fond of (j'aimais bien) mother -- but really that didn't mean much (cela ne voulait rien dire)" (p. 80). His affects appear to him as questionable rather than as inevitable and valid; I came to feel that this aversion (against talking about certain things -- N.L.) had no real substance (je n'ai plus trouvé d'importance á ces répugnances)' (p. 89). He is much aware of the almost total dependence of his affective on his somatic state (cf. p. 80) -- conforming though in extreme fashion) to what is probably a contemporary trend.

While the hero is acutely aware of his atypicality as a "stranger" to the world, he spontaneously subsumes most of his few near-affective experiences in interpersonal relations under general categories. When his lawyer asks him whether he had loved his mother, he replies "yes, like everybody else" (83). When his girl friend asks him "Suppose another girl had asked you to marry her -- I mean a girl you liked in the same way as you like me -- would you have said 'Yes' to her too?" the hero does not find such a hypothesis inconceivable and his emotions towards Marie unique. He answers, apparently effortlessly: "Naturally" (p. 53). In this, he presumably manifests a widely diffused trend in the quality of Western "love" experiences in this century.

It may be surmised that such "generalizing" procedures are in part a defense against the unconscious threat of overwhelming affect. When the hero learns of his mother's death, he arranges for keeping "the usual vigil" (p. 1) beside the body. The owner of his habitual restaurant affirms "there's no one like a mother" (p. 2) and lends him a black tie and mourning band procured for the occasion of an uncle's death.

The hero shows a high degree of detachment towards decisive impacts of his environment on him. During most of his trial he feels as if somebody else is about to be condemned to death. "... He ("one of my policemen" -- N.L.) asked me if I was feeling nervous. I said: No, and that the prospect of witnessing a trial rather interested me" (p. 103). When danger mounts, "the futility of what was happening (tout ce que je faisais d'inutile en ce lieu) seemed to take me by the throat" (p. 132).

---

24. This is in sharp contrast to the intensity of his reactions to external non-personal stimuli -- to the colors (cf. pp. 14, 20, 93), smells (cf. pp. 10, 20), tactile values (cf. pp. 14, 61, 92, 95), sounds (cf. p. 122) of cityscape and landscape. These he knows to be his "surest, humblest pleasures" (p. 132). The hero is also presented as feeling a persistently strong and unbrokenly euphoric sexual attraction towards his girl friend -- almost the only point in which I would question his plausibility. Perhaps the author, so free from many illusions, is here still presenting a derivative of the Western myth on the transcendent position of "love" in human nature.

All value judgments have ceased to be self-evident, as they have in some variants of contemporary empiricist epistemology. There is a tabula rasa where the traditonal ethical postulates stood. But the hero attains at the end a state of exaultation in contemplating the certain facts of his present aliveness and impending annihilation: "It might look as if my hands were empty. Actually, I was sure of myself, sure about everything, far surer than he ⌈the prison chaplain -- N.L.⌉ : sure of my present life and of the death that was coming. That, no doubt, was all I had; but at least that certainty was something I could get my teeth into -- just as it had got its teeth into me (je tenais cette vérité autant qu'elle me tenait)" (p. 151). The cathexis withdrawn from norms is in part displaced to very general aspects of facts.

Choices made, then, appear as quite inevitable and correct (for they have been made) and as quite arbitrary (for they were choices). In his final exaltation the hero comes to feel that "I'd been right, I was still right, I was always right. I'd passed my life in a certain way and I might have passed it in a different way.... I'd acted thus and I hadn't acted otherwise.... And what did that mean? That, all the time, I had been waiting for this present moment, for that dawn ⌈of execution -- N.L.⌉ ... which was to justify me" (pp. 151, 152).

The hero abstains from morally reacting to others as much as to himself (cf. pp. 34, 45). His incapacity for moral indignation is again related to certain contemporary trends. (Cf. Kris and Leites, 1947.)

What are the behavioral counterparts to the hero's valuelessness? His tendency is to minimize overt action, symbolic as well as motor. He tends to react with silence to communications of others, perpetuating the wordlessness of his relations with his mother. He shows a preference for the maintenance of his personal status quo, at any given moment and with reference to his overall mode of life. When an evening conversation imposed on him is prolonged, he feels that "I wanted to be in bed, only it was such an effort making a move" (p. 41). When his employer offers him a Paris job, "I saw no reason for 'changing my life'" (p. 52). Getting out of bed requires an intense effort.

Whenever he contemplates alternative courses of action, he becomes convinced that they lead to an identical result. Thus nothing is a "serious matter (une chose grave)" (p. 53). When his boss offers him a Paris job, "really I didn't care much one way or the other (dans le fond cela m' était égal)" (p. 52). When he is present at a tense underworld encounter which may instantly develop into shooting, "it crossed my mind that one might fire or not fire -- and it would come to absolutely the same thing (tout cela se valait)" (p. 172).

Correspondingly, the hero tends to feel a situation as invariant which according to the judgment of non-"strangers" has varied radically. When his boss, offering him a Paris job, stresses the advantages of a "change of life," "I answered that one never changed his way of life" (p. 52).

"The same thing" to which all conceivable courses of action lead is a negative thing. When the hero accompanies the coffin of his mother to the cemetery in the Algerian heat, he is told: "If you go too slowly there's the risk of a heat stroke. But if you go too fast, you perspire and the cold air in the church gives you a chill" (p. 21). He adds: "I saw ... (the) point: either way one was in for it (il n'y avait pas d'issue)" (p. 21). There is no conceivable intermediate optimal point between too much and too little. Similarly -- and again with the heat in the role of the great depriver -- at a certain point during the morning which ends with the crime, the hero stands before a house he is expected to enter: "...I couldn't face the effort needed to go up the steps and make myself amiable to the women. But the heat was so great that it was just as bad staying where I was. ... To stay or to make a move -- it came to much the same (cela revenait au même). After a moment I returned to the beach" (p. 73) -- a move which leads to the murder.

"One is cooked both ways" because death is the terminal state of any sequence of acts -- which is therefore equivalent to any other sequence. "Nothing, nothing had the least importance, and I knew quite well why.... From the dark horizon of my future a sort of slow, persistent breeze had been blowing towards me, all my life long, from the years that were to come. And on its way that breeze had leveled out (égalisait) all the ideas that people tried to foist on me. ... What difference could ... (it) make ... the way a man decides to live, the fate ... he chooses, since one and the same fate was bound to 'choose' not only me but thousands of millions of privileged people.... Every man alive was privileged; there was only one class of men, the privileged class. And all alike would be condemned to die one day....And what difference could it make if ... he [the prison chaplain instead of the hero -- N.L.] were executed ... since it all came to the same thing in the end?" (p. 152). This indifferentism with the horizon of death acts manifestly as a defense against distress. Despairing of his girl friend's faithfulness, the hero asks in the context of the passage just quoted: "What did it matter if at this very moment Marie was kissing a new boy friend?" (p. 153). The fatherless and motherless (in more than one sense) murderer asks: "What difference could they make to me, the deaths of others, or a mother's love or ... God?" (p. 152). Awaiting execution and faintly hoping for the success of his appeal, the hero attempts with conscious and only partly successful effort to make himself see that "it makes little difference whether one dies at the age of thirty or three score and ten....Whether I die now or forty years hence, this business of dying had to be got through, inevitably" (pp. 142-43).

Presumably the belief in death as annihilation has been, and is, spreading and deepening in Western culture. Reactions to this major trend seem to be (as one would expect) polarized. On the one hand there is an increasing tendency to "scotomize" death, i.e. to minimize its role in conscious awareness. On the other hand, a breakthrough of this awareness may dominate the consciousness of the individual in a somewhat new fashion: The massive fact of death may appear as establishing the pointlessness of life beyond any possibility of mitigation. The tabula rasa as to previous conceptions of Good and Evil may thus be accompanied by a tabula rasa as to previous conceptions of the Meaningful Life.

But the residual certainty of the very fact of life which is accentuated when valuelessness has been established (cf. page 251 above) may become the new meaning-creating factor: If death is annihilation, life -- all we have -- is infinitely precious (a resurgence of the carpe diem theme in "highbrow" speculation which has often accompanied the breakdown of civilizations). This is the metaphysical and axiological aspect of the passage on "certainty" quoted on page 251 above. The sentence quoted "every man alive was privileged" may thus become one denying or affirming the meaningfulness of life according to whether the temporariness or the availability of the "privilege" is stressed. If the positive accent is chosen, the desired though unobtainable "life after the grave" appears as "a life in which I can remember this life on earth. That's all I want of it!" (p. 150). The hero attempts to get rid of the intruding prison chaplain as "I'd very little time left and I wasn't going to waste it on God" (p. 150). But there is a price to this reversal: The affects which the negative view intended to ward off by the depreciation of life reappear. The hero awaiting the coming of the executioners every dawn knows every morning that "I might just as well have heard footsteps and felt my heart shattered into bits" (p. 152). On the other hand intermittent fantasies of survival give him the task "to calm down that sudden rush of joy racing through my body and even bringing tears to my eyes" (p. 143). Thus belief in the meaninglessness of life appears in the hero related to the successful repression of affect, and belief in its meaningfulness to the return of the repressed from repression.

What typical conscious motivations remain available to the hero in his predominant negative phases? The hero tends to choose a certain action "for want of anything better to do" or as "I had nothing to do" or "as a last resource" against the unspecified displeasure of more complete inaction. He tends to comply with demands made on him in a "why not?" fashion. When his pimp acquaintance asks him for a favor "I wrote the letter [requested -- N.L.] ... I wanted to satsify Raymond as I'd no reason not to satisfy him" (p. 41). When the pimp thereupon says "so now we are pals, ain't we? (tu es un vrai copain), I kept silence and he said it again. I didn't care one way or the other, but he seemed so set on it, I nodded and said 'yes'" (p. 41). When his boss offers him a Paris job, "I told him I was quite prepared to go; but really I didn't care much one way or the other" (p. 52). When his girl friend asks him if he would marry her, "I said I didn't mind; if she was keen on it, we'd get married." When she objects to this reaction, "I pointed out that ... the suggestion came from her; as for me, I'd merely said 'yes'" (p. 53).

Presumably the predominance of such "negative motivations" is overdetermined. Affectlessness is here not only a defense against the various fantasied dangers of involvement but also an instrument of aggression against (and contempt for) those persons who expect a fuller response from the hero. The aggression proceeds by spiteful obedience: Demands are complied with in the letter but not in the spirit.

A major "positive" motivation of the hero is sleep, functioning as defense against the overwhelming impact of dangerous stimuli. It makes him feel good to look forward to sleep in a short while. At a certain "evening hour ... I always felt so well content with life (je me sentais content). Then, what awaited me was a night of easy dreamless sleep" (p. 13). "I can remember ... my little thrill of pleasure when we entered the first brightly lit streets of Algiers ⌈returning from his mother's funeral -- N.L.⌉ and I pictured myself going straight to bed and sleeping twelve hours at a stretch" (p. 22).

Where other psychic structures would react with intense affect, the hero tends to react with fatigue and somnolence -- which he often attributes to the external physical rather than to an internal psychic "heat" (cf. pp. 2, 132-33).

To the high tendency towards sleep corresponds the vagueness and poverty of internal and external psychic perceptions during the hero's waking hours (as was implied in footnote 24, page 250 above, his perception of nonhuman aspects of his environment are rich and acute). Low awareness of self is shown in extreme fashion when the hero after a long time in prison suddenly "heard something that I hadn't heard for months. It was the sound of a voice; my own voice, there was no mistaking it. And I recognized it as the voice that for many a day of late had been sounding in my ears. So I know that all this time I'd been talking to myself" (p. 101). Similarly, the hero at important occasions -- where, again, he is apt, projectively, to hold the heat of the day responsible -- fails to hear or to understand correctly what others are saying to him or about him. When his lawyer pleads for him in court, "I found that my mind had gone blurred; everything was dissolving with a grayish, watery haze (tout devenait comme une eau incolore ou je trouvais le vertige)" (p. 312).

More particularly, the hero -- having interfered so severely with his own affects -- is highly inhibited in the perception of affects of others, especially of those having himself as their target. This lack of empathy facilitates the unconsciously aggressive and self-punitive candidness of the hero, which will be discussed below, and which the critics take at its face value as uncompromising honesty. The same trait also induces a poverty of the prognostic horizon. After the hero has witnessed an altercation between the pimp and a policeman, the pimp tells him "he'd like to know if I'd expected him to return the blow when the policeman hit him. I told him I hadn't expected anything whatsoever (je n'attendais rien du tout)" (p. 47).

Affects of others, if perceived, appear "embarrassing" (cf. p. 88). Explicit or implicit demands of others to express empathy (and sympathy) by words responding to their words, or to express other nuances of affect, tend to elicit a "I have nothing to say" reaction. When the hero's girl friend answers his indifferent marriage consent by declaring that she "loves" him because he's a "queer fellow," but that she might "hate" him some day, the hero reports: "to which I had nothing to say, so I said nothing" (p. 53). When the magistrate asks the hero about his "reputation of being a taciturn, rather self-centered person" (p. 82), the hero answered: "Well, I rarely have anything much to say. So naturally I keep my mouth shut." His habitual silence is thus not based on conscious restraint against verbalizing a rich subjectivity, as one recognizes the limitations of words and values privacy. It is a silence expressing subjective void. Only in rare and fugitive instances does this void appear as a disguise of plenitude. At one moment during his trial the hero feels like "cutting them all short and saying: '... I've something really important to tell you.' However, on second thought, I found I had nothing to say" (p. 124).

In many instances the hero has nothing to say because he experiences what others say as meaningless. (One may recall the central importance, in contemporary empiricist epistemology, of the designation of certain types of sentences as "meaningless" -- and hence neither "true" nor "false" -- which had been regarded as "meaningful" before.) This is particularly the case when others talk about the hero's subjective experiences. When the examining magistrate, using an "intimate" technique, tells the hero "what really interests me is -- you!" (p. 82), "I wasn't quite clear what he meant, so I made no comment" (p. 82). When his lawyer asks him whether he had felt grief when his mother died, "I answered that of recent years I'd rather lost the habit of noting my feelings (m'interroger) and hardly knew what to answer" (p. 80). When Marie "asked me if I loved her, I said that sort of question had no meaning really (cela ne voulait rien dire), but I supposed I didn't" (p. 44). When Marie asks again some time later, "I replied much as before that her question meant nothing or next to nothing (cela ne signifiait rien) -- but I supposed I didn't" (p. 52). His sentences on one's own affects appear either as meaningless or as difficult to test -- but never as evidently true or false, a quality which earlier epistemology usually attributed to introspective statements.

The syndrome of affectlessness which I have sketched in the preceding passages is a largely ego-syntonic one. The hero does not share in the historically typical despair about, and revolt against, psychic impotence -- a change which is probably, again, related to contemporary trends. When his boss offers him a Paris job, the hero declares that "my present ... [life] suited me quite well.... I saw no reason for 'changing my life.' By and large it wasn't an unpleasant one" (p. 52). While he is incapable of "explaining" his subjective state, it isn't a problem for him either. Affectlessness is reacted to affectlessly.

Such is the syndrome which dominates the usual life atmosphere of the hero. But besides the affect inhibitions hitherto described the hero shows a set of affect substitutes. Some of them are somatic. When the hero leaves a consciously entirely flat conversation with the pimp, "I could hear nothing but the blood throbbing in my ears and for a while I stood still, listening to it" (p. 42). Other affect substitutes are non-somatic. Certain perceptions of detail, closely associated with the central matters to which the hero does not react consciously, show a high intensity and at the same time unreality. When he is holding a wake at the coffin of his mother without any conscious grief, ten of her friends are with him: "Never in my life had I seen anyone so clearly as I saw these people.... And yet ... it was hard to believe they really existed" (p. 10). At the funeral itself he perceives in a father figure -- the "boy friend" of his mother in the home for the aged -- the somatic image of his affect inhibition: "His eyes were streaming with tears.... But because of the wrinkles ⌈in his face --N.L.⌋ they couldn't flow down. They spread out, crisscrossed and formed a smooth gloss on the old, worn face" (pp. 21-22). The hero is bored by the prosecutor's speech at his trial: "The only things that really caught my attention were occasional phrases, his gestures, and some elaborate tirades -- but these were isolated patches" (p. 124).[25]

Related to such affect substitutes is doubt about details closely associated with central matters. The novel begins with a doubt about a detail of the mother's affectlessly experienced death -- reminiscent of Leonardo's slip (cf. Freud, 1943, Vol. 8, pp. 190-91) in his diary notation of his father's death: "mother died today. Or, maybe, yesterday. I can't be sure. The telegram from the Home says: YOUR MOTHER PASSED AWAY. FUNERAL TOMORROW. DEEP SYMPATHY. Which leaves the matter doubtful; it could have been yesterday" (p. 1)....

I have up to now discussed the hero's defenses against affect. What are the particular affects which have been repressed, and whose repression is secured by the defenses described? I shall suggest that a major affect involved is murderous rage originally directed against the depriving parents.

Most of the evidence for this hypothesis has been neglected by the critics, who have thus not conveyed a full picture of the hero's manifest syndrome. When Edmund Wilson (The New Yorker, April 13, 1946) considers the possibility of of latent destructive tendencies of the hero, he rejects it as incompatible with his affectlessness: "At the moments when he ⌈Meursault⌋ has to decide whether to act in some definite way, he always thinks to himself, 'After all, it will make no difference whether I do or do not do this!' But the fact is that in spite of his

---

25. Some critics mistake such defenses for completions of impulse. Thus Richard Plant (Saturday Review of Literature, May 18, 1946), affirming that the hero's "animal instincts⌈sic⌋are nicely developed" gives as evidence that he notes with extraordinary sharpness "the heat, the faces of his mother's friends, the sharp light in the morgue."

supposed indifference, he does decide one way and not the other. He agrees to write the letter for the pimp [to an unfaithful prostitute on whom the pimp wants to avenge himself -- N.L.] , thus abetting him in an act of malevolence; therefore, he was either not indifferent to the interests of his acquaintance or not indifferent to the pimp's purpose of doing something mean to the girl. And since his killing of the Arab is deliberate ... he is, again, either not indifferent to the welfare of the pimp [whose enemy the Arab, the brother of the unfaithful prostitute, is -- N. L.] or not indifferent to killing an Arab.... These acts of his which are inconsistent with the assumption that he is genuinely indifferent are never accounted for." However, conscious indifference and intense unconscious destructiveness are not only a possible but even a typical combination. (Cf., for instance, Fenichel, 1945, p. 185)....

The hero presumably experiences intense guilt about the death of his mother, towards whom he has felt conscious, though consciously feeble, death wishes (pp. 14, 80). In accordance with his over-all techniques of defense against affect, he has largely repressed guilt feelings. When the magistrate asks him whether he regrets his murder, he answers that "what I felt was less regret (du regret véritable) than a kind of vexation (un certain ennui)" (p. 87). When the public prosecutor accuses him of his lack of guilt feelings about the murder, "I'd have liked to have a chance of explaining to him in a quite friendly, almost affectionate way, but I have never been able really to regret anything in all my life" (p. 127).

Having repressed his guilt feelings, the hero additionally projects the accuser into the outer world. While he consciously feels innocent of his mother's death, he believes exaggeratedly or at least prematurely that others accuse him of it, or of his behavior in connection with it. (As will be seen below, he behaves presumably in part with the unconscious intent of provoking accusations.) He tends spontaneously to react to such accusations apologetically rather than counterassertively. When he fixes up a two days' leave with his employer to attend his mother's funeral, "I had an idea he looked annoyed and I said, without thinking: 'Sorry, sir, but it isn't my fault, you know'" (p. 1). When the warden of the Home in which his mother died briefly recapitulates her history in the Home, "I had a feeling that he was blaming me for something [i.e. sending his mother to a Home -- N.L.] and started to explain" (p. 3). At the wake near his mother's coffin "for a moment I had an absurd impression that they [his mother's friends who are present -- N.L.] had come to sit in judgment on me" (p. 11). When he for the first time makes love to Marie the day after his mother's death and when Marie learns about this death, "I was just going to explain to her that it [his mother's death -- N.L.] wasn't my fault, but I checked myself as I remembered having said the same thing to my employer, and realizing then it sounded rather foolish (cela ne signifiait rien). Still, foolish or not,

somehow one can't help feeling a bit guilty, I suppose   (De toute façon, on est
toujours un pen fautif)" (p. 24). Finally, the public prosecutor at his trail affirms
emphatically that "this man ... is morally guilty of his mother's death," and
adds -- referring to a parricide which is on the court's agenda -- that "the
prisoner ... is also guilty of the murder to be tried tomorrow in this court"
(p. 128). The projected tends to return from projection: when the hero's "cal-
lousness" about his mother's death is shown in court, "I felt a sort of wave of
indignation spreading through the courtroom and for the first time I understood
that I was guilty" (p. 112).

　　Another major manifestation of the hero's intense unconscious rage consists
in the commission of acts which aggress his environment and provoke it into ag-
gressing him, thus alleviating his guilt. The self-destructive aspect of these acts
is only little conscious; and the same is true for the aggressive aspect of some
of them. For example, the hero adopts a "free association" policy in his verbal
utterances, however grave the consequences of this may be. When he is asked
to speak at his trial, "I said the first thing that crossed my mind ... as I felt in
the mood to speak" (p. 129). The hero is consistently and consciously frank, in
words and acts, in expressing the nonconformism corresponding to his affectlessness. (For many of the hero's fictional predecessors the refusal to conform to conventional modes of expressing affect had been related to the awareness of a unique intense nuance of affect which insisted on its own channels.)
He indicates clearly his lack of grief about the death of his mother and refuses
to go through the paces of conventional mourning behavior (p. 31, passim.), his
atheism (p. 85, passim), his lack of response to others as conveyed by silence.

　　The effect, of course, is to stimulate hostilities directed against himself.
But the hero scarcely -- or only belatedly -- recognizes this. He has, indeed,
little empathy for his environment's aggressive reactions to acts of his own
which are interpreted as aggressive. As he represses destructiveness in himself, he denies it in others. When he communicates to his lawyer his unfavorable attitudes toward his mother, the lawyer makes him promise "not to say
anything of that sort at the trial" (p. 80). Thereupon the hero attempts to satisfy
the lawyer: "Anyhow I could assure him of one thing: that I'd rather Mother
hadn't died." He has no awareness of the unfavorable impact of such a communication. On the contrary, a recurrent conscious motivation of his is "to keep out
of trouble," for example, by complying with demands made by others (cf. page
253 above). Similarly, at the trial (where he behaves with resigned passivity and
his usual provocative candor) he has great difficulties in realizing emotionally the
seriousness of the public intent to murder him for his murder. He exaggerates
the mildness of the world, and this is the counterpart to the presentation of the
world as deprivational by withholding: the world isn't sufficiently interested in
me to be out for my skin. (This belief also serves as a defense against panic.)
Thus the imprisoned hero lacks up to a late moment the conviction that he is in

danger: "At first I couldn't take him ⌈the examining magistrate -- N.L.⌋ quite
seriously. The room in which he interviewed me was much like an ordinary
sitting-room ..."(p. 78); "it all seemed like a game" (ibid.); "When leaving, I very
nearly held out my hand and said 'Good-bye!' (ibid.). When a routine of conversations between the magistrate, the hero, and his lawyer has become established,
"I began to breathe more freely. Neither of the two men, at these times, showed
the least hostility toward me, and everything went so smoothly, so amiably, that
I had an absurd impression of being 'one of the family'" (p. 88). When he first
sees his jury, "I felt as you do just after boarding a streetcar and you're conscious of all the people on the opposite seat staring at you in the hope of finding
something in your appearance to amuse them. Of course, I knew this was an
absurd comparison" (p. 103).

Beside chronic covert self-destructive aggressiveness stand major explosions of overt aggressiveness: the murder of the Arab and an assault on the
prison chaplain. A closer analysis of these acts may show how they fit into the
character structure hitherto described. How are the defenses against complet-
ing rage overcome?

1. The aggressions are felt as inexplicable explosions originating outside
the self and overwhelming it. "Then ⌈at a certain point in the protracted ex-
hortation addressed by the prison chaplain to the hero awaiting execution -- N.L.⌋
I don't know how it was, but something seemed to break (crever) inside me,
and I started yelling at the top of my voice. I hurled insults at him.... I'd taken
him by the neckband of his cassock, and, in a sort ecstasy of joy and rage
(colère), I poured out on him all the thoughts that had been simmering in my
brain" (p. 151).

The murder of the Arab is presented as forced upon the hero by the primarily somatic and only secondarily psychic impact of the heat (a projection of
the hero's impulses, we may surmise, onto emanations of the sun, a frequent
paternal symbol): "As I slowly walked towards the boulders at the end of the
beach ⌈where the hero will find his victim -- N.L.⌋ I could feel my temples
swelling under the impact of the light" (p. 73). When he is near the Arab, whose
posture is then entirely defensive, "it struck me that all I had to do was to turn,
walk away, and think no more about it. But the whole beach, pulsing with heat,
was pressing on my back (se pressait derrière moi). All the sweat that had
accumulated in my eyebrows splashed down on my eyelids, covering them with
a warm film of moisture. Beneath a veil of brine and tears my eyes were
blinded; I was conscious only of the symbols of the sun clashing on my skull"
(pp. 74-75). (The sun as inducer of "daze," while a bout of intense motor or
psychic activity is performed, recurs throughout the novel.)

The murder itself appears -- with a projection of destructiveness onto a
target yet more remote from the self -- as a cataclysmic release of violence
in nature: "Then everything began to reel before my eyes, a fiery gust came

from the sea, while the sky cracked in two, from end to end, and a great sheet of flame poured down through the rift" (p. 76).[26]

According to Newsweek (April 15, 1946) the hero "commits murder ... with the utmost casualness." According to Time Magazine (May 20, 1946) "he ... casually pulls the trigger of the revolver."

2. The hero consciously attempts to resist the explosion of aggression. First, he prevents his pimp acquaintance from shooting the Arab whom he later kills. When he walks on the beach in the direction of his victim, "each time I felt a hot blast strike my forehead, I gritted my teeth, I clenched my fists in my trouser pockets and keyed up every nerve to fend off the sun and the dark befuddlement (cette ivresse opaque) it was pouring into me ... my jaws set hard. I wasn't going to be beaten." But the very attempt to resist the consummation brings it nearer: The sun appears at this moment as "trying to check my progress" and thereby leading the resisting hero unknowingly toward his victim. Once confronted with this victim, the sun bars retreat (cf. above), although the hero, taking another step forward, "knew it was a fool thing to do" (p. 75).

3. The hero encounters his victim without knowing that he will do so: "I was rather taken aback" (p. 74).

4. The hero appears to himself as acting in self-defense. His fantasies of being destroyed (suggestive of castration anxieties) go far beyond the real threat. When "the Arab⌋ at a ⌈safe distance and with an apparently defensive purpose -- N.L.⌋ drew his knife and held it up towards me, athwart the sunlight ... "a shaft of light shot upward from the steel, and I felt as if a long, thin blade transfixed my forehead.... I was conscious ... of the keen blade of light flashing up from the knife, scarring my eyelashes and gouging into my eyeballs" (p. 75).

5. The hero has a conscious instrumental motivation in performing the acts leading up to his crime; this motivation is superego-syntonic. He approaches, unknowingly, his victim, who is in the shadow and near water, in search of relief from the sun. Walking on the beach, "the small black hump of rock ⌊behind which the Arab is lying -- N.L.⌋ came into view.... Anything ... to retrieve the pool of shadow by the rock and its cool silence (J'avais envie ... de retrouver l'ombre et son repos) ... I couldn't stand it ⌊the heat -- N.L.⌋ any longer, and took another step forward. I knew it was a fool thing to do; I wouldn't get out of the sun by moving on a yard or so. But I took that step, just one step, forward. And then the Arab drew his knife" (p. 75).

---

26. When violence begins, the projective impulsion by heat ceases: "The trigger gave.... I shook off my sweat and the clinging veil of light (J'ai secoué la sueur et le soleil)" (p. 76).
    The hero then goes on to fire four more shots. This the magistrate, the public prosecutor, and Edmund Wilson (The New Yorker, April 13, 1946) take as a conclusive indicator of "deliberateness." The novel gives no clues on the immediate context of these "loud, fateful rap(s) on the door of my undoing" (p. 76).

6. Guilt-alleviating and anxiety-enhancing factors such as the ones mentioned facilitate the temporary but total return of the repressed rage from repression. The self-punitive significance of such a return has the same effect. The heat driving the hero to murder and hence to his execution "was just the same sort of heat as at my mother's funeral" (p. 75): the hero atones for that funeral by arranging his own. He feels at the end that he is going to be "executed because he didn't weep at his mother's funeral" (p. 152).

In addition, "perhaps the only things I knew about him [the hero's father -- N.L.] were what Mother had told me. One of these was that he'd gone to see a murderer executed" (p. 138). Presumably the hero's own execution is in part for the benefit of this fantasied spectator who "had seen it through," although "the mere thought of it turned his stomach," and who afterwards was "violently sick" (p. 138). (Also "when we lived together, Mother was always watching me" -- p. 3). One may surmise that inducing the father to be sick has the significance of having a sexual relation with him. One may also surmise that being executed in front of the scoptophilic father has an exhibitionistic meaning. One may further assume that this act is an expiation for aggressive tendencies towards the father in general and his scoptophilia in particular: "at the time [when the hero's mother told him the story -- N.L.] I found my father's conduct rather disgusting. But now I understood; it was so natural" (p. 138). Furthermore, the hero identifies himself with a fantasied spectator of executions (his own?) and thus induces an oral scoptophilic and sadomasochistic ecstasy bordering on panic: "The mere thought of being an onlooker who comes to see the show and can go home and vomit afterward, floored my mind with a wild, absurd exultation (un flot de joie empoisonnée me montait au coeur) ... a moment later I had a shivering fit ... my teeth went on chattering"' (pp. 138-39).

These gratifications induce rationalizing elaborations of the fantasy of attending executions: "Often and often [awaiting his own execution -- N.L.] I blame myself for not having given more attention to accounts of public executions. One should always take an interest in such matters. There is never any knowing what one may come to.... How had I failed to recognize that nothing was more important than an execution; that, viewed from one angle, it's the only thing that can genuinely interest a man. And I decided that if I ever got out of jail I'd attend every execution that took place" (pp. 136-38).[27]

7. The hero's extreme aggressions are probably unconsciously intended

---

27. Some speculative points may be ventured here. The hero's interference with his destructive tendencies towards his father is accompanied by an identification with the (projectively) destructive father. In his pre-crisis equilibrium the hero is the consciously unintentional spectator of a number of beatings, and the equally unintentional audience of stories about beatings: He sees or hears an old man living in his house maltreating his dog, the pimp beating his unfaithful girl, a policeman beating the pimp, the pimp beating the Arab and being counterattacked by him. The pimp tells him about previous beatings of the girl and of the Arab. (While these habitual

to extort concern -- be it in the form of indulgences or deprivations -- from a
world whose real or fantasied neglect had induced chronic suicide by affectlessness. This syndrome breaks down when the hero, in the extreme situation of
impending execution, is exposed to affect indubitably directed towards him. He
is then able to drop the image of the world as essentially uninterested in him
and to react with felt affect to perceived affect. Having gotten a rise out of the
world, he can get one out of himself. When at a certain moment of his trial the
hero "for the first time realized how all these people loathed me ... I felt as I
hadn't felt for ages. I had a foolish desire to burst into tears" (p. 112). When
the owner of his habitual restaurant testifies in his favor with moist eyes and
trembling lips, "for the first time in my life I wanted to kiss a man" (p. 116).

8. Presumably, punishment means for the hero -- among other things --
love. In this context the story of Salamano, a degraded old man living in the
hero's apartment house, and his degraded dog, is relevant. (Thinking of Salamano "for some reason, I don't know what, I began thinking of Mother" -- p. 50.)
The spaniel -- of whom the hero's mother had been very fond -- is "an ugly
brute, afflicted with some skin disease -- it has lost all its hair and its body
is covered with brown scabs" (p. 32). The dog's relation to his master is presented as an extreme sadomasochistic one, with most of the overt sadism on
the side of the master. Salamano repeatedly utters death wishes towards the
dog. But when the maltreated spaniel finally escapes (to his death), Salamano
is in despair and expresses unconditional love for, as well as total dependence
on, the lost object.

9. Presumably the "you'll be sorry afterwards" theme just alluded to enters
into the hero's self-destructiveness. In prison he finds only one scrap of an old
newspaper reporting a murder case: A son is murdered by a mother who ignores
his identity. When she learns about it she commits suicide. "I must have read
that story thousands of times. In one way it sounded most unlikely, in another
it was plausible enough" (p. 100).[28]

10. The hero's acts of violence discharge to some extent his destructive
tendencies; hence a diminution of the counter-cathexis which is expended on
interfering with them. Therefore, the degree of the hero's affectlessness de-

---

"affectionate-like" beatings of the girl "ended as per usual," the hero's
love-making to Marie is free from overt destructive admixtures.)
In the murder of the Arab, however, he makes the decisive transition towards an act of violence of his own. On behalf of what may be a degraded
father figure (the pimp) he aggresses (by his complicity in the pimp's revenge scheme) what may be a degraded mother figure (the pimp's Arab
girl) and destroys her brother-defender himself? If so, his murder would
be a suicide not only in its unconscious provocative intent but also in its
immediate significance.
28. If this were a "real-life" case, the exposure of the subject to the story would
be regarded as accidental and his reaction to it as significant. As this is
a fantasy case, both are significant. This point is implicit in certain preceding passages of this paper, e.g. in the discussion of the hero as a frequent spectator of beatings (cf. footnote 27, page 261).

creases during his sojourn in prison. He discovers memory; time had been more difficult to kill in freedom. Now he can express affectionate tendencies towards the punishing world: "I can honestly say that during the eleven months these examinations [by the Magistrate -- N.L.] lasted I got so used to them that I was almost surprised at having ever enjoyed anything better than those rare moments when the Magistrate after escorting me to the door of the office would pat my shoulder and say in a friendly tone: 'Well, Mr. Antichrist, that's all for the present'" (p. 88). After his second act of violence -- directed, this time, against an obvious father figure, the prison chaplain, and rendering his execution doubly certain -- his affectionate tendencies are more fully released and attain the level of serene happiness: "It was as if that great rush of anger had washed me clean (come si cette grande colère m'avait purgé du mal)" (p. 154). After the assault the hero falls asleep from exhaustion. Awakening he experiences a reconciliation with the indifferent world and its prototypes, the indifferent parents; he can love them though he knows they do not love him: "... for the first time, the first, I laid my heart open to the benign (tendre) indifference of the universe. To feel it so like myself, indeed so brotherly." "Almost for the first time in many months I thought of my mother" (p. 153). He "understands" -- and identifies with -- her having played at making a fresh start just before her death by taking on a "fiancé" in the Home for the Aged where she lived. The novel ends with the re-evocation of the father's execution scoptophilia and with a leap from the acceptance of the indifferent world to the acceptance of the punishing world: "For all to be accomplished, for me to feel less lonely, all that remained to hope was that on the day of my execution there should be a huge crowd of spectators and that they should greet me with howls of execration (haine)."

A satisfactory language of aesthetics scarcely exists. If it did, I would attempt to formulate in it a favorable judgment on The Stranger. Assuming such a judgment, it may be surmised that the psychological plausibility (in this case, the "common sense" implausibility) of the content contributes to the aesthetic value of the novel -- which, on the other hand, depends on "formal" characteristics. Among these there is one of general importance which can be particularly well shown in this novel with its unusual terseness and concreteness of style: the high degree of implicitness of the unconscious content layers. That is, the reader is not (as he is in numerous "psychologically oriented" contemporary productions) told in so many words, or obtrusively led to see, connections of the order of those discussed in this paper. Conceivably the author is less than fully aware of these connections and certainly the critics -- and those readers for whom they speak -- are largely unaware of them. The conditions and consequences of the antagonism between explicitness and aesthetic impact -- an antagonism which has, of course, already received psycholanalytic attention -- seem to warrant further speculation and research.

PART SIX

FILM ANALYSIS

A. Movie Analyses in the Study of Culture

Martha Wolfenstein

This paper will be concerned with the analysis of the content of fiction (or entertainment) films in relation to the study of culture. Other kinds of films and other modes of approach will not be discussed. So, for instance, I shall not attempt to deal with propaganda, documentary, or experimental films. I shall leave aside the investigation of such topics as film history, film production, film technique, the relation of visual to sound effects, comparison of the film with other media such as the novel, questions of aesthetic evaluation.

First, I shall consider briefly the theoretical background of film analysis in relation to cultural studies. Second, I shall elaborate and illustrate procedures for the analysis of movie content. (I shall confine myself to questions of interpretation and shall not discuss observational procedure, for instance, with respect to frequency of viewing the same film, methods of note taking, etc.) I shall attempt to indicate how recurrent movie themes are related to variables of dynamic psychology, and how one can on this basis characterize groups of films within a given culture and compare films of different cultures. Third, I shall indicate some relations of movie themes to their cultural context, pointing out certain of the problems involved in connecting movie plots with real-life behavior and character.

1. Background of the Cultural Study of Movies

It is useful to bear in mind the relation of movie plots to stories and dramas in other and older media, and to recognize some of the theoretical antecedents of the recently developed skill of movie interpretation. The analysis of literary and other art forms in relation to their cultural contexts has developed from the convergence of a number of trends in modern thought. Of these the following may be noted here:

a. Philosophical theories of the differences of art styles of different epochs. The German and French romantics attempted to express what they felt to be major and discontinuous differences in the outlook on life of the ancient world and that of the modern world, and connected with them differences in what they called classic and romantic art styles. A late and elaborate expression of this view appeared in the work of Spengler (1918), in which for each of a number of cultures the styles of art, religion, philosophy, science, technology, and social organization were seen as interrelated.

b. The interpretation of folklore as a culture trait. Traditional tales, having been variously interpreted as concealing remote historical happenings, containing allegories or figurative explanations of events in nature, and so on, came increasingly to be regarded as expressions of the attitudes, daydreams, ethics, and mode of life of the people among whom they were told. This approach, as formulated by Boas and by Benedict (1931), parallels on a more empirical level the approach of the romantic philosophers to the productions of historical cultures.

c. Universal psychological motifs as sources of recurrent mythological themes. After Freud had recognized the relation of the Oedipus myth to a universal human conflict, Otto Rank wrote Der Mythus von der Geburt des Helden (1909), in which he showed a common pattern in myths of various sources (of the birth of Buddha, of Jesus, et al.). Rank carried this approach further in Das Inzest Motiv in Dichtung und Sage (1912), in which he also applied the idea that the manner of expressing certain common themes varies through time. The relation of mythology to universal human fantasies has been most elaborated by the school of Jung (cf., for instance, the recent Hero with a Thousand Faces by Joseph Campbell, 1949).

d. Studies of the work of individual artists in relation to their life histories. This was also initiated by Freud (1943), in his study of Leonardo, and has remained the preferred approach to art of the Freudian school (cf., for instance, Marie Bonaparte's book on Poe, 1933; Ella Sharpe's essays on Shakespeare, 1950).

Contemporary cultural anthropology combines something from each of these approaches in interpreting art productions. It looks for regularities running through all the productions of a culture: its religious rituals, secular dances, myths, ornaments, and the like. At the same time it relates these to genetic psychological material drawn from the typical life cycle of individuals of the given culture. The universal psychological motifs serve to guide the observation both of the life course of members of the culture and of their artistic and other productions. The analysis of Balinese dances in their relation to other aspects of Balinese life, and especially to the characteristic parent-child relations, in the work of Margaret Mead, Gregory Bateson (Bateson and Mead, 1942), and Jane Belo (1949) is illustrative.

While a variety of considerations are combined in the analysis of a work of art from the point of view of its cultural relevance, such an analysis is also selective. This selectivity may be expressed in terms of grouping: With what other works are we going to group this one for the purpose of our study? For the purpose of cultural studies, we group the work with others that have been produced by members of the same culture. That we choose to work with this grouping of material does not exclude the usefulness for other purposes of other groupings. A particular work of art may be grouped with other works of the same artist and we may try to see what are his characteristic themes and ways of treating them. It may be grouped with other works of a particular school of art, with other works of its period, with other works in the same medium, with all other productions growing out of human fantasy. According to the grouping we choose we will get formulations of different levels of generality and pay attention to different orders of likeness and variation. The generalizations obtained from one kind of grouping do not preclude those from another. Thus, for instance, we may want to consider Oedipus, Hamlet, and The Brothers Karamazov from the point of view of their common aspect as Oedipal tragedies. If we want to take into consideration the culture and epoch in which these various works were produced, while not denying their common features, we should proceed to analyze the different ways in which they deal with their common problem. For this purpose we should look for relations between each of these works and others of its culture and epoch, and so on.

In the analysis of works of art for the purpose of cultural studies, cross-cultural comparisons, whether explicit or implicit, are indispensable. Without such comparisons we may attribute to a particular culture tendencies that are more widely shared (cf. Spengler, 1918). Thus, for instance, an attempt to reconcile goodness and badness in a woman is common to the literature and the drama of a number of Western cultures (and also, among other things, distinguishes them from cultures in which this emotional problem does not occur). If we want to distinguish between, let us say, French and American cultures, we must analyze the different ways in which they proceed to reconcile goodness and badness in their dramatic heroines. (A useful exercise for the beginner in cultural analysis of films is to compare films of two or more cultures which deal with a common topic such as the one mentioned.)

2. Procedures in Analyzing Movie Content

A general approach to the interpretation of movie content is as follows: (1) We have a set of concepts and propositions from dynamic psychology (e.g. those having to do with Oedipal conflicts). (2) These suggest a number of variables that can be illustrated in film content (e.g. father-son relations). (3) A particular way of handling such a variable in a film constitutes a theme (e.g. the father figure attacking the son figure). (4) Such a theme may be interpreted by applying propositions of dynamic psychology. We formulate a hypothesis about the derivation of the theme from underlying psychological motives (e.g. the son's hostility is projected onto the father).

In practice our observations and interpretations do not necessarily follow this logical sequence. We may observe a theme and subsequently attempt to relate it to variables derived from our psychological presuppositions. We may also be led by our observations to enlarge or modify our general psychological formulations. In other words, there is an interplay between observations and general ideas; the movement between them is in both directions.

To elaborate further on variables and themes, a variable indicates a general area to be observed, such as father-son relations, mother-son relations, father-daughter relations. A theme is the way in which a particular variable is repeatedly concretized in the productions of a particular culture. Thus, for instance, the moral superiority of a son (or son figure) to a father (or father figure) is a theme of American films; the moral superiority of a father (or father figure) to a son (or son figure) is a theme of British films. These two themes represent different positions in relation to the variable of father-son relations. Their relation to a common variable provides a basis for comparison.

A theme is a unit that recurs. That we look for recurrences is not a peculiar point of film analysis, but is rather a requirement of scientific method, which is concerned not with the unique instance but with regularities. In the preliminary phase of our analysis, what we take as a theme is a matter of convenience. It can be anything from a single image to a total plot configuration. Eventually one attempts to work out interconnections among the themes one has observed in the films of a particular culture. The procedure might be described in somewhat this way. To begin with, if we have seen one film of a particular culture, or several, or a considerable number, but have not yet begun any analysis of them, we are apt to have some vague over-all impressions of their atmosphere. If we think of going to see a French film, an Italian, a Russian, a German, or an American film, we will anticipate a certain quality or flavor of each of these experiences, a certain recognizable world, characteristic of each. The aim of our analysis is to substitute for such inarticulate impressions a structured account of what has happened to produce them. In the transition from impressions to analysis, we work with themes of various degrees of particularity and inclusiveness.

We may cite as illustration a variety of themes, and also suggest in part the way they work into larger constructs. A recurrent theme of British films is the image of a bowed blond head. We get some idea of the significance of this image in relation to the recurrent temptation and danger in British films of men destroying women they love. Kracauer (1947) has observed in pre-Nazi German films the often repeated image of a man leaning his head on a woman's bosom (and we may note that this persists in post-World War II German films). This is associated with a total plot theme in which the hero attempts to rebel against a petty and stuffy family existence but fails, and returns to it beaten and chastened. A certain character type may be taken as a theme, as for instance the good-bad girl of American films, or the prostitute redeemed by love in French films. The good-bad girl fits in with the larger thematic constellation of eating-your-cake-and-having-it in American films and the pervasive trend of denying painful experiences. One can have both the attractiveness of the bad girl and the loyalty of the good; and it is not necessary to acknowl-edge any disappointments in love. In the French alternative, even though the prostitute becomes exclusively devoted to the hero, her previous involvement with other men is recognized.

The ways of characterizing certain groups may be taken as themes, as for instance the way in which the police are depicted. In American films the police are often mistaken, and the private investigator must solve the mystery. In British films, the police are almost always right. In both cases, the image of the police corresponds to the image of the father.

The quality of relationships may be taken as a theme. Thus in American films the hero remains tentative in his feelings for an attractive unknown wom-an; if she turns out to be bad, he can always detach himself. In French films, the hero is more apt to become hopelessly bound to the beautiful unknown and is unable to free himself even when he learns of her wickedness. These alter-natives are related to the general tendencies already mentioned to deny love dis-appointments in American films and to evoke them in French films.

One may also take a total plot configuration as a theme, for instance the recurrent plot of American film comedies in which the hero, alternating between delusions of strength and craven apprehensions of weakness, meets with a series of accidental circumstances, or events contrived by others without his knowl-edge, of such a sort that they confirm his fantasies of omnipotence. As a re-sult of the benevolence of the environment he ends up ecstatically triumphant despite his almost complete incompetence.

The level of concreteness or abstractness on which one works is largely a matter of convenience and individual preference. However, it is probably useful on the whole to work initially with themes of considerable specificity, to stay close to the concreteness of the material. Eventually a number of related themes will group themselves together. This may be illustrated from a study of American movies (cf. Wolfenstein and Leites, 1950). One of the most in-clusive themes turned out to be that of false appearances. We found that for-bidden wishes tended to be expressed as false appearances, and the eventual clearing-up of the false appearance had the significance of demonstrating that no one should be blamed or feel guilty for mere wishes. This generalization only emerged after we had observed a number of themes on a lower level of general-ity the interrelations of which were not at first evident. Thus we had observed the theme of the good-bad girl, the heroine who looks promiscuous but turns out to be quite innocent. We had similarly noted the recurrent predicament of the melodrama hero who is falsely accused, who looks guilty, but in the end succeeds in clearing himself. Comedies repeatedly presented situations where to an inquisitive but mistaken bystander a young couple seemed to be having an illicit affair, a husband seemed to be sharing his wife with his best friend, and so on. Presumably we might by an intellectual leap have arrived at the general concept of false appearances at an early stage of our analysis, in which case we would have had to proceed to observe in detail the various subthemes in which this major theme was illustrated. Proceeding in either direction is feasible, but it seems likely that if high-level generalizations are attempted at too early a stage, insufficient attention may be paid to the wealth of illustrative variations.

Within any one film a number of themes are apt to be repeated. For instance, Gregory Bateson (1945)[1] analyzes the two occasions on which the hero confronts death in Hitlerjunge Quex, the first in which his mother commits suicide by turning on the gas and the hero barely escapes, the second in which he is murdered by the Communists. The attendant circumstances of each of these deaths are remarkably similar. Each follows an achievement on the hero's part, and is associated with a beloved woman. Each is represented by a billowing movement on the screen (of gas, of a fluttering flag), and by a change from darkness to light. Each marks a change in the hero's status and is preceded by words of his anticipating a wonderful future. This repeated sequence within the film was underscored by analogous sequences in other Nazi films, and was interpreted by Bateson as expressing a mystical expectation of passing "through death to a millennium."

Similarly, Erik H. Erikson in his study of the film The Childhood of Maxim Gorky (1950a) observes how repeatedly the young hero, confronted with family scenes of intense emotional excitement, watches but does not participate. Thus non-participation is interpreted as expressing resistance to emotional temptations that would bind the young hero to the old way of life. By non-participation he reserves himself for another world of the future.

We may proceed to make more explicit the characteristics of variables and themes used in the kind of film analysis described here (cf. Wolfenstein and Leites, 1950). Any number of other variables besides those so far illustrated might be chosen. For instance, we might observe the number of characters who appear on the screen at any moment. How many and how long are the sequences in which no characters appear, in which one character appears alone, in which only two characters appear, or three characters, or more, and what is the pattern of alternation of such sequences? We should be inclined to say that variables of this sort would be likely to be meaningful for us only in relation to other variables, of more direct psychological import, as, for instance, the emotional significance of being alone, the meaning of the larger group in relation to the individual's wishes, and so on. The main variables with which we work are chosen because they are related to what we presume to be major emotional concerns of the producers and the audiences. On the whole our assumptions about what is emotionally important derive from contemporary dynamic psychology.

---

1.   Selections from this analysis are reproduced below, pages 302-14. -- Ed.

Having observed certain recurrent themes that illustrate a certain variable, we proceed to interpret them in terms of the underlying psychological presuppositions which guided us in our selection of the variable. In this we are advancing hypotheses about the emotional processes in the producers and the audiences. These hypotheses would require verification by more direct study of members of these two groups.

To indicate schematically these interrelations, suppose our variable is father-son relations. Behind our choice of this variable is our knowledge of Oedipal conflicts and their role in emotional development. We find in a certain group of American films that father figures appear as criminal and dangerously attacking; the hero would be justified in killing them in self-defense, but usually someone else does this for him. In interpreting such a fantasy, we regard it as a variety of solution of Oedipal conflicts, one in which a particular combination of defenses has been employed. So, for instance, the Oedipal hostility of the son appears to be projected into the father; it is denied in the son, thus relieving him of guilt. The son is given a moral justification for attacking the father, since the father attacks him first. However, the son does not destroy the father; someone does it for him. His hostility, even though justified, is again projected. Here the mechanism of projection seems to operate to reduce guilt for Oedipal hostility both by denying it and by justifying it. In making such an interpretation we are assuming that this sort of transformation of Oedipal conflicts has gone on in the producers in their invention of such plots and that the film may offer similar emotional solutions to the audiences. (We do not infer that in actual life producers and audiences resolve their Oedipal conflicts in this way. We consider only the derivation and the impact of the fantasy conveyed in the film. We shall have something to say later about the relations between such fantasies and actual character.)

We may now illustrate more fully the relation of a variable to a group of themes. Let us take as our variable a situation in which one character is the onlooker in the relation of a man and woman to each other. If we consider some of the emotional undertones we would expect such a situation to evoke, we note that it is obviously related to Oedipal conflicts. However, it is more specific; it focuses on the situation where the child discovers, or further observes, the relationship between the parents and reacts to the fact of his exclusion from it. We would consider this to be a major background experience contributing to the emotional significance of scenes where an onlooker observes a couple. It is often useful for purposes of observation to choose as our variable a situation of this sort which is close to the level of concrete content. In practice we do not choose such a variable in advance, but decide to work with it when we find that themes illustrating it occur in our material. We have found the variable of the onlooker and the couple frequently illustrated in both American and French films. (British films seem to be less often concerned with it.)

Some of the most recurrent themes dealing with the onlooker and the couple in American films are the following:

1. The hero sees the heroine with another man and suspects that there is some intense relation between them. He later learns that the relation he imagined between them never existed (Gilda; The Big Sleep).

2. The hero observes a couple together but what happens between them is repulsive or pitiable rather than enviable. For instance, the hero sees through the window that the husband shoots his wife and then commits suicide (The Strange Love of Martha Ivers).

3. A comic character sees the hero and heroine together and mistakenly imagines they are having an illicit affair, or sees the hero or heroine with another partner and again imagines an illicit relation. Nothing is really happening between the observed couple (She Wouldn't Say Yes; Guest Wife).

4. A friend of the hero observes the hero and heroine and assumes a bored, little-boyish attitude toward their being so romantic: "Do I have to listen to all this mush?" (Pardon My Past) This is closely related to the instance where a kid brother, not yet eligible for romance, finds the amorous entanglements of an older brother and sister "all very dumb" (Kiss and Tell).

5. A friendly onlooker promotes the relation of the couple. This may be an elderly parental character, but it may even be the heroine's rival for the hero's love who, having lost out, quickly shifts to becoming a friend of the family (Love Letters; The Bells of St. Mary's; Adventure).

To summarize the main trends in this material: The observed couple do not do anything, or if they do it is not anything that could arouse jealousy or envy, but just the opposite. If the onlooker is jealous, he learns that this feeling was ungrounded (the couple did not do anything). More often the onlooker is not affected by what he observes, or thinks he observes. He may be just a comical passer-by, unrelated to the couple. Or he may be a friend, but then he is humorously indifferent to their involvement with each other, or else he may help to promote it.

French films frequently present the following themes in the treatment of the the onlooker and the couple:

1. The hero first sees a beautiful woman alone, thinks of her as pure, and falls in love with her. Later he sees her together with another man with whom she is seriously involved. This disastrous discovery does not undo the hero's attachment to the woman, which proves fatal for him (Panique; La Passionelle; Martin Roumagnac).

2. An onlooker who is debarred from love sees an amorous couple and reacts with despair or rage. A precocious bespectacled twelve-year-old girl, for instance, sees her aunt's lover enter the aunt's bedroom. As the door closes, she bursts into a storm of tears (Le Corbeau). A hideous dwarf or an embittered spinster may react to their experiences as onlookers of others' happiness with vindictive fury (L'Eternel Retour; L'Amour autour de la Maison).

3. A man who has suffered disappointment in love directs a play in which the woman he loves and his successful rival appear as happy lovers while he looks on (Les Enfants du Paradis; Le Silence Est d'Or).

The main tendencies expressed in these scenes are the following: The relation between the observed couple is an intense and enviable one. The onlooker experiences great suffering in observing them. He may already be in love with one of them so that the discovery of their relation is a painful surprise and disappointment to him. But even if he is not closely involved with them, the realization of his loveless and excluded position is extremely bitter. The onlooker's involvement with the couple may be fatal for him, or may move him to destructive rage toward them. The onlooker may re-evoke his suffering by repeating the occasion of it in a dramatic performance.

The French treatment of the onlooker and the couple is in marked contrast to the American treatment. We may now proceed to an interpretation of these alternate themes. If we assume that a major source for fantasies about the couple and the observer is the childhood situation in which the child observes the parental couple and discovers a relation between them from which he is excluded, it would seem that French and American makers of films have handled very differently the emotions evoked by this experience. French films seem to repeat with relatively little distortion the painful feelings involved in the original situation. The observed couple are indeed intensely bound to each other. The onlooker suffers from the awareness of his exclusion. The experience of the little boy who has loved the mother before he became aware of her relation to the father is repeated in the plots where the hero makes a corresponding discovery about the woman he loves, whom he has first seen alone and then later sees with the other man. The difficulty of giving up this loved woman (the mother), the possible disastrous consequence (for the man who cannot free himself from his involvement with the parental couple), the chagrin, the despair, and the murderous rage, are recognizably reproduced. A probable motive for this re-evocation is suggested by the plots in which the hero as dramatist transforms his love disappointment into a play. Through such a transformation one can experience actively what one previously has undergone passively, and one may by going over it inure oneself to the painful experience. Further observations have suggested that this may be a fairly pervasive motive in the formation of plots of French films -- we can reduce suffering from the numerous inevitable frustrations of life by again and again facing the painful situations. In this way our unrealistic wishes may become chastened and our tolerance for frustration be increased. The principle is similar to that of Mithridates, who by taking a little poison every day succeeded in becoming immune to it.

In American film plots the experience of the child with the parents seems to have undergone much more distortion. The device of denial seems to have been extensively applied. Nothing happens between the observed couple, or at least nothing enviable. The onlooker, whether involved with the couple or just a passer-by, is unaffected by envy or jealousy. Though he may himself be loveless, the sight of the couple's happiness does not rouse any longing in him. The sequence of childhood events in which the little boy first loves his mother and then discovers her relation to the father is reversed in the plot where the hero first sees the heroine with another man, then later learns that there is no relation between them. The choice of this sort of solution to an emotional problem is illustrated in other aspects of American films. As we have already remarked, there is a tendency to deny painful feelings or feelings that involve conflict (as, for instance, hostility toward the father). There is a tendency to deny disappointing experiences. Also emotional involvement with the past, with the family one comes from, is apt to be represented as tenuous or easily dissolved. But even more recent attachments, if they threaten to lead to danger or distress, are relatively easily abandoned. The hero does not remain hopelessly bound to a woman who turns out to be bad. He is apt to keep his feeling for her rather tentative until he has investigated her sufficiently. Liability to serious disappointment or frustration appears as much less an inevitable part of life than it does in French films.

To sum up, in the treatment of the onlooker and the couple, French films seem to re-evoke the feelings of disappointment of the child in order to inure us to them. American film plots tend to solve the problem by denying that anything painful has happened. The differences in themes are derived from the choice of different devices for resolving a common emotional problem.

Our actual procedure in the study of films is somewhat less neat and simple than this account may suggest. Scenes involving an onlooker and a couple occur here and there in the scores of films we see. They are recorded along with a large number of other themes and tentatively interpreted in a variety of ways, depending on their varying contexts. As we begin to organize our data, we may decide to group some of it around the variable of the onlooker and the couple. The material we group around this variable will be at least in part relevant to a number of other variables, for instance, goodness and badness in women, the significance of looking. That is, some of the onlooker and couple material will also be classified with other material relating to goodness and badness in women, and so on. Moreover, we will be working throughout on continually modified formulations of a fairly inclusive sort in which we attempt to connect up a large number of themes in French films or in American films. The analysis of the onlooker and couple themes given here is not arrived at until a rather late stage in our over-all analysis of French and American films.

3. Movie Themes and Their Cultural Context

Let us now turn to consider the relation between the psychological processes we take to be characteristic of a particular culture in the development of movie plots and the prevailing real life character structure of the producers and the audiences. On this extremely difficult question we can at least say that the re-lation is complicated and probably not uniform for different cultures. For instance, we have noted that French film plots seem frequently to derive from the motive of inuring oneself to the painful aspects of reality, while American film plots seem to be more often derived from the operation of projection and denial. Can we infer from this that French character is more dominated by the reality principle, while American character gives freer sway to unrealis-tic infantile mechanisms? Such an inference would not be warranted. Ameri-cans may be readier to regress for purposes of fantasy enjoyment. The French, on the other hand, may strive to achieve in art an attitude of wise resignation that they do not necessarily maintain in real-life situations. In other words, the possible relations between character and preferred fantasies are numerous. We cannot simply infer one from the other. It is necessary to have independent evidence on both topics.

We may, however, attempt to indicate, on the basis of admittedly frag-mentary evidence, some possible connections between movie fantasies and character structure. These connections are suggested less for their substan-tive value than as illustrative of the kinds of relations that may be found. In films, as in drama generally, we experience vicariously the carrying-through of violent impulses to a degree that few of us can manage in actuality. This unleashed dramatic violence assumes a variety of forms. For instance, fre-quently in British films (as, for instance, also in many British novels, from Clarissa on) the victim is a woman. We see numerous heroes who are driven by an impulse to destroy the women they love, or for whom this is a terrible temptation, or who, despite their struggles, are carried away by this impulse, or who, though blameless, suspect themselves of such tendencies. A good father figure warns and guards the hero against his destructive tendencies to-wards the woman (cf. Ghost of Hamlet's Father: "Taint not thy mind, nor let thy soul contrive/ Against they mother aught"). One of the indictments against an inadequate father figure is that he fails to prevent the hero from destroying the beloved woman.

We may assume that the kind of defenses that are erected against destruc-tive tendencies are related to the aim of these tendencies, which is variable, and to which fantasies give us a clue. If a major British fantasy of what would happen if destructive tendencies were set loose involves the destruction of a beloved woman, an appropriate defense against such tendencies would be their transformation via a reaction formation into tenderness and protective con-cern for the weak. Some observations of British character tend to suggest that this is a chosen defense against destructiveness. The protection of the weak, as exemplified in the well-known British preoccupation with prevention of cruelty to animals, seems to be a prominent British tendency. In other words, if fantasies as embodied in films show what unopposed impulses would look like, they can give us clues as to why certain defenses have been chosen in the struggle against impulses.

In American films, by contrast, violence appears much more often as an attack against the hero by dangerous and powerful agencies. For protection against violence envisaged in this form, toughness rather than tenderness would seem to be an appropriate character trait. And it would seem that American men do value toughness to a higher degree than is the case with Britons.

These instances suggest one possible kind of relation between chosen fantasies and character, but they also raise many more questions. We should like to know what sort of life experiences, starting with the family situation, have favored such different fantasies of what unleashed violence would look like. In the case of the British, why is male violence aimed to such a degree against women? In the American instance, what has encouraged the projection of destructiveness and consequent justification of toughness? We do not propose to answer these questions here, but raise them to indicate the extent of the problem.

We have suggested one possible kind of relation between chosen fantasies and character structure -- that the fantasies represent impulse completion while the related real-life character is constituted of defenses against these impulses. However, there are other possibilities. In some cases impulses may be carried through to a greater extent in actuality; fiction and life might parallel each other. There is some evidence to suggest that in Russian life there is a distinctive tendency to act out extreme fantasies. Literature and drama would thus tend to repeat or to anticipate actual events. For example, certain novels written in the period immediately following the Russian Revolution anticipated in remarkable detail the later extreme regimentation of life and also the trials of the Old Bolsheviks (cf. Zamiatin's We; Rodonov's Chocolate).

Within a particular culture there may be certain areas where chosen fantasies and actual behavior are complementary, others where they are similar. In American films we find some themes that seem to correspond to real life. There is, for instance, the good-bad girl. This type of heroine, who looks so promiscuous, whose attractiveness is enhanced by her apparent involvement with other men, but who in the end turns out to love only the hero, seems to be a dramatic version of the American popular girl, who is attractive because she dates so many men, but who manages not to get too deeply involved with any of them until she finds the right one.

There is the further possibility that in life certain impulses are carried through while in art defenses against these impulses are expressed. Erikson in analyzing the film of Maxim Gorky's childhood is reminded of certain events of Russian history. There is a scene in the film in which the grandfather, after having beaten the boy, sits beside the boy's bed and tries to conciliate him. Erikson (1950a), recalls in this connection the famous painting of Ivan the Ter-

rible holding in his arms the corpse of his son whom he has murdered. And he
recalls that not only Ivan, but also Peter the Great, murdered his son. We do
not know whether in fact Ivan held his son in his arms after having murdered
him. Possibly this posthumous love, guilt, and longing to undo appears in art
more than in life in Russian culture. The serfs who killed the father of Dosto-
evsky probably did not feel the complicated repercussions of conscience of the
sons of the murdered Karamazov. If this would be the case, we would have an
instance where the crude unleashing of impulse is more extreme in life than in
art. This would be the reverse of the relation we thought might obtain in British
culture, where destruction raged in literature and gentleness was more the rule
in life.

We have considered the following possible relations between fiction and
character: that a similar form of impulse gratification occurs in both; that fiction shows freedom of impulse and character defenses against it, and that conversely impulses are released in actuality while fiction expresses defenses
against these impulses. There is a fourth possibility, that defenses against
impulse are expressed both in fiction and in real-life character. This could
probably be illustrated in some Victorian literature (e.g. Coventry Patmore's
The Angel in the House). Clearly it would be an oversimplification to suppose
that a particular culture might be characterized by a single type of relationship
between fiction and life. One would have to work out, given adequate data, in
which areas which kinds of relationships obtained.

Let us consider briefly the relation between the circumstances of real life
-- for instance, in the kind of family relations that prevail -- and the preferred
fantasies of a given culture. In American life it would seem that children are
encouraged to outgrow and surpass their parents. We do not need to go into the
various factors that contribute to this. We will only remark that it is not considered ideal or adequate simply to reproduce the life of one's parents, to live in
the same house, to pursue the same occupations. The expectation that the children will surpass the parents would seem to contribute to several of the fantasies
we have found to be recurrent in American films. The projection of the son's
bad impulses onto the father may be facilitated by the circumstance that from an
early age the son is encouraged to regard himself as potentially superior to the
father. Similarly, the fact that children are encouraged to strike out on their
own rather than to wait for a paternal inheritance may facilitate the fantasy that
old emotional bonds are easily dissolved. The converse would seem to have
been the case in France, where family property was transmitted and preserved
from generation to generation, and children often had to wait well into middle
age to achieve independence, which only came with the parent's death. The
theme of French films having to do with the difficulty of detaching oneself from
from old involvements may be related to this. What accounts for the preference
for one or another arrangement of family life is a further question, and one we
cannot answer.

In view of what has just been said, we should perhaps qualify our earlier remarks about French and American handling of the onlooker and couple situation. In interpreting these contrasting treatments we implied that different defenses were being employed to cope with the same emotional experience. We should now add that not only in fantasy productions but also in life the original family situation has been treated in different ways. The disappointment that an American little boy feels in discovering the love relation between his parents is qualified from the start by his being treated by both parents as one who is bound to surpass his father. In French families, the childhood experience may well have been more poignant insofar as the little boy felt that it would be long before he succeeded the father, whom he would never surpass. It seems that the fantasies about father figures in American films may be on a more infantile level because in life the son's conscious concern with the father is apt to come to an end as soon as the son is grown up. In France, where the grown-up son was still much involved with his family of origin, the image of the father was apt to be worked over in the light of adult experience, and the more complicated and sympathizable father figures of French films (so often portrayed by the late Raimu) would seem to have developed from this.

To sum up these latter points, which are intended to be merely suggestive, the way in which family and other relationships are styled in a particular culture probably contributes to the preference for certain fantasies. The form the real life relationships assume may be reflected in the favored fantasies. Depending on the defensive structure embodied in prevailing character types, preferred fantasies may coincide with or represent the opposite of actual behavior. Since the possible relations between the preferred fantasies of a culture embodied in films, and other art forms, and actual character are so various one cannot infer one from the other; it is necessary to have independent information on both in order to see how they are related.

B. FIVE ILLUSTRATIONS OF FILM ANALYSIS

Introduction

Rhoda Métraux

In this section of the Manual are presented examples of thematic analyses of fiction films, analyses made by members of Research in Contemporary Cultures and others working on five different cultures, all of them at a distance. The intention is to show, through the presentation of working papers (originally intended for use in discussion) as well as completed research, work of this kind at different stages of completion, made for several purposes and variously inclusive.

So, for instance, the notes on The Tragic Hunt, an Italian film, were the first record of a film seen once as part of a sequence of Italian films; as the notes were intended for later comparison, the record was as complete as possible. In contrast, the notes on two French films, Panique and La Belle et la Bête, made by two different persons, were intended to document a theme of specific interest at the time; here only the relevant details were recorded. (Both films were, however, described more fully by other members of the same working group.) The excerpt from an analysis of seven Cantonese films is from a later stage in the work, when the preliminary material on a number of films was being organized as a whole. The comparison of the Russian film The Young Guard with the novel from which it was taken is based on one or two viewings of the film by several individuals, but depends, in its detail, upon previous knowledge of a large number of Russian films seen and analyzed, and upon long research on the culture (whereas, for instance, the French analyses were made at an earlier stage of research); and whereas all the others were working from positions outside the culture studied, the Russian analyst was working, in a measure, from within, using her own experience and reactions as cues. Finally, the analysis of the German film Hitlerjunge Quex, which is both the earliest in point of time and the fullest, was a first attempt to explore character structure through intensive study of one film in which informants and other materials (films, photographs, written descriptions, etc.) were included as they illuminated the problems presented by this film. These analyses, necessarily brief as presented here and outside the specific contexts in which they were made, are intended to suggest kinds of thematic analysis that can be done in various circumstances -- when a film can be seen repeatedly, when the analyst does not have the language and is dependent upon establishing linkages among the large number of visual clues, when film analysis can be combined (as, essentially, it must be) with other sorts of material. There is not, however, included any analysis in which audience reaction forms part of what is studied -- except insofar as the analyst himself (or herself) has already become aware of significant plot details, images, recurrent symbols, and so on.

Nor have these analyses been worked out, except incidentally, in terms of techniques of film making or the use of sound patterns (voices, music, etc.) or, though they differ in this, the formal aspects of visual imagery. These too, though possibly not singly, are possible approaches to thematic analysis; they do, however, depend upon other combinations of sensitivity and skill. For such work, repeated viewing of single films is necessary and also -- at least as far as sound patterns and their associations are concerned -- close work with sensitive informants. The illustrative analyses given here are intended primarily to be suggestive of methods that can be applied to various aspects of films, to various kinds of films in the study of a culture.

I. Notes on an Italian Film: The Tragic Hunt[2]

Martha Wolfenstein

These notes, recorded shortly after the film had been seen initially, are from a series on Italian films made by the writer who had, at the time, no other systematic data on Italian culture but very considerable experience in film analysis. (Cf. Wolfenstein and Leites, 1950.) This exploratory work on Italian films, undertaken as part of a cross-cultural study of films, was antecedent to work in Research in Contemporary Cultures on Italy. (Cf. "Themes in Italian Culture: A First Discussion," reproduced in this Manual, Part Three, pages 131-40.)

Commenting on the notes, Martha Wolfenstein wrote: "We had seen a little over twenty Italian films before this one. Thus, while we had worked out a number of points about Italian films, these remained in many ways incomplete, fragmentary and uncertain. The points made in these notes, for instance, include the one about good and bad women that I feel quite sure about, along with others that are much more tentative, and also some material that I just record and cannot interpret."

The notes are given here as an illustration of one individual's method of preliminary recording for purposes of analysis. -- Ed.

The scene is the northern Italian countryside in early post-World War II days. A young bride and groom who have just been to a near-by town to be married, and have not yet consummated their marriage, are returning to the farm in a truck that also carries a large amount of money, presumably a government loan which is very vital to the whole community. This money is to pay off the debts of the farmers to the absentee landowner; otherwise their cattle and farm machinery will be taken from them. Two sinister bailiffs of the absentee landowner stand ready to carry out this expropriation if the money is

---

2. Unpublished document RCC-IT 43.

not brought in time. These two bailiffs seem to be identical twins; they are stout men with stocking caps and fur-lined jackets; their faces resemble bull-dogs (cf. the sinister twin assistants of K in Kafka's The Castle).

The bridegroom is kissing the bride in the open back part of the truck, and they are greeted with enthusiastic good wishes by workers going to work early in the morning whom they pass along the way. The bride makes some slight protest about the visibility of their embraces to start with, but this is soon overcome. A crowd of gay well-wishers starts running along behind the truck, demanding wedding candies, which the couple gaily throw to them. The idea of the bridal couple, especially of the virgin bride, and of largesse to the community, seem to be combined here, especially as the truck bearing the couple also carries a large amount of money for the whole farm community. However, this happy and auspicious picture is soon shattered. The truck is held up by a gang of bandits who travel in an ambulance, and both the bride and the money are carried away. The rest of the picture details the flight of the criminal gang, and the pursuit by the farmers who are organized to follow them. The bridegroom re-turns to the farm, the only survivor of his expedition, as the bride has been carried off and the two other men on the truck have been killed. In a struggle with the gang, one of their masks has been ripped off and the hero has seen the face of the man, who turns out to be an old comrade of his from a prisoner-of-war camp, Alberto, who had been his best friend. Alberto warns the hero not to identify him; otherwise the bride will be killed. Back on the farm the bride-groom is questioned in the presence of a large group of people and pretends to know nothing about the gang. It is very quickly grasped by everyone that he knows more than he is telling. Eventually he joins in the pursuit of the gang; he uses the knowledge he has from his previous acquaintance with Alberto to lead them to the abandoned house where the gang is hiding.

The leader of the robber gang is a bad woman who has been a collabora-tionist with the Germans during the war. She is intensely curious about and envious of the young bride. Thus she asks the girl, "How does it feel to be a bride?" The girl replies angrily, "Why don't you get married yourself?" The bad woman laughs bitterly and then says, expressing deep longing that she has not been able to put aside, "Yes, why shouldn't I, why not?" There is a later scene of great physical intimacy between the bad and the good woman. The bride is lying bound on a couch and the bad woman leans over her, lies against her and begs her to confide in her woman to woman about her feelings. She asks the bride whether she has slept with her husband before their marriage. The bride says no but that she would have done anything for him. The bad woman cannot understand this. She is desperately trying to find out the secret by which the good woman holds her man and at the same time is attempting to deny the ap-peal of the good woman. Thus she says to the bride: "He will tire of you; he will come home exhausted from work and go to sleep without looking at you," etc.

Here again is the characteristic acknowledgment of the superior attractiveness of the good woman, which we find in so many Italian films. The good woman has all the charm and mystery and power to bind men to her and to make other women envious of her that in other Western cultures is more likely to be associated with the bad woman. The good girl is here played by the same actress who played the heroine in Without Pity.

The bad woman is depicted as hysterical, megalomaniac, and desperately longing to be loved. She is unfeelingly destructive of others at the same time that she is intensely hypersensitive to any slight to herself and very revengeful. At one point during the flight of the gang in the ambulance, they are stopped by a group of peasants who block the road. The order is given to the driver to drive right through them, but he does not have the nerve. It turns out that the peasants only want the ambulance to take away a wounded man who has been hurt in an explosion of a land mine. Throughout the film, we are aware of the land being full of mines, some of which have already been dislodged, the hero being among the peasants who have devoted themselves to this task of clearing the land, but some of which are exploding off and on throughout the film. The wounded man is delirious, he grabs at the bad woman, trying to embrace her, thinking that she is someone else. In his struggle he tears off her blond wig and we see her close-cropped black hair, which gives away the fact that she has had her head shorn as retaliation for her collaborationism. A coarse German who is a member of the gang laughs uproariously at this revelation. The bad woman is so distraught by this that she opens the door of the ambulance and throws out the dying man.

In a later scene in the gangster's hide-out, the bad woman clings to her lover Alberto, retells the awful scene of her head-shearing, and vows revenge against the leader of her attackers. Alberto, an unemployed veteran who has become desperate at his inability to find a job, has joined the gang out of desperation and does not share the woman's bloodthirstiness. He has been deeply distressed by the killing that occurred in connection with the robbery. The woman, however, had embraced him ecstatically after the killing and told him that he would be a famous gang leader; they will be famous together, their names will be in all the papers. The affair of Alberto with the bad woman is counterpointed to the good relations between the bridegroom and the bride. The bad woman tries repeatedly to persuade Alberto that he should be glad he is in love with a woman like her. Together they will rise above the unrewarding life of the poor. Alberto, although he is intensely bound to this woman, not only by sex but by considerable tenderness, is unable to say that he loves her. This crucial issue of the man's incapacity to love the bad woman comes out in a final climactic scene.

In the hide-out of the gang, we discover that the sinister twin bailiffs are the real masters of the gang. The woman is their agent. The serial numbers on the stolen banknotes are known to the police, and this precipitates the resolve of the gang to exchange the money in haste with black-marketeers who have foreign currency and who are plying their trade on a railroad train. The hide-out of the gang is a deserted country house of rather bewildering interior. There is one rather elegantly furnished room, which belongs to the twin leaders. There is a very disorderly room which belongs to the gang and where odds and ends of things that have previously been stolen are kept. Apparently among objects previously stolen there are two dolls, which one of the gangsters plays with. He shaves off the hair of one of these dolls, and makes her into the likeness of the bad woman.

The army of farmers, led by the hero, now surround the villa. However, the gangsters make their escape by using the bride as a hostage. She is carried along with her eyes bandaged and a revolver held to her back. The hero has a chance to touch her hand as she is let out, but is unable to rescue her. The bad woman recognizes among the farmers the man who led the attack upon her when her hair was shaved off. She taunts him and all of the farmers in a furious and triumphant speech, and she and the gang make off in their car, taking the bride with them. The gangsters shoot at the farmers as they leave, and the farmers shoot back, but no damage is done except that the tires of the farmers' cars are punctured and they cannot continue their pursuit.

There is a scene on an open railway train on which are riding groups of black-marketeers and of unemployed veterans. Here the gang comes in order to make their currency exchanges. The black-marketeers are some of them disguised as jazz musicians, carrying illegal currency in a compartment of a bass drum, while some of them have crates of live chickens. The juxtaposition of the unemployed veterans and the black-marketeers repeats the same combination as the involuntary incorporation of the unemployed veteran Alberto in the robber gang. The veterans are carrying on a campaign of appeal to the peasants. They have a loudspeaker on the train, and as they pass through fields in which peasants are working, they call out complaining about their war hardships, their peace disappointments, and appealing to the peasants to help them find work. In this land-hungry area, where, as we have seen from the farm where the bridal couple lived, the peasants are in the utmost stages of deprivation themselves, it is hard to understand the logic of the soldiers' appeal.

Alberto meets some veterans who recognize him. They all have the same swastika brand on their wrists which the Nazis branded them with. They appeal to Alberto to join them in their campaign. He is anxious to get away from them. In the confusion, some of the money that he is carrying falls from his pocket. When the veterans see it, they turn from him in disgust, saying that indeed he is not one of them. He is deeply distressed by this, and takes the microphone, which he has previously refused, and talks very movingly about the sufferings of the veterans. This speech is entirely convincing to the veter-

ans who had been about to turn against him. This seems to illustrate a recurrent point that one cannot falsify emotional utterances. The fact that
Alberto can speak with such true feeling about his plight as a veteran proves
conclusively to the other veterans that he is one of them. Similarly, in a later
climactic scene, where it is a life-and-death matter for Alberto to tell the bad
woman that he loves her, he cannot do this because he does not love her. The
self-evidence of emotional declarations thus seems to be a characteristic point.
Similarly, earlier, when the bridegroom had refrained from telling all he knew
about the gang because he wanted to protect his bride, it was evident to every
eye that he was not telling everything.

The train with the veterans and black-marketeers is stopped by the police
and the people from the train start clambering off into a V-shaped trough along-
side the railway line. There is a scene of considerable confusion. The hero
and his group come face to face with the German gang member. They are both
pointing their guns at each other and are thus brought to a momentary standstill. This is also a recurrent situation in this film. Neither side beats the
other to the draw, and the two opponents, facing each other at gun point, are
paralyzed from further action. The German diverts his opponents with a simple
ruse, telling them that one of the other gangsters has gone over that way. As
they turn their heads, he runs away. However, we are later told that he has
been shot. We do not see this success of his pursuers.

The hero runs after Alberto, who is escaping through the ruins of a town
where the train has stopped. The hero overtakes him and they have a hand-to-
hand fight in which Alberto refuses to defend himself and the hero repeatedly
knocks him down. However, Alberto, who never entered wholeheartedly into the
activities of the gang, who has been disturbed by the fact that there was blood-
shed in the recent holdup, and who has finally been converted back to his true
moral feelings by his contact with the veterans, now only wants to give the
money back to the farmers. I believe in the scene where the hero repeatedly
knocks him down, Alberto explains finally that he has changed and that he wants
to make restitution.

There is a small shack on an island that was a former Nazi hide-out; there
Alberto and the bad woman now have a rendezvous. The bride is being held
captive there too. Alberto says that all the other members of the gang have been
killed or captured. The bad woman is unaffected by this and repeats her plan
that she and Alberto should go away together out of the country. Alberto tells her
that he has changed, that he wants to give the money back to the farmers. She
says, "Never!" and starts tearing the bills. Meanwile the farmers are approaching the shack. The area through which they are going is still mined and they
are proceeding with considerable caution and slowness. The infuriated bad
woman runs to a switch box which she assures Alberto contains the switch to
blow up the whole mine field. She knows this from her previous visits here

when the shack was German headquarters.

Just previous to this there has been the intense scene between the bad woman and the bride in which the bad woman's longing to be loved has been evoked. The bad woman now stands at the switch, ready to blow up the mine fields and kill all the farmers, and she tells Alberto that she will only refrain from doing this if he tells her that he loves her. Alberto manages to pick up a gun, which he points at her. This is again the recurrent situation of two people standing face to face threatening each other and at a momentary standstill. Alberto is unable to say that he loves the bad woman. She taunts him that he will not shoot her and is approaching the switch closer and closer to the fatal closure. Alberto, before the horrified gaze of the bride, shoots his mistress repeatedly with the revolver and she falls dead, the switch still unclosed. The farmers now enter the shack to receive the stolen money and the captive bride.

Alberto is seated back at the farm surrounded by the whole community of peasants. The bridegroom is pleading with them to let him off. He emphasizes that Alberto was a poor veteran who could not find work. In an earlier scene, in one of the first stages of the pursuit, the hero has entered the ruined apartment of Alberto, and has gone through his papers, which had shown his repeated unsuccessful efforts to find work. The bride also pleads for Alberto, saying that he had saved her life when the other members of the gang wanted to kill her. It is not mentioned that he also saved the life of all the farmers by preventing the explosion of the mine field. In the end, the peasants agree to let Alberto go; the bridegroom suggests to him that near-by a bridge is being built and that Alberto could find work there. There is a diversion as the livestock and farm machinery that had been expropriated by the criminal bailiffs are now returned. The peasants go outside, Alberto goes off alone across the fields. The bridegroom throws a lump of earth at him, which seems to be a friendly farewell gesture. The bride and other peasants join in and we see the lonely figure of Alberto making his way across the field into the sunset.

This film expresses what seems to be a characteristic Italian theme of the extreme emotional disruption attendant on the transition in a girl's life in the loss of her virginity. All the excursions and alarms of the film would seem to have in part the symbolic significance of a celebration of this transition. There was a somewhat similar theme in the French film It Happened at the Inn, where, on the eve of the betrothal of a young couple, there is an extreme disruption of the life of the whole family. A woman is murdered, etc. In French films this disruption attendant on an anticipated sexual consummation seems to express the effect of a family being dislodged from sordid but stable pregenital occupations, notably revolving around property, and lifted to the more moving but unstabilizing levels of sexual love. With the Italians, the disruption seems to revolve around the loss of the young girl's virginity. A recurrent image shows the young girl who is about to make this fateful transition surrounded by men.

In another Italian film, a comedy, One Night with You, the young girl who is about to find love spends a night in a jail cell together with a whole group of men -- her father, her fiancé, the man she has fallen in love with, and at least several others. In Four Steps in the Clouds, the heroine, who has just announced to her family the loss of her virginity, is surrounded in the farmhouse by father, grandfather, the man she pretends is her husband, and several other men. In The Tragic Hunt, the heroine, the bride whose marriage is not yet consummated, is surrounded by the whole gang of thieves. There seems to be a fantasy here that is not completely filled out -- that the girl who loses her virginity should become the property of all the men, that the whole male community should be permitted to enjoy her. This would express the all-or-nothing attitude of the Italians toward female virtue. Between virginity and prostitution there is, in their fantasy, no middle ground. One would be likely to find in this connection the fantasy of the mother as a prostitute, in contrast to the idealized and virginal sister figure. However, I know of no direct evidence on this point as yet. The fantasy of mass rape of the girl who is renouncing her virginity also expresses the fear of not being able to guard the girl's virginity and keep it for her bridegroom. In The Tragic Hunt, between the moment of the marriage when the bride has officially renounced her intention to guard her virginity and the wedding night, there is the inruption of drastic danger and the episode of her kidnapping by the gang. The money that is carried off and then restored is the analogue to the bride's virginity.

Another recurrent theme is that the bad woman is the most direct threat to the good woman. In other films we have seen the bad woman leading or trying to lead the good woman into a life of vice and here we see her directly attacking her life.

The bride on the eve of her wedding night is confronted with the symbolically expressed primal scene in which Alberto and the bad woman face each other, threatening extreme destructiveness; the bad woman expressing her destructiveness toward men by her threat to throw the switch that will kill scores of honest peasants; Alberto threatening her with a gun and killing her. Thus the image of sex as mutually destructive violence is evoked. It is as if for the girl who is about to lose her virginity the most violent associations of sex are brought to the surface. The allusion to the primal scene and early looking experiences is expressed by the fact that the bride is alternately blindfolded and at other times sees more than anyone else. Thus it is she who peeps out the window and recognizes the demonic twins as the gang directors, and of course it is she who witnesses the final fatal violence between Alberto and the bad woman. An effort is made in plotting such films to dissociate as far as possible the sex that involves danger and violence from true love. The sex that is destructive is associated with Alberto, the good man who has gone wrong, and with the bad woman, a betrayer of her country. The feeling is that none of the horrors which attend their relationship can attach to the pure bride. This is in contrast to what would seem to be characteristic Spanish fantasy, in which the truer the love, the more bloody it is apt to be (cf. Lorca and Unamuno). For the Italian fantasy, it would seem that virtue and true love provide immunity to violence, just as departure from virtue means almost immediate exposure to violence.

II. Notes on Two French Films

In each of these brief notes the writer has concentrated on one aspect of the of the film -- the delineation of a father figure. The two films were seen and described during one ten-day period, at a time when the French group in Research in Contemporary Cultures were working specifically on familial relations with particular reference to the position of the father.

The "split image" of the father (referred to in the film notes) was described by Geoffrey Gorer in a preliminary set of statements about French culture,[3] as follows: "French children are taught early about the existence somewhere outside the foyer, of a sinister male mythological figure, to which is attributed excessive violence, destructive sexuality, and other aggressive characteristics (this figure has numerous names -- Ramponneau, loup-garou, Lustucru, le satyre, etc;" the names and stories of various sadistic murderers may also be invoked). This fantasy figure is consequently available as a recipient of all the negative feelings and fears that the young child might otherwise direct onto the image of the father. In most cases it would appear that this psychological safety valve works effectively and the son conceives the father to be succoring, protective, and undestructive." And later: "The displacing of the destructive masculine qualities onto a fantasy figure outside the foyer seems to operate for the daughters as well as for the sons; and as a consequence the father is seen by the daughter as a protective, unfrightening, sexually attractive figure."

Although this formal statement was written somewhat later, the idea of the "split image" of the father had been tentatively worked out when these two films were seen and analyzed. These film notes are therefore illustrations of an intermediate stage of work and show one way in which themes and images drawn from very diverse materials were continually being fitted together -- suggesting new problems or confirming an emergent pattern -- in the process of constructing formulations about a culture. (For purposes of comparison, cf. also "Formulation of a Working Hypothesis: French Dyadic Relationships," Part Three, pages 104-7, and "Interview with a French Couple: Dyadic Relations in the Foyer," Part Four, pages 182-88.) -- Ed.

1. The Father Figure in Panique[4]

Jane Belo

The central figure in this film contains in himself the two aspects of what we have been considering as the "split image" of the father.

On the one hand, this man fits perfectly the characterization of certain aspects of the father figure defined by Martha Wolfenstein:[5] "The father figure is protrayed sympathetically; usually he is the central character. He is shown as suffering, and as causing suffering to others by his love for a younger woman."

---

3. Unpublished document RCC-F 123.
4. Unpublished document RCC-F 113.
5. Unpublished document RCC-F 77.

He is also the bogey described by an informant looking at Card IV of the Rorschach test:[6] "... un monstre, énorme, terrible, prêt d'attaquer quelqu'un, lourd et horrible, marchant pesamment ... une figure et des yeux ... qui vous regardent" (a monster, enormous, terrible, ready to attack someone, heavy and horrible, walking ponderously ... a face and eyes ... which look at you).

In this film, Désiré (as the central character is ironically called) has all the pathos of the older man who loves but who is loved by no one -- neither by his parents nor by his wife, who left him and died. The crowd is hostile to him; it surrounds him in space (knocking into him from all sides in toy automobiles in an early scene at the fair, all converging on him as central figure and butt). In the end, the crime is (falsely) pinned on him by the crowd; it again surrounds him, drives him to suicidal death by falling from a roof.

The hostile feelings of the crowd, of the girl (the real murderer's mistress, whom Désiré loves), of the other citizens, are evoked by his general hairiness, his heaviness, and his "monster" qualities -- he is often "eyes watching you." His behavior includes watching the girl undress, from his window, stopping her on the stairs, luring her to another apartment of his by giving her a card, accosting a little girl of about ten years and offering her an apple. A special point is made of his asking for a saignant steak at the butcher shop (which is translated into English as "bloody," though it might have been rendered just as "juicy").

The stupid butcher later sticks a "beautiful cutlet" under the nose of the same little girl to bribe her into accusing the bogeyman of trying to lure her to his room, but the child steadfastly denies it. Note also that her mother screamed at her, called her indoors, and stood her in the closet for taking the apple Désiré gave her.

When the crowd kicks off Désiré's hat (a well-known trick), the gendarme smiles. At the end, as the crowd surrounds and attacks him, they all are over-come by the same emotion, which is out of control. Even the police are swayed by it, and, though they arrive, it is with the sense that they will not be able to restore order. As Désiré dangles from the roof, the hook and ladder company are called, but they cannot save him. He looks overwhelmingly helpless and pathetic as he turns, swinging in space toward the fireman at the top of the ladder that is just out of reach. Then he falls.

2. Notes on La Belle et la Bête[7]
Geoffrey Gorer

This film is a fantasticated and Frenchified version of the old story of Beauty and the Beast. The relevant material would seem to be the following:

6.   Unpublished document RCC-F 110.
7.   Unpublished document RCC-F 116.

Beauty is the youngest daughter of a widowed man. She has two older sisters who oppress her, make her do the housework, etc., while they go out to enjoy themselves. The two sisters are not diversified in any way, and the conflict therefore looks like that between an elder and a younger sister. Beauty also has a brother, relative age not specified, who tries to protect Beauty from the bad older sisters in a rather ineffectual way, but his sympathy is definietely with her. This brother is pictured as a ne'er-do-well, and he has a friend, a ne'er-do-well like himself, who wishes to marry Beauty, but Beauty refuses him because she does not want to leave her father alone.

The father is nearly ruined and goes to the coast to see if one of his ships has returned. When he sets out for the journey, the older sisters ask him to bring them back a monkey and a parrot, and Beauty asks for a rose, because no roses grow where they live. The father's trip is fruitless, and on the way back he gets lost in a dense and trackless forest and comes to the magic castle of the Beast. Leaving the next morning, the father sees some roses by the door and picks one for Beauty, whereupon the Beast appears for the first time and says that the theft of the rose would usually be punished by death, but that he would give him one chance. If one of his daughters will come in his stead, he can survive.

The father goes back to his family, giving the rose to Beauty. He is prepared to leave after three days to go to the Beast, but Beauty goes in his stead. The vicious Beast is tamed by her charm, but Beauty finds out in a magic mirror that her father is ill and she says that she will die if she is not allowed to go back to look after him. The Beast lets her go and the father recovers.

The ugly sisters, in company with the brother and his friend, plan to rob the Beast, and to prevent Beauty from returning. Beauty, however, does return to the dying Beast, full of compassion. When the friend tries to break into the Beast's treasure house, he is shot by a statue and is transformed into the Beast, while the Beast in turn is transformed into a beautified version of the friend. Beauty and the transformed Beast ascend into Heaven together.

Note. The drama between the sisters and the link between father and daughter are most clearly demonstrated. On the unconscious level it looks as though Beast were a parallel to father rather than to brother's friend (compare the way they both get ill when Beauty is away and recover when she returns). On the overt level, Beast is equated with brother and brother's friend. And it would seem as though the Beast was a personification of le satyre, Ramponneau, Croque-mitaine, etc. -- i.e. of the dangerous aspect of the father's personality.

III. An Analysis of Seven Cantonese Films[8]

John Hast Weakland

The following excerpt from a detailed study of seven Cantonese fictional films consists of a summary statement based on descriptive analyses (not included here) of each of the films. The films were not specially selected for analysis, but included all the Chinese films shown in a four-month period in a commercial theater in New York's Chinatown. As none of the films was seen more than once or twice the emphasis in the anlaysis was upon recurrent features -- whether these were themes, details of plot structuring, character types, etc. At the time the analyst did not know the language and was therefore dependent for his insights mainly upon visual aspects of the films and upon subsequent discussions with Chinese-speaking informants.

Weakland describes his procedure in working on the films in part as follows: "[After reading the English translation to the synopsis several times] I visited the theater and during the showing of the film, notes were made at once whenever anything occurred on the screen that aroused special interest. When noted, these were often mere fragments covering a wide range of subject matter -- a striking shift of mood; a repetition of some feature, object, expression, or detail of structure; emphasis in characterization or custom; or details of technique, such as camera work in beginning and ending scenes. As soon as possible after viewing the film -- usually within a few hours, never more than a day later -- a description of the experience was written up, drawing on the synopsis, the notes, and memory. Everything that could be recalled in the content of the film was included, plus interpretive remarks and questions concerning striking points not fully understood. The film was also discussed with other [Chinese] group members who had seen it, and sometimes additional notes were made at that time."

This film study was undertaken early in the work of the Chinese group in Research in Contemporary Cultures, when the group was engaged in gathering material by various means -- mainly through work with informants and group discussion -- on role relationships, primarily within the family. The film analysis is an example of an effort to increase insight by the use of visual material -- by following the ways in which fictional characters, acting out a plot, were presented to a Chinese-speaking audience. A companion study, based upon popular Chinese stories, was made at about the same time by Virginia Heyer (cf. "Relations between Men and Women in Chinese Stories," Part Five pages 221-34). -- Ed.

1. Roles and Relations in the Family

It is a striking observation that although China is a country where the ideal family is a very large one, a complete family seldom appears, and an extended family is not shown, in the films that were seen. For the most part, the films are concerned only with the incipient family -- the marriage of a young couple.

The father of the young man is usually absent, and references to him indicate father-son antagonism. The girl's father may be present, and he is pictured as a fond and indulgent parent. The mother of either the man or the woman, when she appears in a film, has little relation to the action. Except at the very end of one picture, no mother-in-law is shown in any of these films, but other older women are presented as mean, harsh, and grasping. They are perhaps surrogates for the mother-in-law.

---

8.   Excerpt from an unpublished document, RCC-CH 650. The English titles of the films included in the analysis are as follows: The Red House at Hoy Gok; The Supernatural Sight of a Beautiful One; Sparkling Water's Loving Couple; Doe Sarp Nerng; Beauty Is Skin Deep; The Combined Efforts of Many; The Young Couple.

Actual siblings are almost absent, and children are rarely to be found in the films. Very occasionally two or three young men appear in the same film, but they are usually strongly differentiated -- e.g. hero and servant or comic. Rarely do they have closely similar or competitive roles.

The core of each of these films is the man-woman relationship, and the favored theme is a young man's relation to two types of young woman. The young man is shown as powerless in the face of circumstances. The girls are of sharply contrasting character: one is rather retiring, somewhat nurturing, modest in dress and in manner (particularly she avoids low-necked dresses), and she often seems older than the man and her rival, who is actively enticing, "alluring and dangerous," displays her body (especially her breasts), and may be somewhat Westernized. The man is torn between these two women. Even if he rejects the sexually aggressive one, her actions interfere with his relations to the other woman. If, because of special circumstances (he is drunk, or weak, or is manipulated), he does become sexually involved with the aggressive woman, he usually rejects her in the end and wins the other woman by displaying his need for her nurturing care. In one film, the man marries both girls. This, together with the contrast of the two feminine types, is interesting in relation to the old practice of wealthy Chinese taking a second young wife (often a singing girl) after reaching middle age. The entire constellation of data might possibly be interpreted as follows: The good young woman whom the Chinese man should marry in his youth is maternal, but not fully so. She probably is closer to the child nurse (usually an older sister) than to the mother herself. The alluring but dangerous woman, whom a man might marry later in life, when he is a stronger figure, includes elements of both a younger sister and a daughter.

The clear-cut roles defined for the various types of characters at first seem designed to give an impression of weakness or of strength, but on reflection it would seem more accurate to view them as statements of the behavior necessary or proper for the respective characters in influencing the course of events. There are few available data to indicate whether the Chinese regard the behavior portrayed as "strong" or "weak," or in terms of a strength-weakness dichotomy.

The young men who are the heroes of these films are rather ineffectual. Their fortunes are controlled by older, richer, more powerful men. Against them the young men can feel resentment, but can take no action. A young man is inescapably dependent; his best hope is to gain help from good and friendly older men. Emotionally also the young man is dependent. Typically, an older man or a young woman may assert pressure and induce the young man to act counter to his own feelings. The extent of this emotional dependence varies somewhat from film to film, but it is usually evident even in the exceptional cases where the young man is materially independent.

The older man is presented in several guises. Usually he is a strong figure in comparison with the young man; he may be either good or evil. When he is good, he is depicted as using his strength to respond positively to the vicissitudes of life, to accept responsibilities affecting the welfare of others. It is a matter of goal orientation. The good man accepts and sustains, rather than seeking defined ends. There is some evidence to suggest that even a mature man may be weak -- which, in terms of the films, means that he avoids the responsibilities that fall to him.

The position of the young woman is more complex. Ordinarily, she follows a given role rather strictly. She may be quite submissive to the pressure of the world of affairs, as when she is a singing girl or a cigarette vendor; or she may be active -- sometimes even serving as a warrior -- in the interests of another person (as in The Supernatural Sight of a Beautiful One) for a limited time. But in either case, she holds a powerful weapon in reserve: if a situation becomes emotionally intolerable, she can make this publicly evident by word or deed and then flee the situation -- in extreme cases by suicide (cf. the Chinese pattern of suicide by girls forced by parents into intolerable marriages, and the notes they leave telling the reason for the act). This behavior is striking in two respects -- the outburst is almost always directed against the situation rather than a person, and it is not goal-oriented. It is merely a reaction against an intolerable personal situation, but -- as presented in the films -- it changes the course of events. In contrast, the bad, alluring, but dangerous young woman is a schemer bent on seducing men; here again the evil person is active and goal-oriented.

There is very little material in these films on the role of the older woman. The evil woman who is older closely parallels the evil man -- she is selfish and active. The good older woman is receptive and generous, but is not closely involved in the plot.

2. Time Perspectives[9]

Repetition is a prominent feature, whether it involves a fragment or an important scene. Some of the repetitions are disguised, different characters being involved in a repeated structural or dynamic frame, but more often it is quite open. Repetition may be multiple. At times the repetition is progressive, which then serves to increase the intensity of the situation. In this manner, the film may progress toward a major climax by employing growing cycles of ups and downs and subclimaxes.

The importance of destiny and the inescapable weight of circumstances are stressed, and suggest that the Chinese regard destiny as inescapable, yet

---

9. For a discussion of time perspectives, cf. Bateson, (1945, from which an excerpt is included in this Manual, below, pages 302-14. -- Ed.), Frank, (1936b), and Lewin (1942).

impersonal. Perhaps because it is impersonal and depends on circumstances, it is impossible to change. Related to destiny ideas, but of wider scope, is the presentation of striving and goal-seeking as bad -- evil people are given to such practices and come to no good end; but positive reaction to immediate circumstances -- the requirements of the present situation -- is good. The means should be fostered, the ends ignored -- they will follow naturally from the means. Confucius stresses this idea in his works.

In the usual climax structure, although variations occur, the origin of the central situation is something like this: The young man, through some minor action or behavior intended to be otherwise interpreted, initiates a powerful emotional response in a young woman. Her reactions to him may be disturbing in their intensity if they are direct (as in Doe Sarp Nerng), or confusing or difficult if they operate in reverse (as in The Red House at Hoy Gok, where the girl rejects the man and becomes ill, or in The Young Couple, where the girl rejects the man because of jealousy). Once the emotionally difficult situation is set up, the course is rather clearly patterned. The young man is almost helpless within the tangle of emotions and circumstances in which he finds himself involved. The girl suffers, mentally or physically, often because of the man's weakness, but at times through her own misinterpretations. She endures this for a time, but it grows worse -- often by cyclical swings -- until the breaking point is reached. Then she abandons her passive role and makes a public emotional reaction to the situation -- she fights, faints, or talks -- and then tries to flee. This, though not calculated to do so, brings about a resolution. If the girl's own incorrect ideas were the cause of her trouble, the outburst completes the resolution. If the difficulty was external to her, someone possessing the appropriate power is stimulated by the outburst to remedy the situation. There are a few variations and some struggle against material rather than personal difficulties, but this climax structure seems to be the major one in almost every film.

IV. An Analysis of the Soviet Film The Young Guard[10]

The excerpts given here are from a working paper prepared for group discussion. The original document, which was slightly over 12,000 words in length, consisted of a plot summary (given here), a detailed running commentary on the film, a comparison of the film with the novel on which it was based (given here), and a commentary on the propaganda aspects of the film, by the three analysts who saw it. Related to it is an interview with a Russian informant who had been a friend of Fadeyev, the author of the novel.

Some of the points that came out of this analysis of The Young Guard were: (1) the contrast to Soviet films made during and immediately after World War II, i.e. the disappearance of the optimism that had characterized these earlier

---

10. Unpublished document SSC 102. The Young Guard (from the novel of the same title, Molodaya Gvardiya, by Alexander Fadeyev) was produced by Mosfilm Studios, Moscow, 1949.

films which (like American films made during World War II and in contrast to German and Japanese films of the same period) emphasized the expected survival of the hero; (2) the death of the whole group of young protagonists -- their survival only in the minds of others; (3) the preoccupation with the enemy within -- the Germans, the external enemy, remain stock figures throughout the film; (4) the attempt to rewrite history of very recent events; and (5) the lack of poignancy in scenes involving important propaganda points, in contrast to the liveliness of small details of some personal relationships, and the consequent unreality and unconvincingness of the film as a whole.

The analysis of The Young Guard was one of a series made by the same group over a period of several years as part of the work on Great Russian and Soviet cultures. The comparison of the film and the novel is given here as an illustration of one way in which two versions of the same plot -- in this case in different media -- can be used to gain insight into the treatment of important themes, here involving a sharp change in emphasis within a brief period of time. It illustrates also one way in which a member of the culture (Vera Schwarz), with a highly developed skill, can provide data on that culture by drawing on her own past experience as part of her view of the contemporary situation. -- Ed.

1. Plot Summary[11]

Margaret Mead

The scene is laid in 1942, in Krasnodon, a mining village. A group of young Komsomol girls are out in the open country talking about what they ought to do if the Germans come. Sound of exploding mines, and arrival of planes. The girls rush back; most people are evacuating according to orders; a few decide to remain and work. Scene between Lubya Shevtsova (a Komsomol girl) and NKVD agent. Scenes of the evacuation and group being bombed; entry of Germans. Then a long series of scenes -- German brutality, organized Komsomol sabotage, more brutality, Russian suspicions of the Russians who work as disguised collaborators, growth of the Komsomol group, organization scenes of Komsomols, warning to Komsomol boy, Sergei Tulenin, about one youth, Stakhovich. The Komsomols organize a concert so as to meet at rehearsals; and then to prevent some of them from being carried off as forced labor, they burn down the labor exchange while everyone is at the concert. Beginning of rout of German armies. Stakhovich and two others arrested; brutality of Germans; Stakhovich confesses. Some of the Komsomols leave to cross the line, others stay. Tulenin, who arrives in the Russian lines, is scolded for having kept Stakhovich and because all the others have not come; he volunteers to return; he goes back and is arrested with all the others. Every single one is taken; all refuse to betray the others. Oleg, the Young Guard boy leader, admits his leadership and takes responsibility for everything. Scenes in prison; the Young Guard singing and defiant. Then all are taken out, bleeding from beatings, to a group grave; they stand up in a group, defiant (but the scene of shooting is not shown). The next scene shows the end of the war and a memorial being raised to the Young Guard in the village; children salute, guns are fired, a flag with Lenin and Stalin waves in front of the crowd -- streams out horizontally -- and they are said to live forever in the minds of the people.

11. The plot summary, slightly edited for clarity, is followed in the original document by a detailed discussion of the narrative and by some general comments (one paragraph included here). -- Ed.

General Comment. This film, made in 1948, is the least moving and least convincing of any propaganda picture I have ever seen. It compares most unfavorably with The Peasants and even with Frontier. Well acted, with everything on its side -- youth, beauty, young love -- it rings entirely false. The propaganda points are allowed to obscure the sense of the plot; the enemy are completely lay figures; the whole preoccupation is with the betrayal from within, but, unlike Frontier, the betrayal has no affect for those who are betrayed.

2. Comparison of the Film and the Novel[12]
Vera Schwarz (Alexandrova)

Generally speaking, the film is better than the novel and better than I had expected.

In reading The Young Guard (1945),[13] I was struck by the very beginning of it -- by the details portraying the future members of the underground organization. The novel begins as if in peacetime: Ulyana Gromova, looking at a water lily, is admiring its beauty and perfection -- it looks like an alabaster sculpture and yet is alive, "but so cold": "Look how it is reposing on the water -- clean (chistaya), austere (strogaya), indifferent (ravnodushanaya)." I felt immediately some connection between this description of the flower and the beginning of the novel.[14]

This remark by Ulyana is not in the first scene of the film; only the flower is put in her hair by her girl friend. But looking at the girls without Fadeyev's bored description of every "graceful" and "maiden" (dyevi cheskaya) gesture or smile, I was pleased. Without the author's comments, they behave much more naturally than in the novel.

This comment can be expanded for almost the whole film (with the exception of the older generation, who -- contrary to the novel -- are less impressive in the film). I visualized a provincial town in southern Russia, with all its poverty and low standard of life. This latter is indicated by little details -- the zinc wash-

---

12. This section has been slightly condensed and edited for clarity. -- Ed.
13. The novel The Young Guard (Molodaya Gvardiya) was published serially in Znamya in 1945, and appeared in book form in 1946 and 1947. The 1945 and 1947 versions of the novel have been compared with the film.
14. I must explain this impression. I know much about Fadeyev's youth. In 1917 he was 16 years old, a high school student in southern Manchuria. He became a supporter of the Red Army and joined the Red partisans. His own experiences of that time are very well described in two novels, The Rout (Razgrom, 1928) and The Last of the Udege (Posledniy iz Udege, 1930-41). When I first heard that Fadeyev had gone to the liberated part of the Donets Basin to look at the town of Krasnodon, where the Young Guard had been active, I thought he would be the best writer to write a novel about this organization. He began to write his novel in 1944, just when the Soviet officials, foreseeing the coming victory, were anxious to present this victory as due to the merit of the Communist leadership and at the same time to show that youth is the 1940s was culturally and spiritually more educated than in the 1920s. That is why Fadeyev begins with the unlikely scene of Ulyana Gromova contemplating the water lily.

basin in the corner of the kitchen, the old-fashioned earthernware milk pot (they were the same in this part of Russia during my own childhood), etc.

Oleg Koshevoy (the boy leader) is much better presented in the film than in the novel. Imagine how unlikely is one detail about him in the novel: during the disastrous evacuation he is described not only as well combed, but also as arranging his hair! This is omitted from the film, as is almost the whole evacuation.

The reasons for omitting the evacuation are clear. Before the novel was adapted for the stage and the movies, Soviet official critics expressed their discontent about the too-detailed description of the confused evacuation in the summer of 1942. According to these critics, even though the evacuation looked confusing from outside, it actually had a plan and leadership.

And here I come to speak about the most important discrepancy between the film and the novel. As I said above, the youth in the novel is somehow artificial because of the author's desire to present the heroes of the Young Guard as very intelligent, very cultured, educated people (Valya Borts, for instance, in the scene where Seryozha Tulenin comes to her house, is lying in the garden reading an English novel by Robert Louis Stevenson). The adults behave much more naturally; this is underlined in one detail -- they all speak colloquial Russian (which in this part of Russia is a mixture of Russian and Ukrainian dialects); through this detail they are in some way warm figures.

In the novel all Party officials -- like Shul'ga and Val'ko -- are very confused. Shul'ga commits a great mistake by asking shelter from a worker (Fomin, who is later hanged by the Young Guard) who, after the invasion, joins "the betrayers of the people." Shul'ga not only takes shelter with Fomin, but also invites Val'ko and, in Fomin's presence, talks about the plan of an underground organization.

This confusion served to bring about a very sharp attack upon Fadeyev. In an article in Pravda (December 3, 1947), it is said that such facts were known during the war, but that a writer should show only "typical features" in an artistic work, and such confusion and blindness were never typical of experienced Party members.

Soon afterward, the attack was repeated in Sovietskoye Iskusstvo (December 5, 1947, p. 2) and in Literaturnaya Gazeta (December 7, 1947, p. 2), in an article entitled "The Novel Young Guard and its Dramatization," from which a quotation follows:

As has already been mentioned in our press (in Pravda and Culture and Life), Fadeyev committed a great error, both artistic and historical. It consists in the following: he has shown very convincingly the characters, the ideals, and the relations of the Komsomoltsy, who have been brought up by the Party. But Fadeyev failed in the creation of full-value images of their educators, leaders, all those to whom our youth are indebted (komu obyazana), for all the best they possess: the images of the Bolsheviks (obrazy bol'shevikov). 15

---

15. This phrase is underlined by the author of the critical article.

... The Young Communists in the novel appear, in the essence, more experienced, more self-restrained (vyderzhany), more sensitive (chutkiy) underground fighters than those Bolsheviks who have been assigned for the underground work. In the conversation with the old miner, Kondratovich [this is all omitted from the film] , an honest and devoted Party worker, Shul'ga hesitates: can he trust him or not? And then suddenly he catches himself, that "he had lost in his soul all criteria about whom he could trust and whom he could not trust in the conditions in which he was living."

What is that for a Party leader (kakoy zhe eto partiyniy rukovoditel)? The Soviet people remained Soviet people in the conditions of the fiercest German terror, and Party leaders, underground organizers, knew whom they could trust and were able to make connections with them. Of course, such an underground id Bolshevik can sometimes commit a tragic error. But only a bad, improper (negodnyi) leader can arrive at such a state of full confusion (polnaya rasteryannost) and despair (otchayaniye) that he loses all criteria. Meanwhile, Fadeyev does not think this about Shul'ga. He is rather inclined to interpret his errors as tragic guilt. 16 And although after his failure, when Shul'ga has been put in the German prison, he severely blames himself, in the novel one does not remark an understanding that such a leader as Shul'ga could not manage the task of underground work.

Similar remarks are made in the article about the second Party official, Val'ko, and then the author concludes:

Unfortunately, the whole Party underground organization is represented in the novel by these two men, Shul'ga and Val'ko, if we do not count some other persons who play a secondary role. This brings us, in the essence, to the conclusion that the Party organization as such is not presented in the novel and the group of the Young Guard are acting in isolation. And this means incompleteness in picturing the work of the Young Communists, for most essential in the life of the Komsomol is the very leadership of the Party.

After this attack, which was repeated in many articles of the Soviet press, one can understand why in the film -- unlike Fadeyev's novel -- Shul'ga and Val'ko are presented as experienced Party members who give instructions to Lubya Shevtsova and the others.

There are two kinds of difference between the novel and the film of The Young Guard:

1. One group of differences can be partly explained by the techniques of dramatization, so, in the novel, for instance, most of the important members of the Young Guard ... were buried alive in the coal pit. They were buried together with Stakhovich, who little by little had betrayed all the members of the Young Guard. Finally he became mad and on the day of execution could not walk and was thrown on the motor truck by the German prison guards. Oleg Koshevoy, the leader of the Young Guard, was shot some days later, on January 31, 1943. Lubya Shevtsova was shot on February 7, 1943. In the film, however, the whole group of the Young Guard, with Oleg Koshevoy at their head, are executed on the same day.

In the novel, the description of the last days of their life is preceded by Fadeyev's personal recollections of the time of the Civil War. He describes the

16. Tragic guilt -- tragicheskaya vina. These two words are also underlined by the author of the article and this seems to me very significant; actually this feeling of "tragic guilt" was characteristic for a great number of Party members in the first period of the Soviet-German war.

death of his friend and comrade who had been mortally wounded. (Fadeyev tried to bring him on his shoulders to a safe place and put him on the grass. The friend asked for water; Fadeyev had nothing in which he could bring him water, so he took with him one shoe of the friend and ran for water. When he came back, the friend was already dead; he sat near him and began to cry. Terrible thirst tormented Fadeyev, and suddenly he nestled to the shoe filled with water and began to drink greedily until the shoe was empty.) This episode could have been included in the film as a vision and as a vivid link between the Civil War and the Fatherland War, and I must frankly say I cannot understand why the movie producers missed the opportunity.

The film gives a rather confused picture of how the group of the Young Guard were unmasked. It becomes clear only by reading the novel. The Young Guard existed not so much on the members' fees as on money they got by selling cigarettes, food, etc., on the black market; all these goods they got from their frequent raids on the Germans' trucks. Some of the members had good friends among town boys who sold the stolen goods. One of these boys was arrested selling German cigarettes. The arrested boy first denied any connection with th other people, but later -- under beatings -- gave the Germans three names, among them that of Stakhovich.

It is interesting that Oleg Koshevoy (and behind him Fadeyev) -- although he does not like Stakhovich from the beginning -- is almost objective in his characterization of him. Stakhovich is shown not as a professional villain; on the contrary, as the son of a well-known Communist family, he was, from his childhood. on, accustomed to be considered as someone important. When he was among other people he could even be a hero, fulfill a deed, but left "alone he was a coward" (odin na odin on byl trus). Although Oleg Koshevoy did not trust Stakhovich and was worried when he was caught, he only said (privately) to Ulyana that Stakhovich could not hold out; he then added, "It is not fair to mistrust when you are not sure. Maybe just now he is going through ordeals and we are still free."

2. More important are differences between the film and the novel that refer to the presentation of the relations between the members of the Young Guard and the adults. In the novel, not only do the members of the Young Guard act mostly on their own initiative, but also most of the parents do not know anything about the doings of their children. Some of the parents, suspecting their activities, are frankly displeased. For instance, there is the father of Vanya Zemnukhov. The father behaved himself courageously during the evacuation (he was appointed guardian of the trust administration), but after the Germans occupied Krasnodon he thought it would be wisest to keep quiet and not become involved in any activities (cf. Chapter 38 of the novel). Vanya's mother tried to soften the relations between father and son, and this whole scene reminds one of the one in The Childhood of Maxim Gorky where Grandma tries to make Grandpa's temper milder.

Incidentally, in the novel most of the parents, with the exception of Koshe-voy's mother, are depicted as very old people -- they are rather grandparents than parents. This can be explained by the hard experiences of Soviet life prior to the war.

In the film, the relations between Oleg Koshevoy and his mother are pre-sented with less tenderness than in the novel. I missed one episode that was in the novel but not in the film. Koshevoy once came home late and hoped his moth-er would be sleeping, but she was still waiting for him. Oleg came close to her, knelt before her, and put his head on her knees as he had so often done when he was a child. Looking at her combed head with the heavy braids, he asks, "Shall I free them" (Khochesh'ya ikh vypushchu na volyu)? He calls his mother "my beautiful one" (prekrasnaya moya).

Important small details are missing from the film. For instance, after Victor killed the German sentry, he suddenly turned away from him and began to vomit "with such force that he had to press the sleeve of his left arm on his mouth in order to soften the sound." This vomiting after killing someone I have encountered in some memoirs of Young Partisans who lived in the woods. (For instance, it is described by Tatyana Lagunova (1946) in her recollections, "In the Woods of Smolensk.")

There are also important details in the last days of the life of the Young Guard that are omitted from the film. For instance, when Ulyana Gromova re-ceived a package from home with a clean shirt, she changed her old bloody shirt, made a bundle of it, and suddenly put her head in it and began to weep..

Also significant is the sudden laughter of the Young Guard as they are sitting on the floor of the prison cell, when Maya says, "You kids don't know anything about dialectic." Maya was one of the few among the members of the group who had been a Komsomol member before the war -- she was already a Komsomol at school. Fadeyev's remark that this laughter occurred because "it was so hard to figure out to oneself that such words could be pronounced in prison" seems to me to be a rather legalistic attempt to save this very laughter (i.e. to make it acceptable to Party leaders). I would connect this laughter with the whole previous characterization of the Young Guard members. They often behaved themselves rather as "kids" than as members of an underground "Communist or-ganization."

The oath of Koshevoy and all other members of the Young Guard in the film and in the novel is the same. It ends with the following words:

... If I should break (narushu) this sacred (svyashchennaya) oath under tor-ture or because of cowardice, so shall my name, my relatives, be damned (prok-lyaty) forever and I myself shall be punished by the severe hands of my comrades. Blood for blood, death for death.

The formulation of this oath has something in common with the old conjura-tions in Russian folklore. These conjurations belong to the oldest examples of folk poetry. They were preserved probably because the people who used them had to be careful not to change a single word. Usually such conjurations end: "shall my words be firm, more firm than stone and iron," or "I am locking my words with locks, the keys of which I am throwing under the white stone Alatyr, and as strong as are the clamps in locks, so are my words."

V. An Analysis of the Nazi Film Hitlerjunge Quex[17]

Gregory Bateson

The thematic analysis of the German propaganda film Hitlerjunge Quex represents an initial effort by a cultural anthropologist to apply anthropological techniques to the examination of a fictional film. Made during World War II (1942), the central question of the research was: What sort of people were the Nazis? Today, however, the analysis has a more general relevance as a study of a German view of Germans at a particular time and place. The analysis is important also because being the first and -- even today -- the most detailed of its kind to have been written up, it gave impetus to further thematic analyses not only of films but also of other types of contemporary artistic productions.

Hitlerjunge Quex was produced and first shown by the Nazis in the period of their accession to power, in 1933. Like the slightly earlier Soviet film The Road to Life (which appears to have had some influence on the makers of the German film), but unlike the Soviet film The Childhood of Maxim Gorky,[18] the plot of Hitlerjunge Quex is a contrived one, designed especially for the use to which it was put -- to influence those who saw it in favor of the political ideology of those who had made it.

Unlike some other German films of the 1930s that used indirect means of propagandizing, this film portrayed both "Nazis" and "Communists" on the screen. In discussing why he selected the film for analysis, Bateson (1945) wrote: "To make all these other films available for analysis it was first necessary to establish the basic symbolic equations and this could best be done by analyzing a film which showed the Nazis and their enemies explicitly labeled on the screen. Such a film makes it possible to dissect out the relationship between these two fixed points and the whole range of phenomena -- parenthood, adolescence, maturity, cleanliness, sex, aggression, passivity and death -- which are embraced by the Nazi view of life. Rather few German films meet this requirement" (p. 1). In addition, the film contained a large mass of material on German family life; and the film was a good one -- in the sense of being well acted and as a close-knit artistic unit. Finally, it carried the stamp of official Nazi approval and was known to have been popular with Nazi audiences.[19]

Bateson's analysis is concerned with the interweaving of themes in one fictional film in which the film as a whole is regarded as a single psychological or artistic unit and each event on the screen is seen as set in the context of the film as a whole.

In his methodological introduction to the analysis, Bateson (1945) stated, in part: "A painting, a poem or a dream may give an exceedingly false picture of the real world, but insofar as the painter or the poet is an artist, and insofar as he has complete control of his medium, the artistic product must of necessity tell us about the man himself. In the same way, this film, insofar as it is an integrated work of art ... must tell us about the psychology of its makers, and tell us perhaps more than they intended to tell. It is not possible, however, to

---

17. The selections presented here are from Bateson (1943 and 1945). The full analysis runs to slightly more than 20,000 words of which only brief excerpts are given.
18. For a detailed analysis of this film, and another approach to film analysis, cf. Erikson (1950a).
19. The film was produced by Ufa under Nazi egis. It was shown to Hitler at the Ufapalast in Munich on September 12, 1933, and had its première -- which was made a great occasion -- a week later in Berlin (cf. Kalbus, 1935).

tell in any given case whether the film makers were fully conscious, partially conscious or unconscious of what they were doing, and therefore this question is not asked in the analysis. In the analysis, the film has been treated not merely as an individual's dream or work of art, but also [because it has been created by a group and with an eye to popular appeal] as a myth. We have applied to it the sort of analysis that the anthropologist applies to the mythology of a primitive or modern people" (pp. ii–iii).

In his examination of the film, Bateson made a series of thematic analyses, in each of which the film as a whole is regarded from a particular viewpoint: (1) time perspectives -- an analysis of climax structure; (2) the characterization of the two political groups and the backgrounds in which they are set; (3) the interactions between the various members of the family; (4) the projected family of the future; and (5) the handling of two symbols -- the knife and death -- recurrent in the film. On the basis of these analyses, then, he constructed a series of hypotheses about Nazi character structure and dynamics.

To illustrate the method of analysis there are presented here, following an abbreviated statement of the plot, one excerpt from a summary statement of the principal themes in <u>Hitlerjunge Quex</u> and portions from two sections of the full thematic analysis. -- Ed.

1. Plot Summary[20]

The hero of this film is Heini Voelker, a preadolescent boy, the son of a violent father and a drudge mother. His parents are of the lower middle class and have fallen in the world as the result of the inflation and the father's war wounds.

Heini's father hurts himself in a minor street riot, touched off by the speech of a sinister Communist, Wilde, when two Communist boys have stolen an apple from a vendor. Stoppel, an organizer of Communist youth, helps the father home and helps the mother dress the wound. The father makes a violent scene when the mother refuses to give him money to buy beer. Heini comes home from his work, sees the scene, and secretly gives his mother a mark, which she gives the father. The mother opens the window, letting in the music of the merry-go-round at the fair. Heini asks his mother for a penny for a lottery where he has seen a wonderful knife; she gives it to him. He goes to the lottery and loses.

Stoppel reappears, comforts Heini, and invites him to join a hike of the Communist Youth the next day. Heini accepts.

On the hike Heini is disgusted by the gross behavior of the Communists, especially a Communist girl, Gerda, who forces a kiss on him. He wanders off in the dark and watches a company of Hitler Youth who are celebrating the summer solstice near by. The Nazis find him, accuse him of spying, and send him away. He sleeps by himself and next morning, after watching the Nazis with longing eyes, he goes home to his mother.

He tells his mother how wonderful the Nazis are and sings her the Nazi Youth Song. The father hears him, is furious, and compels Heini to sing the "International," boxing his ears while he sings.

Next day at school Heini again meets Gerda and resists her advances. He approaches Fritz, a boy leader of the Nazis, and is invited home to supper with

---

20. Summarized mainly from Bateson (1943).

Fritz and his sister, Ulla. Gerda vamps Grundler, a weak Nazi boy. At supper Fritz and Ulla invite Heini to come to the opening of their new Nazi clubroom (Heim) in the Communist district. Heini hesitates because he has no house key, and then accepts.

The father has meanwhile enrolled Heini in the Communist Youth and that evening gives Heini a house key so he can go to the Communist local. Heini is distressed by his father's kind tone, but is determined not to go to the Communist meeting.

When Heini goes out in the evening, he meets Stoppel, who tells him that the Communists are going to raid the Nazi "home" (club) and that he is to help. He slips away, but is caught by the police after the raid. The police tell him to "go home to Mother." The Nazis accuse him of treachery.

Next day Stoppel tells Heini he is a hero because he did not inform the police and tells him of a Communist plan to dynamite the Nazi club. Heini telephones to warn Ulla and Fritz, but Fritz will not listen and Ulla hangs up. Heini tries to persuade the police to interfere but they treat him as a child. While he is looking for Stoppel at the fair, there is a violent explosion -- the Nazis have blown up the dynamite -- and Heini returns home singing the Youth Song.

Stoppel threatens Heini's mother and she is in a state of despair because Heini will not make up with him. He is certain now the Nazis will accept him. As he sleeps the mother turns on the gas to kill herself and Heini; the screen is filled with the fumes (which billow like a flag).

Heini awakes in the hospital. The Nazi boys and Ulla bring him a uniform and a mirror in which to admire himself. Later a nurse tells Heini his mother will never come. While he is convalescent, his father and the District Leader of the Nazis visit him and the question is asked, "Where does the boy belong?" The Nazi wins the discussion by a verbal trick and Heini goes to live in a Nazi clubhouse outside the Communist district. Grundler, the weak Nazi, nicknames Heini "Quex"; he resents this and a small fight breaks out among the boys that is quelled by a barked command from the District Leader.

Heini wants to go to the Communist district to distribute leaflets for the 1933 election. Grundler and Gerda treacherously destroy all the available Nazi leaflets. Heini and Ulla work all night to prepare new leaflets and when the work is completed Ulla gives Heini a sisterly kiss. Heini goes to the Communist district to distribute the leaflets. He is hunted and encircled in the dark streets by the Communists who have been waiting to take vengeance. He takes refuge in one of the tents of the deserted fair.

Accidentally he touches a mechanical figure of a drummer and the figure starts to beat its drum, thus betraying him. Heini is stabbed (presumably by Wilde, who has the original knife that Heini coveted). The Nazis come and find Heini dying. His last words are, "Our flag billows before us, it leads ..." The sound track takes up the Youth Song and the flag appears on the screen, giving place to marching columns of Hitler Youth.

2. The Family Constellation[21]

In this plot Heini's conversion to Nazism depends essentially upon the contrast he is shown between the Nazis' picture of themselves and the Nazis' picture of "Communism." But this is not the only message that the propagandist conveys. At the beginning of the film the propagandist seems deliberately to build up an association between the mother and Communism. It is the mother who goes and opens the window and lets in the degenerate music of the fair, and the fair is the setting in which the Communists are most at home. And it is the mother who gives Heini the money to enter the lottery to try to win a knife from this depraved environment. Stoppel, the Communist organizer, is also associated with the mother, joining her in aiding and placating the father. In this way the audience is encouraged to accept, unwittingly, the basic premise that ideology is related to the family structure.

Also at the beginning of the film we are shown Heini as a hero rescuing his mother from the father's violence by self-sacrifice. As the film progresses, we see these self-sacrificing attitudes shifted from the mother to the nation and the position of Communism shifted from its association with the mother to a very much more dramatic association with the father. The basic premise, that ideology is connected with the family structure, is allowed to persist, but the straw-man association between Communism and the mother is smashed when the father compels Heini to sing the "International," boxing his ears in time with the song. In this way the propagandist confers on Nazism not merely the virtue of Heini's preference for it, but also the whole fanatical gamut of emotions that are evoked in the Oedipus situation.

The film as a whole implies that Nazism is the total destruction of the family. In order to create a violent emotional adherence to Nazism the family itself is unscrupulously sacrificed. The one feature of the film which appears discrepant with this treatment is the propagandist's implict and probably unconscious confession that there is another way. The symbol of adult human status, which Heini is not allowed to use, is the house key -- a symbol that while conferring freedom also confers the promise of return to the family.

3. Time Perspectives[22]

The climax structure of any work of art is related to those characteristics of the artist which the psychologists call "time perspectives." All people must impose sense and coherence on the very complex stream of their experience. They must punctuate this stream so that the relations between events may be meaningful. But the type of sense that different types of people impose is known to vary greatly. Some people see themselves as living in a fatalistic universe;

---

21. Excerpted from Bateson (1943).
22. Excerpt, slightly condensed, from Bateson (1945, pp. 8-13).

others see their own behavior as determining the future; others again believe in a a Golden Age, and of these some will put the Golden Age in the past while others imagine it in the near or distant future. Probably it is not given to man to determine which of these time perspectives is "true," because the stream of events to which the perspective is applied includes not only outside events but also his own behavior. His own behavior will be guided by his own time perspective, and thus whatever that time perspective may be, the total stream as he sees it will acquire the appropriate structure.

But since his behavior is shaped in terms of his time perspective, it becomes important to study this. A statement of a man's time perspective is a way of describing his character.[23]

The time perspective of this film is summarized for us in the Hitler Youth Song the words of which were composed by Baldur von Schirach:

> "Our flag billows (flattert) before us!
> We advance (ziehn) into the future man for man!
> We march for Hitler through night and pain (Not)
> With the flag of youth for freedom and bread!
> Our flag billows before us!
> Our flag is the new epoch (Zeit)!
> And the flag leads us into eternity (Ewigkeit)!
> Yes, the flag is more than death!"

Or, in one phrase, we can summarize the time perspective of the film as "through death to a millennium."

In this film there are two cycles of this kind in which Heini goes through death. First, there is his incomplete death when his mother turns on the gas, and second, there is his final death at the hands of the Communists. We must ask, therefore, What sorts of death were these and to what sort of millennium did they lead? The two deaths have a number of features in common:

1. Each follows some conspicuous achievement on Heini's part. The gas death occurs after he has rescued the Nazi boys and enabled them to blow up the Communists' dynamite; the final death follows his successful distribution of leaflets in the Communist district after the Communists thought that all were destroyed.

2. There is a woman involved in both deaths. The gas death is the final episode in Heini's relation to his mother; and the final death follows Ulla's kiss.

3. Each death is represented on the screen by a sort of billowing or waving motion. In the case of the gas death we see the fumes fill the screen and move like heaving waves. In the final death, it is the Nazi flag itself which fills the frame and billows before us.

4. Each death is accompanied by a change in illumination. The gas death occurs in a darkened room and after it the fumes fade away to disclose Heini in a brightly lighted hospital ward. In the final death Heini distributed his leaflets and was encircled by the Communists in darkened streets; he takes refuge in the dark tent of the deserted fair; he is stabbed in the dark. We then see his legs faltering as he comes out of the tent in a half-light, and finally when the Nazis find him dying

---

23. For more detailed and systematic discussion of time perspective, cf. Frank (1939b) and Lewin (1942).

we see full daylight.

5. Each death accompanies a change in Heini's status. By the gas death he shifts from his family home to the hospital, a sort of neutral ground halfway towards Nazism. By his final death he moves from the world of the living to the world of reincarnated heroes.

6. In each death Heini's last words refer to the future. In the gas death his mother says, "Heini, settle your quarrel with him (Stoppel) or else everything is lost (sonst ist alles aus)" and Heini replies, "But Mother, now it is just beginning (jetzt fangt es doch erst an)." In the final death Heini's last words are: "Our flag billows before us... It leads ..."

7. Each death is rather amply predicted. The gas death is predicted by the mother at the beginning of the film when the father comes home hurt. She says, "You'll bring us all into misfortune (Unglück) again." Later while Heini is coming home from the hike we are shown a shot of the mother lighting the gas, and finally just before the event she says, "Everything is lost" (quoted above). The final death is predicted by the District Leader's anxiety, by Stoppel's and Gerda's warnings, and by the heavily weighted scene in which Wilde picks up the knife. Each death is tragic in the classical sense of being the final outcome of an inevitable sequence of events.

These features which are common to the two deaths give us together a rounded picture of Nazi time perspective. To get this picture it is important not to think of these features separately as they are enumerated above, but to combine then into a hazy sense of the total Weltanschauung. The achievement, the woman, the billowing, the change of light, the change of status, and the destiny idea together make up a state of mind that can only very inadequately be expressed in words -- an ongoing state through some sort of orgasmic upheaval to a final millennium.

The final term in the Nazi time perspective is of special interest. The beginning of the cycle, through suffering and effort to individual death, is comparatively common in fanatical cults, but the final goal towards which the Nazi nominally strives is a rather unusual one. It appears to be a sort of multiple reincarnation in this world. Heini's corpse is replaced on the screen, first by the flag and then by columns of marching Nazis, and in this final shot some trick photography has been used so that while we see the innumerable marching figures moving obliquely away from us we also see, faintly superimposed on them and much larger, the waists and thighs of uniformed Nazi figures striding towards us. Even after the passage through death, there is promise of future turmoil, sexual and aggressive.

A similar promise of multiple reincarnation is still more explicit in another Nazi film, Für Uns (1937). This is a documentary account of a Nazi party ceremony in which we see the dedication of sixteen concrete blocks to the memory of the sixteen martyrs of early Nazism. Each block has on it the name of a hero (Hans Schlageter, Horst Wessel, etc.) and the words "ON CALL" (ZUM APPEL). Each block supports a great urn in which flames billow. As a wreath is laid at the foot of each block, the name of the hero is called, and a thousand men somewhere in the stadium answer, "HERE!" The procession goes on to the next hero and again the answer comes back from another section of the stadium.

Before leaving the subject of Heini's deaths, it is necessary to ask why there should be two of them. In this, the film transgresses the ordinary canons of tragedy, but the reasons for this transgression lie in the peculiar social structure Nazism seeks to set up. In place of the more usual type of social system based on the family, Nazism substitutes a system based on what anthropologists call "age grades." The youth of the nation is to be divided into blocks from small boys (Pfimpfen), who are from six to ten years old, up to the fighting units of S. A. The step from each grade to the next is accompanied by an arduous initiation ceremony. (Cf. Ziemer, 1941.)

Initiation ceremonies and other rites that symbolize the passage from one social status to another usually include a symbolic statement of the candidate's death as a member of his former group, followed by a symbolic statement of his aggregation into the new group. Thus in giving Heini two deaths, the propagandist has epitomized a whole social system and a time perspective that envisages repeated symbolic deaths. Heini's final death implies that the long series of symbolic deaths representing promotions from one age grade to another will reach its climax in a real death and multiple reincarnation. His first death by gas tells us that the entry into the age-grade system is itself a passage rite, differing only from other passage rites and initiations in that Heini's mother, instead of mourning the loss of her boy when he leaves the family, is herself killed.

In killing the mother in this way the film does more violence to the conventional folk philosophies than is immediately apparent. It is not only that the film kills off a member of the group which Heini is leaving but, specifically, the mother is the predicter of tragedy, the representative of inevitable fate. This theme is not very striking in this particular film. We hear the mother at the beginning say to the father, "You will bring misfortune on us again," and later she dies, but this combination is not shocking to the average spectator. That this combination may be significant is, however, demonstrated by another Nazi propaganda film, Fahrmann Maria (Ferryman Maria, 1936), an allegory specifically concerned with death.... [In this film a beautiful ferrywoman, Maria, replaces the old ferryman, who has died. She tricks Death of a young male and lures Death into a swamp into which he sinks. The lovers go off together.] The second film leads us naturally to look in Hitlerjunge Quex for a second Destiny or Providence figure who should be a young female, replacing the dead mother.

This role is filled by Ulla. Twice Ulla works like Fate or Providence behind the scenes, to reverse the course of the plot. First, when Heini is caught spying on the Nazi hike, Fritz is angry and sends him away, but after he is gone we hear Ulla's voice saying, "He might have been one of us." The audience is left with the impression that Nazism is inaccessible, and this impression is reinforced by the distant views of the Nazi camp at which Heini gazes next morning. But on the following day Heini has no difficulty in approaching Fritz, who at once invites him to dinner. Later in the film we see another reversal of the same sort when Heini telephones to warn the Nazis about the dynamite and Ulla hangs up under Fritz's orders. Heini is left unable to make contact with anybody, but the explosion occurs. Nothing is said to explain either of these reversals and only one explanation is possible: Ulla, on both occasions, worked like Providence behind the scenes. Thus into the whole notion of death and into the time perspectives there has been infused a sense that death and Providence should be the object of the sort of attitudes the Nazis would direct towards the desirable female. Such a reading of the film will account at once for the use of orgasmic billowing symbols to represent death.

In concluding this discussion of the time perspectives expressed in this film, it is appropriate to consider how this film differs from others. Insofar as a time perspective involves an expectation of change in the course of events, the perspective itself and its implications for character may alter as time goes on. The expected climax may occur, in which case the former time perspective is satisfied and a new one must be constructed. Alternatively the climax may not occur, and some modification must then be introduced into the time perspective to accentuate or relieve the frustration.

When ... we look at a much later film, Ohm Krueger, released in April 1941, we find an entirely different time perspective. This film deals with the story of the Boer War, and the Boers, fighting England, are clearly the model that is held up before the German audience. The film starts after the Boer War is over. We see Krueger as an old man suffering from psychological blindness in a hospital in Switzerland. He is looked after by a young nurse to whom he narrates the story of the war. The film then cuts back to South Africa, and we see the Great Trek followed by disreputable intrigues attributed to Rhodes, Jameson, Chamberlain, Queen Victoria, and others. The war begins with prodigious victories for the Boers and ends with utter defeat. We see the graves of the Boers and then the film returns to Krueger in Switzerland, who predicts that all this suffering will be avenged by some greater nation.

The time perspective implicit in this film seems to be the precise opposite of that of the films of the early thirties. Instead of "through death to a millennium," this later film offers us "through preliminary victories to ultimate defeat" -- a time perspective which probably results from the resemblance between the First and the Second World Wars. We may note, however, that Hitlerjunge Quex and Ohm Krueger are alike in assuming an enormous pendulum swing in the tide of human events.

4. Political Group and Backgound[24]

The very first shot of the film lays the base for the characterization of Communism. It is a close-up shot of a single apple that fills the screen -- a

---

24. Excerpt, slightly condensed, from Bateson (1945, pp. 13-19).

double symbol of food and sexuality. From this the camera trucks back to include the whole heap of apples in the vendor's store and we see two boys, whom
we later discover to be Communists, debating whether to steal the apples. They
are hungry and without money, and suddenly one of them snatches an apple and
runs. The vendor grabs the boy and begins to box his ears.

A second characterization of Communism follows in the same sequence.
Wilde, the sinister Communist agitator, makes a speech beginning, "Workers
(Proleten), hear me. It is not this boy alone who has been boxed on the ears,
I tell you that all of you who are here have had your ears boxed."

Thus in a single sequence Communists are characterized as unstoical in the
face of temptations of the mouth and as making political capital out of purely
human woes. In doing this the propagandist has resorted to two sorts of Biblical
reference: he has invoked the apple and has put Christlike phrasing into Wilde's
mouth.

On the hike, we see the contrast between the ragged disorderly Communists
and the neat and disciplined Nazis, and we are told almost in so many words that
this contrast is a part of the emotional dynamics upon which Nazism rests. A
platoon of Nazis girls in uniform is standing on the station when a disorderly mob
of Communists comes by. At the head of the Nazi girls is Ulla (though the audience does not know as yet that this girl will play a special part in the story).
Just before the arrival of the Communists, Ulla's head hangs drooping forward
in a very unmilitary posture, but when she sees the Communists she suddenly
raises it and holds herself proudly erect. Her gesture implies that the emotional
value of Nazism is not simple and positive, it is also negative; it is a pride in
not being the sort of people that they accuse their enemies of being.

Immediately after this incident, the film begins to develop the themes that
were first suggested by the apple. We see the Communist boy who stole the
apple take chewed food from his mouth and fling it in the face of one of the Nazi
boys, and in later stages of the film we repeatedly see the Communists indulging
in gross eating, throwing their food, passing a half-eaten apple from one to another, smoking cigarettes (the Nazis apparently do not smoke) and drinking
schnapps (the Nazis drink only beer).

The response of the Nazis to this insult of the thrown food is interesting.
For a fraction of a second we see them break their ranks and about to indulge in
a completely disorderly brawl. The District Leader gives a barked command
and they return to attention. But in this fraction of a second the psychological
base for the whole propagandic system is exposed. The Nazi assumption is that
but for the barked command and their veneer of discipline they themselves
would be the same sort of disorderly rabble that they represent the Communists
as being.[25]

25. The general opinion of informants who were in Germany at this time and in
touch with the Youth Movements is that the Leftist groups were slightly
more disciplined than the Hitler Youth.

This assumption reappears again when Heini is living in the Nazi clubhouse. Heini is referred to as "Quex" (or Quicksilver) at a meal, and when he resents this nickname a disorderly brawl breaks out, involving all the Nazi boys. Some of them fight in one cluster and some in another in a completely disorganized manner, until a barked command from the District Leader freezes them into guilty immobility.

In this sense the disorderly characteristics that the film attributes to the Communists are another example of the Nazis' habit of attributing their own real or potential vices to their enemies, and we shall see that the whole characterization of Communism in this film is in a sense a self-portrait of Nazism. It represents what the Nazis think that they themselves would be like without their discipline or -- psychologically speaking -- what they are like under the veneer of that discipline.

The sexual suggestion that was implicit in the apple is also developed on the hike. When Heini enters the compartment on the train, Gerda, the Communist girl, seizes him around the neck and pulls him down onto her lap. His back is towards her, but she forces his face around until she is able to plant a kiss on his lips. Gerda is wearing a boy's cap and as Heini stands horrified she pulls the cap off her head. Heini says, still more horrified, "You are a girl," and she replies, "You notice everything."

This kiss might appear sufficient to smear the Communists with the combined reproach of sexuality and mouthiness, but the propagandist was apparently not satisfied and he borrows a Freudian recipe to drive the point home. We see Stoppel push a peeled banana into Gerda's mouth with the palm of his hand, and this moment is chosen for the others to start to sing the "International."

Later in the camp we see another characterization of the Communists in which again a Freudian recipe is borrowed. They play a buttocks-slapping game (Schinkenklopfen). The boy who stole the apple is held bent over so that he cannot see who slaps him. Gerda supplies the slap and then self-consciously looks the other way. The boy guesses correctly that she is the guilty one, and she in turn is grabbed by the crowd and held while the boy spits on his hands preparatory to taking his revenge. Heini at this point turns away disgusted....

In contrast to the Communists the Nazis are almost colorless. We see their parade-ground smartness, we see them dashing into the sea to bathe; but these behaviors are rather the negative of the excesses that are attributed to Communism, and throughout one is left with the feeling that Nazi life is empty. On three occasions we see them eat -- on the hike and in the Nazi clubroom and at the home of Fritz and Ulla -- but except on the hike, where the Nazi eating is contrasted with the throwing of food by the Communists, their eating habits

---

26. An official propaganda photograph of the "Strength through Joy" movement shows that this identical game of Schinkenklopfen is commonly played on Nazi picnics.

are not specifically used to characterize them. In the Nazi clubroom the meal is merely the setting in which Heini's nickname is given him, and at the home of Fritz and Ulla it is the whole upper-middle class background that is significant rather than the eating.

We have noted that the contrast in terms of orderliness is based on the Nazi habit of referring their own disapproved weakness to their enemies, and two types of evidence are available to show that the same is true of the sexual contrast.

The first evidence is of the same general type as that which we used in the case of orderliness-disorderliness. The Nazis used the premise that they them-selves would be disorderly but for their discipline, as an argument in favor of their whole system; and in the same way they employ the argument that they would be sexually depraved. The story of Grundler's fall is propagandic in this sense.

The story begins on the morning after the hike, when he and the other Nazis are distributing leaflets. Gerda, under Stoppel's orders, contacts Grundler, asking him for a leaflet and then for another and another till he gives her all he has. Then she throws all the leaflets into the river and starts a flirtation with Grundler by asking him for a cigarette. A few minutes later she says she wants Turkish delight. He asks where they can get this, and she says, "At the fair." We then see Grundler falling in step with Gerda on the way to the fair. Later we see them dizzily riding the horses in the merry-go-round, and the camera stoops to pay special attention to the swinging legs of the boy and girl. From this point on Grundler's uniform becomes more and more slovenly, and finally, under Gerda's influence, he enters into a plot to destroy the entire supply of Nazi leaflets. He brings the leaflets on a barrow to a rendezvous with Gerda and together they throw all the bundles of leaflets into the flowing river.

The inclusion of Grundler in the film can partly be explained as a bid for "truthfulness," an attempt to make the audience say to themselves, "Yes, the film is not an idealized picture of Nazism because after all they do show a bad Nazi," and of course the propagandist can safely show this bad Nazi because the showing is accompanied by disapproval of Grundler's weakness. Actually, how-ever, they have shown a Nazi who is not only bad but deteriorating, and thus, consciously or unconsciously, they have again preached that Nazism has a double quality. On one side Nazism may have the fine overpurity of comradeship (Kamaradschaft), but this purity carries with it on the other side the tendency to deteriorate in a particular direction.

This is by no means the same sort of double nature as that which is attrib-uted to man by the more familiar Christian sects. The Christian dualisms have always assumed good and bad elements within the individual man; they may have insisted that the good side needed external help from Church or minister, but they have never seen man as a mechanical creature who should be passive vis-à-vis an external disciplinary authority. In the Nazi view -- and the same is true of the handling of temptation and depravity in many pre-Nazi German films -- man's nature will respond almost mechanically to bright lights, the whirl of circuses, and city life. He will inevitably be sucked down into a swamp.[27]

The second type of evidence, which shows that, in attributing a certain sort of sexuality to the Communists, the Nazis are merely describing the worst side of their own nature, is indirect. If the Communists were merely represented as different from Nazis, then the film maker could claim that he was simply giving an objective picture. But these "Communists" are not simply different from Nazis, they are a systematic opposite of the Nazi ideal. This relationship is, of course, what we should expect if the attributes of "Communism" are psychologically rooted in the Nazi character, and while it is conceivable that this relatedness might be due to coincidence such a coincidence would be unlikely.

The clearest indication that "Communism" as here depicted is only the obverse of Nazism comes from the make-up of the two girls, Gerda and Ulla. Gerda, the Communist, is more heavily female in her head and torso. Her hair strays loose; she continually expresses her sexual desires and frustrations with gestures of the lips; and her breasts are evident through her sluttish blouse. But in contrast to this femaleness in her head and torso, her legs are usually clothed in slacks. Ulla, on the other hand, is the precise reverse of this. She wears a skirt, but from the waist up she is progressively more boyish. Instead of a blouse she wears a Nazi shirt open at the collar and loosely held with a tie. She has straight blond hair, bobbed and severely parted. She wears a beret.

This contrast may be summarized by saying that if Gerda's head and torso were set on Ulla's legs a complete female figure would result; whereas Ulla's torso on Gerda's legs would give us a complete boy. They are not just two people, different one from the other; they are a pair of people, each systematically related to the other. Gerda is a postadolescent female with male legs and Ulla is an adolescent or preadolescent boy with female legs.[28] The same type of systematic contrast occurs also between Heini's father and the District Leader, and again between Heini and Grundler. It is evident, however, that the likelihood of these three systematic contrasts being all of them due to coincidence is very small, and we may take their systematic nature as evidence for the fact that the depiction of the Communists is a function of the Nazi character.

Lastly, we cannot leave the consideration of the contrast between Nazism and Communism without examining the backgrounds in which these two political

27. Actual death in swamps occurs rather frequently in German films. The case of Fahrmann Maria has already been mentioned. And in Friesenot a girl is punished for sexual relations with a Communist by being led to the edge of a swamp where she must commit suicide. The film suggests that this punishment is a traditional custom among the peasants of this old German colony in Russia.
28. In Nazi youth films the camera rather frequently provides shots of the backs of the legs of boys, showing the bare inside of the knees.

groups are set. The film makers went out of their way to blacken Communism by photographing the Communist scenes in a poor light. Even Heini's home is murky and sinister; the fair so much frequented by Communists is poorly lit; and the room in which the Communists meet is clouded with tobacco smoke. In contrast to this, the home of Fritz and Ulla and the Nazi clubroom are brightly lit, and on the hike we see Heini progress from the murky Communist camp through darkness to the scene in which the Nazis celebrate the solstice, where their beacon fire gives bright contrasts of illumination. When he is dismissed as a spy, Heini retires into the darkness, but next morning he is shown a brilliant scene of the Nazis on the beach in the morning sunlight.

In general these shifts between light and darkness are satisfactorily wover. into the plot, but at the very end of the film one shift from darkness to light seems arbitrary. We see Heini encircled in the darkened street and he is killed in the dark, but when the Nazis come to pose beside his dying body it is broad daylight.

In addition to darkness, the background of Communism is characterized by various kinds of spinning objects -- the merry-go-round, the lottery wheel, and spinning targets in the shooting booth. It appears that the Nazis' conception of the sort of sexuality which they attribute to the Communists is closely linked with feelings of dizziness. Man, the mechanical puppet, is endlessly liable to be swept off his feet into some sort of whirlpool.[29]

In addition to the use of these dizzy symbols, Communism is twice characterized by the river. This occurs at the beginning and the end of the story of Grundler's fall. First we see Gerda throw Grundler's leaflets over her shoulder into the river, and finally we see Grundler and Gerda together throwing the main supply of leaflets in bundles into the water. Probably the appropriateness of this symbol derives from some notion that Communism sweeps all good things away.

There is clearly a rather close relationship between the hypnotic fascination that comes from staring at waves and that which comes from looking at spinning objects, and this relationship is probably another facet of the relationship we have already noted between Nazism and the Nazi characterization of Communism. There is, however, an important difference between waves and spinning objects. Waves contain an illusion of progress, of forward movement, but spinning objects evidently get nowhere. It is possible that the waves used to characterize Nazism are related to the endless marching that has such great fascination for Nazis and which appears in almost every Nazi film. Only in its endlessness does this marching resemble the spinning of the symbols associated with Communism.

---

29. This type of symbolic treatment of temptation is also common in pre-Nazi German films (e.g. Variety, The Street, Sunrise).

PART SEVEN

PROJECTIVE TESTS

A. THE USE OF PROJECTIVE TESTS IN GROUP RESEARCH

Margaret Mead

The use of projective tests in the study of culture at a distance is subject to rather severe limitations. If we wish to emphasize the application of comparable methods to the study of cultures distant in time and inaccessible in space, the method is obviously applicable only to the latter. We cannot give a Rorschach test to Napoleon or Lenin. Also, where the results of tests are coded so that the test stimulus and the response are never again considered as a whole, this is a drawback for group research, where a multidisciplinary group is to work simultaneously on the materials. Here such tests as the Rorschach or the Szondi contrast with tests in which the response forms the kind of whole that can be shared by a group, as is the case with the Horn-Hellersberg Drawing Completion test or Margaret Lowenfeld's World Game and Mosaic tests or, to a lesser extent, the story responses to Thematic Apperception cards, which can be considered more independently of the stimulus card than is possible with the Rorschach. Another difficulty lies in the esoteric nature of interpretation for tests like the Rorschach, in which not only a general knowledge of psychoanalytic theory but also detailed experience with test administration and interpretation are necessary. This means in practice that the clinical psychologist who is administering the projective tests can communicate only conclusions to the other members of the group. Where pictures are drawn or mosaic patterns are made, the whole group can, independently of the detailed procedures of administration and interpretation, work on the results. [1]

A second drawback to the use of projective tests of the Rorschach type is the very large expenditure of time involved in order to arrive at contentless abstractions about amount of anxiety or degree of security. Where comparable or less highly coded methods are used, especially by the anthropological type of interview, the same abstractions can be arrived at, based however on rich contentful material that communicates with other workers in the group;

---

1. This procedure was used in 1950, when members of Research in Contemporary Cultures acted as consultants for Dr. Margaret Lowenfeld in working out the cultural components in American performances on the Mosaic test, performances which, to the analyst accustomed to European responses, often seemed to have no pattern. Through this group work, the consultants -- without having gone through a long apprenticeship in learning to give and interpret the test -- could distinguish some essential contrasts; i.e. the way Americans responded to the space allowed for the design, the way Europeans implicitly asked, "What was the intention of the maker of the test pieces -- obviously as design elements?" while Americans treated the whole as a test rather than as a design; the greater use of color made by Americans, etc.

comments on the frequency of animal responses, for instances, have no such concrete reverberative quality. Viewed from the standpoint of economy, projective tests that yield little cultural content are almost prohibitively expensive.

A third drawback is the effect on informants. Great care must be taken in timing the administration of tests so as neither to disrupt an interview sequence nor to establish transference that is inconvenient in the project setting. As there are great differences among individuals in their responses to the projective test experience, it is difficult to standardize any kind of routine; constant consultation is necessary where informants are to be tested who are at the same time working with other members of the research group. In the two illustrations given here, Dr. Abel used subjects from within the Research in Contemporary Cultures group of informants and also protocols from another project. Dr. Hellersberg worked entirely within the project. The use of Rorschach and Thematic Apperception tests among the small number of French informants was even more subject to disturbances in interviewer-informant relations, though the results were fruitful for this particular group. [2]

A fourth objection is the quasi-clinical position of these tests, which complicates the degree of sophistication that members of the research team are permitted to acquire. On the principle that it is very difficult, if not impossible, to think even in the most superficial way about the responses to a test one has not taken, it was arranged that workers in Research in Contemporary Cultures who had never taken the tests that were to be used (i.e. Rorschach, Thematic Apperception, Horn-Hellersberg) should be given them; subsequently they were confronted with the administering clinicians' refusal to give any interpretation to the individuals who had taken the tests. While this particular difficulty could be overcome, it is symptomatic of the confusion between therapy and research that surrounds any use of these tests, which were designed for diagnostic purposes in therapeutic contexts and have never been properly reassessed or redesigned for research purposes.

On the positive side, the following considerations may be advanced. Individuals with great skill and experience in the use of any one of these tests find them extremely congenial research tools. If such a trained clinician enters a research team and is willing to give up the clinical diagnostic therapeutic approach for a research approach, he or she may be expected to contribute more important insights than might be the case if a less familiar technique for the exploration of personality were to be used. However, this amounts to saying that if a member of a team already knows how to use projective tests, it is worth while to have them used. It is not an argument for adding a clinical psychologist to the team for this specific purpose.

A case may also be made for the usefulness of projective methods as a way of orienting the research worker in handling his own unconscious motiva-

2.   For a report on this research, cf. Abel, Belo, and Wolfenstein: "An Analysis of French Projective Tests," in Métraux and Mead (1953).

tions and in analyzing unconscious elements in the cultural materials being studied. But this is rather an argument for certain kinds of research training than for the research usefulness of the tests.

A final case for the use of these tests is that they present a highly formalized and relatively exact way of coding materials so that they can be communicated to other projective-test workers. As the number of workers in the field of culture and personality who have used projective tests is fairly large, it is probably worth while to have some test results that have been co-ordinated with the results of all the other types of research, to add to this pool of shared knowledge of cultural variations in test responses.

But from the standpoint of exploration, or Stage 1 of this type of research, our experience in Research in Contemporary Cultures lent no support to any preference for the use of projective tests as compared with the use of the free interview by experienced interviewers. Tests would more appropriately be used for Stage 2, that of validation and verification, when patterned responses to standardized situations can be used to test the original hypotheses, just as comparable analyses of closed bodies of documentary material can be used for purposes of validation.

The most important methodological finding from the Research in Contemporary Cultures experience with the use of projective tests is Dr. Abel's: that for the use of these tests to delineate cultural regularities it is necessary to have at least two groups -- male and female, native-born and reared versus native-born and foreign-reared, etc. This means in effect that to adapt projective tests as a tool in cultural research, the comparative method, which assigns equal status to the cultures or cultural elements compared, must be substituted for the essentially normative character of clinical diagnosis, in which each subject's degree of pathology is assayed against some hypothetical "normalcy."[3]

In the two illustrations that follow, these various contrasts are brought out. Both studies are based on Chinese materials and were made at the same time. by research workers in one research group. Both Dr. Hellersberg and Dr. Abel were skilled in the use of the respective tests; one could be shared with the group and contained rich cultural content, the other is presented in a form that is actually only completely intelligible to Rorschach specialists. Dr. Hellersberg's article illustrates the interplay with other types of cultural materials; Dr. Abel's illustrates the use of contrasting groups to provide a comparative basis for her cultural interpretations.

---

3.   In this connection it is interesting that some of the most fruitful work done by Dr. Irving Hallowell's group has come from comparisons between the more and the less acculturated. In illustration of the contention that these tests yield nothing that cannot be arrived at by other methods -- as far as cultural analysis is concerned -- cf. the formulations of Ray Birdwhistell on two groups of Kutenai, in his paper "Personality Dimension and Kutenai-White Contacts," given at a meeting of the American Anthropological Association (1951).

B. TWO ILLUSTRATIONS OF THE USE OF
PROJECTIVE TESTS WITH CHINESE SUBJECTS

I. Visual Perception and Spatial Organization: A Study of Performance on the Horn-Hellersberg Test by Chinese Subjects[4]

Elisabeth F. Hellersberg

This paper is part of a study of cultural stability and acculturation as these are reflected in performance on the Horn-Hellersberg drawing test by seventy adult and child subjects of Chinese birth or background. Of the adults tested, thirty were born in China. The tests were administered by Dr. Hellersberg and other members of the Chinese group in Research in Contemporary Cultures, and were analyzed by Dr. Hellersberg. This is a qualitative study, based on a small number of tests from a group of subjects selected mainly in terms of their availability and willingness to co-operate. Many of them were informants who were interviewed at considerable length on various aspects of Chinese culture.

A comparison of performance on the test by China-born subjects who had been in the United States for varying lengths of time and by American-born subjects with a Chinese background indicates that there is a Chinese configuration in content and form. In terms of this test, it was found that with acculturation there are progressive changes both in content and form, but that the form elements (organization of space, use of wholes, use of perspective, etc.) tend to be the more stable.

Dr. Hellersberg describes the test briefly,[5] as follows:

The test consists of four pages. On the first three pages are twelve squares, in each of which there are a few lines taken from Western paintings. The directions given the subject are: Take your pencil and draw a picture in every square, utilizing the given lines. The subject may draw whatever he likes in any sequence he desires, turning the square in any direction. He is asked to write a caption under each picture. When he has finished the twelve squares with lines, he finds on the last page a square without lines; here he can draw unrestrictedly. An interview follows in which the subject is asked to give information on every picture; i.e. why he has drawn these themes and what the details of the drawings mean to him.

In every performance of this drawing completion test we can discern three levels. The first and second can be described and later measured and evaluated; the third does not permit a quantitative evaluation:

1. On the first level we may observe the conscious content with which the subject deals in drawing and in describing the purpose of his drawings in the interview.

2. On the second level we may discern the way in which the subject organizes and utilizes space. Here one deals with form elements and the way in which the subject expresses his relationship to reality.

3. On the third level are revealed the unconscious mechanisms that determine the content and form of what is drawn and the explanations given by the subject.

The portion of the study reproduced here is concerned with the first level, with the analysis of content and the manner of dealing with reality. -- Ed.

---

4. Excerpt from an unpublished document RCC-CH 662.
5. For a detailed discussion of this test, cf. Hellersberg (1950).

1. Description of Content and Manner of Dealing with Reality

Chinese Realism. The objects the Chinese subject draws appear concrete and practical. He makes numerous references to his immediate surroundings and to places where he has lived in the past. Thus in this test he gives a cross section of his recent experiences. To these he adds the emotional, political, and economic struggle through which he has lived. Every test provides a flow of concrete information on the Chinese people. Many pictures are filled with emotional and philosophical reflections on events and objects, thus revealing a variety of attitudes toward life, nature, other people, and daily events.

1. For instance, a woman subject who did child-welfare work during the Japanese occupation draws pictures that do not show skill or aesthetic value, but with every line she recalls another incident -- such as an old ancestral temple that served as an orphanage for children who had lost their parents. She drew also her home village and a garden of memory where flowers are presented to statues. In the interview she described the people fleeing over the railroad tracks, or the waterfall that soaked all the clothes and mattresses overnight. Another of her pictures shows a blanket on which children pinned paper flowers to decorate it. They used to improvise plays using these blankets as curtains. The informant remembered how the children carried dozens of dogs and cats and chickens with them for company. She remarked on the outstanding resilience of Cantonese children who, disguised as beggars, led some Japanese onto a bridge which was then blown up. This Resistance battle was inspired and directed by the grandmothers.

2. Another subject was a Chinese scholar who had been in the United States for four months. He was worried about the future of China. He drew a devil who descended on two officials. "They [the officials] did crooked business," he commented. He drew a chrysanthemum, which symbolized for him the wise man who retired from his office at an old age. The informant said, "This chrysanthemum is a spirit, the high spirit of the individual, not so easy to be interfered with." He quoted a poem written by a man when he resigned from his position "because he did not like to associate with officials." The informant pointed out that this poet saved his dignity by retiring from office. He devoted his time to contemplation and meditation. In another picture the informant drew a city wall and beyond it the large world with rain and sunshine. "Birds are coming forward to the wall. It is a symphony." And he goes on, "In my way, 'symphony' means that rain and sunshine go on together," meaning that they complement each other. Then he continued, "Raining is pessimist; the birds represent the hope and the savior." These Chinese informants do not delve in the sad things of life alone. They need one feeling tone to complement the other....We see here the mixture of concrete presentation with the symbolic interpretation. In this explanation the informant named contrasting

elements that he related to each other. This makes for "symphony" -- harmony.

3. Another subject was an official, a sophisticated man who expressed doubt that any psychologist could find out anything about his character. He drew a chicken and commented on it, "I like to see a chicken trembling -- no pity. It is just a fact, no emotion." He immediately went on to talk about a letter he had written to a friend who had tried to commit suicide; he wrote him, "A man like you must not accept defeat." And he continued, "I might have drawn a heroic-looking bird, but my pen happened to be making strokes that suggested a freezing chicken." One cannot escape the impression that the suicidal friend and the chicken he likes to see trembling have some relation in his mind; at least his remark of "no pity" is an accurate statement of his attitude. Later he drew the legs of a fat man sitting on a toilet. The character of this informant is different from that of most the other Chinese we tested, but without doubt in its anal-sadistic trends it must represent some characteristic variation.

Feeling Tone. The quotations demonstrate that these Chinese informants do not mind expressing feelings. On the contrary, feeling tone is frequently present and related to objects. A falling leaf is often referred to; i.e. "a leaf in autumn skies which falls from the skies." Or when pictures of mothers are drawn, there may be reference to "a reflection of universal love." There is continual reference to the quietness and beauty of nature, to which one can return whenever one wishes. Folk poems are quoted and added to the drawings. The informants explain that they have poems that are as common as folk songs are to Western man. Looking at high mountains, at waterfalls, or over the great expanse of quiet lakes -- these are scenes which are often repeated. They give deep satisfaction. I was also amazed at the sincere feeling-participation in whatever happens in the world politically. Even the most withdrawn scholar had one or two references to political events in his test. For instance, subjects call their pictures "Symbol of Truman's U.S.A., the Atomic Bomb," or "The Chinese War, the Symbol of Unity," or "How Majestic Is China." Compared with these Chinese subjects, Americans -- in this drawing test -- appear politically indifferent.

Ethical and Philosophical Viewpoints. There are also frequent references to the world as it should be and the way men can live in it. An informant said, "One should be able to live any place and like any place. All is in the mind. When one has peace of mind, one should enjoy any place." And later the same informant said, "I believe that everyone should be a universal, a world citizen." This introduces a third sort of theme that is recurrent: each of these Chinese informants appears to be a kind of practical philosopher. The meaning of human relations and the principles that govern them are real to him. This is not merely theory. How consistently expressions appear that explain symbolic "meaning" is indicated in the evaluation of the content of the drawings.

2. Evaluation of the Content of the Drawings

For the evaluation of the content of the drawings we have used a chart on which the content is recorded (cf. Chart A, page 327). The items drawn can be tabulated on this chart according to various qualitative characteristics of reality. This means that one can make a qualitative distinction between con- crete references to actual physical experience, the reality of everyday life, on the one hand, or the vanishing of this concreteness in emotional subjectivity, in fantasy distortion, on the other. Sometimes a loss of concrete reference to reality experience takes the form of abstraction, a sort of surrealistic playful- ness; sometimes the subject merely scribbles meaningless lines. For instance, a subject who draws a house may say, "I saw it yesterday," or he may comment, "It is just my imagination." Chinese informants frequently remark about their pictures, introjecting some feeling -- "I like this type of house." If such an emotional reference is made in the description of the picture, we assume that the object has been selected for drawing because the subject wants to incorpor- ate some feeling in his drawing.

At the bottom of Chart A nine varieties in the qualitative characters of presenting reality are enumerated. [6] These nine categories represent the various ways in which people in our culture area have presented pictures. These nine categories are, of course, only a selection of the possibilities for drawing objects.

On Chart A a number of areas have been blocked out; these indicate how the material recorded on the chart is used clinically for diagnostic purposes. Of the several areas delineated, [7] one of the most important for testing the ability to function normally of an individual in our culture, is that called the "Objective Zone." Looking at Chart A, it is evident why this area has been so designated. In our culture several functions, such as the economic and political, are dependent upon rational thinking. So, for instance, an individual cannot make a living without sharing, at least to some extent, rational concerns. After many years of experience in administering the test, we have found that efficient participation in the activities of our adult world can be predicted for an individual if 36% of all items drawn by him appear in this Objective Zone.

Testing our Chinese informants, it was found that the results differed from those of members of our own culture essentially in this respect. Of

---

6.   Cf. Chart A. On the left side are listed 40 items (e.g. Everyday life, Home; School, Work, Vocation, etc.) -- objects frequently drawn by sub- jects who have been tested in the northeastern part of the United States. From left to right on the Chart are nine columns on which the items drawn are tabulated, depending upon how they are described by the subject, that is, depending upon how the item described is related to reality. (Cf. key to Columns I-IX, below chart.) This chart is used to record and evaluate the content of the drawings with the descriptions of them given by the subject.
7.   Cf. page 328, the key to the zones indicated on Chart A.

thirty adult China-born subjects whom we tested, only four had 36% or more items in the Objective Zone. Two of these latter were engineers, one was an economist, and one had attended American schools since early childhood. (Form elements and the manner in which the pictures were organized, which character-ized our other informants, also diminished in three of these four tests.) Vari-ous exceptions to this seem to confirm the points we wish to make.

Lack of "objective concern" is, in our culture, shown only by individuals who are immature, emotionally disturbed, or mentally ill. Functioning in their own culture, these Chinese subjects showed positive characteristics. The lack of "objectivity" in our rational terms does not indicate defect in these subjects. Rather, it indicates that any established norm of a psychological test must be regarded as relative. Knowing this, the procedure of comparative testing is fruitful as it leads to the recognition of features and characteristics of a culture different from ours.

In fact, in the Chinese tests there is definite compensation for this lack of "objectivity." This is found in the Subjective Zone -- particularly in Column IV (Emotional values concerned with own person; integrated to objects). "Emotion-al expressiveness" (integrated to the object) is one of the dominant ways in which the Chinese subjects present their surroundings or their past experiences. (Cf. descriptions above, for examples.) The Chinese subjects are lavish in the expression of feeling and in emotional participation. One recognizes this in the titles of the pictures and also in the interviews.

Besides the frequent expression of feeling tone, there is another outstanding phenomenon, namely, a clustering of items in Column VII (Transferred reality; intended symbolism that is not conventional). Needless to say, "conventional" in the sense of Chart A refers only to symbols we regard as conventional for individuals within the area in which the norm was established. (The cross, the American flag, the four-leaf clover, the Valentine heart, the "V for victory" sign, are a few such conventional symbols.)

All other items with symbolic meaning drawn in the test are regarded as "unconventional" and such themes and items are tabulated on Chart A in Column VII. The use of such "unconventional" symbols may have various meanings in clinical interpretation. [8]

However, there are people -- in our Western cultures -- who lack sufficient "objectivity" and who instead delve in a search for meaning in unconventional symbolic presentations. Such people have been found to be either immature or emotionally disturbed, or, in still more severe cases, they are in a process of

8. It has been found, for instance, that individuals of Eastern European
    Jewish background who are in the process of acculturation in the United
    States, and who have found positive ground in the American scene, are
    likely to draw pictures with symbolic meaning.

mental deterioration of a paranoid character. Their drawings represent a desperate search either to find themselves or to find a meaning in the world or in events around them. Therefore, in our culture clustering in Column VII is a symptom of mental distress rather than of normality. (Cf. Chart A, in the Subjective Zone, Columns VII - IX indicate the subject's "Loss of Reality Contact.")

In contrast, many of the Chinese whom we tested revealed a paramountly symbolic approach to the world around them without appearing to be disturbed persons. They filled many objects with meaning and preferably drew things to which a common meaning was attached. These might be a pine tree, the lotus flower, the chrysanthemum, towering mountains, waterfalls, or vast expanses.

We must repeat here that studying a culture always implies the observation of one culture from the point of view of another. Each observation, each evaluation and interpretation, can only be given in terms of a comparison of one culture with another, and is only "relative" in terms of the other culture.

The description "Transferred reality; intended symbolism that is not conventional" (which is our heading for Column VII) is already inadequately used when applied to our Chinese informants. The Chinese symbolic expressiveness is rarely "unconventional" in their own sense, but it is so in ours. We have not the same body of symbolic and philosophical reference to objects around us.

The expression of philosophical and ethical ideas is, for Chinese, part of everyday life. It is not merely a pastime or a hobby or one of many highly specialized activities. The child learns common philosophical phrases as part of his early education, just as he also has learned to walk and to feed himself. He uses such phrases as part of his daily speech without special thought; this obviously has structural meaning. The first reader (the Three Word Classic, traditionally written by Wang Yin Ling in the thirteenth century), on each page of which are three characters forming a sentence, is in content a treatise on man, nature, the good and the bad, on social responsibility, and on social relationships. This first reader presents the ideas of sages who lived centuries ago. The maxims are guides to daily living and are commonly quoted. Hence when a Chinese informant incorporates meaning into many objects, this is not an idiosyncratic expression, but part of the learned, shared behavior of his culture.

When test material from subjects born of Chinese parents is plotted on Chart A, there are two outstanding features: the clustering of items in Column IV and in Column VII. These indicate that the China-born subject's way of presenting material in drawings and his relationship to reality differ from ours in at least two aspects. The first is the expression of feeling tone; the second is the tendency to philosophize. These seem to be compensation for what, in terms of our culture, may be considered a lack of "objectivity."

"Emotional values concerned with own person; integrated to objects" (Column IV) is, of course, a method of dealing with reality that is also found in normal American subjects. However, in the test material of Chinese subjects, it occurs several times more frequently.

We assume then that these activities, feeling and philosophizing, not only occur in connection with the test drawings of Chinese subjects, but also are essential responses to the life around them. (So also when Chinese informants discuss Chinese art, they stress yun [resonance] and ch'i [spirit] as basic concepts that guide painting.) And we are led to conclude that the clusterings in Columns IV and VII are indicative of the way these Chinese subjects deal with reality around them. They are indicative of their way of being objective; that is, object-related.

In general, from this material we anticipate that if we were to rebuild Chart A in order to test Chinese subjects in China and to develop a norm for clinical use in Chinese culture, we would most probably start with the hypothesis that the two aspects which have been discussed are essential features -- as essential as "rational objectivity" is in our culture for the performance of tasks or as a reflection of the subject's relation to reality.

It is likely that, using the test in China, we would find as we found in the tests of our China-born subjects, that items listed in the left margin of Chart A between Lines 11 and 23 (which occur in our Subjective Zone), would be drawn more frequently than the items listed on Lines 1 to 10 of the chart (in our Objective Zone). These latter are items that contribute to a more rational objectivity; in our culture we may even say that they make a rational objective approach possible.

We conclude, therefore, that in building up a "norm" for Chinese subjects -- that is, a norm for the representation of reality in this test -- we would perhaps define an area on the chart covering Lines 11 to 23 and Columns IV to VII. Although this lies within our Subjective Zone, this area would make up the Chinese objectivity or object relationship.

This is, of course, a hypothesis. The data on which the hypothesis is based come from the tests of Chinese subjects who are in an acculturation situation. From them we can only infer what we might expect to find about their way of dealing with the world around them in a study of Chinese subjects in China. [9]

---

9.   In the following sections of the complete paper, data are presented on differences in the selection and the presentation of content by Chinese informants who have been in the United States for different lengths of time. See also above, pages 323-24, the references to the test results of the four Chinese subjects with divergent training. -- Ed.

CHART A *

	I	II	III	IV	V	VI	VII	VIII	IX
1 Everyday life, home									
2 School, work, vocation									
3 City and country									
4 Modern techniques, science	OBJECTIVE								
5 Hobbies, pers. interests									
6 Politics, world events	ZONE								
7 Human figures, whole									
8 Man in motion, groups									
9 History and old time									
10 Foreign countries				EXPRESSIVE			LOSS		
11 Childhood memory									
12 Parks and gardens									
13ₑ Trees, plants, flowers									
14 Landscape				AND			OF		
15 Mountain and rocks									
16 Sea, flowing water, boat									
17 Sun, moon, stars									
18 Human heads				EMOTIONAL			REALITY		
19 Animals (mammals)									
20 Snakes, reptiles									
21 Fish									
22 Birds, insects				ZONE			CONTACT		
23 Horizon									
24 Funny stories									
25 Fairy tales, myths									
26 Parts of human body									
27 Explosion, accidents									
28 Fire, lightning									
29 Rushing water									
30 Blowing wind									
31 Clouds, smoke									
32 Map and top views	REPRESSIVE AND								
33 Fences, bars, screens	RATIONALIZATION ZONE								
34 Shading as screen									
35 Shaded skies									
36 Destruction, decay, etc.									
37 Horror, morbid elements	DANGER ZONE								
38 Closures									
39 Spider web, etc.									
40 Scribbling									

* Adapted from Hellersberg (1950).

Key to Columns I-IX

Column I. Related to own life experience and direct observation
II. Related to present daily events (not personally contacted)
III. Learned about, read about, seen in movies
IV. Emotional values concerned with own person; integrated to objects
V. Day or night dream -- mere fantasy product
VI. Emotional outburst -- mere expressionistic
VII. Transferred reality; intended symbolism that is not conventional
VIII. Surrealism, abstraction or distorted reality
IX. Mere lines without meaning, no attempt to interpret, functional
play

Key to Zones

Objective Zone

Subjective Zone, subdivided into:

Emotional expressiveness (Lines 11-30, Columns IV, V, VI)
Topics permitting emotional projections, emotional perspectives
to reality

Repressiveness, rationalization (Lines 31-34)
Emotional avoidance, rational control, rigidity, neuroticism

Danger Zone (Lines 35-38)
Overpowering anxiety, severe repression, defeatism, beginning
retreat

Loss of Reality Contact (Columns VII, VIII, IX, Lines 39-40)
Different types of retreat: symbolism, abstractions, distortions,
no meaning (details of this omitted)

CHART B

Hypothetical Chinese "Objective" Zone

	I	II	III	IV	V	VI	VII	VIII	IX
Line 11 - - - - - - -									
Line 23 - - - - - - -									

II.   Some Aspects of Personality of Chinese as Revealed by the Rorschach Test[10]

Theodora M. Abel and Francis L. K. Hsu

The purpose of the present investigation was to look for some of the aspects of personality of Chinese subjects as revealed by the Rorschach technique. [11] This small Rorschach study is limited to Chinese residing permanently or temporarily in an alien urban society far from the heart of their culture of origin. By exposure to and contact with non-Chinese modes of life and American cultural media, these Chinese subjects may be considered more or less acculturated. Some of them had been born in the United States, spoke Chinese only hesitatingly, and had never been to China. Others had lived in the larger cities of the Chinese eastern seaboard, and had consequently experienced a variety of cultural patterns prior to their coming to the United States. But all of our subjects had been raised by China-born parents who carried with them their traditions, their system of family and social organizations, their attitudes toward rearing of children, their approved patterns of fitting their offspring, male or female, into a role of life expected of an occupant of a given small or extended family, clan or group position in China or in a Chinese community in the United States.

In order to make for a clearer focus of comparison we included among our subjects only two groups, those who had been born and educated in the United States and those who had been born in China and had received their school and some of their college education there prior to coming to America. We also had one more variable, that of sex, so that we might make a comparison of Rorschach results for males and females born in China and overseas with the possible effects of differential treatment of the sexes in China and in Chinese communities in the United States. All we could hope to find, of course, were some leads and insights, not an over-all picture of Chinese personality.

Our groups consisted of 15 China born males (CBM), 12 China-born females (CBF), 10 American-born males (ABM) and 19 American-born females (ABF),

---

10. Reproduced from Abel and Hsu (1949). This is an excerpt from the original paper.
11. The investigation was carried on as part of Columbia University Research in Contemporary Cultures. The authors had access to Rorschach protocols collected by Dr. Helen Davidson and Miss Leona Steinberg in connection with an extensive project carried on by Dr. Hsu and sponsored by the Viking Fund (now the Wenner-Gren Foundation). About two-thirds of the protocols used in the following analysis came from this source. The others were administered by Dr. Abel, who is responsible for all the Rorschach interpretations. Dr. Hsu contributed much valuable information concerning Chinese culture and personality. (In field work of a later date, Dr. Hsu has collected about 105 Rorschach protocols and 80 TAT records among the Chinese in Hawaii. The analysis and conclusions on these materials will be published in a forthcoming book. Cf. also Hsu, 1948 and 1951. -- Ed.)

ranging in age from 20 through 39, with half of the China-born subjects distributed in each of the two decades, two-thirds of the American-born females in the
decade 20 to 30, and all of the American-born males in the younger decade.

The tests were adminstered to the subjects, some in 1945, and the rest in
1948, by three women examiners. The sex of the examiner has to be taken into
account as a possible factor in influencing test results of Chinese male and
female subjects.

In treating the results we not only handled the material in the usual Rorschach manner of analyzing the approach, the determinants, and the content [12]
but we looked for quality of content and content sequence, and to some extent
we tried to emphasize the influence of culture on personality as revealed by the
test responses.

1. Content Analysis

Analyzing the content of the responses to the blots is one of the most
fruitful means of getting at the ways in which the world is viewed by subjects,
and the kinds of interpersonal relationships they envisage or maintain. The
ways in which human beings are imagined and perceived in the blots, that is,
the kinds of human beings they are and, more particularly, the ways in which
they appear to be acting or behaving, especially when two figures are seen
opposite each other, give us some insight into the ways in which the subject
taking the test conceives of other people in relation to himself, how he feels
toward others and-or how he considers other people react to him. Attitudes of
hostility, friendliness, wariness, fear, dependency, may be expressed by projecting such attitudes into perceived blot figures.

Our four groups perceive human figures in the blots in the following
amounts: CBM, 13%; ABM, 15%; CBF, 13%; ABF, 24%. Thus we see that the
ABF perceive human forms a good deal more frequently than do the other
groups. The ABF also give the highest percent human movement (13.1% as
compared with 9.9% for CBM, 11.9% for ABM, and 11.4% for the CBF). But
it is in the kinds of human beings perceived and in the manner in which these
people are described that we obtain the clearest picture of differences in our
four groups.

Let us see what the people projected into the blots are doing. Among the
China-born males, out of 37 human movement responses there are only 6
(16%) where in the description of the act there are implied feelings of aggression or fear of aggression directed against oneself or against the outside
world. In these 6 cases, however, there is toning down and modulation of the
aggressive impulses, or the figure who is the aggressor is dehumanized (e.g.
toning down, Card III, "Men pulling or bargaining or making an oath"

---

12. The scoring technique employed was essentially that of Klopfer (Klopfer
     and Kelley, 1942).

[of friendship]; Card II, "Wrestling in China, no feet, red hats, but it's before wrestling begins"; or dehumanization, Card VII, "Dogs arguing; they are jealous," Card III, "devils carrying an ax").

There are three other instances where aggressive impulses are implied, but where no overt human movement is involved (Card II, "Man, head off, dying"; II, "Bears fight, head off, dying or [modulated] walking at edge of pond"; II, "Animals, head off, blood"). Out of the 31 cases of human movement not yet accounted for in this group of CBM, 11 instances describe people who stand and face, or do something where the implied action is controlled rather than impulsive or outwardly aggressive (act polite, think, look); 3 describe dependency, or people bent over; 14 do something active, such as dance, swim, skate, carry; 3 describe people as talking.

The same way of projecting human movement characterizes the ABM. Out of 28 instances of human movement, only in 3 is aggressiveness or hostility suggested, and here again it is modified in some way (Card III, "Men dance or beat drums"; III, "Men or women clapping or having tug of war"; III, "Creatures, tongue out, hanging by hair"). One subject gives an additional answer (given later in the inquiry) to Card V, in which he sees a girl with back turned going to strike. Among the other instances of human movement in this group, 3 are described as co-operative (e.g. carrying kettle, holding hands); 4 just stand or sit passively. In the 18 other instances, extensor, but nonaggressive, movement is described as dancing, cooking, hands up over head. But for the ABM there seems to be a quality expressing fear, or the precariousness of life, much more than among the CBM. People are not just described as dancing, skating, and doing "graceful" things, but rather there are instances such as "gnome leaning backward, but he is pregnant"; "gorilla leaning back"; "dolls bent over"; and a denial (Card IX), "No, it is not a witch riding." Also in some of the animal-movement responses there is implied the feeling of danger and insecurity: "birds trying to get a foothold" (Card II); "raccoon trying to crawl on mushy ground" (Card VIII).

Let us now see the way in which the girls perceive human movement in the blots. The CBF give 59 M responses. In no case are any two humans described as attacking or moving aggressively against one another (in one instance puppies are seen "fighting and bleeding" [Card II]). Among these 59 M responses, 12 indicate dependency, such as bent, kneeling, praying, supplicating, baby lies, legs up; 2 people trying to hang onto something or get across a cliff. There are hardly any descriptions of stance and facing, as we saw among the CBM. There is one instance of a man sitting on the bank of a stream. In all other cases, there is extensor activity, such as dancing, jumping, clapping, exercise, swimming, picking fruit, posturing in a dance. In several cases there is what we should describe in America as a childlike quality, "playing tricks," "mimicking," "playing cute but naughty feeling," "splashing," "pogey-stick jump."

In great contrast to the CBF are the ABF. These girls have 87 M responses. Out of 87, there are 21 (about 25%) where aggression or fear of aggression is expressed or at least indicated, either through attack, implied threat, or through an authoritarian or evil figure. For example: "Cannibals hold pot--cut up bloody matter"; "Giant or girl coming down on you"; "drumbeating"; "police raise arm"; "evil eye glances"; "witch shoot rays"; "men pull"; "insects argue." There are 7 cases expressing dependency: "Buddha bent"; "priest prays"; someone lies "hand on mouth"; "foetus sucks." Compared with the CBF, where there is on the average one dependency instance per girl, only one-third of the ABF cases give even one dependency instance. On the other hand, each girl among the ABF gives at least one example of aggression-fear, whereas, as we have seen, there is no single instance of this mode of response among the CBF.

The other M responses are extensor: dance, skate, pledge, run, wave arms. The quality is not as playful as is that of the CBF. Also there crept into the movement descriptions of the ABF a few types not expressed at all by the CBF, such as curiosity -- "look in mirror," "peer in periscope"; or love -- "cupids hold candle," "silhouette of two lovers," "legs rushing around."

We must remember that the aberrant position in Chinese culture is to express hostility, while in the United States it is deviant for a male, and to some extent for a female, at least an adolescent one, not to show some outwardly aggressive behavior. "Acting polite," "to think and look," fit into rules of proper conduct as envisaged by Chinese culture.

Thus it is the American-born Chinese girls who approach to a greater degree the accepted American pattern than do the American-born Chinese males. But in so doing they seem to have conflict; they become cautious and oversensitive (large number of Fc responses), are in doubt or conflict (m responses), and feel guilt (additional Fm scores). The ABF may be battling in their fantasies with authoritarian figures, trying to be accepted in the American pattern but having conflict or difficulty in fitting into an American way of life as they see it around them and also not deviating too much from a pattern of behavior expected of Chinese girls. China-born girls, on the other hand, appear to be in much better balance, less in conflict with authority and living out their fantasies and interpersonal relationships with less tension, less feelings of guilt, and less sensitivity about doing the right and wrong thing.

In yet another way of envisaging human forms do the American-born girls approximate the American cultural pattern. These ABF, as we have seen, perceive many human beings (131 responses in all). Their predominant mode of response is to see people, usually male figures, as "man" or "butler." They also see women, girls, or they see parts of people, legs, arms, and, more commonly, heads of people. They do not describe these people further as to chronological age or particular characteristic. About one-half their responses are of this nature. In addition, about one-fifth of their responses are mythological in character (goblins, elves, Santa Claus, Red Riding Hood). On the other hand, the CBF (who give 81 human responses) do not see so many mythological figures, only 6 out of 81. They see real people, as do the ABF, but less often. However, for the CBF these people are not just designated as people, men or girls; they are frequently described in greater detail in terms of age and physical characteristics such as "there is a baby," "a baby boy," "a foetus," "someone pregnant," "someone with big belly," "fat woman," "skinny girl," "a doll," "a young girl," "a little child," "a boy," "someone dying," "lady with crooked head," "man with hump," "old man," "old lady"; 22.5% of the human responses of the CBF are described in this way, while only 9% of the human responses of the ABF are so characterized.

We might hypothecate some of the reasons for the differences in quality of human response by saying that the China-born girls have a greater acceptance of people in various stages of development and those with a variety of bodily characteristics, whereas the American-born girls are greater "admirers" of what they consider the more acceptable people (young adults, male and female) -- at least those acceptable and glorified in the current American scene. When the ABF see human forms in the blots in a manner unacceptable to them, those they do not admire or in whom they are not interested, they relegate them to mythology. This manner of viewing human beings, of calling old people dwarfs, old women witches, children as impish or fairylike, someone of small stature as goblin or elflike, is a characteristic American cultural pattern. In China old people are venerated, children are not a different "species" from adults, but are young adults. People, when they are accepted, are not just glorified as movie idols. The China-born girls live closer to a way of life where people of all ages are accepted as part of the family group. The ABF follow the American ideal pattern of what constitutes a desirable human being.

Animal responses in these Chinese records do not offer any characteristic which appears to be significant for discussion except that the percentage frequencies of such responses are higher for both male groups than for the China-born and American-born girls (45% for CBM, 46% for ABM, 35% for CBF, 34% for ABF). The lower A frequencies for the females are in keeping with their greater expansiveness and flexibility of response in general; they not only give more responses, but vary the quality and the type more than do the males.

Two other types of content are of particular interest in comparing the ways in which they are handled by our four groups. These are the anatomy responses and those dealing with nature (including plants, flowers, trees, landscapes, mountains, rocks). All four groups give about the same frequency of anatomy responses (5% - 7.8%) a frequency that cannot be considered excessively high in

terms of what is found among the Rorschachs of Americans. [13] The nature
responses are more frequent than are the anatomy ones for all groups except
the ABM (CBM 13%, CBF 15%, ABM 7.6%, ABF 13%).

In the quality of the anatomy and nature responses, and in the sequence of
these responses, we find our male groups differentiated from each other, and
our female groups differentiated from both male groups. And yet more significant is the sequence of responses where we get some indication of the ways
in which the girls handle themselves in the world in which they live.

Our first comparison has to do with the manner in which the two male
groups project anatomy meanings into the blots. We counted the number of
times the frame of the body (bones, pelvic girdle, spinal cord) was referred to,
and the number of times internal organs were mentioned (intestines, lungs,
viscera, kidneys, etc.), and found the two girl groups gave approximately an
equal number of hard anatomy or soft anatomy responses (about 50% responses
in each category). In the case of the males, however, the CBM gave mainly
bony structure (in the proportion of bony structure 15, soft anatomy 2), while
contrarily the ABM gave nearly all soft anatomy answers (in the proportion
body structure 3, soft anatomy 18).

This same difference in quality of response between China-born and
American-born males can be seen when we compare their responses to Card VI.
On this card the CBM stay more on the surface of the blot; 14 out of 15 subjects
see the surface as structured in some way, or as impenetrable ("shell," "hard
object," "jade," "fan"). Only one of the 15 sees anything beneath the surface (an
X-ray). Among the 10 ABM, only 2 report perceiving a structured surface. One
rejects the card entirely, and 7 penetrate the surface of the blot and see something down in the center as "deep canyon with mountain stream in it," "electric
ray fish who has pierced his victim," "electric charges coming out from a radio,"
"butterfly caught in some gluey substance."

It has been suggested by Rapaport that reference to bony anatomy indicates
blocking and rigidity, while visceral references carry some disguised sexual
or perhaps aggressive connotations. In view of the responses of our ABM, not
only in terms of the kinds of anatomy but in view of their manner of handling the
"sex" card, it looks as though they had a greater disturbance in the sexual
sphere, including fear-hostility components, than do the CBM. The responses
the American-born males give to Card II further enhance this interpretation.
In Card II only 2 of the ABM give the popular animal response. What they perceive are such things as "sea animal stinging its prey," "explosion," "foxhole,"
"internal organs." One subject rejects the card. Or they interpret the small
projecting center detail as "nail clippers," "gear teeth," "pliers," suggestive of
an "aggressive" tool or weapon. We must remember that the American-born

---

13. In an average-sized record of 20-25 responses, one to two anatomy re-
    sponses have no pathological weight. (Cf. Rapaport, 1946, p. 298).

males whom we tested were living in Chinatown in New York City and that any difficulties they may experience in their sexual adjustments are bound to be intensified by the abnormal sex ratio (small number of Chinese females) in that area, as well as the difficulties they have in relating to non-Chinese girls.

If the China-born males have any difficulties of an emotional nature (sexual or interpersonal), they have them well under control. As we have seen, they perceive bony rather than soft anatomy; they keep on the surface of and structure the blot in their interpretations of Card VI; they respond in general to color in a controlled and conforming manner with less CF and less pure color than do the American-born males. But in Card II, seven of the CBM give responses associated with blood (e.g. "animals fight," "animals dying," "man dying," "ox slaughtered," "open wound" (W), inside of "mouth showing tonsil operation" (W̃), and "people swearing oath in blood"). In China swearing brotherhood in animal blood has a pleasant rather than an unpleasant connotation. But this does not preclude the possibility that using the color red in this card (II) as a "blood" interpretation is not entirely without an undercurrent of aggression -- fear which has been disguised by structuring the situation as a friendship one. [14]

Among the four instances in which the "popular" animals are seen by the CBM, only two see whole animals in motion, and in one of these cases the animals are running away from each other; one sees animal heads without movement, and the fourth perceives embryo animals. Again, in Card VI, we find a suggestion of some anxiety or conflict in the CBM, for 6 of them interpret the blot as smoke, "a house on fire" or a "house burning"; 2 give evasive map responses, and one calls the blot a "broken-up turtle" (poor form). Only 5 perceive a human or humanlike figure in the blot. These responses, as well as those in Card II, though not conclusive, do suggest the possibility that at least some of the China-born males may at times feel considerable anxiety or the weight of unsolved emotional conflicts, but in no way are they as overwhelmed by their disturbances as are the American-born males. They are living in a relatively more stable emotional atmosphere and where life is less difficult for them than it is for the ABM, a place where they have a definite role and status position.

In a previous preliminary report we spoke of the Chinese as moving between something inside the body (anatomy response) and out to the world of nature. At that time only a small number of the American-born records had been mainly used as a basis of study. In using the larger sampling, which included more individuals, both male and female, both American and China-born,

---

14. Dr. Abel is responsible for this last interpretation. Dr. Hsu does not believe that the blood response indicates hostility on the part of the China-born males. Only deep analytic procedures can give us a final answer on this point.

we have found that it is only the girls, the China-born to the greatest extent, the American-born somewhat less, who show this type of sequence, moving from an anatomy to a nature response. The following percentages show to what extent this is true: among the China-born females, 75% of the anatomy answers are followed by a nature response as the last response to a card. One half of these responses go immediately from anatomy to nature (including landscape, plant, tree); the other half give an intermediate response of person or animal before ending up with nature. Of the other 25% anatomy responses, 17% are followed by some response which does not have nature for its content, while 8% are not followed by any other response. Among the American-born girls a little lower percentage, 58%, move from anatomy to nature (40% directly, 18% after giving an intermediate human or animal content), 16% move from anatomy to some content not nature, and 26% give no subsequent answer.

Among the males there is no such sequence. The CBM never give a nature response following an anatomy one, either directly or after giving an intermediate response. They follow anatomy responses with no consistent pattern. The same is true for the American-born males. In two instances only among the ABM is anatomy followed by nature, and once this nature is a "map with mountains." In other words, with the exception of these two illustrations of anatomy-to-nature sequence on the part of the ABM, this characteristic sequence is one followed by the girls, both CBF and ABF, but in a more pronounced manner by the CBF.

Another difference between the males and the females lies in the kinds of nature perceived. The girls envisage a greater vista on the blots more often than do the males. They move more often out to a landscape world of mountains and plains, seashore and river banks; 45% of the nature responses of the CBF and 44% of those of the ABF are of this kind. Only 30% of the CBM are those describing landscape. The ABM give landscape 36% of the time, but never once is their description of landscape an expansive vista, or even a real landscape. Their responses here again refer to penetrating the blot, such as a "foxhole," "a deep sea where you see the depth," "canyons with deep gorge looking in," or an abstract map of land and wind. This type of response on the part of the ABM again suggests their greater sexual and aggressive disturbances, as it did in the anatomy responses and in their responses to Card VI.

A tentative explanation of the reason why the girls move in a sequence from anatomy to nature and to a more expansive type of nature is in order here. As we know from interview material and from the literature, the Chinese are not taught to feel shame about the body and its functions as are children in some other cultures, as they are in America; nor are they given strict, early toilet training. But even though anatomy responses are not equated as readily with anxiety feelings as they have been found to be among Americans and Europeans, it looks as if the Chinese girls prefer to move away from their perceptions of anatomical parts and organs to another area. As we have seen, the girls turn from an anatomy response to one of nature a great majority of the time. Also the girls perceive nature in the blots two or three times as frequently as they do anatomy. It is suggested, then, that their greater security lies out in the visual field of nature, often landscapes, and that in this way the girls remain in balance, moving from a less secure, perhaps anxiety-ridden, area to one of relative security. The significant role nature plays in the life experience of Chinese can be attested by the predominance accorded nature in the field of art, and by the many festival holidays attendant upon seasonal changes.

The males do not have the same device as do the females, for they do not move from an anatomy response to one of nature. But the China-born males to some extent protect themselves from their problems by never penetrating inside the body (only perceiving bony structure) and by remaining on the surface of Card VI (sexual card). As do the girls, they perceive nature quite frequently, three times as often as they do anatomy, so it is possible that they also prefer, or feel more secure in perceiving, some aspect of nature rather than anatomy. In addition, in describing nature the CBM make use of color, whereas in only one instance do they associate anatomy with color (color being indicative of getting close to experience and feeling emotionally toned in some way to stimulation impinging on the organism). Thus the CBM have a good deal of control over their impulses and can thus behave in "proper Chinese" ways, those dictated by the culture in which they are reared. But the CBM do have some outlets for expressing their feelings; they are not entirely pliant and controlled. They give many nature responses and in so doing they do not shy away from color. Also, they take pleasure in the oral sphere, which we shall discuss later on. But they are not as "open" as are the girls who can perceive anatomy, internal organs as well as bony structure, who use color spontaneously, and who move freely from this area of anatomy to a more secure one in nature.

The ABM are not like the other groups. They do not move from anatomy to giving nature responses as do the girls and, unlike the CBM, they give many fewer nature responses (nature as well as anatomy responses comprise only 7% of their total responses). Also they perceive almost only internal organs when they do perceive anatomy, contrary to the CBM, and they associate color with anatomy. In addition, their nature responses often have an anxiety-ridden connotation, such as penetrating into a hole or something deep (ravine or cave), a type of nature never once given by the female or CBM groups. It looks as though these males do not feel secure in relation to their bodies, particularly in relation to their sexual and aggression-fear impulses, about their sex roles, their acceptance as people in relation to Americans, in relation to China-born Chinese, and in relation to girls. They do not move out to nature, to an expansive landscape; they do not shift from an anatomy to a nature response. Nor do they remain as controlled as do the CBM, by remaining on the surface of experience, such as seeing only bony anatomy and hard or surface structures (Card VI). Also, as we have seen, the human movement responses of the ABM are colored more with suggested fear and hostility feelings than are those of the CBM. It looks as though the ABM live closer to a threatening world fraught with dangers from without (relationship to people) and from within (emotions of anger, rage, fear).

The final content category we propose to consider in the present investigation is that of orality. Oral responses in some form are not predominant, but are at least in evidence, in the Rorschach records of our groups under consideration. It is known that the Chinese readily gain satisfaction from the oral sphere and that it is also a channel through which they give satisfaction to others. Responses were scored as oral if they described food or its preparation, seeking of food, or where an open mouth, teeth, or lips were perceived.

Both groups of girls averaged two oral responses per person; the CBM averaged one and one-quarter, and the ABM had on the average one and one-half expressions of orality per person. The number of individuals giving no oral response is small: 2 for each of the two China-born groups and the ABF. Each of the 10 ABM gave at least one oral answer. The oral responses in all the groups include the use of color in from one-third to one-half the responses. In addition, shading in the response (e.g. "dark colors inside walnut") is also employed to some extent. Both groups of girls are somewhat more expansive than are the males in the frequency with which they project orality, but then they have been consistently more expansive in all their responses, in number, use of human movement, and color. Interestingly enough, the China-born males, who have consistently shown the most constriction and control in mode of response, make use of color in the oral area relatively more often than do the girls. Of the 19 oral responses of the CBM, 11 are associated with color. This suggests that the CBM are freer in expressing their feelings when they can channel these feelings into the oral sphere. Responding to color prior to form, as do the Chinese (including the CBM) when describing food, indicates their ability to express their emotionality freely and spontaneously in this area. As is known, the Chinese have no emotional problem of eating or taking alcohol. They learn from childhood not to be guilty about eating food. They are breast-fed, weaned slowly, and not deprived of food in childhood. The males may be given more food and delicacies than the girls. Among adults banquets and overeating to the point of feelings of great fullness are considered desirable. Chinese literature abounds in descriptions of feasts and banquets.

Descriptions are often vivid when the ink blots were interpreted as food. For instance the CBF speak of "fried shrimps and bread crumbs," "yuyu" for soup, "fluffly candy," "cherry juice dripping down"; the ABF tell of "doughnut puff," "fried and dropped in fat," "kidneys wrapped in fat," "pink cotton candy," "egg out of shell"; the CBM refer to "edible green vegetables," "fruit juice flowing from fruit"; the ABM speak of "frying eggs," "meaty part of lobster claw," "fried fritters."

But all of the answers we have classified under the heading of orality are not those about food. It is in the other types of orality that we can see differences among the groups, the ABF standing out in a different focus from the other three groups. It must be noted, however, that in all four groups, the food category predominates (a category in which we have included the preparing of food). Among the CBF, 70% of their oral responses relate to food and its preparation; 56% of the oral responses of the ABF do so. Among the CBM 80% of their oral responses, and among the ABM 80% of these responses, relate to food and cooking or gathering food.

A second oral category is that where the mouth and teeth are described in some dynamic manner, as "open mouth," "sardonic grin showing teeth," "teeth alone," "red lips." It is this category in which the ABF, and only this group, reveals a number of such responses. There is only one response of this kind for the CBF, four for the CBM, three for the ABM, but fifteen for the ABF. As was pointed out earlier, the ABF was the only group that saw eyes or faces peering or suggesting some unpleasant mode of expression. It would seem that the ABF utilize some aspect of orality not just for pleasure but as a possible means of defense or retaliation. They project their feelings of guilt, or their fears of retaliation, and they exert an implied oral mode of defense.

2. Conclusions

Students of Chinese personality and informants interviewed in investigations on Chinese culture have repeatedly stressed the fact that the formal relationships the Chinese maintain with people, the control they show over their impulses, and the balance they keep between the self and the world around (nature), is related to the role each person is expected to play throughout his life. It is felt that if one approaches strangers too closely, reveals excessive spontaneity and impulsivity, one loses one's role and one forsakes one's equilibrium.

Judging from the Rorschach protocols, our China-born groups, male and female, fit into this Chinese cultural pattern of controlling their impulses and maintaining a pliant but to some degree distantiated role in interpersonal relationships. The Chinese-born girls, however, show greater flexibility in their responses than do the China-born males; they have a less rigid status role to maintain; they are not as responsible as are the males for "following in the shadow of their ancestors." In accepting their less challenging role they have found a way of life, of equilibrium and balance between themselves and the larger world around them. But in maintaining this balance, they do so at some sacrifice, experienceing some intermittent feelings of depression or sadness, but ones which by no means are severe or overwhelming. For both China-born males and females, in the area of nature and especially in that of food, there appears to be freedom for enjoyment and for expressing emotionality in a spontaneous manner. It is in nature where security is found, and in the oral sphere in which satisfaction is sought.

The American-born males, as attested by informant material, have a less clear-cut role in society than do the China-born males. They are more uncertain, less sure of the direction in which their lives should or could lead. They are breaking away from a more traditional way of life, and are attempting to fit into the prescribed American pattern. To achieve this goal, their paths are beset with difficulties beyond their control, influences working against them within both the smaller Chinese community and the larger enveloping American society. In their Rorschach responses these American-born Chinese males seem highly disturbed emotionally, since they give frequent anxiety signs or those suggesting repressed and unsatisfied feelings of rebellion. They appear particularly in a dilemma in the sexual sphere without being able to work out their difficulties in this area.

The American-born girls on the Rorschach appear to be the ones with the most overtly expressed difficulites of adjustment; their protocols indicate that they have hostile-fear feelings toward people, that they are to some degree aware of their inner conflicts, that they have feelings of guilt, and are extremely sensitive about the opinion of others. From interview material it has been found that the American-born girls are in a difficult position in America, as are the American-born males, a position of belonging to and not being accepted wholeheartedly by either Chinese or American groups. But the test does show that these girls can marshal their resources better than do the American-born males who acted as subjects in the test. They face their conflicts more squarely; they rebel but stand up to authoritarian figures; they handle their sexual preoccupations more directly, even though in so doing their feelings of guilt are aroused. They are not as pliant and as controlled in emotional expressiveness as are the China-born, nor as dependent and placid in accepting their role in life as are the China-born girls. What is more, in spite of their anxieties, their feelings of guilt, and their aggressive impulses, they are able to maintain equilibrium and balance between themselves and the outer world almost to the same extent as do the China-born girls. In addition, they are able to do much more about facing and overcoming their difficulties than do the American-born males, who must feel at times quite torn apart and driven by overwhelming forces within themselves and from the enveloping environment.

PART EIGHT

IMAGERY

RESONANCE IN IMAGERY

Rhoda Métraux

The study of imagery is an intensely personal and yet a rigorously formal approach to a culture. Every cultural analysis is to a greater or lesser extent built upon work with imagery, but working at a distance, removed from any first-hand contact except through our informants, our most immediate experience of the culture is through our own perception of imagery and of the complex uses made of it by members of the culture. Consequently, we are likely to work with imagery more deliberately and self-consciously than is necessarily the case when an anthropologist is in the field and later works with his own notes, keeping the field situation as his point of reference. As in other approaches to a culture, the methods used to analyze imagery are based on the assumption that the details are consistent and form a coherent whole, and it is the aim of any such analysis to organize the details -- the images -- in such a way that the final delineation is an accurate statement of the configuration of a given culture. To understand and to describe how the world is perceived and what the people are like who so perceive it through imagery, it is necessary to learn to know the cultural models on which imagery is based and through this to work out how one image echoes and reinforces and counterpoints another. For this echoing relationship of images I have chosen the term resonance, and in this discussion I shall be concerned primarily with some methodological problems of using resonance in imagery for studies of culture at a distance. For my discussion of subjective aspects of such an analysis my most certain guide is my own experience, individually and as a member of a group, of work on American culture and on two cultures studied at a distance (France and Germany) and two peasant cultures observed in the field (Mexico and Haiti); in addition I shall refer to the work of other people where I know it well enough. For illustrations I shall depend mainly on verbal sources of imagery, and this for two reasons -- because of the inherent difficulty of transposing auditory or motor or tactile imagery from other sources into verbal form, and because verbal materials are those with which I am most familiar.[1] However, it should be remembered that the language of speech

---

1. Since the position I am taking in this discussion is that analyses of imagery depend for their accuracy upon the exact specification of each person and item involved, it seems necessary to add that I myself grew up in a bilingual home (American and German), that I have spent much of my life with people who are bi- and multilingual (mainly English, French, Spanish, German, and Russian), that my original scholarly training was in the field of English literature, and that my first work with imagery in different modalities (apart from work with literature) was as a student of European history.

and writing is but one source of imagery.[2] Collingwood (1938) in developing his theory of imagination uses language "to signify any controlled and expressive bodily activity" (p. 241), and speaks of the "language of total bodily gesture" (p. 246). In doing so, he assumes the interrelatedness of posture and gesture and speech, and so on, which is one aspect of the interrelatedness of images in different modalities. Studies of resonance in imagery are studies of imagery in different modalities.

The approach is multifaceted and derives in part from types of analysis that have been developed for studies of artistic products and of process and style, and in part from anthropological field work. I hesitate to call it a specific method, as it is rather a way of working that is integral to various cultural analyses as different from one another as are, for instance, Dorothy Lee's work with Wintu·¹ and Trobriand linguistic materials (1940, 1944, 1949, 1950), Martha Wolfenstein's and Nathan Leites's film analyses (1950), Nicolas Calas's analyses of modern art, Margaret Mead's work with the Arapesh (i.e. with Unabelin, 1949b), Gregory Bateson's and Margaret Mead's analysis of visual aspects of Balinese culture (1942), Margaret Mead's and Frances Macgregor's study of body posture (1951), Erik Erikson's analysis of Hitler's imagery (1950), the work of Theodora Abel and others on Chinese, Mexican, and French Rorschach responses (1949, 1951, 1953), and Nelly Hoyt's studies of Russian folklore -- where the differences among them are not only in the choice of material and method of work but also in the special frame of reference. Different as they are, these studies have in common the fact that the analysis is worked out within the context of a whole culture and in this they exemplify the approach which I am describing and differ from most studies of individual artists, let us say, or from studies of style and of creative process as such. While studies of the latter kind have contributed very considerably to our understanding of how to work with a particular sort of material and to our thinking about special problems of method, the differences in aim limit their specific applicability to cultural analysis.

What distinguishes the approach with which I am here especially concerned is its inclusiveness: Excellence of work depends upon the combined use of many materials -- interviews, oral and written literature, films, painting, and the plastic arts, etc. -- no one of which, with the exception of interviews with informants, is irreplaceable, but each of which contributes to the richness and complexity of the results. The choice of material depends mainly upon the problem on which such a study focuses and upon the person making the analysis. For the exploration of a culture the materials used must cover a fairly wide range and so must not have been created by and intended only for special groups in the culture (though materials of this kind are exceedingly valuable as part of a larger selection); additionally, it is essential to have sufficient diversity so that one can work on imagery in several modalities. Work with verbal sources

_____

2.   For convenience, sake I shall use several terms that ordinarily refer to speech (e.g. _statement_); except where otherwise specified these are intended to refer to any form of communication.

of imagery -- speeches, novels, short stories, textbooks and technical books, autobiographies, and folk and fairy tales, etc. -- is a necessary part of such a study as it provides a means of formulating plot and theme and of cross-check-ing hypotheses based on other types of imagery. But analyses of oral and written liberature alone are entirely insufficient, as is work with any other single type of material. Consequently, this approach is one that can be used only by an individual who finds combined analyses congenial, and it is perhaps best suited to group research.

Irrespective of other sources, studies of imagery ultimately depend, it seems to me, upon work with informants.[3] There are several reasons for this. First, the living individual is the most complex unit with which one can work on a culture at a distance, and an informant can give one a holistic view of a culture that one can obtain from no other single source.[4] Second, just because this is so, an informant working with a skillful interviewer continually in-creases the range and sharpens the focus on detail as he reacts not only to the interviewer but also to his own introspections. Third, informants provide a bridge for the research worker to other sources of imagery, guiding and cor-recting his perceptions and associations to them -- very often by nonverbal communication.[5] So, when I come across a figure of speech which I do not understand or with which I have no immediate empathy (which comes to the same thing), I find that the difficulty often can be quickly solved in interviews where I can see as well as hear my informants. For instance, in reading Ger-man child-care literature I found that although it was easy to classify kinds of rebellious behavior, I could not conceptualize the idea of rebellion or grasp the implications of the phrase generally used. (The German word for rebellion,

---

3. There are, of course, exceptions, e.g. Dorothy Lee's work with Trobriand linguistic materials (1940, 1949, 1950). But Trobriand culture had been studied in great detail and -- since Malinowski himself believed that a new language could be analyzed only as a form of behavior -- the texts (1935, Vol. II) had been so carefully placed in context that it was possible to use his own material, descriptive as well as analytic, for an alternative inter-pretation. Therefore, rather than saying that work with living informants is essential to any study of the imagery of a culture, it is probably more ac-curate to say that extended, intensive interviewing adds immeasurably to the analyst's flexibility and certainty of interpretation. For one example on a limited scale, cf. Martha Wolfenstein's analysis of Soviet newspaper stories and of informants' comments on the stories (Part Ten, pages 331-48).
4. Cf. in this Manual, Margaret Mead's discussion of work with informants (pages 41-49) and also my own introduction to Part Four (pages 143-52). In the methodological introduction to "The Record of Unabelin..." (Mead, 1949b) cf. the discussion of temperamental congeniality between investigator and informant.
5. It is, of course, one of the great difficulties of work on a culture distant in time -- as it is of studies of the creative work of artists of other eras -- that the modes of communication are limited and that the analyst has to re-construct the links among them. One interesting attempt to bridge time and culture -- and so to use his own cultural position for interpretation -- is Madariaga's study of Hamlet (1948). I shall not attempt to discuss the special problems involved in work on a culture distant in time.

Auflehnung, literally means leaning upon, and the phrase sich gegen jemand auflehnen -- to rebel against someone -- literally means to lean up against someone. As an American, this seemed to me a contradiction to the idea of rebellion as a form of activity.) However, when I asked German informants to describe what the phrase meant to them, their posture visibly stiffened and they made warding-off gestures with their hands held stiffly and close to their bodies. Essentially, it was not their verbal explanations -- which more or less coincided with those I had read -- but their bodily reactions that illumined and suddenly gave meaning to a whole series of images I had noted but had not been able to organize around the idea of rebellion. Where the phrase itself had been puzzling and the explanations of what a rebellious child did (sulked, said nothing, ran away, acted with punctilious correctness, etc.) were apparently very conflicting, I could immediately empathize with the posture and gesture and later, recreating the postural reaction for other informants, found that it evoked images for them which I could check against my own. The essential point, if I can formulate it verbally, is that the rebellious person walls himself in and forces this closedness against the person whose intrusion he is attempting to ward off. (Thus, for Germans, the person who -- during the Nazi regime -- "did nothing" could regard himself and could be regarded by others as an active rebel.) In this particular instance, in working with informants there was a real shift in the mode and level of communication. The main point, however, is that free interviewing concretely re-creates a circular actor-audience relationship. This double sense of the individual as a whole (represented here by the informant and the interviewer) and of the culture (exemplified by the informant and by all the source material used) as a whole and as the constant point of reference is perhaps one of the most valuable contributions made by anthropologists to studies of imagery.

Otherwise the materials on which such studies are based are not easy to categorize. There are, however, three main criteria for selection in terms of the material itself. First, it is necessary to know the source as a way of placing each image within its meaningful context. Therefore the most suitable materials for analysis are likely to be those provided by identified individuals (literary materials of various kinds, projective tests and other projective materials, illustrations, paintings, cartoons, comic strips, dance interpretations, and so on) or by identified or identifiable small groups (films, acted plays, ballets, advertisements, and so on). The traditionally anonymous materials of a culture -- riddles and proverbs, nursery rhymes and lullabies, folk and fairy tales, only to name some that are verbal sources of imagery -- are mainly useful when they are commented upon or are referred to illustratively by informants. But the highly stylized imagery of tales, of ceremonies, of architecture, or of ways of handling landscape, etc., can be used independently of informants providing one works with the idiosyncratic features of versions that occur in the culture studied.[6]

Second, any single piece of material -- irrespective of its complexity -- must form a whole unit of some kind, whether it be a single sentence that stands independently, a cartoon, a still photograph with its caption, a novel, a church service, or a collection of songs or anecdotes. Thus a carved frieze or a photograph of a detail of that frieze (where the photograph has been made by a member of the culture) may equally well be regarded as a whole unit in the sense in which I mean this.

And third, for work with imagery the source must, generally speaking, be one within the culture itself. As a rule, secondary sources on a culture should be rejected and, where it is necessary to work with selections (anthologies, collections of photographs, etc.), it is preferable to choose those made by and for members of the culture. This criterion is necessarily subject to considerable modification. French chromolithographs arranged in a Vodou sanctuary in Haiti are striking illustrations of the Creole selection and handling of fragmented detail. Chateaubriand and Karl May, each writing about "America," give one magnificent French and German images. French jitterbug dancers at the height of this fashion in Paris, revealed in their tight and highly stylized version of the dance an emphasis upon formal structure that contrasted sharply with the American emphasis upon patterns of motion. Thus the subject matter itself cannot be narrowly defined. The problem of working with translated materials and of making translations is an extremely complex one which I shall not discuss here, except to say that work on imagery can be done only by someone who has a good knowledge of the language or who can work continuously with a linguistic informant who shares the analyst's aims and who is a member of the culture studied.[7]

But there are also materials and techniques of analysis which must be rejected out of hand. As verbal sources of imagery, I would consider unsuitable all questionnaires (and methods of interviewing) in which the question determined the form of the answer or in which the answers consisted of disconnected phrases or outlines, etc., and all those which were not recorded verbatim. I would reject also methods of analysis of any kind where the results were so phrased that one could not go back to the detail in its original context -- for

---

6.   Cf. Margaret Mead's discussion of this point in this Manual (pages 26-8). For examples of such work, cf. Ruth Benedict's "Child Rearing in Certain European Countries" (1949) and her paper on Rumanian conceptions of their own history, in this Manual, Part Ten (pages 405-15).
7.   The Russian and Chinese groups in Columbia University Research in Contemporary Cultures are examples of such combined work, where the fact that some members of the group did not speak the language was used as a way of giving special focus and sharpness to work on linguistic detail.

someone working on imagery, the Rorschach interpretation is meaningless without the specific protocol on which it is based, and the quantified results of interview analyses are meaningless without a detailed knowledge of the interviews
themselves. Here I do not mean to infer that the interpretations are not of great
value (for they may give us access to levels of experience we cannot otherwise
reach and may also suggest structural relationships that are not readily perceived and that are of great importance), but rather that the research worker
must also know the detailed material on which the interpretation is based.[8] I
would also regard as unusable any method of analysis that depended mainly upon
arbitrary categorizations of imagistic material because of the excessive likelihood of distortion.[9] It is my own experience as an anthropologist that projective
materials cannot be used independently of other sources and that even when they
are part of some larger combination on one culture, they become much more
meaningful for work on imagery when one also has some cross-cultural basis for
comparison. (This is, in fact, simply another way of stating that what one works
with in the imagery of a culture is the idiosyncratic features of one's material
-- both in the details that occur and in the way in which the details are organized
as a whole.) The two dangers to be guarded against in the selection of materials
and techniques of anlaysis are, it seems to me, distortion and distantiation. And
the chief aim in the selection of material and of ways of working on it is the
preservation of its immediacy and integrity.

When one is analyzing a culture and therefore the images of a great many
individuals -- informants, authors, painters, actors in plays and in films, the
skilled and the unskilled, people who "think" with images and others who turn
them into abstract counters -- the detail with which one works is extraordinarily
rich and diversified, far richer than one's own individual system, and yet whatever
techniques of analysis one may use in the interests of precision and clarity, one
is oneself the chief instrument by which synthesis is achieved. The imagery in
such a synthesis will differ from one's own and from that of any one of the individuals studied in being both less rich and more tightly organized. From my
own point of view -- since the two sets of controls within which I can work are

---

8. Thus, in discussing linguistic analyses in field work, Malinowski writes: "At
    times it is necessary in ethnographic description resolutely to go beyond the
    verbal and even ... beyond the conceptual outfit of the natives.... The ethno-
    grapher has constantly to go beyond the native outlook and introduce certain
    categories which are not native. At the same time, in building up his con-
    cepts the ethnographer must never go beyond native facts" (1935, Vol. II, pp.
    18-19).
9. Some methods of analysis are sufficiently delicate that, used by a sensitive
    and experienced research worker, the fact of distortion is clearly recorded
    and can be taken into account. So, for instance, in working with Chinese sub-
    jects, Elisabeth Hellersberg found that their responses to the Horn-Hellers-
    berg drawing test could be accurately recorded and interpreted when the
    method of interpretation was modified to fit Chinese categorization of experi-
    ence. Cf. her discussion of this point in this Manual, Part Seven (pages 320-
    28).

(1) the material itself and (2) my own ability to perceive and integrate -- the
introduction of other and external categories of selection is confusing and complicates the task of making a synthesis. There is undoubtedly an idiosyncratic
element in this; for another analyst the problem of preserving immediacy may
rather be that of previous familiarity or unfamiliarity with the culture -- which,
in my own case, seems to be quite irrelevant.

The analysis of imagery is inevitably a partial approach to a culture. It is
possible, in a sense, to start the analysis at any point and then to work out in
any directions that the material itself leads one. (This means that whatever
point of entry into the culture has been selected, one's further selection of material will be determined in part by the questions raised in the analysis of the
first material. My own preference is to read widely and casually but to work
quite intensively on small pieces of material, following out several independent
lines, and then to select new material at the points at which I begin to find convergence or apparent discrepancy.) But whatever one's starting point, what one
is working towards -- as I understand the analysis of imagery -- is a statement
of the configuration of a culture. (Cf. Bateson, 1936; especially Chapters III and
XVI.) Consequently, as one is trying to formulate the premises and the emotional emphases of the culture through imagery it is necessary also to analyze the
material in terms of significant themes.[10] The following brief illustration from
work on American imagery (cf. Métraux, 1951) is intended to demonstrate how
image and theme are interwoven in one kind of synthesis:

In American culture, figures of speech modeled on the body and on machinery are used interchangeably. We build calculators, electric eyes, electric
brains, iceboxes that think for themselves, and computers (and now, doubling
back, speak of human computers), and we cannibalize older machines to repair
newer ones. Likewise we say of a man that he is a live wire, or a dynamo of
energy, or a dud, that he gets all steamed up, that he shifts into high gear, or that
he slips a cog; we say also that a man is a smooth operator, that he sparks an
activity, or we suggest that someone spin the dial and so change the conversation
-- here combining the man and the machine and the action performed. American
attitudes towards health include treating the body in much the same way that a
good machine should be treated. Body parts should be cared for and repaired,
the body should be inspected from time to time by experts to locate hidden trouble, and most body parts are regarded as reparable or replaceable. This is in
keeping with the conception of the body as something which, like a machine --
and the natural environment -- can be manipulated and arranged and freely
altered, and so also preserved from destruction.11

10. For a discussion of thematic analysis, cf. Martha Wolfenstein's "Movie Ana-
    lysis in the Study of Culture," Part Six (pages 267-80).
11. This view contrasts sharply with that of the British, who "see the world as a
    natural world to which man adapts, in which he assumes no control over the
    future, but only the experienced foresight of the husbandman or the garden-
    er, who plants the best seed and watches carefully over the first green
    blades" (Mead, 1948a; p. 219). It contrasts also with the view of the French,
    for whom one image representing the total personality of the growing child
    is the plant which the gardener (the parent and the educator) manipulates
    in various ways to bring about the most desirable growth and the best fruit-
    ing in maturity (cf. Métraux and Mead, 1953).

The conception of the body as something which can be worked on is reflected in current advice to American mothers to allow their infants to explore their own bodies as they also explore the rest of the safe world around them (Wolfenstein, 1953). Such images of the body are also intricately related to our attitudes towards time -- to our emphasis upon movement rather than structure, upon gradients rather than fixed points. So the body is invoked in images of slump and recovery, and the assembly line is invoked in a discussion of labor-management relations: "The disputes of any moment are over a temporary delineation of a moving line" (Tannenbaum, 1951; p. 161). Our attitudes towards the body, towards machinery, and towards movement are sometimes combined in moving visual images -- in an electric billboard advertisement where flashing lights repeatedly enact the scene of a young man offering a girl a box of candy, or in a three-dimensional advertisement showing a hand endlessly pouring out a refreshing cup of tea, etc.[12]

In the discussion thus far it is evident that I am using the term image in a very vague way. I shall not attempt to make any strict definition, both because I am not here concerned with problems of the codification of experience or with philosophical problems of the nature of reality and because it seems to me premature to attempt a definition of what an anthropologist means by image in reference to a culture. It should be clear that I am not using image as it is used in rhetoric to refer to figures of speech -- though figures of speech are verbal sources of imagery that give us not only content but also clues to ways in which images are formally structured and combined in any system.[13]

For my present purpose it is sufficient to say that imagery is an expression of the perceptual system shared by the members of a society -- that imagery has a selective and stylizing effect upon the perceptions of an individual member of a society, that it is used selectively by any individual, depending upon his innate capacities and cultural experience, and that it is both stabilized and continually modified as images are grouped and patterned in communication between individuals. Image then, as I am using the term, stands for any unit in the perceptual system through which individuals are related to one another in a culture. A gesture, a rhythmic figure beaten on a drum, a design sketched on a jug, a line of melody, words describing the prickling feeling of fear -- each of

---

12. For purposes of comparison it is important to add that American attitudes towards the body and towards machinery are also related to attitudes towards manipulation -- for Americans mastery is properly directed towards the exercise of power over things and is suspect and dangerous when directed towards the exercise of power over persons. This dichotomy is very different from that made by the French for whom (except in special circumstances) the imputation of human qualities to anything nonhuman or non-human qualities to any human being are equally threatening to human dignity. American imagery differs also from the German where, for instance, mechanical models and images derived from machines when applied to individuals threaten to destroy the wholeness of the person and so the individual as a person. (In German culture such images can also be given positive affect.) So in these three cultures images which are superficially somewhat similar but which are linked together in quite different ways, reflect different attitudes towards the human body, towards mechanization, and towards the hierarchical relationships between human beings and things.

13. On figures of speech, cf. Brown (1927). On the formal structure of metaphor, synecdoche and metonymy, cf. figure on p. 118, which can equally well be applied to nonverbal and to verbally expressed images.

these evokes and communicates an image in a different modality. Grouped together in one context each echoes and reinforces the other. Separately or together they may evoke and echo other images with which they are associated in the same or in other modalities. Thinking in terms of the sources of imagery, a motor image, for instance, can be evoked kinesthetically and visually by a person's gestures, by a painting or a statue, or descriptively in speech: "He walked heavily, like a man in thick boots." Each of these also echoes the other.

Thus as an image may be evoked in different modalities, I use resonance in imagery to refer to systematic relationships between images within and among different modalities -- visual, auditory, kinesthetic, tactile, and so on. Resonance is concerned both with the content of discrete images, of clusters of images, and of complexes of images and with the structural properties of images and their relationships to one another in one or in several modalities. I use image cluster as it is used by Armstrong (1946) to refer to a series of images that are grouped and associated with each other. By image complex I mean images in two or more modalities that together form a unit. Since cluster and complex as here defined refer rather specifically to content, it is perhaps necessary to add that both have formal aspects. Thus similes and metaphors are restricted forms in which a cluster of images can be expressed in verbal form.[14] The formal aspect of an image complex is, I think, rather a matter of sequence, of which simultaneity is a special case.

This definition of image is an open one in which I have not differentiated in any way between those images which are evoked by literal statements and those which are evoked by analogy. For work on the imagery of a culture it seems to me entirely necessary to keep this openness, since, as the analyst works, he must continually shift back and forth between intended literal statement and analogy. Thus if one considers these two verbal statements -- "He was tall and gaunt and kindly" and "Lincoln was the green pine, Lincoln kept on growing" (Benet, 1933; p. 84) -- the first is a factual description while the second is a metaphor. Yet for an American either may evoke a series of Lincolnesque images with their various associations, and if one is working on characterization, the first is as relevant as the second as an image-evoking phrase.

Similarly in French culture a description of a beggar seen trudging along a road, a burlap bag cast over his shoulder (cf. Interview IV, page 182), or a strange old man portrayed in a film (cf. the description of Désiré in Panique, pages 289-90), or the melody of a lullaby about Lustucru (a childhood bogey), or the pictures of Babar's disguised elephant soldiers (Brunhoff, 1934; pp. 44-45), or the indefinite Rorschach blot visualized as "the heavy boot of a Russian" -- all of these evoke images associated with the conception of le monstre and with the

---

14. For an image that is constructed in quite a different way, cf. the discussion of the "not-so: so" image in three brief papers in Part Five (pages 242-48). I shall refer to this image again later in this discussion.

disturbed feeling of <u>une menace imprécise</u> (a vague menace), and all -- irrespective of their phrasing in their original contexts -- are relevant to our understanding of the French definition and handling of danger. (Cf. Métraux and Mead,
1953.)

When an anthropologist is working on a new and unfamiliar culture, it is not
always possible, at least initially, to distinguish between literal and figurative
statements. This can be illustrated by the four following sentences, which I have
translated from the original Haitian Creole:

    1. Gédè is here. (Gédè is the name of a god.)
    2. Gédè is dancing in the head of Ti-Jo. (Ti-Jo is a man.)
    3. The milk mounted to her head and made her crazy. (Said of a woman
believed to be insane.)
    4. The mother gave her cold to her baby. (Said by myself, an American.)

The first and the third of these sentences are, for the Creole speaker, simple statements of fact. The first means that the god, Gédè, has possessed a man
or a woman and is now literally present, dancing and enjoying himself. The
second sentence is a synecdochic phrasing of the same fact. The third sentence
is an explanation of cause and effect: a nursing mother was so badly frightened
or angered that the milk literally mounted to her head and made her incurably
insane. The fourth sentence, an explanation which I offered to some Haitian
peasants, was greeted with disbelief and slightly anxious amusement; since it
was incredible that any mother would make her own child sick (would act with
deliberate malevolence towards her own child) and since, in any case, no one
would in her presence accuse a mother of doing so, the Creole listeners treated
what I said as a nonsense statement, and laughed.

The first three sentences and the <u>response</u> to the fourth provide clues to the
Haitian Creole perception of the world. But the sentences can be interpreted --
and the statements classified as having a literal or a figurative meaning -- only
if the analyst's initial point of reference is not his own system of perception but
rather (his own system held in suspense) the context in which the Creole images
occurred. Given an illustration from a culture in which it is evident that some
of the premises about reality are different from our own, the necessity of classi-
fying images according to the system of that culture becomes obvious -- and
therefore also the necessity of not <u>prejudging</u> how they are to be clasified in that
or in any other culture.

As the analyst works, he also continually combines in his own mind images derived from the most various sources and in the process of doing so it is -- for the
moment -- irrelevant whether, for instance, a detail of posture or a memory description of a child being bathed was intended to have literal or figerative meaning. I give
these two examples as a pair -- one a description and a re-enactment of details of
posture seen on a stage, the other a passage from Tolstoy's recollections of his
earliest childhood -- because each evoked (though at widely different times) in the
minds of those who watched or listened or read another set of images -- of the swad-

dled Russian infant, described by Russian informants and seen in Russian pictures.

The first sequence took place at an early Russian group meeting:[15]

An American described and reproduced the actors' gestures which he had seen: "... gestures of holding in the body and holding in the chest ... movement of whole body, head going forward and trunk going down." The Russians present echoed his presentation in a long series of postural and verbal responses that included various images of closure. These in turn were picked up and associated by another participant to his informants' descriptions of swaddling.

The second illustration is from an analysis made by a Russian of the child-hood recollections of several Russian authors.[16] This analyst had not been a member of the group in which the first sequence occurred. The passage from Tolstoy consists of a pair of extended memory images (1913, Vol. I, pp. 319-22):

Here are my first recollections, which I cannot arrange, not knowing what was before and what afterwards; about some of them I don't know if they were dream or reality. Here they are. I am tied. I want to free [my] hands but I cannot do it and I am crying, weeping, and my cry is unpleasant to myself but I cannot stop. Someone is staying with me. And all is in half-darkness. But I remember that there are two [persons] . My crying impresses them, they are worried because of my crying but they don't unbind me, which is what I want, and I am crying louder. It seems to them this is necessary [that I remain tied] while I know this is not necessary, and I want to prove it to them, and I break into crying which is repugnant to me, but is irrepressible. I feel the injustice and the cruelty, not of the people because they are sorry for me, but of fate, and I feel pity for myself. I don't know and will never learn what it was -- whether I was swaddled when I was sucking and drew out my hand, or whether I was swad-dled when I was more than one year old in order not to let me scratch myself when I had shingles, or whether I collected many sensations in one reminiscence, as happens in a dream. But it is correct that this was my first and strongest sensation of life. And I remember not so much my cry, not so much my suffer-ing, but the complexity, the contrariness of the sensation. I want freedom, it doesn't hurt anybody, and I who need it so much, I am weak and they are strong...

The second image follows immediately upon the first:

The other sensation is a pleasant one. I am sitting in a trough and I am surrounded by a new but not unpleasant smell of some substance which someone is rubbing on my little body. Probably it was bran and probably it was in the water and in the trough, but the freshness of the sensation of the bran awoke me and for the first time I became aware of and began to like my little body with its ribs visible to me on my chest, the smooth, dark trough, the nyanya's hands with rolled-up sleeves, and the warm, steaming, swirling water, and its noise, and especially the sensation of the smooth wet rims of the trough when I passed [my] little hands along them.

---

15. I have reconstructed this sequence from the minutes of a Russian group meeting in 1947, from my memory of having the gestures described and shown to me a day or two later, from marginal notes in the minutes, and from a conversation about the meeting with one of the participants. It is of course impossible to reproduce verbally the gestures which were of such importance. The description which I have quoted is also referred to in the introductory note to the Russian group discussion in Part Three (page 107).
16. The passage from Tolstoy was translated by Vera Schwarz (Alexandrova) in a working paper written in 1949, about two years later than the first example given. It was used again in a discussion of image clusters two years later, in 1951. I have included all the relevant dates here to illustrate continuity over a long time-span. The original paper is an unpublished document, RCC-R 217.

This passage led back to and was incorporated into informants' images of swaddling. Then at a later date, the structure and handling of positive and negative affect in the two images suggested the "not-so: so" double image cluster of Russian folk poetry (which then had been related to rumor forms), indicating how narrative and poetic style echo each other as expressions of a mode of thought. Thus one image cluster played into several others in different ways (in content and form), irrespective of the particular source of each.

The difficulties of reconstructing the steps of a synthesis -- even when I try to retrace steps I have taken myself -- are very great, and it should be understood that the sequences I have given here are not in fact reconstructions but merely schematic arrangements intended to suggest the circularity of the process and the way in which the analyst works with images evoked by many kinds of material, some intended to be literally descriptive, some figurative.

In the final analysis it is essential to distinguish between literal and figurative statements, between the kinds of images evoked by one and by the other (and to know how such images converge), and between the uses of imagery in one and another modality, but to attempt to do so from the first would be self-defeating. At least theoretically I can distinguish between (1) the stages of work when I am trying to "see how things fit together" -- when I have, in a sense, "memorized" a great mass of material -- and then I am dependent mainly upon my own remembered perceptions and associations, and (2) the stages when I am trying to analyze structural relationships and then I am dependent mainly upon my detailed knowledge of the sources of the images with which I have been working. The two processes are by no means sequential, one following on the other in some orderly fashion, and it is very likely that other analysts use quite different systems of organization. Actually, it is a matter of emphasis at any moment, since a disciplined study of imagery is based on one's ability to know the detail in context. I have made the separation, however artificial it is, because for me the process of analysis is a dual one of synthesis and definition in terms of the culture studied, and both depend on a conception of what an image is that is open and inclusive.

In studying imagery the unit with which one works is, in fact, seldom -- if ever -- a single, discrete image; rather what one works with, or more exactly, what the anthropologist seems to work with, is image clusters and image complexes. There is, however, a very real difference in this respect between work done in the field and that done at a distance. The fieldworker living in a community continually combines observations of behavior with informants' comments on behavior and descriptions, etc. (cf. Bateson, 1947b). Consequently, the fieldworker continually moves back and forth between different kinds of image clusters and the actual unit of his observation is a complex of images.[17] That is, for

---

17. This is, I think, the implicit point of Malinowski's insistence (1935, Vol. II) that a language must be studied directly in context as a form of action. In

the observer, visual and motor and tactile images and the images evoked by
speech are integrated parts of one whole -- of which any part (a gesture, or a
tone of voice, or a phrase, or a figure of speech, or the design of an object, or
the relative positions of two persons, etc.) or any combination of parts can provide him with a link to another image complex. The following description of a
gesture illustrates this point:[18]

The witch figure in Bali wears long curved fingernails, and when children
enact the witch their hands are curved inward in a clawlike attacking gesture.
We originally accepted the witch as a menacing, attacking figure only, until we
saw a woman in a temple ceremony possessed by the witch, Rangda, and onlookers said they could identify the possessor by the way in which the woman's hands
were held. These hands, sharply shadowed against a wall, were not clutching,
attacking hands but hands bent back with spread fingers. When we followed up
this contradiction with informants we were told that the witch's hands were held
in a position called kapar -- the position of a child who was startled or of a man
as he fell from a tree. This in turn provided the clue to the witch as not only
fearful but afraid -- an embodiment of the fear which she inspired.

The detail linking one image complex to another (like the image of the witch's
hands) may be one that informants are, at least in some cases, fully conscious
of, or it may be used without special awareness (as people use tone of voice in
patterned ways to indicate more than the words alone convey), or it may be a
detail that has significance for the fieldworker though not (in any conscious way)
for the people of the culture. Generally speaking, the way in which an anthropologist selects the kind of clues he uses is considered to be idiosyncratic and "intuitive"; that is, the deductions are made so rapidly that consciousness of the
steps is abbreviated. But when two persons compare notes on a single event
observed by both (or more likely notes on a long series of events), it becomes
apparent that where one has been especially aware of gesture patterns, the
other has taken his clues majorly from tones of voice, and so on. However, we
do not have very much direct and explicit evidence of how particular anthropologists use an image complex or go about the task of building up larger clusters
of images. This seems to be equally the case as far as linguists are concerned,
but for a different reason -- i.e, the formality with which the problem of selection is defined by them (cf. Harris, 1951).

Nevertheless, it is clear that the situation changes considerably when the
analyst is working at a distance and has little opportunity to make any but the
most limited observations. The unit is then much more partial. One way of
describing the difference would be to say that when one can make continuing
observations the fusion of images in different modalities is explicit, whereas
when one is working at a distance the fusion is more or less implicit. Or one
might say that it is like the difference between seeing a play enacted, on the one

---

any event, it is the generalization that I made from my discussions with
him about language in 1940, before I had done any field work.
18. Excerpt by Margaret Mead from an unpublished draft write-up of Balinese
field notes.

hand, and, on the other hand, only reading it or only hearing it read, or seeing it enacted only as a pantomime or only as a shadow play. For each of the partially rendered versions the audience must supply the missing parts. Similarly, when a German informant says, "She came into the room and sat down on the sofa," this statement has implicit in it a series of images related to the probable age and status of the woman who sits on the sofa and of the other women present -- images of posture and gesture and tone of voice, etc., and these in turn may evoke other images related to the idea of having the right thing in the right place (or in the wrong place), etc. The images are present in the mind of the German speaker and are communicated perhaps by tone of voice to the German listener, who will then comment, "Naturally!" or "Who did she think she was!" -- depending upon the particular images conveyed. By getting the informant to describe what such a statement meant to her (or to him) and was intended to convey to a listener, some of these implicit images can be made explicit.

But for much of his work the analyst is dependent upon literally disconnected pieces. Thus on Monday he may discuss a problem of parent-child relations with Informant A, an elderly woman speaking about her own childhood 50 years ago in a village she has not seen for 40 years; on Tuesday go to an exhibition of children's drawings; on Wednesday go to see a group of folk dancers; on Friday read a collection of short stories, including some about family life; and on Sunday discuss paintings seen two weeks earlier and a film seen a month earlier with Informant B, a recently arrived visitor from the country studied. It is then part of the analyst's own work to link up described behavior, gesture, tone of voice, etc. -- not as they necessarily were implicit in the partial image complexes that were noted but as they could have been. Even when, on some succeeding occasion, direct confirmation is obtained through some other combination, I think this distinction must be made. The necessity of constructing image complexes suggests one reason why, at least for the anthropologist who is accustomed to working with sets of related images, films have been so important for work on cultures at a distance. For films do provide carefully selected image complexes (in terms of simultaneity of sight and sound and motion and sometimes color, etc.) which one may or may not get from verbal sources (where, in any case, one has to deal with the necessary conventions of lineal presentation), and which one cannot get from many other kinds of material.

Thus a major task in working with imagery in a study of culture is the re-creation of wholeness in one's units by constructing image complexes and linking together clusters of images.[19] If I have emphasized the point that in work done at a distance one is inevitably working with implicit clusters of images -- which is so obvious as to be taken for granted by an anthropologist with field experience and by anyone who is trained to work with documentary materials -- I have

19. These are, of course, cross-cutting units -- built up from details taken at
    least in part from various sources.

done so not only to indicate qualitative differences between those situations where one can and those where one cannot make continuing observations, but also to place in proper perspective the work of the analyst as an individual studying the imagery of a culture. Actually, the difference between field work and work done at a distance is, in this respect, often more apparent than real, but what is involved can be seen more clearly in the latter than in the former situation.

To describe what is done without including the individual who is making the analysis has very little meaning. It is a commonplace that every observation must include the observer who is making it. Another way of stating this is to say that the analyst of imagery uses his own system of perception to understand the perceptual system of the culture studied. As I understand the analysis of imagery, it is one's disciplined conscious awareness of the two systems within which one is working that makes this such a rigorously formal approach to a culture.

Over time, as one explores a culture, identifying new images and images in new contexts, one's perceptions alter so that, from being able to perceive and evaluate in terms of one's own habitual system, one becomes able to perceive and reproduce more or less accurately the pattern of a system that has been mediated by the images of members of the other culture. This involves a continual awareness of meaning to oneself and of meaning to the other person (the informant, the author of a book, the makers of a film, etc.), where one set of meanings (one's own) is firmly structured and rich in associations while the other is (for oneself) initially fragmentary and fragile, consisting of design elements that may all too easily be distorted because one does not yet know the larger design. Analysis therefore involves locating imagery precisely and at the same time avoiding any very definite commitment about the ways in which images are linked together until by combination and synthesis -- as one begins to catch the resonances -- one discerns and can project the over-all design.

To construct the unfamiliar pattern one is dependent upon one's own sensitivities to sight and sound and movement, to figures of speech and tone of voice, to gesture and plastic representations, to proportional and color relationships, to external configurations and to one's own proprioceptions for one's awareness of imagery and ability to transpose from one to another modality following the styles of the culture. Part of one's work consists in learning to modulate one's own sensory perceptions and to alter the organization of these perceptions so that one can perhaps make finer distinctions between colors or, on the contrary, can group together colors (and this in a new way) which one is accustomed to distinguishing; so that one can locate emotions in parts of one's body that one has hitherto not associated with, let us say, fear or anger or curiosity; so that one can accept as literal, statements which in one's own culture one would regard as figures of speech, etc. And part of one's work consists in learning to perceive and so to build up new image clusters (and these perhaps in new forms)

congruent with one another but different in content and form from those one has
hitherto known.

In effect, it is not a question of enlarging one's own conceptions -- which is
rather the process involved in acculturation and, in another way, in creative
work -- but of organizing another system which, like one's own, is ultimately
based on the organism's reactions to stimulation within and outside the body.
That is, one learns not so that one can become but so that one can construct a
type of personality (actually, of course, more than one), not so that one can acquire but so that one can construct a way of perceiving the world. And neither
the personality nor the image of the world is based on one's own total experience,
but upon one's total empathy with others' experience as it is mediated by imagery.
So it is very different to have learned about relative hierarchy by having grown
up in or by having immigrated into a culture where no two persons are symmetrically equated with each other, and to understand the implications of having always to place oneself vis-à-vis persons above and below oneself by empathy
with one's informants and by the feeling given by the images in which this situation is expressed.

In such a study, the image of the world that is constructed is -- however
exact -- different from that perceived by any individual in the culture because it
is essentially schematic and is defined by the images of many individuals, not by
the total experience of any one of them. When one is working with an informant,
for instance, one is not only continually adjusting oneself to the fine alterations
in posture and tone of voice and to the statements of an individual, but also continually making "mental" comparisons between the gestures of affirmation or
denial or doubt made by this individual and those made by others, or between
the figures of speech that this person uses and that others have used to describe
themselves as children, or to describe their grandfathers, or the arrangement of
a house, or how joy or contentment are experienced. It is this attempt to synthesize by comparison that makes objective one's own subjective empathy with
any one individual.[20]

---

20. On this point, cf. especially the methodological introduction to "The Record
of Unabelin..." (Mead, 1949b). It appears that the anthropologist works by
means of comparison even when the focus of attention is on a single individual as a representative of a culture, e.g. Crashing Thunder (Radin,
1920), or Sun Chief (Simmons, 1942), or Jim Picard (Devereux, 1951), or
Unabelin. The use of comparison is implicit in the anthropologist's traditional statement about working with "the last two old men in a culture." In
a strict dyadic relationship (one-informant-one-anthropologist) where the
anthropologist had recourse to no other sources of information, he could
compare only (1) earlier and later statements made by the informant, and
(2) the informant's statements and his own experiences (including his experiences of the informant and of informants in other cultures). Theoretically the situation is qualitatively altered in any triad (one-anthropologist-
two-informants, two-anthropologists-one-informant). Two research workers interviewing one informant can at least make progressive comparisons
between two sets of insights on the one individual. While in practice this

Similarly, as one reads a novel, or looks at a painting, or reads a manual on child care, or works with a set of Rorschach protocols, one continually compares and synthesizes -- remembering the gesture that accompanied a verbal statement in a film, visualizing the description given by an informant, and so on. And again one's own empathy, without which one could not work at all, is made objective through the process of comparison and synthesis.

As one works, one includes in the comparisons made between individual versions of a common figure of speech (or gesture or visual image) the associations from other sources that come to one's mind. So, in working with French informants on the idea of the stranger -- the person who does not belong and who has no roots in the place where he is (who is déraciné) -- their comments recalled to my mind the dangers that are said to beset the child who ventures out of the home alone -- the gypsies and gendarmes and beggars described by other informants, the characterizations of orphans and adopted children in novels and in legal discussions, the evocation of fanciful monsters in Rorschach protocols, the descriptions of Germans in their daytime and nighttime behavior during the occupation of France, and so on. What one does in each case, it seems to me, is to make comparisons between the descriptions given by several persons and then, rather tentatively, to listen for (this is how I phrase what I do, at any rate) other associations that fit together with them -- so using one's total empathy to construct a synthesis.

Thus the perception of imagery depends in the first place upon the special sensory combinations with which the individual analyst habitually works. But analysis depends also upon training and experience which, on the one hand, enable one to refine one's own perceptions and to some extent to make up for one's deficiencies,[21] and, on the other hand, help one to develop and use flexibly the

---

may not be a tenable work situation, it has important implications for group research where the number of informants may be limited or where, for some other reason, several persons work with one informant (cf. the discussion of the organization of group research in Part Three, pages 85-101).

21. Thus, while the ability to work with intricate rhythmic patterns in music may be relatively unimportant in some cultures, it is very important in the culture of peasant Haiti, where rhythmic figures (in drumming), dance designs, the images of the gods (mediated by songs and by the actions of those who are possessed by the gods), symbolic drawings, etc., are all parts of one loosely integrated complex. A person who, like myself, finds it difficult to identify complicated rhythmic figures and even more difficult to distinguish between variations of one such figure is at a disadvantage and probably will never learn -- personally -- whether the drummers are as individualistic in their interpretations of drum figures representing the gods as are other performers (e.g. the dancers and those who draw the stylized drawings representing the gods). In this case the deficiency is not one that can be made up for by training. There is therefore a gap in my material of which account must be taken even though the problem of individualism can be solved by means of careful work on other types of imagery more suited to my abilities.

skills necessary for making delicate comparisons. Consequently, no two individuals will work precisely in the same way on the imagery of the same culture,
for each will bring to the study a unique combination of abilities and skills,
modified by the experience each has already had in working on other cultures.
And, even when both share in the same material, the final synthesis which each
constructs will reflect an individual relationship to the culture [22]

Furthermore, individuals differ greatly in their own conceptions of how
they assimilate the imagery on which they are working and in their special
awareness of the process of assimilation. On this subject we have autobiographical accounts by creative artists and considerable indirect information about
work processes based on studies of successive versions of a piece of writing
(cf. Arnheim, et al., 1948, for one example), of preliminary sketches for paintings, of successive works by one artist (cf. Spurgeon, 1935; Armstrong, 1946;
Sharpe, 1950; Sewell, 1952), or from combinations of observation and introspection (cf. Collingwood, 1938, 1939). But at least as far as subjective aspects of
the work process is concerned, published accounts by and about research workers are exceedingly meager. My own understanding is based mainly upon a
combination of introspection and discussion at various times with people whose
work I was editing or translating into English, or whose research materials I
was attempting to synthesize into some kind of whole intended to represent the
work of a group of which I was a member and not merely of two or five or ten
individuals' work reinterpreted by myself. Thinking about these more or less
introspective accounts of how a point was worked out and how relationships
were established within the material, I have no doubt but that the process of
assimilation differs fundamentally as between the creative artist and the research worker. The problem of the creative artist is to re-create and communicate an experience which is essentially personal and interior to himself.
The research worker, on the contrary, is concerned with understanding in
order to communicate to others systems which are external to himself -- what
he is attempting to communicate is not a generalized account of his own experience (which would be perhaps an appreciation of another culture) but rather an
account of the way in which others experience the world, organized in a particular way, i.e. through the medium of his own disciplined consciousness.
I would like to suggest very tentatively that one difference between the two

---

22. One vivid illustration of such individual differences in style is provided by
film recordings made by several fieldworkers of the same event, such as
the films made by Gregory Bateson, Jane Belo, and Colin McPhee of Balinese
ceremonials. Where two of them recorded the same event, the recordings
overlap, but the styles are identifiably individual -- in terms of length of
sequence, inclusiveness, the handling of movement in time and space, the
manner of relating small detail and the larger whole, etc. Each communicates a different view of the culture, not conflicting but presented in a different perspective.

kinds of activity -- creativity and research -- is not in the relative subjectivity of the one and objectivity of the other (for these are, however one defines them, common to both the artist and the research worker), but in the research worker's awareness and use of _multiple_ systems and in his habit of defining his own position in relation to each. The few illustrations which I can give that suggest both the differences and the likenesses among research workers in the way in which they handle this kind of awareness are necessarily based on my own experience and on the experiences of a few individuals with whom I have been able to discuss the problem.

I myself can attend to and retain most precisely visual and kinesthetic and tactile imagery, and I am likely to transpose imagery in other modalities into combinations of these. In working with verbal sources of imagery, my ability to concretize is intensified by listening to or actually saying the words, but my ability to synthesize is intensified by seeing them written. When I try to reconstruct a scene or to imagine a new one, I tend to listen for the voices and visualize the gestures of a group of people whom I think of as being external to myself and with none of whom I specifically identify. But in working out a structural problem I tend to feel the structural relationships in my muscles as a way of then visualizing them as abstract patterns. As might be expected, my memory for sequence is unreliable, but it is accurate for clusters.

Another anthropologist describes the process of assimilation as one in which he creates an "internal society" with "multiple voices" that carry on "multiple conversations" in his own mind. Another describes her way of working by saying that she creates multiple models and groups of persons in each of which "I have a position." Still another anthropologist seems in some way to ingest the culture so that, in effect, her own body becomes a living model of the culture on which she is working as well as of the culture of which she is herself a member, and she continually tests out relationships in terms of her own bodily integration. And another describes the process as one of "receiving and sending kinesthetic sets, strengthened by auditory patterns -- largely pitch, intonation and stress rather than words ... I muscularly feel in rhythmic patterns the activities of others -- singly or in groups -- reading them as I read written material, in chunks, consciously registering only shifts of cadence or expectancy violations, internalizing the rest which is relatively easy to recall." This anthropologist also works in terms of patterns which he regards as being as external to himself.

These are, of course, more or less metaphoric descriptions of how these particular anthropologists feel they control and organize their perceptions -- how they react to a mass of detail and organize their reactions into one related set. Although each of them does so in a different way, all of them create some form of internal model so that, imaginatively, their perceptions are given a certain internal objectivity. It is important to make this point because it is a

restatement of the conception of the analysis of imagery as a process that results in a construction, and provides some subjective evidence that such a construction represents neither an extension of oneself nor an incorporation into
one's own perceptual system of a new series of perceptions. Through the use
of such a model, the analyst is enabled continually to specify his own position
to himself and, indirectly, to others, and to distinguish between "what I feel" and
what he knows through empathy "a Frenchman (or a Russian, or a Pole, etc.)
feels like when ..." -- though he has participated in both as a sentient being.

When I work, I use my sensitivity to visual imagery as a way of picking up
clues; another analyst uses his sensitivity to auditory patterns or to patterns of
motion, etc. But each of us responding, for instance, to a new cluster of French
images will say (though certainly not in so many words) something like "From
where I stand (using the kind of model I do) this is how I think this bit fits into
a French image of the world," testing any new piece of information against
both other material and one's own internal model. This is what I mean by
working within a double set of controls and this highly disciplined use of subjective processes is the reason why, in the end, work of this kind is essentially
very formal. The construction I make and that made by another anthropologist
will differ in terms of the kinds of clues we habitually use and of models with
which we work, but providing we have chosen our material carefully and have
worked with some clear model, trusting our own perceptions, the two constructions will match, and, taken together, will be a more complex statement of the
configuration of a culture.

An accurate delineation of a cultural configuration depends also upon precise attentiveness to levels of consciousness and to the preferred modalities of
perception so that in the end one can phrase one's construction in such a way
that it includes the kinds of articulateness of a given culture not only in terms
of what members of that culture can state directly, what they handle metaphori-
cally and symbolically, and what is not expressed by them -- or what is disallowed in communication -- and can only be inferred, but also in terms of the
modalities of imagery that are combined and given emphasis in communication.
This brings us round the full circle back to the material on which the analysis
is based, for our phrasing in this respect will depend entirely upon our knowledge of the source of each detail and of the contexts in which details occurred.
And, finally, the success of our analysis can be tested only through the responses of members of the culture who, if we have caught the resonances of
their imagery, can understand and accept the unfamiliar as well as the familiar
in our image of their culture.

PART NINE

END LINKAGE: AN ANALYTICAL APPROACH

A. HISTORY OF THE APPROACH

Margaret Mead

This part of the Manual is designed to demonstrate the interplay between theoretical formulations, the use of these formulations in organizing new material, the application of the organized material to particular applied problems, and the way in which a fruitful formulation of this sort is itself subject to modification as the theoretical climate changes. In "Morale and National Character," which proved to be the first formulation of the approach now called the study of national character, by Gregory Bateson, earlier formulations of sex-differentiated ethos, which had been developed through intensive field work in primitive societies (Iatmul, Arapesh, Mundugumor, and Tchambuli; cf. Bateson, 1936, and Mead, 1935), were elaborated into a more inclusive model by adding the patterning of parent-child relationships also. On the basis of some very preliminary work on German character and personal experience of English and American cultures, this formulation of end linkage was used to make a first statement about types of contrast among Western societies. The Anglo-American formulation of reversed spectator-exhibitionism relationships between parents and children was then intensively elaborated in the work I did during World War II in interpreting American attitudes to the British, a part of which is briefly summarized in the first illustration (pages 379-82). In 1943, Ruth Benedict, in working out the pattern of Thai culture from literature and a very few informants, used the contrast between the ethos of men and women as an analytical tool; a brief excerpt from this study is given here as the second illustration (pages 382-86). When work in Research in Contemporary Cultures was inaugurated, a preliminary manual was prepared which included the formulation of end linkage as a basic tool. Natalie Joffe's paper on "Non-Reciprocity among East European Jews" (pages 386-89) is a more explicit application to many facets of the culture of East European Jews. Between her paper, which was written in 1948, and Rhoda Métraux's analysis of the spectator role in French culture, written in 1951 (pages 390-93), lie other research and theoretical developments, e.g. the explicit development of cybernetic theory (cf. Ruesch and Bateson, 1951; Mead, 1949f), Gregory Bateson's further application of the concepts of schismogenesis, end linkage, and cybernetics to Balinese culture (cf. Bateson, 1949), and Rhoda Métraux's field work and subsequent organization of Haitian material within this theoretical structure (cf. Métraux, 1951, 1952a, 1952b).[1]

---

1. For other illustrations of the use of end-linkage formulations in this Manual, cf. in Part Ten, Geoffrey Gorer, "Japanese Character Structure and Propaganda" (pages 401-2), and John Hast Weakland, "Chinese Family Images in International Affairs" (pages 421-26).

The end-linkage formulation has the advantage of including both the biologically given (the dependence of human infants at birth and the complementary physical functions of the two sexes) and properties of interaction inherent in all human groups, such as initiation-response, learning, and social differentiation among individuals by role and status. It provides a starting point for analysis of any culture, no matter how complex, since degrees of complexity are provided for in the formulation. Like the use of the psychosexual development of the child to order material when the living society is inaccessible, this approach makes it possible to anchor a variety of observations -- on relationships between employer and employee, speaker and audience, teacher and pupil, etc., all subject to enormous social modification -- to biological constants of the dependency of the human infant and the sexual differentiation of human beings.

The principal development since the original formulation in 1942 has been a systematic and explicit inclusion of the detailed steps within the interaction patterns originally described as dominance-submission or as exhibitionism-spectatorship between parents and children.

B. FORMULATION OF END LINKAGE

Gregory Bateson

Scientific inquiry has been diverted from questions of this type [i.e. questions related to the study of national character] by a number of trains of thought which lead scientists to regard all such questions as unprofitable or unsound. Before we hazard any constructive opinion as to the order of differences to be expected among European populations, therefore, these diverting trains of thought must be examined.

It is argued that not the people but rather the circumstances under which they live differ from one community to another; that we have to deal with differences either in historical background or in current conditions, and that these factors are sufficient to account for all differences in behavior without our invoking any differences of character in the individuals concerned. Essentially this argument is an appeal to Occam's Razor -- an assertion that we ought not to multiply entities beyond necessity. The argument is that, where observable differences in circumstances exist, we ought to invoke these rather than more inferred differences in character, which we cannot observe.

The argument may be met in part by quoting experimental data, such as Lewin's experiments (unpublished material), which showed that there are great differences in the way in which Germans and Americans respond to failure in an experimental setting. The Americans treated failure as a challenge to increase effort; the Germans responded to the same failure with discouragement. But those who argue for the effectiveness of conditions rather than character can still reply that the experimental conditions are not, in fact, the same for both groups; that the stimulus value of any circumstance depends upon how that circumstance stands out against the background of other circumstances in the life of the subject, and that this contrast cannot be the same for both groups.

It is possible, in fact, to argue that since the same circumstances never occur for individuals of different cultural background, it is therefore unnecessary to invoke such abstractions as national character. This argument breaks down, I believe, when it is pointed out that, in stressing circumstance rather than character, we would be ignoring the known facts about learning. Perhaps the best-documented generalization in the field of psychology is that, at any given moment, the behavioral characteristics of any mammal, and especially of man, depend upon the previous experience and behavior of that individual. Thus in presuming that character, as well as circumstance, must be taken into account, we are not multiplying entities beyond necessity; we know of the signifi-

_____
2.   This is an excerpt from Bateson (1942b, pp. 74-89).

cance of learned character from other types of data, and it is this knowledge which compels us to consider the additional "entity "

A second barrier to any acceptance of the notion of "national character" arises after the first has been negotiated. Those who grant that character must be considered can still doubt whether any uniformity or regularity is likely to obtain within such a sample of human beings as constitutes a nation. Let us grant at once that uniformity obviously does not occur, and let us proceed to consider what sorts of regularity may be expected.

The criticism which we are trying to meet is likely to take five forms. (1) The critic may point to the occurrence of subcultural differentiation, to differences between the sexes, or between classes, or between occupational groups within the community. (2) He may point to the extreme heterogeneity and confusion of cultural norms which can be observed in "melting-pot" communities. (3) He may point to the accidental deviant, the individual who has undergone some "accidental" traumatic experience not usual among those in his social environment. (4) He may point to the phenomena of cultural change, and especially to the sort of differentiation which results when one part of the community lags behind some other in rate of change. (5) Lastly, he may point to the arbitrary nature of national boundaries.

These objections are closely interrelated, and the replies to them all derive ultimately from two postulates: first, that the individual, whether from a physiological or a pyschological point of view, is a single organized entity, such that all its "parts" or "aspects" are mutually modifiable and mutually interacting; and second, that a community is likewise organized in this sense.

If we look at social differentiation in a stable community -- say, at sex differentiation in a New Guinea tribe[3] -- we find that it is not enough to say that the habit system or the character structure of one sex is different from that of another. The significant point is that the habit system of each sex cogs into the habit system of the other; that the behavior of each promotes the habits of the other.[4] We find, for example, between the sexes, such complementary patterns as spectatorship-exhibitionism, dominance-submission, and succoring-dependence, or mixtures of these. Never do we find mutual irrelevance between such groups.

Although it is unfortunately true that we know very little about the terms of habit differentiation between classes, sexes, occupational groups, etc., in Western nations, there is, I think, no danger in applying this general conclusion

3. Cf. Mead (1935), especially Part III, for an analysis of sex differentiation among the Tchambuli; also Bateson (1936), for an analysis of sex differentiation among adults in Iatmul, New Guinea.
4. We are considering here only those cases in which ethological differentiation follows the sex dichotomy. It is also probable that, where the ethos of the two sexes is not sharply differentiated, it would still be correct to say that the ethos of each promotes that of the other; e.g. through such mechanisms as competition and mutual imitation. (Cf. Mead, 1935.)

to all cases of stable differentiation between groups which are living in mutual contact. It is, to me, inconceivable that two differing groups could exist side by side in a community without some sort of mutual relevance between the special characteristics of one group and those of the other. Such an occurrence would be contrary to the postulate that a community is an organized unit. We shall, therefore, presume that this generalization applies to all stable social differentiation.

Now, all that we know of the mechanics of character formation -- especially the processes of projection, reaction formation, compensation, and the like -- forces us to regard these bipolar patterns as unitary within the individual. If we know that an individual is trained in overt expression of one half of one of these patterns, e. g. in dominance behavior, we can predict with certainty (though not in precise language) that the seeds of the other half -- submission -- are simultaneously sown in his personaltiy. We have to think of the individual, in fact, as trained in dominance-submission, not in either dominance or submission. From this it follows that where we are dealing with stable differentiation within a community, we are justified in ascribing common character to the members of that community, provided we take the precaution of describing that common character in terms of the motifs of relationship between the differentiated sections of the community.

The same sort of considerations will guide us in dealing with our second criticism -- the extremes of heterogeneity, such as occur in modern "melting-pot" communities. Suppose we attempted to analyze out all the motifs of relationship between individuals and groups in such a community as New York City; if we did not end in the madhouse long before we had completed our study, we should arrive at a picture of common character that would be almost infinitely complex -- certainly that would contain more fine differentiations than the human psyche is capable of resolving within itself. At this point, then, both we and the individuals whom we are studying are forced to take a short cut: to treat heterogeneity as a positive characteristic of the common environment, sui generis. When, with such a hypothesis, we begin to look for common motifs of behavior, we note the very clear tendencies towards glorying in heterogeneity for its own sake (as in the Robinson Latouche "Ballad for Americans") and towards regarding the world as made up of an infinity of disconnected quiz-bits (like Ripley's "Believe It or Not").

The third objection, the case of the individual deviant, falls in the same frame of reference as that of the differentiation of stable groups. The boy on whom an English public-school education does not take, even though the original roots of his deviance were laid in some "accidental" traumatic incident, is reacting to the public-school system. The behavioral habits which he acquires may not follow the norms which the school intends to implant, but they are acquired in reaction to those very norms. He may (and often does) acquire patterns the exact opposite of the normal; but he cannot conceivably acquire irrelevant patterns. He may become a "bad" public-school Englishman, he may become insane, but still his deviant characteristics will be systematically related to the norms which he is resisting. We may describe his character, indeed, by saying that it is as systematically related to the standard public-school character as the character of Iatmul natives of one sex is systematically related to the character of the other sex. His character is oriented to the motifs and patterns of relationship in the society in which he lives.

The same frame of reference applies to the fourth consideration, that of changing communities and the sort of differentiation which occurs when one section of a community lags behind another in change. Since the direction in which a change occurs will necessarily be conditioned by the status quo ante, the new patterns, being reactions to the old, will be systematically related to the old. As long as we confine ourselves to the terms and themes of this systematic relationship, therefore, we are entitled to expect regularity of character in the individuals. Furthermore, the expectation and experience of change may, in some cases, be so important as to become a common character-determining factor[5] sui generis, in the same sort of way that "heterogeneity" may have positive effects.

Lastly, we may consider cases of shifting national boundaries, our fifth criticism. Here, of course, we cannot expect that a diplomat's signature on a treaty will immediately modify the characters of the individuals whose national allegiance is thereby changed. It may even happen -- for example, in cases where a preliterate native population is brought for the first time in contact with Europeans -- that, for some time after the shift, the two parties to such a situation will behave in an exploratory or almost random manner, each retaining its own norms and not yet developing any special adjustments to the situation of contact. During this period, we should still not expect any generalizations to apply to both groups. Very soon, however, we know that each side does develop special patterns of behavior to use in its contacts with the other.[6] At this point, it becomes meaningful to ask what systematic terms of relationship will describe the common character of the two groups; and from this point on, the degree of common character structure will increase until the two groups become related to each other just as two classes or two sexes in a stable, differentiated society. (Cf. Bateson, 1935.)

---

5.   For a discussion of the role played by "change" and "heterogeneity" in melting-pot communities, cf. Mead (1942a); also Alexander (1942).

6.   In the South Seas, those special modes of behavior which Europeans adopt towards native peoples, and those other modes of behavior which the native adopts towards Europeans, are very obvious. Apart from analyses of "pidgin" languages, we have, however, no psychological data on these patterns. For a description of the analagous patterns in Negro-white relationships, cf. John Dollard (1937), especially Chapter XII, "Accommodation Attitudes of Negroes."

In sum, to those who argue that human communites show too great internal differentiation or contain too great a random element for any notion of common character to apply, our reply would be that we expect such an approach to be useful (1) provided we describe common character in terms of the themes of relationship between groups and individuals within the community, and (2) provided that we allow sufficient time to elapse for the community to reach some degree of equilibrium or to accept either change or heterogeneity as a characteristic of their human environment.

1. Differences Which We May Expect between National Groups

The above examination of "straw men" in the case against "national character" has very stringently limited the scope of this concept. But the conclusions from this examination are by no means simply negative. To limit the scope of a concept is almost synonymous with defining it.

We have added one very important tool to our equipment -- the technique of describing the common character (or the "highest common factor" of character) of individuals in a human community in terms of bipolar adjectives. Instead of despairing in face of the fact that nations are highly differentiated, we shall take the dimensions of that differentiation as our clues to the national character. No longer content to say, "Germans are submissive," or "Enlgishmen are aloof," we shall use such phrases as "dominant-submissive" when relationships of this sort can be shown to occur. Similarly, we shall not refer to "the paranoidal element in German character," unless we can show that by "paranoidal" we mean some bipolar characteristic of German-German or German-foreign relationships. We shall not describe varieties of character by defining a given character in terms of its position on a continuum between extreme dominance and extreme submissiveness, but we shall, instead, try to use for our descriptions some such continua as "degree of interest in, or orientation towards, dominance-submission."

So far, we have mentioned only a very short list of bipolar characteristics: dominance-submission, succoring-dependence, and exhibitionism-spectatorship. One criticism will certainly be uppermost in the reader's mind, that, in short, all three of these characterisitics are clearly present in all Western cultures. Before our method becomes useful, therefore, we must try to expand it to give us sufficient scope and discriminatory power to differentiate one Western culture from another.

As this conceptual frame develops, no doubt many further expansions and discriminations will be introduced. The present paper will deal with only three such types of expansion.

2. Alternatives to Bipolarity

When we invoked bipolarity as a means of handling differentiation within society without forgoing some notion of common character structure, we considered only the possibility of simple bipolar differentiation. Certainly this pattern is very common in Western cultures; take, for instance, Republican-Democrat, Political Right-Left, sex differentiation, God and the Devil, and so on. These peoples even try to impose a binary pattern upon phenomena which are not dual in nature -- youth vs. age, labor vs. capital, mind vs. matter -- and, in general, lack the organizational devices for handling triangular systems; the inception of any "third" party is always regarded, for example, as a threat to our political organization. This clear tendency towards dual systems ought not, however, to blind us to the occurrence of other patterns.[7]

There is, for example, a very interesting tendency in English communities towards the formation of ternary systems, such as parents-nurse-child, king-ministers-people, officers-N.C.O.'s-privates.[8] While the precise motifs of relationship in these ternary systems remain to be investigated, it is important to note that these systems, to which I refer as "ternary," are neither "simple hierarchies" nor "triangles." By a pure hierarchy, I should mean a serial system in which face-to-face relations do not occur between members when they are separated by some intervening member; in other words, systems in which the only communication between A and C passes through B. By a triangle I should mean a threefold system with no serial properties. The ternary system, parent-nurse-child, on the other hand, is very different from either of these other forms. It contains serial elements, but face-to-face contact does occur between the first and the third members. Essentially, the function of the middle member is to instruct and discipline the third member in the forms of behavior which he should adopt in his contacts with the first. The nurse teaches the child how to behave towards its parents, just as the N.C.O. teaches and disciplines the private in how he should behave towards officers. In psychoanalytic terminology, the process of introjection is done indirectly, not by direct impact of the parental personality upon the child.[9] The face-to-face contacts between the first and

7. The Balinese social system in the mountain communities is almost entirely devoid of such dualisms. The ethological differentiation of the sexes is rather slight; political factions are completely absent. In the plains, there is a dualism which has resulted from the intrusive Hindu caste system, those with caste being discriminated from those without caste. At the symbolic level (partly as a result of Hindu influence) dualisms are much more frequent, however, than they are in the social structure (e.g. Northeast vs. Southwest, gods vs. demons, symbolic Left vs. Right, symbolic Male vs. Female, etc.).

8. A fourth instance of this threefold pattern occurs in some great public schools (as in Charterhouse), where the authority is divided between the quieter, more polished, intellectual leaders ("monitors") and the rougher, louder, athletic leaders (captain of football, head of long room, etc.), who have the duty of seeing to it that the "fags" run when the monitor calls.

9. For a general discussion of cultural variants of the Oedipus situation and the related systems of cultural sanctions, cf. Mead (1940b), also Róheim (1934).

members are, however, very important. We may refer, in this connection, to the vital daily ritual in the British Army, in which the officer of the day asks the assembled privates and N.C.O's whether there are any complaints.

Certainly, any full discussion of English character ought to allow for ternary, as well as bipolar, patterns.

3. Symmetrical Motifs

So far, we have considered only what we have called "complementary" patterns of relationship, in which the behavior patterns at one end of the relationship are different from, but fit in with, the behavior patterns at the other end (dominance-submission, etc.). There exists, however, a whole category of human interpersonal behavior which does not conform to this description. In addition to the contrasting complementary patterns, we have to recognize the existence of a series of symmetrical patterns, in which people respond to what others are doing by themselves doing something similar. In particular, we have to consider those competitive [10] patterns in which individual or group A is stimulated to more of any type of behavior by perceiving more of that same type of behavior (or greater success in that type of behavior) in individual or group B.

There is a very profound contrast between such competitive systems of behavior and complementary dominace-submission systems -- a highly significant contrast for any discussion of national character. In complementary striving, the stimulus which prompts A to greater efforts is the relative weakness in B; if we want to make A subside or submit, we ought to show him that B is stronger than he is. In fact, the complementary character structure may be summarized by the phrase "bully-coward," implying the combination of these characteristics in the personality. The symmetrical competitive systems, on the other hand, are in almost precise functional opposite of the complementary. Here the stimulus which evokes greater striving in A is the vision of greater strength or greater striving in B; and, inversely, if we demonstrate to A that B is really weak, A will relax his efforts.

It is probable that these two contrasting patterns are alike available as potentialites in all human beings; but clearly, any individual who behaves in both ways at once will risk internal confusion and conflict. In the various national groups, consequently, different methods of resolving this discrepancy

---

10. The term "co-operation," which is sometimes used as the opposite of "competition," covers a very wide variety of patterns, some of them symmetrical and others complementary, some bipolar and others in which the co-operating individuals are chiefly oriented to some personal or impersonal goal. We may expect that some careful analysis of these patterns will give us vocabulary for describing other sorts of national characteristics. Such an analysis cannot be attempted in this paper.

have developed. In England and in America, where children and adults are subjected to an almost continuous barrage of disapproval whenever they exhibit the complementary patterns, they inevitably come to accept the ethics of "fair play." Responding to the challenge of difficulties, they cannot, without guilt, kick the underdog.[11] For British morale Dunkirk was a stimulus, not a depressant.

In Germany, on the other hand, the same clichés are apparently lacking, and the community is chiefly organized on the basis of a complementary hierarchy in terms of dominance-submission. The dominance behavior is sharply and clearly developed; yet the picture is not perfectly clear, and needs further investigation. Whether a pure dominance-submission hierarchy could ever exist as a stable system is doubtful. It seems that in the case of Germany, the submission end of the pattern is masked, so that overt submissive behavior is almost as strongly tabooed as it is in America or England. In place of submission, we find a sort of parade-ground impassivity.

A hint as to the process by which the submissive role is modified and rendered tolerable comes to us out of the interviews in a recently begun study of German life histories.[12] One German subject described how different was the treatment which he, as a boy, received in his South German home from that which his sister received. He said that much more was demanded of him; that his sister was allowed to evade discipline; that whereas he was always expected to click his heels and obey with precision, his sister was allowed much more freedom. The interviewer at once began to look for intersex sibling jealousy, but the subject declared that it was a greater honor for the boy to obey. "One doesn't expect too much of girls," he said. "What one felt they ⌈boys⌉ should accomplish and do was very serious, because they had to be prepared for life." An interesting inversion of noblesse oblige.

4. Combinations of Motifs

Among the complementary motifs, we have mentioned only three -- dominance-submission, exhibitionism-spectatorhsip, and succoring-dependence -- but these three will suffice to illustrate the sort of verifiable hypotheses at which we can arrive by describing national character in this hyphenated terminology.[13]

---

11. It is, however, possible that in certain sections of these nations, complementary patterns occur with some frequency -- particularly among roups who have suffered from prolonged insecurity and uncertainty; e.g. racial minorities, depressed areas, the Stock Exchange, political circles, etc.
12. Gregory Bateson, unpublished research for the Council on Human Relations.
13. For a fuller study, we ought to consider such other motifs as aggression-passivity, possessive-possessed, agent-tool, etc. And all of these motifs will require somewhat more critical definition than can be attempted in this paper.

Since, clearly, all three of these motifs occur in all Western cultures, the possibilities for international difference are limited to the proportions and ways in which the motifs are combined. The proportions are likely to be very difficult to detect, except where the differences are very large. We may be sure ourselves that Germans are more oriented towards dominance-submission than are Americans, but to demonstrate this certainty is likely to be difficult. To estimate differences in the degree of development of exhibitionism-spectatorship or succoring-dependence in the various nations will, indeed, probably be quite impossible.

If, however, we consider the possible ways in which these motifs may be combined together, we find sharp qualitative differences which are susceptible of easy verification. Let us assume that all three of these motifs are developed in all relationships in all Western cultures, and from this assumption go on to consider which individual plays which role.

It is logically possible that in one cultural environment A will be dominant and exhibitionist, while B is submissive and spectator; while in another culture X may be dominant and spectator, while Y is submissive and exhibitionist.

Examples of this sort of contrast rather easily come to mind. Thus we may note that whereas the dominant Nazis preen themselves before the people, the czar of Russia kept his private ballet, and Stalin emerges from seclusion only to review his troops.[14] We might perhaps present the relationship between the Nazi Party and the people thus:

Party	People
Dominance	Submission
Exhibitionism	Spectatorship

while the czar and his ballet would be represented:

Czar	Ballet
Dominance	Submission
Spectatorship	Exhibitionism

Since these European examples are comparatively unproved, it is worth while at this point to demonstrate the occurrence of such differences by describing a rather striking ethnographic difference which has been documented more fully. In Europe, where we tend to associate succoring behavior with social superiority, we construct our parent symbols accordingly. Our God, or our king, is the "father" of his people. In Bali, on the other hand, the gods are the "children" of the people, and when a god speaks through the mouth of a person in trance, he addresses anyone who will listen as "father."[15] Similarly,

14. This paper was written during World War II, in 1942. The formulation would now be amplified (in regard to the Russians) to include the mirroring quality of Russian behavior -- Stalin reveiwing troops wearing pictures of Stalin, the speaker joining the listeners in applauding his own speech, etc. -- Ed.

15. Cf. Bateson and Mead (1942), published after this article was written. For a further discussion of Balinese culture using this model cf. Bateson (1949). -- Ed.

the rajah is <u>sajanganga</u> ("spoilt" like a child) by his people. The Balinese, further, are very fond of putting children in the combined roles of god and dancer;
in mythology, the perfect prince is polished and narcissistic. Thus the Balinese pattern might be summarized thus:

High Status	Low Status
Dependence	Succoring
Exhibitionism	Spectatorship

And this diagram would imply, not only that the Balinese feel dependence and
exhibitionism and superior status to go naturally together, but also that a Balinese will not readily combine succoring with exhibitionism (that is, Bali completely lacks the ostentatious gift-giving characteristic of many primitive
peoples) or will be embarrassed if forced by the context to attempt such a combination.

Although the analogous diagrams for our Western cultures cannot be drawn
with the same certainty, it is worth while to attempt them for the parent-child
relationships in English, American, and German cultures. One extra complica-
tion must, however, be faced; when we look at parent-child relationships instead of at relationships between princes and people, we have to make specific
allowance for the changes in the pattern which occur as the child grows older.
Succoring-dependence is undoubtedly a dominant motif in early childhood, but
various mechansims later modify this extreme dependence, to bring about some
degree of psychological independence.

The English upper- and middle-class system would be represented diagram-
matically thus:

Parents	Children
Dominance	Submission (modified by "ternary" nurse system)
Succoring	Dependence (dependence habits broken by separa- tion -- children sent to school)
Exhibitionism	Spectatorship (children listen silently at meals)

In contrast with this, the analogous American pattern seems to be:

Parents	Children
Dominance (slight)	Submission (slight)
Succoring	Dependence
Spectatorship	Exhibitionism

And this pattern differs from the English not only in the reversal of the spectatorship-exhibitionism roles, but also in the context of what is exhibited. The
American child is encouraged by his parents to <u>show off his independence</u>.
Usually the process of psychological weaning is not accomplished by sending
the child away to a boarding school; instead, the child's exhibitionism is played
off against his independence, until the latter is neutralized. Later, from this
beginning in the exhibition of independence, the individual may sometimes go
on in adult life to show off succoring, his wife and family becoming in some
degree his "exhibits."

Though the analogous German pattern probably resembles the American in the arrangement of the paired complementary roles, certainly it differs from the American in that the father's dominance is much stronger and much more consistent, and especially in that the content of the boy's exhibitionism is quite different. He is, in fact, dominated into a sort of heel-clicking exhibitionism which takes the place of overt submissive behavior. Thus, while in the American character exhibitionism is encouraged by the parent as a method of psychological weaning, both its function and its content are for the German entirely different.

Differences of this order, which may be expected in all European nations, are probably the basis of many of our naïve and often unkind international comments. They may, indeed, be of considerable importance in the mechanics of international relations, inasmuch as an understanding of them might dispel some of our misunderstandings. To an American eye, the English too often appear "arrogant," whereas to an English eye the American appears to be "boastful." If we could show precisely how much of truth and how much of distortion is present in these impressions, it might be a real contribution to interallied co-operation.

In terms of the diagrams above, the "arrogance" of the Englishman would be due to the combination of dominance and exhibitionism. The Englishman in a performing role (the parent at breakfast, the newspaper editor, the political spokesman, the lecturer, or what not) assumes that he is also in a dominant role -- that he can decide in accordance with vague, abstract standards what sort of performance to give -- and the audience can "take it or leave it." His own arrogance he sees either as "natural" or as mitigated by his humility in face of the abstract standards. Quite unaware that his behavior could conceivably be regarded as a comment upon his audience, he is, on the contrary, aware only of behaving in the performer's role, as he understands that role. But the American does not see it thus. To him, the "arrogant" behavior of the Englishman appears to be directed against the audience, in which case the implicit invocation of some abstract standard appears only to add insult to injury.

Similarly, the behavior which an Englishman interprets as "boastful" in an American is not aggressive, although the Englishman may feel that he is being subjected to some sort of invidious comparison. He does not know that, as a matter of fact, Americans will only behave like this to people whom they rather like and respect. According to the hypothesis above, the "boasting" pattern results from the curious linkage whereby exhibition of self-sufficiency and independence is played off against overdependence. The American, when he boasts, is looking for approval of his upstanding independence; but the naïve Englishman interprets this behavior as a bid for some sort of dominance or superiority.

In this sort of way, we may suppose that the whole flavor of one national culture may differ from that of another, and that such differences may be considerable enough to lead to serious misunderstandings. It is probable, however, that these differences are not so complex in their nature as to be beyond the reach of investigation.

C. FOUR APPLICATIONS OF END-LINKAGE ANALYSIS

I. Applications of End-Linkage Formulations to Anglo-American Relations in World War II[16]

Margaret Mead

When an attempt is made to use anthropological methods to strengthen a relationship between peoples of two contemporary cultures, still different problems arise. Here the focus is not upon points of vulnerability, which may be breached, as with the enemy, or strengthened, as for members of occupied countries, nor upon traditional strengths and coherencies to be enhanced, and weaknesses and contradictions to be guarded against, as in work in own culture. Instead, our efforts have to be directed toward finding areas of agreement which can be used as a background for the acceptance of differences which are causing specific friction and tension. Research and resulting communications are focused upon a relationship, and the nodes selected for emphasis are defined in terms of that relationship, not in terms of the emphasis within the whole culture pattern of each society. For instance, if foreign policy is to be discussed and the foreign policy of one culture is most congruent with upper-class values, while in the other it is most congruent with middle-class values, this asymmetry would be consciously explored, perhaps to the neglect of any exploration of the exactly corresponding class in the other country, because of its lack of immediate relevance to the problem in hand.

As illustrative material for such an operation, I shall draw upon my own experience in working on Anglo-American relations, and particularly use data upon the areas of friction and misunderstanding between American troops and British civilians in Britain in 1943.

In the initial steps I depended upon the formulations of symmetrical and complementary schismogenesis, developed by Gregory Bateson (1942a; 1942b), in which the United States and Britain were both diagnosed as relying upon the stimulas provided by a greater strength in the opponent (symmetrical pattern) rather than the stimulus provided by relative weakness (complementary pattern). With this approval of symmetrical relationships shared by both the United States and Britain was associated a common moral disapprobation of bullying, picking on someone who was smaller, throwing one's weight around, etc.

In addition to the original statement of this diagnosis, I had elaborated, before going to England, the American version of·adequate provocation to attack, under the formulation of "the chip on the shoulder,"[17] in which I stressed that that the American boy, reared by women, was given a deep doubt of his essential

16. Reproduced from Mead (1948a; pp. 210-11, 312-17).
17. Cf. Mead (1942a), Chapter IX, "The Chip on the Shoulder" (pp. 138-58).

aggressiveness, combined with a lack of pattern for exercising it, in contrast
to the British boy, reared by older boys and men to combine a belief in his innate aggressiveness with an obligation never to use his full strength unless
pushed into an extreme position in which he could turn at bay. The famous
"backs to the wall" order of Haig in World War I to the British, and reported
exhortations of General Patton to his men, emphasizing the difficulty of the
task, but also the fact that the enemy was on the run and the United States
Army had the best equipment in the world, are conspicuous examples of the
way in which military leaders have intuitively relied upon these different pat-
ternings of a basically symmetrical schismogenic attitude. Phrased colloquial-
ly, the underlying similarity became, "Both British and Americans believe that
the strong have an obligation not to abuse their strength. We both hate bullies,
and conversely, those who cringe to bullies."

The second theoretical formulation was the hypothesis of end linkage
(Bateson, 1942b): that the way in which parent-child relationships are patterned
in respect to such behaviors as succoring-dependence, dominance-submission,
and exhibitionism-spectatorship provides a learning situation for the child which
patterns his subsequent behavior in situations where these behaviors are involved. Specifically, in Anglo-American relationships, the exhibitionism is reversed, in Britain it is Father who exhibits to his children; he is the model for
their future behavior. Father does the talking, provides the model, and before
a very quiet and submissive audience, in accordance with the keen ethical disapproval of overuse of strength. Father underplays his strength, understates
his position, speaks with a slight appearance of hesitation in his manner, but
with the cool assurance of one who knows. In the United States this position is
reversed, and at the American breakfast table, it is not Father, but Junior,
who talks, exhibits his successes and skills, and demands parental spectatorship and applause, with an insistence that can be clamoring and assertive, because after all he is speaking from weakness to strength. The American background for this reversal was explored (Mead, 1942a) and in the spring of 1943
we tried using the contrast in a radio program, in which samples of parent-
child behavior at the breakfast table were followed by excerpts from American
and British public speeches.[18]

18. This program was given as part of the series, "Science at Work" of the
    American School of the Air of the Columbia Broadcasting system (cf.
    "Science at Work," 1944). The two speeches ran as follows:
    British Lecturer:
        "Ladies and Gentlemen ... I have been asked to talk to you tonight about
    British war production. We have, of course, improved. Our over-all fig-
    ures for the past year show a definite increase. But it is, I think, in planes
    that the picture is most striking. Our largest bombers, which incidentally
    carry four times the bombload of yours, are now coming quite satisfactorily
    into production."

For lecturing in Britain, these two formulations of symmetrical schismogenesis and end linkage provided both a theoretical background for understanding
and material for interpreting one of the acute points of friction between British
and Americans. This point was British repudiation of American "boasting" and
American repudiation of British "arrogance." It lent itself particularly well to
use on the lecture platform and over the radio, as tone of voice was the principal
medium in the demonstration. By a little careful interviewing in each new area
in Britain, I could get verbatim, and therefore acceptable, statements of the
British objections. "The trouble with the Americans is that when they are good
at something they say so." "The trouble with the Americans is that they talk
so much about what they are going to do; we don't talk, we just do it" (from the
Scots). I could then rely upon the lecture situation, itself one in which the exhibitionistic role of the lecturer and the spectatorship role of the audience was
defined, to provide me with additional illustrative material. I could quote from
the chairman who in presenting me, putatively in the parental role on a British
stage to a great tired audience who had come out in the blackout on a freezing
Sunday night in Scotland, said, "Be as kind to the audience as you can, Dr.
Mead"; or I could refer to the whole institution of the "vote of thanks," in which
the British audience, after sitting, docile and respectful while the lecturer
plays Father, re-establishes the balance by the paternalistic tone in which the
proposer of the vote of thanks addresses the now seated lecturer.

Explanations of behavioral differences which stressed upbringing were
easily acceptable to the British, because of the strong cultural emphasis upon
"character" as something which is acquired in the course of the right education
rather than an innate possession of any individual or class of individuals. It was
possible to show that whenever an American spoke, he spoke as he had learned to
speak when he was small and so would put that irritating overstatement into his
voice which the British called "boasting." Whenever a Briton spoke, he spoke
as he had heard his father and other elders speak, as the strong and assured,
carefully pulling his punches with that irritating understatement in his voice
which the American called "arrogance." It was possible to show how the words
understatement applied to the British and boasting applied to the Americans,

---

American Lecturer:
"Well, ladies and gentlemen ... I see I'm down on the program to talk to
you tonight about Alaska. I can think of one good reason why I know something about that country. It's because I've had to make upwards of 20 to 30
trips there, summer and winter in the past fifteen years.
Two or three of these trips, I might add, were by dogsled, far off the
beaten track. On at least one of them, I nearly lost my life. But the thing I
want to tell you folks about tonight is the change that's come over Alaska
since our boys went in there. Yes sir ... mass-production methods and the
Good Old American qualities of hard work and initiative are showing results up there these days. I predict that five years after this war finishes,
we'll be spending summer in Alaska the way we used to spend winter down
in Florida. That's a tip, folks."

emphasized the virtues of British behavior and devalued American, while by using the parallel words <u>understatement</u> and <u>overstatement</u>, both British and American behavior could be put in a common frame, that of habits learned in childhood.

II. Male Dominance in Thai Culture[19]

Ruth Benedict

The most revealing of all Thai summaries of male and female character is the proverb which is on every tongue: "Man is paddy; woman is rice," i.e. man is the seed rice able to reproduce itself, woman is rice polished for eating. As Thai women informants said, "She can only be swallowed once," "she can't reproduce unless a man comes to her." But a man "can produce by himself." An informant illustrated with a "rice" (woman) as a kernel inside a closed circle; of "paddy" (man) as a short straight line with arrows radiating out from him. The proverb is used in the education of girls to teach them to guard their virtue -- for they can only be "eaten" once; i.e. by one man. In the education of boys, it bears testimony to their superiority; they are the "seed" which produces the harvest.

In spite of all the freedom of Thai village women and of the wives of officials, the one superiority -- fertility -- which is ascribed to them by most peoples is not theirs by Thai definition. They provide a nest for the child in the womb and nourish their husbands, but they have not the virtue of creativity in themselves.

Yet they can nourish their husbands well. As men say in Thailand, "A play friend is not equal to a die friend and a boy friend is not equal to a girl friend," i.e. a man is a fair-weather friend, but from a woman one can expect loyalty till death. When a man courts a girl, he selects one to whom, in the Thai phrase, "he can trust his life in sickness and his obsequies after death." It is the woman -- not the husband, as in our Episcopal marriage service -- who must "cherish ... till death do us part."

This is the great Thai daydream, and it is the betrayal of this daydream that is usually elaborated in story and proverb and simile. A woman who does not satisfy this dream, since she has no other justification in living, has betrayed her kind. The Thai say: "A male elephant, a crocodile, and a loving wife, put not your trust in these." They say: "Three days' absence from home and your wife is another's."

The best statement of what men hope and fear for in their wives is the writing of the Siamese philosopher quoted by Young (1900; pp. 86-88).

1. Some wives are to their husbands as a younger sister. They look to their husbands for approving smiles as the reward of their kind and affectionate forethought. They confide in him and feel tenderly toward him. And when they

19. Reproduced from Benedict (1952, pp. 44-48). This paper was written in 1943.

have once discovered the wish, the taste, and the ideas of him whose approval they respect, they devote themselves thoughtfully and assiduously to the realization of his desires. Their own impulsive passions and temper are kept under strict control lest some hasty word should mar the harmony of their union.

2. Some wives are to their husbands as an elder sister. They watch sedulously their husband's outgoings and incomings so as to prevent all occasion for scandal. They are careful as to the condition of his wardrobe and keep it always in order for every occasion. They are diligent in preserving from the public gaze anything that might impair the dignity of their family. When their lord and master is found wanting in any particular, they neither fret nor scold, but wait patiently for the time when they can best effect a reformation in his morals and lead him toward the goal of upright manly conduct.

3. Some wives are to their husbands like a mother. They are ever seeking for some good thing that may bring gladness to the heart of the man for whom they live. They desire him to be excellent in every particular, and will themselves make any sacrifice to secure their object. When sorrow or trouble overtakes them, they hide it away from the eyes of him they love. All their thoughts center round him, and they so order their conversation and actions that in themselves he may find a worthy model for imitation. Should he fall sick, they tend him with unfailing care and patience.

4. Some wives are to their husbands as a common friend (i.e. "play friend"). They desire to stand on an exactly equal footing with him (i.e. they give tit for tat). If ill-nature is a feature in the character of their husbands, they cultivate the same fault in themselves. They will quarrel with him on the slightest provocation. They meet all his suggestions with an excess of carping criticism. They are always on the lookout for any infringement of what they deem their rights, and should the husband desire them to perform any little service for him, he must approach the subject with becoming deference or their refusal is instant and absolute.

5. Some wives wish to rule their husbands. Their language and manners are of a domineering nature. They treat the man as if he were a slave, scolding, commanding, and forbidding with unbecoming asperity. The husbands of such women are a miserable cringing set of men.

6. Some wives are of the robber kind. Their only idea in getting married is the possession of a slave and the command of the purse. If there is money in the purse, they are never satisfied until they have it in their own grasp. Such wives generally take to gambling and staking money in the lottery, or purchasing useless articles. They have no care as to where the money comes from or by whose labors it is earned, so long as they can gratify their own extravagant and ruinous fancies.

7. Some wives are of the murderous kind and possess revengeful tempers. Being malicious and fault-finding, they never appreciate their own homes and families, and are always seeking for sympathies from outside. They share their secrets with other men, using their pretended domestic discomfort as a cloak for their own vice and an excuse for their greatest misdeeds.

The wives who are on a female pattern are all "good"; they are "younger sister," "elder sister," and "mother." They will be "die friends," and in looking for a wife a man looks for one who will reproduce his relations with the women of his family. Yet Thai men are so rarely impotent that it is not a subject of gossip, not even a cursing accusation. These wives who follow the pattern of their husband's mothers and sisters are submissive and ideal.

The wives who take their prototype from males are "bad." From the whole context and from the whole description of Thai concepts and behavior in this memorandum, this is evidently not because of taboos separating the respective spheres of the sexes but is, rather, a projection upon women of all the non-hierarchal relations between men. These latter are relatively "difficult" in Thailand. First there is the "play friend" type who returns evil for evil and will

do her husband no "little service" unless he pretends deference. Then there is
the domineering woman who orders her husband about, and he becomes a "miserable cringing" being. The "robber kind" are out for money and interested only
in spending it at their whim. Only the last and "murderous kind" betray their
husbands by taking lovers. Wandering sexual fancy is only characteristic of
one out of four "bad" wifely types which disturb a man's peace.

The man's attitude toward the relations of the sexes is given symbolic elaboration in the national game of kite-flying -- which is played exclusively by men.
This game is carried out with a skill which all observers have admired. It is a
"courtship" of a female kite and a male kite. The female kite is a four-sided
diamond shape and goes up with a lilting motion to the accompaniment, in any
exhibition game, of a dancing tune from the orchestra. There is a special orchestra for the female kite and another for the male kite when it finally comes
up to "court" the female. The man who flies the female kite stays in one part
of the field, and his kite is not allowed to cruise. Presently another kite-flyer
from another end of the field sends up his male kite. This is a much heavier
kite, perhaps six times as big, in the shape of a five-pointed star. It ascends
higher than the female kite and cruises toward the female to "capture" it. It
must not get too close to the body of the little kite or its balance would be upset,
and it would "lose"; then the male kite's orchestra would play a lamenting tune
and if the female kite has an orchestra, it will play triumphantly. But the string
of the male kite has attached to it, up toward the kite, two small curved twigs of
bamboo which project out in four points. The female kite has a slacker cord attached to its string up in the air, and into this loop the male kite must get its
tentacles. It swoops down on the dancing female kite and, if it is successful,
drags her in triumph to its end of the field where they both fly entangled to the
triumphant music of the male kite's orchestra. She is "his."

The male is the huge, heavy kite, the female the little, dancing one. The
male is the cruiser, the female is anchored. The male pulls her into his orbit
and flies with her in triumph; if he gets too close to her and falls, it is "she" who
caused his fall, and "she" triumphs. "I have never, I think, seen the Siamese so
serious, with attention so riveted, as when they assemble in thousands every
afternoon for hours at a stretch to fly their kites. That for them is the real
business of life" (Campbell, 1902, p. 107).

The game well symbolizes the relation of men and women. Men are not
doubtful of their masculinity -- which is here symbolized in the kite's size and
shape and activity. Men mark their kites with their insignia or name and may
have three or four at hand to continue the game if one falls or is damaged. The
object of the game is to keep a "wife" within their orbit and both male and female
"flying"; if "he" falls, it is the woman's fault, and "she" has won. But attacking
her too closely -- perhaps it would be fair to say dominating her, or possessing
her, in the European sense -- would mean, in the kite game, falling to the ground

and being defeated. Thai men assume that she is small and fragile and has no "game" to play unless a man "captures" her. It is the same statement under another simile which they make in "Woman is rice, but man is paddy." Success, for the man, depends upon skilled maneuvering and a not too close approach to the body of the other kite -- on one's own wits, in daily life, and one's canny skepticism about others.

The plots of their impromptu "sings" show the rules of the game between men and women as they are thought to work themselves out in Thai behavior. After the male leader has sung the invocation, the answering female leader invokes dead women leaders to assist her " in making men humble and discomfited, in fact to make her victory over them absolutely crushing." It is again the "contest" of the kite game. The most popular ways in which the "sing" may develop is "contending for a lady" or contending for a man. In the first form, described by Prince Bidyalankarana (1926), the husband is urging his wife to return to him no matter what her infidelities; "despite her faithlessness his love for her is as deep as ever, and he implores her to abandon her lover and return home to husband and child." It is not necessary for the husband to defend his "honor"; he wants her within his orbit. In the plot of contending for a man, the man finds himself "an unhappy fellow who stands between two sharp tongues." He has lost the initiative to the women, and the story only ends when he is once more paired with one of them. Obviously, the "crushing victory" for which the women ask is pre-eminence in repartee; they do not seek a "defeat" of men in the sense of humiliating them.

The high place of the male in his world is powerfully reinforced in real life by Buddhist teachings and by the male prerogative of the monkhood, from which women are unconditionally excluded. But the Buddhist doctrine of man's superiority is divorced from sex; by definition the monk is asexual. Among the Thai this operates merely to remove from men a possible source of anxiety; they do not have to prove their virility by affairs with women or even by their relations with their wives. They are, in Pallegoix's words, "almost passionless" -- and one man in twenty is at any given time unquestionably chaste, since he is in a monastery -- yet impotence is hardly recognized except that it is admitted that it might be found in a psychopath. King Mongkut retired to a monastery for more than twenty years, and when he came out, at forty-five, he fathered more than eighty children. This is regarded as natural, and the enforced celibacy of the monk is regarded as equally unneeding of remark; it is not considered as a serious frustration. Even today reformers speak of the harm not eating after midday may do to a delicate constitution, but they do not speak of sex frustration.

The villagers, especially in later life, enjoy bandying insults and they have a language for this which is obscene in their sense. It accuses the other person of sexual irregularities, even of incest. This is what is referred to when they speak of "the mouth of a market woman," but the older men take active part also. The more usual form of insult, however, is a delicate manipulation of respect terms and gestures; the least shade of difference carries the insult.

III. Non-Reciprocity among East European Jews[20]

Natalie F. Joffe

All of the following remarks apply only to in-group behavior. The obligations enjoined on a Jew not to take interest on a loan, to keep an open house, and to support the various community enterprises do not necessarily function in his relationship to the Gentile world. It would be hard to envisage this society without its operating in a Gentile milieu -- it is indeed almost impossible to conceive of its existence without a strong out-group, because its economic base lies in distribution of, and more recently manufacture of, commodities rather than in agriculture.

For a society within the framework of the Western cultural tradition, East European Jewish culture exhibits a minimum of reciprocal behavior. Wealth, learning, and other tangible and intangible possessions are fluid and are channeled so that in the main they flow from the "strong," or "rich," or "learned," or "older," to those who are "weaker," "poorer," "ignorant," or "younger." Therefore all giving is downward. This mechanism is conceived of as a way to perpetuate the community and to maintain the status quo, the society never being thrown out of balance through internal crises. All higher status, with the exception of sex, is achieved and achievable, and even sex-typed status (that of husband-father and wife-mother) are achieved categories additional to the ascribed one of sex.

The good things of the world are infinite and acquirable. They are those things which confer higher status and are acquired not for themselves alone but for transmission, and the flow is always from the strong to the weaker -- a process that might best be compared to the second law of thermodynamics.

Since Jews do not constitute a land-identified community,[21] and there is no concept of "retirement" (absolute age always is deferred to), little emphasis is placed upon the common virtue of building up a patrimony or a landed estate to be passed on to one's heirs for the establishment of a dynasty; it is also possible that this position is reinforced by the fact that the vast majority of Jews living under shtetl conditions were extremely poor and there was a very slim margin between adequate support for a family and near-starvation, which al-

---

20. Unpublished document RCC-J 127. Cf. also Joffe (1949), which is an expanded study of the same subject.
21. "Jews constitute a 'people-identified' community. The community consists of any ten adult men. It is of interest to note that stars play little part in the orientation and spatial concepts of the Jews." (Comment by Dr. A. I. Hallowell, at a meeting of the American Ethnological Society on "Spatial Recognition in the Psycho-dynamics of a Culture," January 13, 1948.)

lowed practically no latitude for savings; instead, money is more apt to be given
to the young people at the time of marriage for the foundation of a new family
unit. What remains to be passed on at the time of death is usually minimal --
the seat in the synagogue, a pair of candlesticks, some books or jewelry.

To the Jews, even the most orthodox, death is an occasion of unmitigated
grief, and all of the reminders of the bereavement are disposed of as soon as
possible. (In New York, for example, it is usual for the family of the deceased
to move as soon as possible from the apartment where the death occurred.) The
clothing of the dead person is given away, not thrown away or sold. There seems
to be some idea that cloth, being soft and permeable, has some of the personality
of the dead person, and it is disrespectful for the members of the immediate
family to think that they can fill it. Metal, being hard, is less liable to be im-
bued with this aura, so jewelry is saved and worn, as are household effects.
Heirlooms like a samovar or candlesticks are valued, for they show that the
family in the past was rich enough to have them; but there are few of them.

It is mandatory for the good things of life to be shared or to be passed
downward during one's lifetime, so the miser is never respected; instead he is
openly criticized, and his behavior is deplored and condemned. It is one of the
greatest blessings in the world to put what you have at the service of others,
be it wealth, learning, or children. Indeed, the concept of the good deed, the
Mitzvah, is not voluntary -- it has been enjoined upon every Jew by God. It is
only through these acts that you are assured of entrance into Paradise. These
duties are not construed as a burden, but rather as a source of joy. The
Mitzvah has been so worked into the structure of the society that it serves as
a channel through which property, learning, and the like are diffused downward.
For example, it is a Mitzvah for a wealthy man to marry off an orphan girl, so
he furnishes her with a dowry, negotiates for the marriage and supplies the
wedding feast. Or fostering of learning is a Mitzvah, therefore if you are
learned, you expound the Torah to others, or, failing that, support the seminary. To take money for such acts has a low prestige affect, which may explain why the Malamed (teacher) is despised.

It is shameful, however, to receive succor of any sort from those who are
inferior to you in any status. To receive any of the aforementioned implies
that you are in a position to be controlled, for the reciprocal of the downward-
giving is deference. Children must defer to adults, the young to the old, the
ignorant to the learned, women to men. To accept things means that you are
inferior to the donor, which may in part explain the contempt the Jews have
for those who take bribes, because, by acceptance, they become "subadult." It
is not shameful to accept from your equals -- it is preferred. This may cast
light on the fact that the old prefer to live in squalor, where they can be "their
own bosses," rather than with children who can supply creature comforts, or
favor living in a home for the aged rather than to be beholden to an individual.

The following lists illustrate (1) some points of transmission from those of higher status (donors) to those of lower status (recipients) and some forms of deferent behavior expected of the latter; and (2) some points of symmetical behavior, give and take between equals. Types of donor-recipient relationships are summarized in Chart A (page 389).

1. Points of Transmission; Donors and Recipients

Mitzvah (good deeds)	Deference

I. Adult to child, older to younger

  a. Support
  b. Hanukah-Gelt
  c. New holiday clothing
  d. Education and learning
  e. Dowry and marriage
  f. Care for orphans
  g. Mediate ethical standards

I. Child to adult

  a. Deference
  b. To marry and have children (parental)
  c. To say Kaddish (prayers for the dead, primarily for parents)

II. Learned to ignorant

  a. Transmission of learning
  b. Accessibility to those who seek to learn
  c. Support of institutions of learning
  d. Settlement of points of law
  e. Mediation between Jews and Gentiles

II. Ignorant to learned

  a. Deference and docility

III. Rich to poor

  a. Support
  b. Free matzoths
  c. Free meals, kest
  d. Linens for the newborn
  e. Arrangement of marriage for an orphan
  f. Care of the sick
  g. Burial and care of cemetery
  h. Talmud, Torah, Yeshiva, etc.

III. Poor to rich

  a. Deference

IV. Husband to wife

  a. Support
  b. Assurance that wife will get into Heaven

IV. Wife to husband

  a. Deference
  b. Feeding and caring for husband and children
  c. Working so husband can study
  d. Mediation with mundane world
  e. Supplying husband with Mitzvahs

V. Dead to living

  a. Advice in times of crisis
  b. Mediation in the afterworld

V. Living to dead

  a. Burial of the dead
  b. Maintenance of the cemetery
  c. Prayers for the dead (Kaddish)

VI. Host to guest

  a. To keep an open house
  b. To feed and care for guests (especially on Sabbath and holidays)

VI. Guest to host

VII. Well to sick
  a. To care for the sick
  b. To offer them things

VII. Sick to well

2. Symmetrical Behavior: Give and Take between Equals

I. Woman - Woman

a. Exchange of <u>Schalochmones</u> (sweetmeats) at Purim; the exchange is calculated not in terms of identity but of unlikes so grouped as to be equated.
b. Mothers-in-law dance together at weddings; mothers-in-law brag to each other.

II. Man - Man

a. Care during illness (a temporary condition)
b. Support of the aged
c. The <u>Minyan</u>, etc.
d. Burial

CHART A

Points of Transmission: Donors and Recipients

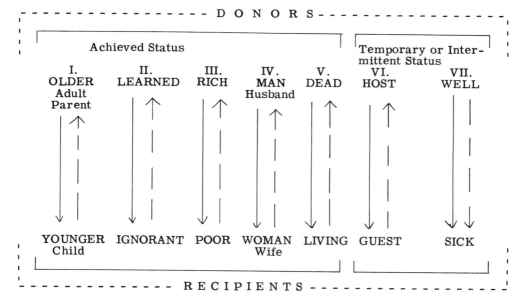

Legend
<u>Mitzvah</u> (good deeds) _____
Deference _____ ____ ____ ____

IV. A Note on the Spectator in French Culture

Rhoda Métraux

Spectatorship and the position of the spectator are highly stylized in French culture. Whereas <u>looking</u> is regarded by the Chinese, for example, as an active occupation and by Americans as a passive one, it seems to have the double possibility for the French. Spectatorship in French culture may be active, as in the case of the critic who passes judgment on what he sees; or it may be passive, as in the case on the one hand of the apprentice who learns by watching the performance of a master, or on the other hand of the person who is involuntarily prevented from participating in what he sees.

Involuntary non-participation in what is seen provides a dramatic theme in which the problem may be resolved in opposite ways: (1) the passive spectator (e.g. an unattractive or helpless older man watches a younger man with a woman to whom he himself is attracted; a young man watches an experienced older man with a woman to whom he himself is attracted; a woman watches her husband with a younger daughter-like girl; a girl watches a sister with a man to whom she herself is attached, etc.) may enter into hopeless, destructive, or self-destructive rivalry with the person whose place he (or she) would like to take;[22] or (2) the spectator may, on the contrary, be stimulated to re-enact what has been seen -- or the suggested possibilities -- with another, more available person.[23]

Both of these situations, it would seem, derive from the spectatorship characteristic of the learner; in both, the spectator -- like the apprentice -- is in a subordinate position to those who are seen. When this brings about a reversal of expected roles -- i.e. an individual who is normally in a superordinate position is made to be a passive spectator -- this may be an essential tragic (or sometimes comic) element in the situation.

The active spectator, in contrast, is regularly in a superordinate position; that he does not necessarily act out his role is then a matter of his own choice. So, for instance, as an active spectator, the critic compares what he sees -- the novel, the painting, the actor, etc. -- with standard or model productions, acting in this respect as the mentor of the artist who may be an innovator; at the same time he instructs the passive audience -- the general public -- in how

---

22. Among recent French films in which this theme has been explored, cf. <u>Les Enfants du Paradis</u>, <u>Le Silence Est d'Or</u>, <u>Le Corbeau</u>, <u>Panique</u>, <u>Marie du Port</u>, etc. The theme of the spectator in French films has been treated extensively by Martha Wolfenstein and Nathan Leites in "Plot and Character in Selected French Films: An Analysis of Fantasy" (Métraux and Mead, 1953).

23. This possibility is used repeatedly with comic effect in French films. So, for instance, a young man may be shown watching an attractive woman singing on a stage; he then turns to kiss his sweetheart. It is also used in French advertisements, where looking may be combined (e.g., in advertisements for perfumes and foods) with another kind of sensory experience.

to see the work of art or the actor's style, and so on, and how to place it in its context of other work.[24]

There is also a third possible position for the spectator in French culture: that of the onlooker who voluntarily abstains from participation in that he withholds the expression of judgment and affect -- the laissez-faire position of the mature individual who observes la vie humaine without commitment or comment. The problems of this position, in terms of intellectual and affective commitment, have been explored by various writers (Sartre, de Beauvoir, Camus, etc.) in recent years.[25] As a possible position for the mature individual, voluntary non-participating spectatorship must be paired with one position of exhibitionism -- that of the superordinate individual who is looked at, but who does not, ideally, take part in action (e.g. the President of the French Republic).[26]

The two types of active and passive spectatorship first described suggest that there are in French culture two forms of actor-spectator relationship, and that these involve a reversal of superordination and subordination and a different definition of "spectatorship" and "exhibitionism" for each type. The third type (with its non-participating exhibitionist opposite) suggests the importance in French culture of situations in which non-participation (in the sense of overt expression of feeling, etc.) is a form of regularly expected behavior.

With this in mind, we may now turn to the foyer and to the relationship between parent and child in the home to look for models of the actor-audience bipolarity. French relationships tend to be of an exclusive dyadic nature; tend, that is, to be relationships between pairs of individuals. Geoffrey Gorer has described the foyer as follows:[27]

A married couple, together with their children, constitute a foyer; a foyer consists of a nexus of dyadic relationships -- relationships between pairs of individuals -- each of which by its existence gives strength, richness, and significance to the others. All relationships tend to be of an exclusive dyadic nature; valued emotional complexity develops in those situations where the whole group are interconnected through mutual relations over a long stretch of time.

Thus in discussing relationships in the foyer, one must consider not only the pair who make up any one dyad, but also the expected relationship of the third person to a dyad, and vice versa (i.e. on the one hand, the pairs of husband-

---

24. See, for example, the discussion of the function of criticism by the French critic Henri Peyre (1944). The artist himself may, however, reverse the position of the critic, as when an informant, a French-trained artist, comments that "critics were always hanging around the artists' cafés, trying to find out what it was all about, so they would know what to write." (Unpublished document RCC-F 210.)
25. Nathan Leites (1947) has discussed a special aspect of the problem in connection with his analysis of Camus's L'Etranger (reproduced in this Manual, Part Five, pages 248-63). -- Ed.
26. An understanding of both aspects of this position is essential to any discussion of contemporary French neutralism in international politics.
27. Unpublished document RCC F 123. For a detailed description of expected French family relationships, cf. Métraux and Mead (1953).

wife, mother-son, father-son, etc.; on the other hand, the relationship of son
to mother-father, of mother to father-son, etc.).

In the earliest relations of parent and child in the family, the father's role
is almost entirely one of distant spectatorship, with the major interaction that
of mother and child.[28] It is the mother who "teaches" the child to learn (to be
receptive and responsive) and who, when the child is still too young to talk,
may respond in its stead so that it is provided not only with models of initiative (the adult position) but also of response (the child's position). As the child
gains in autonomy, it learns better to respond -- rather than (as is expected
of the American child, for instance) to experiment and explore on its own behalf. Therefore it learns also to expect that initiation and response are paired.
Learning is acquired by repeatedly following the correct models provided by
elders who have the skills, and understanding is expected to follow upon, rather than to be a necessary condition to, learning. This especially emphasizes the
passive position of the learner, the apprentice. Later, when the child no longer
requires nursery care, a special relationship may develop between father and
son[29] and, still later, if the daughter is "chic et caline," between father and
daughter, to both of which the mother is a spectator.

But, most important, the child is expected to be a quiet spectator of the
interaction between father and mother. ("Father" and "mother" are used here
advisedly, as the child is excluded from various aspects of the marital relationship. So, for instance, both the parents' sexual relationship and their discussions of financial problems and plans are kept from children. As one woman informant said: "When you speak of the family, you say 'father' and 'mother'" [not 'husband' and 'wife'] .) At table, when the child eats with its parents,
it is told: "Mange et tais-toi" -- "Eat and be quiet" -- while the parents converse and, through their conversation, provide the child with a model for the
enjoyment of food.

Later, the school child may be called upon by the parents to perform for
them (especially for the father), or it may be included to a certain extent in
conversation, where, again, it exhibits what it has learned. In such situations
the parents (especially the father, with the mother providing a link between the
two -- both supporting the father and protecting the child) become the spectators of the child's activity. But unlike the child who is learning and who is
expected to be a noncritical spectator, the parents as spectators judge the

---

28. This is, of course, not peculiar to the French family.
29. French male informants seldom speak of having had an intimate relation-
    ship to their father, but such an early relationship may prefigure the later
    one between teacher and student, etc. In French autobiographies (Gide,
    Loti, etc.), it is the breaking-off of such an early affectionate relationship,
    viewed retrospectively after the death of the father, that is sometimes re-
    garded as particularly significant.

child's performance -- comparing the child not to other actual children but to what the child should be becoming.[30]

Thus, briefly, the two positions of spectatorship are built up in the family, one based on the child learning by watching its parents (and by responding to them), the other based on the parents' (especially the father's) watching the learned behavior of the child and responding to its exhibition with praise or criticism.

Returning now to the position of the uninvolved spectator, we may also consider the "outsider" to any of the dyads. In fact, the dyadic relationships of the foyer are such that the "outsider" himself is involved in an exclusive relationship with each of the members of any dyad and he is an "outsider" only to the extent that each dyad has its area of privacy, of interests and information, of feeling and comment, not shared with others. And the security of everyone depends upon this area of privacy being maintained by all. Thus each individual is at some time a spectator who is expected not to intrude upon, not to comment upon, the activities of another pair of individuals. The assumption is not that he will not have his private views and feelings, but rather that he will not air them in such a way that the relationship between another pair is threatened or disturbed. For, as visualized by the French, the danger of intrusion comes not from within but from outside the closed circle of the family. (But the pathology of looking is undoubtedly based upon such unauthorized looking and being looked at.)

Thus the patterned relationships in the foyer and, among these, the relationship of parent and child, provide us with one set of models for the several positions of the spectator in French culture. Further elaboration would require examination of other linked relationships systematically related to these family models.

---

30. French informants regularly emphasize that each child in the family is (or should be) treated differently from the others -- one being given adult books to read, the other not, at the same age, etc. -- in terms of personality differences. (Such statements must be regarded as retrospective comments on what the child desired as well as on what may have happened.)

PART TEN

APPLICATIONS OF STUDIES OF CULTURE AT A DISTANCE

A. POLITICAL APPLICATIONS OF STUDIES OF CULTURE AT A DISTANCE

Margaret Mead

The approach described in this Manual has been used for a variety of political purposes: to implement particular governmental programs within a country, to facilitate relationships with allies, to guide relationships with partisan groups in countries under enemy control, to assist in estimating enemy strengths and weaknesses, and to provide a rationale for the preparation of documents at the international level. All these uses involve diagnosing the cultural regularities in the behavior of a particular group or groups of people that are relevant to the proposed action -- whether this be the dissemination of a propaganda statement, issuing an order against fraternization, a threat of a certain type of reprisal, an introduction of a new international regulation, or a like matter. The diagnosis is made for the purpose of facilitating some specific plan or policy, and at least implicitly, includes predictions of expected behavior that may make such a plan or policy successful or unsuccessful.

Diagnosis and prediction are always concerned with the regularities in the behavior of a group of people who are members of a common culture and with the behavior of individuals with respect to these particular regularities. For instance, during World War II, it was possible to say what was the likelihood of Japanese surrender in groups which did and did not contain officers, but not to predict what any given single Japanese soldier would do, although the limits of his behavior might be fairly accurately indicated. The larger the number of individuals about whom a prediction is to be made, the more useful the method is. As it is concerned with regularities in behavior that are to be attributed to having been reared in, or subsequently inducted into, a common culture, this method also applies better to moderately long ranges of time -- that is, during the first few days an event of unprecedented scope may produce a degree of disorganization for which cultural prediction is difficult.[1] Whenever prediction is required for several years ahead, trends have to be included within the regularities, and these trends may be altered or reversed by events outside the system, such as the appearance of an unusual insect pest that destroys the principal crop of a country, or conquest by a foreign power, and so on. The length of time to which

---

1. So in World War II, for instance, while it was possible to predict types of panic reaction to the first major bombings of German cities, it was not possible to know what measures had been taken to prevent or deal with panic, or to predict a panic reaction in a specific instance. Over time, however, it was possible to work out patterns of reaction to different sorts of bombing in particular areas, or reactions of people in one city when another was bombed, and so on, and so to increase predictive skill.

a cultural prediction can usefully be applied has to be determined for each specific case in which the method is being used.

The second set of considerations is the nature of those persons or authorities or agencies who are to use the diagnoses and predictions provided by the study of culture, whether made at a distance or by field studies within an accessible society. Every prediction must include the ability of those who would use it to act upon the advice given about how to strengthen their own population, improve relationships with allies, defeat an enemy, or facilitate the functioning of international bodies. For example, a cultural analysis may show that workers in a factory, soldiers in an army, members of the merchant marine, and so on, would produce more or would display higher morale if given more self-government. However, a belief in the inability of these same workers or merchant marines to use such self-government efficiently may be an integral part of the executives' or officers' ability to lead. If any change is to be made, it must be one that will be congruent with the beliefs and attitudes of the officers and executives as well as with the potentialities of the rank and file for greater achievement. Similarly, recommendations for educational campaigns among a population -- to increase voluntary enlistment, or the purchase of war bonds, or the acceptance of rationing, or the facilitation of safety measures -- must not only include the relevant cultural diagnoses about the expected behavior of those to whom the educational and propagandic material is to be directed, but must also be couched in terms that can actually be effectively implemented by those who are to write the pamphlets, make the speeches, plan the broadcasts, and so on. And here too, the larger the number of people involved in putting a cultural diagnosis into practice, the more the cultural regularities in their behavior have to be taken into account. Where it is possible to plan a course of action that involves no change, but only the utilization of some regularity in the behavior of the implementing group, then it is an advantage to have a large group involved. For example, on the whole, Scots, in terms of their Scottish version of British culture, are less likely inadvertently to irritate an American audience or group than are English people. Where Anglo-American relationships are in a delicate state of balance and better feeling is essential to the implementation of some common policy, it is possible to make the blanket recommendation: "Send Scots to the United States." If, however, it is necessary to recommend some change in the tone of voice or in the approach -- as might be the case when, instead of asking for Scots, changes in the tone of voice of English public-relations officials were necessary -- this will be the harder task, and the larger the number of such officials who must be implicated in the change, the harder the task will be, up to the point at which such a large group is involved that the new behavior can become institutionalized. For example, when armed forces are quartered in a friendly country, the incorporation in their behavior of changes in manners to prevent offending the residents of the country will be far more difficult than will be the indoctrination of a small group of consular officials. But, in time, it may be possible to make certain altered behaviors part of the regular army procedure on such matters -- for example, not giving twenty-four-hour leave in an area where the local population feel that part of such a leave will inevitably be spent at the expense of the virtue of the young female population.

A further consideration in regard to those who are to use cultural advice is that when the advice goes against the rooted beliefs of the implementers, it can be used best by small groups who combine power with narrow, well-defined objectives -- such as getting a bridge built or getting a particular unit to surrender. The most conspicuous historical example on a large scale is the case of the the Japanese emperor in World War II. A small group with power, who saw their principal task to be that of ending the war, could take cultural advice about the Japanese that was deeply antipathetic to American culture as a whole, with its rooted belief that all monarchy is bad.[2] Equally well-founded cultural advice on postwar Germany, which had to be implemented not over a few days by a small group with great power, but over several years by a large army of occupation, had almost no effect.

Policy-making advice has, therefore, not only to take into account the cultural regularities of those who must implement a decision, but also -- where the advice goes against a belief or a prejudice -- the actualities of the situation. The power of the implementers, their number, and the speed with which they can act are all relevant variables. While individuals with power may, in emergencies and to accomplish well-defined goals, be able to lay aside part of their cultural inheritance, the disallowed cultural prejudices are likely to reassert themselves very quickly. Over a longer time span and where many people are involved, only such changes as are genuinely congruent with the culture of the implementers, as well as with the culture of the other group or groups involved, can be expected to be undertaken voluntarily and to be carried out effectively.

Also, it is worth considering to what extent it is possible for those who have an understanding of the cultural regularities of another group -- one which, however, they keep hidden from that group -- to manipulate members of the group in question. The fear of such manipulation repels one type of person in a democratic society, while others who have been given specific strategic tasks to perform may be attracted to it.[3] In general it may be said that cultural understanding of another group that is accurate, but which that other group are themselves unwilling to recognize, is highly useful to anyone wishing to conduct operations involving members of the understood group, but that -- in these circumstances -- secrecy is on the whole irrelevant. Cultural understanding of the sort discussed in

---

2.   Cf. Geoffrey Gorer: "Japanese Character Structure and Propaganda" (below, pages 401-2).
3.   For further discussions of this point, cf. Bateson (1952), Mead (1949a), Appendix II, and Taylor (1947).

this Manual can be achieved only within a frame of reference that recognizes the internal consistency of the premises of each human culture and also recognizes that much of this consistency is unconscious; that is, is not available to the average member of the culture. Ideological systems that refuse to analyze each culture on its merits are so resistant to this type of cultural understanding that it is impossible for those who accept such systems to make direct use of cultural analyses. So, for example, a cultural analysis of Bolshevism is, it would seem, quite unusable for a convinced Bolshevik, who, if he were to accept it, would have to give up the absolutism on which his motivation depends. Similarly, deep cultural attitudes which are not so ideologically defined -- such as the American preference for the substitution of machinery for manual work and delight in elaborate mechanical devices -- are equally resistant to analysis, even when the price paid for such resistance is great -- as in the relative efficiency at certain periods of American and Russian tanks. Only a concerted effort, over a long period, by a very large number of people who are concerned to publicize a needed change, can alter such deep attitudes.

These statements of limitation apply primarily to constructive change. It is possible to do considerable damage by revealing to a people the negative and disallowed aspects of their cultural motivations. It is just here that great precautions need to be taken against modern forms of quite open psychological warfare that play upon cultural weaknesses not by the use of concealed sources and "black" devices, but by frankly avowed "white" devices, against which, however, any population is relatively helpless unless counterdefenses can be systematically mobilized.

The following seven illustrations provide specific instances of the application of anthropological principles to political problems of different types. Each is necessarily only a brief excerpt from a longer study, and the analyses themselves were of different degrees of completeness and specificity. The first three are from wartime work on Japan, on Rumania, and on United States relations with an ally, Great Britain. The others are taken from more recent work on three other cultures, and, directly or indirectly, stem from work done in Research in Contemporary Cultures.[4]

---

4. Additionally the following selections in other parts of this Manual are also from such applied studies: the excerpts from Gregory Bateson's analysis of Hitlerjunge Quex, in Part Six (pages 302-14), and in Part Nine his discussion of end linkage (pages 367-78), Margaret Mead's application of end-linkage formulations to Anglo-American relations (pages 379-82), and Ruth Benedict's analysis of male-female relations in Thai culture (pages 382-86). These are all from studies made during World War II.--Ed.

B. SEVEN APPLICATIONS OF STUDIES OF CULTURE AT A DISTANCE

I. Japanese Character Structure and Propaganda

Geoffrey Gorer

1. The Dichotomy of the Universe[5]

It will be remembered that the Japanese boy has to be continuously sub-servient and deferent toward his father and elder brothers, but may be aggressive and commanding toward his mother and sisters. Because of this differential treatment received from and allowed toward his two parents, the Japanese boy grows up in a divided universe where he must continuously use careful discrimination. To the male part of the universe -- that is, all males of superior age and status -- he must respond obediently, passively, and unquestioningly, following the patterns that they lay down and taking orders they give; only by so doing will he be safe and rewarded; any other action invites drastic punishment. Complementarily, as he grows older he will learn that younger men and men of lower status will give him the unquestioning obedience that he gives others. The male universe is an ordered pattern in which reward is gained by compliance and a full knowledge of relative status. From the Emperor (with his divine ancestors as his superiors) to the newborn infant (with the outcastes as his inferiors) every male has his exact place in this male world; upward aggression will be punished directly by those affected, excessive downward aggression by mockery from those above. The male universe gives assurance and safety, but little indulgence; it administers heavy punishments for deviance, controls the sanctions and all the secondary rewards. One must comply with the patterns of the male universe. Resistance and aggression are dangerous.

In contrast with this male world of dominance and submission, there is the female world from which come all the primary gratifications (food, drink, warmth, sex) and which can be controlled, and forced to yield up its gratifications, by aggression or threats of aggression. The male world gives orders and expects obedience; the female world threatens and pleads, but can always be made to yield if the male is sufficiently strong and persistent in his aggressions. The female world is loved, ill-treated, and despised.

This division of the world of the male Japanese into two contrasting aspects is fully developed in Japanese symbolism and philosophy. Female is "dark" and "passive," male "light" and "active"; the land is male, the sea female, the sun male, the moon female, and so on. But this dichotomy has still further implica-

---

5. Reproduced from Gorer (1943a; pp. 119-21).

tions. The growing child sees the universe in terms of its parents and this original division is never fully dissipated by later experience. It seems certain
that to the contemporary Japanese other races and societies are viewed as either male or female; as groups to be followed and obeyed implicitly, or as groups
to be forced to yield to aggression or threats of aggression. Further, it appears
historically as though in the nineteenth century England and America were
viewed as indubitably male, and therefore to be obeyed and copied as much as
possible but that in the last forty years, the sex of these groups has been first
questioned, and then reversed. The defeat of the Russians in 1905 probably originally called in question the "virility" of the whites and this uncertainty was increased by the willingness of the Anglo-Saxon to negotiate, to bicker and yield,
instead of commanding, in the next twenty years. Finally, in the invasion of
Manchuria, and subsequently, the Japanese found that the Anglo-Saxons showed
all the female characteristics; they cajoled and threatened without carrying out
their threats; they constantly yielded to a show of aggression, each time vowing
that that concession would be the last; they parleyed; they allowed their nationals
to be ill-treated or insulted without retaliation; they were feminine, and would
therefore yield the primary gratifications ("raw materials") if enough aggression
were used. On December 7, 1941, this theory was put to the test; and the demo-
cracies still held their feminine role. Most convincing of all, they asked for
mercy, declaring Manila an open city; and just as on such a plea the angry boy
will destroy his mother's hair-do and break her precious pins, so in response
did the Japanese destroy Manila with special attention to buildings of religious
or symbolic importance.

2. Original Recommendation about the Japanese Emperor[6]

It seems to the writer that neither the Mikado himself nor the abstract
Throne should ever be attacked; indeed they should never be mentioned other
than respectfully. Attacking the Mikado would be like attacking the Pope for
medieval Catholics; it would merely excite anger against foolish sacrilege. Japanese society is inconceivable for the Japanese without a ritual head; and, as
with the Papacy, the present holder of the office is relatively unimportant. If,
however, the sacred dignity of the Mikado is admitted, then all the people with
real, as opposed to ritual, power can be attacked in their every action, for bringing the Emperor into contempt, for trafficking in the Emperor's name, for betraying the Emperor and taking power for themselves. The whole period of the
Shogunate is full of characters who mistreated the emperors, forced them to ab-
dicate, stole from them, etc.; contemporary history as it is taught in schools emphasizes the importance of the Emperor and the unworthiness of many of the
Shoguns.

6. Reproduced from an unpublished report prepared late in 1941 at the Insti-
    tute of Human Relations, Yale University. An abbreviated version of this
    report (not including the passage reproduced here) was distributed in 1942
    (cf. Gorer, 1942).

II. Some Problems of Cross-Cultural Communication between Britain and the United States: Based upon Lecturing in Britain and the United States during World War II.[7]

Margaret Mead

The problem of communication in a language which was theoretically mutually intelligible, supposed to be "one language," presented a number of difficulties which could be partially resolved by reference to cultural differences. In all probability the greater the difference between the languages of the pair of cultures with which one is attempting to work, the more automatic warnings are provided to the translator. But between English and American, and between other cultures similarly related through a common tradition and a still somewhat intelligible pair of languages, language confuses rather than clarifies, and other sorts of clues are necessary.

Two systematic observations made it possible to communicate better. The first was analysis of the difference between the American and the British sense of a scale of values. Americans tend to arrange objects on a single scale of value, from best to worst, biggest to smallest, cheapest to most expensive, and are able to express a preference among very complex objects on such a single scale. The question "What is your favorite color?" so intelligible to an American, is meaningless in Britain, and such a question is countered by "Favorite color for what? A flower? A necktie?" Each object is thought of as having a most complex set of qualities, and color is merely a quality of an object, not something from a color chart on which one can make a choice which is transferable to a large number of different sorts of objects.

The American reduction of complexities to single scales is entirely comprehensible in terms of the great diversity of value systems which different immigrant groups brought to the American scene; some common denominator among the incommensurables was very much needed, and oversimplification was almost inevitable.[8] But as a result, Americans think in terms of qualities which have unidimensional scales, while the British, when they think of a complex object or event, even if they reduce it to parts, think of each part as retaining all of the complexities of the whole. Americans subdivide the scale, the British subdivide the object. Americans are able to describe a room in terms of its "color scheme," where the British eye would retain a sense of some fifty elements involved in the whole interior pattern, even when speaking of a square inch of the rug. From this British insistence on complexity flows, naturally enough, an insistence upon uniqueness and an unwillingness to make comparisons.

---

7. An excerpt, reproduced from Mead (1948a; pp. 217-20).
8. Mead (1942a), Chapter VII, "Brothers and Sisters and Success" (pp. 54-70).

Discussions as to the relative merits of cities, which Americans make happily in terms of size, wealth, or some other common denominator, seem to the British either meaningless or as irrelevant boasting. In turn, the British refusal to provide statistics on the size or the wealth of a city seemed to the Americans to be either obscurantist or unfriendly. In Anglo-American contacts of all sorts, committee meetings, teaching situations, etc., it was important to watch the misunderstandings which arose along these lines, as the British voted the Americans oversimplifying when they harped on some exact statement of a position on a numerical scale, and the Americans voted the British inaccurate, if not engaged in deliberate falsification, when they quoted the population of Bengal with an error of ten million with the statement that "it doesn't matter," because they were concerned with the relative, not the absolute, size of one Indian province.

Another sort of misunderstanding which influenced communication was the difference between the British and the American sense of the real world. The British see the world as something to which man adapts, the American as man-controlled, a vast malleable space on which one builds what one wishes, from blueprints one has drawn, and when dissatisfied simply tears the structure down and starts anew.

The great sense of mechanical control of the environment, product at least in part of an empty continent and the Machine Age, extends to American attitudes toward crops and animals, which are again something to be planned for, streamlined, increased or decreased at will, and even, to a certain degree, to human beings, who can be, if not completely molded by man-made devices, at least sorted mechanically into simply defined pigeonholes. In contrast, the British see the world as a natural world to which man adapts, in which he assumes no control over the future, but only the experienced foresight of the husbandman or the gardener, who plants the best seed and watches carefully over the first green blades. Man is seen as the junior partner of God, expressed either in conventional or more contemporary forms, but still the junior partner of forces to which he can adapt but which he cannot control. He can "only handle one link in the chain of destiny at a time."

The humility of this phrasing has its own forms of arrogance, as in Milton's "God is decreeing to begin some new and great period ... what does He then but reveal Himself to His servants, and as His manner is, first to His Englishmen."

Vis-à-vis this state of mind, ordinary American figures of speech implying control and mechanism not only fail to communicate but actually establish barriers.[9] It was necessary to drop the familiar figures of an America converting for full production, laying down blueprinted acres of factories six months ahead of schedule, and streamlining labor-management relations, and use instead the

9. When lecturing in Great Britain.

figures of speech of horticulture, to speak of "planting the seed" in "carefully prepared ground," of an effort which even when skill and experience were used to their utmost, still depended in final outcome on forces with which man could co-operate but which he could not control.

Roads and buildings in Britain which have been there a long time become part of the natural world, not something to be swept aside lightly for a new plan. This was difficult for Americans to understand, who often found that a badly bombed city, once the rubble had been cleared away, which was still a wounded landscape to the British, looked to them very much like any American city, in eternal process of rapid transformation, in which the old was torn down with hardly a sign of regret.

The very different sorts of self-consciousness about all social process had also to be analyzed and allowed for: the American's willingness to think about the immediate future and his unwillingness to think very far ahead; the British unwillingness to let too great a degree of self-consciousness interfere with the smooth flow of highly disciplined habitual behavior but their greater willingness to think ten years ahead; the sudden shift in British attention which permitted them to attribute to themselves, retrospectively, a degree of planfulness which they would have repudiated at the time as paralyzing. I was at first confused by these contradictions -- by being told in one breath that to think about the next week's plan would be unthinkable and that in some earlier operation of exactly the same nature "we were very clever," and infinitely cunning. Once the contrast was clear, it was possible to discuss the past when any detailed dissection of motive and behavior was desired, and the far future if articulate goals came into question.

III. History as It Appears to Rumanians[10]

Ruth Benedict

No attempt will be made in this memorandum to repeat easily accessible facts of Rumanian history. It is necessary, however, to present Rumanian history as it appears to Rumanians. For historians, the problem is to present the event as nearly as possible as it actually happened, and they have brought together data with this end in view; for our purposes, the way in which history is taught in schools, the powerful folk myths of the Rumanian past, are also of primary importance. The very selectivity is significant. Similarities and contrasts between the objective facts and the Rumanian interpretation are also important. In addition, a statement of their view of their history gives an opportunity to state the most relevant occurrences in their past.

---

10. Reproduced from Benedict (1946c; pp. 4-12). The work was based upon interviews and published literary materials, and was done in 1943.--Ed.

Rumanians are likely to plot their history around a series of heroes -- Rumanian heroes, in spite of the fact that this list of illustrious leaders goes back to Alexander and Trajan. Alexander the Great is not only Rumanian, he is Christian. Riding on his great white horse, he led his legions against the barbarians of the known world -- and planted the Cross. Alexander is a glorious compensation for the centuries when the barbarian conquests swept over Rumania; he is the mythical golden age of the past, which succeeding centuries could not obliterate.

Trajan, too, is a living folk hero, not as a Roman emperor subduing a distant outpost populated by their own ancestors, but as the founder, the "papa," of Rumania. The Romans' century and a half of rule in their trans-Danubian province of Dacia is the rallying point even today of Rumanian nationalist feeling, for it gave Rumania, alone among the peoples of Eastern Europe, a basically Romance language. Rumania is completely surrounded by Slavic-speaking peoples -- Russians, Poles, Ruthenians (of Czechoslavakia), Serbs, and Bulgarians -- and on the west by Hungarians speaking a language allied to that of Finns and Turks. Rumanians see their history as a long struggle during which they have preserved their Roman tongue and their identity against conqueror after conqueror, and hence the myth that makes Trajan the father of Rumania is nationally indispensable.

Racially they see themselves as the true representatives of the Roman Empire in the East. Even today the origin of the Rumanians is a football of political nationalism. The Rumanian version is that when the Roman legions withdrew before the migrations of the barbarians, and when Goths, Huns, Slavs, Avars, Bulgars, and Mongols took possession of the plains century after century, "Rumanians" maintained themselves in the mountains, their true homeland, ready to decend in the thirteenth and fourteenth centuries and later to re-establish themselves as the dominant peoples. Hence, too, all the scattered peoples of the Balkans who have retained a Romanized dialect in the mountains of Epirus and Macedonia and Pindus are "Rumanians" -- lost tribes separated from their motherland. They claimed, even when Greater Rumania was intact, 600,000 Rumanians in Russia, 300,000 in Yugoslavia, 30,000 in Hungary, and 50,000 to 60,000 in Bulgaria (cf. Bolitho, 1940; pp. 113). This dogma is sacred even though the spoken language of Istria or of the Pindus is unintelligible to Rumanians, and even though the physical anthropology and the culture of the "Rumanian"-speaking Macedonians contrast strongly with that of the population near Bucharest.

Trajan and his conquest of Dacia, also, is still advanced as the basis for Rumanian territorial rights in Transylvania. For Trajan's Dacia was not in the plains of the Old Kingdom; it was on the Carpathian bastion. Hence Transylvania becomes the cradle of the Rumanian race. Every school child knows this and is taught to die to retain or reclaim his homeland.

For a thousand years after Roman withdrawal from Dacia there is a complete blackout of Rumanian history. No historical record mentions Latins (Vlachs) in this region again until the thirteenth century. "For a thousand years we have no trace whatsoever of those Romanized Dacians. All of a sudden they appear in the year 1222 in Hungarian documents concerning Transylvania under the name of 'Vallachian communities.' Where had these people been all this time? That is what historians have called the enigma of the Middle Ages" (Pribichevich, 1939; p. 37). This "enigma," however, does not necessarily refer to a unique event. It is only a special instance of what occurred in the mountainous regions of Southeast Europe during the invasions that swept over the plains: any old inhabitants of the land who remained on the plains were speedily overridden or gradually absorbed, and only those who took refuge in the mountains preserved their identity. Balkan and Carpathian peoples, Romanized under the Caesars, escaped from the barbarians to small mountain valleys and maintained themselves; there is no historical necessity that they should all have been of the same race or tongue. To this day Latin-based dialects have persisted in many regions, even in Switzerland. The fact, however, that only in Rumania did they achieve statehood has fostered the idea that these Latin-based dialects, whether they are found in Istria or Dalmatia or Greece, are evidence of unity with the modern nation Rumania, the true heir of Roman civilization in Eastern Europe.

When the curtain rises again upon Rumanian history, four heroes are preeminent to the Rumanians in the late fourteenth, fifteenth, and sixteenth centuries. They personify resistance to the encroachments of great powers; Hungary and, more than all, the Turks.

The first of these is Mircea the Old, Prince of Walachia from 1368 to 1418. The Turks defeated the Serbian army at the famous field of Kosovo in 1389; four years later the last trace of Bulgarian independence was overthrown, and a few years later the Turks also defeated the Hungarians. No wonder, then, that during the reign of the minor voivods of Walachia, the name of his country first appeared on the register of vassals of the Sublime Porte, and that the year before his death, Mircea had to acknowledge its suzerainty by an annual tribute, meantime surrendering Dobrogea to the Turks (cf. Seton-Watson, 1934; pp. 32-34). Soon after, additional annual tribute of 500 children to be reared as Turkish Janissaries was also required of Walachia (cf. Stratilesco, 1907; p. 24). This nonmilitary tale of helplessness and defeat is not interpreted in Rumania -- as Kosovo is in Balkan states -- as a national martyrdom, and Mircea is no symbol of martyrdom; Mircea the Old is presented as a ruler who when all the rest of Christendom laid down its arms and submitted to the Turks, fought and fought and fought again against the Turks. He is a national savior. So, too, his Moldavian contemporary, Alexander the Good, another popular hero, fought the Hungarians and checked their expansion across the Carpathians.

Stephen the Great (1460-1504), grandson of Alexander the Good, outshines the earlier heroes. Constantinople fell to the Ottomans in 1452, and Stephen organized resistance to the new order with the full support of an army drawn from a relatively free peasantry whose right to the soil depended on their military service. He called upon them to fight for their own land. Stephen took the initiative in capturing strong strategic points from the Turks, and when Hungary, alarmed at his aggressiveness, sent armies against him instead of against the Turks, he overcame them and turned again to oppose the Turks. The Pope called him the Athlete of Christ, and he commemorated his victories by building some forty churches, many of which are still standing as famous fifteenth-century relics (cf. Seton-Watson, 1934; pp. 41-49). Stephen the Great marks the high point in Rumanian valor and strategy and social solidarity. When in World War I King Ferdinand offered his troops the most valued possible reward to induce them to continue fighting when Russia withdrew, the phrase was that he would give them land "like Stephen the Great" (cf. Mitrany, 1930; p. 107). When today the peasant sings of the glory of his country, he sings of Stephen (Stratilesco, 1907; pp. 21-22):

Stephen, Stephen, the great lord,
Has no equal in the world
Except the Splendid sun....
The whole world is in amaze:
The land is small, the land is strong,
And the foe cannot advance.

Michael the Brave lived less than a century later (1593-1601), and he was also a military hero. But conditions had changed in Rumania. Michael fought with mercenary forces and his supporters were the Moldavian princes who longed, like Michael, to free themselves of the payments they were required to make to the Porte. For this it was necessary to unite the small principalities of the region -- and Michael therefore set out on a career of conquest of Walachia and Transylvania. He fought, that is, not against the Turks but against the Christians. During his eight-year meteoric career he won these battles and, as every Rumanian child knows, "united all Rumanians." But it was a union of conquest, not a league voluntarily entered into to oppose the Moslem. His statue stands in the central plaza of Bucharest and is the proper place for nationalist demonstrations.

The other fact about Michael the Brave is stressed by historians as different as Rosette, Seton-Watson, Mitrany, and Stratilesco, but is not mentioned in Rumanian schools: he wrote serfdom into Rumanian law. Rumania had no feudalism, in the Western European sense, in medieval times, and, as has been said, Stephen fought with a free peasantry. In Rumania there was no theory that overlords owned the land and the peasants on it. A princelet, domn, if he wished to settle peasants even on uncultivated land, had to get the permission of the commune -- i.e. village or villages of peasants, which alone had title to the land; the overlord had a right only to tithes on produce, honey monopoly, profits of mill and tavern, direct taxes, a small number of work days per year. Michael not only bound all Old Kingdom peasants to the land and reduced them to the position of serfs; "in Transylvania he deliberately threw himself into the arms of the Magyar nobility and helped them to suppress the Rumanian peasantry, which had risen in the belief that he was coming to their aid" (cf. Seton-Watson, 1934; p. 621). The career of Michael is only one illustration of the way in which subjection of the peasant population was increased under Rumanian masters; mitigations occurred at periods of national impotence or under direct pressure of international events. Rumania, however, ascribes it to foreigners.

The last great traditional hero is Tudor Vladimirescu, who lived more than two centuries later and led a brief revolt in 1821. For a century the domn had no longer been a Rumanian; Constantinople had adopted a policy of letting these positions out on a three-year basis to wealthy Greeks, both because Rumanian princelets were, from the Porte's point of view, too troublesome and because Greeks could afford to pay higher prices for the privilege. Because these rich Greeks lived in the Phanar, a wealthy district in Constantinople, the eighteenth century is called the Phanariot period in Rumania. It came to the point where it was a question whether the Old Kingdom would be completely Hellenized (cf. Seton-Watson, 1934; p. 192). The old "dues" were increased -- corvée labor was always small in comparison with other countries -- and when peasants had a poor harvest, etc., they fell into debt slavery. The people, still predominantly sheepherders, fled deeper into the Carpathians, and many men joined the haiduk, the popularly supported brigands who had tired of paying tribute and who kept rendezvous in the mountains. The haiduk bands, as elsewhere in Southeast Europe, owed loyalty only within the band and to their leader. Vladimirescu can be called a legitimate haiduk who, with the aid of Russia, which was at the time warring against the Turks, succeeded in rallying such popularly supported outlaws, as well as villagers. "Our rising," he wrote, "is directed only against the boyars,[11] who have devoured our rights" (cf. Mitrany, 1930; p. 24). He made no distinction of nationality, but instead distinguished between tyrannical and non-tyrannical boyars. Nevertheless, because of the dominance of the Phanariotes, the movement was predominantly anti-Greek, and when the rebels succeeded in occupying Bucharest, even though Tudor was murdered by order of a Phanariot militia chief, his Russian ally forced the Turks to end the Phanariot regime, and under Russian auspices the two provinces of Moldavia and Walachia were granted autonomy.

The era of great wealthy estates and a half-nourished peasantry, however, had by no means ended. The nineteenth century is the high point of misery for the Rumanian peasant.

---

11. The boyar in Rumania is the equivalent of the feudal landowner in other European countries, and can for the last century be translated "rich land-owner." For Vladimirescu's time, it has to be translated "the powerful, who collected the peasants' dues."

The first official autonomous act of Moldavia and Walachia at the end of the Russo-Turkish War of 1829 was the adoption of the Organic Statutes, which for the first time established the principle that land itself belonged to the boyar, the landowner, who only granted use of it at his will to the peasant, and the Statutes allowed the owner new and excessive powers (cf. Mitrany, 1930; pp. 27-41). Even the Czarist Russian negotiator, Kisselev, protested and tried to modify the severity of the Statutes (cf. Seton-Watson, 1934; p. 210; Mitrany, 1930; pp. 33-34).

The great European liberal upheavals of 1848 hardly touched Rumania, though they did benefit the Rumanians living in Translyvania; their status had been that of serfs, and they were freed by Hungary in 1848. In Rumania itself feudal serfdom, in any of its Western forms, though it was favored by the boyars at various times and under various rules, was not folk custom (cf. Mitrany, 1930; p. 47, fn. 17); the Rumanian economic curse has been sharecropping and what amounted to debt slavery for the peasants. These had been inherited from the Phanariot period, and native boyars now stepped into the old Greek privileges. A great change in livelihood patterns favored the extension of these exactions in the mid-nineteenth century at the time of the Crimean War. This was the new market for wheat and corn to satisfy which the black-earth plains of Moldavia and of certain regions near Bucharest were admirably fitted. The traditional economy of Rumania had been sheep-herding, supplemented by cereals, and the mountain valleys were the favored locale. The plains had been largely used for summer pasturage. Now, however, boyars could make great profits from the work of sharecropping or wage-paid peasants on the plains. Pastoral land was restricted cumulatively through the nineteenth century, the exactions of the Rumanian boyars multiplied, and even the coup d'état reforms of Cuza (1864) -- the so-called emancipation of the serfs -- in effect only left the peasants more at the mercy of the boyars (cf. Mitrany, 1930; p. 547). What the reforms would have needed to be effective was not "emancipation of serfs," but some amelioration of the debt slavery which conscripted their labor. The reforms failed, too, partly because Cuza's advocacy of them -- they were intended to curtail the power of the boyars -- made his position untenable in Rumania, and a palace revolution resulted in the importation of the Hohenzollern Carol I as prince, and later king, of Rumania (lately formed coalition of Moldavia and Walachia).[12] One of the first acts under this regime was to sanction use of the military to compel the peasant to work upon the boyars' land and to deny the peasant appeal to any court.

---

12. Rumania became an independent kingdom through the good graces of the Congress of Berlin, but this treaty of 1878 -- which ended Turkish sovereignty in Rumania -- is remembered by Rumanians as "when we lost Bessarabia." In fact, they lost the three southern provinces of Bessarabia, where the population is almost solidly Ukrainian -- certainly not Rumanian.

"Between 1870 and 1906 the rents paid by 67.6% of the peasant tenants had risen by 100%; those of 13.8% of them by more than 300%; and those of 3.3% by over 500%. For the land held in métayage, which they cultivated with their own seed, animals, and implements, the peasants were found to be paying one-half to two-thirds of the harvest, and a variety of additional charges in labor and in kind.... Under the pressure of such circumstances the peasants were driven to borrow from the landowners and tenants. M. D. Nenitescu declared that an official inquiry conducted in 1901 established that for such loans 60% had come to be regarded as a 'friendly' interest; but that sometimes the landlords took from the peasants 125%, 250%, 365%, and even 528% in the form of labor dues" (cf. Mitrany, 1930; pp. 83-84).

This is the background for the peasants' revolt in 1907, in which 10,000 peasants were put to death. However, "nothing more positive came of the fierce rising of 1907 than a revised and enlarged edition of the existing agrarian laws. The men who were to interpret and apply them remained the same, and, beyond a passing flush, the temper and habits of Rumanian public life were hardly affected by the peasants' show of despair. Occasionally some politician felt moved to confess that 'everything remains as it was'" (cf. Mitrany, 1930; p. 90). Only in 1917 when her ally, Russia, was abandoning the Eastern Front and Rumania had to act desperately to keep her troops from going home as the Russians had, did the King make promises to the army which involved crucial expropriation of privately owned lands. This promise could not be carried out during the war, and it is estimated that out of a population of 7,000,000, 800,000 to 1,000,000 were war casualties (cf. Seton-Watson, 1934; p. 519). She had, however, fought on the side of the Allies, and she emerged with a territory increased by 20%, having gained Transylvania, Dobrogea, Bessarabia, Bukovina, and part of the Banat.[13] There was an equal increase of population. The consequences of the war and the Russian Revolution in contiguous territory made some fulfillment of Rumania's agrarian promises essential, and from 1918 to 1921 radical expropriation of lands and reallotment to peasants were carried out. Compensation paid by the state to the landlords speedily became valueless because of the depression, and landlords were reduced to poverty. As for the peasants, they "were made to pay its real value several times over by means of indirect contributions. They escaped the selfish exploitation of the large owners only to fall under the stepmotherly tutelage of a mercantilist state" (cf. Mitrany, 1930; p. 574). "The ambition to create a national industry was coupled with a policy of making agriculture pay for it" (cf. Mitrany, 1930; p. 576).

---

13. Popular irredentist feeling was strong in protest against the part of the Banat that went to Serbia by the Treaty of Trianon. Rumania, in spite of preferential treatment, was thoroughly estranged by the deliberations at Versailles (cf. Seton-Watson, 1934; p. 539).

During the late 1920s a Peasant Party grew up under the leadership of the Transylvanian statesman Julio Maniu. In the relatively free election of 1928 this Peasant Party came into power and Maniu became Prime Minister. Townsmen and the upper class had for the first time apparently lost control of the administration, but, as events showed, they need not have been fearful. The great State patronage system only drew the new incumbents into its toils. The depression also created grave difficulties, and the peasants regarded the Peasant Party as having failed.

It was in this situation that the great peasant-based popular movement grew up in Rumania -- the Iron Guard. This is famous in England and America as the great pro-Axis party in a country whose upper class and whose king were pro-French. But the Iron Guard contrasts strongly with Nazism in Germany or the Croix de Feu in France. The hero and idol of the Iron Guard was the peasant Codreanu. He was a calm and powerful person with benign countenance who always wore Rumanian peasant dress -- only Mihalache, right-hand man in Maniu's Peasant Party, retained peasant dress in the world of public affairs, and he roused endless peasant enthusiasm sitting silent on his horse at gatherings. In course of time, the Iron Guard came to include representatives of the "best people," some people attracted to it because it was pro-Axis, and a Left Wing accused of being Communist. But its strength was its mass basis -- its peasants. It was organized in "cells." Its program called for reformation of the monarchy's corruption and abuses -- and it was at the same time royalist. It was pro-Axis, but it preached defying Hitler and fighting Hungary to get back the area of Transylvania given to Hungary in 1940; it was passionately irredentist on every frontier. It was anti-Semitic; except for Cuza's anti-Semitic party, it was the only Rumanian party so heedless of the support of the Western Powers that it made anti-Semitism official. Rumania was doubtless the most anti-Semitic country except Poland, and it was therefore a popular plank. The Guardists were "more anti-English than Hitler." And they also preached a better Rumania and built community houses and hostels, repaired churches and peasants' houses, and carried out co-operative activities on public works. They marched and shouted and demonstrated and gave to the populace a sense of common goal and of group strength.

"The violent deeds with which the Capitano (Codreanu) had been connected never hurt his prestige with the Rumanian people. To the Rumanian people the Capitano remained a saint and a martyr and the apostle of a better Rumania. Even skeptical ones who did not agree with him in political matters still grew dreamy-eyed remembering Codreanu" (cf. Waldeck, 1942; pp. 35-36). He was killed during Carol's purge of the Iron Guard in November 1938, along with hundreds of his followers. His party had in the previous year's elections returned enough votes to be the second strongest party in the country, and Carol had countered by abolishing the constituion and the party system. It was easy to oppose the Iron Guard as irresponsible riffraff unfit to govern, and to show that they had used violence against their opponents. And as Codreanu said, if he came to power, he would make an alliance with Germany in forty-eight hours. But it is important to recognize the movement as a genuine popular movement put down by the King.

With the fall of France less than two years later, Carol's pro-French foreign policy was no longer possible, and General Antonéscu became dictator, collaborating with Germany, with the remnants of the Iron Guard sharing the power. Carol and Lupescu fled the country, and for several months the gendarmerie of the Iron Guard arrested and killed whoever they would in Bucharest and in many other parts of the country. "Rumanians were terrified at their capacity for excess." No one knew who would be next. It hampered German schemes in the "raw materials field," and Hitler sided with Antonéscu and took to Germany Horia Sima, leader of the Iron Guard. From now on, Rumania depended on German-supported order; all semblance of a popular movement had been disarmed.[14]

Rumanians follow several leitmotifs in interpreting this history. First, bad Rumanian conditions are due to foreigners and have improved under the national Rumanian state. This theme has several different forms: (a) Rumanian independence has lifted the peasant slowly but surely out of an original serfdom under barbarians, Turks, and Phanariotes; Rumanian peasants are submissive "like sheep," and all the benefits they have been given by the state were given out of goodness of heart. This is the view of several well-placed and intelligent Rumanians interviewed, but others make a different interpretation; (b) Rumania had her own rulers from the thirteenth to the seventeenth centuries, and people were free then; the peasants lost their status under foreigners; the first act of the United Principalities was Cuza's "emancipation of the serfs," and periodically before and after World War I agrarian reform was forced upon the state by peasants' revolts or, in 1917, fear of such revolutionary uprisings as Russia's. They stress, as historians do, that there were five peasant revolts in the reign of Carol I (1866-1914). These informants stress the initiative taken by the hard-pressed peasants and the fear inspired in the state by their violence; they look to the peasants for initiative in further improvements which will bring back Rumanian freedom as in the golden age of the thirteenth to the seventeenth centuries. These differences in interpretation are significant, but they agree in nationalistic emphasis; they agree in putting at one pole conditions under Rumanian rule and at the other conditions under foreign dominance. This attitute is expressed in many other connections, and many informants gave as the reason why so few Rumanians migrated to America to improve their

---

14. This paper was written in November 1943. -- Ed.

condition: "Why should we think there would be any improvement if we trusted ourselves to foreigners? Rumania has always suffered from the foreigner." Applied to their history, this interpretation omits or minimizes the remarkable continuity in Rumanian conditions from 1700 on, whatever the national affiliations of the group that held the whip handle; even in the eighteenth century, the country's problem was not feudalism in its Western form but Phanariot exactions from the peasants and their consequent debt slavery. Just so, in the 1920s the leader of the Agrarian League reiterates that in his day the Rumanian evil was "serfdom to the banking trust. Free labor, but taxed and coerced trading -- that is the modern method of serfdom" (cf. Mitrany, 1930; p. 547). For two centuries the trouble had been fundamentally the same: the peasants' "dues," taxes, and indebtedness. Those who benefited from the system have been Turks, Greeks, Jews, and Rumanians; Rumanians certainly did not take less than the others.

In most other European countries, in the Middle Ages, and later, the nobles had to strive against a king -- and they did so in the name of liberty. The peasants, however, feeling that the nobles (landlords) lived at their expense, sympathized with the kings. This was reasonable, for centralized power was built up in those centuries by limiting and controlling the landlord's power over his serf. But in Rumania there were no noble feudal families with hereditary tenure; there were only incumbents who bought their positions and had to get rich from the peasantry as fast as possible before their tenure was withdrawn to be given to a higher bidder. "The Sultan (later it was the Rumanian state), weighed on the prince, the prince on the boyars, and the boyars on the peasants. There existed a hierarchal tyranny" (statements of M. Thouvenel, French Ambassador, about 1800). Rumania has not even in 1943 arrived at a different alignment of internal politics, though the race and the nationality of those who weigh upon the ultimate producer have changed and are now the latter's conationals.

Second, another theme Rumanians select in discussing their history is irredentism -- which for the period after World War I becomes the Greater Rumania theme. This irredentism is not based on their national state's past glory, as is Poland's or Hungary's. Rumania became an independent state only in 1878, with a Hohenzollern king because no native prince was tolerated by the rest. They have no great campaigns of conquest to hark back to; their stand against the Turks in 1877 and their engagements against the Germans at Marari and Maracesti in the summer of 1917 are their modern subjects of military glory. Irredentism in Rumania is ethnic, and claims all speakers of Roman-based dialects. It is exceedingly fierce. The treaty of 1878, which gave them national independence, is "when we lost Bessarabia"; the Treaty of Trianon, when they doubled their territory and population, is sour to them because they lost the part of the Banat below the Danube. To the Rumanian soldier, the campaign in 1919 against Béla Kun and the Communist threat in Hungary was "to get back Transylvania." Germany's permission to Hungary to take back part of it again in 1940 stirred the bitterest feelings of that tragic year, and Russia's previous grab of Bessarabia and Bukovina had roused emotions of the same order. When Rumania's troops fought later on the Eastern Front, they were "retaking Bessarabia," and, for interest, the territory beyond. Every child knows the quatrain:

> From the Dniester to the Tisza
> Every Rumanian has wept to me
> That he cannot endure
> The injustice of foreign misrule.

Irredentism is a passion in many present-day European states, and the fact that the Rumanian version is based on language and not on conquest fell in with post-World War I theories of self-determination and the currently accepted practice of counting minorities by the language they speak. Our interest at this point is in the fact that Rumania's irredentist passion, though equal to Hungary's and Poland's -- the two pre-eminent irredentist states -- does not look back, like theirs, to a time when their strong state ruled over subject peoples. It is the irredentism of a state less than a hundred years in existence; Hungary's irredentist arguments meet Rumania's at no single point.

Third, implicit in the foregoing leitmotifs is an entirely genuine lack of consciousness that Rumania has at all crucial points in her history as an autonomous kingdom been a pawn in the hands of stronger states. In some other states where this has been true it has become a major grievance; Rumanians do not recognize it even as a grievance. The autonomy of Moldavia and Walachia was set up in 1829 by Russia at the end of the Russo-Turkish War under her jurisdiction; Bismarck made Rumania a state at the Congress of Berlin in 1878; Greater Rumania was set up as a buffer state by the Great Powers at at the Treaty of Trianon. All these events and many others are in the Rumanian view "when we achieved independence," "what we won by our battles at Marari and Maracesti," etc. The fact that national efforts or organization to achieve these goals were never very marked or persistent -- except in the realm of negotiations -- does not figure. Rumanians have a strong tendency to see in history justification for thinking of themselves as "big shots," and they find it difficult or impossible to admit their own powerlessness or bad management or failure.

IV. Courage: Cumulative Effects of Sacrifice[15]

Sula Benet

Suffering and death are accumulated as capital with which to redeem Poland. John Gunther, in his column "Inside Europe Today" (1949), "wrote: "One Pole we met put it this way with bitter vigor: 'You in the West may have the highest standard of living in the world. We Poles have the highest standard of death.'" Repeatedly Polish soldiers fight far from their native soil for a foreign

---

15. Reproduced from Benet (1952; pp. 40-50).

country, and for a cause very indirectly connected with the welfare of Poland. This presumes that a Pole is the "knight of freedom," and will fight wherever a a fight for freedom takes place. Their spilled blood is not wasted on the country where it falls. In the last analysis it will be credited to Poland.

In a song about Monte Cassino during World War II, speaking about great Polish losses, there is a popular passage:

> The Pole married honor....
> This land belongs to Poland,
> ⌐because of the blood spilled there⌐
> Though Poland be far away.
> Freedom is measured by crosses.

And in an unpublished poem Broniewski says clearly:

> Through the sea of the Caspian
> Through the sand of Libya
> We wander directly to Poland.

It isn't so very direct, at least on a geographical map, but on the psychological map of Polish imagination, such a route of march is very well understood.

One of the most-beloved military leaders whose memory is still very dear to the hearts of the Poles was Kosciuszko. He was not a victorious leader. On the contrary, after a brief success in the war with Russia, he suffered defeat under Maciejowice, and this defeat concluded the uprising. Another beloved general was Pulaski, who also suffered defeat. There were many others: Sulkowski, who died in Egypt; Traugut, a leader of the uprising of 1863, who was hanged on the gallows in Warsaw, and others. What is so striking in these names is the fact that although they suffered defeat, their glory was not dimmed; on the contrary, their popularity was magnified. It seems that the measure of greatness in a leader is not gauged by Poles as it is by other peoples. It is not the victory that is important, but other values. Most of the above-mentioned leaders fought with foreign enemies on foreign soil. Kosciuszko and Pulaski later on took part in the war of the American Revolution. Sulkowski and Poniatowski fought in the army of Napoleon. This list could also be extended to include Dabrowski, Kniaziewicz, and others of Bonaparte's army. Also Wroblewski and Dabrowski, who fought in Paris in 1870, and so on up to the well-known battles of the Poles at Tobruk and at Monte Cassino during World War II.

To be a political martyr is the highest ethical achievement in the life of an individual. The famous poet Mickiewicz said in the Books of the Polish Pilgrimage and the Polish Nation (1911):

> He who stays in his fatherland and endures slavery in order to preserve life loses fatherland and life. But he who leaves his fatherland to defend liberty at the peril of his life will save his fatherland and will live eternally.

After the defeat of the insurrection of 1830-31, the political émigrés discussed the responsibility for this uprising. Those who condemned the uprising were very few. The whole discussion was concerned with the details of the organization and the course of events. The interesting point is that the people who had led the uprising were not condemned for the failure, but because in the end they had surrendered instead of fighting until death came. Slowacki (192-) in "Gród Agamemnona" (The Grave of Agamemnon) says sarcastically that those who saved their lives were "half-knights." According to a traditional story, Mickiewicz, speaking to one of the generals of the uprising, was arguing with him that they should all die to the last man, to which the general is said to have replied, "Perhaps so that you could write poetry about it afterward." A Polish song called "Warszawienka" says, "Today is your ⌊Poland's⌋ triumph or death."

These two facts: (1) that the military leaders died defeated, and (2) that the Poles fought on foreign land and under foreign leadership: are related to an important aspect of Polish thinking; that is, that the measure of success is not so much the achieved goal and the results of the battles as it is the conduct during action, and the demonstration of the indomitable qualities which in Poland spell honor.

It is easy to establish one characteristic -- that the concrete goal, which is freedom, is remote and very generalized. But the emphasis is on defense. It is not so important to achieve as it is not to surrender. A Pole does not conquer, he defends. At one time he defends Christianity, at another, Western civilization or Western culture against Russia, etc.

The individual is very deeply concerned with the honor of the small unit or segment of life with which he is engaged, where he can reinforce all those values which are so important to him -- not to give in, not to compromise. At the same time he does not feel responsible for the larger units of which his is only a small part. Thus a synchronization of the whole, according to observers, is very difficult to achieve.

One example of this concern with the small unit is illustrated by the legend about Poniatowski, the head of the Polish unit in the army of Napoleon. The order was given for him to retreat, but any retreat, regardless of the emergency, would have been considered dishonorable. Upon receipt of the order to retreat, Poniatowski gave his men a command to advance, and he himself led the way to his death by jumping into the rapids, with the words, as tradition has it: "God has entrusted me with the honor of the Poles, and only to God can I give it back."

In Polish interpretation of their history, the story of Poniatowski approaches very closely the ideal of the Polish man, and therefore such episodes are very dear to the Polish heart, and they are invoked constantly. Without fail they produce a response of boundless pride. This bravado is exactly what appeals so much to the emotions. For example, the storming of Samosierra in Spain during the Napoleonic Wars, the fearless attacks of Polish cavalry on German tanks, the storming of Monte Cassino in World War II -- these are the epitome of bravery to the Poles. We should say a few words about Samosierra. A Polish unit in the army of Napoleon called themselves the "Knights of Freedom" in the war being fought against Spain, but it must be remembered that the defenders of Samosierra were people who were fighting on their own soil against aggressors, so that actually the Poles did not fight for freedom, but were themselves the "enemy" of freedom. It looks as though the end result is not important; the importance lies in how men conduct themselves in a given situation. This is why retreat -- under any circumstances -- is impossible. Poles identify honor with bravado, regardless of the price they pay for it, and regardless of the total situation. Very often this manner of thinking leads to great misunderstanding. For instance, in 1940, the French decided to give up Paris without further fighting, but the Polish units refused to capitulate and moved forward toward the German army. The retreating French soldiers turned over their arms to the "mad" Polish. This caused a lack of co-ordination within the whole plan. The Poles were not moved by any idea of "strategy and politics"; they only knew that their honor did not allow them to capitulate.

During the "blitz" in London, Polish air units were sent aloft to fight the Germans. The Poles were reckless both of their own lives and of the planes. Although the English appreciated their bravery, they could not afford to lose the planes and were forced constantly to curb the enthusiasm of the Poles.

There have been other misunderstandings between the Poles and their allies. Poles fighting in foreign lands consider that they have a mission to fulfill. Their allies, usually much more sober and considerate of the over-all picture, treat the Poles as poor relations. Both sides cling stubbornly to their points, and the conflicts repeat themselves with tragic regularity; the Poles who fight abroad in the role of "soldiers of freedom" are left out and are always on the losing side, and because the allies want to settle their affairs, they return to normal life, while the Poles constantly remember the unattained goal. Their allies regard them as lunatics, maniacs, and adventurers. The Poles think of their allies as too sober, too commercial, too much given to compromise.

In the very busy thoroughfare the Place de l'Alma in Paris stands the monument of Mickiewicz. The statue represents a pilgrim clad in Biblical costume, holding a staff in his hand. One gets the feeling that the tragic pilgrim is remote, lonely, and lost in the midst of the busy traffic about him.

The everyday life of a nation, one could say, is not occupied just with wars, and the values discussed above must be those of only one group. We could say that those values are the ideals and are not applicable to everyday life. This is true, but nevertheless these values receive attention not in extraordinary circumstances only. On the contrary, since they are so integrated into home life and school education, they leave their imprint in every sphere of the people's activities. One may also say that not all Poles have these ideals, that after alll the people are divided into groups, into political parties, live in different regions. This is also true. There is an even greater division into groups than one might expect. However, in studying the various groups, one is surprised to find that all have some very important values in common. For instance, the Left Wing group, especially the Socialists, whose programs were supposed to be based on rational principles, supported the nationalist movement and the hopeless uprisings.

The uprisings of Kosciuszko, at the end of the eighteenth century, were supported by the folk element, the city people as well as the peasants. (Tradition has it that Kosciuszko wore peasant dress though he was a nobleman.)

The uprising of 1830 was provoked by military officers who were at that time also considered Left Wing. The rebellion against the Czar in 1905 was organized by the militant Socialist Party. Opposed to these terrorists of 1905 were the National Democrats, who represented the Right Wing. They included more of the wealthy element and the city bourgeoisie, who were more reserved and less adventurous. But there is an interesting point here, which was commented upon by a Polish writer who was also oriented toward the right. He said that from his Right Wing democratic group came heroes who were organizers of uprisings and rebellions, among them Kosciuszko. The contradiction is only superficial, because politics and programs are one thing, the sentiments of the people are something quite different. The truth is that the bourgeoisie, quiet and balanced, who dislike risk, in their dreams and fancies really have the other ideal. This ideal is so strongly linked with national tradition that it needs only a spark to start off a conflagration. This is what happened during the last war.

There is a characteristic Polish version of an anecdote of World War II:

A group of parachutists were in a plane preparing to make a practice jump. The Englishman was asked to jump first. He asked, "Does Mr. Churchill know that I am about to make this jump?" They answered, "Yes." The Englishman continued, "Does the King know about it?" The answer was, "No." "Then," said the Englishman, "I shall not jump." The Frenchman was next invited to jump, but he replied that he had a petit diner to attend that night. The Czech, next in line, inquired if the movie cameras were shooting the jump, and when told that they were not, he refused to jump. At this, the soldiers began to quarrel with the officers about who was supposed to jump first. Someone said, "The Poles are cowards." With that the Poles came forward one by one and leaped from the plane without the protective parachutes.

This isolation of bravado from the whole context very often leads to the loss of any hierarchy of values. A small thing looks like a very large one when sacrifice and bravado are involved. This divorce from reality also brings about vagueness and generalization as to the real goals. There is also a failure to analyze the goals -- they are not precise. In such an intellectual and emotional climate it is easy to induce people to become interested in very generalized programs. To the foreign observer this is extremely confusing. It can also be dangerous. For example, the idea of democracy and freedom and equality is basic, but with just a small amount of manipulation this simple concept may become a very complex and dangerous one. The anti-Semitic pogroms are cases in point.

In connection with this we should mention one important feature: fideism (faith). Slogans are not analyzed -- they are believed in. Consequently, once the slogan is invoked, anything that accompanies it will be believed and taken en bloc.

Strong voices of criticism have been raised in literary and historical circles in an attempt to do away with messianism and unrealistic traditional ways of

looking at historical facts. The debunkers were the "great Europeans." They attacked the works of Sienkiewicz and demonstrated that the victorious battles of
Sienkiewicz' novels actually never took place, and that the behavior of his heroes
did not correspond to the true behavior and slogans of sixteenth-century Poland.
But the entire body of Polish traditional historians rose in protest against the
debunkers, and insisted that it was necessary to educate Polish youth in the spirit of nationalism and patriotism.

The transition from romanticism to realism and from national to social interests became a marked feature of intellectual evolution and of public life only
after the catastrophe of 1863. "Positivism" became a fashionably intellectual
slogan. "Organic work" -- meaning day-to-day efforts at social, economic, and
educational improvement -- was made the program of national effort, in place of
political conspiracy.

There are many discussions on realism in Poland today, and with good reason too, but the trouble is that nobody knows what realism means. Poland does
not afford a favorable climate for cultivating such extreme realism.

This is an abstract from an article written by Mark Zulawski under the
title "Warsaw" (1946), which shows how conscious the Poles themselves are of
their tendencies:

We find with great easiness the words and slogans which in our minds
correspond to the present situation. In our minds ... but what is in the mind of
other people, people of conscience and bravery in other European countries,
citizens of other towns? For them our slogans and our phrases were and always
are unintelligible. They are terrified by the bloody mist that surrounds our
brains. We speak always about blood, about sacrificing our lives, that from
blood and ruins are born new values, about ashes. The greater part of Polish
professional intelligentsia, those people who inherited the squires' ⌐nobility as
a whole⌐ mentality, for foreigners these people are almost pathological objects.
Those are people who are always ready to die, to spill blood. They produce and
bear physical sufferings. Those people in difficult situations know how to find
only one escape ... death. It may be that this is only a survival of our long
slavery, the school which gave us situations which cannot be solved. It is possible. But the most surprising fact is that it is precisely those features of our
culture of which we are especially proud, and we are annoyed when other people
want to esteem us for other virtues, for the industriousness and honesty of our
peasants, for the skill and endurance of our laborers, for our traditional tolerance, for our science and art.

I should like to give here a rough translation of a fragment of a poem by a
great Polish poet, Juljan Tuwim (1944; pp. 11-12):

To Those Doomed to Greatness

Sometimes from everyday mythology
Suddenly from a corner, from a vision, from an inner understanding,
From a color, a line, a melody,
In a flash of recognition--the Fatherland appears before you.
She[16] comes so undeniably,
So unmistakably, so uniquely,
That you recognize her in an echo,
You see her in a shadow --

---

16. In Polish, "Fatherland" is always referred to as "she."

She is yours, your own, alive.
And this feeling is much stronger than the power
Of Batorych, Chrobrych, Jagiellonow [great Polish kings,]
Than pompous books on history,
Than the divine babbling
Of bards and poets.
O those bombastics of history
That rhyme so easily both victory and glory,
Those geese cackling behind fences
About their capitolian ancestors!
O those historio-Sophians
Warmed by the pathos of history,
Winged nags harnessed to the wooden cart of history,
Again they have dragged Poland
Along "Roads," "Missions," and "Predestinations,"
Again every little puppy, every news vendor,
Every man in the street,
Grows fat on the grease of ancient glory.
Once and for all, the devil take the "Roads!"
In place of history exaggerated,
Perhaps for a change we could have some botany or geography?
Away with you, misleading bard,
Who summons noisy history's muse.
You cannot cover with Matejko canvas
Poland's misery, her nakedness, her wounds,
To greatness you would like to doom her,
To predestination, falcons, swords,
While her people wear patched pants and worn-out shoes;
You would lead the people with your pen on stretched historic roads,
While in cold and hunger the people fester in filthy huts,
While they tighten their belts on their empty guts
Or lose them, torn out on the bloody road to greatness....
We reject historic checks
Payable on Mars in a hundred years.
Let us have cash on the table!
Today's events, everyday affairs,
Banknotes of joy--not numismatics--
And billions of coins of happiness!
And the beautiful theater of history
The Fatherland can keep in her museums.
We are a simple people, a modest people,
Not supermen, not giants,
We pray God for another power,
For another road to greatness.

V. Chinese Family Images in International Affairs[17]

John Hast Weakland

The Chinese tendency to think in terms of analogy to the family system applies also to their way of thinking about international relations. Even under Chinese Communism, discussion of international affairs is not in pure Marxist language. Such discussion still includes evident, specific family imagery, and also other expressions which, though making no immediately evident family reference, are best comprehended by considering them in relation to Chinese family patterns.

---

17. Reproduced from Bunzel and Weakland (1952; pp. 185-94).

A specific example of family imagery in Chinese Communist writing is
given in reading material recently prepared for use in the elementary schools
in China (cf. Chen, 1950; pp. 326-26):

The capitalist world is like the feudalistic big family. The United States
is the Big Brother. France, England, Italy, the others are little brothers.... The
brothers appear to be in harmony but are actually engaged in rivalry and antagonism.... The socialistic world is different. The Soviet Union is the Big
Brother of the progressive family.... There is no exploitation, no oppression.
Look at the Peoples Republics in Eastern Europe!.... The Soviet Union enabled
them to establish independent states and helped them in construction work....
Is not the Soviet Union a kind and loving Big Brother? Dear readers, we are
indeed fortunate because we live in the new socialistic world. We must, under
the leadership of the Soviet Union, resolutely protect the peace of the world and
not allow the capitalists of the capitalistic world to hurt our Big Brother.

Such imagery is not confined to children's books; similar thinking appears
in Chinese Communist newspaper references to South Korea as the "younger
brother" of the United States, and to North Korea as the "younger brother" of
China. (Cf. China Daily News, New York City.)

In the passage quoted, the image of international relations presented is one
of two families of brothers. There is no mention of any paternal figure among
nations, nor of any group of nations organized on what we have called the paternalistic family pattern. However, since the capitalistic world is termed as like
the "feudalistic big family," it seems that the essential image of organization is
as much (or more) that in groups of actual brothers in a joint-family household
as it is that in "brotherhood" social organizations. Nevertheless, this imagery
stresses similarity and parallel relationships -- co-operation within each
"family" of nations, rivalry between them -- rather than complementary relationships within one larger whole.

The description given of the "capitalistic world" indeed seems similar to
what the Chinese joint family of brothers often was in fact: "The brothers appear to be in harmony but are actually engaged in rivalry and antagonism." But
the "progressive family" is seen as very different; it realizes the old Chinese
ideal and dream of perfectly harmonious relationships. This thinking resembles
Chinese Communist thinking about the family system and the national government: Even though two systems are organized on the same fundamental pattern, all trouble and evil are attributed to one of them alone -- the "family" of
the "capitalistic world" has a monopoly on human difficulties -- while perfection is attributed to the other example of the same pattern. (The two, of course,
are not recognized as the same by the Chinese Communists.) There is a projection of all that is wrong onto one example, and idealization of the other, with
little recognition of the pattern itself as underlying both sides of the picture, and
little consideration of altering or modifying it.

The passage quoted also presents the Soviet Union and China in the relationship of "elder brother" and "younger brother" within the "progressive family,"
and the implications of this may be examined. In the sphere of the actual fam-

ily in Chinese culture, an elder brother should receive obedience and respect from a younger brother, and in turn should make sacrifices on behalf of the younger and be solicitous for his welfare. Information from interviews on Chinese culture indicates that the position of younger brother is an envied one, with the elder brother seen as assuming responsibility and taking care of the younger, but not able to enforce any demands. It would seem that the quotation, picturing the Soviet Union as the elder brother who gives assistance and China as the younger brother who grows up to fulfill his family role more adequately, fits the ideal of the relationship of brothers rather well. It is not clear from this quotation whether the Chinese Communists believe their "elder brother" will be able to enforce any demands upon them or not, but there appears to be little indication in these contemporary statements that any demands at all were expected.

This vision of the position of "younger brother" in relation to the Soviet Union also fits in with the Chinese tendency to idealize certain situations. What will occur when -- as it almost certainly will -- the Soviet Union does not play the role of "elder brother" properly and makes demands that the Chinese Communists can neither overlook nor deny -- this is not fully predictable now. It will depend in part on what benefits are in fact derived from the Soviet Union, on the relationships of the Chinese Communist government to non-Communist countries, and on the security of its own position within China. However, it is expectable that even if the relationship between the Soviet Union and the Chinese Communists becomes very difficult, the Chinese Communists will continue to represent it as very harmonious as long as possible, just as dissent among the brothers of a Chinese joint family is concealed from the public until a break-up of the household reveals the actual state of affairs.

A very important feature of recent Chinese thought, both Nationalist and Communist, on international relations has been protest against "inequality" and demands for greater "equality" with other nations. In Chiang Kai-shek's China's Destiny (1947) the "inequality" of China when compared to Western Powers and Japan, especially as expressed in the various "unequal treaties" giving these Powers special privileges in China, is presented as practically the sole cause of all China's troubles (cf. Chapters II-III, passim); and Chiang wrote very favorably of the greater "equality" reached during World War II, when China's Western allies canceled such treaties and signed new "equal" treaties (cf. Chapter V). Sun Yat-sen also wrote of the necessity for China to align herself with nations "who treat us on the basis of equality" (1927; p. vii). A Communist version of this theme (Fang, 1950) claims Chinese and Soviet equality in certain economic agreements as against former unequal agreements in British-Chinese and American-Chinese enterprises:

When we compare the contract of the Kailan Mining Company [Sino-British] with present Sino-Soviet agreements, we can see that the principle of equality shown in the new agreements is simply incomparable.

And Mao Tse-tung states (1939; p. 2):

The various peoples of the Chinese nation are never willing to bow their
heads to the oppression of the outside world ... they only approve of co-operation under equal terms.

Although the meaning of these terms "inequality" and "equality" as used by the
Chinese is complex (and is markedly different from their meaning for Americans),
it seems that it is possible to clarify this meaning, and to show that it also has
some connection with Chinese patterns of the family and of human relationships
in general.

For Chinese, "inequality" appears to involve particularly a fear that the occupant of a position of superior power will use that power to take advantage of
the occupant of a weaker position, especially to make demands on the services
or resources of the weaker without making a reciprocal return. Such a fear
appears not only in regard to relations between nations, as described above, but
also in regard to relations between individuals. For example, Chinese movies
give prominence to scenes in which an employer takes advantage of a servant
who is powerless to defend himself;[18] or a son is pressed by his father into a
marriage that will benefit the father's interest (as the son sees it; the father
sees it as necessary for the social or material well-being of the family), but
which prevents the son from marrying a girl he loves.[19] The fear essentially
seems to be that a relationship will be one-sided and to the advantage of the occupant of the more powerful position, rather than mutually advantageous, as relationships should be according to Chinese ideals. Such a relationship can be
maintained only by coercion, for the Chinese view is that if the occupant of a position of authority does not perform his role properly, then no allegiance is due
him on any other grounds: If the emperor does not act as an emperor should,
then he is not truly an emperor. He no longer has the "mandate of Heaven." In
regard to the specific case of China's international relations, the very existence
of the relationships with the Powers implies coercion, as China wanted to be
separate, not part of such a system, and certainly not an inferior and weaker
part.

This leads to an examination of the meaning of "equality." This is not the
reverse of "inequality" as just described; that is, it is not the situation existing
within a properly functioning system of complementary roles. Such roles are
different and are of different status, whereas the Chinese word for "equality"

18. Cf. "An Analysis of Seven Cantonese Films," in Part Six of this Manual
    (pages 292-95). -- Ed.
19. This is a major theme of the famous Chinese novel The Dream of the Red
    Chamber (Ts'ao Hsueh-Ch'in, 1929), where the son resists taking the im-
    perial examinations and making a proper marriage, which would lead to
    governmental office and continuation of the family line and fortune. In a
    modern version, in the film New Red Chamber Dream, the same theme is
    presented in terms of a marriage that would benefit a business enterprise
    run by the father.

(p'ing teng) literally means "equal level." Equality, it would appear, exists or
is approximated only between two or more separate occupants of similar roles.[20]

In regard to the question of "equality," the Communist view of an international family of brothers may suggest a significant advance from earlier "inequality" either as pictured by Chiang or in the Communist writings about "imperial-
ism" in China. It seems that in the Chinese view there are comparative degrees of
"equality," even though the two terms as analyzed above seem qualitatively different. This, however, is like a question of family relationships considered
earlier: if two brothers only are thought of, they are not equal but in an unequal
and complementary relationship to each other; yet from a different viewpoint the
relationship between elder and younger brother -- in comparison to that between
father and sons -- involves relatively much more of equality, similarity, and independence of action. Thus China's newly envisioned position as younger brother in a family on equal terms with the family of the Western Powers, and with
only an elder brother over one even in own family, may seem a considerable
gain in "equality."

It should be pointed out, however, that the desire for "equality" is, very probably, only one half of the pattern of Chinese conceptions of international relations, the side appropriate to China's situation in recent years. The position of
"equality" in a way is far below China's position of former times as a great imperial Power, and below China's aspirations of even the last century, about
which Sun Yat-sen wrote (1927):

In its age of greatest power, the territory of the Chinese Empire was very
large, extending northward to the north of the Amur, southward to the South of
the Himalayas, eastward to the China Sea, westward to the T'sung Lin.... When
China was strongest, her political power inspired awe on all sides, and not a
nation south and west of China but considered it an honor to bring her tribute
(p. 35).
Before China was subjugated, she had a very cultured people and a powerful
state. She called herself the "majestic nation," the "land of famous letters and
objects," and looked on other countries as barbarian; she thought she was situa-
ted in the center of the world and so named herself the "Middle Kingdom" (p. 66).

Even late in the reign of the declining Manchu dynasty, China attempted to treat
envoys from England as tribute-bearers, and dreamed during the Boxer Rebellion of casting out foreign "barbarians" completely. Dr. Sun also envisioned not
merely "equality" but a return of China to her position of great power (1927;
pp. 146-48):

Japan studied from the West for only a few decades and became one of the
world's greatest Powers. But China has ten times the population and thirty times
the area of Japan, and her resources are much larger than Japan's. If China
reaches the standard of Japan, she will be equal to ten Great Powers.... If China
gets only as far as Japan, she will have the strength of ten Powers in her one
state, and will then be able to recover her predominant national position.
After China reaches that place, what then? A common phrase in ancient
China was, "Rescue the weak, lift up the fallen." Because of this noble policy

20. In this connection, cf. "Interview with a Chinese Scholar: Friendship," in
    this Manual, Part Four (pages 192-98). -- Ed.

China prospered for thousands of years, and Annam, Burma, Korea, Siam, and other small states were able to maintain their independence [largely as tributary states of the Chinese Empire].... If we want China to rise to power, we must not only restore our national standing but we must also assume a great responsibility towards the world.... Only if we "rescue the weak and lift up the fallen" will we be carrying out the divine obligation of our nation. We must aid the weaker and smaller peoples and oppose the Great Powers of the world.... Then will we be truly "governing the state and pacifying the world."

Perhaps, then, internationally as well as in the nation and in the family, the position of equality is attractive if one is but a unit among others, some of them stronger. A certain freedom and independence also then seem desirable. But it is even better, if possible, to be the center that rules the whole; then control and obedience, the proper performance of various roles, are seen as the desirable kinds of behavior -- are seen by the central figure of authority, at least, as leading to the good of all concerned.

VI. The Soviet Style of Chess[21]

Leopold H. Haimson

It is in the spirit with which Soviet players approach the chess situation that both Western and Soviet commentators have found the most distinctive characteristics of the Soviet school of chess.[22]

The perfectly valid generalization is frequently made that Soviet masters view chess as a struggle, as a battle of intellects and wills, in which the attack necessarily must be assumed -- in which victory depends upon keeping or wresting the initiative from the opponent. As Michael Botvinnik, the present world champion, puts it (1951; p. 39):

People of different character play chess -- some more actively, others more passively. But among Soviet players there are no completely quiet players. Basically, we strive for the initiative, for the attack; and in defense, for the counteroffensive.

The view that chess is a struggle in which the initiative must be wrested and/or held, while indeed characteristic of Soviet players, is by no means a unique feature of the Soviet school of chess. The distinctive feature of the approach of Soviet masters really lies in a further assumption -- in their belief that the two decision-making capacities that are pitted against each other in a chess game are limited and vulnerable. Since both the participants are considered to be intellectually and psychologically vulnerable, the outcome of the game may be wholly or partly decided by the degree to which the decision-making capacity of each of them is taxed and strained in the course of the game.

---

21. Reproduced from Leopold H. Haimson, The Soviet Conception of Action, in Theory and Practice (a book now in preparation). The article has been condensed for reproduction here.

22. I am indebted for some of the conclusions presented here to a series of conferences with Mr. Reuben Fine, an American chess master and commentator who has had considerable experience in playing against Soviet masters in the past fifteen years.

In order to understand their rationale for this assumption, it is necessary to consider another aspect of the thinking of Soviet chess masters -- their evaluation of the relative significance of positional and combinational play.

Soviet chess commentaries stress the importance of positional considerations -- in the deployment of the chess pieces and in the occupation by them of the main lines of attack -- but they emphasize as well that from such positional considerations no abstract universal rules are to be derived (cf. Botvinnik, 1951; pp. 49ff.). Positional considerations are relative to specific concrete positions, and the conclusions to be drawn from them must always be regarded as provisional in nature.

The denial by Soviet masters of the existence of universal positional laws, of the availability of any universal strategic criteria that might automatically be applied to all game situations, impels them to search continuously for new variations, for innovating countermoves against the schemes of development that are currently favored. In his monograph on Soviet chess, Botvinnik suggests that the development and testing of such innovations is a necessary element in a player's preparation for an important match.

The belief of Soviet players in the limited and provisional character of existing knowledge about positions has driven them to search continuously for new approaches to the game. But as far as the actual game situation is concerned, this belief has also had an almost opposite effect: it has impelled Soviet masters to consider the chess game, and particularly its opening phase, as a struggle for familiar and psychologically suitable positions. Since all knowledge about chess is necessarily spotty, since all criteria of positional validity are per force provisional, the Soviet player must attempt to force his opponent into positions that are familiar and psychologically suitable to himself and -- if possible -- unfamiliar and psychologically unsuitable to the opponent. Botvinnik states (1951; p. 11):

Every master [must] direct the course of the game into a channel which is suitable and habitual for him. In order to confine [bind] the struggle to such a style, one must, first of all, impose one's will on the opponent, one must wrest the initiative in the battle.

Another element enters into this definition of the chess game as a contest of wills. Soviet masters stress the vulnerability of the decision-making capacity of the player not only in the light of the limited information available to him, but also because he is expected to make his decisions under battle conditions and against time pressure.

The stress that Soviet masters consequently place on the elements of familiarity and psychological preparedness in the ability of a player to solve the problems created by his opponent's moves is expressed in almost every single one of their discussions of chess tournaments and matches.

Tied to the conviction of Soviet masters that all positional knowledge is necessarily provisional and limited is another distinctive feature of their style --

the emphasis laid on the development of relatively short-range combinations. The distinction between the combinational orientation of Soviet players and the "positional" style of most Western masters is a quite subtle one.[23] It is not that Soviet masters ignore or minimize the importance of positional considerations. Botvinnik's very definition of the nature of combinations -- with its positional overtones -- is evidence enough for this (1951; p. 27):

What is the content of chess combinations? From the very first, the chess player learns that there exist habitual material relationships among the pieces: e. g. that the rook is stronger than the knight, that the bishop is equal to three pawns, while the rook is roughly equivalent to a bishop and two pawns. The greatest art in chess is to find possibilities which lead the game into positions in which the usual quantitative relationships among the pieces no longer obtain.

Thus the combinational player must gain positional advantages as the necessary points d'appui for the development of his specific combinations against the opponent's pieces. Unlike the positional player, who, at least in the openings and in the middle game, is inclined to threaten pieces for the sake of positional advantages (i.e. in order to occupy space), the combinational player attempts to gain these positional advantages (i.e. occupies space) during the early phases of the game in order to develop his threat against the pieces. Ultimately, the difference between the two styles is a matter of relative emphasis and relative timing.

We have observed that Soviet chess doctrine advances two major objectives: (1) that the Soviet player is to gain the material or psychological initiative by forcing his opponent into positions that are more familiar to the Soviet master than they are to his adversary; and (2) that the Soviet player is to exploit this initiative for the development of powerful combinations against his opponent's pieces. Let us now consider how these objectives are specifically implemented -- with the white as well as with the black pieces -- in the various phases of the chess game.

As far as the opening phase of the game is concerned, the selection of a specific system of openings in a match or a tournament is rarely based on any general analytical rules, on any abstract view of the game as a totality. It is usually founded not on a comparative evaluation of all possible openings, but on a study of the opponent's favorite style and predilections, and on an estimate of the Soviet player's own strengths and weaknesses.

As might be expected, the opening styles followed by most Soviet masters vary significantly, depending on whether they are holding the white or the black pieces. With the white pieces, which entitle the player to the initiative of the first move, they are inclined to depend on familiar and thoroughly tested openings. With the black pieces, which give the opponent the advantage of the first move, they resort more frequently to the use of new variations -- even when they

---

23. The development of the Western "positional" style of chess under the influence of Steinitz and others was discussed by the author in an earlier part of the paper that is not reproduced here. -- Ed.

are aware that these variations contain certain over-all positional weaknesses.

In spite of the stylistic differences that I have discussed, the <u>objective</u> pursued by Soviet players with whites and with blacks is essentially the same. It is to seize or to maintain the psychological and material initiative -- to gain the "positional" advantage -- on the basis of which a combinational attack can be mounted against the opponent's pieces. Thus, as Botvinnik points out, the Soviet chess doctrine requires that -- with both whites and blacks -- the openings be "tied to the development of combinations in the middle game" (p. 51; p. 46).

When one considers the actual games of Soviet masters, it becomes apparent that the realization of this general objective depends on the preservation or gain of <u>an advantage in tempo</u> over the opponent.

When they are playing with the white pieces, Soviet masters generally attempt, during the opening phase of the game, to commit their opponents to a static and passive defense. As soon as this goal has been attained, the offensive is usually shifted from its original positional objectives to the exploitation of the positional weaknesses that may have appeared as a result of the opponent's defensive commitments in the other sectors of his front, or, more frequently, it is turned into a series of direct combinational attacks against the opponent's exposed pieces.

As Soviet commentators frequently point out, the success of such tactical shifts hinges not only upon the surprise that may be inflicted on the psychologically committed opponent but also, and especially, on the more tangible superiority of tempo that may have been achieved as a result of his initial defensive commitments.

When the black pieces are used, the advantage in tempo has to be <u>wrested away</u> from the opponent; and Soviet players are consequently more inclined in this instance to direct the game from the very beginning into tense and complex positions and to introduce in this process new and relatively untested variations. The opponent may be compelled thereby to diagnose positions quite different from those he had originally expected -- and this in battle conditions and under the relentless pressure of the clock. If the opponent chooses to stick to his original strategic plan, he will have to make -- in haste -- the necessary adjustments imposed by the unexpected positional complexities that have arisen. If, on the other hand, he chooses to abandon his original plan, he may thereby allow the psychological -- and possibly the material -- initiative to pass to the Soviet player. In either instance, it is hoped, the opportunity will have been created for the black pieces to gain the all-important superiority of tempo.

The combinational counteroffensive style with the black pieces that I have just described probably constitutes the major contribution that the Soviet school has made to chess thinking, and David Bronstein has been the most brilliant exponent of it. In the 1951 world championship match, he won four out of his five victories over Botvinnik in this fashion, a most remarkable percentage of victories with black pieces. (Cf. particularly the fifth, seventeenth, and twenty-first games of this match.)

Botvinnik, as well, is an advocate of counteroffensive tactics and of vigorous combination play with the black pieces, but he is attuned to the restrictions that may be present in any concrete position; indeed, he may well be considered as one of the great masters of positional play. This degree of awareness of positional considerations is not manifested by some of the younger Soviet chess masters, in spite of all the injunctions of the "leaders" of the Soviet school.

So profound is the distaste of these players for any extended "passive defense," so great is their need to play for victory rather than for a draw, that they are blind, in many instances, to the limitations inherent in certain positions. As Winter points out, this was the negative side of Bronstein's aggressive and imaginative play with the blacks in the world championship match (Winter and Wade, 1951; p. 24):

> This dynamic quality of Bronstein's chess contains its own weakness. Occasionally, he fails to realize that the conditions inherent in a position render tactical combinations an impossibility, and this lack of objectivity cost him the seventh and nineteenth games, when dour defensive play instead of counterattack would probably have secured a draw.

Such, then, is the price that young Soviet players such as Bronstein have frequently had to pay for the boldness and aggressiveness of their style of play with the black pieces. But it must be kept in mind that the emphasis laid by Soviet chess theorists on the positional requirements for the development of combinations constitutes a specific warning against this very tendency.

In the preceding discussion, I have attempted to outline the distinctive characteristics of the style of Soviet chess masters -- the grounds on which it is valid, I believe, to speak of a school of Soviet chess. I have observed that fundamental to the approach of Soviet masters to the game is the definition of the chess situation as a battle between the limited and vulnerable decision-making capacities of two specifically human antagonists -- rather than a contest of abstract principles and strategies.

It is apparent from the foregoing that the style of Soviet chess masters reflects with remarkable faithfulness the definition of man's interaction with his environment that underlies the Soviet ideal of "conscious activity."

The world of the Soviet chess master -- like that of the model of the new Soviet man -- is a world of conflict in which the actor must seek to impose his will upon the situation. But the offensive, the initiative that is required of him, can and must be taken only in a situation which, at the very least, is more familiar to the actor than to his opponent. As much as possible, the real objectives of the attack should be defined only after the opponent has been psychologically and/or materially committed to a set strategy of attack or defense, and after this strategy has been successfully diagnosed by the Soviet player.

These are the concrete frames of reference -- the tangible signposts -- that

are required to guide the activity of the new Soviet man in chess, just as much
as in other aspects of contemporary Soviet life.

VII. The Soviet Image of Corruption[24]

Martha Wolfenstein

In the Soviet press there regularly appear articles exposing various forms
of corruption. These contrast with the larger number of articles that vaunt the
great and continuing achievements of the Soviet people in all fields of material
and intellectual work or call for still higher levels of achievement. In the articles on corruption this high moral atmosphere is relaxed, and we get a picture of
various unregenerate characters perpetrating large or small swindles with confidence, enjoyment, and success. These articles are usually written as feuilletons, in a heavily satirical style; the escapades of the malefactors sometimes
achieve a level of high comedy. While literary and dramatic criticism insistent-
ly demand the depiction of ideal types, these feuilletons perpetuate the genre of
older Russian and early Soviet satire (e.g. of Gogol, Ilf and Petrov). This is
permissible as an exposure of actual scandals; the pieces are ostensibly report-
age, names are named and corrective measures are demanded. After an interval of some weeks or months follow-ups appear in which relevant agencies state
that they have confirmed the findings reported in the articles and have taken appropriate measures, usually far from extreme.

In the first part of this study I shall analyze the characteristic plots of the
scandals in the Soviet press, indicating the forms of malfeasance, the types of
characters involved, the life atmosphere that is evoked, the conflict between
crook and critic, and the suggestion of omniscience at the top level. In the second
part, I shall discuss interpretations of these scandals given by Soviet DP's, and
the presumable intentions of the regime in exposing corruption in the particular
form chosen.

1. Scandals in the Soviet Press[25]

a. Forms of Malfeasance

The malefactors may be classified under three main heads: <u>nonperformers</u>,
who maintain nonfunctioning enterprises at considerable cost; <u>embezzlers</u>, who
subvert public property for their own advantage; and <u>grabbers</u> of various sorts

---

24. This article is based on work done for the Center for International Studies,
    Massachusetts Institute of Technology.
25. This section is based on all the feuilletons dealing with corruption (42 arti-
    cles) that appeared in translation in <u>The Current Digest of the Soviet Press</u>
    during 1951. The original feuilletons appeared in various Soviet newspapers,
    mainly <u>Pravda</u> and <u>Izvestia</u>. For a list of references to the feuilletons
    cited in this and the following section, see below, page 448. This list includes
    references (1-27), as given in the text after a title.

(accumulators, impostors, junketeers, coercers, bribe-takers), who manage to get money and other benefits in illegal ways.

Nonperformers. "In a Peaceful Backwater" (1) describes a lecture bureau in Novosibirsk which reports great and expanding activity to the delight of the City and Executive Party Committees. In fact no lectures are being given. Fees for lectures are listed in the names of persons who know nothing about it, and are collected by those running the bureau.

A similar scandal on a higher level is reported in "Soft Berth" (2). A bureaucrat maintains a trust whose functions have been made superfluous as a result of reorganization. He should have asked for abolition of his trust, but he could not give up the grandeur of his position, nor its material perquisites and opportunities for patronage.

"Jugglers" (3) describes a new combine for the manufacture of refrigerators in Kemorovo. The first director assembles a large staff, then absconds with funds. A new director reorganizes the staff and draws up the first year's accounts. Nearly 200,000 rubles have been expended; not a single refrigerator has been produced. The director is unperturbed. He decides to expand the production plan for the next year and to ask for more than twice the amount.

Embezzlers. In "Technology of the Hairpin" (4) a man from Moscow, vacationing at a nearby village, happens to notice in a notions store that all the hairpins are light-colored. Moved with sympathy for brunettes, he starts to manufacture brown hairpins, getting a farm woman to dip the light-colored ones in brown lacquer. He disposes of them through a friend who is chairman of the local notions store. However, he is not long satisfied with this small-scale operation. He draws others in, obtains materials and large-scale equipment; "galvanizers, automatic and semi-automatic punches, electric motors and even presses weighing several tons." He then invites the local farm chairman to tea; the tea is 100 proof and there is plenty of good food. The farm chairman agrees to provide workers for hairpin manufacturing. Next the houses of collective farmers and communal property are rented for the enterprise. After three years the farm is declining, but hairpin manufacture is booming. Some of the farmers protest. The chairman retorts: "'So you oppose hairpins? ... You're enemies of culture!'" (In an unpublished paper on "Images of Soviet Lower Depths," Vera Schwarz has pointed out how asocial characters use official slogans in a mocking way.) By a highhanded procedure the chairman is re-elected, and the hairpin business goes into a further expanding phase.

"In the Country Seat of the Cherkasovs" (5) describes the operations of the director of a sugar combine who with his wife is doing a little illegal business in pigs. The Cherkasovs become depressed when they find that the collective farmers are underselling them. Then, however, they get a brilliant idea: "What if ordinary pork could be transformed into some more refined product? And soon a variety of salami called Cherkasovka appeared on the Rybnitsy market.... The

cost of this speedily growing concern was met by the state, and was officially
described as 'expenditures incurred in sugar distillation.' Yet the specialists
in sugar distillation were dismissed for 'lack of accommodation' and replaced by
storemen and agents who knew their way around the pork and salami business."
Cherkasov regularly sends "material tokens of respect" to his superiors, who
"never failed to remark, 'What an obliging, what an exceptionally considerate man
is our Filipp Faddeyevich!'" An inspection commission from the Sugar Beet
Trust throws the Cherkasovs into a panic. However, due no doubt to the inter-
vention of their protectors, the only consequence is that they are to be transferred
to another sugar trust, where they foresee that they can set up a bigger and better salami business.

In "Near Barnaul" (6) a collective farm chairman rents communal land to
city people. Similarly, in "Pal Mitya" (7) a collective-farm chairman hands out
garden plots to nonfarm people. In "Changing Wine into Water" (8) a director of
a meat trust regularly claims short weight in meat deliveries, and carries on an
illegal trade in meat and fat. "A Bubbly Business" (9) reports the mysterious
disappearance of thousands of bottles of champagne.

Grabbers: Accumulators. "On the Quiet" (10) tells of a chief engineer of a
municipal administration who obtains authorization to plan streetcar lines,
power installations, etc. He holds multiple jobs and even collects unused vaca-
tion pay from several agencies while he goes off to the seaside. He shows limit-
less anxiety to please his superiors, who manifest their appreciation in frequently rewarding him with bonuses and additional fees. The chief of the Control and
Inspection Administration finds that the engineer has in recent years got nearly
150,000 rubles under false pretenses. The City Executive Committee now recom-
mends that he be prosecuted, but no action is taken.

Impostors. A man who poses as an old friend of Gorky and implies that he
is very close to the Minister of Education is described in "A Grab-All on the
Faculty" (11). He offers his services as professor, lecturer, writer, journalist,
and lectures on all subjects, but his favorite theme is "Love, Friendship, and
Comradeship." His life is at variance with the lofty sentiments he expresses.
When he is accused of being mercenary, he defends himself: "'When I am lecturing, I do not think of money, I am completely absorbed in my work. The thought
of money comes only after the state of spiritual ecstacy.... I realize that this
trait of mine is ugly. I am combating it, but am unable to get rid of it at once.'"
A similar character is described in "Zealous Pen" (12), a "hopeless ignoramus
and militant graphomaniac" who has occupied the position of staff propagandist in
a research institute of agricultural machine building for over two years.

Junketeers. A Crimean town where a health resort is to be built is the subject of a geological study because of the sliding of the soil. "Abrasion in a Health
Resort" (13) reports how visiting specialists come yearly from the north to discuss with the local authorities the possible causes of the landslide. They carry

on their speculations while sunning themselves on the beach. Students preparing dissertations come along and draw advisers' fees. Each new specialist starts to survey the situation all over again. This has been going on for ten years and no conclusions have been reached. The writer of the article suggests that rain water carried away the top soil due to clogged sewers. None of the geologists would have noticed this, however, as they only come in the sunny season.

Coercers. In "At Home and on Duty" (14) a lieutenant of militia evicts tenants to take their flat himself. He proceeds to expropriate the neighbors' gardens and produce. Then he decides he needs larger quarters; he wants to take over the neighboring flat, which is occupied by an old woman. He gets a cold attic for the old woman, who, however, does not want to move. He then stuffs up her chimney so that her flat is filled with smoke and she leaves.

Bribe-takers. Bribing of officials is incidental to many of the forms of malfeasance already described. There are additional instances such as that described in "In Exchange for Shashlyk" (15). At a Turkmenian agricultural technicum, degrees are given in exchange for "a ram or any other valuable object." For the possessors of such goods the undertaking of a long course of study becomes unnecessary. Soon it becomes known that there are three miracle-workers (the venal officials of the technicum) who can give one in a moment all the wisdom taught in the school.

b. Types of Crooks

A characteristic of some of these swindlers that is repeatedly mentioned is that they are plump and well fed. Pal Mitya, the farm chairman who is disposing of collective property so freely, is portly and red-cheeked (7). A similar farm chairman is "stocky" and gives an "impression of good health" (6). Mrs. Cherkasov, who is rushing off to market to sell a pig, is a "plump lady" (5). These characters are usually jovial, crude, brazen, and untroubled. However, on occasions when things go wrong or exposure seems imminent, they may reproach each other or become panicky or depressed (5).

Another characteristic appears in officials in more urban centers who are confronted by critics (the story of such critics and their difficulties will be considered later). These officials are irritable, excitable, and vindictive. They are blustering and threatening toward the critics who oppose them, and relentless in retaliation (16, 17). Officials who suppress the work of innovators are pictured in a similar way.

On a higher level, the bureaucrat who values not only the profits but also the prestige of his position is described in this way (2). He "furnishes his study in the style of one of the numerous Louis, places on his desk a massive cast-iron inkstand depicting wrestlers preparing for a bout, and hangs notices around the walls making categoric demands on visitors: 'Do not come without appointment,' 'When you have finished your business, leave'" (2).

An impostor shows yet other characteristics: "a stealthy gait, ingratiating mild manners, arrogant, oily eyes, and amazingly facile hands" (11).

Thus we find a variety of negative traits: fat complacency, wallowing in the pleasures of the flesh, irritability and personal vindictiveness, grandiosity and love of display, and insinuating deceptiveness. All these traits are opposed to the ideal Bolshevik character, which eschews present gratification, demonstrates firm emotional control, does not descend to personal animosities, is contemptuous of unnecessary display, and never attempts to ingratiate.

c. Life Atmospheres

Two alternative life atmospheres are noticeable in these stories of swindlers: one of Oblomovism combined with euphoria, the other of crude enterprise and great activity.

In the first case, no work is accomplished, but there is plenty of good food and drink. In "Reeds Were Whispering" (18) an inspector comes to a factory that is markedly deficient in its output. He is escorted to the office. "'And what is this?' he asked severely.

"'Well, a chicken, cucumbers ...,' Manager Kosarev explained. 'Please have a rest and eat something. After that you will have more strength for business.'

"The plant manager did not have to spend a long time convincing his superior, soon they were having a friendly chat while the bad quality of production, the failure to fulfill the plan, and the exhausted account in the State Bank were forgotten.

"When evening came and the workers were leaving the plant they could hear two blurred voices singing:

"'Reeds were whispering ...'"

In "Mefody Golubets & Co." (19) Mefody Golubets maintains a farm that has no legal status and has never even been registered. He devotes himself to providing local officials with grain to fatten their geese or with pigs at bargain rates: "Comrade Fillipov likes goose with apple sauce or fried turkey with buckwheat gruel as an entree.... Once he ⌊Golubets⌋ found out that Yevgeny Nikolayevich Malyarevsky, a high-ranking official, had a high respect for pork chops. And so, one cloudless day, Golubets had a pig for Yevgeny Nikolayevich."

A similar atmosphere of nonproductivity and gratification pervades the story of the geologists sunning themselves at the Crimean resort (13).

In contrast to this there are the stories of bustling and successful, though illegal, enterprise. The hairpin and salami businesses already cited are examples. Where legal operations show delays, inefficiency, etc., and are repeatedly excoriated and exhorted in the press on these grounds, the illegal undertakings seem to be run with great energy and success. On a more individual basis, the impostors and the engineer with the multiple jobs show a similar incessant activity, though here the output is negligible.

A striking characteristic of the lives of these swindlers is the brazenness and openness with which they carry on their illicit activities. The director of a meat trust tells an employee to draw up a statement that the meat delivery is 339 kilograms short. The employee objects that this is not true.

"'Go on, write that statement,' said Manto threateningly. 'You are working here, and you'd better learn how wine can be turned into water.'" When the employee becomes indignant, he is told his services will not be needed (8).

When, in "Troublesome Character" (20), a chief mechanic takes it into his head to criticize the poor production in his organization, his superior tells him to resign or he will be dismissed with a bad character reference. As the chief mechanic refuses to resign, his superiors demote him in the hope that he will get offended and leave. "Everything was arranged according to standard procedure, quite crudely and obviously."

All these alleged aspects of the lives of crooks, satiated inactivity or energetic private enterprise, together with brazen unconcern for secrecy, must contrast sharply with the usual lives of Soviet citizens.

d. Slight Deprivational Impact

It is striking that in most of these stories no point is made about anybody's suffering as a result of the crooks' operation. (Any critic who attempts to interfere is made to suffer, but that is incidental, not a direct result of the illegal operation.) In the main, what is shown is that the crooks and their collaborators are prospering and may even be benefiting others. Presumably the illegally manufactured hairpins and salami, for instance, met a definite need.

It is sometimes stated ironically that the crooks are moved by concern for others. Mefody Golubets, who maintains an illegal farm and is so zealous in providing good food for local officials, "sympathizes with delicate palates" (19). Such feeling for others' needs is probably considered patently cynical in the context of self-seeking greediness. But it is also probably regarded as intrinsically implausible in a culture where, as other articles bring out, concern with satisfying the consumer is slight and where there is overt pleasure in frustrating him. (There are stories, for instance, of uncomfortable train journeys and bad hotel accommodations in which the effect of material inadequacies is greatly aggravated by the brusque and malign behavior of the attendants.)

There are only a few instances in which the activities of the crooks are made out to be directly deprivational to others. In one such case, "Summer People" (21), a seaside camp for Pioneers is taken over by the families of local bureaucrats. They eat up the food that is supposed to be for the campers. As a result the bureaucrats' children gain five or six kilograms in weight in the course of the summer, and the other children gain only 500 or 700 grams. Thus the writer does not go so far as to say that the deprived children actually lose; they only gain considerably less than the others. In other instances, people are illegally deprived of their apartments, (14, 22). In yet another case, "Advertisement and Reality" (23), people who send money to a mail-order house but never receive

what they have ordered are said to suffer "disappointments and injured feelings."
Where farm plots are rented to outsiders or collectively raised pigs are sold illegally, the farmers presumably suffer, but this is not made explicit. In the majority of cases there is not, even on an implicit level, any identifiable victim of
the crooks' activities.

Perhaps we may understand this absence of stress on any deprivational effects in the following way. The writers of these articles, while exposing malefactors, must at the same time maintain the compulsory view that everyone is
well-off in the Soviet Union, no one is suffering. So, for instance, the account of
the mail-order house that fails to fill any orders (23) is turned into a demonstration of the high level of living. What are the people ordering? "What they want
is cameras, radios, opera glasses, musical instruments, paint, bicycles, watches,
and soccer shoes. These are all objects meeting the cultural needs that develop
when prosperity and happiness have entered a man's home. The very nature of
these orders attests to the material well-being of the Soviet people and to the
variety of their cultural needs." Thus, by a curious logic, the fact that nobody is
getting these luxuries is taken as proof that they have everything else they could
want.

e. Martyrs of Criticism

Corruption works partly through the bribing of higher-ups (of which I have
cited numerous instances), partly through the intimidation of subordinates.

Mutual amnesty is another important factor in the system of corruption.
This is a secular variant of "Judge not that ye be not judged." Stalin has castigated this as a "family way" of dealing with organizational problems: "Ivan
Ivanovich, a member of the leading top of such and such an organization, has, let
us say, committed a grave mistake and spoiled matters. But Ivan Fyodorovich
does not want to criticize him, to proclaim his mistakes, to correct his mistakes. He does not want to do so, as he has no wish to create enemies for himself. 'He has committed a mistake and spoiled matters -- well, so what? Who
does not commit mistakes? Today I spare him, Ivan Fyodorovich [Stalin confuses the two names] and tomorrow he will spare me, Ivan Ivanovich. For where
is the guarantee that I won't make a mistake?'" (Speech at 15th Party Congress,
December 3, 1927. Cf. Stalin, 1946-51, Vol. X, p. 329.)

In the otherwise smoothly working system of corruption the active critic is
a "disturber of the peace," a "troublesome character." These terms are used by
the feuilletons ironically, but they obviously also make sense quite literally. (We
may recall that according to Bolshevik doctrine it is a lamentable weakness of
human nature to want a peaceful and undisturbed existence.) The retaliation
against such critics is relentless. As they have violated the rule of mutual amnesty, every effort is made to expose some error in their work. Even if none
is found, they are demoted, fired, expelled from the ranks of Party candidates.
Frequently they are prosecuted for slander.

Party candidate Neznanov, in "It Happened at Raksha" (17), continually writes to the newspapers exposing plundering of collective-farm property, illegal dealings in pigs, etc. The public prosecutor is furious at this nuisance, accuses him of being a crook, an embezzler, and a plunderer. Neznanov is expelled from the ranks of the Party candidates. Members of the District Party Committee, when questioned afterward, say that perhaps they trusted the prosecutor too blindly, "'but whatever you say, Neznanov is a suspicious character.' 'Why?' 'He keeps writing to provincial organizations and newspapers.'" The prosecutor continues to pursue Neznanov on a variety of fabricated charges. "It started as a civil suit for damages, but the 'case' gradually 'swelled' and ever new evidence against Neznanov kept accumulating. Then the civil suit for damages became a 'criminal case.'"

In "Unpartylike Attitude toward Criticism" (24), a sergeant home on leave notices irregularities in the local veterinary center, and writes to the newspaper. The director of the veterinary center denies the charges and the newspaper retracts. The director then sues the sergeant for libel. The sergeant, however, has by now returned to his unit. "Contrary to all common sense," his father is brought into court on the libel charge. The father protests that while everything said about the veterinary center was true, it was not he who said it. Nevertheless, he is sentenced to one year of corrective labor. This is a "case of vengence for criticism unparalleled in our society."

In "Disturber of the Peace" (25), a projected tubing shop in a subway construction is very inefficiently organized. There are delays and waste; the directors keep obtaining new time limits and not meeting them for six years. An engineer put in charge of the tubing shop begins exposing the inefficiency in Party meetings and writing to the press. There is an inspection, but nothing happens: the inspector feels warmly toward the director but coldly toward tubing. Finally, work starts, but a machine breaks down. The directors now raise great hue and cry against the engineer, blaming him for bad work, and though the machine is quickly repaired, he is thrown out.

Thus the stories regularly end with the apparent defeat of the critic. Though he gamely continues his struggle, the odds against him seem massive and overwhelming. An isolated figure, he suffers the repercussions of his criticism; he is demoted, thrown out, entangled in threatening law suits.

f. How Is It Found Out?

With the excellent organization of corruption through bribery, intimidation, mutual amnesty, and counterattack against critics, it remains somewhat of a mystery how these scandals come to be known to the top level and so to be exposed in Pravda or Izvestia. The process of investigation is never revealed. This is no doubt in part related to Stalinist secrecy about intelligence department procedures. But it also seems to express more deep-lying feelings about knowing and guilt.

The articles express a double attitude about the concealment of the crimes they describe. On the one hand, it would seem as though these crimes could be concealed indefinitely. On the other hand, there are recurrent vague statements that everything eventually comes to light. Speaking of the illegal farm of Mefody Golubets, the writer exclaims: "And a farm is not a needle -- it cannot be concealed in a haystack!" However, this seems to be contradicted by the "seven years of the existence of this illegally born 'invisible' farm" (19).

Where officials of the technicum are trading diplomas for rams, we are told, "all these shady transactions could not, of course, remain hidden." The collegium of the relevant ministry passes a resolution to punish the officials and confiscate the bogus diplomas. However, months pass and nothing happens. (This is a recurrent theme in these stories and elsewhere in the Soviet press; endless resolutions are passed and nothing is done about them. It is only resolutions proceeding from the very top level that have power to transform life. Resolutions on all lower levels are apt to be spoken of with contempt as ineffectual, and officials are continually castigated for mistakenly thinking they have accomplished something in passing a resolution.) Thus the revelation of what was hidden led only to a resolution that was forgotten (15).

However, the fact that the hidden crimes are exposed in <u>Pravda</u> and <u>Izvestia</u> demonstrates that despite all venality, inadequacy, and obstruction on lower levels these things become known at the top. The suppression of the process by which they become known, together with the vague warning that everything must come to light, produces the illusion of omniscience at the top level. It is undoubtedly important to the Soviet elite to maintain this illusion of their omniscience in the minds of their subjects, and probably also in their image of themselves. In the film of the Battle of Stalingrad, Stalin looks at the map, which immediately opens up to the scene of the actual battle; he gives his directions as if he could see every detail of what is going on.[26]

The apparently isolated and ineffectual struggle of the virtuous and courageous low-echelon critic against his vicious and powerful superiors is seen from the top. It is through the intercession of the top leadership that the obscure hero or heroine will be vindicated. This exemplifies an older Russian pattern that has been perpetuated in Stalinism: the alliance of the leader and the people against the corrupt bureaucracy of intervening levels. (Unofficial anecdotes often express just the opposite: It is Stalin who is starving the people, etc.)

Aside from the utility of maintaining that the leadership is omniscient, there would seem to be a deep-lying Russian belief that true knowledge is omniscience. Empirical ways of thinking, which stress the detailed steps through which something happens and the detailed clues by which it is found out, have had less time

---

26. Cf. also the discussion of omniscience in "The Image of the Leader in Soviet 'Post-October' Folklore," Part Five (pages 234-42). -- Ed.

to take hold in Russia than in the West. The ideal of knowledge remains much
more an immediate and complete revelation of the core of events, of the soul of
another person. This is related to the great stress on motives rather than on
means. One sees this in older Russian literature, such as The Brothers Karamazov. There is no crime investigation in the Western sense of assembling
clues and reconstructing how the crime was committed. Ivan, once he confronts
his own guilty motives, understands everything. The omnipotence of motives is
implicitly assumed. In the Moscow trials, there was no reference to how the
crimes of the defendants were detected. Material clues adduced to substantiate
alleged acts were minimal. (Contrast the prominence of the typewriter, the
pumpkin, etc., in the Hiss trial.) The emphasis on motives and goals was greater than on means, with the double implication that once the bad motive exists,
the most extreme acts inevitably follow, and that where there have been bad acts
there must have been bad motives behind them. (On the esoteric level the latter
point was not believed, but was regarded as important in convincing the masses.
This esoteric use, however, suggests that the belief that nothing happens without having been willed may persist in the Bolsheviks on a less conscious level.)

In the stories about the crooks, another aspect that contributes to the impression of omniscience at the top is the reproduction of private conversations.
The stories are written in a literary style, replete with dialogue -- the writer
relates, and the reader can listen in on, the conversations of these crooks among
themselves. Fictional writing, which these stories approximate in style,
assumes the viewpoint of omniscience. But presumably from the Russian point
of view omniscience is not only a literary convention but a credible attribute of
the authorities. From the viewpoint of omniscience, the crooks are known. This
is enough. Their punishment, if not immediate, is inevitable. In Tolstoy's
phrase, "God knows the truth but waits."

g. Follow-Ups

Some weeks or months after the publication of a story of corruption a brief
paragraph appears reporting the follow-up. It is regularly stated that the article
has been discussed and investigated by some appropriate organization, a city
or province soviet executive committee or a ministry, and the report has been
found to be entirely correct. As to the malefactors and their various allies, protectors, etc., they mainly get off with a warning or a reprimand. Less often they
are dismissed from their posts or expelled from the Party. Occasionally a case
is referred to the prosecutor, or a prosecutor who has been postponing action is
instructed to proceed. Sometimes it is only stated that steps have been taken to
improve the work of an agency that up until now has been operating on a fraudulent basis.

As to the victims, mainly the persecuted critics, it is frequently stated that
they have been compensated, reinstated in their jobs, or that reinstatement has

been advised. However, there is some incompleteness and casualness here. Thus in the case of an engineer who was fired for criticism, while his superiors were reprimanded, it is not said whether he was reinstated (25). In the case of the father of a critic who was sentenced to a year of corrective labor, the follow-up tells us nothing further about his fate (24).

2. Readers' Reactions and Intentions of the Regime[27]

We may wonder what impression these stories of corruption make on the Soviet reader. Reactions of Soviet DP's suggest that such stories may be subject to considerable reinterpretation (though of course we do not know to what extent these DP's may be atypical in relation to the predominant Soviet public). In the view of these informants, the images of both crook and critic are transformed. Explanations are offered as to the duration of malfeasance and the timing of exposure. The uncertainty of punishment evokes a wide range of feelings and apprehensions. I shall take the responses of these informants as the starting point for speculations about further possible impacts of publicized scandals on Soviet citizens, and also about the intentions of the regime in publishing such stories.

a. The Crook Is No Villain

The reactions of former Soviet citizens were obtained to two feuilletons, "Disturber of the Peace" (25), and "In the Country Seat of the Cherkasovs" (5). In "Disturber of the Peace" the directors of a projected tubing shop have for six years delayed getting the shop going. Informants believe that this prolonged nonfunctioning was the case, but that it was not the fault of the directors. They were probably unable to obtain the materials they needed. One informant calls attention to the dates: 1944 et seq. At that time it was impossible to obtain metal equipment without a very high priority, which this shop probably lacked. This shifting of emphasis to the date illustrates the way in which Soviet readers frequently interpret newspaper articles, as shown from other interviews. By a displacement of emphasis to a detail not stressed by the writer they achieve a reversal of the intended meaning.

The nonperformance of the directors of this particular shop is seen by the informants as involved with the whole hierarchy of related agencies. Higher organizations failed to provide needed supplies. These particular directors were singled out because a scapegoat was needed. An older Russian feeling of communal responsibility may underlie these reactions. It seems arbitrary to focus blame exclusively at any one point. These feelings probably correspond to present Soviet reality; that is, the directors of such a shop are dependent on a large

---

27. The following material is based on interviews with six Soviet DP's. The interviewing was done in Russian and the newspaper articles were presented to them in the original.

network which they cannot control. However, the existence of such underlying feelings of communal guilt may contribute to the creation of corresponding social forms. The attempt to single out an individual malefactor and hold him exclusively responsible represents a countertendency. This may express the Westernizing trend in Bolshevism, the attempt to inculcate a strong sense of individual responsibility. This has not taken hold in the DP's interviewed, who see the individual on whom punishment falls as a scapegoat arbitrarily chosen out of an indefinite number who are equally guilty.

In the story of the Cherkasovs, the director of a sugar-beet enterprise is raising pigs and manufacturing salami on the side. Again the informants believe this, but they see it in a different light than that in which it is presented. They suppose the director needed the salami for barter in order to get equipment he could not otherwise obtain. He probably sent some of the salami to his superiors not as a bribe but as a sample of the product he was turning out. Here we see the operation of a translation rule observed by Leites and Bernaut (n.d.) in connection with the indictments in the Moscow trials. A certain act that was committed originally in an acceptable context (e.g. on orders from the regime) is placed for purposes of inculpation in an entirely different context (e.g. as an act of conspiracy against the regime). In the case of the salami manufacture, the readers show facility in translating backward; that is, displacing the identical act from a bad to a good context.

Another device of inculpation which is rendered null by the readers is the substitution of a vague general term for a specific act. The Cherkasovs are said in the story to be maintaining their pigs at state expense. Translated into concrete terms by our informants, this means that they are feeding the pigs on the waste products of the sugar-beet industry. This is no crime at all, but simply practical, thrifty, and enterprising.

As in the case of the nonfunctioning tubing shop, so also here, informants do not believe in the isolation of the alleged malefactors. They think that Cherkasov's doings were well known to his superiors, carried on with their approval and collaboration.

Thus by a variety of devices the reader may reverse the moral judgment of the feuilleton, substituting exculpation for inculpation of the alleged malefactor. However, our informants, who are DP's, emphasize anti-regime attitudes. Their way of decoding and reversing newspaper articles may represent only one sector of the Soviet public. We may therefore speculate on other possible reactions, those of less critical citizens. The spectacle of sin rampant is sometimes ritually evoked for the delectation of the virtuous, as in the traditional sermons of the New England preacher. In a similar way, the devoted Soviet citizen may enjoy the stories of satiated crooks wallowing in illegality. In older Russian satire, of which the feuilletons in the Soviet press are in many ways a continuation, the careers of crooks were a subject of amusement and delight. (In contrast to this,

our DP informants do not imagine the alleged crooks of the feuilletons having any
pleasure, but rather shivering in their boots as they anticipate retribution for
shortcomings that are beyond their control.)

For the Soviet citizen living in conditions of hardship and scarcity, the exposure of particular thieving or inefficient officials, presented as exceptions,
may have the effect of diverting blame from the regime. The reader is given a
legitimate target for his discontent. For the worker who feels that his superior
is taking advantage of his position, these exposés may give the assurance that the
official will not get away with it forever. To the lowly it may offer the consola-
tion of demonstrating the hazards of high position. Also, since in these exposés
officials and Party men are shown denouncing each other, this may convey to the
common worker that they are not a closed club united against him.

b. The Critic Is Not a Hero

In the feuilletons the critic from below who exposes the crooks is a righteous,
plucky, isolated individual who dares, and often bears the brunt of, retaliation
from those he attempts to expose. According to our informants, his motives are
much more self-seeking, and the risks he runs are much less. Thus the engineer
who in "Disturber of the Peace" defies the threats of his superior and even sacrifices his position to expose bad work, is seen by informants as a shrewd ca-
reerist who will gain promotion and get credit with the Party. He will probably
take the place of the director he exposed.

In the case of the Cherkasovs, where it is not explicitly stated that they were
denounced, the informants readily supply this missing piece. They adduce the
following possible motives for denunciation: personal revenge, having been passed
over in the distribution of gifts, and seeking advancement; an envious Party secretary may have wanted to prevent the director's getting a new position; hungry,
envious workers may have been infuriated by the director's taking a pig from the
communkhoz (communal property); Party men from whom denunciations are required may have written to the local newspaper; a worker may have been ambi-
tious to break into print as a rabkor (worker-correspondent).

Where in the official picture the critic is a lonely hero, informants see him
as inspired by a Party official or someone else higher up. He is being used, acting on instructions, running little or no risk. In the official picture, the good man
on the lower level fights the good fight, suffering, maligned, mistreated, and
alone, because he cannot see wrong flourish and not raise his voice against it.
One day the powerful ones at the top see his struggle, hear his cry, and intervene to punish his wicked tormentors and give him his due reward. This version utilizes a traditional Russian fantasy of the alliance of the people and the
leader against the wicked bureaucrats who intervene between them. In the version presented by our informants, the relationship between the leadership and
the good little man is a less mystical and less noble one. The leadership uses the
lower-echelon critic as a tool. Just as the individual crook was seen as arbi-

trarily isolated from a larger network in which he was enmeshed, so the individual critic is seen as involved in a larger scheme. The desperate struggle of the individual critic appears as a dramatic fiction. The alleged crook appears not as a wicked individual, but as one who is hard pressed in a vast system which he cannot control and maneuvering as best he can to meet impossible requirements. The critic emerges as an agent in a complicated scheme of controls. It is equally arbitrary to assign blame to one and credit to the other.

The dramatically evoked hostilities between critic and crook may also be a fiction. In "Disturber of the Peace" (25) angry conversations are related in which the director threatens the engineer who is exposing him, while the engineer remains resolute in his righteous opposition. An informant imagines that this relation may have been quite different. The critic "may be a decent man who had no choice but to follow orders. He will probably 'sit' next if conditions are beyond improvement. [The informant supposes that the critic will replace the deposed director, who will have been sent to prison.] It is possible that between the engineer and the director there was an entirely different kind of conversation before the latter's arrest. They may have shaken hands, with the engineer expressing his regrets that he had been instrumental in the fall of the director, and the director expressing his good wishes that the other might not fall into his shoes."

The malcontents thus oppose to the moral simplicities of the official view, with its sharp opposition of black and white, the older Russian moral intricacies, the mutual involvement of each with all, the paradoxes in the depths of the human soul, the mysterious affinity of good with evil. Again, we do not know how widespread such reactions are, to what extent they are those of only a small minority.

It may be added here that while the critic is generally presented in the Soviet press as a very positive character, there are exceptions. Thus occasionally a fraudulent critic or a false accusation is exposed. A piece called "Gossipmonger" (26) indignantly exposes a bogus critic. A man named Stroilov, in Kuibeshev, once convicted for shady dealings, is furious against the prosecutor and becomes a worker-correspondent castigating others' wickedness. He picks up old women's gossip in the market place and in corridors of public buildings and writes enormous volumes of complaints and warnings. "It would appear that the town of Kuibeshev is entirely inhabited by scoundrels, rogues, embezzlers and fornicators, and that there is only one irreproachable honest, thoroughly Soviet man on Kuibeshev soil -- Stroilov himself." His accusations are not confirmed. Such slanderers of "our wonderful people" should be held criminally liable. It is stated that Stroilov manages to live without working; thus it seems to be suggested that he lives by blackmail. He projects his own vices. And he is motivated by revengeful feelings toward the prosecutor, who will appear delinquent in his duties if he does not pursue the endless cases exposed by the critic.

In "A Case Bogged Down in Formalities" (27), the wife of an injured worker pathetically appeals against heartless bureaucrats who tax her as an unmarried person because they cannot find the record of the marriage. Some weeks later Izvestia prints a correction of the mistake. A checkup shows that the officials were wrongly accused of red tape. The pretended victim was trying to get tax cuts by fraud. The editorial board has given a strict reprimand to the author of the feuilleton.

Thus, according to the official view, the exceptional bad critic is guilty of the motives (self-seeking, jealousy, revenge, etc.) that the discontented reader ascribes to critics generally. Perhaps the reader with the penchant for reversing would interpret the instances just cited in this way: the accused were guilty but have managed through influence to turn the tables on their accusers. The one officially presented as the bad critic might thus be turned back into the martyr of criticism.

c. Duration of Malfeasance and Timing of Exposure

The feuilletons picture illegal activities as going on over a period of years. Though they warn that such activities cannot go on forever, the situation as they describe it appears a stable one. The malefactors seem securely entrenched, bribing superiors and intimidating inferiors. However, the situation is envisaged by informants as far from stable. In a steadily worsening situation a point may be reached where concealment is no longer possible.

As informants have pointed out, the motives for denunciation are more manifold than those usually acknowledged in the press. Also these motives are systematically utilized by central agencies that support the critic. It has been repeatedly remarked by informants that articles exposing malefactors appear as part of a comprehensive campaign in which there is a cracking-down on a whole profession or type of shortcoming. Deficiencies that may have been condoned in various localities will then have to be exposed by local officials.

That an illegal operation has continued for years may suggest to the Western reader considerable safety and impunity for the operator. Our ex-Soviet informants, however, picture the operator as mainly apprehensive, waiting for the blow to fall. The exposure of an illegal operator after many years may have a positive impact on the ordinary Soviet reader. He may feel that though his superiors have been getting away with things for a long time, they will yet be caught.

As presented in the press, illegal operators are first exposed, their activities satirically elaborated, without a word about their being caught or penalized. It is not until the follow-up, after an interval of some weeks, that action on the case is reported. The manifest explanation is that the appropriate agencies must investigate and confirm the story, which, being done with all due legality, takes time. Also, we may suppose that the illegal operator must first be thrown out of the Party, since it is undesirable to prosecute a Party man. Those who wish to prosecute a particular official may await the expose in the central press that they can then use against him.

Some of our informants have their own view of the time relation of these events. They suppose that by the time the exposé appears in the central press the illegal operators will have been long since arrested; they are already "sitting" (i.e. in prison); they have already been sentenced to twenty-five years in Siberia. These readers in effect deny the methodical process of investigation implied in the interval between the exposure and the follow-up in the press. The exposé that is manifestly forward-looking, a challenge to corrective action, appears to these readers as a post-mortem on a closed case.

d. Ambiguity of Punishment

When the story of an illegal operator is first told in the press, his punishment remains unspecified and even on the manifest level uncertain. In the interval until the follow-up appears, the reader is thrown back on his own fantasies as to the fate of the malefactor. Leaving the story thus unfinished may be a powerful stimulus to guilt and fear in the reader. This indefiniteness may have a more terrifying effect than any specification. Moreover, the precise degree of punishment may be unimportant. What is certain is that the illegal operator has become liable to some penalty -- even if he only has a very uncomfortable time for some months struggling to extricate himself.

When the follow-ups appear, the punishments mentioned are usually moderate -- in the main reprimands, sometimes dismissal. Our informants are inclined to think that this is still only part of the story. The director who has been dismissed will have this fact inscribed in his workbook. He may not be able to get another position. He may be pursued further on other charges. Informants tend to anticipate much more severe penalties than those specified in the follow-ups. However, forced labor, for instance, would be passed over in silence. If more severe punishments are imposed than those acknowledged in the press, there would then be a counterpoint between mild words and harsh acts, especially in view of the jocose tone of the feuilletons. The effect might be one of mocking cruelty, the torturer maintaining a bantering tone while his victim struggles in the toils. (The opposite of this combination occurs in recent Soviet foreign policy, where strong words have accompanied mild actions.)

However, there is also the possibility that after the great purges of the 1930s, punishment became for a time less severe. It has also been frequently remarked that in the shortage of trained personnel, such men could not be spared. An informant adduces this in the case of Cherkasov; as a needed expert he might very likely be transferred to another post. Stories of arrested officials who have returned are widely known, as well as stories of arrested scientists treated with great consideration and given every facility to continue their work. The position on the preservation of personnel has been a double one. The loving conservation of prized personnel by the older Bolsheviks was followed by the devastating waste of the purges, after which trained persons were again for some years handled with care.

The ambiguity of punishment thus allows the imagination to range the gamut between fear and hope. If you are caught, God knows what may happen -- and yet the condemned do sometimes return. The latter possibility corresponds to an old Russian belief that nothing is irreversible. This appears, for instance, in a theme of Russian folklore, that of the dead czars who were believed still to be alive and who would one day return.

e. Intentions of the Regime

A major intention of the regime in exposing corrupt officials may be to justify the elaborate system of inspection and control. By relating the stories of malefactors, the regime says in effect: Look what would happen all the time if we did not have the controls we do have. In older Russian writing on the theme of human weakness, religious regeneration was sometimes called for; sometimes bad social conditions were blamed. Neither of these alternatives is usable today. In the souls of many there are bourgeois residues, tendencies to go with the stream instead of against. These are tendencies the earlier Bolsheviks strove and inveighed against, which are sometimes said to be no longer present in the true Soviet man. However, in the guise of bourgeois residues enough bad tendencies remain to require a binding system of controls. The exposure of the sort of thing that would happen in the absence of such controls justifies the system. In the feuilletons, inspection officials frequently fail to rectify a bad situation; prosecutors fail to pursue malefactors. This demonstrates the need for other agencies to check on inspectors, prosecutors, etc. Bolshevik leaders since the beginning of the Soviet regime have maintained the necessity of a suppagency to watch over bureaucracy.

In the main, the stories of corruption do not deal with major industries, and there may be a tendency to locate such activities in outlying or backward regions. By this displacement of emphasis onto nonessential areas, the impression is avoided that there is corruption in the core of Soviet productive life. The propagandist is caught between two requirements: to show the need for controls and to minimize the misdoings. If the corruption reported is peripheral, this might seem to weaken the implied justification of the central and over-all control system. However, to the Bolshevik way of thinking, a small internalized bad object may destroy the massive whole; it cannot be excessively militated against.

f. Relation to Pre-Soviet Satire

The controlled press of Czarist times permitted a considerable amount of leeway for liberal writers to express in satirical form their criticisms of bureaucratic corruption and other defects of the regime. The satirist there expressed the protest of a minority against the established order. The feuilletons of the Soviet press continue stylistically the tradition of this earlier satire. However, there is a reversal of position. The satire is now used by the authorities on behalf of the established order against the exceptional and the deviant.

Pre-Soviet satire appealed in a general way to the conscience of the reader; whether, when, and how it might be acted on remained indefinite. The feuilleton in the Soviet press is an explicit directive to action. Relevant agencies should proceed at once to prosecute the named malefactors. Editors are responsible for seeing that such action follows the exposés they publish.

The rationale of the feuilletons, in which a literary piece is a directive to specific action, embodies the general Soviet position on art, an extreme version of Platonist aesthetics. In literature and drama no major characters should be presented whose example could not be put literally into practice. A direct continuity between literature and life is assumed; what one sees in the theater one will go out and do. If in the feuilletons negative characters are presented, the context is presumably that of the rogues' gallery or police line-up, which may be supposed to preclude the readers' identification. The practical appeal is to control agencies and to popular approval of their activities.

All the following references are to issues of The Current Digest of the Soviet Press (Vol. III, 1951). References to the Soviet newspapers in which these feuilletons originally appeared are given in The Current Digest translations.

1. "In a Peaceful Backwater" (No. 35, pp. 36-37; follow-up, No. 41, p. 37)
2. "Soft Berth" (No. 29, p. 36)
3. "Jugglers" (No. 16, p. 27)
4. "Technology of the Hairpin" (No. 20, pp. 32-33; follow-up, No. 23, pp. 32-33)
5. "In the Country Seat of the Cherkasovs" (No. 29, p. 42; follow-up, No. 36, p. 36)
6. "Near Barnaul" (No. 12, pp. 40-41; follow-up, No. 20, p. 33)
7. "Pal Mitya" (No. 20, p. 26; follow-up, No. 32, p. 36)
8. "Changing Wine into Water" (No. 30, p. 26)
9. "A Bubbly Business" (No. 32, p. 35)
10. "On the Quiet" (No. 25, p. 26; follow-up, No. 32, p. 36)
11. "A Grab-All on the Faculty" (No. 34, p. 36)
12. "Zealous Pen" (No. 25, p. 32)
13. "Abrasion at a Health Resort" (No. 19, pp. 23-24)
14. "At Home and on Duty" (No. 19, pp. 24-25; follow-up, No. 24, pp. 25-26)
15. "In Exchange for Shashlyk" (No. 29, p. 42; follow-up, No. 36, p. 36)
16. "I Won't Stand for It" (No. 30, pp. 26-27)
17. "It Happened at Raksha" (No. 35, p. 29)
18. "Reeds Were Whispering" (No. 38, pp. 24-25)
19. "Mefody Golubets & Co." (No. 27, pp. 33-34)
20. "Troublesome Character" (No. 38, p. 24)
21. "Summer People" (No. 21, pp. 26-27)
22. "The Grigory Orlovsky Case" (No. 33, pp. 23-24)
23. "Advertisement and Reality" (No. 21, p. 34; follow-up, No. 25, pp. 32-33)
24. "Unpartylike Attitude towards Criticism" (No. 29, p. 33; follow-up, No. 32, p. 34)
25. "Disturber of the Peace" (No. 33, pp. 27-28; follow-up, No. 38, p. 29)
26. "Gossipmonger" (No. 24, p. 37)
27. "A Case Bogged Down in Formalities" (No. 17, p. 22; follow-up, No. 27, p. 35)

APPENDIXES

APPENDIXES

Appendix A

Recommendations for the Organization of Group Research

Columbia University Research in Contemporary Cultures involved the participation of some 120 people in work on seven cultures (China, Czechoslovakia, the East European Jewish shtetl, France, Poland, pre-Soviet Great Russia, Syria) over a four-year period, from 1947 to 1951. The research was done mainly between 1947 and 1950; the final year of the project was devoted to writing up materials and to some work on special problems by small, specially formed groups. On the basis of this experience, the following summary recommendations can be made for the organization of multidisciplinary groups to do exploratory work (Stage One, as described in the Introduction to this Manual[1]) on cultures at a distance in time or space.

1. The total group should provide for as much opportunity as possible for cross-cultural comparison, by

a. Simultaneous work on more than one culture

b. Including as participants individuals who have worked on other cultures

c. Including as participants members reared in other societies or with experience of other societies

2. The total group, and any groups within it, should be constructed on a flexible, open-ended, non-hierarchical basis. Participation should depend upon genuine interest and should be of many types, subject to changes of various sorts. This may obtained by

a. A non-hierarchical structure[2]

b. Flexible work procedures (cf. below on government-financed research) concerning time, etc.

c. Senior participation which is either voluntary or, if paid, brief, so that voluntary work and devoted overtime work can be given without resentment, and unsatisfactory written work can be rejected without guilt

d. A method of participant choice which is individual and stresses the total personality, including the state of training, type of ability, and so on, of the would-be participant

e. Avoidance of part-time participation in which the number of hours or the days of work are rigidly specified and must be fitted into inflexible schedules of the same sort in clinic or consultation room. Such rigid schedules do not fit in with the rhythms of this type of work and engender resentment from those participants who give their time without counting the hours. Highly paid psychiatrists and clinicians fit in better as senior volunteer participants where whatever time they are able to give is appreciated.

3. Materials collected or analyzed by the group should be completely shared in a usable form, processed so that each member can have a copy, and marked with an appropriate numbering system for ready reference.[3]

---

1. Cf. page 7.
2. For one example, cf. The Chart of the Structure of Research in Contemporary Cultures, Part Three (page 90).
3. While the system used in Research in Contemporary Cultures has been line numbering by page, it has been pointed out that, if materials are to be duplicated often, numbering by sentence throughout a paper (or, in work with

4. Verbatim records should be kept of all group discussions. Mechanical recording, ideally combined with having the ultimate transcriber present during the discussion, and with transcriptions in a form which can be distributed to each·member of the group, seems to be the most satisfactory method at present.

5. The project should be financed and administered in a way compatible with the above procedures. This has several implications, i.e.

a. The financing should be below the level of aspiration and planning of the group members, so that the gap between resources and aspiration is filled by extra effort and devotion.

b. The financing should be such that changes of plan are possible -- so that new people can be added, new consultants sought -- in order to preserve the sense of flexibility.

c. The bulk of the funds should be used to implement research rather than to pay the salaries of senior people. Money should be adequate for clerical work, for editing, for duplicating materials, for paying informants where this is necessary, for giving graduate students subsistence. Senior people should be attracted by interest in the problem and the facilities for research. One skilled clerical editorial worker per three full-time research workers, over the whole duration of the project, would seem to be a workable ratio (except during an intensive write-up stage). Provision in the project plans for a competent editor and for extra clerical workers (who would work periodically on a part-time basis when materials are being written up, rather than continuously) is a virtual necessity.[4]

d. It is essential in projects financed under government grants or contracts, or by foundations or institutions which are so large that very elaborate accounting and personnel procedures are necessary, that there also be some "free funds." These free funds should be at least in a ratio of one to twenty (one part free funds to twenty for which a strict accounting must be given). These free funds are needed to

i. Employ people who are unemployable in formal terms, e.g. aliens

ii. Pay for unorthodox acts and items (such as taking flowers to an informant, working on Sunday, buying two copies of the same book, paying for telephone calls in odd categories, etc.)

iii. Absorb all disputable elements in a contract at once without wasting time in discussion. Such small disputable, disallowed items can take a wholly disproportionate amount of staff time all along the line.

iv. Tide over periods between contracts, which the largest institutions are often unwilling to do.[5]

---

informants, numbering by interchanges) may be a more practicable method, especially for the selective memory of the visual-minded who may persist in remembering a point as being "halfway through X's second interview with the goldsmith at the top of the page."

4.   Experience has shown that it is almost invariably uneconomical to bring in temporary editorial or clerical assistants who are totally unfamiliar with the work that is being done and the individuals who are doing it. One method of handling the problem is to include as volunteers in the group one or two individuals with, for instance, professional editorial experience, who are interested in the research problem and who are paid during a period when they do editorial work. The ratio of editorial and clerical workers to full-time research workers, and the amount of periodic additional assistance that is necessary, will vary depending upon individual members of the research group -- e.g. how many can type up material in semifinished or finished form, how many do not type at all, how many may require assistance because of language difficulties, and so on.

5.   Some institutions turn back part of the overhead derived from contracts to permanent research groups to be used for such free funds for purposes of this sort. Alternative arrangements are small, incorporated nonprofit organizations which can build up a reserve by performing services to which

6. The project should be conceived broadly and generously enough to allow for a considerable amount of failure. This is particularly necessary because

    a. The use of volunteers means inevitable changes in personnel.

    b. When there is an applied aim, any opportunity for a participant to obtain better access to the country being studied must be taken advantage of, which means loss of personnel and the disruption of plans.

    c. Dependence upon individuals who are émigrés, foreign students, or political refugees, etc., as workers on an inaccessible area means, at the present time, dependence upon individuals who have undergone traumatic experiences, a certain number of whom are seriously disturbed. Some of them may break down, leave their work unfinished, and so on.

    d. Emphasis upon a field where psychoanalytic concepts are important means that a considerable number of participants will be attracted to psychoanalysis, or will be in analysis. It also means the participation of senior people with therapeutic responsibilities. Although it is possible to make project rules, such as "No therapy within the project" or "All those who go into analysis must report this to the convener or director," such rules break down in practice almost as completely as would rules about falling in love or not quarreling. As a result, eddies of unaccountable feeling between analysands, between would-be analysands and possible therapists, and so on, are bound to develop and may be disruptive.

7. Such projects cannot be expected to succeed inside governmental agencies but should be contracted for to outside organizations, as the organization of any government office itself is completely incompatible with this kind of work.

8. In projecting forward future uses of the materials accumulated in such a project, it must be recognized that the raw materials can be used only in the way they were intended to be used -- as a whole. They are not suitable for cutting up, coding, or casual quotation by those who have not taken the time to acquaint themselves with all the given materials on a given culture and the sequence in which these were collected. This means that their continued usefulness for future work will be dependent upon the type of custodial care that is provided for at the conculsion of research at a particular stage.[6]

---

their members contribute voluntarily, and for which payment is made to the organization. A third alternative is fixed-price contracts for which payment is made for a report, or a series of reports, where no specification is made as to how the money is to be expended.

6.   A permanent file of the Research in Contemporary Cultures working papers, published materials, and so on, has been established under the custody of the Institute for Intercultural Studies, 15 West 77th Street, New York 24, New York, where it will be available for research use by qualified individuals and organizations.

Appendix B

Participants in Columbia University Research in Contemporary Cultures and Successor Projects[1]

Theodora M. Abel	Geoffrey Gorer	James Mysbergh
Susan Viton Anderson	Daniel H. Gray	Joan Nicklin
Tomoe M. Arai	Leonard Guttman	Genoeffa Nizzardini
Ann Arcaro	Leopold H. Haimson	Irene Norton
Conrad M. Arensberg	Barbara Harris	John Orton
Freda Arkin	Elisabeth F. Hellersberg	Roger Peranio
Mark Atwood	Helen B. Henry	Vincenzo Petrullo
Alex Bavelas	Elizabeth G. Herzog	Evelyn R. Richmond
Jane Belo	Hazel Hester	David Rodnick
Ruth Benedict	Virginia Heyer	Elizabeth A. Rodnick
Sula Benet	Nelly Schargo Hoyt	Marion Marcovitz Roiphe
Elsa Bernaut	Hsien Chin Hu	Celia Stopnicka Rosenthal
Roman Bernaut	Margaret Huger	Irene Rozeney
Theodore Bienenstok	Ruby S. Inlow	Bertram H. Schaffner
Michel M. Borwicz	Alicja Marja Iwanska	Shepard Schwartz
Joseph Bram	Natalie F. Joffe	Vera Schwarz (Alexandrova)
Julie Buhler	Carol Kaye	Eli Shouby
Ruth Bunzel	Rose R. Kolmetz	Milada Souckova
Elena Calas	Ruth Landes	Rosemary Spiro
Nicolas Calas	Ruth Hallo Landmann	Gitel Poznanski Steed
Naomi Chaitman	Edith Lauer	Adolf F. Sturmthal
William K. C. Chen	Eleanor Leacock	Ina Telberg
Louise Giventer Cohen	Elsie Choy Lee	Lucy Mary Toma
Herbert S. Dinerstein	Leila Rozelle Lee	Stephan Toma
May M. Edel	Percy Lee	Ruth Valentine
Zekiye Suleyman Eglar	Nathan Leites	Y. C. Wang
Erik H. Erikson	Paulette D. Leshan	Anna Wu Weakland
Ralph Fisher	Michael Luther	John Hast Weakland
Rose Shirley Flood	Frances C. Macgregor	Marion Weidenreich
Denise M. Freudmann	Margaret Mead	Eric R. Wolf
Helen T. Garrett	Alfred Métraux	Martha Wolfenstein
Paul L. Garvin	Rhoda Métraux	Rose Wolfson
Ellen L. Godwin	Philip Mosely	Mark Zborowski
Joseph Gordon	Warner Muensterberger	Rosalind A. Zoglin

---

1. This list is not inclusive.

BIBLIOGRAPHY[1]

** Abel, Theodora M. 1948. "The Rorschach Test in the Study of Culture, "Rorschach Research Exchange and Journal of Projective Techniques, XII, No. 2, 79-93.

** ------, Jane Belo, and Martha Wolfenstein. 1953. "An Analysis of French Projective Tests." In Themes in French Culture: Preface to a Study of French Community by Rhoda Métraux and Margaret Mead (in press).

------, and Renata A. Calabresi. 1951. "The People as Seen from Their Rorschach Tests." In Life in a Mexican Village by Oscar Lewis. Urbana: University of Illinois Press. Chapter 13, pp. 306-318.

** ------, and Francis L. K. Hsu. 1949. "Some Aspects of Personality of Chinese as Revealed by the Rorschach Test," Rorschach Research Exchange and Journal of Projective Techniques, XIII, No. 3, 285-301.

* ------, and Natalie F. Joffe. 1950. "Cultural Backgrounds of Female Puberty," American Journal of Psychotherapy, IV, No. 1, 90-113.

Abraham, Karl. 1909. "Traum und Mythus. Eine Studie zur Völkerpsychologie," Schriften zur angewandten Seelenkunde, Heft 4. Vienna: Deuticke. Eng. trans. 1913, "Dream and Myths," Nervous and Mental Disease Monograph Series, No. 15.

------. 1912. "Amenhotep IV (Ecknoton). Psychoanalytische Beiträge seiner Persönlichkeit und der monotheistischen Alter-Kultus," Imago (Berlin Psycho-Analytical Society), Band 1, Heft 4, 334-360.

------. 1942. Selected Papers of Karl Abraham, trans. D. Bryan and A. Strachey. London: Hogarth Press and The Institute of Psycho-Analysis.

Acton, Harold, and Lee Yi-Hsieh. 1941. Glue and Lacquer, trans. from the Chinese. London: Cockerel Press.

Alexander, Franz. 1942. Our Age of Unreason. Philadelphia: Lippincott.

* Arensberg, C. M., et al. 1953. Techniques and Cultures. Washington, D.C.: Foreign Service Institute, U.S. Department of State (in press).

Armstrong, Edward A. 1946. Shakespeare's Imagination, A Study of the Psychology of Association and Inspiration. London: Lindsay Drummond.

Arnheim, Rudolf, et al. 1948. Poets at Work. New York: Harcourt, Brace.

Asch, S. E. 1951. "Effects of Pressure upon Modification and Distortion of Judgments." In Groups, Leadership and Men, ed. Harold Guetzkow. Pittsburgh: Carnegie Press. Pp. 177-190.

Bateson, Gregory. 1935. "Culture Contact and Schismogenesis," Man, XXXV, 178-183.

------. 1936. Naven. Cambridge: Cambridge University Press.

------. 1937. "An Old Temple and a New Myth," Djawa, XVII, 1-18.

---

1. This bibliography includes references throughout the Manual, theoretical works relevant to the field of culture and personality, particularly to the special division of this field called national character (starred once), and publications directly related to Columbia University Research in Contemporary Cultures and successor projects (starred twice), whether these are by members of the projects or are critical reactions to them.

Bateson, Gregory. 1941a. "The Frustration-Aggression Hypothesis," Psychological Review, XLVIII, No. 4, 350-355. Reprinted 1947 in Readings in Social Psychology, eds. Theodore M. Newcomb, Eugene L. Hartley, et al., pp. 267-269.

------. 1941b. "Experiments in Thinking about Observed Ethnological Material," Philosophy of Science, VIII, No. 1, 53-68.

------. 1942a. "Some Systematic Approaches to the Study of Culture and Personality," Character and Personality, X L, 76-84. Reprinted 1948 in Personal Character and Cultural Milieu, ed. Douglas G. Haring, pp. 71-77. (Revised Edition, 1949, pp. 110-116).

------. 1942b. "Morale and National Character." In Civilian Morale, ed. Goodwin Watson. Boston: Houghton Mifflin. Pp. 71-91.

------. 1942c. "Social Planning and the Concept of Deutero Learning." In Science, Philosophy and Religion, Second Symposium, eds. Lyman Bryson and Louis Finkelstein. New York: Conference on Science, Philosophy and Religion. Pp. 81-97. Reprinted 1947 in Readings in Social Psychology, eds. Theodore M. Newcomb, Eugene L. Hartley, et al., pp. 121-128.

* ------. 1943. "Cultural and Thematic Analysis of Fictional Films," Transactions, The New York Academy of Sciences, Ser. 2, V, No. 4, 72-78. Reprinted 1948 in Personal Character and Cultural Milieu, ed. Douglas G. Haring, pp. 78-84. (Revised Edition, 1949, pp. 117-123.)

------. 1944a. "Pidgin English and Cross-cultural Communication," Transactions, The New York Academy of Sciences, Ser. 2, VI, No. 4, 137-141.

* ------. 1944b. "Cultural Determinants of Personality." In Personality and the Behavior Disorders, II, ed. McVeigh Hunt. New York: Ronald. Pp. 714-735.

* ------. 1945. An Analysis of the Nazi Film Hitlerjunge Quex. New York: Institute for Intercultural Studies (mimeographed).

* ------. 1946. "The Pattern of an Armaments Race. I. An Anthropological Approach. II. An Analysis of Nationalism." Bulletin of the Atomic Scientists, II, Nos. 5-6, 10-11; Nos. 7-8, 26-28. Reprinted 1948 in Personal Character and Cultural Milieu, ed. Douglas G. Haring, pp. 85-93. (Revised Edition, 1949, pp. 124-132.)

* ------. 1947a. "Atoms, Nations, and Culture," International House Quarterly, XI, No. 2, 47-50.

------. 1947b. "Sex and Culture," Annals, The New York Academy of Sciences, XLVII, Art. 5, 647-660. Reprinted 1948 in Personal Character and Cultural Milieu, ed. Douglas G. Haring, pp. 94-107. (Revised Edition, 1949, pp. 133-146.)

* ------. 1949. "Bali: The Value System of a Steady State." In Social Structure Studies Presented to A. R. Radcliffe-Brown, ed. Meyer Fortes. Oxford: Clarendon Press. Pp. 35-53.

* ------. 1952. "Applied Metalinguistics and International Relations," Etc., X, No. 1, 71-73.

* ------, and Margaret Mead. 1941. "Principles of Morale Building," Journal of Educational Sociology, XV, No. 4, 206-220.

* ------, and Margaret Mead. 1942. Balinese Character: A Photographic Analysis. New York: Special Publications of The New York Academy of Sciences, II.

Bavelas, Alex. 1951. "Communication Patterns in Task-Oriented Groups." In The Policy Sciences, eds. Daniel Lerner, Harold D. Lasswell. Stanford: Stanford University Press. Pp. 193-202.

Belo, Jane. 1949. "Bali: Rangda and Barong." American Ethnological Society Monographs, No. 16. New York.

Benedict, Ruth. 1922. "The Vision in Plains Culture," American Anthropologist, XXIV, No. 1, 1-23.

------. 1923. "The Concept of the Guardian Spirit in North America," Memoirs of the American Anthropological Association, No. 29, 1-97.

* ------. 1928. "Psychological Types in the Cultures of the Southwest." In Proceedings, Twenty-third International Congress of Americanists, pp. 572-581. Reprinted 1947 in Readings in Social Psychology, eds. Theodore M. Newcomb, Eugene L. Hartley, et al., pp. 14-23.

------. 1931. "Folklore." In Encyclopedia of the Social Sciences. New York: Macmillan.

* ------. 1934. Patterns of Culture. Boston: Houghton Mifflin.

------. 1935. Zuni Mythology. 2 vols. Columbia University Contributions to Anthropology, No. 21. New York: Columbia University Press.

* ------. 1938. "Continuities and Discontinuities in Cultural Conditioning," Psychiatry, I, No. 2, 161-167. Reprinted 1948 in Personality in Nature, Society and Culture, eds. Clyde Kluckhohn and Henry A. Murray, pp. 414-423.

* ------. 1943. "Recognition of Cultural Diversities in the Post-War World," Annals, American Academy of Political and Social Science, CCXX-VIII, 101-107.

* ------. 1946a. The Chrysanthemum and the Sword. Boston: Houghton Mifflin.

* ------. 1946b. "The Study of Cultural Patterns in European Nations," Transactions, The New York Academy of Sciences, Ser. 2, VIII, No. 8, 274-279.

* ------. 1946c. Rumanian Culture and Behavior. New York: Institute for Intercultural Studies (mimeographed).

* ------. 1948. Patterns of American Culture. A lecture delivered to members of the United Nations Secretariat, Columbia University foreign students and International House residents at International House (New York), February 21 (mimeographed).

** ------. 1949. "Child Rearing in Certain European Countries," American Journal of Orthopsychiatry, XIX, No. 2, 342-350.

** ------. [1950.] "The Study of Cultural Continuities," and "An Outline for Research on Child Training in Different Cultures." In Towards World Understanding. VI. The Influence of Home and Community on Children under Thirteen Years of Age. Paris: Unesco. Pp. 5-13, 15-25.

* ------. 1952. Thai Culture and Behavior, an Unpublished War Time Study Dated September, 1943. Data Paper, No. 4. Southeast Asia Program, Department of Far Eastern Studies, Cornell University. Previously issued 1946, New York: Institute for Intercultural Studies (mimeographed).

Benét, Rosemary and Stephen Vincent. 1933. A Book of Americans. New York: Farrar and Rinehart.

** Benet, Sula. 1951. Song, Dance and Customs of Peasant Poland. New York: Roy.

** ------. 1952. Patterns of Thought and Behavior in the Culture of Poland. Columbia University Research in Contemporary Cultures (dittoed).

* Berger, Morroe. 1951. "'Understanding National Character' -- and War," Commentary, XI, No. 4, 375-386.

Bernard, Claude. 1878. Les phénomènes de la vie, 2 vols. Paris.

Bidyalankarana, Prince. 1926. "Rhyme Making and Singing in Rural Siam," Journal of the Siam Society, XX, No. 2, 101-127.

** Bienenstok, Theodore. 1950. "Social Life and Authority in the Eastern European Jewish Shtetl Community," Southwestern Journal of Anthropology, VI, No. 3, 238-254.

** ------. 1951. "Antiauthoritarian Attitudes in the Eastern European Shtetl Community," American Journal of Sociology, LVII, No. 2, 150-158.

Birdwhistell, Ray L. 1952. Introduction to Kinesics. Washington, D.C.: Foreign Service Institute, U. S. Department of State (mimeographed).

Boas, Franz. 1897. "The Social Organization and the Secret Societies of the Kwakiutl Indians." In Report of the U. S. National Museum for 1895. Washington, D. C. Pp. 311-737.

Bolitho, Hector. 1940. Roumania under King Carol. New York: Longmans Green.

Bonaparte, Marie. 1933. Edgar Poe, étude psychanalytique. Paris: Denoel et Steele.

* Booth, Gotthard C. 1946a. "Variety in Personality and Its Relation to Health," Review of Religion, X, No. 4, 385-412.

* ------. 1946b. "Organ Function and Form Perception: Use of the Rorschach Method with Cases of Chronic Arthritis, Parkinsonism and Arterial Hypertension," Psychosomatic Medicine, VIII, No. 6, 367-385.

Botvinnik, M. 1951. The Soviet School of Chess (Sovetskaya shakhmatnaya Shkola). Moscow.

Bowra, C. M. 1952. Heroic Poetry. London: Macmillan.

* Brickner, Richard M. 1942. "The German Cultural Paranoid Trend," American Journal of Orthopsychiatry, XII, No. 3, 544-545; No. 4, 611-632.

* ------. 1943. Is Germany Incurable? Philadelphia: Lippincott.

Brown, Stephen J. 1927. The World of Imagery. London: Kegan Paul, Trench, Trubner.

Brunhoff, Jean de. 1934. The Travels of Babar. New York: Random House.

Bunzel, Ruth. 1932. "Introduction to Zuni Ceremonialism." In U. S. Bureau of American Ethnology, Forty-seventh Annual Report ... 1929/30. Washington, D. C. Pp. 467-544.

** ------. 1950. Explorations in Chinese Culture. Columbia University Research in Contemporary Cultures (dittoed).

** ------, and John Hast Weakland. 1952. An Anthropological Approach to Chinese Communism. Columbia University Research in Contemporary Cultures (dittoed).

Calas, Nicolas. n.d. The Garden of Delight of Hieronymus Bosch (in preparation).

Campbell, J. G. D. 1902. Siam in the Twentieth Century. London: E. Arnold.

Campbell, Joseph. 1949. The Hero with a Thousand Faces. New York: Pantheon Books.

Camus, Albert. 1942. L'Etranger. Paris: Gallimard. The Stranger, trans. Stuart Gilbert. New York: Knopf, 1946.

Cannon, W. B. 1929. Bodily Changes in Pain, Hunger, Fear and Rage. New York: Appleton.

Cannon, W. B. 1932. The Wisdom of the Body. New York: Norton.

Carmichael, Leonard (ed.). 1946. Manual of Child Psychology. New York: Wiley. Second Edition, 1953 (in press).

Chapple, Eliot D. 1949. "The Interaction Chronograph: Its Evaluation and Present Application," Personnel, XXV, No. 4, 295-307.

------, and C. M. Arensberg. 1940. "Measuring Human Reactions: An Introduction to the Study of the Interaction of Individuals." Genetic Psychology Monographs, XXII, No. 1, 3-147.

------, and Carleton S. Coon. 1942. Principles of Anthropology. New York: Henry Holt.

------, and W. C. Vaughn. 1944. "A Clinical Method for Studying the Factor of Human Relations in Disease," Journal of Laboratory and Clinical Medicine, XXIX, No. 1, 1-18.

Chekhov, Anton. 1903. Complete Works (Polnoye Sobraniya Sochinenii). St. Petersburg: A. Marx.

------. 1907. Complete Works (Polnoye Sobraniya Sochinenii). St. Petersburg: A. Wolf.

Chen, Theodore Hsi-en. 1950. "New China, New Texts," Current History, XIX, No. 112, 321-327.

Chiang Kai-shek. 1947. China's Destiny. New York: Roy.

Cobb, Edith. n.d. The Ecology of Imagination in Childhood (MS.).

"Code of Ethics of the Society for Applied Anthropology." 1951. Human Organization, X, No. 2, 32.

Collingwood, R. G. 1938. The Principles of Art. Oxford: Clarendon Press.

------. 1939. An Autobiography. London: Oxford University Press.

Crespi, Leo P. 1950. "The Influence of Military Government Sponsorship in German Opinion Polling," International Journal of Opinion and Attitude Research, IV, No. 2, 151-178.

Current Digest of the Soviet Press, III. 1951. Ann Arbor, Michigan: Joint Committee on Slavic Studies.

Dal, V. 1903. The Dictionary of the Living Great Russian Language (Tolkovyi slovar Velikorusskavo Yazyka). St. Petersburg.

Dallin, David J. 1951. The New Soviet Empire. New Haven: Yale University Press.

Davis, Allison, and John Dollard. 1940. Children of Bondage. Washington, D. C.: American Council on Education.

------, and Burleigh and Mary Gardner. 1941. Deep South. Chicago: University of Chicago Press.

Deloria, Ella. n.d. Dakota Family Life (MS).

Deutsch, Karl W. 1950a. "Comment." In Perspectives on a Troubled Decade, Science, Philosophy and Religion, 1939-1949, Tenth Symposium, eds. Lyman Bryson, Louis Finkelstein, and R. M. MacIver. New York: Harper. Pp. 93-94.

------. 1950b. "Nationalism, Communication, and Community: An Interim Report." Ibid. pp. 339-365.

Devereux, George. 1951. Reality and Dream. New York: International Universities Press.

* Dicks, Henry V. 1947. See Rees, J. R.

* ------. 1950. "Personality Traits and National Socialist Ideology," Human Relations, III, No. 2, 111-154.

* Dicks, Henry V. 1952. "Observations on Contemporary Russian Behaviour," Human Relations, V, No. 2, 111-175.

** Dinerstein, Herbert S. 1952. Leadership in Soviet Agriculture and the Communist Party. Santa Monica, Calif.: Rand.

* Dollard, John. 1935. Criteria for the Life History. New Haven: Yale University Press. Reprinted 1949, New York: Peter Smith.

* ------. 1937. Caste and Class in a Southern Town. New Haven: Yale University Press.

------. 1943. Fear in Battle. New Haven: Yale University Press.

------, L. W. Doob, N. E. Miller, and R. R. Sears. 1939. Frustration and Aggression. New Haven: Yale University Press.

------, and N. E. Miller. 1950. Personality and Psychotherapy, An Analysis in Terms of Learning, Thinking, and Culture. New York: McGraw-Hill.

* DuBois, Cora. 1944. The People of Alor. Minneapolis: University of Minnesota Press.

Eberhard, Wolfram. 1937. Chinese Fairy Tales and Folk Tales. London: Kegan Paul, Trench, Trubner.

** Embree, John F. 1950. "Standardized Error and Japanese Character: A Note on Political Interpretation," World Politics, II, No. 3, 439-443.

** Endleman, Robert. 1949. "The New Anthropology and Its Ambitions," Commentary, VIII, No. 3, 284-291.

Erh-nu ying-hsiung chuan (Tale of Son and Daughter Heroes). 1935. Shanghai.

* Erikson, Erik H. 1943. "Problems of Infancy and Early Childhood." In Cyclopaedia of Medicine, Surgery and Specialties. Second Revised Edition. Philadelphia: Davis. Pp. 714-730.

* ------. 1945. "Childhood and Tradition." In The Psychoanalytic Study of the Child, I, eds. Anna Freud et al. New York: International Universities Press.

** ------. 1950a. Childhood and Society. New York: Norton.

* ------. 1950b. "Growth and Crises of the 'Healthy Personality.'" In Symposium on the Healthy Personality, ed. Milton J. E. Senn. Second Supplement to the Transactions of the Fourth Conference on Infancy and Childhood. New York: Josiah Macy, Jr. Foundation. Pp. 91-146.

Fadeyev, Alexander. 1928. The Rout (Razgrom). Third Edition. Moscow: Zemlya i Fabrika.

------. 1930-1941. The Last of the Udege (Posledniy iz Udege), 4 vols. Moscow.

------. 1946 and 1947. The Young Guard (Molodaya Gvardiya). Moscow: Publishing House of the Central Committee of the Allsoviet Komsomol Union. Serial Publication, Znamya, 1945.

Fang Hung. 1950. "An Economic Survey of the Three Sino-Soviet Joint Stock Companies," Chinese Press Survey, X, No. 4, 99-101. Translated from Kuan Cha (Peking), May 15, 1950.

Fenichel, Otto. 1945. The Psychoanalytic Theory of Neurosis. New York: Norton.

* Foerster, Heinz von (ed.). 1951. Cybernetics, Transactions of the Seventh Conference, March 23-24, 1950. New York: Josiah Macy, Jr. Foundation.

* Foerster, Heinz von. 1952. <u>Cybernetics, Transactions of the Eighth Confer-</u>
<u>ence, March 15-16, 1951</u>. New York: Josiah Macy, Jr. Foundation.

* ------. 1953. <u>Cybernetics, Transactions of the Ninth Conference, March 20-</u>
<u>21, 1952</u>. New York: Josiah Macy, Jr. Foundation.

Foeth, A. 1912. <u>Complete Works</u> (<u>Polnoye Sobraniya Sochinenii</u>). St. Petersburg: A. Marx.

Ford, Clellan S., and Frank A. Beach. 1951. <u>Patterns of Sexual Behavior</u>.
New York: Harper and Paul B. Hoeber.

Fortune, R. F. 1932a. <u>Sorcerers of Dobu</u>. New York: Dutton.

------. 1932b. <u>Omaha Secret Societies</u>. Columbia University Contributions
to Anthropology, No. 14. New York: Columbia University Press.

Frank, Lawrence K. 1939a. "Cultural Coercion and Individual Distortion,"
<u>Psychiatry</u>, II, No. 3, 2-27.

------. 1939b. "Time Perspectives," <u>Journal of Social Philosophy</u>, IV, No. 4,
293-312.

* ------. 1948. <u>Society as the Patient</u>. New Brunswick: Rutgers University
Press.

* ------. 1951. <u>Nature and Human Nature</u>. New Brunswick: Rutgers University Press.

------, et al. 1948. "Teleological Mechanisms," <u>Annals</u>, The New York
Academy of Sciences, L, 187-278.

Freud, Anna. 1946. <u>The Ego and the Mechanisms of Defense</u>, trans. Cecil
Baines. New York: International Universities Press.

Freud, Sigmund. 1938. <u>The Basic Writings of Sigmund Freud</u>, trans. and ed.
A. A. Brill. New York: Modern Library.

------. 1940-1950. <u>Gesammelte Werke</u>. London: Imago.

------. 1943. "Eine Kindheitserinnerung des Leonardo da Vinci." In <u>Gesam-</u>
<u>melte Werke</u>, VIII, 128-211.

* Fromm, Erich. 1941. <u>Escape from Freedom</u>. New York: Farrar and Rinehart.

* ------. 1948. <u>Man for Himself</u>. New York: Rinehart.

** Garvin, Paul. 1949. "Standard Average European and Czech," <u>Studia Lin-</u>
<u>guistica</u>, III, No. 2, 65-85.

* "Germany after the War, Round Table -- 1945." 1945. <u>American Journal of</u>
<u>Orthopsychiatry</u>, XV, No. 3, 381-441.

Gesell, Arnold, and Catherine S. Armatruda. 1945. <u>Embryology of Behavior</u>.
New York: Harper.

------, Frances Ilg, et al. 1943. <u>Infant and Child in the Culture of Today</u>.
New York: Harper.

------, Frances Ilg, et al. 1946. <u>The Child from Five to Ten</u>. New York:
Harper.

Giles, H. A. 1908. <u>Strange Stories from a Chinese Studio</u>. Second Revised
Edition. Shanghai: Kelly and Walsh.

Ginzberg, Louis (ed.). 1909. <u>The Legends of the Jews</u>, trans. from German
by Henrietta Szold. Philadelphia: Jewish Publication Society of
America.

** Goldman, Irving. 1950. "Psychiatric Interpretations of Russian History, A
Reply to Geoffrey Gorer," <u>American Slavic and East European Re-</u>
<u>view</u>, IX, No. 3, 151-161.

Gorer, Geoffrey. 1938. Himalayan Village. London: Michael Joseph.

* ------. 1940. "Society as Viewed by the Anthropologist." In The Cultural Approach to History, ed. Caroline F. Ware, pp. 20-33.

------. 1941. "The Myth in Jane Austen," American Imago, II, No. 3, 197-204.

* ------. 1942. Japanese Character Structure and Propaganda, A Preliminary Survey. Second Edition. New York: Institute for Intercultural Studies (mimeographed).

* ------. 1943a. "Themes in Japanese Culture," Transactions, The New York Academy of Sciences, Ser. 2, No. 5, 106-124. Reprinted 1946 in Science News, No. 1, 26-51.

* ------. 1943b. Burmese Personality. New York: Institute for Intercultural Studies (mimeographed).

* ------. 1946. "Japanese Character," Science News, No. 1, 26-51. Harmondsworth, Middlesex: Penguin Books.

* ------. 1948. The Americans. London: Pearn, Pollinger and Highan. The American People. New York; Norton.

** ------. 1949. "Some Aspects of the Psychology of the People of Great Russia," American Slavic and East European Review, VIII, No. 3, 155-166.

* ------. 1950a. "The Erotic Myth of America," Partisan Review, XVII, No. 6, 589-594.

** ------. 1950b. "The Concept of National Character," Science News, No. 18, 105-122. Harmondsworth, Middlesex: Penguin Books.

* ------. 1950c. "Some Notes on the British Character," Horizon, XX, Nos. 120-121, 369-379.

** ------. 1951. "Swaddling and the Russians," New Leader, May 21, pp. 19-20.

** ------, and John Rickman. 1949. The People of Great Russia. London: Cresset Press. New York: Chanticleer Press, 1950.

Gorky, Maxim. 1938. Lenin, Stalin, Creations of the Peoples of the USSR (Lenin, Stalin, tvorchestvo narodov SSSR). Moscow.

* Gottschalk, Louis, Clyde Kluckhohn, and Robert Angell. 1945. "The Use of Personal Documents in History, Anthropology and Sociology," Social Science Research Council Bulletin, No. 53, New York.

Gunther, John. 1949. "Inside Europe Today," New York Herald Tribune, February 8.

** Haimson, Leopold H. 1951. The Ideal of "Conscious Activity." Some Aspects of Decision Making and Communications in Soviet Theory and Practice. Columbia University Research in Contemporary Cultures (dittoed).

** ------. n.d. The Soviet Conception of Action in Theory and Practice (in preparation).

* Hallowell, A. Irving. 1945. "The Rorschach Technique in the Study of Personality and Culture," American Anthropologist, XLVII, No. 2, 95-110.

* ------. 1951. "The Use of Projective Techniques in the Study of the Socio-Psychological Aspects of Acculturation," Rorschach Research Exchange and Journal of Projective Techniques, XV, No. 1, 27-44.

* Hanks, L. M. 1949. "The Quest for Individual Autonomy in the Burmese Personality," Psychiatry, XII, No. 3, 285-300.

* Haring, Douglas G. 1946. "Aspects of Personal Character in Japan," Far
        Eastern Quarterly, VI, No. 1, 12-22. Reprinted 1948 in Personal
        Character and Cultural Milieu, pp. 355-365. (Revised Edition, 1949,
        pp. 396-407).

* ------. (ed.). 1948. Personal Character and Cultural Milieu. Syracuse. Re-
        vised Edition, 1949. Syracuse: Syracuse University Press.

Harlow, Harry F. 1949. "The Formation of Learning Sets," Psychological
        Review, LVI, No. 1, 51-66.

------. 1950. "Analysis of Discrimination Learning in Monkeys," Journal of
        Experimental Psychology, XL, No. 1, 26-39.

Harris, Z. S. 1951. Methods in Structural Linguistics. Chicago: University
        of Chicago Press.

Hartmann, H., E. Kris, and R. M. Loewenstein. 1949. "Notes on the Theory
        of Aggression." In Psychoanalytic Study of the Child, III-IV. New
        York: International Universities Press.

Hebb, D. O. 1949. The Organization of Behavior. New York: Wiley.

Hellersberg, Elisabeth F. 1950. The Individual's Relation to Reality in Our
        Culture, An Experimental Approach by Means of the Horn-Hellers-
        berg Test. Springfield, Ill.: Charles Thomas.

Henry, Jules and Zunia. 1944. "Doll Play and Pilaga Indian Children,"
        American Orthopsychiatric Association Research Monographs, No. 4.
        Reprinted 1948, abridged, in Personality in Nature, Society and Cul-
        ture, eds. Clyde Kluckhohn and Henry A. Murray, pp. 236-251.

* Henry, William E. 1947. "The Thematic Apperception Technique in the Study
        of Culture-Personality Relations," Genetic Psychology Monographs,
        XXXV, No. 1, 3-135.

Herzog, Elizabeth G. 1947. "Pending Perfection: A Qualitative Complement
        to Quantitative Methods," International Journal of Opinion and Atti-
        tude Research, I, No. 3, 31-48.

Hilgard, E. R., and D. G. Marquis. 1940. Conditioning and Learning. New
        York: Appleton-Century-Crofts.

Hohman, L. B., and Bertram Schaffner. 1947. "The Sex Life of Unmarried
        Men," American Journal of Sociology, LII, No. 6, 501-507.

Holmberg, Allen R. 1950. Nomads of the Long Bow. Publication No. 10,
        Institute of Social Anthropology, Smithsonian Institution. Washington,
        D. C.

Hsu, Francis L. K. 1948. Under the Ancestors' Shadow. New York: Columbia
        University Press.

------. 1951. "The Chinese of Hawaii: Their Role in American Culture,"
        Transactions, The New York Academy of Sciences, Ser. 2, XIII,
        No. 6, 243-250.

Hughes, Everett C. 1943. French Canada in Transition. Chicago: University
        of Chicago Press.

Hull, Clark L. 1943. Principles of Behavior. New York: Appleton.

* Hutchinson, G. E. 1944. Review of Gregory Bateson and Margaret Mead:
        Balinese Character, and of Rebecca West: Black Lamb and Gray Fal-
        con, in "Marginalia," American Scientist, XXXII, No. 4, 290-291.

* ------. 1950. Review of Margaret Mead: Male and Female, in "Marginalia,"
        American Scientist, XXXVIII, No. 2, 282-289.

** Inlow, Ruby Strand. 1948. "Some Implications of Research in Contemporary Cultures for the Education of Social Workers." In Regional Planning for Social Work Education, ed. Lora Lee Pederson. Nashville, Tennessee. Pp. 71-81.

Jakobson, Roman. 1939. Le développement phonologique du language enfantin et les cohérences correspondantes dans les langues du monde. V Congrés International de Linguistes. Bruges.

* Joffe, Natalie F. 1948. "The Vernacular of Menstruation," Word, IV, No. 3, 181-186.

** ------. 1949. "The Dynamics of Benefice among East European Jews," Social Forces, XXVII, No. 3, 238-247.

Kalbus, Oscar. 1935. Vom Werden deutscher Filmkunst. Altona-Bahrenfeld: Cigaretten Bilderkunst.

* Kardiner, Abram. 1939. The Individual and His Society. New York: Columbia University Press.

* ------. 1945. The Psychological Frontiers of Society. New York: Columbia University Press.

* Kecskemeti, P., and Nathan Leites. 1945. Some Psychological Hypotheses on Nazi Germany. Library of Congress, Experimental Division for the Study of Wartime Communications, Document No. 60. Washington, D. C. (mimeographed).

Klein, Melanie. 1948. Contributions to Psycho-Analysis, 1921-1945. London: Hogarth Press and The Institute of Psycho-Analysis.

* Klineberg, Otto. 1944. "A Science of National Character," Journal of Social Psychology, XIX, 147-162.

* ------. 1950. "The Tensions Affecting International Understanding, A Survey of Research," Social Science Research Council Bulletin, No. 62. New York.

Klopfer, B., and D. M. Kelley. 1942. The Rorschach Technique. New York: World Book.

Kluckhohn, Clyde. 1938. "Participation in Ceremonials in a Navaho Community," American Anthropologist, XL, No. 3, 359-369.

* ------. 1949. "Personality in Culture." In Mirror for Man. New York: Whittlesey House, McGraw-Hill. Chapter 8, pp. 196-227.

* ------, and Florence. 1947. "American Culture: Generalized and Class Patterns." In Conflicts of Power in Modern Culture, Seventh Symposium, Conference on Science, Philosophy and Religion. New York: Conference on Science, Philosophy and Religion. Pp. 106-128.

------, and Henry A. Murray (eds.). 1948. Personality in Nature, Society and Culture. New York: Knopf.

Kracauer, Siegfried. 1947. From Caligari to Hitler. Princeton: Princeton University Press.

Kris, Ernst, and Nathan Leites. 1947. "Trends in 20th Century Propaganda." In Psychoanalysis and the Social Sciences, I, eds. Géza Róheim, et al. New York: International Universities Press. Pp. 393-409.

Kriukova, M. S. 1937. "Knee-Length-Beard and the Clear Falcons," Novyi Mir, No. 5. Moscow.

------. 1938. Legend about Lenin (Skazanie o Lenine). Moscow.

------. 1941. "Chapai." In Bylini ... , I-II, ed. M. S. Kriukovoi. Moscow.

Kriukova, M. S. 1945. "The Legend about Lenin." In Folk Tales of the People of the Soviet Union, trans. Gerard Shelley. London: H. Jenkins.

Kroeber, A. L. (ed.). 1953. Anthropology Today. Chicago: University of Chicago Press.

* LaBarre, Weston. 1945. "Some Observations on Character Structure in the Orient: The Japanese," Psychiatry, VIII, No. 3, 319-342.

* ------. 1946. "Some Observations on Character Structure in the Orient: The Chinese," Psychiatry, IX, No. 3, 215-237; No. 4, 375-395.

** ------. 1948. "Columbia University Research in Contemporary Cultures," Scientific Monthly, LXVII, No. 3, 239-240.

Lagunova, Tatyana. 1946. "In the Woods of Smolensk," Novyi Mir, Moscow.

* Lamb, Robert K. 1950. "Entrepreneurship in the Community," Explorations in Entrepreneurial History, II, No. 3, 114-127.

* ------. 1952. "Political Elites and the Process of Economic Development." In The Progress of Underdeveloped Areas, ed. B. F. Hoselitz. Chicago: University of Chicago Press. Pp. 30-53.

** Landes, Ruth, and Mark Zborowski. 1950. "Hypotheses Concerning the Eastern European Jewish Family," Psychiatry, XIII, No. 4, 447-464.

Lasswell, Harold D. 1930. Psychopathology and Politics. Chicago: University of Chicago Press.

------. 1935. World Politics and Personal Security. New York: McGraw-Hill.

------. 1937. "The Method of Overlapping Observation in the Study of Personality and Culture," Journal of Abnormal and Social Psychology, XXXII, 240-243.

------. 1938. "Provisional Classification of Symbol Data," Psychiatry, I, No. 2, 197-204.

------. 1948a. Power and Personality. New York: Norton.

------. 1948b. The Analysis of Political Behavior: An Empirical Approach. London: Kegan Paul, Trench, Trubner.

------. 1951. The Political Writings of Harold D. Lasswell. Glencoe, Ill.: Free Press.

------, and Abraham Kaplan. 1950. Power and Society. New Haven: Yale University Press.

------, and Nathan Leites (eds.). 1949. Language and Politics. New York: George Stewart.

Latzko, E. A. 1911. Bylini. Moscow.

* Lee, Dorothy. 1940. "A Primitive System of Values," Philosophy of Science, VII, 355-378. Reprinted 1947 as "A Linguistic Approach to a System of Values," in Readings in Social Psychology, eds. Theodore M. Newcomb, Eugene L. Hartley, et al., pp. 219-224.

* ------. 1944. "Linguistic Reflection of Wintuᶜ Thought," International Journal of American Linguistics, X, No. 4, 181-187.

* ------. 1949. "Being and Value in a Primitive Society," Journal of Philosophy, XLVI, No. 13, 401-415.

* ------. 1950. "Lineal and Non-Lineal Codification of Reality," Journal of Psychosomatic Medicine, XII, No. 2, 89-98.

Lee, Jon. 1940. Chinese Tales Told in California. MSS Series, No. 1, WPA, California State Library, San Francisco.

* Leighton, Alexander H. 1945. The Governing of Men. Princeton: Princeton University Press.

* Leighton, Alexander H. 1949. Human Relations in a Changing World. New York: Dutton.

* ------, and I. Opler. 1946. "Psychiatry and Applied Anthropology in Psychological Warfare against Japan," American Journal of Psychoanalysis, VI, No. 1, 20-34.

Leighton, Dorothea C., and Clyde Kluckhohn. 1947. Children of the People. Cambridge: Harvard University Press.

* Leites, Nathan. 1947. "Trends in Affectlessness," American Imago, IV, No. 2, 89-112.

* ------. 1948a. "Trends in Moral Temper," American Imago, V, No. 1, 3-37.

* ------. 1948b. "Psycho-Cultural Hypotheses about Political Acts," World Politics, I, No. 1, 102-119.

** ------. 1951. The Operational Code of the Politburo. New York: McGraw-Hill.

** ------, Elsa Bernaut, and Raymond L. Garthoff. 1951. "Politburo Images of Stalin," World Politics, III, No. 3, 317-339.

** ------, and Elsa Bernaut. n.d. Ritual of Liquidation (in press).

* ------, and Martha Wolfenstein. 1947. "An Analysis of Themes and Plots," Annals, The American Academy of Political and Social Science, CCLIV, 41-48.

* ------, and Martha Wolfenstein. 1951. "Movie Psychiatrists," Complex, No. 4, 19-27.

Lenin and Stalin in the Poetry of the Peoples of the USSR (Lenin i Stalin v poezii narodov SSSR). 1938. Moscow.

* Levy, David M. 1937. "Sibling Rivalry," American Orthopsychiatric Association Research Monographs, No. 2.

* ------. 1946. "The German Anti-Nazi: A Case Study," American Journal of Orthopsychiatry, XVI, No. 3, 507-515.

* ------. 1947. New Fields in Psychiatry. New York: Norton.

* ------. 1948. "Anti-Nazis: Criteria of Differentiation," Psychiatry, XI, No. 2, 125-167.

Lewin, Kurt. 1942. "Time Perspective and Morale." In Civilian Morale, ed. Goodwin Watson. Boston: Houghton Mifflin. Pp. 48-70.

* ------. 1948. Resolving Social Conflicts, Selected Papers on Group Dynamics, 1935-1946, ed. Gertrud Weiss Lewin. New York: Harper.

* Lindesmith, A. R., and A. L. Strauss. 1950. "A Critique of Culture-Personality Writings," American Sociological Review, XV, No. 5, 587-600.

Linton, Ralph. 1923. "Material Culture of the Marquesas Islands." Bernice P. Bishop Museum Memoirs, VIII, No. 5.

* ------. 1945. The Cultural Background of Personality. New York: Appleton-Century.

* ------. 1951. "The Concept of National Character." In Personality and Political Crisis, eds. A. H. Stanton and S. E. Perry. Glencoe, Ill.: Free Press.

* Lipkind, William O. n.d. A Community Study of the Town and Kreis of Miesbach, Germany (MS.).

** Little, Kenneth L. 1950. "Methodology in the Study of Adult Personality," American Anthropologist, LII, No. 2, 279-282.

Lorge, Irving, et al. 1952. "Evaluations of Rational Decisions," American Psychologist, VII, No. 9.

Lowenfeld, Margaret. 1951. An Objective Method of Study of Children and Adults (MS.).

* Lowie, Robert H. 1945. The German People, A Social Portrait to 1914. New York: Farrar and Rinehart.

McClelland, David C. 1951. "Measuring Motivation in Phantasy: The Achievement Motive." In Groups, Leadership and Men, ed. Harold Guetzkow. Pittsburgh: Carnegie Press. Pp. 191-205.

* Madariaga, Salvador de. 1928. Englishmen, Frenchmen, Spaniards, An Essay in Comparative Psychology. London: Oxford University Press.

------. 1948. On Hamlet. London: Hollis and Carter.

Malinowski, Bronislaw. 1915. "The Natives of Mailu," Transactions of the Royal Society of South Australia for 1915 (Adelaide), pp. 494-706.

------. 1922. Argonauts of the Western Pacific. New York: Dutton.

------. 1927. Sex and Repression in Savage Society. New York: Harcourt, Brace.

------. 1935. Coral Gardens and Their Magic, 2 vols. London: Allen and Unwin. New York: American Book Co.

Mao Tse-tung. [1939.] The Chinese Revolution and the Communist Party of China. New York: Committee for a Democratic Far Eastern Policy (mimeographed).

Mayakovsky, V. 1928. "Communist March." In The Order to the Army of Arts, II, 173. Moscow-Leningrad.

* Mead, Margaret. 1928. Coming of Age in Samoa. New York: Morrow.

* ------. 1930. Growing Up in New Guinea. New York: Morrow.

* ------. 1935. Sex and Temperament in Three Primitive Societies. New York: Morrow.

* ------. (ed.). 1937. Cooperation and Competition among Primitive Peoples. New York: McGraw-Hill.

* ------. 1938. "The Mountain Arapesh. I. An Importing Culture," Anthropological Papers, American Museum of Natural History, XXXVI, Part 3, 145-349.

* ------. 1939. From the South Seas. New York: Morrow.

* ------. 1940a. "The Mountain Arapesh. II. Supernaturalism," Anthropological Papers, American Museum of Natural History, XXXVII, Part 3, 317-451.

* ------. 1940b. "Social Change and Cultural Surrogates," Journal of Educational Sociology, XIV, No. 2, 92-110.

* ------. 1941a. "Administrative Contributions to Democratic Character Formation at the Adolescent Level," Journal of the National Association of Deans of Women, IV, No. 2, 51-57.

* ------. 1941b. Review of Abram Kardiner: The Individual and His Society, in American Journal of Orthopsychiatry, XI, No. 3, 603-605.

* ------. 1942a. And Keep Your Powder Dry. New York: Morrow.

* ------. 1942b. "An Anthropologist Looks at the Teacher's Role," Educational Method, XXI, No. 5, 219-223.

* ------. 1942c. "Customs and Mores," American Journal of Sociology, XLVII, No. 6, 971-980.

* ------. 1942d. "The Comparative Study of Culture and the Purposive Cultivation of Democratic Values." In Science, Philosophy and Religion, Second Symposium, eds. Lyman Bryson and Louis Finkelstein. New York: Conference on Science, Philosophy and Relgion. Pp. 56-69.

* Mead, Margaret. 1943. "Anthropological Approach to Dietary Problems," Transactions, The New York Academy of Sciences, Ser. 2, V, No. 7, 177-182.

* ------. 1944a. The American Troops and the British Community. London: Hutchinson.

* ------. 1944b. "What Is a Date?" Transatlantic, No. 10, pp. 54, 57-60.

* ------. 1946a. "Professional Problems of Education in Dependent Countries," Journal of Negro Education, XV, No. 3, 346-357.

* ------. 1946b. "Research on Primitive Children." In Manual of Child Psychology, ed. Leonard Carmichael, Chapter 13, pp. 667-706. Second Edition, 1953 (in press).

* ------. 1946c. "Pouvoirs de la femme: Quelques aspects du rôle des femmes aux Etats-Unis," Esprit, No. 11, 661-671.

* ------. 1946d. "The American People." In The World's Peoples and How They Live. London: Odhams Press. Pp. 143-163.

* ------. 1947a. "The Application of Anthropological Techniques to Cross-National Communication," Transactions, The New York Academy of Sciences, Ser. 2, IX, No. 4, 133-152.

* ------. 1947b. "Fundamental Education and Cultural Values." In Fundamental Education, Common Ground for All Peoples. Paris: Unesco. Pp. 132-154. New York: Macmillan.

* ------. 1947c. "On the Implications for Anthropology of the Gesell-Ilg Approach to Maturation," American Anthropologist, XLIX, No. 1, 69-77.

* ------. 1947d. "The Concept of Culture and the Psychosomatic Approach," Psychiatry, X, No. 1, 57-76.

* ------. 1947e. "The Mountain Arapesh. III. Socio-Economic Life. IV. Diary of Events in Alitoa," Anthropological Papers, American Museum of Natural History, XL, Part 3, 159-420.

------. 1947f. "The Implications of Culture Change for Personality Development," American Journal of Orthopsychiatry, XVII, No. 4, 633-646.

* ------. 1948a. "A Case History in Cross-National Communications." In The Communication of Ideas, ed. Lyman Bryson. New York: Harper. Chapter 13, pp. 209-229.

* ------. 1948b. "The Contemporary American Family as an Anthropologist Sees It," American Journal of Sociology, LIII, No. 6, 453-459.

* ------. 1949a. Male and Female. New York: Morrow.

* ------. 1949b. "The Mountain Arapesh. V. The Record of Unabelin, with Rorschach Analyses," Anthropological Papers, American Museum of Natural History, XLI, Part 3, 289-390.

* ------. 1949c. "Collective Guilt." In Proceedings of the International Conference in Medical Psychotherapy, III. International Congress on Mental Health, London, 1948. New York: Columbia University Press. Pp. 57-66.

* ------. 1949d. "Character Formation and Diachronic Theory." In Social Structure, Studies Presented to A. R. Radcliffe-Brown, ed. Meyer Fortes. Oxford: Clarendon Press. Pp. 18-34.

** ------. 1949e. "Two Projects," Human Organization, VIII, No. 11, 28.

* ------. 1949f. "Psychologic Weaning: Childhood and Adolescence." In Psychosexual Development in Health and Disease, eds. Paul Hoch and Joseph Zubin. New York: Grune and Stratton. Pp. 124-135.

* Mead, Margaret. 1950a. "Some Anthropological Considerations Concerning Guilt." In Feelings and Emotions, The Mooseheart Symposium, ed. Martin L. Reymert. New York: McGraw-Hill. Pp. 362-373.

* ------. 1950b. "The Comparative Study of Cultures and the Purposive Cultivation of Democratic Values, 1941-1949." In Perspectives on a Troubled Decade, Science, Philosophy and Religion, 1939-1949, Tenth Symposium, eds. Lyman Bryson, Louis Finkelstein, and R.M. MacIver. New York: Harper. Pp. 87-108.

* ------. 1950c. "Unique Possibilities of the Melting Pot," Social Welfare Forum, Official Proceedings, 76th Annual Meeting, National Conference of Social Work, June 12-17, 1949. New York: Columbia University Press.

------. 1951a. "Anthropologist and Historian: Their Common Problems," American Quarterly, III, No. 1, 3-13.

** ------. 1951b. Soviet Attitudes toward Authority. New York: McGraw-Hill.

** ------. 1951c. "Columbia University Research in Contemporary Cultures." In Groups, Leadership and Men, ed. Harold Guetzkow. Pittsburgh: Carnegie Press. Pp. 106-118.

* ------. 1951d. The School in American Culture. Cambridge: Harvard University Press.

** ------. 1951e. "What Makes Soviet Character?" Natural History, LX, No. 7, 296-303, 336.

** ------. 1951f. "The Study of National Character." In The Policy Sciences, eds. Daniel Lerner and Harold D. Lasswell. Stanford: Stanford University Press. Pp. 70-85. "L'Etude du Caractère National," trans. J. G. and P. H. Maucorps. In Les "Sciences de la Politique" aux Etats-Unis. Cahiers de la Fondation des Sciences Politiques, No. 19. Paris: Librairie Armand Colin, 1951. Pp. 105-132.

* ------. 1952. "Some Relationships between Social Anthropology and Psychiatry." In Dynamic Psychiatry, eds. Franz Alexander and Helen Ross. Chicago: University of Chicago Press. Pp. 401-448.

** ------. 1953a. "National Character." In Anthropology Today, ed. A. L. Kroeber, pp. 642-667.

* ------. 1953b. "Cultural Bases for Understanding Literature," PMLA (in press).

* ------, (ed.). 1953c. Cultural Patterns and Technical Change. Paris: Unesco (in press).

------, Eliot D. Chapple, and G. Gordon Brown. 1949. "Report of the Committee on Ethics," Human Organization, VIII, No. 2, 20-21.

** ------, and Frances C. Macgregor. 1951. Growth and Culture, A Photographic Study of Balinese Childhood. New York: Putnam.

* Merton, Robert K. 1951. "Selected Problems of Field Work in the Planned Community," American Sociological Review, XII, No. 3, 304-317.

Métraux, Alfred. 1940. "Ethnology of Easter Island," Bernice P. Bishop Museum Bulletin, No. 160.

------. 1951. Making a Living in the Marbial Valley (Haiti). Paris: Education Clearing House, Unesco (UNESCO/ED/OCC/10).

* Métraux, Rhoda. 1943. "Qualitative Attitude Analysis: A Technique for the Study of Verbal Behavior." In Report of the Committee on Food Habits, 1941-1943. "The Problem of Changing Food Habits," National Research Council Bulletin, No. 108. Washington, D. C. Pp. 86-94.

** ------, (ed.). 1950. Some Hypotheses about French Culture. Columbia University Research in Contemporary Cultures (dittoed).

Métraux, Rhoda. 1951a. Kith and Kin, a Study of Creole Social Structure in Marbial, Haiti. Unpublished Ph.D. dissertation, Columbia University, New York.

** ------, (ed.). 1951b. A Report on National Character. Prepared for the Working Group on Human Behavior under Conditions of Military Service, Research and Development Board. Columbia University Research in Contemporary Cultures (dittoed).

------. 1952a. "Some Aspects of Hierarchical Structure in Haiti." In Acculturation in the Americas, Proceedings of the 29th International Congress of Americanists, II, ed. Sol Tax. Chicago: University of Chicago Press. Pp. 185-194.

------. 1952b. "Affiliations through Work in Marbial, Haiti," Primitive Man, XXV, Nos. 1-2, 1-22.

** ------, and Margaret Mead. 1953. Themes in French Culture, Preface to a Study of French Community. Stanford: Stanford University Press (in press).

Meyer, Donald R., and Harry F. Harlow. 1949. "The Development of Transfer of Response to Patterning by Monkeys," Journal of Comparative and Physiological Psychology, XLII, No. 6, 454-462.

Mickiewicz, Adam. 1911. Books of the Polish Nation and the Polish Pilgrimage (Ksiegi Narodu i Pielgrzymstwa). Lwow: Dzieta.

Miller, N. E., and John Dollard. 1941. Social Learning and Imitation. New Haven: Yale University Press.

Mitrany, David. 1930. The Land and the Peasant in Rumania. New Haven: Yale University Press.

* Mittelmann, Bela, Harold G. Wolff, and M. P. Scharf. 1942. "Emotions and Gastroduodenal Functions: Experimental Studies on Patients with Gastritis, Duodenitis, and Peptic Ulcer," Psychosomatic Medicine, IV, No. 2, 5-61.

* Mosely, Philip E. 1940. "The Peasant Family: The Zadruga, or Communal Joint Family in the Balkans and Its Recent Evolution." In The Cultural Approach to History, ed. Caroline F. Ware, pp. 95-108.

** ------. 1951. "Some Soviet Techniques of Negotiation." In Negotiating with the Russians, eds. Raymond Dennett and Joseph E. Johnson. Boston: World Peace Foundation. Pp. 271-303.

** Muensterberger, Warner. 1951. "Orality and Dependence: Characteristics of Southern Chinese." In Psychoanalysis and the Social Sciences, III, eds. Géza Róheim et al. New York: International Universities Press. Pp. 37-69.

Murdock, George P. 1949. Social Structure. New York: Macmillan.

Murphy, G. 1947. Personality, A Biosocial Approach to Origins and Structure. New York: Harper.

Newcomb, Theodore M., Eugene L. Hartley, et al. (eds.). 1947. Readings in Social Psychology. New York: Henry Holt. (Revised Edition, 1952, eds. G. E. Swanson, Theodore M. Newcomb, Eugene L. Hartley, et al.)

** Norton, Irene. 1950. "How an Understanding of Cultures Can Aid the Day Care Center," Understanding the Child, XIX, No. 4.

* Orlansky, Harold. 1949. "Infant Care and Personality," Psychological Bulletin, XLVI, No. 1, 1-48.

Peyre, Henri. 1944. Writers and Their Critics. Ithaca: Cornell University Press.

* Plant, James S. 1937. Personality and the Cultural Pattern. New York: The Commonwealth Fund.

Pribichevich, Stojan. 1939. World without End. New York: Reynal & Hitch-cock.

Proceedings, First Colloquium on Personality Investigation, Held under the Auspices of the American Psychiatric Association, Committee on Relations in the Social Sciences, December 1-2, 1928, New York City. 1928. Baltimore: Lord Baltimore Press.

Proceedings, Second Colloquium on Personality Investigation, Held under the Joint Auspices of the American Psychiatric Association, Committee on Relations of Psychiatry and the Social Sciences, and of the Social Science Research Council, November 29-30, 1929, New York City. 1930. Baltimore: Johns Hopkins Press.

Prutkov, Kuzma. 1933. Complete Works. Moscow: Academi.

Quong, Rose. 1946. Chinese Ghost and Love Stories. New York: Pantheon Press.

Radcliffe-Brown, A. R. 1930. "A System of Notation for Relationships," Man, XXX, No. 93, 121-122.

Radin, Paul. 1920. Crashing Thunder, Winnebago Indian. Berkeley: University of California Press. New York and London: Appleton, 1926.

Rank, Otto. 1909. Der Mythus von der Geburt des Helden. Leipzig: Deuticke.

------. 1912. Das Inzest-Motiv in Dichtung und Sage. Leipzig: Deuticke.

------. 1914. The Myth of the Birth of the Hero, trans. F. Robbins and S. E. Jelliffe. New York: The Journal of Nervous and Mental Disease Publishing Co.

Rapaport, David. 1946. "Diagnostic Psychological Testing," II. Menninger Clinic Monograph Series, No. 4. Chicago: Year Book Publishers.

* Rees, J. R. 1947. The Case of Rudolph Hess. London: Heinemann.

* Report of the Committee on Food Habits, 1941-1943. 1943. "The Problem of Changing Food Habits." National Research Council Bulletin, No. 108. Washington, D. C.

* Report of the Committee on Food Habits. 1945. "Manual for the Study of Food Habits." National Research Council Bulletin, No. 111. Washington, D. C.

Richardson, F. L. W. 1941. "Community Resettlement in a Depressed Coal Region," Applied Anthropology, I, No. 1, 24-53.

Richardson, L. F. 1939. "Generalized Foreign Politics," British Journal of Psychology Monograph Supplement, No. 23.

* Riesman, David. 1950. The Lonely Crowd. New Haven: Yale University Press.

* ------. 1952. Faces in the Crowd. New Haven: Yale University Press.

* Rodnick, David. 1948. Postwar Germans. New Haven: Yale University Press.

* ------, and Elizabeth. n.d. Czechs, Slovaks and Communism (MS.).

Róheim, Géza. 1930. Animism, Magic and the Divine King. London: Kegan Paul, Trench, Trubner.

* ------. 1932. "Psycho-Analysis of Primitive Types," International Journal of Psycho-Analysis, XIII, 1-224.

------. 1934. Riddle of the Sphinx. London: Hogarth Press.

------. 1943. "The Origin and Functions of Culture." Nervous and Mental Disease Monograph Series, No. 69.

------. 1945. The Eternal Ones of the Dream. New York: International Universities Press.

* Róheim, Géza. 1950. Psychoanalysis and Anthropology. New York: International Universities Press.

* Ruesch, Jurgen, et al. 1946. "Chronic Disease and Psychological Invalidism, A Psychosomatic Study." Psychosomatic Medicine Monograph, No. 9.

* ------, and Gregory Bateson. 1949. "Structure and Process in Social Relations," Psychiatry, XII, No. 2, 105-124.

* ------, and Gregory Bateson. 1951. Communication, The Social Matrix of Psychiatry. New York: Norton.

* Sapir, Edward. 1950. Selected Writings of Edward Sapir, ed. David Mandelbaum. Berkeley and Los Angeles: University of California Press.

* Sargent, S. Stansfeld, and Marion W. Smith (eds.). 1949. Culture and Personality, Proceedings of an Interdisciplinary Conference. New York: Viking Fund.

* Schaffner, Bertram. 1948. Father Land. New York: Columbia University Press.

* Schneider, David M. 1947. "The Social Dynamics of Physical Disability in Army Basic Training," Psychiatry, X, No. 3, 323-334.

** Schwartz, Shepard. 1951. "Mate-Selection among New York City's Chinese Males, 1931-1938," American Journal of Sociology, LVI, No. 6, 562-568.

"Science at Work." 1944. Education, LXV, No. 4, 228-238.

Seton-Watson, R. W. 1934. A History of the Rumanians from Roman Times to the Completion of Unity. Cambridge: Cambridge University Press.

* Seward, Georgene H. 1950. Review of Margaret Mead: Male and Female, Psychology Bulletin, XLVII, No. 3, 280-282.

Sewell, Elizabeth. 1952. The Field of Nonsense. London: Chatto and Windus.

Sharpe, Ella Freeman. 1937. Dream Analysis, A Practical Handbook for Psycho-Analysts. London: Hogarth Press and The Institute of Psycho-Analysis.

------. 1950. Collected Papers on Psycho-Analysis, ed. Marjorie Brierley. London: Hogarth Press and The Institute of Psycho-Analysis.

Shaw, Lau. 1945. Rickshaw Boy. New York: Reynal & Hitchcock.

** Shub, Boris. 1950. "The Soviets Expose a Baby," New Leader, June 17, pp. 11-12.

Simmons, Leo W. (ed.). 1942. Sun Chief. New Haven: Yale University Press.

Slowacki, Juliusz. 192-. Works (Pisma). Warsaw: Haskler.

Sokolov, I. M. 1950. Russian Folklore, trans. Catherine Ruth Smith. New York: Macmillan.

Spengler, Oswald. 1918. Der Untergang des Abendlandes. Munich: Beck.

* Spindler, G. Dearborn. 1948. "American Character as Revealed by the Military," Psychiatry, XI, No. 3, 275-281.

Spurgeon, Caroline F. 1935. Shakespeare's Imagery and What It Tells Us. Cambridge: Cambridge University Press.

Stalin, Joseph. 1946-1951. Works (Sochinenya), 13 vols. Moscow.

Stoll, E. E. 1937. Shakespeare's Young Lovers. New York: Oxford University Press.

Stouffer, S. A., et al. 1949-1950. Studies in Social Psychology in World War II, 4 vols. Princeton: Princeton University Press.

Stratilesco, Tereza. 1907. From Carpathian to Pindus. Boston: J.W. Luce.

** Sturmthal, Adolf. 1948. "National Patterns of Union Behavior," Journal of Political Economy, LVI, No. 6, 515-526.

* Sullivan, Harry Stack. 1940-1945. Conceptions of Modern Psychiatry. Reprinted from Psychiatry, III, No. 1, 1940, and VIII, No. 2, 1945. Washington, D. C.: William Alanson White Psychiatric Foundation.

* ------. 1948. "Towards a Psychiatry of Peoples," Psychiatry, XI, No. 2, 105-116.

Sun Yat-sen. 1927. San Min Chu I, trans. Frank W. Price. Shanghai: China Committee, Institute of Pacific Relations.

Tannenbaum, Frank. 1924. Darker Phases of the South. New York: Putnam.

* ------. 1946. "The Balance of Power in Society," Political Science Quarterly, LXI, No. 4, 481-504.

------. 1951. A Philosophy of Labor. New York: Knopf.

Taylor, Edmund. 1947. Richer by Asia. Boston: Houghton Mifflin.

Teffy, N. A. [N. A. Buchinskaya]. 1912. Humorous Stories (Yumoristicheskie rasskazy). St. Petersburg: Shipornik.

Thompson, Laura. 1950. Culture in Crisis, A Study of the Hopi Indians. New York: Harper.

Thorndike, E. L. 1932. Fundamentals of Learning. New York: Teachers College, Columbia University.

Tocqueville, Alexis de. 1835. De la démocratie en Amérique Bruxelles. Democracy in America, 2 vols. New York: Knopf, 1945.

Tolstoy, Leo. 1913. Collected Works (Polnoye Sobraniya Sochinenii). Moscow: I. D. Sytin.

Trager, George, and H. L. Smith. 1951. An Outline of English Structure. Studies in Linguistics, Occasional Papers, No. 3. Norman, Oklahoma: Battenberg Press.

Tsao Hsueh-Chin. 1929. The Dream of the Red Chamber (Hung Lou Meng), trans. Wang Chi-chen. London: Routledge.

Turgenev, I. 1898. Complete Works (Polnoye Sobraniya Sochinenii). St. Petersburg: A. Marx.

Tuwim, Juljan. 1944. Before the Day (W Przededniu). New York: Penzik.

United States Strategic Bombing Survey. 1947. The Effects of Strategic Bombing on German Morale. Washington, D. C.

Waldeck, Rosie G. 1942. Athene Palace. New York: R. M. McBride.

Wang Chi-chen. 1944. Traditional Chinese Tales. New York: Columbia University Press.

* Ware, Caroline F. (ed.). 1940. The Cultural Approach to History. New York: Columbia University Press.

Warner, W. Lloyd, and Paul S. Lunt. 1941. The Social Life of a Modern Community. Yankee City Series, I. New Haven: Yale University Press.

------, and Paul S. Lunt. 1942. The Status System of a Modern Community. Yankee City Series, II. New Haven: Yale University Press.

------, and Leo Srole. 1945. The Social Systems of American Ethnic Groups. Yankee City Series, III. New Haven: Yale University Press.

------, and J. O. Low. 1947. The Social System of the Modern Factory. Yankee City Series, IV. New Haven: Yale University Press.

** Weakland, John Hast. 1950. "The Organization of Action in Chinese Culture,"
    Psychiatry, XIII, No. 3, 361-370.

** ------. 1951. "Method in Cultural Anthropology," Journal of the Philosophy
    of Science, XVIII, No. 1, 55-69.

Weber, Max. 1930. The Protestant Ethic and the Spirit of Capitalism. Lon-
    don: Allen and Unwin.

Whiting, John W. M. 1941. Becoming a Kwoma. New Haven: Yale University
    Press.

Wiener, Norbert. 1948. Cybernetics. New York: Wiley.

------. 1950. The Human Use of Human Beings, Cybernetics and Society.
    Boston: Houghton Mifflin.

* Wilbur, George B., and Warner Muensterberger (eds.). 1951. Psychoanalysis
    and Culture. New York: International Universities Press.

Winter, W., and R. G. Wade. 1951. The World Chess Championship: 1951,
    Botvinnik vs. Bronstein. London: Turnstile Press.

** Wolfe, Bertram D. 1951a. "The Swaddled Soul of the Great Russians," New
    Leader, January 29, pp. 15-18.

** ------. 1951b. "Swaddling and the Russians," New Leader, May 21, p. 20.

** Wolfenstein, Martha. 1950. "Some Variants in Moral Training of Children,"
    In Psychoanalytic Study of the Child, V. New York: International
    Universities Press. Pp. 310-328.

* ------. 1953. "Trends in Infant Care," American Journal of Orthopsychiatry,
    XXIII, No. 1, 120-130.

* ------, and Nathan Leites. 1950. The Movies, A Psychological Study. Glen-
    coe, Ill.:. Free Press.

* Wolff, Harold G. 1947. "Protective Reaction Patterns and Disease," Annals
    of Internal Medicine, XXVII, No. 6, 944-969.

Young, Ernest. 1900. The Kingdom of the Yellow Robe. Second Edition.
    London: Constable.

** Zborowski, Mark. 1949. "The Place of Book Learning in Traditional Jewish
    Culture," Harvard Educational Review, XIX, No. 2, 87-109.

** ------. 1951. "The Children of the Covenant," Social Forces, XXIX, No. 4,
    351-364.

** ------, and Elizabeth Herzog. 1952. Life Is with People, The Jewish Little
    Town in Eastern Europe. New York: International Universities
    Press.

Ziemer, Gregor. 1941. Education for Death, The Making of the Nazi. New
    York: Oxford University Press.

Zulawski, Mark. 1946. "Warsaw," New Poland, January. New York: Polish
    Information Service.

INDEX

Abel, Thedora M., 89, 318-19, 335 n., 344;
    quoted, 228 n.; section by, with Hsu,
    329-40
Adolescence, studies of, 88, 134 n.
Affectlessness, trends in, 248-63
Alexander, Franz, 39 n.
Alexandrova. See Schwartz, Vera
American Museum of Natural History, 6 n.
Anthropologists, methods of, 10, 15, 18-31,
    41-53, 92-93

Bali, 25, 50, 59, 148 n., 268, 355, 360 n.,
    372 n., 375-76
Bateson, Gregory, 8-9, 23, 35 n., 59, 70,
    268, 272, 344, 360 n., 365; quoted, 12-
    13; sections by, 302-14, 367-78
Bavelas, Alex, 35 n.
Belo, Jane, 234 n., 268, 360 n.; section by,
    289-91
Benedict, Ruth, 6, 8, 15, 21, 26-27, 35 n.,
    63, 66, 89, 92, 219, 268, 365; sections
    by, 382-86, 405-15
Benet, Sula, 89, 92, 151; section by,
    415-21
Bernard, Claude, 40
Bibliography, 455-74
Bidyalankarana, Prince, quoted, 385
Boas, Franz, 15, 42 n., 45, 268
Bonaparte, Marie, 268
Botvinnik, Michael, quoted, 426-29
Britain: attitudes, 19-20, 349 n.; con-
    trasted with U.S.A., 24-25, 27-28,
    33 n., 377, 379-82, 398, 403-5
Bunzel, Ruth, 35 n., 45
Burma, 27

Calas, Nicolas, 344
Campbell, Joseph D., 268; quoted, 384
Camus, Albert, novel by, 151, 248-63
Cannon, W. B., 40
Caroline Zachry Institute of Human De-
    velopment, 134 n.
Chapple, Eliot, 35 n.
Chess, Soviet style of, 426-31
Chiang Kai-shek, quoted, 423
Children, 66-68, 77-78; Chinese, 158-62;
    French, 182-88, 290, 390-93; German,
    302-14; Italian, 134-38; Jewish (East

European), 387-88; Polish, 153-54,
    179-81; Russian, 167; Syrian, 170-76
China, 115-24, 150-51, 157-62, 192-98
    221-34, 292-95, 320-40, 421-26
Columbia University Research in Contem-
    porary Cultures, 6, 8 n., and passim
    through 453; list of participants, 454;
    organization of, 87-99, (chart) 90
Community Service Society, New York
    City, 98
Congruence, 42, 62-64
Conrad, Joseph, 19
Co-operation, definition of, 373 n.
Corruption, Soviet images of, 431-48
Council on Intercultural Relations, 97
Courage (Poland), 156-57, 415-21
Culture: definition of, 22, 58; of living
    communities, 49-53; national, 7, 23-24
Culture area, 26-28
Culture at a distance, 3-49; applications of,
    395-448; skills needed in study of,
    10-18; theory and methods derived
    from other disciplines, 34-40; theory
    and practice of, 18-34
Culture character structure, 4-6, 22, 33-34
Culture complex, definition of, 27
Culture traits, 26-27
Cybernetics, 39-40

Davidson, Helen, 329 n.
Deloria, Ella, quoted, 42-43 n.
Deutsch, Karl W., 24
Dollard, John, 35 n., 39 n.
Drama, interpretation of roles, 205-15
Drawing tests. See Tests, Horn-Hellersberg
Dubois, Cora, 35 n.

East European Jews. See Jews, East
    European
End linkage, 363-93
England. See Britain
Erikson, Erik H., 35 n., 38, 272, 278-79, 344

Fadayev, Alexander, novel by, 295-301
Family relationships: British, 376; Chi-
    nese, 421-26; French, 105-7, 182-92,
    391-93; German, 305; Japanese, 401;
    Jewish (East European), 387-89